COLLECTING MATCHBOX DIECAST TOYS

DIECAST TOYS THE FIRST FORTY YEARS

Seventy five regular wheel models on a Lesney display unit.
Also shown on the left is a Rag and Bone Cart (circa 1949), a Matchbox
Convoy model (circa 1987), the rare Y4 Duesenberg 'J' Town Car (circa
1976) and the Y12 Model 'T' Ford Van in Arnott's
livery (circa 1982).

COLLECTING MATCHBOX DIECAST TOYS

THE FIRST FORTY YEARS

KEVIN McGIMPSEY & STEWART ORR

With chapters written by Nigel Cooper, Paul Carr
and Wolfie Ginsburg

BASED ON AN ORIGINAL IDEA BY

GERRY TEKERIAN

Published for Matchbox International by

MAJOR PRODUCTIONS LIMITED

**COLLECTING
MATCHBOX DIECAST TOYS
The First Forty Years**
was written by Kevin McGimpsey
and Stewart Orr.

First Edition Copyright © 1989.

ISBN: 0 9510885 1 3

Published by Major Productions
Limited, 42 Bridge Street Row,
Chester, England, Great Britain.

Word Processing by M. Quayle
Secretarial Services, Chester
Book Cover by T. Smith,
Chester Design Studios, Chester
Photography by C. Brickwood,
C.B.A., Newbury
Typesetting by T. Bailey,
Ark Typesetting, Newbury
Reproduction by Colorfields, Eaton
Socon, Cambs
Book Designed by
Bernard Crossland, Thame
Printing by
BPCC Hazell Books Ltd, Aylesbury
First printed May 1989 (7,200)
Second printing November 1989 (5,250)

OUR THANKS

The Publishers would like to thank the following
contributors for their help and expertise:

Brian Bailey	Everett Marshall
Philip Bowdidge	Charles Mack
Paul Carr	Don Milne
Nigel Cooper	Robert Newson
Rock Cramer	Joe Recchia
Fred Diehl III	Bob Rusconi
Horace Dunkley	Ron Slyder
Les Duplock	Jim Smith
Bob Gamble	Patrick Talbot
Wolfie Ginsburg	Jack Tempest
Eric Goldsmith	Mike Thomas
David Henley	John Torrance
Tiffana Lam	Patrick Williamson
Ken Li	Takuo Yoshise

The publishers would like to thank the following for
their direct and valuable information. Where their
direct contributions to the book appear their names
are mentioned in italics, in alphabetical order:

John Allen, *Concept Design Engineer,
Lesney Products/Matchbox Toys Ltd.*
Noreen Arberry, *Industrial Engineer,
Lesney Products/Matchbox Toys Ltd.*
George Carey, *Manufacturing Director,
Lesney Products/Matchbox Toys Ltd.*
Derek Grundy, *Senior Quality Engineer,
Lesney Products/Matchbox Toys Ltd.*
Martin Hickmore, *Research & Development
Department, Lesney Products/Matchbox Toys Ltd.*
Keith Lister, *Quality Assurance Manager, Europe,
Matchbox International.*
Jack Odell O.B.E., *Co-founder of Lesney Products.*
John Simmons, *Toy Development Engineer,
Lesney Products/Matchbox Toys Ltd.*
Leslie Smith O.B.E., *Co-founder of Lesney Products.*
Sidney Sullivan, *Manager of the Research &
Development Department, Matchbox Toys Ltd.*
Gerry Tekerian, *Marketing Manager,
Lesney Products/Matchbox Toys Ltd.*
Graham Ward, *Managing Director of Promod
Ltd,and an Appointed Stockist.*
David Yeh, *Founder of Universal Matchbox Toys.*

SOURCES

Lesney News
Published as an in-house
magazine by the Lesney
Publicity Department
from 1968.

Lesney Scene:
A further supplement to
Lesney News.

Matchbox Collectors' Club:
The official quarterly
newsletter published by the
Fred Bronner Corporation
between 1966 and 1982.

*Railway Modeller
Magazine:*
A respected magazine for
model railway enthusiasts.

Miniature Auto Magazine:
A model car enthusiasts
journal.

*Miniature Autoworld
Magazine:*
A model car enthusiasts
journal.

Games & Toys Magazine:
A magazine published for
the toy trade.

CONTENTS

PREFACE

It is with great pride that we are celebrating the first forty years of Matchbox toys. It is indeed fitting, therefore, to record this in a book of such distinction. This book pauses for a moment to reflect on all the activities that have taken place over the last four decades; to muse with the people who were involved and responsible for providing so much joy to millions of children around the World; and to reflect with those 'children' who have grown up with Matchbox toys and who still derive great pleasure from them.

A contemporary photograph of David C.W. Yeh, Chairman of Universal Matchbox

The compilation of this book has been a monumental task; researching and verifying the facts as they happened and interviewing many of the people involved not least Leslie Smith and Jack Odell without whom there probably would not be Matchbox toys as we know them today.

Whilst famous marques such as Bugatti and Duesenberg are no longer manufactured, they still live through the detailed and accurate Matchbox Models of Yesteryear collection, together with all the other vehicles in the "Matchbox" Series, Convoy, Superking and Sky-Buster ranges.

Now that DINKY has also been included into the Matchbox family, we eagerly look forward to the years ahead, and plan to ensure the Company and its products continue to give pleasure to millions of people.

I hope you will enjoy this book and find its chapters informative and interesting.

Many thanks to everyone involved.

David C.W. Yeh, Chairman

INTRODUCTION

There can hardly be a child born in the Western World after 1945 who hasn't at one time or another played with Matchbox toys.

"I had one of those when I was a child." "I used to have lots of Matchbox toys, but my mother gave them away." Phrases such as these are heard all over the World when collections of Matchbox toys are seen in homes, old toy shops, toy museums and toy shows.

This book has been written by two Matchbox toy enthusiasts, assisted by a team of experienced collectors, to celebrate the first forty years of Matchbox and Lesney toys. It should interest collectors and general transport enthusiasts alike.

This is the first time that a book has been written on the subject of Matchbox toys, which has the support and assistance both of Mr Jack Odell O.B.E. and Mr Leslie Smith O.B.E., the two principal founders of Lesney Products, and of Mr David Yeh, the chairman of the Universal Corporation, the owners of the Matchbox business since 1982. The book contains much hitherto unpublished, first-hand information, which I'm sure will be new even to the most ardent collector or historian.

The entire history of Lesney and Matchbox Toys is covered and it may not be too long before a contestant on an international quiz show chooses Matchbox as a specialist subject. Special attention has been given, in separate chapters, to the various ranges of toys produced over the last forty years, including early Lesney toys, the "Matchbox" Series 1-75, Models of Yesteryear and King Size and Superkings.

The two co-founders of Lesney Products: Leslie Smith O.B.E. and Jack Odell O.B.E.

There is also a fund of information on the international aspects and markets of Matchbox and, although the book has been written in the United Kingdom, the intention has been to take a global, and not an insular, approach.

Finally, it may be useful to record that a roadsign from the A4/1 Accessory Pack, (which is 5 cms/1.6 inches high) has been used in the many excellent photographs taken specially for the book to indicate the size of the models shown and that the dimensions of the models have been given throughout in both centimetres and inches.

I have collected Matchbox toys since the mid-1950s and I was delighted to be asked to introduce this book. I believe that the proprietors of the Matchbox International Collectors' Association (M.I.C.A.), Kevin McGimpsey and Stewart Orr, and their team of specialist writers, have produced a major work, which is not only enjoyable to read but also contains a large amount of new and detailed information on Matchbox toys.

Patrick Talbot

1 The Kohnstam Connection

EARLY GERMAN INFLUENCES 1875 TO 1959

◀ The 'Waltzing Couple' is now regarded as one of the classic clockwork tinplate toys. Made in 1905 and attributed to Günthermann, it was distributed as a Moko toy. When wound, the toy perfectly simulated a waltzing movement.

Many diecast collectors are not fully aware why the name Moko once appeared on the familiar Matchbox style yellow boxes in which the famous "Matchbox" Series were originally marketed to the public.

The story of how the three ex-servicemen from World War II developed their highly successful business from humble beginnings just after the war is described in Chapter Two. The fact that the names Moko Lesney appeared on the packaging meant nothing to most people and the majority of the customers who bought the models probably never gave the matter a second thought.

Moko was actually the trademark of an old established firm of toy merchants M. Kohnstam & Co. and was derived from the first two letters of the two names of the founder, Moses Kohnstam. He is believed to have originally come from Czechoslovakia. He was a kindly man who possessed shrewd business acumen. Moses Kohnstam, who lived in Germany, noted with interest the steady increase in the number of toy manufacturers as a result of the healthy expansion in worldwide trading being experienced by Germany towards the end of the 19th century. Germany was beginning to supply the world with many goods; toys represented a significant portion of this trade and there was a good future for any enterprising businessman.

Moses Kohnstam decided not to become a manufacturer but to start in business as a wholesaler of toys in the small town of Fürth, close to the city of Nüremberg in Bavaria, where most of the country's toy business was centred. He had reasoned –

correctly, as it transpired – that many of the smaller firms coming into being would need someone to take care of the distribution side of their business. The great majority of Germany's toy manufacturers had set up in and around Nüremberg. There were many good reasons for this, the main one being that there was an excellent concentration of skilled workers available in the area which could be of great use in the production of tin plate toys. Nüremberg had been for many years the home of the clock-making industry and of manufacturers of other small items, including musical instruments. The clock-makers, in particular, were suffering from a serious decline in trade as a result of the importation of cheap watch mechanisms from America and the work – not entirely dissimilar – offered by the new toy factories was very welcome.

The future looked good and the production of clockwork powered tinplate toys, aided by the

9

opening of conveniently situated tin mines in Bavaria, was to continue successfully right up to the world trade depression of the 1920s. Business was good for Moses Kohnstam, too, as his firm could offer the busy industrialists the combined services of advertising, wholesaling, packaging, and distribution throughout Europe, leaving them to concentrate on production. Under the trade-name Moko the firm became a toy factor of some importance.

The business commenced in 1875 and eventually Moses Kohnstam had storage space at his offices in Nüremberg plus all the necessary facilities to distribute toys from several of the leading manufacturers. These toys were sometimes sold under the actual makers' name, whilst others would be offered bearing the Moko label, with Kohnstam receiving commission from the manufacturers on every toy sold.

As part of his work in developing the scope of his business outside Germany, Moses Kohnstam often visited Britain where there was a great demand for toys from Germany although local manufacturers were not too happy about the flood of German manufactured goods which were pouring into the country, just as Japanese imports were later to do in the 1960s. In 1880 Moses Kohnstam was a cofounder of the Manchester Toy Week, which became a regular event and was welcomed by toy wholesalers from the North of England and its inauguration created what is regarded as the forerunner of the present day Harrogate Toy Fair held every January.

By 1894 Moses Kohnstam was represented by offices in London, at 24 Milton Street EC (later EC2), as well as in Fürth, Milan, and Brussels. The firm's catalogues were packed with play-things of every kind and included a vast

range of toys and novelties; mouth organs, accordions and concertinas. The consumers were eager to buy the cheap goods churned out by the continually improving mass-production methods. Moses Kohnstam handled all classes of toys, right down to the humble tinplate Penny Toy once sold by pavement traders and nowadays eagerly sought after by enthusiastic collectors. The firm marketed the products of many prominent German manufacturers, including the tinplate marvels offered by that most revered firm of German toymakers, Gebruder Märklin. The source of some of Kohnstam's toys is not certain and many of the suppliers have not been identified, but it is known that he received goods from such toymakers as S. Günthermann (trademark S.G.), Georg Mangold (trademark GAMA), Gebrüder Einfalt (trademark Technofix), Adolf Schümann (trademark A.S.) and Richards (trademark Rico).

Between the 1920s and 1930s the Moko catalogue pictured a wealth of toys and, besides an amazing variety of tinplate playthings, there appeared boxes of lead soldiers, toy telephones, dolls' house furniture, air rifles, miniature gardening sets, dolls' bathrooms (with electric light and running water!), toy theatres, soldier outfits for children, sparking novelties, small musical boxes, toy gramophones, toy horse-drawn carts made from wood, rocking horses, pedal cars, toy castles, toy stoves, dolls' tea-sets, miniature shops, composition miniature animals, Noah's Arks, dolls' furniture, pewter altar ornaments, wooden sailing boats, celluloid novelty toys, novelty-filled Christmas stockings, electric motors, pull-along soft animals, cinematographs, dolls of all sizes, toy typewriters, toy sewing-machines, lithographed figural showcards for shop window display, and even animated

novelty figures for shop windows. The terrific selection of tinplate toys shown in the Moko trade brochures of this time included a huge variety of clockwork animated figures, many carpet toys, fire-engines, aeroplanes, airships, merry-go-rounds, toy locomotives (both clockwork and steam powered), toy boats, railway stations, stationary steam engines with animated accessories, trams, and tinplate motor cars. Many of the examples shown were from recognizable toy makers, such as the Double Billiard-Player toy by Georg Levy, the Santa Claus car by Tipp & Company, and the flywheel operated cars by J. L. Hess.

The wholesaling of dolls and cuddly toys began around 1909 when Moses Kohnstam registered the trademark Cupid (No. 312593) to be used to define a certain range of dolls being marketed. The registration of a patent of a design of a baby's bottle followed in 1910. Known as 'Mother's Darling', the bottle was supplied in two versions for separate distribution in Britain and in Germany. The British version featured a flag bearing the name Moko and carried the legend:

'– quiet and good, requires no nursing attention or food'.

However, the firm continued its main business wholesaling tin toys and, just prior to the outbreak of World War I in 1914, an example of a tinplate novelty from their catalogue was a Railway Keeper's

Timepiece which also doubled up as a waterproof match holder. Business came to a standstill with the outbreak of hostilities and the London office was taken over by the British Government for use as a Lord Roberts Memorial Workshop. M. Kohnstam & Co. was wound up in 1914.

Moses Kohnstam died in 1912 at the age of 72 leaving three sons – Julius, Willi and Emil. Julius went

Two clockwork tinplate vehicles made in Germany during the late 1920s. The Flying Police Squad Car features a battery operated searchlight and was made by Richards of Bavaria. The original Moko price label is still attached. This toy retailed in the U.K. at 2s. 9d. (13p). The green closed limousine features moving pistons and is attributed to Georg Mangold. The Moko trade mark can be seen on the radiator.

to England in 1890 and founded the London branch office. In 1912, immediately after the death of his father, Julius opened a doll factory under the name Keen & Son in part of the Milton Street premises, using imported German-made heads. One of the dolls produced was known as 'Vera'. His supply of toys came from the head office in Fürth and were mainly marked Moko. In 1920, Julius established a doll and toy manufacturing business under the name of James Garfield & Co. which lasted until 1927. On 31 December 1923 a new company known as J. Kohnstam & Co. Ltd., was incorporated. This was the business that was to have a direct link with Lesney some two decades later. Two superb examples of German made clockwork tin toys which were marketed by J. Kohnstam & Co. Ltd., were a tinplate Flying Police Car, manufactured by Richards of Bavaria, and a saloon car with moving engine pistons which carried the Moko name on the radiator grille and was, in all probability, made by the firm of Georg Mangold. Typical clockwork novelty toys imported into England by J. Kohnstam & Co. Ltd., included the teetering Penguin Waiter who tried his best to balance a bottle of soda-water on a tray as he wobbled along, and the toy clockwork tinplate elephants produced by Blomer & Schüler.

In 1933, Julius established a doll making company in Aylesbury, in Buckinghamshire, under the name Dollies Ltd., in a bid not only to expand business, but to build a financially secure base for the rest of the Kohnstam family still living in Nazi Germany. Willi and Emil stayed in Germany until 1933, at which time the office was closed down because of the political situation. Emil left for England to join his brother in 1934, leaving Willi behind. Jack Odell a co-founder of Lesney Products vividly recalls Richard Kohnstam explaining how his family had managed to escape from Germany in the 1930s. *Odell:* "Emil came to England in 1934 when the problems started in Nüremberg in Germany . . . The Jewish people had been thrown out of Poland . . . many of them were toy makers

and they all ended up in Germany. They soon realised that they were going to get thrown out of Germany also, so their community leaders chose several leading business men to go to England – one of them was Emil, and under the guise of the doll factory opened up by his brother Julius, Emil established himself in England as a toy importer. Companies in Germany began to send him millions of toys for distribution in England and they were all bought by him from his suppliers at half price! Part of the profit he put into the bank and so built up large accounts. That money then bought property in London to help house many of the German Jews who fled Germany in 1937 and 1938." Other families doing the same kind of thing were the Reeves family of Mettoy, later associated with Corgi.

In 1935 Julius died at the age of sixty-two and Emil remained in charge of the business. Julius's only son Richard began to form his own business in 1938 but with the war looming up he stayed with Emil at J. Kohnstam & Co. Ltd. It survived World War II with some difficulty but managed to stay in existence by making and marketing simple games.

Richard Kohnstam served in the Royal Artillery during the war and became a glider instructor, later working in intelligence. When peace returned he gave up the idea of setting up on his own and decided to concentrate on the marketing and distribution of diecast toys with his Uncle Emil. Emil and Richard registered the trademark Moko in England in 1949. Richard was well-educated and he could speak several languages fluently. He never lost the common touch. One of his often cited beliefs was: "The success of a product in the toy market is directly proportional to the amount of pleasure the consumer receives, i.e. play value." Another was: "People are

more important than products and if the people behind the product are good, then the rest will follow." Richard's instinct was such that if he was to tell a manufacturer that he had got it wrong, there was never an argument!

In 1946 to further expand his business interests Richard Kohnstam contacted several of the many toy manufacturers who had set up business in the north of London, such as Charbens and Benbros. He became interested in the new firm of Lesney Products who had commenced business in 1947. Lesney had decided to make toys and turned to Emil and Richard Kohnstam, who at this time were located at Clerkenwell Road in the City of London, for help and advice.

Odell: "One of the people that I used to work for in industrial castings before I made toys was Charbens. Charles Reid and Dicky Kohnstam knew each other before the war . . . he was selling their stuff and my name was mentioned to Kohnstam." Richard Kohnstam, because of his background, had developed strong commercial links in Europe. He would annually visit the toy fairs in Germany, France and Italy. At the Nüremberg Toy Fair, for example, he would have a tent containing a huge range of toys from several British toy manufacturers, and would accept orders from the European wholesalers. Thus began the famous Moko Lesney connection and an understanding was reached whereby Lesney would manufacture the toys whilst Moko in the main – (there were other rival toy factors who had good working relationships with Lesney) – would carry out almost all the packaging, advertising, distribution, and selling of the new range. It was also agreed that, when Kohnstam bought toys from Lesney to sell abroad, he would pay Lesney within seven to

ten days thus ensuring a good cash flow for Lesney.

By the mid 1950s J. Kohnstam & Co. Ltd., had also marketed several non-Lesney diecast toys, including a diecast Drummer Soldier with a clockwork mechanism, a revolving Fairground Carousel, a Crawler Bulldozer, a Crawler Tractor, a Crane, a Hayrick; and a large scale model of a Ruston Bucyrus Excavator. One of the more valuable non-Lesney Moko toys was a superb space toy which was part of the 'Konstrukta Range' – which was similar to a Meccano construction set.

There was no Moko involvement in the very early Lesney toys, such as the Aveling Barford Diesel Road Roller, the Crawler Bulldozer, the Crawler Tractor, the Soap Box Racer, and the Cement Mixer. J. Kohnstam & Co. Ltd., however, acquired the rights from A. Gilson to manufacture a Muffin Junior Puppet, and Lesney were given the project (For further details please see Chapter Three). Jumbo the Elephant, the Prime Mover, Bulldozer and the Small Coronation Coach were also Lesney toys of the early 1950s that had a Moko involvement.

Whilst he was associated with Lesney, Richard Kohnstam continued to involve himself with other British toy-making firms and was responsible for the launch of another character toy, Prudence the Kitten. Amongst other Moko toys were the Farmette series and in 1955 a figure of a girl on a scooter.

The involvement with Lesney led to the "Matchbox" Series of 1953, the Major Packs of 1957 and the Gift Sets from both ranges. It was agreed that the name Moko would be placed alongside the name Lesney on the boxes. This enabled Moko to promote the models more confidently.

Leslie Smith, a co-founder of Lesney Products, remembers Richard Kohnstam recalling his

J. Kohnstam & Co. Ltd., was not confined to simply distributing Lesney products during the 1950s. This display illustrates just some of their other lines.

was to select a target city, book a hotel room, and set out his wares to display to all the likely customers he could round up in the area. He was the ideal person for the requirements of Tamiya, knowing the business so well, and having the necessary excellent command of foreign languages. He also bought the business of Colonel Stewart Beattie with its well-known chain of shops that specialised in model and hobby products.

Richard Kohnstam died in 1985, the last of a line of specialist toy wholesalers. He had obviously inherited the drive and expertise of his grandfather. There was no doubt that old Moses would have been proud of his grandson, especially for the leading part he had played in putting the famous "Matchbox" Series on the path to success. Much of the history of the company's successful days reflected the marketing guidance he had provided. He had relieved Lesney of the chores of packaging, distribution, and advertising which allowed them to spend more money on developing moulds for their essential new products. He had presented the firm with the idea of 'Jumbo the Elephant', a direct copy of the popular toy from Blomer & Schüler, and was also responsible for their creation of the popular television character toy of 'Muffin the Mule'. He had marketed for them the extremely successful miniature 'Coronation Coach' which sold over one million pieces and, using the well-respected name of Moko, had been highly successful in the marketing of the "Matchbox" range in general. He had also helped to develop the idea of matchbox style boxes in which to present the Company's models and the use of the name "Matchbox" itself, an idea which certainly appealed to the members of the public!

early days in Germany to Jack Odell when Moko used to distribute little wooden dolls in matchboxes as a novelty range of toys. This memory cemented the idea already thought of by Jack Odell of packing the diecast miniatures into cartons designed to resemble matchboxes. Unbeknown to Smith and Odell, Emil and Richard Kohnstam registered the trademark "Matchbox" in late 1954. This did not please Lesney when this registration was discovered. In 1958 Emil Kohnstam died at the age of seventy-seven, and by the following year Lesney was able to buy out Richard Kohnstam and with it the full title to the name "Matchbox", along with the sales rights and

the design registrations. The name Moko was dropped and by 1961 appeared no longer on the cartons.

It appears that Richard Kohnstam had intended to retire from business in 1959 but he must have decided against this as he almost immediately set himself up in business as Richard Kohnstam Ltd. and registered the trademark "Riko". He continued working for Lesney until 1960 when he set up a hobby import business on White Lion Street, Islington, and secured the agen-

cies of two of Germany's leading toy manufacturers, Märklin and Faller. *Railway Modeller* March 1963: "We were interested to see on the excellent stand of Richard Kohnstam Ltd., a wide range of continental imports, with particular emphasis on the famous range of Märklin, Faller and Bürsch products." In 1968 he was asked by the Japanese toymaking firm of Tamiya, who had taken a small stand at the Nüremberg Toy Fair, if he would spearhead their business in Europe. He tackled the job in his usual energetic manner – just as he had done so when working with Lesney – by filling his car boot with samples and driving off to the Continent. His method

A Review of the Company

THE FIRST FORTY YEARS

◄ An artist's impression of the Rifleman Public House. No photographs are known to exist and the building was demolished soon after being vacated by Lesney.

BIOGRAPHIES PERSONALITIES AND EARLY PRODUCTS

Leslie Charles Smith was born on 6 March 1918. As a boy he was interested in tinplate clockwork toys, building bricks and, towards the end of his childhood, Meccano. His family did not spend vast sums on his toys, and in the main they were bought from shops such as Woolworths. Soon after leaving school be obtained a job as an office boy with the firm of J. Raymond Wilson Co. which specialised in shipping British goods to Australia, New Zealand and Europe. Leslie Smith later transferred to the buying department which involved the procurement of carpets and textiles. On several occasions before the war, Leslie Smith had visited France, Belgium, Italy and Holland. Following the outbreak of World War II, Leslie Smith then aged 22 joined the R.N.V.R. (Royal Naval Voluntary Reserve) as a Signal Rating. He soon became a Lieutenant and saw action in the North Sea and at the Dieppe Raid. He completed a tour on motor–gunboats patrolling from Yarmouth to the Hook of Holland, followed by action in North Africa, the Sicily Landings, Salerno and the D–Day Landings in 1944.

Leslie Smith's job had been held for him by Wilsons during the war – this was standard practice as anyone with a job before the war was entitled to return to it upon the cessation of hostilities. However, Leslie Smith did not anticipate being with this company for the rest of his life. *Smith:* "One of the advantages of the war was that it opened your mind much wider as to what the world consisted of – not just your local activities."

Just a few months after being demobbed Leslie Smith met up with an unrelated school friend called Rodney Smith. Rodney Smith was born on 26 August 1917 and had served with the Royal Navy as a Petty Officer. Once demobbed, he went back to his pre–war job with Die Casting Machine Tools Ltd. (D.C.M.T.) – a diecasting company based in Palmers Green, North London. The two Smiths met up on several occasions and talked about their futures. They both felt that it would be sensible to do something on their own, but the problem was exactly what to do. *Smith:* "Rodney Smith said 'All I know at D.C.M.T. is die-casting – should we get involved with this?'." Leslie Smith agreed that this could well be the direction to go in, even though he for one knew nothing about diecasting.

As with any new venture the Smiths had to ask themselves many questions – "Should we really start this, how do we start and what are we going to call the business?". The name Lesney was derived from a combination of their Christian names. *Smith:* "As his name was Rodney and I was Leslie we just broke up our names to form Lesney. Let's call it Products as we didn't know what we were going to make." The partnership of Lesney Products came into being on 19 January 1947.

Following the war there was not much money about and London was full of young demobbed 'entrepreneurs' looking for ways in which to make a living. *Smith:* "One never had much money. During the war you just got your payments and you couldn't actually save for anything". However, each of the Smiths had received a £300 war gratuity and although Rodney Smith had spent some of his already, Leslie Smith postponed his marriage for a year, as he could no longer afford to get married and start up in business at the same time. By pooling together their gratuities the Smiths were able to purchase their first diecasting machine from D.C.M.T.

The next problem was to find premises, not an easy task as many buildings in London had been partly demolished or were in a desperate state of repair. Rodney Smith gave up his job with D.C.M.T. and concentrated on finding premises.

He soon found a condemned public house known as 'The Rifleman', Union Row, N17 on the boundary between Edmonton and Tottenham in North London, at a rent of £2 per week. The Smiths set about putting the place right – this involved an extensive clear out of rubble and fittings and repairing a very leaky roof. Their one and only brand new, post–war diecasting machine was placed in the saloon bar!

They needed work desperately and were fortunate to receive an

order to make 10 to 20,000 string-cutters which were crude components made up of an old razor blade and a diecast holder. They had the mould for the holder made by a local tool maker as the Smiths did not have either the equipment or the expertise to make their own. Unfortunately the firm that made the mould also made a copy for themselves with the result that orders for further string-cutters never materialised for Lesney.

The Smiths had only been working together for a few weeks when Rodney Smith introduced a friend named John William Odell (known as Jack) to Leslie Smith. Jack Odell was working for D.C.M.T. at the time. He was an engineer by trade and had served with the Royal Army Service Corp and the Royal Electrical Mechanical Engineers in the war. During the North African campaign Odell on his own initiative often stripped damaged or wrecked military vehicles of all useful components and used these to keep his own vehicles on the road. His radio call sign during war operations was 'Lledo'! Jack Odell had been born on 19 March 1920 and left school at the age of thirteen to work for Simms Motors who made starters and motors for the car industry. *Odell:* "I had started engineering when I was fourteen, and after nine months at Simms I found it so boring it wasn't true. I think it was because I was born to be an engineer that I found it boring . . . I had many other jobs too . . . I worked in a cinema and was an estate agent for several years . . . Never really made a go of anything and I think I was quite pleased when I found that for the first time somebody wanted me, and it was King George."

When Jack Odell was de-mobbed the first person he turned to for employment was Sidney Ambridge who was Managing Director of D.C.M.T. Ambridge

gave Odell a job in the tool room and paid him 3s. 3d. (16p) an hour. At one time Ambridge lodged with Odell at Odell's mother's house. After nine months at D.C.M.T. Odell realised he could make castings as well as D.C.M.T. and he became anxious to start on his own. Odell travelled up to Bedford, some fifty miles north of London, and bought a quantity of ex-army machinery at £60 a unit. He had already secured orders for his dies which he anticipated making with his new machinery. When he arrived back at his premises in Harringay, the local council intervened and told him that he had no right to set up an industrial diecasting firm within a residential area. The only person that Odell knew who might be able to help was Rodney Smith whom he had got to know when Rodney was at D.C.M.T. Odell met the two Smiths at The Rifleman and explained the problem. *Odell:* "Rodney said to me, if you want to pay the £2 a week rent you can wire up your equipment here and start using it" The two Smiths envisaged a lean patch once their string cutter job had been completed. *Odell:* "They were stuck with a £2 a week rent, a new machine, and they couldn't get moulds made. There was also an eight week gas strike". Odell installed his machines and began making his tools to fulfil his own orders. His first tool, for which he received £100, was completed within twenty-one days. Rodney Smith sampled this tool for Odell on his machine. The General Electric Company (G.E.C.) were shown the casting of Odell's hook ceiling plate by an electrical distributor who had seen the tremendous potential for such a component. G.E.C. placed an order for ten thousand units with the distributor who had told G.E.C. that the component belonged to his company and so the name Lesney

never appeared on any of the castings. In the light of this huge order the two Smiths asked Odell to join them as a full partner. Leslie Smith anticipated that with the injection of Jack's equipment, Lesney Products would have just about enough tooling machinery. *Smith:* "Another step forward – I always thought it better to have two engineers rather than one". An agreement was drawn up between the three partners. Leslie Smith continued to work for J. Raymond Wilson Co., but devoted all his spare time to Lesney. *Smith:* "I did not work full time for Lesney Products because we only had a limited amount of money. When you start any new venture, you are obviously not making money, you are just scrambling around trying to survive." Leslie Smith did much of the book–keeping, accounts and some selling. Rodney had the job of diecasting and Jack that of making the moulds. Jack was particularly interested in experimenting with a new form of tooling for his pressure diecasting process. This revolutionary process was to produce virtually flash free castings and eliminate most of the need to fettle, i.e. remove the excess metal from the castings. The way forward for Lesney was via this new technique of clean automatic diecasting.

By early 1948 Lesney had thirty-five different industrial moulds and dies. The work force consisted of eight employees and the three partners. *Odell:* "When I first started working with Lesney we were in a small corrugated shed with a corrugated iron roof . . . there were six small hand presses mainly worked by hand. The Rifleman lay about thirty or forty yards off the road and it was a very small pub with just one bar downstairs, a parlour behind, three little rooms upstairs and, of course, a cellar. The cellar was very useful because that's where we had the presses." Lesney were soon to discover that industrial diecasters received little or no new work during the last quarter of the year. Companies such as G.E.C. informed Lesney through the electrical distributors network that although they were not cancelling any of their orders, there was no need for any more components until January of the next year. *Odell:* "Any money we had made in the first nine months could then be lost in the next three – all we could do was clean the windows and the machinery". However, in late 1947 Sidney Marks of M.Y. Dart, who were toy manufacturers, placed an order with Lesney to make a diecast component for a toy cap gun. This order certainly helped the Lesney cash flow but even more importantly demonstrated to the three partners that their diecasting skills could be turned to other products. *Smith:* "We thought to ourselves that perhaps we should be making toys and this could help even out our year's production". In early 1948 anticipating the expected October to January lull Lesney tried a new venture. *Odell:* "We got one or two Dinky toys and we made similar ones for about a third of the price, they eventually sold at 2s. 11d. (14.5p) and they sold extremely well".

Jack Odell made the moulds, the first of which was a Diesel Road Roller, and this was quickly followed by a Cement Mixer and a Crawler Tractor. The toys were packed one dozen to a box and Leslie Smith secured a contract initially with Woolworths but later with national wholesalers. *Smith:* "The Dinky Range was to our minds the very upper class quality to go for. All their distribution was through toy shops and by direct selling. A toy shop was very proud if it was a Dinky distributor. Many toy wholesalers and retailers would have liked to sell Dinky but they

were not allowed to unless they were a recognised distributor. So when the trade saw our early toys they said: 'This is what we want . . . we can now have products similar to the ones up the road'."

Lesney Products was incorporated as a private company on 9 March 1949 in the business of selling toys and diecastings, with Odell and the two Smiths as the Directors. Further premises were needed. *Smith:* "Shortly afterwards we took more premises up in Enfield and put some of our diecast machines in there to cater for the industrial side of the business." In 1949 Lesney vacated The Rifleman (it was later demolished) and moved to 1A Shacklewell Lane, Dalston, E8.

In late 1950, with a view to the forthcoming Festival of Britain, Lesney invested some of their profits into new moulds to make the Royal State Coach. Unfortunately, the Korean War intervened and in March 1951 the Government placed a ban on the use of zinc for the making of toys. *Odell:* "We were not able to use our stocks of zinc for toys as it was rationed and on the banned list. Whatever you had been using you only now got a quarter, but only to be used for vital products." *Smith:* "So we had to shrink back as a company because we had been making these large toys and that had given us a nice bit of trade. The electrical component side had begun to fade away because so many other people had started up and because the zinc diecasting was found to disintegrate into dust due to the reaction between the zinc electrical components and the lime in plaster." In 1951, Rodney Smith announced to his fellow directors that he could see no future in Lesney and that he did not want any further involvement. *Smith:* "I think one felt at the time it was an era and we just had to adjust ourselves to that. We had to get rid of some

A contemporary photograph of the two co-founders examining some of their models in the early 1960s.

staff to bring down the overdraft and make it a break even situation." Rodney Smith turned to chicken and duck breeding – there was certainly a demand for fresh meat and duck eggs as Britain was still in the throes of food rationing. However, things did not work out as rationing ended very soon after he had begun this venture, and he further found that he could not compete with the new forms of commercial battery breeding. Rodney then set up in business dredging up weeds from the River Thames and selling them to Woolworths as floral decoration. Soon afterwards he turned to pig breeding, but when this too did not work out he turned back to his best skill – that of diecasting and joined the London firm of toy factors, Morris & Stone (London) Ltd. in 1954. Rodney had sold his Lesney shares to Leslie Smith and Jack Odell for £8,000 and he used the residue of this lump sum as his contribution to the venture which was called R. Smith (Diecasting) Ltd. In 1958 Rodney sold his shares to his fellow directors and emigrated to Australia.

Lesney had, fortunately, built up a good stockpile of zinc before the embargo, but with no more electrical component orders materialising they found them-

selves with tons of valuable zinc, but no work. Odell paid a visit to a rival diecasting firm who were making components for the motor car industry and received an order to make castings for them. He purchased more machinery and the company enjoyed a boom time making castings for this firm on a contract basis. *Odell:* "We could charge what we liked, because we had the zinc and nobody else had". Imperial Smeltings, a subsidiary of Rio Tinto Zinc, supplied all Lesney's and Meccano's raw material at this time.

On 6 February 1952 King George VI died and the country prepared itself for the Coronation of Queen Elizabeth II in 1953. The Korean War Armistice was signed in May 1952 and a few weeks later the zinc embargo was lifted. As zinc was plentiful once again Lesney decided to produce a large Coronation Coach using the moulds which were made in 1951 for the Festival of Britain Coach. The large coach was a great success with over 33,000 pieces being sold.

Jack Odell then designed a new mould and produced a miniature Coronation Coach. Richard

Kohnstam of J. Kohnstam & Co. Ltd. was given sole rights of distribution. The miniature coach was a phenomenal success with over one million pieces being sold. What were Lesney to do with the consequent revenue and with the fact that in just a few years they were fast becoming a household name?

THE BIRTH OF THE "MATCHBOX" RANGES

Jack Odell saw the way forward for Lesney by creating a range of miniature diecast models. During late 1952 he had experimented with various ideas. His breakthrough came with a completed brass prototype of a small road roller. *Odell:* "My oldest daughter had just started school and the kids were restricted in what they could take to school to play with. The school only allowed them to take a matchbox size container to school. They used to put terrible things in them like beetles and chrysalises. I said 'Look, you just can't do that'. She tried putting the Coronation Coach inside her box, it would not go and that rang a bell with me . . . If I could make a model or toy that would go inside her box she could take that to school. I gave her the brass roller for her box and all the kids came round that night and they wanted one too." As the brass roller had cost Odell some £5 to make he told the children that he could not afford to make them all one. *Odell:* "I then thought and told them I'll make a very simple mould and I'll cast a few." Jack Odell did as he had promised and produced a mould for £100. An assembled prototype was shown to Leslie Smith and Richard Kohnstam who both agreed that

"Matchbox" means different things to different people!
A Lesney News *cartoon from 1969*

this was a most exciting development. Richard Kohnstam asked to be allowed to distribute the new range. Jack Odell was convinced that there was an immediate market for miniature toys. *Odell:* "With a Dinky toy, if you put it into a little girl's hand it looked too big and was too heavy and cumbersome, but when you put the little Diesel Roller in a girl's hand, to her down there, it was a big toy!"

Richard Kohnstam liked the idea of having the miniatures packaged and sold in a matchbox type box. He vividly remembered a range of wooden dolls and furniture that had been made by a German toy company and sold by Moko during the 1920s. These had been very popular at the time and it seemed right that the same type of packaging be adopted by Lesney. *Smith:* "Dicky said to Jack, well let's keep them in matchboxes – toys in matchboxes used to be very good in those early days." By coincidence Jack Odell, during the discussions, picked up a box of matches made by the Norvic Match Co. Ltd, Susice, Czechoslovakia. He opened the box and placed the prototype inside. *Smith:* "We

An example of miniature figurines with their matchbox containers, a range of toys that the Kohnstams had imported from Germany in the inter-war period

liked this Scandinavian type design and that was the birth of "Matchbox". The idea and the concept was sealed there and then. The "Matchbox" Series was about to be launched. In late 1954, neither Smith nor Odell realised that J. Kohnstam & Co. Ltd had registered the name "Matchbox"!

The first four models were made by late 1953 and by early January 1954 the Kohnstam stand at the Harrogate Toy Fair was proudly displaying the first four "Matchbox" miniatures – The Aveling Barford Road Roller, the Muir Hill Site Dumper, the Cement Mixer and the Massey Harris Tractor. The Muir Hill Site Dumper was a scaled down version of a large scale dumper truck that had been considered, but never got past the tooling stage (for further information see Chapter Three). *Odell:* "The toy wholesalers in November 1953 told us 'Sorry we can't sell them, people say they look like they have come out of Christmas crackers.' They were priced at 1s. 6d. (7.5p) and we thought to ourselves 'what can we do?'.

Suddenly in January, the kids had money in their pockets and when they went into a toy shop, they found that they could at last buy a toy for 1s. 6d. (7.5p) that was a complete toy." All of a sudden Lesney found the wholesalers wanting the toys. *Odell:* "They wanted hundreds of gross." *Smith:* "Yes, the bus was the turning point in my mind . . . a bus is always popular." Further additions to the "Matchbox" Series in 1954 and 1955 were the Quarry Truck, the Horse Drawn Milk Float, the Caterpillar Tractor and the Dennis Fire Engine. The fire engine and bus were not based on earlier larger Lesney toys.

Although the name 'Moko' was featured on the boxes, the models themselves did not have any mention of Moko. *Smith:* "We thought that if we were ever going to have a fight with Kohnstam we should stop putting Moko on the moulds and just have Lesney. At least in a dispute the most expensive part of the business, the moulds, would belong to Lesney."

In 1954 Odell persuaded Smith to leave his other job and come into Lesney full–time. Leslie Smith had of course been working at Lesney on a regular basis, as and when he could doing the wages, administration, sales, marketing and exports. *Odell:* "I was completely on my own – hiring and firing, making tools, getting sales and running the place. Our turnover was £250,000 and I had one hundred people working for me. One day I had to go to Les and say to him that I was killing myself with the workload and that he was either in full time or I had to look for a manager. Les went back and spoke with his wife Nancy and decided to come in."

Smith realised that Kohnstam had successfully tied up the domestic market. *Smith:* "I began to build up the export side

Fred Bronner in the 1960s. The Fred Bronner Corporation had been bought by Lesney circa 1964 - total cost £261,000.

– that was always my strategy, as I realised that we could not just survive in the United Kingdom." *Odell:* "Les was very much export minded . . . " In the same year Fred Bronner, an enterprising toy salesman from New York, U.S.A., formed a company called the 'Fred Bronner Corporation' to handle the importing, marketing and selling of imported toys including "Matchbox" in the U.S.A. Originally he had to share distribution with other toy importers such as Daniel Jacoby. By 1956 the Bronner organisation was given exclusive rights to the "Matchbox" Series. Lesney bought a further factory at 38 Barrett's Grove, Stoke Newington, N16 near Shacklewell Lane, in 1955. This factory was situated next to a disused church which was also used as a warehouse. Lesney used Barrett's Grove until 1959.

By 1956 Lesney were making considerable profits. *Odell:* "We had so much money that our accountant told us we had to lose or get rid of £250,000 – at that time it was like being a millionaire on a desert island, as I only had about £18 in the bank. One of the big problems was that we had made too much money and this money was in the bank and if we drew it out, the sur–tax directive would be a killer". Lesney decided to buy a factory even though they did not really need it. A local estate agent took them to a vacant building at 59 Eastway, Hackney Wick, London, E9. Both Smith and Odell arrived at the factory straight from the production line dressed in their white coats. The vendor implied to Smith and Odell that they didn't look like candidates who had a quarter of a million pounds. By chance Lesney and the vendors banked at Barclays of Dalston. Odell and Smith offered the vendor £200,000 and a phone call was made to Barclays. *Odell:* "The bank manager said to him 'If it's those two characters Odell and Smith they have twice as much money as you have, so don't be rude to them'. We got

him to throw in all the spraying equipment." The factory was bought and although it wasn't occupied at once, the Eastway factory eventually housed a foundry with eighty machines and a workforce of over one thousand.

The Models of Yesteryear range was started at Barrett's Grove and was introduced in 1956 although it was not advertised until 1957. The name Yesteryear was conceived by Odell because the range was to be a reflection of the past. *Odell:* "I said to Les, 'I'm going to make a new range and call it Yesteryears' he said 'don't be stupid, there is no such word.' He went and got a dictionary and Yesteryear wasn't in it, but it is now! He didn't want to know, but in the end it happened". The word is now an accepted part of the English language. Odell had become slightly disenchanted with the "Matchbox" Series, and felt that he needed a new engineering challenge. *Odell:* "I loved the older stuff, but the "Matchbox" Series were slabs . . . We were running out of ideas . . . Just one piece things and I wanted something I could put more detail into and make more interesting. As an engineer I loved Showman's Engines, Allchin Traction Engines, buses and fire engines." In the same year Leslie Smith had discovered from a trade journal that Kohnstam had registered the word "Matchbox". *Smith:* "I said, crumbs he can't do that." *Odell:* "I went to Kohnstam and said 'I'm not going to make any more Matchbox – I'm going to scrub the word Matchbox and call them the Lesney Series. I will mill the Matchbox name off the bottom and I'll throw the boxes away!' We sought legal opinion and found that we could not re-register the name . . . we could only share the name." The Kohnstams agreed to have "Matchbox" re-registered in both parties' names. *Smith:* "Richard would sell and we would make." However, Smith and Odell were not really happy with this arrangement and Lesney started to review their involvement with J. Kohnstam & Co. Ltd. *Odell:* "Once we had registered in both our names we knew it wouldn't be long before we separated from them." Richard Kohnstam was not offered any involvement with the new Yesteryear Range.

The first three Yesteryears were shown at the 1956 Toy Trade Fair, although Lesney had nearly brought the range out in 1955. *Smith:* "We were going to bring out the new models a year before but we probably had enough work on with the "Matchbox" Series – it tended to hold one back". There was no immediate Yesteryear strategy. *Smith:* "It was all fits and starts with Yesteryears – there wasn't a schedule of so many a year. It was only later on, we thought 'we've got a range now so we had better have a policy'. We got to Y16 and decided to go back again." Boxes similar in design to the "Matchbox" Series were produced by a local firm called Boxes Ltd. In the same year Mettoy introduced their Corgi range. *Odell:* "At the Harrogate Toy Fair, Les and I were walking down the hall towards their stand . . . Mettoy asked us to leave their stand . . . it was the worst thing they could have done as it made us more determined to beat them and turn out cheaper and better stuff."

Leslie Smith's main aim up to 1959 was to open up new markets. Kohnstam until 1959 had sole rights for the "Matchbox" Series (and later Major Packs) for Europe and some other parts of the world. Smith dealt direct with Australia and New Zealand, as this market was well known to

him from his days in the textile world. Fred Bronner had been given the sole rights to North America. However, with only three Yesteryears, Smith realised that he would not be able to go to all the world markets and expect a positive response. *Smith:* "We said to Richard 'Right you've got your network in certain parts of the world and it makes sense for us to join forces'. We used his people. If Kohnstam didn't have an agent, then I would trace somebody and send samples. An order would come back, and in those days there was great trust and open credit . . . I can't recall having a single bad debt."

1957 saw the launch of a new range – Major Packs. These larger models made to the same scale as the miniatures were a compromise between the early Lesney toys and the "Matchbox" Series. *Odell:* "We just wanted a bigger toy and a bit more turnover . . . we wanted a variation . . . they were very good." The Major Pack series gave Lesney the opportunity to exploit a gap in the market. The first Major Pack to appear was the Caterpillar DW20 Earth Scraper. This was very much a natural subject for Lesney to make and could never have been reproduced for reasons of scale in the "Matchbox" Series. The Major Pack series were produced for ten years and were eventually withdrawn in 1967. Several of the models were continued in the King Size range that had been started in 1960. *Smith:* "Somehow they weren't the right size. They were lorries, transport vehicles, and then we thought we ought to bring out cars and drop the Major Packs." In total there were fifteen different Major Pack models in a series numbered from M1–10. As with the miniatures, Richard Kohnstam was given the sole rights of distribution and hence the Major Pack boxes, up to and around 1961, reflected the Moko involvement.

THE DISSOLUTION OF MOKO/LESNEY

With the very successful launch and continued success of the Yesteryear range, Lesney became disgruntled at having to include J. Kohnstam & Co. Ltd. in their affairs. As the Yesteryears were selling well Lesney asked themselves if they really needed to be involved with J. Kohnstam & Co. Ltd any longer. *Smith:* "I think we thought to ourselves, what do we need a factor for – it was niggling at us." Before the days of the "Matchbox" Series it had been a tight deal with J. Kohnstam & Co. Ltd. As toy factors they worked on 17.5% – this was tight for the factor as he had to give cash discounts, pay carriage, and employ salesmen. Lesney attempted to cost by product, but at the end of the day only knew by their feelings whether a product had been successful. *Smith:* "We felt it in our guts – not very scientific. The spraying cost so much, the cost of the axles to buy in, metal and box costs. Lesney always set the retail price, i.e. 2s.11d (14.5p), and then worked backwards." Pricing was very tight and this forced Lesney to look at the percentage taken by Kohnstam.

Lesney were also disappointed that Richard Kohnstam had not exploited the export markets. *Smith:* "Richard was to my mind stifling us on the export side. He couldn't keep up with the pace and we wanted to grow!" *Odell:* "We had been growing so fast they wouldn't spend the necessary money to keep up with us . . . for some time they just refused to spend more money." Odell was told of a problem in South Africa – local retailers were only able to buy Matchbox if they agreed to buy other toys also handled by J. Kohnstam & Co. Ltd. *Odell:*

"When I came back we decided that we'd paddle our own canoe. We had to buy him out to get our name back." Lesney anticipated going public in 1960 and wanted to buy J. Kohnstam & Co. Ltd. before doing so. *Odell:* "I flew out to see if it was true that Kohnstam was using our product as a premium. When I got back from South Africa they said to us 'You are going too fast . . . do you want to buy us out?'." In 1959 Lesney paid Richard Kohnstam £80,000 for the balance of the "Matchbox" trademark and warehouses and offices situated at Clerkenwell Road, City Road and Pentonville Road. Four years later Lesney also bought out Fred Bronner and made his organisation a division of Lesney. Fred Bronner was placed in charge of this division – which included warehousing facilities, and office space totalling just over 93,000 square feet, with the main office situated on 120 East 23rd Street, New York.

Up until this time Lesney advertising and marketing had been handled by Dorland Advertising Ltd. Both Odell and Smith had established a good working relationship with Dorland's senior accounts executive – Mr Peter Webb. He was eventually persuaded to leave Dorland and join Lesney. *Railway Modeller* October 1960: 'Our congratulations go to Mr Webb on his recent appointment as advertising and publicity manager for Messrs. Lesney Products & Co. Ltd . . . Among other duties he will assist in determining new models . . . Mr Peter Webb has always been interested in model railways.' *Smith:* "He brought in another dimension to the firm . . . great marketing skills . . . much more professional in his approach." The combination of Webb's skills and enthusiasm for model railways led to high sales being achieved in the "Matchbox"

Series, Major Packs and the early Models of Yesteryear. *Railway Modeller News Special* June 1959: "Matchbox cars, we feel, need no introduction to the majority of our readers, for, as we know from many a Railway of the Month, these vehicles appear on most 00 gauge layouts, not to mention several TT systems as well.

The reasons are not hard to find. First and foremost, with the exception of some of the earliest models in the series, the cars are virtually 4 mm scale, so close indeed that only hair–splitting checking can find any discrep-

ancies. The second point is that, despite their small size the detail and finish on these vehicles is superb, while the price 1s. 6d., is most reasonable.

Their Yesteryear series has, if anything, proved even more popular with modellers because the prototypes chosen are all outstanding examples of historical vehicles. These models retail at varying prices around the 2s. 6d. mark." Soon afterwards model railway enthusiasts were encouraged to send off for a specially prepared listing that detailed the scales and sizes of the entire range of models. It is apparent that Peter Webb was able to influence the *Railway Modeller* so that scarcely a bad review of a new model was printed. His influence can also be detected in the number of models produced at around the scale of 00 following his appointment.

THE COMPANY GOES PUBLIC

Lesney went public in 1960. *The Times* 23 September 1960: "One of the more interesting industrial companies to enter the stock market is Lesney Products die-casting engineers, makers of the "Matchbox" Series of toys.

This company is coming to the public for the first time next Thursday with an offer of 400,000 ordinary 5 shilling shares at 20 shillings each, at which price they will yield £6.5s.0d on a forecast dividend of 25%. On the limited profit of £300,000 this dividend would be covered 4.8 times on the capital currently being issued. Brokers are Montagu Loebl, Stanley and Co. About 80% of the Lesney production is devoted to small toys mainly the "Matchbox" Series of diecast miniature road vehicles. These are produced in quantity terms of millions and over half the output is exported to more than ninety overseas territories. The remaining 20% of the business is in small light commercial diecasting.

The company has under construction a new factory building, (Lee Conservancy Road often referred to as simply Hackney), which is scheduled for completion at the end of this year – which will increase productive capacity by about 125%. The entire cost of this is being

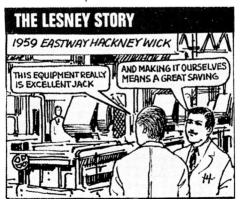

financed by internal resources. Bearing in mind the influence this is likely to have on future profit and the growing toy markets necessitated by the rising birth rate, and higher incomes, it will be fair to assume a modest premium when dealings begin."

The Times reported a few days later that the Lesney offer was 'oversubscribed'. *The Times* 1 October 1960: "For its offer of 400,000 five shilling ordinary shares in Lesney Products, Montagu, Loebl, Stanley & Co. received 12415 applications for 6014440 shares." *Odell:* "We had to go public in 1960 because we had so much money in the bank that the tax man was going to get the lot. We had to do it quickly because once twenty five per cent of the shares were in public hands, the sur–tax umbrella went . . . it was all to do with the tax laws."

In 1962 Smith and Odell became joint managing directors of Eastway Zinc Alloy Co Ltd., which in turn supplied zinc to Lesney.

The company's continued success through the 1960s was aided by its comprehensive penetration of outlets which could sell their products successfully. In many ways their competitor's (most notably Dinky) adherence to chosen stockists enabled Matchbox to be the obvious choice for outlets such as Post Offices, newsagents, tobacconists, gift shops and department stores, all supplied by wholesalers or as direct accounts depending on turnover.

Lesney's policy of trying to give value for money married to an affordable price meant that the acquisition of a toy could be an impulse purchase, bought nearly anywhere and not the object of a special visit to a toy shop. The ranges of toys covered the market from less than 2s. 0d (10p) up to

10s. 0d (50p) and hence represented formidable opposition to companies such as Dinky and Corgi. In 1966 Lesney were awarded their first Queen's Award to Industry. Over 3,600 people were employed at Lesney and a record 100 million models were made and sold per year. The *1966 Pocket Catalogue:* 'Enthusiasts of all ages through-out the world collect and enjoy "Matchbox" models today and it is a true but amazing fact that if the models from a year's work in the Lesney factories were placed nose to tail, they would stretch from London, England to Mexico City – a distance of over 6,000 miles.'

In 1966 the Fred Bronner Corporation launched their own Collectors' Club which by 1972 had recruited over 50,000 members.

During 1967 and 1968 Lesney had a turnover of twenty eight million pounds, the profit on which was five million pounds. *Odell:* "We were in the Guinness Book of Records that year . . . we made more profit with capital employed than any other company in England."

The building of a new factory at Edmonton started in June 1967. Within two years the 108,000 square feet plant was completed, 20,000 square feet of which was just for the Matchbox Motorway production lines. *Lesney*

News December 1968: "At Edmonton arrangements have been made to facilitate the storage of six of Lesney's fourteen foot double-decker buses . . . This will ensure (for the high quality local workforce) direct transport to and from the factory and warehouses.'

Leslie Smith and Jack Odell were both awarded an O.B.E. in 1968 and Lesney Products were also awarded a further Queen's

Sir Gerald Templer presenting Lesney's second Queen's Award to Industry in 1968.

Award to Industry. To celebrate this milestone Lesney produced a plated version of the Y13 Daimler and attached it to a Wades porcelain ashtray. It was labelled: 'Presented by the Board of Directors to each member of the company in appreciation of the combined efforts necessary to obtain the company's second Queen's Award for Export.' Leslie Smith also went to the Tokyo Toy Fair in this year.

Lesney News 1968: "Mr Smith has just returned from his trip to Japan where he headed a trade mission of fourteen British toy manufacturers. Mr Smith says: "Indications are that sales of 'Matchbox' toys in particular are expanding in step with Japan's national growth".' In the same year Lesney donated several models to the Helium Centinnial Committee. *Matchbox Collectors'*

A mass of "Matchbox" toys being shown to Her Majesty in 1969 by Mr Smith accompanied by Mr Tapscott, the Company Chairman.

Club 1968: "A special assortment of "Matchbox" models were sealed in four time capsules in Amarillo, Texas in conjunction with the Helium celebrations (1968). The four capsules will be opened in 1993, 2018, 2068 and 2968. The chairman of the Smithsonian Institute selected the assortment of twenty-one "Matchbox" models as being the most accurate and most representative of today's vehicles."

Fourteen factories were employing over six and a half thousand employees by 1969. Lesney were awarded a further Queen's Award to Industry. In November 1969 Her Majesty the

Her Majesty walking down Lee Conservancy Road with Mr Tapscott followed by The Duke of Edinburgh

Queen accompanied by His Royal Highness the Duke of Edinburgh visited the Lesney factories at Hackney.

THE AMERICAN CHALLENGE

In England the output per week was running at 5.5 million models, and over one million industrial diecastings. Models were being exported to 130 countries with 40% going to the U.S.A. In fact, just over 80% of the total production was exported. However, disaster was about to occur. *Smith:* "To give Fred Bronner his due, he reported rumours that Mattel had got something big and special. We thought 'what can they bring out that is so special – four wheels and an axle – we'll be all right'. And when the toy fair came – Yes! they had it, they had this Hot Wheels thing going round and round on a loop and then you'd see the Lesney

car going !" *Odell:* "I was in America at that time and all you could see on the T.V. was 'Hot Wheels'. Mattel launched them with ten million dollars worth of advertising."

Fortunately, the new axle that enabled the Mattel miniatures to go so fast had not been patented. Although Odell was opposed to introducing Superfast wheels he told his team to develop something similar. In the interim period, Lesney lost ground in the

U.S.A. to Mattel, but, of course, Mattel did not have the quantities of stock to serve all the markets. Lesney needed finances to develop and produce their new 'Superfast' range. *Smith:* "All the Hot Wheels were made in Hong Kong with cheaper labour – a bit of wire going through and welded by hand. We couldn't compete labour wise, so we had to produce new special automatic machinery . . . we were on the ropes as it were because until

A contemporary cartoon from Lesney Scene 1972.

then we had had great cash flow, and now suddenly it started to disappear".

Odell: "Our sales in the U.S.A. fell from U.S. $28 million to U.S. $6 million the following year. Of course, we had expanded well in advance with more people, computers, factories and distribution points . . . that year we lost money."

Mr Paul Tapscott, who was then Lesney's Chairman, went to the bank and unsuccessfully tried to secure a £2 million overdraft. After much discussion, Tapscott secured a loan of £1.5 million. *Smith:* "It was enough to hold us through the difficult period, plus the expenditure of all the new machinery . . . but it took us over eighteen months to get the Superfasts right." *Odell:* "It cost us millions of pounds to build the machinery to do Superfast and to change all the moulds as well as the hot stamping machines for the bits on the wheels." Even so, Lesney received their fourth Queen's Award to Industry in 1970. Mr Roy Mason, the then President of the Board of Trade wrote to Lesney: "To have received four Awards in five years is a remarkable achievement."

Lesney News January 1970: 'The festive season departed full of good cheer for both Lesney and the many children who bought Superfast this year.

'Yes! Superfast topped the pops in being the most wanted Christmas stocking filler in Great Britain . . . Superfast, since its introduction in August, has been overhauling the substantial lead established by 'Mattel' with the Hot Wheels cars."

Lesney began developing their first six plastic kits in 1971. Although they were expensive to develop, the plastic kits have since proved themselves to be one of the most profitable lines and they are still being produced

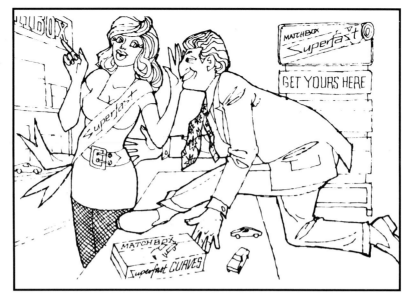

"Superfast refers to the toys – not me sir" Lesney News *September 1972.*

to this day. In the same year Lesney had successfully converted the majority of models in the "Matchbox" Series to 'Superfast', but they had accumulated short term losses of £700,000.

In the same year Fred Bronner retired from his position as President of the Lesney U.S.A. organisation. *Matchbox Collectors' Club 1971:* "With a smile on his face and a twinkle in his eye, Fred Bronner even looks as if he belongs in the toy business. But his life has not been all fun and

games. He grew up in Vienna, the son of middle class parents. He received his law degree from the University of Vienna . . . in 1938 he had to flee from Austria. Speaking only German he went to Paris and then to Trinidad. The Bronners came to the U.S.A. in 1945. One day an advertisement in an English magazine caught Fred Bronner's attention and prompted him to send for his first "Matchbox" samples to offer in the U.S.A. So in 1954 he founded the Fred Bronner Corporation

(later to be renamed Lesney Products Corporation) . . . He became so successful that today the name Bronner is synonymous with the "Matchbox" Series in America's toy trade. Mr E. D. Harrowe became the new President of Lesney which had by now moved into a new 200,000 square foot plant in Moonachie, New Jersey.

FURTHER GROWTH IN THE 70s

A new Lesney factory with a floor area of 150,000 square feet on a fourteen acre site had been opened in Rochford, Essex in 1969. By 1971 it had a total work–force of one thousand and was producing thirteen million Superfast wheel sets per week. *Smith:* "These were anxious days but we were helped by the fact that Mattel never had the broad range of Lesney nor could they supply the world's needs. Our own world–wide export coverage helped to reduce the impact of Hot Wheels." *Odell:* "Les decided that everything had got to be Hot Wheels . . . I didn't think that it was actually

The Architect's illustration of the Lesney factory in New Jersey, 1969.

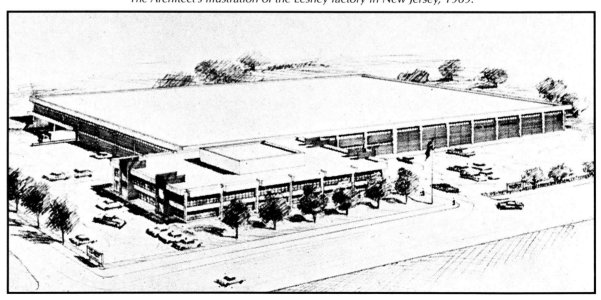

necessary to change all our stuff because it was such a big market . . . we would still have made a lot of money."

To reinforce in children's minds the idea of Superfast toys Lesney entered the world of Formula Two motor racing. *Matchbox Collectors' Club* 1972: "The car carrying the "Matchbox" name in the newly developed Surtees Team Formula Two, designed and built by the Surtees Organisation . . . Racing for the chequered flag will be John Surtees (four times World Motorcycling Champion and a former World Racing Champion) and Mike Hailwood (nine times World Motorcycling Champion). The "Matchbox" Formula Two will be racing from 12th March through to 15th October in sixteen different events in seven different countries."

In the same year Lesney introduced Cascade the first of many diversified "Matchbox" products. It was marketed as a

John Surtees streaking home in his new "Matchbox", 1975.

family game and comprised a mechanism that propelled steel balls into 'thumper' drums."

Odell decided to resign as joint Managing Director in 1973. He was offered an honorary title of Deputy Chairman for which he received a pension, and with the exception of attending new development meetings, stayed out of the day–to–day running of Lesney Products.

Leslie Smith became sole Managing Director until 1980. *Odell:* "I basically had a sabbatical for seven years and played golf a few times a week. I had ten holidays a year to make up for all the holidays I never had."

Between 1973 and 1979 Lesney Products continued to make good toys and healthy profits. The Rola-matic Miniatures had been introduced by early 1973. This was a new and innovative concept whereby specific new models were given features which worked when the vehicle was pushed forwards.

Production at Lesney stopped in the first quarter of 1973 because of a nationwide power strike which lasted eight weeks, quickly followed by a rare strike at Lesney by the members of the Fettling Shop. Then two disasters struck the Rochford factory: First a fire which not only burned down a large part of the plant and the majority of the plastic components and then a flood which made most of the remaining machinery inoperable. Production priority was given to Superfast and consequently the production of the Yesteryear range was stopped. Although they were advertised as being in the shops, no Yesteryears ap-

peared in the domestic market during 1974 and were not released in the U.S.A. until 1975. *Matchbox Collectors' Club* 1973: 'There are four new Models of Yesteryear but that is not the whole "new" story. Yesteryears are virtually all new because every model has been repainted in vibrant new colours plus the old plastic wheels have been replaced with real rubber ones. The window package has also been changed to co–ordinate with the colour of the car in the package.' *Matchbox Collectors' Club* 1974: "We have not discontinued Models of Yesteryear, but due to the shortage of materials in England we were

By 1975 Lesney was developing and diversifying into non-diecast products.

The all-new mechanized, family fun game from "MATCHBOX". From the baffling climb up the Spyro-Lift to the final count in the Score Pit, Cascade is pulsating action and continuous excitement. Watch the steel balls fly over the Thumper Drums. Release any number at a time. Let them all fly at once for a full Cascade. Play 1-2-3 Cascade, High Roller, Time Trial, and Cascade 10. Every Cascade set comes complete with 10 steel balls, Spyro-Lift, Thumper Drums, Score Pit, Re-load Ramp, layout mat and game rules. There's nothing like it!

unable to put this series into production . . . we hope to have them available later this year." In fact it was not until 1975 that Yesteryears were on general release. *Lesney Scene* Spring 1977: "The recently released official 1976 figures for Lesney Products & Company Ltd show a record sales improvement from £43.5 million to £56.4 million."

Between 1974 and 1977 Lesney continued to develop and diversify. By late 1975 a huge advertising campaign had been launched by Lesney promoting the latest Matchbox product – Fighting Furies. These were fully

jointed action dolls and included Captain Pegley and Hook. The adventure ship Sea Fury was also made as part of the range, which included a vinyl carry–case which became a bridge and deck of a Spanish Galleon when unfolded.

The company of Lesney Products became a holding company in 1977 and moved its headquarters to 93 Burleigh Gardens, Southgate, North London. Leslie Smith was appointed as the Group Managing Director and the Chairman of three newly formed U.K. Subsidiaries. Reproduced

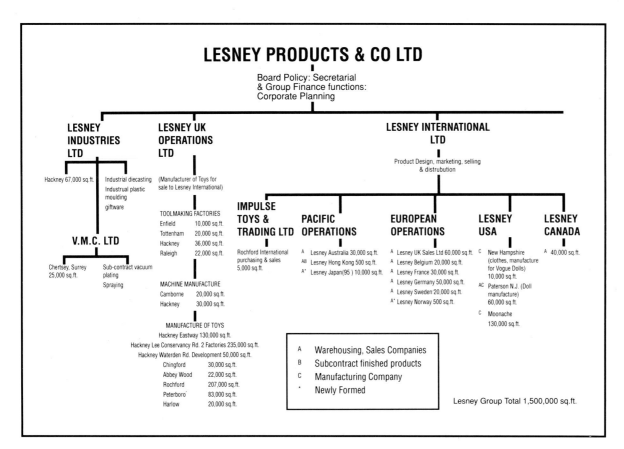

LESNEY PRODUCTS & CO LTD
Board Policy: Secretarial & Group Finance functions: Corporate Planning

LESNEY INDUSTRIES LTD
Hackney 67,000 sq.ft.
Industrial diecasting
Industrual plastic moulding
giftware

V.M.C. LTD
Chertsey, Surrey 25,000 sq.ft.
Sub-contract vacuum plating
Spraying

LESNEY UK OPERATIONS LTD
(Manufacturer of Toys for sale to Lesney International)

TOOLMAKING FACTORIES
Enfield 10,000 sq.ft.
Tottenham 20,000 sq.ft.
Hackney 36,000 sq.ft.
Raleigh 22,000 sq.ft.

MACHINE MANUFACTURE
Camborne 20,000 sq.ft.
Hackney 30,000 sq.ft.

MANUFACTURE OF TOYS
Hackney Eastway 130,000 sq.ft.
Hackney Lee Conservancy Rd. 2 Factories 235,000 sq.ft.
Hackney Waterden Rd. Development 50,000 sq.ft.
Chingford 30,000 sq.ft.
Abbey Wood 22,000 sq.ft.
Rochford 207,000 sq.ft.
Peterboro' 83,000 sq.ft.
Harlow 20,000 sq.ft.

LESNEY INTERNATIONAL LTD
Product Design, marketing, selling & distrubution

IMPULSE TOYS & TRADING LTD
Rochford International purchasing & sales 5,000 sq.ft.

PACIFIC OPERATIONS
A Lesney Australia 30,000 sq.ft.
AB Lesney Hong Kong 500 sq.ft.
A* Lesney Japan(95) 10,000 sq.ft.

EUROPEAN OPERATIONS
A Lesney UK Sales Ltd 60,000 sq.ft.
A Lesney Belgium 20,000 sq.ft.
A Lesney France 30,000 sq.ft.
A Lesney Germany 50,000 sq.ft.
A Lesney Sweden 20,000 sq.ft.
A* Lesney Norway 500 sq.ft.

LESNEY USA
C New Hampshire (clothes, manufacture for Vogue Dolls) 10,000 sq.ft.
AC Paterson N.J. (Doll manufacture) 60,000 sq.ft.
C Moonache 130,000 sq.ft.

LESNEY CANADA
A 40,000 sq.ft.

A Warehousing, Sales Companies
B Subcontract finished products
C Manufacturing Company
* Newly Formed

Lesney Group Total 1,500,000 sq.ft.

---

above is a table showing the company's structure, taken from Lesney Scene.

Trading in the group throughout 1977 and 1978 continued to be very profitable. Lesney Products were awarded their fifth Queen's Award to Industry in 1977. The Lesney Products Group had a total worldwide work–force of six thousand. In a message to the work–force the Chairman Mr Leslie Smith wrote: 'Although the current year has started cautiously, I cannot see any reason why we cannot continue our success.'

In late 1977 an old building opposite the Eastway plant was bought, redesigned and partly rebuilt to house under the same roof the two-hundred-and-fifty members of the Design Development, Machine Tool Development and Press Tool

sections in Waterden Road. On 20 September a new 80,000 square feet factory at Peterborough was opened.

In 1978 a further freehold factory was purchased at Hall Lane, Chingford, Essex, which was used to consolidate the work of both the Tottenham toolroom and the Ladysmith Road, Enfield toolroom and the existing Chingford factory. Lesney also purchased a further diecasting business, Metal Castings (Worcester) Ltd, which in the main made aluminium castings. In the same year Lesney acquired A.M.T., a manufacturer of plastic construction kits in the U.S.A. which was to be complementary to the company's own U.K. plastic kit business. *Lesney Scene Summer* 1978: "Mr Leslie Smith commented 'Apart from obtaining substantial new businesses in the U.S.A. we hope to

extend distribution of the A.M.T. kits, which are mainly larger scale highly detailed trucks, vans and cars, in other markets, especially Europe'." The A.M.T. project immediately suffered production problems as A.M.T. were in the process of resiting the factory from Detroit to Baltimore.

Whilst it lasted, Lesney marketed the A.M.T. range as a separate range of Matchbox plastic kits. *Tekerian:* "If you took a look at the ranges, Matchbox plastic kits were predominently airplanes, small cars, motorbikes, ships and military vehicles. A.M.T. kits on the other hand didn't compete with Matchbox kits because they were into trucks and larger scale cars and Star Trek." When Lesney went into receivership in 1982 A.M.T. was not bought by Universal, but instead by Ertl.

Other acquisitions in 1977 included Vogue Dolls. The *Sunday Times* 1978: "Lesney bought the rundown Vogue Corporation for a modest (undisclosed) sum from Tonka, revamped the range from heads to frillies . . .'It's working out to be a fantastic investment' Smith enthuses 'Turnover was a few hundred thousand dollars. Now we're talking in millions.' Lesney invested some $750,000 developing its U.S. foothold in this staple sector of the toy business, and is already budgeting for Ginny Doll sales of about $5 million . . . Smith has no doubt that 1978 will be a very good year for Lesney'." Lesney earned a profit after tax for the period ending January 1978 of £5.4 million. During the same period the turnover had risen from £55.4 million to £88.9 million.

For the period ended January 1979 the company's operating profit decreased from £9.9 million to £6.8 million because of the cost of financing the A.M.T. acquisition and increased interest charges, but it should be remembered that at this time the toy trade in Britain was in turmoil. The recession led to a severe reduction in disposable income for the purchase of toys. In 1979 the famous Meccano group went into liquidation and soon afterwards Mettoy was involved in a management buy–out.

THE RECESSION BITES

Despite being able to fend off many of the effects of the recession, the economic reality of Britain at that time could not be ignored. In January 1980 the company commenced a programme of rationalisation and steps were taken to make employees redundant. In February 1980 the company's bankers required a report on the financial state of the company and as a result of this an executive chairman Gordon Hay and a financial director Maurice Alberge were appointed in addition to the then existing management. The executive chairman asked Jack Odell to come out of retirement. A meeting was set up between Odell and the bankers, and Odell was asked to rejoin Lesney to supervise the diecast/engineering side of the business. Odell only agreed to go back for one year and was appointed joint Vice Chairman. After three weeks Odell reported: "It's like being the Captain of the Titanic – the whole thing's going down." Odell eventually stayed on until the receivers were called in.

Following extensive negotiations with its bankers Lesney granted fixed and floating charges over the whole of its undertaking to a consortium of bankers on 7 July 1980. In the same year Leslie Smith and Jack Odell were approached by David C.W. Yeh (their eventual successor) to manufacture for Lesney using his Far East resources, i.e. Universal. *Yeh:* "Leslie was concerned that we would steal his technology. He wouldn't listen to his own man in Hong Kong, Peter Olsen the Managing Director of Lesney International, who liked my idea . . . their production costs were far too high."

Yeh had found this reasoning to be illogical because, in his opinion, Far East technology was far ahead of anything in the West. Later that year Olsen was, however, authorised by Lesney to approach Yeh to produce for them a series of Walt Disney character toys. Initially, two Japanese cars were made in Hong Kong as a trial to see if they could match the quality. To

appease U.K. toolmakers they were called No. 76 and No. 77. Lesney had discovered that the cost involved in making these toys made it impossible to produce them in the U.K. Yeh took on the job and delivered it to Lesney at the agreed price and on time.

In 1981 Olsen left to join Yeh at Universal. Yeh had already forecast the demise of Lesney. "The reason why the Matchbox diecast line was not competitive was that all their products came from England, whereas their competitors' products came from the Orient. Their price at Lesney, starting with higher production costs and followed by export duties, did not allow enough of a profit margin for Lesney to do advertising." This, of course, was more true for the goods going into the U.S.A. as opposed to goods going into the E.E.C. which did not attract onerous duties.

Yeh also believed that the American market had performed badly because Lesney had not catered for that market with a range of American cars, whereas Lesney's main competitors had young consumers in the U.S.A. who were more likely to buy an American car rather than, for example, an Austin Mini, which, although popular in Britain was virtually unheard of in the U.S.A.

Draft accounts prepared to 31 January 1982 showed, on sales of £72.4 million, an operating loss of £7.5 million before extraordinary costs of redundancy, which totalled an additional £1.04 million. The company ran into severe creditor pressure in early 1982. The sales figures in early 1982 were in line with budget, but during April and May they fell below.

Various freehold properties were disposed of and a total of £500,000 approximately was applied to reduce the bank borrowings.

Throughout 1982 negotiations for the sale of the company were taking place. An early potential purchaser had agreed to give a decision by 28 June 1982. However, the banking consortium indicated in early June 1982 that they would not be justified in making further advances without a firm commitment by the intended purchaser. This was not forthcoming and the company requested its bankers to appoint a Receiver and Manager.

In 1982 Lesney had a workforce of 3,500 and had six operating plants within the United Kingdom as well as over five hundred employees and several operations in twelve other countries.

On 11 June 1982 R.D. Agutter and G.T.E. Parsons, of Peat Marwick Mitchell & Co., were appointed Joint Receivers and Managers. *Tekerian:* "We knew they were coming . . . you've never seen people empty their desks of their personal possessions so fast . . . it was a traumatic but funny situation, you knew that your life was in turmoil and yet people reacted in a funny way. We all went to the pub for lunch, and then came back to meet the receivers."

The Times 12 June: "Lesney Products, the Matchbox Toy makers which has been trying to trade out of a liquidity crisis for almost two years, went into receivership yesterday. But the group, which employs 3,500 people on six sites will continue to trade while joint receivers Mr Guy Parsons and Mr Richard Agutter will attempt to sell the business as a going concern. Lesney, under its new Chairman Mr Gordon Hay who was brought in as a company doctor, had been talking to three or four potential buyers for several months."

It was hoped that these negotiations would be completed

before conditions worsened, but at a board meeting on Thursday the directors decided to call the banks and ask for more money. Without extra cash they knew there was a risk of breaking the law and trading while knowingly insolvent. The first alarm bells rang out in 1980 when a slump in demand and a strong pound brought profits down to a loss of £3.6 million. Mr Paul Tapscott, of stockbrokers Montagu, Loebl, Stanley & Co, which first brought Lesney to the stock market in 1960, stepped down as Chairman and was replaced by Mr Hay.

Mr Maurice Alberge was appointed Finance Director of Accounts. Ernst and Whinney were asked to report on the company to banks. A second report by Price Waterhouse was commissioned seven months ago and that is understood to recommend a sale."

The majority of Lesney's assets were transferred into a 'shell' company called Matchbox Toys Ltd. However, the liabilities remained with Lesney and the Receivers began to look for buyers of Matchbox. Even though the bank was owed money, a further loan was agreed upon to enable Matchbox Toys to maintain production in anticipation of Christmas sales. *The Times* 18 September: 'Matchbox hope – A joint receiver of the collapsed toy group Lesney Products said yesterday that prospects looked good for the sale of the manufacturing and marketing of toys as a going concern. Mr Richard Agutter has set up a new company, Matchbox Toys, to assist an eventual sale. At the same time the receivers sold off Lesney Industries to a management buy-out group headed by Ron Perryman, the Managing Director of this Lesney subsidiary.'

THE UNIVERSAL TAKEOVER

David Yeh had flown to London to make a bid for Lesney Products even though he realised that negotiations were still underway with another company. *Yeh:* "Lesney had a history of being able to sell anything it could make until Mattel came along in 1968 with Hot Wheels. Mattel made their product in Hong Kong, obviously much cheaper than it could be made in England.

"They shipped the product to the U.S. duty free while Matchbox was paying 12% or 13% duty. At the time we were the smallest company in the race for Lesney." Other companies interested included Mattel and Fisher Price.

The negotiations with Fisher Price fell through and Yeh believed that he was in with more than an evens chance of succeeding. Yeh told the receivers that he was only interested in acquiring Lesney if one of the two remaining factories were sold off (Rochford or Lee Conservancy Road, Hackney).

Yeh submitted his offer of £16.5 million and at the same time moved his board of directors from Hong Kong to London so that they could liaise directly and immediately with Gordon Hay and the banks. The Midland Bank considered Yeh's offer and his attached conditions and ordered the receivers to accept it forthwith.

An agreement was signed on the 24 September 1982 and Universal headed by David Yeh became the new owners of Matchbox; by signing the agreement Universal had doubled its size. *Yeh:* "It was

the bargain of the year . . . it was the bargain of the century . . . I didn't realise just how valuable a trade name it was."

The Times 25 September 1982: "Hong Kong group buys Matchbox – Matchbox Toys, part of the crashed Lesney Products Co., has been sold to Universal International (Holdings) of Hong Kong. Mr Guy Parsons said yesterday that the price was "very substantial" but warned that there was no hope for any recovery for shareholders. Neither he nor the buyers, whose world toy sales total more than £100 million a year, would disclose the figure.

Mr David Yeh, Universal Chairman said the deal gave Universal a United Kingdom manufacturing base "from which we can penetrate the Common Market".

Mr Robert Simpson, who moves in as Matchbox Managing Director, said "Universal intended to go ahead with the previous board plans to reduce Matchbox operations into one manufacturing plant." At present there are two factories at Hackney and Rochford, Essex, each employing about one thousand people."

Odell had approached the receivers and bought a quantity of machines, tooling and equipment from them. He later founded his own new diecasting company trading under his old wartime radio call–sign 'Lledo'!

The Universal Group was owned and controlled by Mr David C.W. Yeh who was born in Shanghai, China, on 3 September 1929. He was raised in Shanghai and studied Banking and Finance at St. John's University. He left university to become a trainee at Hong Kong's Chekiang First Bank.

After six years in the bank his banker father, who had moved to Hong Kong from Shanghai

before the communist take over, persuaded Yeh to go into the plastics business. *Yeh:* "I left China when its economy was booming . . . I left because my father had a job in Hong Kong so I had to follow.

If it wasn't for that I probably would never have left Shanghai . . . nobody could have known that within a year or so the country would fall into the hands of the communists (1949)". Yeh then became a plastics salesman selling German plastic raw material to Hong Kong companies. *Yeh:* "I knew at that time it was a plastics world . . . "

During the mid 1950s just as the "Matchbox" Series was becoming established, David Yeh heard that the Louis Marx toy company were planning to establish a manufacturing plant in Hong Kong. Yeh arranged an interview with Louis Marx himself and was offered the job of manager working directly with Louis Marx. Yeh regarded his time with the Marx organisation as being his apprenticeship to the toy industry.

Yeh: "Louis always talked about Matchbox . . . he even came out with a similar line but in plastic and not diecast . . . they were also put in a type of match box and they sold pretty well for two or three years, especially in America, but they were crude.

"Matchbox was already very popular . . . I remember reading about the Coronation Coach of 1953 . . . " Yeh stayed with the Marx organisation for eight years. *Yeh:* "Louis was the first American who had the vision that the Far East was going to be the production base for toys in the future . . . he had gone to Japan first and then Hong Kong . . . I got all the necessary coaching from Louis directly... "

In 1964 Yeh used his U.S.

$10,000 savings to launch his own company – Universal Doll Dress and Universal Traders. He set up a factory in Hunghom and leased fourteen sewing machines. His company manufactured doll dresses and by using many of the contacts made at Marx turned over U.S. $200,000 in his first year. In 1967 one of the only two diecast toy companies in Hong Kong came up for sale; Yeh bought this company Modern Diecasting for H.K. $80,000 and renamed it Universal Diecasting. In the same year he created a further new company – Universal Manufacturers Limited – in Taiwan, which made wooden toys. In 1987 the company was still in existence, although its emphasis had shifted to high technology electronic toys.

In 1971 the Universal Group began plastic manufacturing in Hong Kong. One year later Universal International (Holdings) Ltd (U.I.H.) was formed to consolidate the marketing and manufacturing activities of the continually growing Universal Group. The shareholders of U.I.H. formed a sister company called Uni-Investors Ltd, which acquired a 100,000 square feet factory building which in turn was leased to Unitoys.

The Universal Group then began to look for ways to increase their sales in the U.S.A. Yeh realised that by being a sub–contractor he was vulnerable to market forces. His price always had to be competitive and better than his fellow sub–contractors, and he felt that to ensure the future success of Universal he had to establish a marketing company in the U.S.A.

In 1977 Kidco Inc. was formed in Chicago to market and distribute Universal Products in the U.S.A. The following year

Uni–Investors Ltd bought 80% of L.J.N. Toys Ltd, which was a small toy importer and distributor in New York.

L.J.N. had been losing money but it did own a couple of exclusive licenses, one of which was for the Extra Terrestrial (E.T.) figure, the star of Steven Spielberg's hugely successful film 'E.T.'. Yeh reacted quickly to the film, produced the figures and then quickly dropped the project as he had learned already in the toy industry that fads and fashions come and go too quickly.

In 1980 the Universal Group acquired further factory space (100,000 square feet) in Macau, under the name of Macau Toys Ltd. The Macau government were successfully recruiting a variety of manufacturers to the peninsula, all being tempted by inexpensive labour and no duty tariffs. The following year a further company was created – Macau Diecasting Toys Ltd and the majority of Universal's Hong Kong operations were transferred to Macau.

In 1983 with Matchbox International only three months old, it was agreed that the research and development of the Matchbox diecast ranges be retained by the R & D Department in Enfield, Middlesex.

Models of Yesteryear would still continue to be made at the Rochford factory in Essex, along with the successful Matchbox plastic kits. *Tekerian:* "The return on investment for a plastic kit is very low compared to a diecast model, but, having said that, plastic kits are really amongst the most profitable ranges that Matchbox has ever had." The factory at Hackney which had closed down was put on the market for sale by the Receiver. It was finally sold in 1988 for use as single manufacturing units and extensive alterations took place Universal then put into operation their plans to get

Matchbox back up and running. The tools for the Matchbox Miniatures were moved to Macau and by May 1983 the first shipment of Macau–produced diecast Matchbox cars left for the world.

Soon afterwards the entire Superking range was also being made in the 169,030 square feet Macau factory. In early 1987 Matchbox moved the production of the Yesteryear range from Rochford to Macau, and by mid 1987 everything that had anything to do with the manufacture of Matchbox diecast was in the Far East save for the Research and Development, which was kept at Enfield. The Rochford factory was kept open and produced the Matchbox plastic model kits and pre-school products – to supply the local markets and to save on the cost of shipping these bulky items from Asia to the Western markets.

Within three years of the takeover Matchbox was making a U.S. \$6 million profit. In 1986 Matchbox Toys were declared the number one top seller in Europe and although Lesney had abandoned the Japanese market Matchbox were now making significant in-roads into that potentially untapped market. By acquiring Matchbox and relocating the entire manufacturing to the Far East, Yeh had achieved two basic criteria: reduction of production costs to remain steady and competitive and the creation of a low risk income generating all year round world–wide business. *Yeh:* "I didn't think I could get into the Chinese market that quickly if I didn't have Matchbox . . . Matchbox gave me a franchise to go anywhere I wanted to go."

In 1986 Matchbox Toys Limited (U.K.) began negotiations through Kenner Parker to buy the Dinky trade mark. By early 1987 through brilliant nego-

tiations a deal was completed for a relatively low price. *Yeh:* "Kenner owned it and when Airfix went under I asked them for a price for Dinky.

They gave me a ridiculous price and I said I wasn't interested. Then, after a few more years, Kenner had difficulties and then I got it for a much lower price." To protect the Dinky Trade Mark, a series of Matchbox Miniatures were packaged in Dinky blister packs.

The first Dinky prototypes were shown at the Harrogate Toy Fair in January 1988. *The Financial Times* 21 December 1987: "Dinky, one of the most evocative names in toy making, is being reborn as a brand for miniature cars.

Matchbox intends introducing a range of diecast metal miniature vehicles branded as Dinky later next year. However, the new Dinkys will be manufactured in Asia, almost certainly at the huge diecasting plant in Macau, operated by Matchbox, part of the Universal Holdings Group of Hong Kong.

Matchbox makes all its diecast models in Macau and China. This year it ended diecast model manufacturing in the U.K. when in transferred production of its Yesteryear range from its Rochford plant in Essex. Matchbox, the world's largest producer of diecast toys, purchased the Dinky name this year from Kenner Parker, the U.S. toy company. Mr Gerry Tekerian, Matchbox Marketing Manager for the U.K. said that the new range would be 'collectable'.

The company had to start "from scratch" with the Dinky range because there were no production moulds. Mr Tekerian declined to give further details on the scale of the new models, their styling or packaging. Dinky was a victim of the spate of company collapses that

changed the face of the U.K. toy industry in the early 1980s."

Mr Yeh believes that to survive and grow Matchbox Toys must expand. Matchbox Toys will be leading the way into the 1990s with new ideas for the toy world.

Matchbox Toys will not just be regarded as being a diecast toy manufacturer, as was seen in 1986 and 1988 when Matchbox Toys purchased the licence to produce two Rubik's games, one of which, Rubik's Magic Puzzle sold over eight million pieces in 1986/1987.

In 1988 Universal Matchbox is regarded as being one of the world's leading manufacturers of toys and produces diecast models sold in one hundred and twenty countries throughout the world.

In 1986 Universal Matchbox turned in net sales of U.S. \$257 million and made a net profit of U.S. \$16.7 million. Mr David Yeh believes that the biggest untapped toy market in the world is China. China has just over three hundred million children and Universal Matchbox has already begun to build financial and cultural bridges with China. A Matchbox collection will be put on permanent display in Shanghai's Children's Palace in 1989. *Yeh:* "I know that from a collectors point of view Matchbox has probably been the most collected toys in the world. Whenever I am talking with anyone and I mention Matchbox it is instantly recognised, and most people then say 'When I was young I played with Matchbox!' I am proud to be the owner of Matchbox."

In 1988 Universal Matchbox employs over five thousand staff world–wide and has manufacturing plants in Hong Kong, Macau, China and Rochford, Essex. Universal Matchbox subsidiaries are found in England, West Germany, Spain, Italy, France, Japan, U.S.A. and Australia.

3 The Early Lesney Toys

FINDING THE WAY 1948 TO 1957

◀ A display of the main colour variations to be found on the early Cement Mixer. In the foreground are two of the Road Roller variants. The example featuring a flywheel is particularly rare.

For nearly a decade (1948 to 1957) Lesney Products made an ad hoc series of toys that are now regarded by enthusiasts as being one of the most collectable Matchbox ranges.

These early Lesney toys (fifteen in total) were never part of a marketing strategy, unlike, for example, the "Matchbox" Series that was developed as an ideal range to cater for the needs of youngsters. No-one at Lesney took the responsibility for the overall marketing of these early toys; instead each one was regarded as an individual project, and seldom did anyone regard the latest toy as being an important step forward. It is only in recent years that these fifteen toys have been classed together and referred to by collectors as The Early Lesney Toys. The majority of these toys had great play value backed up with realism, size, durability and vivid colours. However, with high development costs, short runs and valuable space taken up for storage and materials, the range only existed for nine years.

The first four toys had a road making theme, the Diesel Road Roller, Cement Mixer, Crawler Tractor and Crawler Bulldozer. They were all made between 1947 and 1949, and the fact that Richard Kohnstam of J. Kohnstam & Co. Ltd., (Moko) had not yet begun toy factoring for Lesney is the main reason why none of these toys were sold with boxes. There was, however, one exception, and that is discussed below.

The Aveling Barford Diesel Road Roller was first made in 1948. It measured 4.25" in length and 2.5" in height (10.8 cms x 6.35 cms). *Smith:* "In 1947 we were approached by many companies to make certain diecast components and one chap (Sidney Marks)

asked us to make a toy cap gun. We then thought to ourselves that we should be making toys as the orders on the gun were quite substantial and it would help to even out our year's production as commercial work tended to have bursts and then lulls of activity." Jack Odell decided to base his first Lesney toy on the then current Dinky Road Roller. This is hardly surprising as Britain, between the immediate post-war years and the mid 1950s, was heavily involved in a massive road building programme and this type of toy, even if Dinky had already produced one, was felt to be an ideal way in which to capture the imagination of young children. *Smith:* "In 1948 we decided to invest in some moulds – Jack designed them for the Aveling Barford". *Odell:* "It was one of the best sellers that Dinky had at that time and it was almost the limit of our machine size in those days". The roller was made at The Rifleman pub and was eventually withdrawn in late

1949. During that small period of time four distinct casting versions appeared in an array of different colours.

The earliest models consisted of a body casting with a separate roof featuring the words 'Made in England' underneath; the roof had front and rear supports with a strengthening 'X' between the rear struts, there was a towing hook at the rear of the body and two large hollow rollers at the rear and a smaller front hollow roller cast in two halves supported by a rotating cage. Unlike the Dinky Road Roller, the Lesney toy did not have a baseplate. The basic colour scheme was a green body and roof with unpainted roof supports and rollers.

However, modifications to the tools had to be made, especially in relation to the inside of the body casting where the rear roof strut pins were inserted. This section was strengthened so that the pins no longer protruded all the way through the thicker casting inside the roof. A dot was cast on either side of the word 'in' under the roof and the strengthening 'X' was deleted from the rear roof support. The outer surfaces of the rear rollers were made more concave and this created a more obtrusive hub. The colour of the body remained green, and the rollers were painted in red.

A little later a 23 mm (.88") flywheel was mounted to the left hand side of the toy. *Odell:* "We put flywheels on and we shouldn't have because it was a diesel roller but all we were doing was making toys and not models in those days." Two main colour combinations exist, either the body and roof in green with a yellow flywheel and rollers in red, or the body and roof in orange, flywheel and the rollers in black. These versions are both rare.

For the final version the fly-

32 *The Early Lesney Toys*

wheel was removed and a major modification was made to the body, i.e. the inclusion of a driver. *Odell:* "We were just trying to create a bit more interest . . . " Axles made out of nails were replaced by axles made out of pins. Several colour combinations exist including body and roof in green with red rollers; body and roof in greyish brown and rollers in red; body and roof in pale green and rollers in red and finally body and roof in red and rollers in green. *Odell:* "We used to send the early toys out to a sprayer and the paint was not very easy to get in those days just after the war . . . there was a shortage of everything. Sometimes we just had to have any green . . . it didn't make any difference to us as they were just put into boxes and then sold to shops."

Lesney Products, in the late 1940s early 1950s, did not have the time or the resources to manufacture individual boxes for their toys. They packaged the rollers in large cardboard boxes, twelve to a box. However, a toy distributor who handled the Lesney roller, Betal (J. & H. Glasman Ltd.), did advertise the toy in *Games & Toys* in January 1950 along with a box that featured the words 'Steam Roller'. It would appear that this box was made by Betal to encourage sales.

Made concurrently with the road roller was the Lesney Cement Mixer. *Odell:* "There was a building site down the road and they were using a cement mixer and we went and drew it up." This toy measured 3.5" (8.9 cms) long and consisted of a 'body' which was a frame structure with a motor housing cast as one piece, a barrel with a separately cast arm riveted to a turning handle and two wheels with a single axle. The legend 'Made in England' was cast onto one side of the arm as the export market was beginning to open up. These components

were painted a variety of colours with the barrel, arm and handle always being the same. The most common combination was dark green body and barrel with red wheels. Other colours include pale green or red bodies, and yellow wheels. There was only one main casting variation. Inside the barrel were four platforms spaced equally around the circumference against which the casting ejectors in the mould bore with an ejector mark circle on each platform. On the early models all four platforms are the same height. On later models one of the platforms was increased in height.

The original price of the large Cement Mixer was 3s. 0d (15p), and as with the Road Roller the Mixer was sold in large cardboard boxes, twelve to a box. *Odell:* "Volume begets value . . . that's why nothing was to scale with each other, we just had to make a box full – volume made up the value". Production of this crude toy ceased in 1950. Jack Odell was not proud of the Cement Mixer. "We were jolly good diecasting engineers but we weren't very good toy makers in those days."

The remaining two toys of the road making theme – the Crawler Tractor and Crawler Bulldozer – were first made in 1948. The tractor, some 4 inches (10.2 cms) in length, was a one piece casting. Detailing was included to show the engine block as well as a small chimney stack and a driving lever. The tractor body was cast singly from three simple tools arranged so that the maximum detail could be afforded to the engine. The hollow wheels, upon which ran the rubber tracks, featured three cut-outs on the inner surface. The wheels were kept in position by axles that were either crimped over at both ends or with a large head at one end and crimped over at the other. Most tractors were issued with a driver whose left

arm was cast folded across his lap and a right arm that was to be placed near the driving lever. Various colour schemes are associated with the tractor: all over pale green, dark green, red, orange or a dull yellow. *Odell:* "In those days when we did them for Woolworths they used to take them in boxes of twelve. They liked a variety of colours in the box . . . yellow ones, green ones, that sort of thing." The rubber treads were usually in black and were made by an outside agency known as the Bryn Wah Rubber Company based in London. The tracks were delivered to Lesney in tubes which were then unravelled and cut up with a knife. *Odell:* "They cost more than the model." The Crawler Tractor was never issued with its own box and was packaged in a similar manner to the Road Roller and Cement Mixer. The Crawler Tractor is regarded as being one of the rarer early Lesney toys.

It was an easy and economical way to enlarge the range by converting the tractor into a Bulldozer. The axles were slightly lengthened and a bulldozer blade and simulated hydraulics were added to the basic tractor casting. The side frames and blade were cast as separate components and the blade then clipped into the ends of the frames by means of two cast-in sockets. There are two known casting variations of the bulldozer. Early toys were fitted with a lifting handle on the left-hand side fixed to the front axle outside the blade frame. This added feature enabled children to lift and lower the blade realistically. The second version of the bulldozer was released in 1950 as part of the Prime Mover set. The bulldozer no longer had the lifting handle but instead had a brass washer to cover the slot in the frame. As the Prime Mover set was being distributed as a Lesney Moko toy, the legend

'LESNEY – MOKO. MADE IN ENGLAND' appeared on the lower reverse side of the blade. A further casting difference between the 1948 and the 1950 versions was that the three cut-outs on the inner surface of the wheels were now filled in. The bulldozer was not issued with the driver as found on the tractor. The later version was nearly always fitted with green rubber treads instead of the normal black. A small run of later bulldozers were fitted with black treads. Various colour schemes are associated with the Crawler Bulldozer – all over pale green, dark green, red, orange, yellow and, for the bulldozer issued with the Prime Mover, bright yellow body, red wheels and blade and with the hydraulics on the blade frame highlighted in gold.

Although otherwise unrecorded, Mr Leslie Smith is convinced that the third model in the 'range' was to have been a Muir Hill Site Dumper approximately the same size as the Road Roller and finished in red and green. Jack Odell remembers that the Muir Hill was made by tool maker Don Rix who started a company with Frank Constable called Condon Productions Ltd. in 1948. *Odell:* "He was my tool maker – he left me and he started making diecastings, but like everybody else during the zinc embargo, packed it in. He made a few but he didn't have the zinc. I bought the mould from him but I never made any." The Muir Hill mould was the inspiration behind the "Matchbox" Series (2a). *Smith:* "We asked Jack to scale down the models of the Road Roller, the Muir Hill and Cement Mixer"

A further new theme was introduced in 1949 – vehicles that could be seen in post-war British streets. The first was a horse-drawn milk cart. The large Milk Cart was first issued in 1949. The length of this toy was 5.4 inches and it was 3.5 inches high (13.8 cms x 8.9 cms). This was the first ever toy to be made at the new factory in Shacklewell Lane. Originally the selling price was 3s. 6d (17.5p) and this eventually went up to 3s. 11d. (19.5p). With

Many early Lesney toys came in various shades of colours. The light green bulldozer and the tan trailer of the large Mover are much sought after colours.

These models were the first to be packaged by Lesney and are illustrated here in their standard colours.

post-war Britain still being affected by petrol rationing, many public related services, out of necessity, used horse-drawn transport. *Odell:* "We felt that kids liked milk carts and we made one because the milkman used to deliver milk to the factory in one."

The body was usually painted in orange, (the same shade as the Crawler Bulldozer), but a few examples have been found in a dark blue. The casting was a very intricate piece of diecasting and included the driver's seating position complete with a foot rest, top rails to ensure the milk crates did not fall off, a double shelf arrangement inside the cart, raised letters 'Pasteurised Milk' on the sides picked out in white, and rear springs with holes for the rear axle. *Odell:* "After we measured the cart we made it wider because

it looked just too thin. All our models were larger than life . . . everyone of them was a caricature of a model and not actually a model."

There are two different body castings. The earliest type had the driver's seat cast close to the top of the cart and in addition the offside front gap between the rail and the top is filled in. Later types had the driver's seat raised up, which created a larger gap between the seat and the top of the cart, and had two casting circles to the rear of the seat. The horse was attached to the cart by fragile shafts. A peg on one side of each shaft secured the horse in place. There are two distinct horse castings. Early horses had a very wide hollow area on the underneath of the horse. Later examples had a much narrower

gap and were consequently heavier. The early horses were painted a most unrealistic metallic grey, whereas later versions were a dark brown with white trim applied to mane, feet and tail. Examples have been seen with gold trim highlighting the collar and middle strap. Lesney were not satisfied with their early castings of horses. *Odell:* "We made absolutely accurate measurements of the horse and that's why it is awful. After that all horses were made about 50% bigger to make them look alive . . . if you bought a Britain's (a long established toy company, still in existence, that specialises in figures and animals) horse in those days it was so good it looked as if it would walk away." The driver, basically like the one found on the Crawler

Tractor, but with two extended arms and no hands, was finished in various shades of white and with or without flesh colour trim applied. It should be noted that two of the model's components, the driver and the horse, were common to the Rag and Bone Cart which is described next.

Each Milk Cart was issued with six metal milk crates, and there are two distinct castings of these. Early crates had two open sides whereas later crates were slightly larger and featured four open sides. As with the driver, various shades of white can be found and some bottle tops were highlighted in red. The Milk Cart was the first early Lesney toy known to have been issued in its own Lesney box. *Smith:* "The Milk Float was a success because it was a recognised thing."

The Milk Cart was followed by a model known as the Rag and

Bone Cart. This was based on a typical totter who would have been seen driving his horse and cart around the post-war streets of London. The cart including the shafts to affix the horse measured just over 5" (12.7 cms). The framework for the horse shafts was affixed to the cart by a rivet beneath the cart. As with the Milk Cart this toy had its own driver (identical casting) who was afforded a foot and back rest. On each side of the cart was featured a high hoarding with the legend "Rag & Bone Merchants". The wheels were secured by axles, one end having a dome and the other crimped. The horse was the same casting as was found on early examples of the Milk Cart, i.e. with a very wide hollow area underneath. Each Rag and Bone Cart came with seven pieces of junk: a man's bicycle frame, the wheel from a mangle, the headboard section of an iron bedstead, a cistern, a tin bath, a bucket and a slatted box open at one end. With the exception of the latter, which was painted in brown-grey, the rest of the junk pieces left Lesney in an unpainted state. The most common paint scheme for the Rag and Bone Cart was overall bright yellow (a similar shade to the Prime Mover Bulldozer) with red wheels including the surfaces and the spokes. Other colours include a pale green (similar to the shade used on the bulldozer) and white. The horse was finished in metallic grey, whereas the driver was found in various shades of brown. Each toy came packaged in its own box, very similar in size and design to the Milk Cart. *Odell:* "I was so disappointed; I made ten gross and they stuck . . . they wouldn't sell. I think we just flogged the last few out. Now I don't know why they didn't sell because the Milk Cart was a marvellous seller and the Rag & Bone Cart just didn't sell at all."

This everyday street range was extended in 1949 with the Soap Box Racer, a miniature replica of a youngster riding on his homemade go-cart. This model, which Smith maintains never went into full production, consisted of a simulated plank of wood and box which described 'Soap' on one side and 'Soda' on the other. Riveted to the front of the racer was a cross-frame with an axle for the small front spoked wheels. The wheels at the rear were much larger. Very little attention was paid to the axles, the ends were just pushed over to prevent the wheels falling off. The upper half of the model was painted in a copper-bronze colour, with the underneath left unpainted. The boy figure was cast separately and was painted overall in dark brown, but with his face, hands and lower legs picked out in a flesh colour. The boy's hands were cast so that they could easily grasp his steering reins, which were represented by an elastic band connected to the front axle via a hole directly above.

A small number of Soap Box Racers were made with blank bases. The other known variation is a Soap Box Racer with the legend 'A LESNEY PRODUCT – MADE IN ENGLAND' cast on the base. These latter models were most probably made for the overseas market and complied with regulations governing manufacturers intending to export their goods. Odell maintains that just over 1,400 Soap Box Racers were produced. *Odell:* "I remember making the mould myself, it was an absolute failure that never made the grade. We made ten gross and then let the wholesalers have them . . . they took a few of them and they were sold." It does appear strange that if the model had been released it was not boxed. Smith is adamant that the Soap Box Racer was rejected by the toy factors and wholesalers as it had no volume value. *Smith:* "We always insisted upon quality from the beginning. This is where we won over all the smaller people around us in the diecast trade. We only had one flop – it was the Soap

Exceptionally difficult to find are the Soap Box Racer, the Milk Cart in blue and the Rag and Bone Cart in green.

Box Racer because it had no volume."

The next toy to appear was unique for Lesney in that it was made from tin and had a clockwork motor. Jumbo the Elephant was first made in 1950 and it retailed for 5s. 11d. (25p). Mr Smith recalled how Richard Kohnstam had shown him and Jack Odell a tinplate clockwork elephant that J. Kohnstam & Co. Ltd., had been importing into England from Germany prior to World War II. He had obtained a recent example of the toy

Lesney as the Korean War was under way and there were strong rumours in the trade that toy manufacturers would soon be deprived of the use of zinc. Richard Kohnstam persuaded them to proceed with the project. Lesney contracted out to a local firm the task of making the pressed sheet metal bodies, the tin litho printing and the clockwork mechanism. The tin body was made in two equal halves which were kept in place by six tin tabs. A simple clockwork motor was fitted

'ambles' forward from side to side forwards.

Mr Smith explained why the legs were diecast and not tin – (Blomer and Schüler elephants had four tin legs). Pride was the real reason behind it – as not one part of the elephant had actually been made by Lesney, who were, of course, attempting to promote themselves as a diecast toy producer. Each leg was individually numbered 1–4, although there was no difference to either front or rear legs. However, the numbering did

to the Blomer and Schüler box, although there was no mention of Lesney on the box. There were two different types of box – both measuring 4.25" x 3.75" (10.8 cms x 9.5 cms). The first type was printed in blue and yellow and made no mention of Moko, whereas the second in red and black did.

Jumbo was only produced during 1950 and 1951. Jack Odell recalls that fifty gross of the toy were made. Lesney were never comfortable with it as a toy and they did not believe that the

Left: The post war Blomer & Schüler tinplate clockwork elephant made circa 1948 in the U.S. Zone of Germany. Right: The Lesney version with box.

elephant, made by Blomer & Schüler, in the U.S. Zone of Germany in 1949. Blomer and Schüler used the 'Jumbo' as their trademark on all their novelty tinplate toys from the 1930s onwards. Lesney were 'playing with fire' by copying it! Early mock-ups were made of the elephant based upon parts of the actual toy but changed so as not to incur charges of blatant copying. Time, however, was against

within the body. The mechanism was ordered from a small local company called Gordon Thoroughgood, who had also supplied the motor for the Moko drummer boy referred to in Chapter One. This mechanism powered a lever and rod with the rod connected to the front and rear legs on each side of the elephant. When wound the levers moved the rods and, balancing rather precariously, the elephant

assist the work-force in assembly. *Smith:* "Well, four legs make an elephant . . . " A piece of grey wool was retained by a tab at the rear of the elephant. Mr Smith confirmed that the wool was bought from a local wool shop just round the corner from Shacklewell Lane, and joked "We got a lot of tails from one ball of wool". Each elephant was packed in its own box – again rather similar in size and design

future lay in clockwork tinplate toys.

The decision to end production was made for Lesney with a complete clampdown on the use of zinc at the climax of the Korean War and no more elephants were made after early 1951.

One of the largest early Lesney toys measuring 13.25" (30.35 cms) was the Prime Mover, Trailer and Bulldozer. It was first made in 1950 but production ceased during the zinc embargo. After the embargo was lifted,

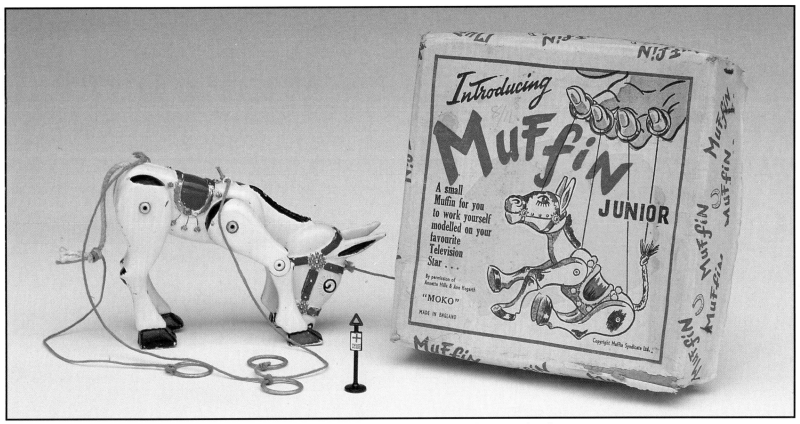

Muffin the Mule was a very early example of a television related toy.

production recommenced in early 1954. The model retailed at 14s. 6d. (72.5p). The set was advertised in *Games & Toys* in September 1953 together with a short reference to "Also The New Matchbox Series."

The Prime Mover itself measured 5" (12.7 cms) in length and was painted in an overall orange colour (the same shade as the Milk Cart). *Odell:* "It was one of the biggest diecastings ever made on our small machines . . . it was far too big but somehow we used to get it out." The mover was made from several castings, one comprising the main body, cab and engine whilst others comprised the rear chassis, loading ramps, the main axle supports, front wings, petrol tanks and driver. The main castings were joined together by crimped-over tongues cast onto the main body, which passed through slots in the rear loading ramps above the rear wheels. The engine was cast with the main body, also painted in

orange but with gold trim applied to the pipes. The engine was concealed by two separate and easily removable engine covers, painted green (a similar shade to the Road Roller). Gold trim was also applied to the rear towing hook and the fuel tanks. Raised letters were cast into the cab doors – 'BRITISH ROAD SERVICES' – and highlighted in white, and also on the area to the rear of the driver's cab – 'MAX 20 MPH No 37'. The driver, a different casting from either the Milk Cart or the Rag and Bone Cart driver but similar to the Crawler Tractor driver, was held in place by a rivet securing his right foot through a hole in the cab's right-hand side. On the underneath of the cab roof was the legend 'MADE IN ENGLAND'. Very late models were not issued with the driver and the locating hole was filled in. Six hollow cast metal wheels, painted grey, were attached to

three separate axles. The wheels measured 28 mm x 9 mm (1.12" x .12"). The trailer measured 8.5" (21.6 cms) in length was normally found in a medium blue colour, although examples do exist in orange or tan (the same shade as found on the Road Roller). The upper surface of the trailer had a diamond non-skid pattern. Underneath the trailer was the cast-in description 'A LESNEY-MOKO TOY', to be found on the left hand side, whilst 'MADE IN ENGLAND' was on the right hand side. The two hollow metal chocks were painted in medium blue and also had a diamond non-skid pattern on their sloping faces. These enabled the bulldozer (already described) to move up onto the trailer. Once again the trailer featured six diecast wheels in grey. The wheels on the trailer were smaller and measured 22 mm x 8 mm. Joining the tractor to the trailer was a separately cast towing

bar. This was issued in several finishes including medium blue; silver or just bare metal. The Prime Mover set was packaged in a large dark blue box with or without two labels affixed to either end. The labels featured 'PRIME MOVER TRAILER AND BULL-DOZER' in red and 'A LESNEY-MOKO TOY MADE IN ENGLAND', with LESNEY-MOKO in blue repeated several times. Jack Odell estimates that some three to four hundred gross were manufactured.

'Muffin the Mule' had been created by Ann Hogarth who formed the Muffin Syndicate. They approached the British Broadcasting Corporation (B.B.C.) in 1946 with their idea of a children's television programme. The show was presented by Annette Mills and was first transmitted by the B.B.C. on the 20 October 1946.

In 1949 Alf Gilson of A. Gilson Ltd. had a factory at 1A

Shacklewell Lane, Dalston, E8, when Lesney were still at The Rifleman on Union Row. Odell remembers Gilson saying, "This place is far too big for me, I only need one floor and part of another area." *Odell:* "We said we'd rent the rest off him." The proprietor Alf Gilson had been an electrician by trade and had diversified into inexpensive diecast toys. He made diecast toys such as tractors, but suddenly found himself with a very good toolmaker who knew everything there was to know about patterns. Alf Gilson saw the potential of these television characters and understood the growing potential of television. Gilson approached the Muffin Syndicate to obtain a licence to manufacture Muffin the Mule puppets. After discussions with Miss Mills he agreed to make a royalty payment in advance. Gilson, however, was not in a position to totally fund the project himself and approached J. Kohnstam & Co. Ltd. He persuaded them to provide the necessary capital to reserve the raw materials and pay 50% of the tooling costs and all of the advance royalties. Gilson's toolmaker made Muffin the Mule. Unfortunately for both J. Kohnstam & Co. Ltd. and Gilson the Korean War intervened and the government imposed a ban on the use of zinc for toys. It is still unclear whether Gilson managed to manufacture any of the puppets prior to the embargo. Advertisements placed by J. Kohnstam & Co. Ltd. in Games & Toys in 1950 and 1951 would suggest that the toy had been made and was available. *Smith:* "He saw no future in the toy trade and so he went to Canada. I believe he sold all his rights to Kohnstam."

A. Gilson Ltd. closed down and Lesney took over the other half of

the factory as they believed that by concentrating on industrial components, such as windscreen wipers, on a sub-contract basis, they could weather the restrictions imposed by the ban.

With the lifting of the zinc ban in 1952, Richard Kohnstam, who had already invested heavily in the Muffin the Mule project, approached Lesney with a proposal that they begin manufacturing the Muffin puppet and Kohnstam would market and distribute the toy. A 5% royalty fee of the retail price was paid to the Muffin the Mule Syndicate. Lesney was not afforded the privilege of being credited with the toy – all boxes merely stated Moko – and there was no manufacturer's mark on the toy.

The Junior puppet was made out of zinc alloy with the body cast in two halves, riveted together internally. The head and neck, once again in two halves, was attached to the body by an internal rivet. The rear hollow legs were pivoted at both the top and the knees. The rear right inside leg bore the inscription 'MADE IN ENGLAND'.

The basic colour of the puppet was off-white, although shades do vary from cream to pure white. Black trim was applied to the hooves, insides of the ears, mane, eyes, nostrils and tops of the legs. The saddle and bridle were in bright red trimmed with gold. This trim varied because of the lack of any quality control. *Smith:* "We used a lot of out-workers who did the painting of the components – they used their prams and filled them up."

The 3 inch (7.6 cms) puppet's tail, made out of locally obtained string, was tied to one of four circular washers made out of zinc alloy. The other strings in a pinkish red colour were attached to the puppet by means of cast in ringlets on the puppet's forehead, neck and back.

The puppet was packaged in a simple cardboard box, the panels of which were stapled together. There were two differently sized boxes during production. The first box measured 5.8 inches square x 1.5 inches (14.8 cms x 3.8 cms), whilst the second box measured 6.5 inches square x 1.7 inches (16.5 cms x 4.4 cms). The front panel on both types featured an attractive drawing of the Muffin Junior with a description to appeal to potential customers 'A small Muffin for you to work yourself, modelled on your favourite television star . . .'

The actual quantities of sales were good. Jack Odell estimates that 50,000 Muffins were made. Production of the puppet was, however, short-lived as Leslie Smith realised that it was at most probably a passing fad. Lesney began winding down the project in 1955 with the death of Miss Mills. *Smith:* "Oh, it was a tremendous success and it surprised even us at the sheer volume – it was a very good line. I often wonder how many dining room tables Lesney indirectly damaged as a result of Muffin dancing up and down on its four strings . . ."

In 1950 some of the profits made from the Cement Mixer and Road Roller project were used to fund a new idea for Lesney, the manufacture of a large State Coach which was to be a souvenir to celebrate the forthcoming Festival of Britain in 1951. The large coach measuring 15.75 inches (40 cms) was made at the Shacklewell Lane Factory in 1950. *Smith:* "The coach was never meant to be a child's toy in any sense – purely a souvenir. The Festival was an attempt by the Government to cheer up the public and it was a stir to get Britain back – Come on you visitors, come and see us".

Very detailed and accurate drawings were produced. In fact, Jack Odell commissioned a woodcarver to make the patterns. Odell had seen some of his work in a local church. Odell used all his engineering skills to make four tools. Production began in late 1950 at the Shacklewell Lane premises, producing the impressive looking coach containing King George VI and Queen Elizabeth, pulled by four pairs of large greys handled by four riders. *Odell:* "With the Festival of Britain coming up, I bought a pantograph . . . a three dimensional pantograph . . . it cost the earth but it could make fantastic shapes and I decided to make a State Coach."

The first version of the coach, made initially in 1950 to commemorate the Festival of Britain, was stopped more or less at once due to the outbreak of the Korean War. *Odell:* "I made only about a dozen castings. We were not able to use zinc for toys as it was on the banned list. Whatever you were using before you now only got a quarter. The moulds for the Coronation Coach were put under the four legs of a work bench . . . it was a bit low and it gave me backache!"

The main body of the coach was comprised of two equal halves crimped together at the top of the rear section, from within the coach, and at the top of the front section, once again from within the coach. The front and rear pairs of Tritons were slid into place between the curved extension arms of the coach and secured by a nail which was then crimped at one end.

The wheels were then placed directly beneath the pairs of Tritons on their own crimped axles. The front pair of wheels was further riveted to the underneath of the Tritons enabling them to have a restrictive pivot. The roof was placed on a non-permanent basis to rest on a ridge formed under

Lesney Coronation Coaches. The King's body is just visible within the large coach on the right.

the coach. The two royal figures were cast onto a seat inside the coach. Not much detail was afforded to their legs – in fact neither the King nor the Queen was given feet! The casting did not mention by whom or where the coach was made.

The horses were not made from pressure fed castings of zinc but were slush mouldings in lead, which produced a more pliable product, i.e. much softer and less brittle than diecast zinc. Lesney did not have the resources to make the horses themselves; so they contracted the job out to Benbros, who were located in Walthamstow. Lesney had previously considered the Barrett brothers who were trading under the name of Barrett & Sons in Holloway, London, N7. *Odell:* "Barretts tried to make them – they made a mould but they were not successful. The horses were in lead, I daren't have lead in my place because you've only got to get a penny weight of lead in a pot with two tons of metal and the metal goes useless – falls to bits." The hollow horses were joined to the square 10 inch (25.4 cms) long horse-bar by panel pins crimped at one end, and disguised by a diecast housing member on either side of the horse-bar. The horses, which when picked up would be prone to rotating, were further secured by wire pins which passed through the horses, which had loops and which in turn held in place the gold linked chains running on either side of the four pairs of horses to the bracket on the front axle. The horse-bar ended in a hook which fitted into the same bracket by way of a tailor-made oval slot.

The 1950 State Coach was only ever produced in a gold finish. All examples seen of the gold coach have roofs which were painted underneath. A small quantity only were made because of the clamp down on the use of zinc in the toy trade due to the Korean War. Some of the coaches undoubtedly were 'stolen' from Lesney, but none were officially released. The balance were taken off the assembly line and put into storage.

In 1952, with the forthcoming Coronation of Queen Elizabeth II, Lesney saw an opportunity to recoup their expenses incurred in making the tools and moulds for the 1950 State Coach. *Odell:* "One day I woke up and my wife said 'You're a lucky fellow' I said 'Why?' and she said 'The King died . . . you've got a Coronation Coach and there will be a Coronation in twelve months'."

A few days after the King died zinc came off ration and Lesney were back in the business of making diecast toys. The tools and moulds were quickly reinstated and production began almost immediately. An estimated 300 coaches were made and assembled until it was discovered by an assembly line foreman that the coach still had the two royal figures inside. Lesney realised that this oversight would make them look unprofessional; so production ceased at once. The tools were modified in two ways:

The male figure was cut off at the waist, leaving only a tell-tale sign of his legs still visible in the coach.

The words 'Made in England' were cast onto the middle of the right hand drop beneath the coach.

The double figure coaches were released by Lesney and mixed up with the single figure coaches. In total Lesney Products made 33,000 of the large coaches. Unlike the 1950 version, the 1953 Coach was found in three distinct colours: gold paint, gilt plating and silver plating. Undoubtedly the silver coach is by far the scarcest of the three 1953 versions. Lesney did not have the vacuum coating process in the early 1950s. *Odell:* "The idea was that they were going to be plated with silver nitrate . . . but they used to go black . . . we

got a lot of rejects so in the end, because the demand was there, we painted them in gold."

The horses were painted in many shades of white varying from pure white to a more creamy shade. All horses had grey manes, tails and hooves with red, white and gold blankets underneath gold saddles. The blinkers and reins were finished in black, and the four outriders were finished in black riding hats, flesh coloured faces and hands, red tunics, white breeches and black boots.

The horse-bar and hook was usually finished in pure white, but once again examples in either gold or even bare metal have been found. Although rather obscure it is perhaps worth stating that a pin rather than a nail was used on the gilt coach to secure the front and rear axle. Obviously there was no marketing of the 1950 Coach because production had to cease so quickly.

However, for the 1953 Coronation Lesney decided to give the toy factoring firm of Eisenmann & Co. Ltd. (instead of J. Kohnstam & Co. Ltd.) the majority of the coaches. Eisenmann & Co. Ltd. took out an advertisement in Games & Toys magazine in September 1952. Richard Kohnstam would have liked more. *Odell:* "I would only let him have two dozen gross a week because I couldn't let down my other regulars." However, Kohnstam did so well with the coach that from then on Moko was given exclusive rights for the home market.

The Coronation Coach was packaged in a red coloured cardboard box – 16" in length x 2.5" wide and 3.5" in height (40.6 cms x 6.4 cms x 8.9 cms). The box was in fact too low as many coaches have been found with the ornate decoration on top of the roof damaged; invariably the box roof has been pierced by this

part of the coach's roof. On top of the box lid was glued a white label bearing a coloured picture of the coach and the words 'Coronation Coach – Made in England, Lesney Products & Co. Ltd. London'.

The dimensions of the label varied between 6.2 cm) wide and 5.6 cm wide. Each box contained a cardboard tongue to protect the horses and an abundance of pink coloured tissue paper to ensure that the coach was not damaged in transit. Some 1953 Coronation Coaches have been found in boxes as above, but with a further label covering up 'Lesney Products & Co. Ltd. London' and reading instead 'Morris & Stone (London) Ltd.' The coaches inside these boxes were Lesney made.

Sam Morris started up his toy business in 1946, not originally as a diecast firm, but as a toy factor and wholesaler. It is known that by 1949 Sam Morris was having toys made for him by other toy firms which he sold under his own company's name. It is believed that because Eisenmann & Co. Ltd. were only selling the large coach within the United Kingdom, Sam Morris saw potential in the United States. Sam Morris placed an order through Lesney for a few thousand large Coronation Coaches, relabelled the red boxes with his own markings and distributed them in America.

The immediate success of the large Coronation Coach inspired Lesney to invest heavily in new tools for a miniature Coronation Coach. This little souvenir sold over one million pieces, and gave Lesney not only the finances to create the "Matchbox" Series in late 1953 but, just as importantly, the confidence to do so. This small coach was the last of the early Lesney toys to have any Moko involvement.

In 1953 Lesney were only one

of many small toy makers in the North-East of London. Other toy makers included Jack and Nathan Benenson (Benbros), and Charles and Benjamin Reid (Charbens), but there was not much separating them in equipment capacity or range. However, the Lesney miniature Coronation Coach was the product that established Lesney and pushed them way ahead of their contemporaries. Just look at what Lesney wrote about themselves in the 1966 Pocket Catalogue:

"It all began in 1953 with a miniature diecast model of the Coronation Coach with its team of eight horses. In Coronation Year over a million were sold, and this tremendous success was followed by the introduction of the first miniature vehicles models packed in matchboxes."

Jack Odell is credited with the idea of scaling down the already assembled large State Coach and issuing a miniature Coronation Coach for the masses of people who showed an interest in the forthcoming Coronation. "The young children would never have seen a Coronation before, and it was an item that I thought would attract people as a souvenir to take away with them after visiting London!" The small coach was also made at Shacklewell Lane. It measured 41 mm in length, excluding the horses, and sold for 2s.11d. (14.5p).

The tools were quickly developed and made by Jack Odell. *Odell:* "I got the patterns for the large coach ... they were about three to four to one up for the big one, and I reduced the pantograph down to ten to one which was as small as it would go, and ran round a piece of perspex and put some plasticine in it and felt that was about the right size." Some members of Lesney's management and workforce were sceptical that such a large coach could be reduced to such a tiny piece of diecast and still remain recognisable. Les Smith was adamant that the coach would not be made unless the quality was good. "We were always insistent on quality, always quality, and this is where we won against all the people around us in the diecast toy trade, including Gilson, Benbros and others – if it wasn't right let's not do it"

However, all their fears were allayed when Jack revealed the first shots of the miniature coach. It was agreed immediately that it was good and production went quickly ahead. The coach had one casting variation. On the rear panel of some coaches between the two rear Tritons were cast the words 'ENGLAND'. This was so as to adhere once again to export regulations.

The horses, eight in all, were attached to the pole. A compromise had to be reached over the number of legs. Of course there should have been thirty two, but Lesney could only produce sixteen! *Odell:* "Somebody at the time said 'If you can sell eight horses with only sixteen legs you'll make a million someday'." Four outriders were on the left hand set of horses, all suitably coloured with red blankets on the horses and the riders in smart red tunics, black trousers, black hats and white faces.

The pole affixed to the horses stated that the model was 'A MOKO TOY BY LESNEY BRITISH MADE'. *Smith:* "The word Moko was put on the mould because it was offered as an exclusive distribution product to Kohnstam. This helped to strengthen his sales potential."

The wheels were all crimped onto the axles. Both silver and gold effect coaches have been reported. However, the gold is more likely to be due to tar-

nishing (even though more realistic) rather than design or production line input. The colour of the horses and the pole varied from a bright pure white to a creamier white. The coach was not plated underneath.

Some collectors still get confused when offered the Benbros coach. There had been a close association between Lesney and Benbros. *Smith:* "Benbros made our horses for the large Coronation Coach and they liked our small coach".

The main difference between the Lesney and Benbros models was that the Lesney Coach had blank carriage doors whereas the Benbros Coach had the 'E.R.' insignia in relief.

Les Smith remarked that the Benbros model did not pose a threat to the Lesney Coach, as they were too far ahead in both production and marketing for the Benbros coach to make any significant dent in the Lesney sales.

Odell: "The day of the Coronation I had ten gross of the small coach in stock and I couldn't give them away. I was so sick of the sight of Coronation stuff that after nine months of them lying in a corner I had them moved away and melted down."

The Coronation Coach was packaged in a multi-coloured box. The end flaps showed the Moko involvement with the product. Richard Kohnstam launched it at the Harrogate Toy Fair in January 1953. Kohnstam also advertised it in *Games & Toys* for January 1953, as did the well-known store of Hamleys of London in several Meccano magazines of early 1953. The box has been credited with being the first type of "Matchbox" with its side panels showing the words 'Coronation Coach – a perfect miniature'. No box variations have been reported.

An advertisement for the

miniature Coach in *Games & Toys* in June 1953 stated that 500,000 had been sold in the first sixteen weeks of production, and also told the trade that there were also 'Four new models in preparation' (a reference to the forthcoming "Matchbox" Series models).

With over one million pieces sold, this was the breakthrough needed by Lesney to give them the capital to ensure rapid expansion.

The miniature Coach appeared on many cakes during the festivities of the 1953 Coronation and this was the start of the name Lesney becoming a household name. However, the Miniature Coach is also significant for two other reasons. Lesney saw the obvious market leaders in diecast toys as being Dinky. *Smith:* "The use of a better zinc and thinner castings, as used in the production of the Miniature Coach, showed Lesney that they could compete with Dinky – Finer casting in comparison with Dinky was one of our successes, and we got it from seeing the thin casting on the small Coronation Coach. "Our whole approach was to make thin castings that were quite capable of standing up to play. By 1953 the quality of zinc was so good it allowed us to produce the thin castings whereas Dinky tool makers only knew from their tradition that the castings must be 'X' thickness."

Secondly, the success of the small coach revealed to Les Smith, who was in charge of marketing, that here was a major factor to success – quality toys in quantity. *Smith:* "When we did the small coach we began to see the advantages of volume. We could make other items the same way, and we showed our first miniatures at the Harrogate Fair in 1954." *Odell:* "The money made on the small Coronation Coach was put into a separate

banking account as I wanted to keep the profit separate . . . I wanted to make a small range of miniatures . . . I was sure that they would sell."

The Bread Bait Press, which was not, of course, a toy, was produced from 1954 until 1957 and was designed by Jack Odell to cater initially for his own fishing needs. It measured 5.3 cm high, was made at the Shacklewell Lane factory and retailed for 2s. 11d. (14.5p). The Bread Press, a device for the sole use of fishermen, was conceived in its entirety by Jack Odell as he had long realised that fishermen needed a way to make durable bait.

Smith: "Yes, Jack was keen on fishing and as subcontractors we used to make a part of a fishing rod and we thought we should make a press of some sort. Jack, who was keen on fishing said 'All right, I'll make one'".

There were three basic parts to the Bread Press: a rectangular frame made out of zinc diecast and painted bright red, a butterfly head attached to a long screw, both in bright diecast, and finally the press itself which was in two equal halves, in bright diecast, both halves featuring a pin-sized hole. Some presses were issued with parts or all of the mechanisms painted green.

The aim of the Bread Press was stated on the box to give 'perfect satisfaction every time' and it achieved this primarily by preventing 'the bait from crumbling'. There are two known versions of the Bread Press; common to both versions is the engraved panel on one side of the rectangular frame – 'LESNEY BREAD BAIT PRESS – MADE IN ENGLAND PAT PEN'.

The Bread Press was never distributed through toy factors but instead Lesney approached a Fish and Tackle retail shop on the Camden Road, Holloway,

The Bread Bait Press guaranteed 'perfect satisfaction every time'.
The Covered Wagon, the last early toy, was primarily for the American market.

London, (Milbournes), and offered them exclusive rights. *Smith:* "He had it for a time, didn't sell too many and so after twelve months we gave it to everyone else." For this exclusive distribution early Bread Bait Presses were cast with the legend 'MILBRO'.

Other authorities believe that the outlets where many of the presses were sold was in fact called Millard Bros Ltd, which was a local sports goods distributor. Their trademark was 'Milbro'. However, once this exclusive distribution agreement with either Milbournes or

Millard had been terminated, Lesney deleted the name from the tool and so post-1955 Bread Presses have no mention of Milbro.

The Bread Press box was designed along similar lines as the miniature range, i.e. a small matchbox. The front of the box was in yellow with red and black decoration and the back of the box, once again in yellow, had black text on how to use the press.

The end flaps in red had no text but the striker panels were taken up with instructions in both German and French, a sure

reflection of both the international appeal of fishing and the beginning of internationalism for Lesney.

The Bread Presses were sold in batches of 24, neatly packaged in an outer box which could be easily used by the retailer both to display and to dispense the presses. *Smith:* "It wasn't a great line, I suppose fishermen are inclined to keep their stuff. It lasted several years but production ceased in 1957."

It now seems surprising that in 1954 after the successful introduction of the first eight models of the new "Matchbox"

Series, Lesney approached the market from the other end by introducing a new range called 'The Major Scale Series'.

The first model produced for the new range was a Massey Harris Tractor, which was developed during 1952. Although this tractor – specified as No. 1 – was released onto the market, none of the other models were. As the Major Scale range did not materialise, the Massey Harris Tractor has been classified by collectors as an early Lesney toy!

The Massey Harris tractor was first issued in 1954 and came about because one of the Lesney toolmakers had a brother working at Massey Harris. Lesney sold the first run of tractors to Massey Harris who ran a promotion featuring the model. There was no mention of Major Scale Series on the early boxes. The tractor measured 8 inches (23 cms) in length and was just over 5.5 inches (14 cms) high. Lesney had recently developed larger capacity machines with these bigger toys in mind. Pre-production samples revealed a weakness in the steering mechanism which was quickly strengthened. The tractor re-tailed for 17s 6d (87.5p). It was made in two equal halves and joined together by rivets on the base and the side in the area of the front wheel axles. No detail was spared including a large bucket seat, steering wheel and

Above: The only model to be actually issued in the Major Scale Series.

Below: The Euclid Quarry Truck was never released. The miniature version gives a clear impression of the larger toy's actual size.

exhaust pipes. The body was painted in red and shades varied from early bright red to later models that had a more orange hue. The legend 'MASSEY HARRIS 745D' was cast into both sides of the body and was highlighted in white while several parts of the engine were detailed with gold paint. The steering wheel has been found with either a red or a beige finish. The wheels were always painted beige including the front wheel steering mechanism. Black rubber tyres were fitted to each wheel, which also featured the legend 'MADE IN ENGLAND BY LESNEY' on both sides. These were made by an outside agency called Poppy. The majority of rear axles were of the usual riveted end, but several later tractors were fitted with axles kept in place by screw heads.

Each tractor came packaged in its own box of which there are known to be several types. Once the promotion with Massey Harris was over Lesney added the words 'No. 1 in Major Scale Series' to the boxes.

Production of the tractor ceased in 1955, although it took at least two years before Lesney stock was exhausted. *Smith:* "It was a very successful product with at least two or three hundred thousand being made. From the beginning I was sending samples worldwide and got orders back." Advertisements for the tractor were carried in *Games & Toys* in April 1954 and March 1955.

The No. 2 was to have been a large Euclid Quarry Truck measuring 11 inches (27.9 cms). *Ward:* "One certainly does exist – one was offered to me for several thousand pounds, I know that it went to an overseas collector, three or four years ago." No. 3 was to have been a very large Diesel Road Roller – approximately 9 inches (22.8 cms) in length. *Odell:* "Yes, the Quarry Truck had two wheels at the front and four at the back. I only made three or four Quarry trucks and two Rollers. All three Major Scale Series were shown to the trade at the British Industries Fair in 1955. There had already been a Moko advertisement in *Games & Toys* in April 1955 advertising the Euclid Truck.

The only known example of the proposed Fowler Big Lion Showman's Engine, circa 1955.

Smith: "We also did a Euclid Lorry, because when we saw the tractor we thought we had better go for that size – it looked all right to us." This lorry, however, was never actually sold (even though the trade had been advised of its imminent arrival and that it would be selling for 25s. 9d. – (129.5p). But what happened to the Euclids seen at the 1955 Fair? Smith: "I can still see the one we had filled up with rubbish and paint. We had had an awful job to get the axle right – it was so large and bent so easily. It was a super model, but we realised when we got the "Matchbox" Series going that they took up too much space . . .'
Odell: "At that time the "Matchbox" Series was going so fast I had to retool all the time. The tools were being run day and night and they were getting old. Then I would make a larger one and in a better way. There was so much money in it compared to the larger scale toys we dumped them. We never got round to making them."

The No. 4 in the series was to have been a model of the Fowler Big Lion Showman's Engine. Progress on the tools for this project was made throughout 1955 and eventually arrived at the stage of producing tooling for all the ancilliary components. These included the front and rear wheels, the side lights, the canopy supports, the steering wheels and the brake wheel. The finished model would have measured 4.5 high, 8.25" long and 3" wide (11.5 cms x 20.5 cms x 8 cms). It was the model's anticipated finished weight and the probable cost in materials which caused the project to be abandoned. Simmons: "It was when they saw the weight that it would have been they thought again. Zinc was still not that easy to obtain and the model would also have been expensive. The plans were later used to produce the Y9/1 Showman's – Jack loved steam driven engines. I remember Ken

THE EARLY LESNEY TOYS 1948 – 1957					
	DATE OF ISSUE	TITLE	FACTORY SITE	PACKAGING	SIMILAR TO "MATCHBOX" SERIES
(1)	1948	Aveling Barford Diesel Road Roller	The Rifleman	Unboxed	1a
(2)	1948	Cement Mixer	The Rifleman	Unboxed	3a
(3)	1948	Crawler Tractor	The Rifleman	Unboxed	8a
(4)	1948	Crawler Bulldozer	The Rifleman	Unboxed	18a
(5)	1949	Horse Drawn Milk Cart	Shacklewell Lane	Boxed	7a
(6)	1949	Rag and Bone Cart	Shacklewell Lane	Boxed	
(7)	1949	Soap Box Racer	Shacklewell Lane	Unboxed	
(8)	1950	Jumbo the Elephant	Shacklewell Lane	Boxed	
(9)	1950	Prime Mover, Trailer and Bulldozer	Shacklewell Lane	Boxed	15a, 16a, 18a
(10)	1951	Muffin the Mule	Shacklewell Lane	Boxed	
(11)	1952	Large Coronation Coach	Shacklewell Lane	Boxed	
(12)	1953	Small Coronation Coach	Shacklewell Lane	Boxed	
(13)	1954	Massey Harris Tractor	Shacklewell Lane	Boxed	4a
(14)	1954	Bread Bait Press	Shacklewell Lane	Boxed	
(15)	1955	Covered Wagon	Shacklewell Lane	Boxed	

EARLY LESNEY TOYS NEVER RELEASED

	DATE OF ISSUE	TITLE	FACTORY SITE	SIMILAR TO "MATCHBOX" SERIES
(1)	1949	Muir Hill Site Dumper	Shacklewell Lane	2a
(2)	1955	Euclid Quarry Truck	Shacklewell Lane	6a
(3)	1955	Diesel Road Roller	Shacklewell Lane	1a or 1b
(4)	1955	Fowler Showman's Engine	Shacklewell Lane	(MOY 9/1)

Wetton saying that he had a few pieces of the components."

The last early Lesney toy to be made was the Covered Wagon in 1955. It was similar in size and concept to the small Coronation Coach. When first marketed in the U.S.A. it was numbered 59 in the "Matchbox" Series with a price of 59 cents. However, the number was dropped in 1957 and was replaced in the "Matchbox" Series in late 1958 by a Singer Van.

The Covered Wagon measured 124 mm (4.88") in length and comprised a wagon with a separate metal canopy, four wheels and a driver with a separate horsebar and six horses (and unlike the small Coronation Coach all the horses had a full complement of legs). The horsebar featured the legend 'MADE IN ENGLAND BY LESNEY' on its upper surface.

The horsebar was attachable to the wagon by means of a circular 'eye', which fitted neatly to the hook on the wagon situated below the driver. The six horses were cast onto the horsebar and a rider was cast onto the leading left side horse. There was just one casting variation. Early Covered Wagons were fitted with water barrels which were cast to a connecting rod which slotted into position on either side of the wagon. As a money saving exercise later models were issued without this component and the slots in the wagon were filled in. The horsebar and horses were painted in dark brown and shades of brown were common.

The horses had white tails and faces, whilst the outrider wore a tan shirt and cowboy hat with a red necktie. Early toys had horses

trimmed in gold. The wagon itself was green (a similar shade to the Cement Mixer) and the canopy was produced in various shades of white through to cream.

The water barrels were generally bright red, but some were painted brown. Each Covered Wagon came with its own box similar in design to the small Coronation Coach box.

Whilst describing the Covered Wagon as 'A Perfect Miniature' the box did not mention Moko. Odell: "We sold them wholesale and not just for the U.S.A. . . . they didn't sell very well." The Covered Wagon was not deemed a great success. Smith: "It was not top of the pops – there was a horse and so it was limited in appeal." The Covered Wagon, originally priced at 2s. 11d (14.5p), had been withdrawn by 1957.

The Production of a Matchbox Toy

'MASTERS OF OUR OWN QUALITY'

LESNEY PRODUCTION

With the sudden success of the three early miniatures Lesney found themselves with insufficient production facilities. Larger premises had been found in nearby Stoke Newington, Lesney having already moved from their original small works in Tottenham, North London. The industrial diecasting business also expanded quickly and in 1957 the works moved to Hackney, London E9. By 1961 Lesney were employing 1,300 people in a specially constructed factory in Hackney covering a floor area of 110,000 square feet. Further large factories at Lee Conservancy Road and Rochford were opened in 1964 and 1969. By the mid 1960s Lesney were producing 2,000 tons of zinc-alloy diecastings annually, 85% of which were Matchbox vehicles and the remainder industrial components such as car door handles and hinges.

In hindsight it is thought that the success of Lesney was because of the high quality of the models, their finish and their design as well as Lesney's precision diemaking. These high standards caught the imagination, not just of the toy trade and the public, but also of the engineering industry. In December 1961, a trade magazine called *Mass Production* ran a full feature on the production processes employed by Lesney.

In 1961 there were some one hundred and twenty different models available in the various Matchbox ranges. These were produced at the rate of one million per week. In one afternoon in 1961 the factory produced more Y15 Rolls Royces in miniature than the number of full-size Rolls Royce cars produced since the foundation of Rolls Royce Ltd in the early 1900s.

Once a week a meeting of marketing men and development engineers would select and discuss models that they thought could be included in the ranges over the next one, two or three years. *Odell:* "I started my week with this meeting on a Monday morning . . . it was the most important meeting of the week because it was the new model meeting and the research and development meeting." During the 1960s this meeting would include Leslie Smith and Jack Odell along with their fellow director Bert Bastock. The Chief Designer Fred Rix, (who eventually retired in 1979), and Ken Wetton the Chief Model Manager always attended. Other members of staff needed for these very important meetings included senior representatives from the R. & D. Department, Publicity and the Drawing Rooms. *Smith:* "In the early days it was done in two seconds, but as we got bigger we had more formal meetings . . . about a half dozen of us." Eventually a list of some sixteen models would be agreed upon to develop in the next six months, after examining photographs of the actual vehicles and in some cases the technical drawings supplied by the motor industry. The list of possible models was then handed over to a team of model makers.

As the Matchbox ranges began to evolve, so Lesney nominated special teams to co-ordinate the ranges. *Smith:* "They would each do their own research, go round and ask people, travel to toy fairs and so on. Soon we developed, let's say, for the "Matchbox" Series ten new models to launch next year." The team leaders would then submit their ideas. *Smith:* "Jack and I would sit at a table and there would be a presentation . . . we might say 'no! that's no good – come back again!' until we thought O.K., we'll accept that one and that one".

It took several weeks to craft by hand a replica of a Matchbox model. The model makers cut them out of solid blocks of perspex, and, where necessary, incorporated brass. The work involved many hundreds of hours of painstaking craftmanship. These prototypes had to be completely accurate replicas of the proposed finished production models. *Odell:* "We used to make the models as they should be . . . but then we might add an eighth of an inch of perspex in between to widen it out . . . we would say 'That looks a bit long or too short' . . . we might then cut it up again." Eventually these replicas were shown to the development engineers and once it had been agreed that they were up to standard the replicas

Ken Wetton at work. He was responsible for many of the models that appeared in the 1960s and early 1970s.

were handed over to the drawing office. A draughtsman then carefully drew out the many parts of the model, necessarily accurate to a millimetre and accurate to scale, from the information supplied to him from the Research and Development Department. Skilled pattern makers then hand-carved from wood or resin minutely accurate patterns. These patterns were made three to four times larger than the workshop drawings so that any error in the shape or measurement could be detected at once.

When the pattern was finished, it was split in two, so that the reverse impression could be taken. This reverse impression, known as a 'cataform', was the basic shape from which the model would eventually be diecast. At the same time the

draughtsman critically checked all measurements with his original drawings. A resin cast was made from each part. These casts are known as 'the female of the species' and it was from these large plastic moulds that a quarter-size die was carved out of solid steel.

A highly skilled pantograph operator cut the delicate outline of the new model in high quality chrome-vanadium steel. The operator ran a sensor stylus over the contours of the mould, the tiny needle of the cutter bore out an exact quarter-size replica from the block of steel. Senior toolmakers then checked the dies at every stage to ensure that a high degree of accuracy had been maintained throughout their construction. Upon completion the die was then bedded down – a laborious and highly-skilled job

whereby the die was fitted into a complete mould and the mould was filled with molten metal to ensure that it was not leaking. The mould was then baked in an oven for two days at temperatures in excess of 1,000°C to harden it.

This hardened mould was then 'tried out' in the foundry, minor adjustments were made to it where necessary to make good any necessary improvements. Finally, the mould was examined by the Progress Tool Room. *Lister:* "The R. & D. was at one time set up at Higham's Park and we would all drive up there from Rochford . . . they had their own diecast machine there and we would try out the mould and make a report." Early 'shots' of the casting were put together – sometimes even painted and presented at the next selection meeting. The mould was then ready to be used by the diecasters in the toy foundry.

Up until 1956 all the castings were made on hand-operated machines. *Odell:* "It just wasn't possible to go out and buy an automatic diecasting machine. I don't think there was a machine available anywhere in the world . . . they all thought it was too dangerous to pump molten metal into dies automatically with the risk of burning people." The moulds had been opened and closed by hand. Odell realised that there was a need for automatic diecasting machines. *Odell:* "I had to perfect a safe machine; so to stay ahead of the competition I built in the safety and designed the machine around it . . .without total safety if the cycle went wrong with the mould opening it could squirt a lot of molten metal all round the place." Several dry runs were successfully carried out. *Odell:* "I got the mould on ("Matchbox" Series 35a the Marshall Horse Box) and at that time I had forty hand-operated machines in the foundry. We lit the machine –

the moment came when I had to press the button for it to start working automatically . . . all of a sudden all the other machines stopped . . . I looked round and the whole foundry was empty, they were all looking through the windows and they thought if someone was going to get burned it wasn't going to be them . . . I pressed the button and the castings started coming out. That was a very important day in the diecasting world. I knew then how the man felt who had just done the first four minute mile. Once we had achieved this the world knew that they had to do it also to stay with us."

But why was it that Odell had to design his own automatic diecasting machinery? During the mid 1950s with the output of the "Matchbox" Series reaching an unthought of level, Odell and Smith had decided to invest heavily in new diecasting machinery. Odell had driven up to Wolverhampton to visit a supplier with the intention of purchasing twelve new machines. *Odell:* "He looked at me and laughed and then told me that they only made twelve machines a year eleven of which were already sold to the Metal Box Company . . . You can have one in eleven months time. I was shattered, it was the end of the world". On his drive home Odell designed in his head an automatic diecasting machine. He ran into the factory that evening and told two of his colleagues to ring up their wives and make their excuses. *Odell:* "I must put this down, I have just designed a diecasting machine and I must get it on paper". They swept the floor and cleared the walls and using chalk Odell drew out the many components of his machine on the floor and the walls. By eight o'clock that night Odell had drawn out his plans. *Odell:* "We had to put barrels around the drawing so that nobody would walk on it or rub it

A contemporary photograph from one of the foundries.

out the next day, and I remember when I got there the next morning some clown had placed a hat with a few coppers in it just as if someone had done a drawing on the pavement for money!". A draughtsman then made an accurate drawing of the machine. Three weeks later Odell took the first shot off that machine. During his time at Lesney, Odell went on to make fifteen hundred diecasting and injection moulding machines, at an average cost price

of £900 and £1,300 respectively. In the toy foundry molten zinc alloy was continually poured into the backs of the diecasting machines from giant six ton furnaces. In 1961 there were eighty diecasting machines at the Hackney factory, all designed and made by Odell and his engineers. By 1966 there were more than one hundred and fifty. They were all capable of making fourteen shots per minute and some were capable of making 7,000 sets of

castings in a day. Some of the multi-impression moulds produced up to 100,000 castings per week compared with the slower production of King Size models that reached 35,000 per week.

By late 1955 Odell had made his first two hundred diecasting machines (Mark III) which were in turn scrapped in 1958 to be replaced with his Mark IV design that was capable of taking larger dies. By 1962 Lesney couldn't purchase enough zinc to maintain their production runs; so Odell designed a plant for alloying zinc. A subsidiary of Lesney, known as Eastway Alloy Zinc Co. Ltd., eventually went on to produce six hundred tons of zinc per week, of which two hundred and fifty tons were used by Lesney; the balance was sold to other diecasting companies. Wearing their now famous white coats Odell and Smith worked on the factory floor, modifying existing machines and developing new ones, and any of the work-force with a problem could approach them immediately. *Odell:* "On Monday afternoons I managed to get round three of the factories. Tuesday was quite a good day because I could get round another four or five. Wednesday morning I did two and on Wednesday afternoons there were the usual directors' meetings or accounts meetings. Thursdays were for visits to factories that I needed to visit more than once . . . this left Friday . . . I would do everything on Friday that I had not managed to do during the week." Improvements were always being introduced and the use of standard die blocks made the switching of production on any machine a matter of a few minutes' work

From the diecasting lines the castings travelled on conveyors to the barrelling installation in the fettling shop. It was here that Lesney's close attention to precision diemaking began to repay the high initial costs. The castings were so clean that they were virtually flash-free and, after about one to three minutes in the barrels, they had burnished themselves without any chips or liquid additives. *Grundy:* "Only in very exceptional circumstances did the tumbling have to extend to eight minutes." All overflows and ejector lugs had also been removed. The castings were then emptied into biscuit tins for storage prior to tipping onto conveyor belts to be sorted by female workers, who each picked out a particular part from the batch, with the scrap metal passing along the conveyor direct into the foundry for remelting.

The sorted components were transported by an ingenious apparatus that conveyed them at ceiling height round to the degreasing and priming departments. In the early 1960s Lesney degreased the castings in trichloroethylene, but this was later changed to a phosphate solution.

Above: An interior view of one of the foundries.　　　*Below: Sorting out castings - rejects were recycled.*

'Jo' at work.

castings were given three separate coats of paint. Adjacent to every spray shop was an up-to-date paint laboratory which had a team of technicians who continually tested the paints. Every twenty minutes fifty painted castings were picked at random from the conveyors for a quality control check. The castings, still on their spindles, then proceeded in double file into the oven entrance in the centre of the booth where they were baked at 300°F.

Even in the early 1960s the paint shop had a capacity of 250,000 castings a day and over 800 gallons of lead-free paint were used every week. By 1966 the spray shop were using nearly 2,000 gallons of paint per week. By the early 1970s they were using 3,000 gallons per week. *Odell:* "By the early 1960s we were up and running and we hit a million a day, that's total toys." Models requiring accurate painting on such details as tail lights and radiator grilles were conveyed to a line of twenty-eight specially constructed machines. The female operators took a model in each hand and pushed one end of the model into one of four

After degreasing, the castings proceeded to the spray machines. For the main spraying process the castings were laid out in batches on a wire link belt (known as the traverse) on which they moved at ten feet per minute under sixteen spraying heads. These heads swept to and fro across the path of the castings. The sprayed castings then passed into a tunnel oven with a recirculating hot air system.

Two-tone models were masked and sprayed in a separate automatic booth. Castings with intricate surfaces such as bodies were mounted on rotating spindles known as the Spindle Automatic Spray Machine (this machine was also known as the 'Jo' after J. Odell). As the spindles entered the booth from each side, a lug just above the conveyor sprocket sent them spinning beneath nine stationary spray guns. With either process, all the

The traverse sprayer in action.

Just some of the many injection moulding machines in the Plastics Department.

openings. Two openings sprayed silver paint onto the exact frontal area required and two sprayed on spots of red to represent the rear lights. These twenty-eight operators could finish the front-ends and rear-ends of 10,000 models a day. *Smith:* "We had a whole line of workers just doing gold work who were skilled at it. They would just get the brush and it was done."

This more professional approach to finishing had replaced the 'out-

worker' system which had been adopted between 1948 and the late 1950s whereby casual labourers were paid for work done on a weight basis, i.e. one bin of painted components would be worth 'X' pence. *Smith:* "Outdoor workers would arrive with their prams. As we got bigger it got harder to control the quality – some of them got up to all sorts of tricks, such as putting a brick at the bottom of the bin and dumping the toys around the corner. In the end we decided

that's the end of outdoor work . . . we ought to be able to handle it ourselves and then we would be the masters of our own quality."

The plastic department produced the needed components such as seats, windows and wheels. This department was originally sited at the Eastway factory, but was moved to Lee Conservancy Road in 1964. A further facility was installed during the late 1960s at Edmonton and Harold Hill. During the late 1960s the Lee Conservancy factory

produced in excess of 50 million plastic components each week.

Each of the machines – over eighty of them in 1970 – was similar in design to the diecasting machines, i.e. material was injected into the mould which formed the component. The plastic granules which were pre-coloured were fed through a hopper into a heated cylinder where they were then forced out under pressure into the mould. Lesney could produce ten different grades of plastic and a total combination of over sixty colours. The eighty or so plastic injection moulding machines could make over 1.25 million wheels and tyres every day. Each batch was quickly, yet thoroughly, inspected as it was ejected from the mould. *Arberry:* "It was rumoured that if all the plastic moulding machines cycled at the same time at Lee Conservancy Road, they would all fall through the floor into the packing department."

All the finished component parts, either diecast or plastic, were then sent from the many separate factories such as Rochford and Edmonton for storage in the Number One factory at Lee Conservancy Road. The flow of these components to the twenty or so assembly lines was the function of the Production Control team. They would organise the calling in of parts for loading onto four separate overhead conveyor systems, which automatically unloaded the parts onto the designated production lines. In 1970 Lesney were producing six million toys per week and each toy had an average of twelve component parts!

On arrival, the various components were assembled in a flow-line method. As the car body travelled along, such parts as windows, interiors, steering wheels, suspension and spare wheels were added. Each part was fixed by machines which pressed or spun over the rivets to give extra strength to the model. *Grundy:* "From 1966 automatic wheeling machines were built at approximately ten per month. By 1968 there were approximately seven-hundred-and-fifty special purpose machines at the Lee Conservancy factory, all built by Lesney, such as: pinfeeds, presses, spray and label machines and hubbing equipment etc." However, mistakes were often made during assembly as several different models and their com-

Above: The Packaging Department in action.
Left: How wheels emerged from the Plastics Department.

ponents would come down the assembly line at the same time! *Arberry:* "In 1969 a radical change took place in the assembly of Lesney toys. Instead of the famous flow-line a new concept was introduced called 'work-enlargement'. The assembly lines were phased out over a period of time and replaced by individual machines where an operator would make most or all of the toy. This meant that instead of 'production runs' and stockpiling a portion of the range, the whole range could be made in smaller quantities per week, but the whole year through, thus ensuring year round availability . . . gone were the days when Les Smith on a walk through the assembly area would be heard to say 'Pick up that card it costs a farthing (.25p) a piece'."

As Lesney became more and

more professional, so with it came streamlining and standardisation. This cut down on the expense of producing unique components and made the assembly of models easier. *Smith:* "Professional people came in and would say 'You ought to standardise this . . . there are too many bits and pieces in a Yesteryear.' There could be six different hand brakes and only one or two slight differences between any of them. We had about eighteen different wheels . . . which at times got mixed up. We tried to agree to, say, two sets of wheels – that's what we tried to do – analyse it and streamline it." During the early 1950s the axle was crimped to retain the wheel which left a tiny sharp blade which could harm a child. Lesney then changed to riveting the axle with a German designed machine. Each of these machines could perform 9,000 operations a day.

Decoration was applied to models, where necessary, by transfers applied by hand on a separate assembly line. At one time these were applied by outworkers who were paid so much a hundred. *Smith:* "Some of our decals were done outside and if it was done wrongly . . . to scrape the wrong decal off was a nightmare . . . you would spoil the paint . . . we had to stop it." The female operators in the factory worked at incredible speed, using the motion of the conveyers to pull each transfer from its backing. Over 100,000 transfers could be applied in one day by this highly skilled team. By 1968 the various labels and insignia were applied by electronically operated machines which could accurately place a label either side of the model simultaneously at speeds of up to eighty models a minute. By 1978 the Lesney factories were trying to use fewer and fewer labels. New tampo printing

machines had been bought from Germany and where possible these were used instead to apply the decoration.

Seven automatic packing machines handled the entire output of the factory. The machine opened up the flat carton, tucked in one end and carried them, open end upward, past the operator who inserted a model in each at the rate of 100 a minute. By 1966 this had increased to 120 items per minute. The machine then tucked in the open ends of the cartons and discharged them in stacks of the right size for the transit cases.

Ultra-modern automatic handling and automatic conveyor systems then moved the finished and packaged models to the transit stores ready for stocktaking, selection and despatching

Above: Boxing up the finished models.   *Below: The final judgement!*

to all the Lesney markets throughout the world.

The quality of the toys was quite clearly superior to that of Dinky. The Lesney directors never failed to be surprised that Meccano had not altered their production techniques to follow suit. The war had forced the need to produce purer materials, especially where zinc alloy was concerned (many armaments had used zinc diecasting). By 1950 the need for substantial diecast mouldings was unnecessary and uneconomical, but this was unnoticed by Meccano.

The growing reputation of Lesney in the early 1960s was such that they were paid a visit by the management of Meccano. *Odell:* "One of their top managers walked around the place and the poor fellow nearly had a heart attack. He said 'Look you are running machines at fourteen shots a minute and some of those are two impressions . . . we are still using machines designed in 1933 . . . we open the mould and put a pair of pliers in, take the casting out and then close it up again . . . we can only do five shots a minute . . . we can't cope with this, will you buy us out?" Odell and Smith declined the offer due in the main to the geographical location of Meccano which was sited in Liverpool.

The wooden pattern for the Y10 Diddler Trolley Bus. The original plastic model is on the right and the final production version is on the left.

MATCHBOX PRODUCTION

Since the creation of Matchbox Toys in 1982 little has changed in the production of a Matchbox toy. The salient differences are shown below.

The choice of new "Matchbox" models is still taken most seriously by Matchbox. Ideas emanate from collectors, the public, the worldwide Matchbox Marketing Departments and the Research and Development team based in Enfield, Middlesex. The ultimate decisions have to be astute as the development costs in the 1980s have now risen into millions of pounds. Matchbox Toys' policy in the late 1980s is to keep the Models of Yesteryear Range limited to 30 models – three or four new models are planned for each year, up to fifteen new Miniatures, six Superkings and, of course, several recolours and reliveries.

The Research and Development team in the main initiate models to be included in the ranges.

Every year they attend the Motor Show held in October, looking for new cars and trucks that have just been launched. They still use photographs and where possible take up-to-date and detailed photographs, measurements and notes. Further aids may include technical drawings or blue-prints if made available by the motor manufacturer. An artist is commissioned to paint the proposed subject-matter on card. This stage is usually reserved for Yesteryears or Dinkys. From this information the project leader in the R. & D. department briefs a model maker to produce a mock-up in resin. A rubber mould is also made to enable duplicate replicas of the resin mock-up to be made. These in turn are sent to the main Matchbox subsidiaries for their initial comments. At least two years in advance, Matchbox Vice-Presidents and Managing Directors of the main subsidiaries meet Mr D.C.W. Yeh to discuss the many proposed models. Specific markets will naturally want their own cars and trucks e.g. Matchbox Toys Germany will argue for Mercedes, B.M.W. and Volkswagen! *Yeh:* "I don't get involved with individual model selection . . . I view the whole range and if I see something missing I remark on this . . . one of the biggest car producers today is Japan, so has the range got a good representation of Japanese cars?" *Sullivan:* "Model selection is a compromise between the various markets . . . the final model selection is taken at the highest level." If the model is given the go-ahead, a draughtsman will produce technical drawings from the resin model. A large master pattern is made from these drawings in wood. The pattern is still made two or three times the size of the final model. When the drawings and pattern are finished, they are examined at a development meeting. *Lister:* "At these meetings we look at all the drawings and indicate where there have to be improvements."

At the same time a member of the Research and Development Department makes final contact where relevant, with the company which owns the livery. For example, company trademarks used recently by Matchbox have been Heinz, Carter's Seeds and Michelin. Matchbox Toys pride themselves on using only authentic trademarks and company colours, and normally seek permission before using them. Some companies have been known to demand royalties for the use of their trade mark. Matchbox Toys, where possible, persuade those who ask for such royalties to consider the free publicity that the model will give them.

Once the mould is under way, the idea is to get castings produced as soon as possible. These

A tumbling machine used to remove excess metal from the new castings.

An internal view of the Macau production plant.

'first shots', as they are called, often lack small areas of detail such as wording on base castings and detail ribs. These are used to assess assembly methods and to enable jigs to be prepared. Some castings are used by the R. & D. for checking and are also sprayed, assembled and decorated by hand using transfers *Lister:* "The earlier you got your first shots, the earlier we at Quality Assurance could test the castings and feed back information to the toolroom that, for

example, the product didn't need any more work done to it." These early models are used for catalogue photography and also for exhibition at the toy trade fairs. Examples of 'first shots' are sent back to the Research and Development Department for checking that the model meets specifications. When they are passed, the factory begins the production of the new model. If for any reason during production a fault or a weakness becomes evident, the tools are removed

and modified. Although this is deemed to be an expensive way in which to ensure that the models will stand up to everyday wear and tear, it does, of course, create collectable variations.

All assembled models passing down the production line are still checked by staff of the Quality Control Department. Every stage of the cycle is double-checked, including the testing of wheels, the paint finish and tampo printing.

Diecast production in the Far East takes place in Hong Kong, Macau and mainland China. Matchbox is the biggest employer in Macau after the government. When demand stretches production capacity to the limit, Matchbox eases the pressure by giving some of the work to outworkers – ironically, just as Lesney did in the early 1950s. Many of the diecast machines are ex-Lesney ones; these have proved to be robust enough to continue making Matchbox toys well into the late 1980s.

In all these ways Matchbox Toys aim to produce the best possible model of the chosen vehicle.

AN ABANDONED PROJECT

With a company as large as Lesney many projects were initiated but were destined never to come to fruition. One such project is described here about which some information has been gathered which will be of interest. It is worth noting that some of these projects started because there was a lull in the Toolroom and some time could be usefully given to reworking old tools to provide something new. In the case of this example, however, it was a completely new idea.

A resin pattern, some of the actual tools and two examples of the Y9 Leyland 3 Ton Subsidy Lorry.

The project in question is that of an airport crash tender which was developed to a very advanced stage at the end of the 1970s. This magnificent model was progressed to the final tooling stages before being abandoned. Originally the model was to have featured flashing lights, a siren and an operating water pump but these features, in particular the water pump, were later abandoned. The water tank proved especially difficult to be made water-tight. The model was destined to be a Super King and would have been assured of being the largest Lesney ever produced.

A magnificent Superking model, sadly destined never to see the light of day.

The Matchbox Regular Range

5

1953 TO 1969

There cannot be many boys in the world who have not at some time played with Matchbox toys. Indeed, an often heard comment in collectors' shops is: 'I had that model when I was a child.' As many millions of these small vehicles were produced over the years, this comes as no surprise. The non-collector is often amazed by the asking price for some mint-boxed models, but it should be remembered that these miniatures were manufactured solely for children to play with and so it is only natural that very few have survived in their original condition.

To explain the origins of one of the most popular range of toys that Lesney ever produced, it is necessary to return to the early 1950s when Lesney was in its infancy. The huge sales of the smaller Coronation Coach in 1953, known to have sold 500,000 models within sixteen weeks, gave impetus to the idea that there was a market for a range of miniature vehicles, although, at this time Lesney was producing the early Lesney toys described in Chapter Three. It was realised that small children had some difficulty holding large scale toys and so it was decided by the company to manufacture some of the early Lesney toys in a much smaller scale. *Smith:* "The miniatures were always to be contemporary and forward looking."

1953

In June 1953 an advert appeared in *Games and Toys* a trade magazine, to announce their four new models. These were to be distributed by the factor Richard Kohnstam, as Lesney were more interested in the production of toys rather than having to go around the world selling them.

The first miniature models were available in tiny quantities at the end of November 1953, and numbers 1 – 4 were shown at the 1954 Harrogate Toy Fair. However, sales of the first four models were not particularly good, partly because shopkeepers were not initially impressed by the tiny models which were disparagingly described by some as having originated from Christmas crackers! Additionally there was more profit per model to be gained from products such as Dinky toys. *Odell:* "They were made about September or October 1953 and we got them into the shops in November and they were absolutely useless! At this time of year the first Lesney miniatures were pronounced as failures." In view of the verdict given by local shopkeepers, Odell only made three moulds for the first three models. When the range expanded and sales increased it was not unknown for some models to have four or five moulds because more than one mould would be run to keep up with the demand.

After Christmas 1953 some children found that whilst they could not afford larger scale models with their pocket money, the new Matchbox toy was easily attainable. *Odell:* "The only thing a child could buy for 1s. 6d (7.5p) was a Matchbox toy or a lead soldier. You can't play with one lead soldier, you need a few, but with one little wheeled toy you can ruin this and scratch that … You have a complete toy."

By March 1954, after this slow beginning, demand began to exceed supply and advertising in the trade magazines helped to stimulate interest. In April, an advertisement placed by Kohnstam proclaimed 'Dignity', referring to the large Massey Harris tractor, and 'Impudence', showing the first four models from the "Matchbox" Series. A further chance to show the range occurred at the British Industry Fair at Olympia which attracted visitors from around the world. This was an annual event held in the spring or early summer and continued until its eventual demise in 1956. It differed from a trade fair, such as those held currently at Earls Court in London and Harrogate, in that the public could also attend. Orders flooded in from South Africa and the United States.

The first miniature model was the Aveling Barford Road Roller (1a). All the models in this chapter have been described using the Matchbox number to which a suffix letter has been added in order to differentiate between models with the same number. The first Road Roller is, therefore, described as (1a) and the second version as (1b). The Roller was descended from the early Lesney toy which, in turn, had owed its

origins to a best selling Dinky model. The first version may be distinguished from the three subsequent Road Rollers by its full length canopy. It was available in either dark or more rarely in light green with gold trim and red rollers. A driver was cast as part of the body and painted in tan. A casting variation soon occurred when the centre section below the roof supports was extended beyond the level of the other two supports. At the same time the ends of the roof were modified from a curved edge design to one with a straight bottom edge.

The Dumper (2a) was the first of three Muir Hill Site Dumpers. It had a dark green body with gold trim and a red bucket. The first issue was fitted with green painted wheels which is now quite difficult to find. Later models had unpainted wheels. The first two dumpers included a tan painted driver who was fitted facing forwards so that he could not see what he was emptying from the bucket! This model was not based upon a released early Lesney toy, although it was in all probability based on the non-released larger scale Muir Hill Dumper as described in Chapter Three.

The Cement Mixer (3a) only appeared in light blue. It could not be moved along easily, but it had a wheel which could be turned to rotate the barrel as on the real mixer. Most of these models were fitted with orange painted metal wheels but models released after 1959 were fitted with grey plastic wheels. It was one of only a few models in the first twenty which was not to be later substantially altered in terms of size, colour or design. There were several minor casting modifications to various components during this model's eight year life, the most noticeable of which was the removal of a handle from the engine casing on later models.

The first miniature Massey Harris Tractor (4a) came in red with spoked front wheels and large mudguards mounted either side of the tan painted driver. Hand applied gold trim was used to make this model more realistic. It was fitted with a tow hook, although Lesney were never to manufacture any form of machinery or implement which could be towed by this tractor.

New models and their usual colour scheme:

1a Aveling Barford Road Roller in green
2a Muir Hill Site Dumper with green body and red dump
3a Cement Mixer in light blue with either orange or grey plastic wheels
4a Massey Harris Tractor in red

1954

The problem of packaging these four miniatures was solved by the introduction of a box the size of a matchbox, hence the creation of the name. The origins of the packaging have already been described in Chapters One and Two.

It was not until the London Bus (5a) was added to the range in mid 1954 that sales expanded rapidly. The explanation for this trend is to be found in the choice of vehicles. The first four models were not vehicles that a child would necessarily recognise immediately. The bus, on the other hand, was a familiar sight to most children. This model featured paper labels which stated 'Buy "Matchbox" Series'. It was by far the smallest Lesney scale model as it measured only 52 mm. It came with and without a number plate recess at the rear whilst the undetailed grille was decorated with gold trim.

The Euclid Dump Truck (6a) was intended to be released in

both the new Major Scale Series and the "Matchbox" Series. There was not the manufacturing capacity at the small factory to allow large toys to continue and in any case the demand for the "Matchbox" Series was fully occupying the workforce. The decision to drop the larger Euclid was not taken lightly, however, for in the April 1955 edition of *Games and Toys* the new large Euclid was advertised together with the new models from 'the famous Matchbox Series'. Perhaps even the wording had not been finalised at that time! The first Euclid Dump Truck, (6a), had an orange body and a grey dump unit. Six metal wheels were fitted to this model; it was deleted from the range as grey plastic wheels appeared and so it is possible for an example to have appeared with the later type of wheels.

By the end of the year a Horse-drawn Milk Float (7a) and a Caterpillar Tractor (8a) became available. These models were also based on the early Lesney toys. Sales at first were rather limited, especially with the Milk Float, because not every child would have been familiar with a Horse-drawn Milk Float. However, sales of the early Lesney Milk Float had been good and there was no reason to suppose that the miniature version would not eventually sell as well. Today the Milk Float commands a higher price than most other original series models as it is more difficult to find in mint condition; the shafts could break and the horse could be easily lost. First versions were fitted with eight-spoke metal wheels but the variants with grey plastic wheels, especially with crimped axles, are harder to find. There are several casting variations on this model. The moulds for the 7a were made by a toolmaker at home in his garage. As the mould was necessarily delicate, he was asked to make four or five at the same time so that if one broke another would be available to take its place. *Odell:* "The large one had been such a good seller we made it the number seven in the "Matchbox" Series. It sold and sold and sold … the little one. I had it retooled at least three times. Every time the toolmaker hadn't much to do I said 'make another Milk Cart'."

The Caterpillar Tractor (8a) was released later as a bulldozer by the addition of a blade. Early variations include yellow painted instead of bare metal rollers, a pale yellow body and an orange body. The usual issue was in plain yellow with unpainted rollers. The driver was originally painted red but subsequently appeared in the body colour, usually with a black hat. Four casting variations appeared in the engine alone, but these were unintentional as parts of the mould broke off under the strain

of prolonged output. Although 8a was included as the final 1954 issue, it did not come in the same type of box as the first seven models which had been packaged in boxes with a script 'Moko'. The Caterpillar's box depicted 'A Moko Lesney' all in the same capital type face.

New models and their usual colour scheme:

5a London Bus in red
6a Euclid Dump Truck with
   orange body and grey dump
7a Horse-drawn Milk Float in
   orange with brown horse
8a Caterpillar Tractor in yellow

1955

Sales further increased with the release of a fire engine (9a) based upon the 1948 Dennis F.2 Fire Engine. It had a fixed ladder and

two large wheels on the escape which could be rotated. Gold trim was applied to the grille, windscreen, fireman's helmet and hose reel.

The Scammell Scarab Mechanical Horse and Trailer (10a) was a familiar sight around Britain's railway stations in the 1950s. The model consisted of a red cab pulling a grey trailer. No major variation occurred with this model which was one of the smallest in terms of scale.

The first ERF Petrol Tanker (11a) was painted in the same dark green colour as the more common version of the Aveling Barford Road Roller, 1a. The green tanker has proved to be one of the rarest regular wheel models. Subsequently it appeared in either dark or light yellow with silver trim applied to the grille and fuel tanks. The green and later red variants were trimmed in gold. The red tanker was the most common version and was

the only variations to sport a small 'Esso' decal which very occasionally has been found on the sides of the tank. The decal exists in two sizes. Initially a flat brace was cast to strengthen the join between the cab and the tank but later a half rounded brace was added.Whilst the Dinky toy range had widely featured constructional models, Lesney expanded their range to other commercial vehicles. Odell preferred model lorries to cars as he felt that they were much better value for money and were more interesting in terms of shape and this partly explains Lesney's reluctance to produce cars in the early days. In addition, it was thought possibly wrongly, that cars would not have the height and width of commercial vehicles and so would not be as popular. The nearest that Lesney came to producing a car before 1956 was the Land Rover (12a) which appeared in green with silver trim and a tan driver. *Odell:* "I've

The rare and more common colour variants on the first trucks, 1955 to 1956.

still got the mould for number twelve . . . Yes, the original . . . It was found in a scrap yard."

In 1955 more commercial vehicles entered the range. The 'O' Type Bedford Wreck Truck (13a) featured a body with cutaway sides. It was painted light brown and decorated with silver trim. The jib and hook were both painted red. There were no casting variations with 13a although it is sometimes confused with 13b which was issued in 1958.

The Daimler Ambulance (14a) was issued with a cream body and silver trim. A few versions have been seen without a red cross roof decal which was a factory mistake.

An early Lesney toy again provided the inspiration for the Diamond T 980/981 Prime Mover (15a) and Transporter Trailer (16a). Although the Prime Mover underwent considerable alterations in the scaling down process, the trailer remained a virtual copy of its big brother. The pair were based upon actual vehicles and the Prime Mover is today one of the most interesting miniatures. Although it may have been a colour trial, a very small quantity of models have been found in yellow. At the end of its production in 1958 the 15a was issued with ten grey plastic wheels and this variation is almost as rare. The orange 15a with six metal wheels remained one of the most common then and one of the least expensive today of all the first series models.

The six wheel Transporter Trailer was a rather plain light brown but it provided good play value with its moveable ramp. A modification took place inside the hinged rear ramp and the area beneath the front of the chassis was strengthened.

Another 'O' Type Bedford provided the cab for a Removals Van (17a) which is a sought after

model possibly because, to many, it epitomises Britain in the mid 1950s. The Removals Van displaying the name of 'Matchbox' on its side was an every day sight and for the collector this vehicle has provided plenty of variations. Originally issued in light blue, the colour scheme was changed briefly to maroon then to light green and finally to dark green on the second version of the van, (17b). The sales had not been particularly high and it was felt that a colour change would help.

The Caterpillar Bulldozer (18a) was the tenth new model to join the range in 1955. The addition of a red blade and arms to the original yellow casting, 8a, was an easy way for Lesney to create yet another best-seller and was a move that had been successful with the early Lesney toy. The axles of this model were made slightly longer than those of the Caterpillar Tractor to accommodate the blade. The driver has been found with either a yellow or a black painted hat and although he was cast as part of the model he was not shown on the box illustration.

1955 – New releases and their usual colour scheme:

9a   Dennis Fire Engine in red
10a Scammell Scarab Mechanical Horse and Trailer with red cab and grey trailer
11a ERF Petrol Tanker in red
12a Land Rover in green
13a Bedford Wreck Truck in light brown with red jib
14a Daimler Ambulance in cream
15a Diamond T Prime Mover in orange
16a Transporter Trailer in light brown
17a Bedford Removals Van in green
18a Caterpillar Bulldozer in yellow with red blade

In 1956 a car was introduced into the range for the first time in the form of an MG Midget TD (19a) and so a new dimension was added to the range which helped to increase sales. This little sports car was an instant success and led the way for further cars. It could be found in either cream or the rarer colour of off-white with red seats and a tan driver.

The ERF Lorry (20a) was a simple open back truck, known in the U.S.A. as a Stake Truck. It ranged in colour from deep maroon to a dark red and its final very short run in 1959 was fitted with grey plastic wheels instead of metal ones, making this variation one of the rarest. The first issue was trimmed in gold but all subsequent releases had silver trim. A colour trial model has been found in light green.

To complement the London bus a light green Bedford Duple Luxury Coach (21a) joined the range. All of these coaches carried 'London – Glasgow' decals above the side windows. There were no major variations to the casting.

The Vauxhall Cresta (22a) was Lesney's first saloon and its choice was simply explained by the fact that Odell owned a real Cresta in a two-tone livery. It was decided that the model should have the same colour scheme. It appeared originally in maroon and off-white and later in dark red and white. The tow hook enabled connection to a caravan or trailer. *Odell:* "The car cost a penny instead of a fraction of a penny to paint because the whole model was first painted by out-workers in white and then, after the fitment of a metal cap, it was oversprayed in maroon. They were all sprayed with paint containing lead but we couldn't export these to Australia unless they were lead free . . . We had to

change the paint and this caused us problems." The two-tone paint scheme was not a complete success as the diecast cap tended to cause a shadow effect to the finish. Although hailed as a major breakthrough the two-tone scheme was not repeated for some time as it was an expensive process with a high scrap rate and used up considerable amounts of paint. This particular model did not achieve a high profit margin and had to be balanced by some of the other cheaper to produce models within the range such as the Prime Mover.

At the same time as the release of the Vauxhall Cresta, a pale blue Berkeley Cavalier Caravan, (23a), was added to the range. It included a red 'ON TOW' and black 'MBS 23' together on an orange background rear decal. Both the tow bar and the axle cover were modified during the very short time this model was in the range. Many of the cars issued in the next few years were fitted with tow hooks so that a child could make his own combinatons.

Construction vehicles always featured strongly in the "Matchbox" Series and the Weatherill Hydraulic Excavator (24a) and its successor 24b were produced for eleven years. It appeared either with an orange yellow or a plain yellow body with a 'Weatherill Hydraulic' rear decal. The bucket could be raised or lowered on both versions. This model was the first to include model numbers cast on to the metal wheels and also the first model to have its number cast on the base. This numbering system occurred because it was part of a family mould. In the manufacturing process a body, base and wheels would all be derived from one small mould. When plastic wheels were introduced in 1958/1959, these could all be of a common type and it was no longer necessary to number the wheels. Although most models

The early construction vehicles featuring the various Road Rollers and some early colour changes. Note the Norvic matchbox on the left.

were fitted with the correct wheels there were inevitably some mistakes. However, it is strange that the first model to have a model number cast on to the wheels, 24a, only featured number 23.

The Bedford 12 cwt. Van (25a) known in the U.S.A. as a Panel Truck was only ever painted in dark blue. The 'Dunlop' decal was the first non-Matchbox advertisement and Lesney had sought and obtained the permission of the tyre company for the advertisement. Dunlop was the first company to pay for its advertising space on a Matchbox vehicle. The fact that this model completed its life in the one guise with only

changes to the wheels from metal to grey plastic and with the decals from orange-yellow to yellow indicates that so long as Dunlop paid for the advertisement and sales were maintained, Lesney were happy to continue with the livery.

The ERF cab was used again for the orange Cement Mixer (26a). It had a barrel which could be revolved and was issued with four metal, grey plastic or silver plastic wheels. The model was in the range for six years and the only casting change of note involved the lengthening of the barrel stem at the front end.

One of the most sought after first series models is the first

issue of the Bedford 'S' type Low Loader with a light blue cab and a dark blue trailer (27a). The colours were similar to those used for the Removals Van, 17a, and Dunlop Van, 25a. The colours were quickly changed to a light green cab and a light brown trailer. The blue cabs were slightly more numerous than the trailers. A few blue cabs with tan trailers have been found. Today this model is classified as extremely rare and as a number of collectors possess the two-tone blue Low Loader it is presumed that it was a short production run rather than a colour trial.

Another Bedford 'S' type cab was used as a Compressor Truck

(28a). It was to be painted in the same way as the Weatherill Hydraulic in that it changed from orange-yellow to yellow. Only metal wheels were fitted to this model.

Two further models for 1956 were replacements, the first of many in terms of increased sizes. A larger Road Roller (1b) had a much shorter canopy but the overall length of the model increased from 49 mm to 57 mm. The question of why the Road Roller and later the Caterpillar Tractor and Bulldozer were all enlarged three times after the initial release is often asked. *Odell:* "As the range gradually developed, certain models with high sales capacity were felt to look too small when compared with the rest of the range, especially where new models were being built to a larger scale and so larger versions were considered and made." These models with a similar theme were continued without being referred to as new models by Lesney and were packaged in the original boxes despite having updated castings. By 1956 it was only a matter of sixteen weeks between having an idea for a new model and getting the model into the shops. It was difficult enough to get boxes for new models ready in time wthout the additional problem of converting them.

The second Double Decker Bus (5b) was also issued in1956, being 5 mm longer than its predecessor. The paper labels of 5a were now replaced by redesigned bright or dull 'Matchbox' transfers for 5b and the hand applied gold trim was later changed to mask sprayed silver trim. The wheels changed from metal to grey plastic and so eventually did the advertisements to the now rarer 'Player's Please' and then to the even rarer 'B.P. visco-static'. The B.P. company was one of a number of companies which paid for the privilege of having their name advertised on Matchbox vehicles. One wonders about the outcry today if tobacco advertisements like 'Player's Please' were to appear on children's toys!

1956 – New models and replacements in their usual colour scheme:

    20a ERF Lorry in maroon
    21a Bedford Coach in green
    22a Vauxhall Cresta in
        maroon and white
    23a Berkeley Cavalier
        Caravan in pale blue
    24a Weatherill Hydraulic
        Excavator in yellow

    25a Bedford 'Dunlop' Van in
        blue
    26a ERF Cement Mixer in
        orange
    27a Bedford Low Loader
        with light green cab and
        light brown trailer
    28a Bedford Compressor Truck
        in yellow
    1b Road Roller in light
        green
    5b London Bus in red

1957

A foldout trade sheet displaying models appeared in 1957, showing the first forty two models. It is unknown when this 1957 sheet actually became available, but in *Games and Toys* the Jaguar XK 140 (32a) was described as 'just one of fourteen new "Matchbox" Series (many for immediate delivery) on show'. Therefore, it is assumed that by then the new models numbered 29 to 42 were in the final stages of production.

The Bedford Milk Delivery Truck (29a) was the second model after the Dunlop van to use the same basic Bedford design. It appeared with a pale brown body and either metal or grey plastic wheels. Later versions had cream crates and bases instead of white, the original colour used. In the U.S.A. where milk rounds were largely unknown, this van was known as a Pop Truck.

The Ford Prefect (30a) was the first vehicle to have a complete model description on the base and so misinterpretation was less likely to occur. The normal colour for this model was light grey-brown with either metal or grey plastic wheels. When the trim was applied by hand, the whole of the rear bumper was painted before the base and tow hook were fitted. With mask spraying the process took place after the model was complete and so the rear

bumper was silver-trimmed on either side of the tow hook. The colour of the Ford Prefect was changed to pale blue towards the end of its life making this colour quite rare. The reason for this was simple. The Prefect was already due for replacement and the light grey brown paint had run out. Rather than order fresh quantities of a colour which may not be used, another colour, in plentiful supply was substituted.

The next release testified to the magnitude of the U.S.A. market as it was an American Ford Customline Station Wagon (31a). The overall colour was yellow, and grey plastic wheels replaced metal wheels during 1958. A colour trial model has been found in red. *Odell:* "The number 31 was a marvellous seller."

The Jaguar XK 140 (32a) was a popular choice of model. It is usually to be found painted in off-white. Towards the end of the model's life the colour scheme was changed to red. There are two distinct shades, orange-red and dark red; and both variants are now quite hard to find. The former colour occurred because the red paint was sprayed over the original white body. This can often be detected when the model is viewed from underneath. Some of the white and all of the red Jaguars came with grey plastic wheels.

The Ford Zodiac (33a) came in a range of colours from dark blue to bright sea-green and eventually with a two-tone colour scheme. Two extremely rare models have also been found in a dark blue colour. By 1960 grey plastic wheels had replaced the metal wheels and early in 1961 the Zodiac appeared in metallic mauve with orange side panels. By the end of that year green tinted plastic windows had been fitted and in the course of events the grey plastic wheels had given way to silver.

The introduction of the

Volkswagen 15 cwt Van (34a) was influenced by the expansion of the third largest market, Germany. There was no advertising, for the orange-yellow or yellow decal proclaimed a ficticious name, '"Matchbox" International Express'. The wheels were normally metal or grey plastic but a few models also appeared fitted with silver plastic wheels.

The ERF Marshall Horse Box, Mark 7, (35a) was known in the U.S.A. as a Horse Pullman. The familiar cab and base was painted bright red and the light brown horse box had an opening door to increase play value. All four types of wheel were fitted to this truck but the silver and black plastic wheel versions are the rarest. *Odell:* "It was made at Barretts Grove … That mould was the first mould to go on my automatic diecasting machine."

An Austin Cambridge A50 (36a) was originally in blue-green, but later it was changed to a pale blue body. It appeared with either metal or grey plastic wheels. All of the A50s should have had red rear lights but in the event the red paint was applied to the rear wings as the rear lights were lower down.

A Karrier Bantam 2-tonner was used as the basis for a 'Coca-Cola' Truck (37a). This truck, like the Weatherill Hydraulic Excavator, 24a and the Bedford Compressor Truck, 28a, came in either orange-yellow or yellow. Lesney had two yellow paint shades and it was of no consequence during the 1950s which paint was used. The crates on 37a were originally uneven but a casting modification meant that the crates appeared as an even load. The decals applied to the sides of the vehicle could be either large or small. The rear decals were always large. Metal wheels were generally fitted to this model, but final releases in 1959/1960 saw the inclusion of grey plastic wheels. Perhaps partly because of the number of collectors who favour Coca-Cola memorabilia, this standard model is one of the more expensive items in the original range.

The same Karrier Bantam was used as the basis for the Refuse Truck (38a). The first release was coloured in an odd grey-brown shade, with the familiar orange-yellow or yellow decals inscribed, 'Cleansing Department'. The body colour was quickly changed to plain grey and could be found with either metal or grey plastic wheels. A final short run saw another colour change to silver when either silver or grey plastic wheels were fitted. Examples with silver plastic wheels are known to exist. The silver rim diminished with time and, of course, there was no point in having trim on the silver version.

The Ford Zodiac which appeared as a saloon as (33a) was also released as a Convertible (39a). Its colour has been difficult to define for it was either in a pale pink or peach initially before developing by degrees to a far richer pink or peach. The first issues had a brown interior and base, which is now rare. This was quickly altered to a green interior. Wheels changed from metal to grey plastic and a final run saw the fitting of silver plastic wheels. The trim was originally applied by hand but later by mask spray. This model was cheaper to originate as certain parts could be copied from, 33a, the saloon version.

Another Bedford cab was used with the seven ton Tipper (40a). The cab was painted red but the tipper changed with time from light to dark brown. Metal wheels gave way to plastic and silver trim diminished by degrees.

The first 'D' Type Jaguar painted in its famous colour of British Racing Green became (41a) with '41' decals applied to the front and rear of the Jaguar.

Decals with '52' applied to the 52a Maserati may have also been applied to 41a. A small final run was fitted with grey plastic wheels but all the other models had metal wheels.

The third version of the Bedford 12 cwt van appeared with the 'Evening News' van (42a). The yellow body had a sign-board with 'First With The NEWS' on the roof, front door decals proclaiming 'FOOTBALL RESULTS' and 'Evening News' on both sides of the van. Metal, grey and, more rarely, black plastic wheels were all applied as well as silver trim to the grille and headlights. It was a popular model as it lasted in the range for almost eight years.

As well as the twelve new models for the year there were also some improvements to the existing range. The second Muir Hill Dumper in the same colours as 2a appeared in a slightly larger scale as (2b). When grey plastic wheels were introduced in 1958 this Dumper was one of the first conversions from metal wheels.

The second Massey Harris Tractor appeared as (4b) and was again coloured red but the light brown driver was cast separately. The size of the model was unaltered but the body was now hollow instead of solid. The front wheels were now solid metal and the mudguards had been removed. The wheels were altered again to grey plastic, front and rear, before the model became one of the first to be completely deleted from the range in 1960.

Another enlargement took place with (10b) the Scammell Mechanical Horse and Trailer. There was a colour change in that the trailer was altered from grey to pale brown and the cab became dark red. After a time the trailer wheels were converted to plastic.

The final change occurred with the Berkeley Cavalier Caravan.

Although the colour for 23b remained the same as for 23a, the modifications were such that the 23b is considered to be a different model. The major differences are that the latter has a full descriptive baseplate; has an open axle; has a lower step below the door and the stud which secures the base is behind the door outline rather than part of the door. In fact 23a was one of the shortest run models being manufactured for only a few months before being replaced. The pale blue body continued for more than two years but just before the wheels were changed from metal to grey plastic, the model was recoloured in lime green. This colour is quite hard to find but one of the rarest colour schemes also occurred with this second type of Berkeley Caravan. Fewer than ten examples of this model painted metallic lime green are known to exist. This should not be confused with the Bluebird Dauphine (23c) which was also painted metallic lime green and may be classified as being quite rare. The tow bar was strengthened twice before the model was replaced in the range in 1961.

1957 – New models and replacements in their usual colour scheme:

29a Bedford Milk Delivery Truck in pale brown
30a Ford Prefect in light grey-brown
31a American Ford Station Wagon in yellow
32a Jaguar XK140 in off white
33a Ford Zodiac in green or two tone metallic mauve and orange
34a Volkswagen Van in blue
35a ERF Marshall Horse Box with red cab and light brown box
36a Austin A50 Cambridge in blue
37a Karrier 'Coca-Cola' Truck in yellow
38a Karrier Refuse Truck in grey
39a Ford Zodiac Convertible in peach with a green interior
40a Bedford Tipper with red body and light brown tipper
41a 'D' Type Jaguar in green
42a Bedford 'Evening News' Van in yellow
2b Muir Hill Dumper with green body and red dump
4b Massey Harris Tractor in red
10b Scammell Scarab Mechanical Horse and Trailer with dark red cab and light brown trailer
23b Berkeley Cavalier Caravan in pale blue

1958

The year heralded the beginning of a change in wheel materials. The shift from metal to plastic was due to cost factors as plastic was cheaper. The metal wheels had to be grenodised grey with an etching finish, which involved extra handling and thereby extra cost, whereas the plastic wheels could be manufactured in one process. Hence, in 1958 both grey and black plastic wheels were fitted for the first time when stocks of metal wheels for a particular model had been exhausted.

The decision to fit either black or grey wheels on a particular model was generally quite relaxed. *Odell:* "A model may look better with black rather than grey wheels. Sometimes we got fed up with seeing the same colour wheels on a model. There were no hard and fast rules." Sometimes on the assembly line a particular wheel would run short and another colour or type would be fitted to complete the production run.

Even in the 1950s there were pre-production or colour trial models and there would be much discussion about the planned production run. Sometimes the pre-production colours would be packaged, planned and distributed to the trade. No-one in Lesney was concerned about such variations for as long as the model was in working order, the consumer would hardly worry about its

Lesney did not take short cuts with regard to tooling but tried where possible to ensure that a model's release coincided with the appearance of a new car. Odell believed that children bought what they saw on the road or what their father drove. Children tended not to buy vehicles which they did not easily recognise. Hence, it could be some years before an unusual

Minx (43a) is generally found today in a two-tone livery. However, the first issue was a very short run in bright green and this variation is now quite rare. The first two-tone colour scheme was a blue-grey bonnet and sides with a pale grey boot and roof with either metal or grey plastic wheels. A colour change in 1960 occurred when the bonnet and sides were painted turquoise

colour shades occurred with generally later models appearing in lighter shades of metallic blue. It was available for six years and during that time it was initially fitted with metal wheels, then grey plastic and finally silver plastic wheels.

The 1.5 litre Series 1 Vauxhall Victor was produced in Luton from February 1957 onwards and at the time was controversial in

The first cars were not fitted with plastic windows but there were several interesting colour changes. The green Hillman Minx (43a) the red Vauxhall Victor (45a) and pale brown Morris Minor (46a) are amongst the rarest regular wheel variations.

colour. In the early days paint spraying took place outside the factory and wrongly coloured models would be more unlikely to be noticed by Lesney personnel. *Smith:* "There was no point in wasting perfectly saleable models." The yellow Prime Mover, 15a, and red Vauxhall Victor, 45a, were probably pre-production models, which proved to be unacceptable in that colour, but were issued for sale.

new car became a new model. In the regular wheel era Odell made the models that he liked and those he believed that children would like. As time went on, particularly towards the end of the 1960s when the Superfast era commenced, this was no longer to be the case.

Numbers 43 to 48 were ready in January 1958. The Hillman

whilst the boot and roof appeared in off-white. Only grey plastic wheels were fitted to this variation.

A metallic blue Rolls Royce Silver Cloud (44a) was the first model to be painted in a metallic colour. It was a slightly more expensive process as another coat of paint was required to obtain the required finish. Various

style as it was a departure from the more traditional Vauxhall appearance. The Lesney version of the Vauxhall Victor (45a) was intended to be red but Berger, Lesney's main paint supplier at the time, suggested a new primrose yellow, a suggestion that Lesney adopted. Fewer than ten red models are known to exist and so this colour must be classified as one of the rarest. It may be differentiated from a repainted model by the absence of a dashboard bar, which is common to all yellow models. All four types of wheel were fitted to this Vauxhall.

During 1960 plastic windows were fitted, initially clear, but generally they are to be found with a green tint.

The Morris Minor 1000 (46a) was another model which is known to have been issued in a trial run colour of pale brown. As with the red Vauxhall Victor described previously, fewer than ten are known to be in collections. The usual colour for the Morris Minor was dark green with metal or grey plastic wheels. Towards the end of the model's life in 1960, blue cars were issued in dark or light shades with grey plastic wheels. When the dark green paint had run out, blue paint was used instead.

A red Trojan 1 ton Van with 'Brooke Bond Tea' decals (47a) had either metal or grey plastic wheels fitted. No major variations arose with this model.

As most of the cars issued to date had included a towing hook it was natural that another trailer besides the Caravan, 23a, should be included in the range. A Meteor Sportsman Mark II Sports Boat & Trailer (48a) featured a light brown deck which varied in shade and a light blue hull upon a black trailer which had either metal or grey plastic wheels. A very small number of trailers were issued with silver plastic wheels. This model did not attract large sales and was replaced after only two years.

A six wheel M3 Personnel Carrier (49a) was the first of ten military vehicles to be issued in a period of two years. It was painted in a traditional olive green. The rear pairs of wheels were rollers inside grey tracks. Some of the final issues were to be found with green tracks. The front wheels changed from metal to grey plastic and finally to black plastic. There was usually

correlation between the wheels and the rollers but examples exist of grey wheels with metal rollers and grey wheels with silver plastic rollers. A bonnet decal featuring a white star in a circle was included on all models though models with metal wheels are known to exist without decals. The body was originally crimped to the base but later a rivet was used. Several minor variations exist around the bogie wheels.

The model proved to be very popular and sold for a period of more than nine years.

Although several models of the first and second series retained their colour scheme throughout their production life, the Commer Pick-up Mark VIII (50a) was certainly an exception. At first it was painted in pale brown with either metal or grey plastic wheels. It then appeared in light brown, a definite colour change rather than a shade difference,

with either grey or silver plastic wheels. The first two-tone version with a red body and white cab has proved to be the rarest. The final colour variation again featured a red body but the white contrast colour was changed to grey. This two-tone version is also quite difficult to find though it was issued with both grey and black plastic wheels. There are several minor casting variations on the Commer Pick-up.

The yellow Albion Chieftain Flat Bed Truck with a pale brown load (51a) originally had 'Portland Cement' decals on the cab doors in a circle and on the truck sides in two lines. Very quickly the decals on the sides of the truck were increased to read, 'Blue Circle Portland Cement'. Both the truck and the load were subject to colour shades, generally becoming darker as time went on. All four types of wheels were fitted, with both the grey and rarer silver plastic wheels even appearing in two sizes.

Sports and Racing Cars

The first model not originally to have grey metal wheels or rollers was a red Maserati 4CLT/1948 Racing Car (52a) which was fitted from the outset with black plastic wheels. A decal with the number '52' was soon applied and later black plastic tyres were fitted to diecast spoked wire wheels to give a more authentic representation. This version in red is hard to find, for there was a colour change to lemon-yellow soon after the introduction of the spoked wheels. As with the second version of the 'D' Type Jaguar, 41b, a few models were fitted with decals bearing the number '3' or '5'. Early Maseratis had cast drivers painted in cream, but some of the later models appeared with a white driver.

The Aston Martin DB2-4 Mark I (53a) was a particular favourite of Jack Odell. He had progressed financially at this time to be able to afford an Aston Martin. Owners of Aston Martins are asked by the company for their preference in colour. Odell chose primrose yellow, a paint used by Jensens. He was contacted by Aston Martin and asked whether he would mind if another customer had his car painted in the same colour. After agreement had been given, Odell was perturbed to hear that a yellow Aston Martin had been seen outside various London night clubs. To avoid embarrassment he decided to have his car resprayed maroon. The model Aston Martin was first coloured in a pleasant light metallic green and may be found with either metal or grey plastic wheels. For a short time before the model was deleted from the range, it was recoloured to a metallic maroon to coincide with Odell's resprayed car. The model had either grey or black plastic wheels.

The Saracen Personnel Carrier (54a) was a model of the standard armoured carrier used by the Royal Armoured Corps and the Infantry. It was appropriately painted olive green and featured a revolving turret. The only body variation involved the antenna base on the upper left side of the body which looked like a step and was missing on later models because of a damaged die.

The D.U.K.W. (55a) was based upon a military vehicle which had been built in the U.S.A., and was used extensively by the British army in World War II. The real vehicle was a 2.5 ton G.M.C. Amphibian Truck which had been a secret weapon until June 1943. Its purpose was to transport supplies and soldiers from ships to the coast. The prototype real vehicle took just thirty eight days to complete and the term D.U.K.W. was its coded serial letters. It was known as a Duck by both the engineers at the G.M.C. works in the U.S.A. and by the soldiers who used it in action during the invasion of Sicily. The Matchbox model had a smaller scale body when compared with the rest of the army vehicles in the series and so it did not sell as well as the larger military issues. The first releases had metal wheels but later either grey or black plastic wheels were fitted. There are no casting variations with the D.U.K.W.

One of the most popular models with regular wheel collectors is the red London Trolley Bus, (56a). The first releases had black poles and these are quite rare, although examples have been found on both metal and grey plastic wheel versions. Models may be checked for authenticity by viewing the underside of the poles through the windows. This should show a black clip fastened through the roof as the poles were painted before assembly. The usual colour scheme was all over red with 'Drink Peardrax' side decals and 'Hampton Court' destination boards to the front and rear.

Metal, grey and black plastic wheels are relatively common today but the variation with silver plastic wheels is harder to find. The Trolley Bus was included in the series for more than seven years with no alteration apart from the described wheel changes.

Jack Odell acknowledges that the pale green Wolseley 1500 (57a) was not one of the best choices for the range. It had no special features and was rather small in comparison with most other models. As silver trim had superseded gold trim after the release of the ERF Cement Mixer (26a) in 1956, it is strange to find some Wolseleys with gold trim. The majority of models being painted with the more usual silver trim. Only grey plastic wheels were fixed to this car. This model is known to fade to yellow-green if exposed to prolonged sunlight.

The A.E.C. 'B.E.A.' Coach (58a) was an interesting choice as it would normally be confined to airfields and probably not recognisable to the majority of children. This may explain why its inclusion in the range was limited to only four years. The coach was always painted dark blue, though shades exist. The first type of decal used showed 'British European Airways' in white lettering. Subsequently blue lettering on a white background was used in the decal except for the 'B.E.A.' logo which was white on a red block. The decals were sized such that they would always be transferred from a roll of decals by machine on to the coach. However, the consistent shape of the model meant that it could easily be placed backwards into the machine in which case the 'B.E.A.' appeared at the rear of 'British European Airways'. Grey wheels were usually fitted for both the silver and black plastic wheel variants are hard to find.

The pale green Ford Thames Van (59a) was issued with orange-red and yellow 'Singer' decals on both body panels. On the side doors the words, 'Singer Sewing Machines', appeared in white within a large 'S' in the same colours as the panel decals. First releases had plain side doors but soon raised door lines were added to enable the decals to be fixed accurately. Towards the end of this model's production the decals were changed to a darker red, but even more noticeable was the change in body colour to a much darker green known as 'Kelly green' in the U.S.A. The van in this colour is quite difficult to find. Grey and silver wheeled versions are more uncommon, making the darker green van with silver wheels a rare piece.

The last new model for the year was a Morris Pick-up (60a). It was a popular model for it remained in the range for almost eight years almost unchanged. The body colour of light blue remained constant throughout. The two line decals were in two sizes. The larger 'BUILDERS' part of the decal was always red but the first decals in smaller lettering, 'SUPPLY COMPANY' were in black. All subsequent smaller lettering appeared in white. The last issues of this model appeared without the cab rear window common to all previous models. All three types of plastic wheels were fitted with the grey wheels fixed to a body without a rear window being by far the rarest.

Although there were eighteen new models for the year, Lesney still had time to enlarge and update eleven of the earlier releases. This had nothing to do with decreased sales, merely a desire to get the range to appear to be more consistent. Of course, the models were of different scales but it was resolved that similar vehicles would be of similar scale. The early size of the carton determined the size of the model and although there was some anxiety when the box was enlarged to accommodate the larger models, this now meant that the smallest vehicles seemed too small for the larger boxes and so these were scaled up. Each model was considered on its merits and if it was decided that a larger model would be an improvement, then replacement occurred.

The third version of the Aveling Barford Road Roller, (1c), was painted either with a light or a dark green body. The metal rollers continued to be red but the towing hook of the preceding models was replaced by a flat tow bar.

The second version of the Caterpillar Tractor (8b) had a yellow body, metal rollers and green tracks. The Caterpillar company were happy for Lesney to feature one of their products as a model as long as due recognition was given. To this end, 'Caterpillar Reg. Trade Mk.' was cast on the base of all subsequent Caterpillar Tractors and Bulldozers as well as on the flaps of some boxes. There are no known casting variations and although it was in production for three years, it is now one of the hardest models to find.

The Dennis Fire Engine (9b) was updated by the addition of a front bumper and the inclusion of the model description and number on the base. Metal wheels were usual for this model although a short run of grey plastic wheels occurred just before it was replaced. It was only manufactured for a short time because 1959 saw the introduction of a more modern fire engine, the Merryweather Marquis (9c). As with the first version, 9a, the 9b model is known to exist with a smaller pair of sixteen spoke escape wheels.

The larger version of the ERF Petrol Tanker (11b) was always painted red. First versions had gold trim applied by hand but this was soon changed to silver trim. Models came with or without an oblong base hole and earlier releases did not have a brace between the cab and tank. All four types of wheel were fitted although silver plastic wheels were by far the rarest.

The second version of the Bedford Wreck Truck (13b) was slightly longer than its predecessor and also included a model number and description on the underside. The crane jib was kept in place by the rear axle, whereas with 13a it had been clipped into position. However, the most noticeable difference concerns the crane box which was extended to give the jib more of an enclosed appearance. Metal wheels were common for this wrecker but grey plastic wheels were also fitted before its withdrawal from the range.

Another Daimler Ambulance (14b) considerably larger in size but otherwise similar in design to its forerunner, was issued with a red cross on the roof of its cream body. Both metal and grey plastic wheels were affixed to this ambulance which later was painted off-white. The final, rarer version was fitted with silver plastic wheels.

A major casting change occurred to 17a at the beginning of 1958 to cause the classification of a second Bedford Removals Van, (17b). Several modifications took place with the new mould: the window between the cab and the body was cast open instead of closed; the radiator grille had six equal bars instead of a mixture of thick and thin bars; the gap between the cab and the body was increased and the roof was flatter in appearance. Early issues were painted light green but later a much darker shade of paint was applied. Metal wheels were eventually replaced by grey plastic and the last type of decal outlined the word 'Removals' in black.

A second yellow Caterpillar Bulldozer (19b) was an obvious addition to the range and the Caterpillar Tractor, 8b, was used as the basis. Indeed, the base may be found cast with either a No. 8 or a No. 18. The rollers were always metal and the tracks always green. Today it is quite a difficult model to find.

In 1958 the original MG Midget TD was replaced by the MG 'A' (19b). Lesney felt that the first car was too small and somewhat dated to fit in with the range and so the replacement, as with the real car, was enlarged and modernised. The car body was painted off-white whilst the cast interior was red. A light brown driver was fitted separately and later castings revealed jacket and pocket outlines. Silver plastic wheels are quite rare on this model, although metal and grey plastic wheels are not so difficult to find.

A replacement Bedford Duple Luxury Coach (21b) was painted first in medium green and later in dark green. Grey plastic wheels were fitted to both variants but metal wheels only appeared with the earlier colour. Again a 'London to Glasgow' decal as on the 21a was used for this model.

At the beginning of 1958 Vauxhall Motors announced a replacement for the Vauxhall Cresta 'E' Series, the saloon which Lesney had modelled as 22a. The new car was the Vauxhall Cresta 'PA' Series and this was quickly introduced into the range. The first version appeared in pink which could be found in various shades up to a rich cream. The Crestas previously produced were not fitted with windows but the major innovation of 1960, the fitment of plastic windows to certain models, applied to (22b) and so pink models with green tinted windows exist in small numbers. During 1960 Lesney produced three different two-tone Crestas. The body was sprayed in one colour and then the lower sides were oversprayed in a contrasting colour. The first two-tone scheme is by far the most difficult to find where the lower half of a pink model was oversprayed in turquoise. This colour scheme is recognised as being one of the rarest regular wheel models. The turquoise overspray was then applied to a model which had been painted in metallic brown. Comparatively, the most common two-tone variant is the Cresta in light grey with a lilac overspray but it should be pointed out that none of the two-tone versions are easy to find in mint condition. When the two-tone scheme reverted to a single colour, Lesney used gold as a body colour for the first time, though of course it had been used for trimming models for some years. The gold model may be found in differing shades but these should not be confused with the copper coloured Crestas which proved to be the final versions before the model was withdrawn from the range in June 1965. Grey plastic wheels were originally fitted and these may be found on all colour variants. Black plastic wheels occurred only on the copper versions whilst silver plastic wheels may be found on the final two-tone models as well as gold and copper Crestas. There are no major casting variations with this model and the windows, when fitted, although varying in shade were always green tinted. This model has proved to be a firm favourite amongst collectors because of the number of variations.

Few collectors would disagree that the second version of the Bedford Low Loader (27b) is one of the most difficult models to find, regardless of any colour, wheel or casting variation. It was issued for less than two years and as it retained the same colour scheme as its predecessor, 27a, retailers and children may not have noticed or been concerned about the (17 mm) size difference. Metal or grey plastic wheels were fitted to the version with a light green cab, but only the second

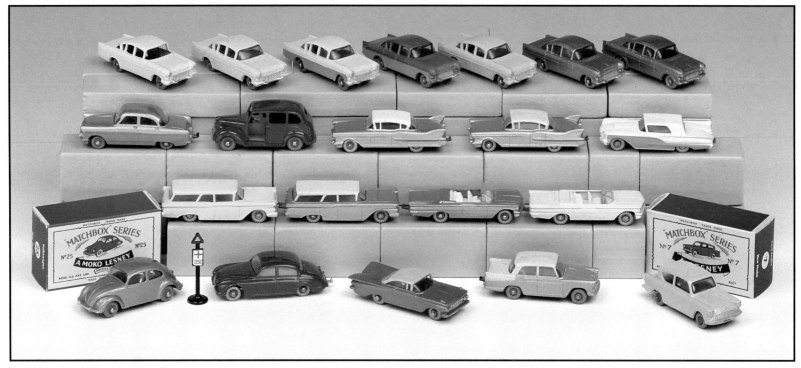

All of the cars illustrated were first issued between 1958 and 1962. The row of Vauxhall Crestas are in the order of their colour changes.

type of wheels were affixed to the dark green cab and trailer which also could vary between light and pale brown.

1958 – New models and replacements in their usual colour scheme:

43a Hillman Minx in blue-grey and grey or turquoise and off-white
44a Rolls Royce Silver Cloud in metallic blue
45a Vauxhall Victor in light yellow
46a Morris Minor 1000 in dark green
47a Trojan 1 ton Van 'Brooke Bond Tea' in red
48a Meteor Sports Boat in light brown and blue with black trailer
49a M3 Personnel Carrier in olive green
50a Commer Pick-up Mark VIII in light brown or red and grey
51a Albion Chieftain 'Portland Cement' Truck in yellow with pale brown load

52a Maserati 4CLT/1948 in red or lemon yellow
53a Aston Martin (DB2-4 Mark I) in metallic green
54a Saracen Personnel Carrier in olive green
55a D.U.K.W. in olive green
56a Trolley Bus in red
57a Wolseley 1500 in pale green
58a A.E.C. 'B.E.A.' Coach in dark blue
59a Ford Thames 'Singer' Van in light green
60a Morris J2 Pick-up in light blue

1c Aveling Barford Road Roller in light or dark green
8b Caterpillar Tractor in yellow
9b Dennis Fire Engine in red with front bumper
11b ERF Petrol Tanker in red (enlarged)
13b Bedford Wreck Truck with reshaped box with light brown body and red jib
14b Daimler Ambulance in cream or off-white (enlarged)
17 b Bedford Removals Van with window in green.

18 Caterpillar Bulldozer in yellow
19b M.G. '1959' Sports Car in off-white and red seats
21b Bedford Duple Luxury Coach in green (enlarged)
22b Vauxhall Cresta in pink, light grey and lilac, gold and copper
27b Bedford Low Loader with green cab and light brown trailer

1959

It had been possible to keep the cost of the range at 1s. 6d. (7.5p) partly because the volume of sales had increased but also because inflation was not a factor during the 1950s. However, by 1959 the company had realised that its product was unique and there was some pressure to increase prices. Whilst relations had always been cordial between the factor and Lesney, feelings became strained

when Lesney discovered that in 1954 Kohnstam had registered the Matchbox name. Following legal advice the name was shared between the two sides but in reality there was a desire to break away from the factor and to set up Lesney's own distribution business. As Kohnstam had enjoyed a 17.5% mark up, Lesney could benefit from this saving and hold down prices. Lesney bought out J. Kohnstam & Co. Ltd. and re-possessed the other half of the Matchbox trade mark. It was to be the end of an era.

In the U.S.A. Fred Bronner had become the sole Matchbox importer. The Matchbox models were popular (not least because of their price) but as there were far more toy manufacturers in the U.S.A., there was stiffer competition. The fact that the U.S.A. was so vast allowed Lesney to expand despite this fierce competition. In order to maximise advertising, Fred Bronner had issued small catalogues to the trade for a number of years. Richard Kohnstam had produced fold-out sheets in the U.K. and now Lesney followed this trend and eight million copies of the 1959 Pocket Catalogue were produced which came after requests from the trade and from customers for a reference book. Lesney, possibly for the first time, had recognised that collectors did exist. However, the two joint managing directors were not collectors, being more concerned that the latest model would be better than the previous one. They had not realised at this time what interest there was from a collectors point of view.

Les Smith was very keen to expand the business and he was concerned that European sales had been held back by the high prices. He knew that if the price set by Kohnstam in Germany of DM 1.75 could be reduced to DM 1, a single coin, then sales could really take

encourage demand, German vehicles entered the range. This was also true in France where, despite trade restrictions, sales increased dramatically after 1961 under the management of Georges Bieber.

Between 1953 and 1959 the range had been marketed mainly to the wholesale trade, although some multiple chain stores like W.H. Smith, Boots and John Lewis were also placing orders for their outlets. This explains why Matchbox toys were to be found in small newsagents. Until this time most of the advertising by Kohnstam had been to the trade, although space was taken in *Toy Trader* and *Games and Toys*. In early 1959 Lesney used the Dorland Advertising Agency whose account executive, Peter Webb, left the agency to join

comics like the *Eagle* and collectors journals such as the *Railway Modeller* was due in no small part to Peter Webb who had a keen interest in model railways. During June 1959 he was appointed as the publicity manager at Lesney and had a hand in determining new models.

Webb's influence may be clearly seen from an advertisement placed by Lesney in the July 1959 issue of the *Railway Modeller:* 'The Matchbox range is so wide and varied, it would be impossible to illustrate them all here, but most of the models are ideally scaled for model railway layouts. The majority of Matchbox stockists carry comprehensive displays of Accessory Packs and Major Packs, including the famous Yesteryear range. A good tip

than the previous practice of using out-workers to apply trim to models. However, in order to reduce costs some parts which had prevously received trim, particularly rear bumpers and later rear lights, were left untrimmed. As the 1960s progressed fewer parts were trimmed and so it is sometimes possible to categorise a model chronologically by the amount and area of trim. The gradual decline in trim application from 1959 onwards is not covered specifically for every model.

The first model released in January 1959 was that of a Mark I Ferret Scout Car (61a) which was used in large numbers as a light reconnaissance and liaison vehicle. It was a good representation although connoisseurs could comment on the lack of headlamps and wireless aerials.

Military vehicles.

off. When the Lesney distributor, Jap Prins, was established it soon became possible to cut the costs dramatically. At the Nüremburg Toy Fair of 1960, large orders were received and this stimulated interest in Germany. Of course, to

Lesney Products as manager of the new advertising and public relations department. The company began to advertise heavily prior to going public in September 1960.

The wider advertising in boys

when going along is to take with you a proprietary scale figure for proportional values.'

By the beginning of 1959 Odell had designed and built mask-spraying machines. These were far quicker and less expensive

The driver was wrongly positioned: he should have been forward and to the left to enable him to take up his correct position in the centre of the vehicle. This would have enabled a commander to stand behind the driver. The light brown driver was sometimes fitted wrongly to face the rear but this would not have been important to the vast majority of purchasers. The Ferret was coloured in the usual olive green with black plastic wheels and either three or four lines of descriptive text on the base. The addition of the words "Matchbox" Series resulted in the four-line base and this was a later addition. Today this is one of the more common first series models.

The A.E.C. General Service Truck (62a) was based upon the 1952 A.E.C. Militant troop or cargo carrier. It was not subject to any casting changes and although illustrated in the first 1959 catalogue as having a black base and grey plastic wheels, only the plack plastic type were used and the body was completely painted in olive green. It was included in the range for only four years and as a result it is one of the rarer military models.

The 3-tonner 4x4 Service Ambulance (63a) became part of the range in March. It appears to have been a copy of the Dinky Toys vehicle. The real model was peculiar in that the cab was definitely based upon a Commer GX and yet the engine was supplied by Ford. This model was sprayed in the usual olive green paint and at first sported a considerable amount of silver trim which decreased when machines were used to mask spray the trim. A large decal with a red cross on a white background was attached to either side and the base may be found with or without a hole. Only black plastic wheels were fitted to this model. As with the General Service Truck, it was not very popular and was only issued for four years.

March heralded the arrival of a Scammell 6 wheel Breakdown Truck, (64a). This truck also bore

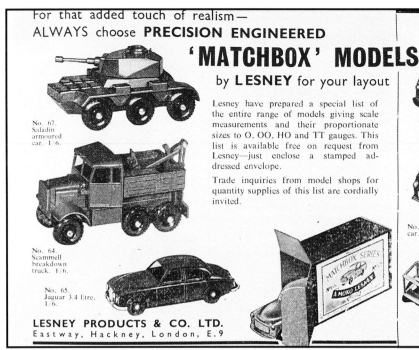

a striking resemblance to a larger scale model made by Dinky. The metal hook on the Scammell was originally painted in the same olive green as the body but later it was made from grey plastic. A few models were fitted with the rarer silver metal hook. There were several small casting variations during this model's seven year life. The box for this model always included a mis-spelling: the word 'Scamell' was spelt with only one 'l'.

The Jaguar 3.4 litre (65a) was the first of two saloons released in April. It had a dark blue body with both silver and red rear trim. Initially the rear number plate was trimmed in silver but, before the model's deletion, only the front grille was decorated. A short run in metallic blue paint occurred in 1960.

The DS 19 Citroen (66a) also joined the range in April 1959 to help sales in France. There was no intense discussion with regard to colour. Smith: "It may have been that yellow was the colour in the spraying machines at the time or when we surveyed the whole range it may have looked short of

This advertisement from the Railway Modeller in 1960 was at pains to stress the suitability of Lesney models for railway layouts.

yellow models." A brief production run included the fitment of silver wheels instead of the usual grey plastic. The model was soon replaced in October 1962 by the Harley Davidson Motor Cycle and Sidecar.

In May a model of the 6x6 Saladin Armoured Car (67a) the standard heavily armoured car operated by regiments of the Royal Armoured Corps became available. It was a sister vehicle to the Saracen Personnel Carrier, 54a, for the prototypes were built on the same chassis and had similar sized engines. Suggestions from military vehicle collectors that the Saladin needed to be in camouflage colours fitted with a searchlight were ignored by Lesney!

Odell was not in the least concerned that the scale when accurately measured was exactly 86:1 and not 75:1 as shown in the pocket catalogues. This model with its rotating turret proved very popular and featured in the range

for more than eight years, one of the longest running regular wheel models. Although Odell admitted that he had perhaps featured too many military models, he had been motivated by the high sales that Dinky Toys had enjoyed in the early 1950s. During the 1950s he noticed that on the six o'clock news army vehicles were being regularly featured and so they would be instantly recognisable to children. By the end of 1959 ten military models had been included in the range. The first ones had sold well in line with sales of the general range and so Odell continued to add further models that he believed would sell well. Perhaps his marketing strategy concerning military models was borne out by the fact that the two models which remained longest in the regular wheel range were the Personnel Carrier, 49a, and the Saladin Armoured Car, 67a, described above.

In June an Austin Mark 2 Radio Truck (68a) maintained the stream of olive green military vehicles. No casting variations are known despite the model's inclusion in

The illustration of delivery vehicles shows the change from the 1954 Horse-Drawn Milk Float (7a) to the 1963 Commer 'Rentaset' Van (62b).

the range for more than six years. If the ERF Horsebox had the first vertically opening door, the Commer 25 cwt Van (69a) released in July, was the first van to feature a sliding driver's door. The van appeared with a maroon body and yellow 'Nestle's' advertisement. Before the model was replaced, the body was recoloured to red and this colour variation is usually harder to find.

Lesney were unable to make up their minds initially when the Ford Thames Estate Car (70a) joined the range in July. The 1959 and 1960 catalogues show two trial run colour schemes. In the first edition of the 1959 catalogue a two-tone dark and light green version is illustrated. In the second edition and in the 1960 catalogue a red and grey two-tone Estate Car was shown. In the event, turquoise and yellow were the two colours used. The earliest releases did

not have windows, but soon clear and then green tinted plastic windows were fitted. All three types of plastic wheel were fitted.

Although it is apparent that Lesney copied certain Dinky toys, nowhere is this more obvious than in the first edition of the 1959 catalogue as an actual Dinky toy is illustrated. The wheels on the Austin 200 gallon Water Truck (71a) were disguised to some extent, but nevertheless the Dinky model was used to illustrate No. 71, probably because the Matchbox model was not ready for the catalogue photographer. The actual issued model has been found with only one casting modification. Originally the rear corners of the base were cast square but later these corners were cut away. The first Matchbox Collector badge, depicting the box for an Aveling Barford

Road Roller was included with first issues of the Water Truck as a gimmick to boost sales on a rather mundane truck. The badge had been advertised in the U.S.A. as being available with the Ford Thames Estate Car, 70a, but it is doubtful whether this actually occurred.

When the Massey Harris Tractor, 4b, was deleted from the range in 1960, it was to make way for a model of the most popular farm tractor of the late 1950s. Although the tractor shown in the first 1959 catalogue was an artist's impression, the Fordson Major Tractor (72a) became available in October in Britain although some models had been released as late as March 1960 in the U.S.A. The body always appeared in the Ford tractor colour of blue. The front wheels were grey plastic whilst grey

tyres were fitted to the orange rear wheels. The wheels and rear tyres then changed to black. Towards the end of the model's inclusion in the range, either black or grey tyres or orange front wheels superseded the solid plastic wheels in order to match the rear wheels. This was the first model to be fitted with separate tyres. Tractors with yellow instead of orange wheels are very rare and seem to have occurred when the yellow wheels from the John Deere Lanz 700 Tractor, 50b, were mistakenly fitted. The Fordson was included in the range for a period of seven years with only one casting modification; the platform around the base rivet on earlier models was replaced by a flat base.

The Leyland 10 ton R.A.F. Pressure Refueller (73a) was available from October. It closely resembled the large Dinky model and was painted in a similar

Any scale you liked as long as it fitted into a box!

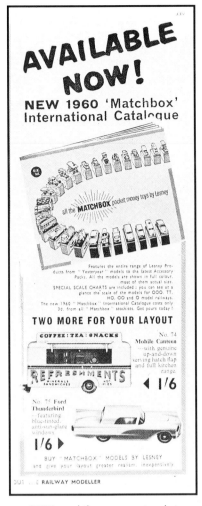
1960, and the range extends to seventy five current models.

shade of R.A.F. blue. The Matchbox model was fitted with six grey plastic wheels although a model with black plastic wheels is known to exist. The thin, flat brace between the box and tank was altered to a thicker, rounded type during the first year of issue. However, the usual version of this truck includes a fully cast brace between the box and tank. All models included an R.A.F. roundal decal on the top of the box section. The Refueller was only included in the range for three years and no other variations are known to exist.

By the end of 1959 several cars with towing hooks had been included in the range and so it came as no surprise when a third type of trailer was released in November. The Mobile Refreshment Canteen (74a) certainly provided interest for railway modellers and collectors. The first version had a white body with a light blue base and the yellow model shown in the 1960

catalogue was a pre-production example. The colour was soon changed to cream and then to pink. The white and cream versions are hard to find and the pink model is rare. The most common body colour was silver, though the base may be found in several shades of blue ranging from pale blue through mid-blue and turquoise to dark blue. All these models came with side and headboard decals. The wheels were usually grey plastic although silver plastic wheels are not too difficult to find. Only one example is known fitted with black plastic wheels. The Canteen was included in the range for nearly seven years and during that time casting modifications took place to the towing bracket and the hinge arm on the batch.

The two-tone Ford Thunderbird (75a) was the first model to be fitted with plastic windows from the outset. Although plastic had been used since 1958 in the

manufacture of wheels, late 1959 was the first time that plastic was used to produce windows. The body was cream coloured with peach or later pink side panels. The base colour varied from dark blue to turquoise on the earliest models, all of which had silver plastic wheels. The base colour was changed to black before the silver wheels were replaced with grey and then black plastic wheels.

The Ford Thunderbird was not advertised in Britain until May 1960, but it had been available in the U.S.A. in September 1959 along with the 66a, Citroen, and before the release of models numbered 67 to 74. The Thunderbird was probably released earlier in the U.S.A. because it was known that sales would be high. The R.A.F. Pressure Refueller and Mobile Canteen, on the other hand, were not released in that country until July 1960.

The Euclid Quarry Truck (6b) was an improved version of the same truck as 6a. The body and

tipper were both painted yellow and there was a 'Euclid' decal on both cab doors. Six black plastic wheels were usually fitted to this truck but a model with grey plastic wheels is known to exist.

The A.E.C. Merryweather Marquis Series III Fire Engine (9c) was faithfully copied by one of Lesney's many competitors. All these models were painted in the bright red colour traditionally associated with Fire Service vehicles. At least two moulds were used for this popular model and on one of the later moulds, the twin rear hose connectors were accidentally omitted during the production stage. Hence, some models have these hose connectors and others do not.

A collection of trucks which were first released between 1957 and 1960. The larger Bedford Low Loader (27b) the three versions of the Karrier Refuse Truck (38a) and three types of Guy Removals Van (46b) are all shown.

The ladders were painted tan originally, then in gold and finally in silver. The latest models with either gold or silver painted ladders may be found with eighteen rungs instead of the seventeen rungs common to all previously issued models. The first models had grey plastic but later black plastic wheels became standard issue. This proved to be an enormously popular model and was included in the range for more than seven years before it was replaced in November 1966 by the Boat and Trailer, (9d).

The second Land Rover (12b) was painted in the traditional military green colour so that it could be used with the other army models in the range. Unlike 12a, this vehicle did not have a driver. It was usually fitted with black plastic wheels but a final run included the fitment of grey plastic wheels. This variation is now hard to find. The steering column may be found either short and thick on earlier models or long and thin on later Land Rovers. The Safari Land Rover replaced 12b in 1965.

The Rotinoff Super Atlantic Tractor (15b) was a model of a huge, incredibly powerful tractor designed and built in England by the son of an eminent Russian engineer, George Rotinoff. It was powered by a Rolls Royce eight cylinder 16.2 litre supercharged engine developing 366 hp. Fewer than fifty real trucks were produced before Rotinoff's death in 1960. Interestingly, the real trucks had sliding doors and lifting the bonnet required the skills of two men. Most of these vehicles entered military service in Britain or Switzerland, but a few were used as heavy haulage machines and it was one of these which Lesney used as the basis for their model. An example of the real tractor's power is that whilst a 100 ton Volvo F12 has trouble pulling a Churchill tank today, the Super Atlantic is still able to pull it even when the brakes are still locked on the trailer. The model was painted in a slightly lighter shade of orange when compared with 15a and there were no casting variations during the four year period of issue. A very small number of models were fitted with grey plastic wheels making this variant quite rare as the vast majority of models had black plastic wheels.

The ERF 68G Truck (20b) with 'Ever Ready for Life' decals was a larger model than 20a and representative of a more modern truck in that it was fitted with eight wheels and contemporary wrap-around cab windows. The model was painted dark blue to which a separate black painted baseplate was fitted. The white decal initially came with an orange outline, but later this was altered to red. There were two minor casting changes which affected the left rear mudguards and the axle posts. All three types of plastic wheel may be found on this model although the version with silver plastic wheels is generally more difficult to find. The model was replaced in April 1965 by the Chevrolet Impala Taxi.

A second version of the Weatherill Hydraulic Excavator (24b) was issued in a larger scale than 24a and with a different arm assembly. The yellow colour scheme was retained and it was still possible for the arms to be raised and lowered. The 'Weatherill Hydraulic' advertisement decal was maintained on the rear of the excavator. The wheels for this model at first were grey plastic but later a different type of black plastic wheel, front and rear, was fitted. With the exception of the wheels and axle ends, the model continued unaltered in the range for a period of more than eight years.

The Ford Thames Trader Compressor Truck (28b) was another enlarged and improved model. Although many of the boxes were not endorsed 'New model' and often the new version continued to be packaged in the same box as its predecessor, the Thames Trader reflected the latest type cab design. Yellow paint was again applied to the whole body although silver trim was used initially on both the cab and the compressor radiator. Later only the cab radiator was mask sprayed. Slight modifications were made to the compressor engine but only black plastic wheels are known to exist on this model.

1959 – New models and replacements in their usual colours:

62a A.E.C. General Service
   Truck in olive green
63a Ford 3 ton 4x4 Service
   Ambulance in olive green
64a Scammell Breakdown
   Truck in olive green
65a Jaguar 3.4 Litre in blue
66a Citroen DS 19 in yellow
67a Saladin Armoured Car 6x6
   in olive green
68a Austin Mark 2 Radio Truck
   in olive green
69a Commer 30 cwt 'Nestle's'
   Van in maroon

70a Ford Thames Estate Car in
   turquoise and yellow
71a Austin 200 Gallon Water
   Truck in olive green
72a Fordson Major Tractor in
   blue
73a Leyland 10 ton Pressure
   Refueller in R.A.F. blue
74a Mobile Canteen in silver
75a Ford Thunderbird
6b Euclid Quarry Truck in
   yellow
9c Merryweather Fire Engine
   in red
12b Land Rover in olive green
15b Rotinoff Super Atlantic
   Tractor in orange
20b ERF 686 Truck in dark blue
24b Weatherill Hydraulic
   Excavator in yellow
28b Thames Trader Compressor
   Truck in yellow

1960

By 1960, one million models were being produced each week by 1,300 employees and Matchbox models were being sent to almost every country. Even 80,000 models had been dispatched to Russia in an order then worth £33,600. In addition to making toys, Lesney were also making half a million commercial diecastings per week including fuel and oil filter heads and hinge components. *Odell:* "We had what amounted to a blank cheque ... there was so much demand."

Representatives were instructed worldwide to accept orders only in gross lots. Sometimes a model would have to wait for six months before issue whilst the orders were all collated so that issue dates could be approximately the same. Lesney had experienced some complaints when they had exported early deliveries to some countries only to find that some wholesalers had imported the models back again so that they could have the latest releases first.

This practice occurred in particular with the Ford Thunderbird.

By the beginning of the year most metal wheels had been replaced with black, grey or silver wheels. Large grey and silver wheels were not usually used because the knit-line was more obvious, i.e. where the two sides of a wheel had been manufactured.

Whilst it may appear that few new models were released in 1960, this was not deliberate as many shops had not received the full range of seventy five models and so advertisements for Nos. 73, 74 and 75 appeared well into the year. In addition many models were being improved without any announcements or advertising.

Although at the beginning of the year the range consisted of seventy five different models, it was never actually policy to limit the range to only seventy five. Lesney felt on reflection that perhaps there were too many military models in the range and that the theme was over-extended. With so many models in the range some vehicles were bound to be poorer sellers than others. In particular wholesalers and retailers complained about the size of the range because of the shelf space that would be taken up if the whole range was stocked. It was then that Lesney adopted a positive policy of withdrawal and replacement through the range. Models were replaced when their sales figures started to drop. A model was never withdrawn simply because the mould had broken.

It was not until July that replacement models were advertised, but they were certainly worth the wait. A Cadillac Fleetwood Sixty Special (27c) had been scheduled to be No. 76. This was revealed on the boxes of the first series of gift sets which had been released towards the

end of 1959. It was therefore necessary to erase the 76 from the base of the model and this was achieved by the addition of a small platform, created by re-cutting the mould deeper, onto which No. 27 was imprinted.

The Cadillac was originally issued in metallic green with an off-white roof and clear plastic windows. This colour scheme is now quite rare for it was quickly altered to a metallic mauve body with a pale pink roof. However, several shades have appeared on this model and it is possible to collect a large number of variations. This is particularly apparent when crimson or black bases utilising silver, grey or black plastic wheels together with clear or green tinted plastic windows are all taken into consideration. It was advertised with a strong, realistic towing hook for coupling-up with other towing Matchbox models. Note also the panoramic windows. A pre-production example is known to exist in yellow.

The Triumph T110 Motor Cycle and Sidecar was originally intended to be number 78 but with the limitation of the range it became (4c) when released in July. It was of a much larger scale than other models. Lesney's motto was 'Volume begets value'. A model in the same scale as the cars may have suited the tiny proportion of model railway enthusiasts but children would have shied away from such a small model when they could see larger items available for the same price of 1s. 6d. (7.5p). The Triumph T110 Motor sold many millions and two moulds were necessary to run simultaneously to cope with the demand. It was an expensive model to produce because of the various parts including the intricate open spokes and so it had to be balanced in the range by cheaper to produce models. *Odell:* "The Triumph was the most fantastic model that Lesney ever made." It proved to be his favourite model. It was advertised in the *Eagle* comic as 'featuring authentic wire-spoked wheels and a three dimensional fully detailed engine'. It was always intended to be

strengthen the ribs connecting the cycle to the sidecar. At a later stage the brace between the mudguard and the sidecar was enlarged.

August heralded the release of an Austin FX3 Metropolitan Taxi,

silver wheels were used towards the end of this model's life. The base of the model also included a platform for the original number 77 and was replaced with 17.

The Foden 15-ton Sugar Container Truck (10c) joined the

In October a Guy Removal Van with Pickfords decals (46b) joined the range. An attractive feature of this model was an opening shutter-type rear door in white plastic. The dark blue body had a decal reading: 'PICKFORDS -

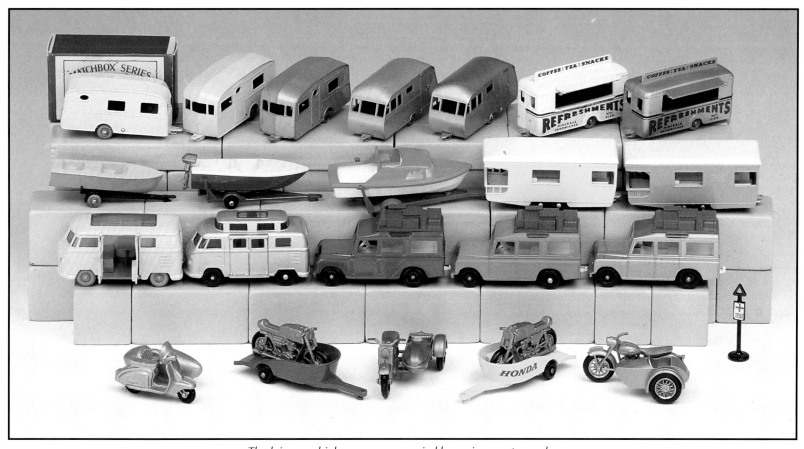

The leisure vehicles are accompanied by various motor cycles.

painted with a steel blue body although an example of a version with a metallic copper body, similar to that of the Harley Davidson, has been seen. This is presumed to be the result of Triumph castings being placed upon the wrong assembly line as the wheels were of the larger Harley Davidson type. An example was also rumoured to have been found in a Harley Davidson box. The mould for the Triumph Motor Cycle and Sidecar eventually broke, but another was quickly manufactured in its place and the opportunity was taken to

(17c). The colour should naturally have been black in line with the usual London cab colour scheme, but Lesney thought that the miniature looked too drab in black. The rest of the world market would not necessarily know that London taxis at this time appeared only in black and it was felt that a brighter colour would be more appealing to children. It was, therefore, decided to opt for a non-authentic maroon. The interior was usually grey although the final run was in a distinctly paler shade. Grey wheels were fitted originally but

range in September. It was a marvellous piece of model engineering and came complete with intricate and realistic decal advertisements. Painted in an authentic dark blue, its rear decal initially featured a crown above the rear advertisement. All three types of plastic wheels were fitted to this truck with the silver ones being the hardest to find. There are several minor casting variations with this model involving every section of the body whilst the final decal type included the red lettering in a fluorescent style.

Removers and Storers – Branches In All Large Towns' in three separate lines. Pickfords commissioned Lesney to produce a distinctive model with only two lines of lettering omitting the 'Branches In All Large Towns' and respacing the remaining two lines. These were usually given away by Pickfords to customers using their services from 1962 onwards. The model sold well and was available for eight years but there was a colour change to a green body during the mid 1960s . Near the end of the model's life the Bournemouth based department store of Beales also gave away about 3,000 of these vans to customers who spent above a certain sum in the store. They were recoloured exclusively for the promotion to a light brown body packaged in a distinctive white box with 'It's a pleasure' labels. As the company owned subsidiary stores around the Bournemouth area, these were known as Bealesons. Hence, the name on the side of the van featured 'Beales-Bealesons' so that the model could be given away to customers in both the main Bournemouth store and its subsidiaries. The models are generally accepted by collectors as Lesney produced models, although Jack Odell could not recall ever seeing one and doubted whether the machines would have been stopped to produce a few thousand models. *Odell:* "A special order would have needed to have been around the million figure as demand was so high that there was no place for special orders." The assembly, painting and application of decals were therefore performed elsewhere. It was perhaps fortunate with this model that nothing beyond a splayed clip needed to be spread in order to hold the base in place. These models are now sought after by many collectors and often command quite high prices for mint and boxed examples. Unfortunately, there have been some darker coloured fakes made of this model with angular rather than rounded decals.

The first model with an opening engine cover was the rear-engined, Volkswagen 1200 Sedan (25b). Though first advertised in July, it did not appear until October. It was the second release of the year to have a steel blue body. The new colour had been recently introduced by a supplier. *Smith:* "The normal Lesney policy with smaller models was to usually

Good value by today's standards - Christmas gifts from Lesney.

paint them in light colours in order to make the model look larger." The clear windows were superseded by green tinted replacements and either grey or silver wheels were fitted. Though the real car lays claim to the longest period of productivity, in that it was designed and built by Porsche before World War II and is still manufactured today in South America, the Matchbox model was included in the range for less than four years. Lesney were able to manufacture, during this relatively short period of time, far more examples of the Beetle than the total output of the world's most produced car over a period of five decades.

Despite the fact that only six new models appeared as replacement models during the year, there were several upgraded versions of familiar items. The third bus was a redesigned A.E.C. Routemaster (5c) in a larger scale. The normal decal advertisements were either 'Players Please' or 'BP

visco-static', but both 'Peardrax', from the Trolley Bus, 56a, and 'Baron of Beef' decals have also been noted. Unfortunately, it has been difficult to determine if these rare decals were put on at the factory. The original 'Baron of Beef' decals were applied by Lesney following an order from a London restaurant for buses which could be given to customers. As the buses were given away for more than three years from 1962 until 1965, several are known to exist. However, surplus decals were later sold to collectors and these may have been privately applied. Although No. 5 had been cast into the destination boards of the two previous buses, this was the first London bus to have the number included as part of the text on the baseplate. The final releases included criss-cross markings on the inside of the roof and there was a minor modification to the axle supports. Either grey or black plastic wheels were fitted.

No. 13 acquired the reputation of being an ill-fated model. *Odell:* "Somehow the person making the Wreck Truck always ended up getting the sack . . . The hook was not right. It got so that no-one wanted to make it." There did not appear to be too much wrong with the revised Ford Thames Trader Wreck Truck, (13c). It continued the tradition of wreckers at this number and was not considered to be a big enough change by Lesney to either call new or originally pack in a box different from that of the Bedford Wrecker, 13b. It had a red body with decal advertisements of 'Matchbox Garages', with or without an outline around the decal. The wheels were either grey or black plastic although the grey ones are the more difficult to find. The jib was initially of open lattice work but later this was cast fully closed whilst the boom could be in red or silver metal and later grey plastic.

A second trailer to be towed by

The advertisement reads:

IDEAL CHRISTMAS PRESENTS FOR ALL RAILWAY MODELLERS

PRECISION ENGINEERED 'MATCHBOX' MODELS

by LESNEY

Marvellous gifts for giving— even better to receive

MATCHBOX PRESENTATION SETS

No. 3. Car Transporter set 12/11.

No. 4. Commercial vehicle set 12/-.

MATCHBOX MODEL No. 74. Mobile canteen 1/6.

YESTERYEAR SERIES

No. 13. Sante Fe general locomotive 2/9.

No. 14. "Duke of Connaught" 4-2-2 locomotive. 2/9.

MAJOR PACK No. 6. Pickford 18-wheel transporter 3/11.

Lesney Products & Co. Ltd., Eastway, Hackney, London, E.9

A wide variety of trailers were always present in the range and some typical combinations are depicted.

the Prime Mover was called the Super Atlantic Trailer (16b) to complement the Super Atlantic Tractor, 15b, which had been available the previous year. The first version which can be quite difficult to find came with a light brown body and tow bar with grey plastic wheels. The whole model was soon recoloured orange but later the tow bar appeared in black or was left unpainted. The orange painted trailer was also fitted with

grey plastic wheels but subsequently these were superseded by black plastic. There was no longer a hinged ramp with this model and perhaps it was, therefore, less interesting than the first trailer. It lasted for only three years before being replaced by the Scammell Snow Plough.

A second American Ford Station Wagon, (31b), joined the range

during 1959. A Ford Fairlane replaced the Ford Customline. The same yellow colour was retained and the body did not appear to be significantly different. Lesney did not announce the updated version as a new model and so wholesalers, retailers and probably most purchasers did not concern themselves with the difference. Closer inspection would have

revealed clear or later green tinted plastic windows and twin instead of single headlights. A few models have been found without the windows fitted. Today a mint example of the yellow version commands a comparatively high price even though it was available for some time before the change to a two-tone livery of metallic green body and pink roof. Both colour versions may be found with either a crimson or a black base. Black plastic wheels were fitted only to the two-tone version and this may be hard to find but both grey and silver plastic wheels may be found on both colour variations. A slight modification was made to the area around the towing hook. A Lincoln Continental replaced the Station Wagon in 1964.

The second version of the 2 ton Karrier Bantam Coca-Cola Truck (37b) emerged in 1960. There is sometimes some confusion with the number of variants. It is now generally considered that the model without a base, 37a, bene-fitted from a casting modification only when the uneven crates were altered to allow the mould to run better. 37b is, therefore, usually accepted as the truck with a base. The body only appeared in bright yellow but the rear decal comes in two distinct sizes. Many casting changes to the cab design may be recognised such as the re-designed radiator and steps below each door. Grey or black wheels were usually fitted although very rarely silver plastic wheels have also been found on this model.

A larger version of the 'D' Type Jaguar (41b) was released in 1960. It retained the dark green body of its predecessor and the front scoop which was at first cast open was soon filled in. The usual decal number was '41' but both '5' (from the Y5/1 Bentley) and '6' (from the Y6/2 Bugatti) are known to exist. When the first models were made available, they were fitted with solid grey plastic wheels. Later this changed to black tyres on wire wheels and a very short final run saw the fitment of black tyres on red wheels making this version quite rare.

1960 – New models and replace-ments in their usual colour scheme:

27c Cadillac Fleetwood Sixty Special in metallic lilac and pink

4c Triumph Motor Cycle and Sidecar in steel blue
17c Austin Metropolitan Taxi in maroon
10c Foden Sugar Container in blue
46b Pickfords Removal Van in blue or green
25b Volkswagen Sedan in steel blue

5c Routemaster Bus in red
13c Thames Trader Wreck Truck in red
16b Super Atlantic Trailer orange
31b Ford Fairlane Station Wagon in metallic green with pale pink roof
37b Karrier Coca-Cola Truck with base in yellow
41b 'D' Type Jaguar in green

1961

Lesney continued their technical improvement of the range during 1961 with models which had been available for some time now being sold in upgraded versions often with two-tone liveries and windows. This concept had proved to be successful with the second version of the Vauxhall Cresta which had first been released in the U.S.A. in August 1960. Other models were to feature these improvements in 1961. Lesney were their own fiercest critics and were always looking for ways to improve their products. Rival toy companies were growing and so the makers of Matchbox were keen to remain the market leaders and any innovation was considered. Metallic paint cost a little more to purchase and to apply but if the change stimulated demand or enhanced the visual impact of a model, this was all to the good. This was reflected in the price, however, with the first increase since 1953. From February 1961 the cost of models in the range in the U.K.

rose from 1s. 6d. (7.5p) to 1s. 8d. (8p), which, of course, included purchase tax!

In January 1961 the American Ford Fairlane Station Wagon (31b) which, like its predecessor, the Ford Customline, had always been painted yellow, was now issued in the two-tone colour scheme of metallic green and pale pink. The Ford Zodiac, 33a, which could be found in several shades of green was now briefly available in metallic mauve and orange. During the year this was improved further by the addition of windows. Two other models, the Vauxhall Victor, 45a, and Thames Estate Car, 70a, remained in their old colours but were fitted with windows.

Lesney aimed to release at least one new model each month in order to stimulate interest with children and collectors of all ages. One of the first releases for 1961 was the third issue Caravan, a Bluebird Dauphine, (23c), featuring an opening door. The first release proved to be the hardest model to find as it was painted in metallic lime green, the same colour as the final version of the previous 23b, Berkeley Caravan. The usual colour for this caravan was metallic mauve and it was fitted with the three wheel types of grey, silver and black plastic. It was available for five years and during this time was strengthened in several places by thicker braces. However, perhaps the most interesting feature is that some time during its issue it was fitted with a green tinted window insert. Only two models are known to exist with this fitting and one is currently on permanent show in the Chester Toy Museum. It is presumed that this was a prototype and that Lesney decided against its inclusion for this vehicle.

In February the Chevrolet Impala Sedan (57b) replaced the Wolseley 1500. It appeared in two-tone blue and included

Vehicles to suit every taste.

windows and a towing hook. Early versions had clear windows but these soon gave way to green tinted ones. The base may be found painted either blue or black. First issues had silver paint masked sprayed to the front and the rear, as well as red rear lights, but during the early 1960s in the interests of economy the rear end remained blue with no added decoration.

In the early 1960s scooters were a relatively cheap form of transport most popular with the younger generation. By itself a scooter would be difficult to play with and so a sidecar was fitted to the pale metallic green Lambretta TV 175, (36b). It replaced the Austin A50 and like the Chevrolet was in the range for five years. Odell was very critical of the model because

Above: A second set of construction vehicles issued between 1958 and 1964.

of its casting and what he thought to be poor sales potential. However, the model was included in the range for more than five years and so perhaps his worst fears were not recognised in sales terms.

March brought the release of a Ford Anglia (7b) one of the most popular cars on Britain's roads during the 1960s. Like the real car it featured an inward sloping rear window. It was only available in pale blue although earlier versions sported more silver paintwork and red rear lights. The Anglia was fitted with grey, silver or black plastic wheels. It replaced the Horse Drawn Milk Float and remained in the range for six years.

The first European truck to appear in the range was also released in March. It was a Magirus-Deutz Crane Truck (30b) and the normal colour scheme was a silver body with an orange jib and hook. Models have been found with a tan body and either a red or orange jib with a matching

Below: An Austin Cambridge for 1s. 8d. – Pocket Money Toys!

hook. These versions are presumed to be colour trial models. Grey, silver and black plastic wheels were all fitted whilst the colour of the metal hook changed from orange to silver and finally to grey plastic. There are numerous small casting changes with this model. Perhaps the most noticeable being the rear of the crane which was originally open at the rear but was later closed. *Odell:* "This Crane Truck was a fantastic seller." At this time Lesney were pleased to point out that all of their models were now finished in lead-free paint, a fact which may well have interested careful parents.

Two-tone metallic paint proved to be popular during 1961 and April saw the release of a two-tone green Farina Austin Cambridge (29b) which took the place of the Bedford Milk Float. This model had green windows and a towing hook and was fitted with all three colour wheels. The amount of trim declined during its five year inclusion in the range.

Although the 1950s style of luxury coach like 21a and 21b, could still be commonly seen as real vehicles on Britain's roads, a new type of coach was emerging, quite distinctive from the old. Thus (40b) the Leyland Royal Tiger Coach, was added to the range to replace the old Bedford Tipper. This model also featured windows and a polychromatic steel blue finish. Early versions had red rear lights and this coach may be found with all three wheel versions. The model was the longest yet produced in the range and had to be fitted into a longer than normal box. The actual vehicle was an experimental body version and really rather obscure for an everyday road vehicle.

The next two miniatures became available in July 1961. They were old themes in a new format. The pale green Milk Delivery Truck (21c) was a Commer and came

complete with cream or white moulded bottles in miniature crates. The cab was fully glazed, originally in clear but more usually with green windows. Bright advertising signs on the roof and doors changed during its seven year inclusion in the range, from a bottle to a cow design. All three wheel types occurred but the grey wheeled version is much harder to find. At the time of printing the catalogue the model was not ready and so an artist's impression of a Milk Float in blue with a sliding door and a yellow flat roof, quite unlike the actual model, was substituted.

A Bedford TK Tipper (3b) replaced the Cement Mixer. It had an opening tailboard and a super-detailed chassis. The cab was always painted grey but the tipper changed from maroon to red during its six year life. The red and tan version shown in the 1961 catalogue was only an artist's impression. It is to be found with both grey and black wheels.

August saw the release of two models, both of which included for the first time a major component made from plastic. An up-dated Cement Mixer (26b) now mounted on a six-wheel Foden chassis instead of the former ERF body, featured a revolving plastic container. For a very short period this container was made in either light or dark grey plastic and this is rare today as the usual run had an orange container. For the first years of its life this model had grey wheels but later black wheels were fitted. Casting modifications occurred when it became necessary to strengthen the chassis beneath the barrel.

The second August issue, the (48b) trailer with removeable plastic sports boat, which was advertised to sail and float, was another update on the previous all metal version. It featured a tiny outboard motor which could be moved up or down for use on a river or during transportation. The trailer could be found in either

dark or light blue, normally with black plastic wheels but there was a short run with grey plastic wheels. The colours of the detachable boat were red and either cream or white and as the colours were reversible, either the deck or the hull could be found in red. The engine was plated in either gold or silver. Neither of the boats and trailers proved to be very popular. The 48a lasted three years whilst 48b with a plastic boat was produced for five years.

In 1961 the third versions of the Caterpillar Tractor (8c) and Bulldozer (18c) were issued. They were considerably larger at 48 mm and 58 mm than 8b and 18b. They were fitted with metal as well as silver and black plastic rollers, with the silver versions being the most difficult to find. By this time all models had been manufactured with numbers on their bases. However, the Caterpillar moulds were used for both 8c and 18c and so to avoid confusion, the number was deleted. First issues show the complete number which could be either an 8 or an 18. The erasure of the number was not perfect on one of the two moulds and so part of the number could be seen on some of the later releases. At either end of the section bearing the description, Lesney England, two small strengthening braces were added to later models.

No further models were issued during 1961, despite the fact that line drawings in the catalogue of the future Aston Martin Racer, (19c), and the Volkswagen Caravette, (34b), indicated that they would soon become available.

1961 – New models and replacements in their usual colours:

23c Bluebird Dauphine Caravan in metallic mauve
57b Chevrolet Impala in two-tone blue
36b Lambretta Scooter and Sidecar in pale metallic green
7b Ford Anglia in pale blue

30b Magirus-Deutz Crane Truck with silver body and orange jib
29b Austin Cambridge in two-tone green
40b Leyland Royal Tiger Coach in steel blue
21c Commer Milk Delivery Truck in pale green
3b Bedford TK Tipper with grey body and either maroon or red tipper
26b Foden Cement Mixer in orange
48b Sports Boat in red and white & blue trailer

8c Caterpillar Tractor in yellow
18c Caterpillar Bulldozer in yellow

1962

There was another price increase in February 1962 to 1s. 9d. (9p). However, the models intended for release during the year showed that the small increase was being put to good use with even more detailed features. In addition, the old style boxes were replaced during the year with boxes showing the models in full colour instead of a line drawing.

In February, the second car to have an opening engine cover became available. Following the Volkswagen Sedan, 25b, in 1960 with a rear opening engine cover, the 3.8 litre Jaguar (65b) featured an opening bonnet which revealed a detailed silver-grey engine. Initially the body was painted metallic red with silver wheels and green tinted windows, but later releases were in plain red, of which shades exist, with silver, grey or black wheels. As the die wore, so the final models had a grille of re-duced size and the grille badge, visible on the earlier models, gradually wore away.

The new Jaguar was joined in the range by the metallic green

A superb model of the 3.8 litre Jaguar introduced to coincide with the launch of the actual car in 1962.

Aston Martin DBR 5 Grand Prix Racing Car (19c) replacing the two previous M.G.'s. Its size was larger than was originally intended because the scale on the pantograph was set wrongly. Subsequently, models were made to fit in with this larger scale. It was another first for Lesney in that the intricate wire spokes cast on the wheels were claimed to be the smallest and finest produced at that time. The driver was originally in grey plastic and then later in white. The decal number was normally '19', but numbers '52', '5', '3' and '41' from other models have been reported. Although the model was intricate in detail it was one of the shortest lived models of the

1960s, being issued for only three years. In April a fourth American car was included in the range, a Pontiac Convertible (36b) not least because the U.S.A. was now Lesney's largest overseas market. It superseded the Zodiac Convertible and was metallic violet in colour with a red steering wheel. The body was later changed to yellow and eventually the steering wheel became part of the interior in cream or off-white. The base also changed from crimson to black. The yellow version came with all three types of wheels, but the rarer metallic violet version was only fitted with grey or silver plastic wheels.

In May, the 1962 catalogue

showed several of the new issues for the earlier part of the year as well as the fourth and largest version of the Aveling Barford Diesel Road Roller, (1d). This green model had red plastic rollers and maintained the tradition of a road roller at No. 1 until 1967, a period of fourteen years. No trim colour was applied and the driver was painted in the same colour as the body. It had a separate baseplate which came with or without a hole. The final verison included two base rivets and revised base lettering with some of the text moved to the underside of the roof.

The ambulance theme connected with No. 14 was continued in May, but the Bedford TJ Lomas (14c) was issued with a fully fitted cream or white interior revealed by twin opening rear doors. It also had 'L.C.C. Ambulance' and a red cross decal on each side. A possible trial run version of this model has been found with a red cross on the roof as advertised at the time in *Railway Modeller*. This may have been the original idea because cast roof guidelines for the application of a decal were provided on the roof on early models, although in the event a decal was not applied. All three wheel types were applied to this model although black wheels are by far the most common. Most of these new models were being fitted with plastic windows but this did not occur with the Lomas Ambulance. A driver's bench was part of the interior moulding, but there was no steering wheel.

The long awaited Volkswagen Devon Caravette Motor Caravan (34b) finally made its appearance in June 1962 and proved to be well worth the wait. It was advertised as having 'a double-coat, lead-free, stove-enamelled finish and tinted windows'. The opening doors revealed a very detailed interior with seats, table and washbasin. The pale green body was complemented by a

darker green interior. One of the interior doors and both windows were subject to casting changes but perhaps the most noticeable modification concerned the interior which was changed from being riveted to the base to an all-in-one casting so that the interior became part of the base casting. The Caravette came in all three plastic wheel versions and was issued for five years. As explained previously, sometimes a model would have to wait six months before issue whilst the orders were collated to ensure a simultaneous release date worldwide, and this may have been the case with 34b.

July brought the arrival of an updated Dumper described as a Muir-Hill Dumper (2c) with 'Laing' decals on the driver's door. This model was the first to be packaged in a fully coloured picture box. Within a very few months the whole range was similarly boxed. The dumper body was red and the tipper green although this was a late colour change by Lesney as the first box and the several catalogues show this model illustrated in the reverse colours. This catalogue example was a pre-production model. The Dumper existed for five years with no major changes.

By August 1962, Lesney claimed to have sold over 20,000,000 miniature items of contractors' equipment. To increase this achievement the Hillman Minx was replaced by an Aveling-Barford TS250 Tractor Shovel (43b) with working arms to raise and lower the bucket and new style, extra large wheels. The body remained in yellow throughout the model's six year life but the shovel, base and driver could be either yellow or red. This resulted in four possible colour permutations. The all-yellow version, as shown in the 1963 catalogue and on the first box is probably the most difficult to find together with the version with red shovel and red driver.

The 'E' Type Jaguar (32b) was released in September and reflected a tremendous increase in detail in comparison with its predecessor, the XK 140 Jaguar. Whereas 32a had just a body and base, the 32b 'E' Type boasted

Two more models were replaced in October. The B.E.A. Coach gave way to an International Drott Excavator (58b) whilst the 66a Citroen was substituted by a third model with a sidecar, this time a Harley

seller and it was included in the range for just over three years.

The Harley Davidson, a beautiful model, lasted slightly longer, four years, and now commands one of the highest prices in mint condition for a

covered the parts so evenly. Component suppliers often worked very closely with us and were keen to assist in maximising sales." Sales of the Harley in the U.S.A. were expected to be high because the real motorcycle orig-

Emergency vehicles were always included in the range.

fourteen individual parts. The off-white interior fittings included a steering wheel, seats and a luggage shelf whilst the cast wire wheels were plated. A high-gloss paint finish in metallic red completed the beautifully contoured appearance. Initially, the Jaguar was fitted with green tinted windows as advertised in U.S.A. magazines, but very soon these gave way to clear windows. The Jaguar was not replaced until February 1968 even although some Lesney personnel believed the model to be somewhat undersized.

Davidson Motorcycle and Sidecar, (66b). The two models being removed were sold in colour picture boxes for a very short time until their withdrawal and are amongst the rarest in this type of box. The Drott had working arms which could raise and lower the bucket and rubber tracks. Originally the model appeared in red with a silver engine but later versions were in orange and finally with an orange engine. A short run of the red excavator had silver rollers but the general issue was fitted with black rollers. The model was not a particularly good

standard model. It was illustrated on the box and in the 1963 catalogue in blue but it was actually released in metallic copper, a colour obtained through the use of a vacuum plating process. *Smith:* "At this time Lesney were experimenting with different paints and finishing processes. Sometimes a paint manufacturer would indicate to us that a new type of paint was available which may well suit a particular model. In the case of the Harley, the paint used covered the intricate details completely, whereas a more conventional paint may not have

inated from there, but, perhaps because of the colour, did not meet expectations. Equally, perhaps, Lesney had saturated the market by having two motorcycles and a scooter in the range at the same time.

November saw the release of the first Ferrari racing car, (73b). It represented the latest rear-engined Formula 1 racer with the characteristic shark's nose front end, megaphone exhaust pipes, an authentic decal of the famous prancing horse insignia with a No. 73 racing number and, true to tradition, the wire wheels which distinguished Ferrari from all of the other conten-

SUPER NEW "MATCHBOX" VALUE

14 individual parts make up this great new model priced at only 1/9. Just look at some of these features:

★ BEAUTIFULLY CONTOURED SUPER-DETAILED DIECAST BODY

★ UNBREAKABLE PLASTIC TYRES ON PLATED "SEE-THROUGH" WIRE WHEELS

★ UNIQUE HIGH-GLOSS DOUBLE STOVE-ENAMELLED PAINT FINISH

★ CLOSE-FITTING CLEAR WINDOWS WITH "OPEN" DRIVER'S WINDOWS

★ INTERIOR FITTINGS INCLUDE SEATS, LUGGAGE SHELF, STEERING WHEEL, ETC.

NEW - AT ONLY 1/9

New "Matchbox" Series No. 32 "E" TYPE JAGUAR length 2⅝ inches. Scale 65 : 1

MORE VINTAGE VALUE THIS MONTH

New "Models of Yesteryear" No. Y-8, 1914 Sunbeam motor-cycle with Milford sidecar

Superb silvered finish. Handlebars actually steer. Plated wire wheels. Packed in new, full-colour box with historical notes. Length 2⅝ in., scale 34 : 1. Price 4/-.

1962 full colour catalogue showing over 130 models now available at your "Matchbox" store. In case of difficulty, write direct, sending 3d. stamp, to Dept. RM6, **Lesney Products & Co. Ltd.,** Eastway, London, E.9

A 1962 advertisement extolling the virtues of the latest Jaguar to join the range.

ders in the 1962 Grand Prix races. The driver for 73b was the same one as for the Aston Martin Racer.

1962 – New models and their usual colour scheme:

- 65b Jaguar 3.8 in red
- 19c Aston Martin DBR 5 Racer in metallic green
- 39b Pontiac Convertible in metallic violet or yellow
- 1d Aveling Barford Road Roller in green with red plastic wheels
- 14c Bedford Lomas Ambulance in white
- 34b Volkswagen Caravette in pale green
- 2c Muir Hill 'Laing' Dumper with red cab and green tipper
- 43b Aveling Barford Tractor

Shovel in yellow and red
- 32b 'E' Type Jaguar in metallic red
- 58b Drott Excavator in red
- 66b Harley Davidson and Sidecar in metallic copper
- 73b Ferrari Racer in red

1963

In 1963 Lesney announced one of the largest expansion programmes ever undertaken in the toy industry. A new factory in Lee Conservancy Road added another 200,000 additional square feet of floor space to the 110,000 square feet of the existing factories in nearby streets at the Eastway group of factories. The new

building was to cost in the region of £1,000,000 and completion time was expected to be within eighteen months. The factory was to be one of the largest toy producing factories in Europe with more than one hundred and fifty automatic diecasting machines being designed, built and installed by Lesney's own engineers. By this time more than 60% of Lesney's products were being exported.

In February 1963 a Police Car entered the range as a replacement for the D.U.K.W. It was a Ford Fairlane (55b) and was representative of the Police cars familiar in a television series, imported from the U.S.A. It was initially painted dark blue, now quite a rare colour, but very quickly altered to metallic blue. The Fairlane had a cream plastic interior and a red roof light with bonnet and door Police badge decals. The wheels were normally black although both silver and grey wheeled cars have been found.

The sensation of the year depicted on the front cover of the 1963 catalogue was to be a Mercedes Benz 220SE coupe (53b) which was claimed to be the first model saloon car with opening doors. This feature was possible because the doors were held in place by an interior moulding. Early models were in maroon whilst later releases were red. A colour trial model has been found

Opening doors with no unsightly gap – competitors take note!

FANTASTIC "MATCHBOX"!

- Opening Doors • Seats • Steering Wheels
- Windows • Authentic Transfers

Here's REAL New Year pocket-money value at only 1/9

New "Matchbox" Series No. 53, Mercedes 220SE Coupe. 1/9.

New "Matchbox" Series No. 55, Police Car. 1/9.

Stop Press! Terrific new 24-page full-colour "Matchbox" International Catalogue now available at your "Matchbox" stockist. In case of difficulty write direct, sending 3d. in stamps, to: Dept. RM1, **Lesney Products & Co. Ltd.,** Eastway, Hackney Wick, London, E.9   Telephone: AMHurst 0541

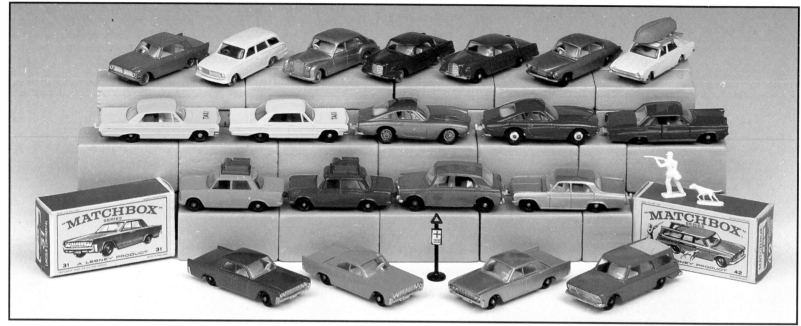

Below: By 1963, Lesney had introduced innovative features to add play value to their toys.

in gold. All three types of wheel may be found. The model was the longest miniature yet produced and had to be fitted into a longer than normal box. It replaced the 53a Aston Martin and was issued for five years.

March saw the release of a Commer 'Lyons Maid' ice-cream van, (47b). A short run of metallic blue which is now quite difficult to find, was later changed to blue and finally to cream. It featured considerable internal detail including freezers, authentic transfers and a salesman with an ice-cream at the ready. There were three different kinds of decal for both the van sides and roof. The salesman actually came in three different sizes because three different interior plastic moulds were used. The van was fitted with black wheels throughout its five year life with the exception of a very short run with grey wheels. The base was secured either by a clip or a rivet. To make way for this model, the Trojan 'Brooke Bond Tea' van was withdrawn from the range.

May brought the introduction of

another first for Lesney. The Ford Zodiac was replaced by a Ford Zephyr 6 (33b) which featured clear windows, cream seats and a steering wheel. It also featured spring suspension on all four wheels, which were to be found in grey, silver or black plastic. The body came in various shades of sea-green and earlier releases featured red-painted rear lights.

To accompany the Zephyr, a Vauxhall Victor Estate Car (38b) was released to replace the Refuse Truck. Although shown on the box and in the catalogue in blue, it was only available in yellow with initially a red and later a green interior. Silver trim was applied but as usual diminished with time. Both interior variations were fitted with the three wheel variations. The opening rear door was, of course, another new play feature.

Another Ford Fairlane was released in June to replace the 'Singer' van. This model had not previously been announced and so it is presumed that it was a

sudden decision to use the same vehicle as 55b in a change of colour and guise, in that it was now a red Fire Chief's car (59b) instead of the Police car. At the same time a large Matchbox Fire Station was manufactured and so this car complemented the release. The red Fairlane came with door and bonnet decals in two sizes. Although the interior was ivory, the roof light was white. Black plastic wheels were normally fitted but grey plastic wheels have also been found. Silver wheels have also been reported.

In July a cream Commer T.V. Service Van (62b) was added to the line. Replacing the General Service Truck, it came complete with three plastic television sets, a ladder, an aerial and a working rear roller shutter door. During most of its five year life it advertised 'Rentaset' in red script lettering but shortly before it was deleted, green 'RADIO RENTALS' advertisements were substituted. The windows were always of green plastic but whereas earlier models had the black painted baseplate connected to the body by means of base clips, front and rear, later releases included a rivet at the front. There were also minor casting changes concerning the ladder rests. Although most vans had black wheels, both variations were available with grey wheels in very small numbers. This is often a difficult model to find complete because the small parts were originally part of one plastic red moulding on a sprue. As soon as they were separated, it was easy for the small televisions to be lost as they were carried loose in the back of the van, whereas the ladder and aerial could be secured to the roof of the van.

In August a 6-wheel Euclid Quarry Truck (6c) replaced the earlier version. The model looked as though it had ten wheels but, in fact, the heavy duty rear wheels were of a single moulding. Later

individual wheels were fitted. All were of black plastic although there are variations in design, particularly with the front wheels. The tipper body could be fixed in any position. The model was originally decorated with silver trim but this was dropped before the model's deletion in 1968. There are a number of minor casting variations with this truck affecting the body, chassis and base.

In September 1963 a Scammell Mountaineer Snowplough (16c) entered the range where it remained for six years. It replaced the Rotinoff Super Atlantic Trailer and although originally shown in the 1963 catalogue in yellow with a grey blade and a 'Scammell' decal, it was released with a grey cab and an orange tipper with either orange and white or red and white stripes on the blade. The base came with or without a hole and the steps to the cab could be found open or closed. A model with grey plastic wheels is a rare variation for these were only fitted in small quantities towards the end of this model's life. Black plastic wheels are usually associated with this model.

The final issue of 1963 was a Dennis Tippax Refuse Truck (15c) with opening tailgate, replacing the Rotinoff Tractor in November. It had a dark blue cab and grey container displaying a 'Cleansing Department' decal which could be either angled or square ended. The container may be found with, or very rarely without, a small front hole. Before it was deleted from the range after a life of five years, labels replaced decals and the silver trim was dropped. All models were fitted with black wheels.

1963 – New models and their usual colour scheme:

55b Ford Fairlane Police Car in metallic blue
53b Mercedes 220SE Coupe in maroon or red
47b 'Lyons Maid' Ice Cream Van in blue or cream

33b Ford Zephyr 6 in green
38b Vauxhall Victor Estate Car in yellow
59b Ford Fairlane Fire Chief's Car in red
62b T.V. Service Van in cream
6c Euclid Quarry Truck in yellow
16c Scammell Snowplough
15c Dennis Refuse Truck in dark blue and grey container

1964

The Leipzig Award for outstanding design and construction was made annually to specific companies exhibiting at The Leipzig Toy Fair held behind the Iron Curtain in East Germany. In 1964 Lesney were given the Award for their "Matchbox" Series. Although the sales in these Socialist countries were comparatively low, Lesney knew it was important to be present at the toy fair each year with their new products.

In 1964 the price of the range was increased to 1s. 11d. (9.5p) each. The theme for the new models was working suspension as revealed in the 1964 catalogue. Two new cars were advertised with this feature in advance literature as well as new models of a pick-up and a truck.

In January the first release for the year appeared in the form of a Jeep Gladiator Pick-up, (71b), with suspension. It was painted red and had opening doors with either a plastic or a metal door spring. This model had black wheels and a black base which came with and without a patent number. The green interior was fairly common in Europe but soon all models had white interiors.

February saw the release of a Rolls Royce Phantom V (44b) with opening boot. Its colour varied between a light metallic mauve and silver grey. A cream interior, suspension and a black base was

common to all variations, but silver trim was not applied to later models. All three types of plastic wheel were fitted. Although a Rolls Royce was usually included in the range, it had not been a great seller. This was certainly true of the Phantom for it was only produced for three years. A pre-production model is known to exist in green.

One of Odell's favourite models joined the range in March, the Foden, Hoveringham Tipper, (17d). Although the windows shown in the 1964 catalogue were not fitted, this may be explained by the fact that eight-wheelers were always expensive to produce because of the amount of assembly work involved. The red body carried an orange tipper with large 'Hoveringham' decals and green or white plastic springs were fitted over the first and third axles until this feature was dropped from the final releases. Early models had black bases but later versions had red bases. Slight modifications affected the tipper stop and the area around the axle holes.

In April the Military Ambulance was replaced by an Alvis Salamander 'Foamite' Airport Crash Tender (63b) although it was not until November that it was released in the U.S.A. It was an attempted reproduction of a typical Airport Crash Tender which would have been used to spray an aircraft fire with foam. Unfortunately for the connoisseur, Lesney had wished to maximise play value and this led to the main body being derived from a Pyrene vehicle and the roof detail originating from the Foamite Tender. Of course, this did not affect the huge demand for this new variation of fire appliance. This model came with a ladder, hoses and two plastic nameplates which had lugs to fit into holes on the sides of the model. The front and rear pair of the six wheels were sprung although this was abandoned on later versions.

Commercial vehicles. The 'Aral' Tankers were produced for the European market.

Most models had gold foam hoses but a few were fitted with silver hoses. The springs on the base of the model were either white or green.

Two new models were introduced into the range in May. The first was a B.P. Petrol Tanker with a Bedford TK cab (25c) which tilted forwards to reveal a steering wheel, seats and an engine which had been cast as part of the base. This feature was included purely for play value as the real Bedford TK did not have a tilting cab! However, it is known that this feature had been considered for the real vehicle when prototypes were being developed. It could have been coincidence or possibly Lesney had some advance information about a new Bedford TK! Models with grey plastic wheels are rare, as the general issue had

black wheels. Another first with regard to this vehicle was that it later appeared in blue and white instead of yellow-green and white featuring blue 'Aral' decals for the German market. This colour change for an overseas market reflected the huge demand in Europe and today the blue version is a sought after variation. The tanker replaced the Volks-wagen Sedan and was issued for four years.

Another issue for May was a Mark Ten Jaguar (28c) complete with suspension. The real car had been available since 1961 and was quite a common sight, at least on Britain's roads, by 1964. Although shown in blue in the catalogue and on the box, the release colour was a light metallic brown and featured black plastic wheels. A boxed version with grey wheels has been found in South Africa,

but this may have been a colour trial model. The opening bonnet revealed an engine which was painted the same colour as the body. Towards the end of this car's four year period of inclusion in the range, the engine was left unpainted because the bonnet was assembled before painting. The Jaguar superseded the Compressor Truck.

The Taylor Jumbo Crane (11c) replaced the ERF Petrol Tanker in June. It was usually found in all over yellow with a red double chain hook. When the weight box was painted red, a few hooks appeared with single chains in either red or yellow plastic. The jib was subject to a number of casting changes, the model being available for five years.

August saw the release of a combination Tractor and Trailer. The green John Deere Lanz 700

Tractor (70b) was fitted with yellow wheels and steering wheel. Either grey or black tyres were fitted. The Tipping Trailer (51b) was in the same shade of green and it too was fitted with either grey or black tyres on yellow hubs. Three yellow plastic barrels were included as a load.

In September, a Snow-Trac (35b) joined the range. The model was based on a detailed example of a Swedish vehicle and came with a red body, silver base and grille and green tinted windows. White rubber tracks were fitted around the six black plastic wheels. A white decal with 'Snow-Trac' was originally applied by hand to the side of the vehicle, but when labels generally replaced decals it was found that the labelling machine could not apply the labels properly because the area in question was recessed. A number of models exist without any description until the die was modified to include cast lettering.

In the same month a Lincoln Continental (31c) continued the American theme on. It featured spring suspension and an opening boot. It was coloured originally in a dark metallic blue which appeared in lighter shades as time progressed. There was a colour change to a turquoise in the late 1960s and a few examples exist of this Lincoln with regular wheels but in the Superfast colour of metallic lime green. The turquoise variation with Superfast wheels is one of the rarest changeover models.

The Caterpillar Tractor again was reviewed as the range had continued to grow in size over the years and as demand was still high, it was decided for a third time to make a new, larger model. The new model (8d) is easily differentiated from the previous releases because on this occasion no driver was cast. The yellow body colour was retained with either a large or a small exhaust stack and with or without a base hole. Green tracks were again fitted to black plastic rollers. This model was only manufactured for a period of two years before being replaced by the Ford Mustang.

The Caterpillar Bulldozer (18d) was also enlarged and the details given for the Caterpillar Tractor are equally applicable for the Bulldozer with the exception that silver plastic rollers were originally fitted before a changeover in black plastic rollers. The Bulldozer was not withdrawn from the range until 1969.

1964 – New models and their usual colour scheme:

71b Jeep Gladiator Pick-up in red
44b Rolls Royce Phantom V in light metallic mauve
17d 'Hoveringham' Tipper in red and orange
63d Airport Crash Tender in red
25c Bedford 'B.P.' Tanker in lemon, white and green
28c Mark Ten Jaguar in metallic brown
11c Taylor Jumbo Crane in yellow
50b John Deere Tractor in green
51b Trailer in green
35b Snow-trac in red
31c Lincoln Continental in metallic blue
8d Caterpillar Tractor in yellow

18d Caterpillar Bulldozer in yellow

1965

On 1 January 1965 the range in the U.K. was increased in price by a penny to two shillings (10p). The original 49c in the U.S.A. remained until 1966, when it was increased to 55c. Two million models were being produced weekly by a workforce of three thousand. The company could not keep up with demand and it was difficult to select models to be dropped from the range in the light of such good sales. However, two vehicles were released in January. By now it was usual for Lesney to produce two identical moulds for each die. This allowed the casting

The later regular wheel construction models represent a wide cross-section of real vehicles.

machines to have a double output. Each die was expected to produce at least five million trouble free models.

Although the Studebaker Lark Station Wagon (42b) had been released in the U.S.A. in November 1964, it did not appear in Europe until the new year. This model displayed a sliding roof over the rear compartment and a white plastic hunter complete with rifle and hound. Early models were painted completely in blue but as time went by the sliding roof became progresively lighter in colour until this part became a separate shade of blue.

The Hatra Tractor Shovel (69b) was painted orange with grey tyres on orange hubs. The tyres were soon changed to black and for a time the hubs were red until the whole model was changed to yellow. Some crossovers have been noted in colours between the body and shovel as well as red wheels on yellow bodies and vice versa but these have not been easy to find and have been produced by accident.

The Ford Corsair (45b) complete with green plastic roof rack and boat, was released in February. It was only ever painted in a pale primrose yellow and featured a red interior and tow hook as well as suspension. The brown boat displayed on the first box for this model never appeared. A short run of this model had a silver grey painted base. A Corsair with a white interior is on display at the Chester Toy Museum but this is a pre-production model.

Also in February an ultra-modern Trailer Caravan (23d) with a detachable roof revealing a detailed pale blue interior became the fourth caravan in the range. Although the first box of the model depicted a blue body, it was available in yellow initially and later in pink. The red interior

shown in the 1965 catalogue was a pre-production colour.

April saw the appearance of the second Chevrolet Impala, on this occasion as a New York yellow-cab (20c) in either light or dark yellow. This taxi incorporated a driver as part of the detailed interior which was usually cream but could be found in red. The bonnet displayed a taxi decal which was later replaced by a label. The taxi always had clear rather than the tinted windows of the 1965 catalogue. Examples of grey plastic wheels rather than the normal black plastic wheels have been found, but these are very rare. An early short run had a silver-grey rather than an unpainted base.

The second model of this month was a Dodge Wreck Truck, (13d). The cab was shown on the box and in the catalogue in green with the body in yellow with a grey plastic hook. This very rare colour scheme has been verified, although some forgeries were produced in the factory some time later with crimped axles and labels and so detection is comparatively easy. The common version is in reverse colours with a yellow cab and green body. Later versions had red hooks and final issues had labels.

Although the Ferrari Berlinetta (75b) was shown in the 1965 catalogue in blue, it was in fact painted in metallic green. The first release in May had a silver grey base whilst all subsequent models had unpainted bases. Originally the wheels were tyres fitted to wire wheels, but these were dropped in favour of tyres on solid silver wheels. The Berlinetta was one of those rare models whose body appeared in the new Superfast colour of red but which was issued in tiny quantities with regular wheels. This variation is extremely rare.

In June the fourth red London Bus (5d) was issued. It is immed-iately recognisable as it was fitted

with a white plastic interior and was slightly larger than 5c, the earlier A.E.C. Routemaster. The base came with either a five or four line description. Lesney applied both 'B.P. Longlife' decals and redesigned 'B.P. visco-static' decals or labels. In addition, the 'Baron of Beef' decals added by Lesney and 'Pegram' labels applied by the firm of shop-fitters with Lesney's permission com-pleted the number of authentic advertisements. The casting around the rear of the bus was later strengthened as was the base area around the axles.

A sporting theme commenced with a red Pontiac Grand Prix Sports Coupe (22c) which featured opening doors, a centre console as part of the grey plastic interior, a tow hook and suspension. The earlier bases came without patent numbers and the door springs were altered from plastic to metal. The model continued into the Superfast era in 1970.

In July a model of Jim Clark's famous Formula 1 Lotus Racer with a Coventry Climax engine (19d) appeared in traditional British Racing green with yellow stripes and plated engine and exhausts. The plastic driver remained in white although the bonnet and side number '3' could be a decal, a label or a mixture of both. In the G4 Gift Set the Racer came with an orange body with either decals or labels.

In the same month the Fiat 1500 (56b) fitted with a roof rack joined the range. It is probably one of the most common regular wheel models to be found and, of course, the real vehicle can still be seen today as a Lada with only minor alterations. However, in the G1 Gift Set, this Fiat was painted in all over red with tan luggage and is considerably harder to find than the normal green version.

August saw the release of an 8-wheel Faun Crane Truck (30c) with a green body and orange revolving jib. One variation involved a red

hook instead of the normal yellow hook. A model with a turquoise body was found in a G6 Gift Set.

The Crane Truck was accom-panied by a white S & S Cadillac Ambulance, (54b). This had red cross decals, which were later replaced by labels in two sizes, and blue tinted windows and red roof lights as well as a detailed white interior and suspension.

In September the BRM Formula 1 Racer (52b) was released to com-plement the Lotus Racer. The new model replaced the Maserati and had a plated engine, exhaust pipes and suspension. The first model was painted blue but red versions appeared in G4 Gift Sets. The number five on the nose and sides came originally in decal form but later as a label. The blue BRM was fitted with a No. '3' decal for a short time.

A short wheelbase Mercedes Coach, (68b), was released in September. This coach was shown in the 1965 catalogue in dark blue and white, colours which never materialised. The first box showed a dark green and white version and a colour scheme of turquoise and white was to be found mainly in the U.S.A. in small quantities. The more common colour scheme is an orange body and a white plastic top. It had detailed plastic seating which came in two sizes. The axles can be found either open or closed.

The final release for 1965 was a red and yellow Grit-Spreader (70b) on the new Ford 'D' series chassis. It featured a novel black or grey plastic rear tab pull which could be opened or closed to allow gritting to take place as on the real vehicle. It included a plated grille and tinted windows. Most releases had a pale yellow container but a few later models were painted in bright yellow.

1965 – New models and their usual colour scheme:

42b Studebaker Lark Station Wagon in blue

49b	Hatra Tractor Shovel in orange or yellow
45b	Ford Corsair in pale primrose
23d	Trailer Caravan in yellow or pink
20c	Chevrolet Impala Taxi in yellow
13d	Dodge Wreck Truck in

1966

1966 saw the first price increase for the range in the U.S.A. as well as the formation in April of the first U.S.A. Official Collectors' Club which published a quarterly newsletter. The Club was run by

and Jack Odell over a period of more than twenty years. The dates for first release of models from 1966 onwards vary tremendously from country to country. Often there was as much as a six months gap before all countries received their new models. The dates given below

way to a blue body whose luggage could be brown or red-brown. A tiny quantity of the gold superfast models appeared with regular wheels.

Another January release was the Fire Pumper Truck (29c) based on a U.S.A. vehicle. It originally advertised 'Denver' decals on the

The whole range of buses and coaches produced by Lesney between 1954 and 1969.

75b	Ferrari Berlinetta in green
5d	Routemaster Bus with seats
22c	Pontiac GP in red
19d	Lotus Racer in green
56b	Fiat 1500 in green
30c	Faun Crane Truck in green and orange
54b	Cadillac Ambulance in white
52b	BRM Racer in blue
68b	Mercedes Coach in orange and white
70b	Ford Grit Spreader in red and yellow

yellow and green

Lesney Products Corporation in New Jersey and reported on the latest releases and attempted to answer members questions. The year was memorable for Lesney not least because of the honour associated with receiving the Queen's Award to Industry for outstanding export achievements. Lesney was the only toy firm to gain this recognition and when the Award was granted again in 1968 and 1969, it was testimony to the achievement of Les Smith

are for the first known releases in the U.K.

The first release for the year was the Safari Land Rover (12c), another vehicle to continue a theme. It was described in *Miniature Autoworld* in January 1966 as being "finished in flamboyant green with white anti-glare seats for tropical climates!" The model included windows, steering wheel, suspension, a towing hook as well as brown plastic, roof-mounted luggage. The green version gave

cab doors but these were later dropped as it proved impossible to fit labels accurately on to the doors. The Fire Pumper came complete with plastic hoses and ladder on a red body which included blue windows and dome light.

January also saw the inclusion of a Land-Rover Fire Truck (57b) in the range. Originally a plastic base lever could operate or deactivate the suspension for this model, but later the lever was deleted. The detailed rear control panel varied according to the particular mould used in manufacture. Labels replaced decals during the model's life and a tiny number of models were fitted with grey plastic wheels instead of black.

It is difficult to state categorically which regular wheel model had the highest sales because no matter what the model, demand always exceeded supply and so larger sales were gained from the vehicles whose moulds ran the fastest. *Odell:* "The best selling miniature of all time was the Ford GT 40 Racing Car." February saw the introduction of (41c). It was finished in the U.S.A. colours of white with a blue bonnet stripe and red interior. The rear plated engine, visible through a transparent cover was complemented by a jewelled exhaust and authentic, semi-reclining red seats. Final releases had a bonnet label superseding the decal. Two rarities occurred with the Ford GT. Firstly, the red wheels rarely seen on 41b were fitted for a short time and during 1966 a yellow bodied version appeared in the G4 Racetrack Set. The real car was known as the GT 40 because it was just 40 inches high from the ground.

Another car available from February was the MG version of the very popular BMC 1100 saloon (64b) a common sight throughout Britain in the 1960s. Although advertised in a flamboyant maroon, it was in fact released in green with plated bumpers, grille and headlights. The usual features were improved by the addition of a driver and a dog lying on the rear seat with its head through the rear side window.

Two trucks appeared in February, both detailed with silver plated plastic grilles, bumpers and bases. However, these plastic parts were soon changed to metal on the Dodge Cattle Truck, (37c). The cab was yellow whilst the plastic body, in medium or dark grey, included an opening tailgate over which two white, oversized bulls could pass to fill the body space. The blue Leyland Flat-bed Truck with site hut, (60b), carried a yellow and green plastic hut. It had blue windows and remained unchanged in terms of colour when Superfast wheels were later fitted.

In March the Mercedes 230 SL (27d) appeared as a faithful replica of the German sports car. It featured opening doors and a detailed red plastic interior. It was painted in off-white or cream although a colour trial model is known to exist in green.

A Daimler Fleetline rear-engined, double-decker bus (74b) available from April 1966 can be found in cream, green or red, in each case displaying 'Esso Extra Petrol' advertisements. These were in decal form on the first cream buses but all later buses had labels applied. The Fleetline included a detailed white plastic interior and suspension as well as a Daimler grille badge.

The Opel Diplomat (36c) was originally shown in turquoise on early boxes when available in May 1966, but in fact it was only ever issued in gold with a white interior. It featured an opening bonnet revealing a chrome plated, or, more rarely, a grey plastic engine. It is another of the more common models still comparatively easy to obtain today. A colour trial model has been found boxed and painted in turquoise.

The release for June was a Leyland Pipe Truck (10b) which typified Lesney's innovatory ideas. A red flat-bed truck with side supports held six grey plastic pipes which could be connected together to form a line. Although the grille and base were normally chrome plated, they could be found in unplated plain white plastic. First releases were inscribed under the cab with 'Leyland No. 10', but all later versions were recast with 'Ergomatic cab', so that the base could be used for other Leyland and A.E.C. trucks with different numbers.

In July 1966 the unusual Alvis Stalwart (61b) joined the range, the real vehicle was the successor to the D.U.K.W. for the British army. It was a prototypical vehicle which was equally at home on land or in the water. On close inspection the propelling ducts and fire extinguisher can be recognised. The suspension on this model can be clearly seen when it is propelled over undulating surfaces. The 'B.P. Exploration' colours of green, white and yellow in decal or label form were chosen as being more attractive than military green. The first issues had smooth beds on the carrier but all subsequent versions had ribbed beds. The wheels were normally green but yellow ones were available for a short time prior to the model's deletion from the range in 1971. It was one of the very few models to continue in the range unaltered when most other vehicles were modified for Superfast wheel fitting. This amphibious vehicle was re-released in 1978 in Twin Pack TP 16 with one-piece regular black wheels in military colours. Pre-production versions of this model have been seen in metallic green.

September saw the emergence of two more Dodge trucks. The six-wheel Dodge based on a forward controlled chassis was the basis for the Stake Truck, (4d). It was initially released with a yellow cab and blue stakes but the colour of the stakes soon changed to dark green. After this model was deleted from the Superfast range in 1971, it later reappeared as MB71 in 1978 as a four-wheel Cattle Truck complete with two bulls. In the 1980s it reappeared in several colours with a trailer as a Twin Pack and in 1988, twenty two years after it was issued, it was recoloured in green in the MC7 Farm Set.

The Dodge Dump Truck (48c) with a tipping body was built on the normal six-wheel chassis.

Chrome plated plastic parts brightened up an otherwise plain red body. This also applied to the base which could be either full length or short with three rivets or only one.

October saw the arrival of a G.M.C. Greyhound Coach (66c) which had a silver-grey body and a white interior. As all models had to fit standard Matchbox boxes, it was necessary for the Greyhound bus to be shortened. In comparison with the real coach, one pair of panoramic side windows was missing. The first release had clear windows and blue-edged decals with slanted ends. Later orange tinted windows were fitted and grey-edged labels replaced decals. These may be found either slanted or squarely cut.

In the same month a CJ5 Jeep (72b) appeared with a yellow body, black tyres on yellow wheels, a red plastic interior and a black base. It carried a spare tyre at the rear. The yellow paint varied in shades from pale lemon to very bright yellow. A colour trial version with a white interior is on permanent display at the Chester Toy Museum.

A Ford Galaxie Police Car (55c) replaced the smaller Ford Fairlane. The Galaxie appeared with a white body, a cream interior and driver and a blue roof light. Decals were applied to both the bonnet and doors. The roof light was quickly altered to red, making the version with a blue roof light quite rare. Decals were replaced by labels, first on the bonnet and then on the doors. This Police Car remained in the range for only two years.

The same body was used on the Ford Galaxie Fire Chief's Car (59c) except that it was, of course, coloured red with Fire Chief decals. The roof light was always blue. For two years the Fire Chief's Car shared the same unpainted base with the Police Chief's Car in that both had a base inscribed No. 55/59. When 55c was replaced, the Fire Chief's Car was modified to show only No. 59

A wide variety of farm vehicles were produced between 1957 and 1969. The red and white Commer Pick-up (50a) the orange Ford Tractor (39c) and the Fordson (72a) with yellow wheels are all rare models.

on a raised platform. Labels again replaced decals and crossovers between the two are known.

A Ford Mustang Fastback (8e) was released in November. It had a white body with clear plastic windows revealing a red interior. Its black plastic wheels with silver hub caps were replaced by black tyres on silver wheels and soon after the silver trim on the grille was discontinued. Finally, an orange body with a red interior appeared very briefly before Superfast wheels were introduced. A metallic blue colour trial model is known to exist. The Mustang model was unique because below the driver's door a lever could be moved backwards or forwards to steer the car. It was probably not a

great success because no other vehicle in the range used this mechanism.

The final release for 1966 was a blue and white Bertram 31 Cabin Cruiser on a blue two wheel trailer, (9d). The cruiser, with a clear windscreen, was made from plastic which enabled it to float. The Boat and Trailer continued for many years into the Superfast era, changing colour only when included in a Twin Pack. The major moulding difference is that the boat came with and without lugs on the side of the deck. Colour trial models have been seen with a turquoise trailer and a

boat with a green hull and a white deck. The colour trial version which can be seen at the Chester Toy Museum is in red and grey.

1966 – New models and their usual colour scheme:

12c Safari Land Rover in green or blue
29c Fire Pumper Truck in red
57c Land Rover Fire Truck
41c Ford GT Racing Car in white
64b M.G. 1100 in green
37c Dodge Cattle Truck
60b Leyland Site Hut Truck in blue with yellow and green hut

27d Mercedes 230 SL in white with red interior
74b Daimler Bus in cream, green or red
36c Opel Diplomat in gold
10d Leyland Pipe Truck in red with grey pipes
61b Alvis Stalwart in white
4d Dodge Stake Truck in yellow with green stakes
48c Dodge Dump Truck in red
66c Greyhound Coach in silver
72b CJ 5 Jeep in yellow
55c Ford Galaxie Police Chief
59c Ford Galaxie Fire Chief
8e Mustang in white
9d Cabin Cruiser in blue and white and blue trailer

By the beginning of the year production figures had reached an amazing 2.5 million models per week with almost 75% of the total output exported. During this time, when Britain was faced with

windows. A noticeable casting variation can easily be seen with regard to the hinge on the loader. Earlier models have this enclosed whilst later variations have a cut away section.

The Volkswagen Camper (34c) came with a silver body, amber windows, orange plastic interior

cross country vehicle commonly used by N.A.T.O. forces during the 1960s for military manoeuvres. The colour scheme originally comprised a tan body and a turquoise base. A model has been reported with a red base and tan body but the usual replacement colour was of a light blue body

May saw the introduction of a Ford Tractor (39c) and a 4-wheel Hay Trailer (40c). The tractor was in the traditional Ford colours of a blue body and yellow wheels and engine cover. In 1967 all-over blue tractors came as a group of three on the King Size, K20 Tractor

Some of the cars produced in the late 1960s featured 'Autosteer'. The illustration depicts these and other cars released from 1966 onwards.

economic difficulties, it was indeed an achievement for a toy company to regularly break sales records year after year.

Two new models available in January were the Ford 'D' Series Refuse Truck (7d) and a second Volkswagen Camper. The Truck came with either an orange-red or an orange body, a grey plastic container and an unpainted metal loader. This model had a double tipping action and suspension and was finished with green plastic

seating and a black base. The double side doors opened and there was an authentically raised roof panel with skylight. The major variation with regard to this Volkswagen motor caravan is that after a time the raised roof was lowered to be only slightly above normal roof height. Although this Camper continued in the range until 1971, it was not modified to accept Superfast wheels.

The Mercedes Unimog (49b) was the civilian version of the rugged

with a bright red base. All models had black tyres on yellow wheels.

The Rolls Royce Silver Shadow (24c) was a new car in 1966 and Lesney were the first company to produce a miniature model. It was finished in metallic wine red with a detailed ivory interior. The boot opened and the radiator was plated. The wheels originally had silver hubs but these were later altered to tyres on silver wheels. A colour trial model has been found in silver.

Transporter. Finally, in 1972, as part of BMX-2 Tractor Transporter Set, three all over orange tractors were carried. The trailer was in blue with yellow wheels and detachable raves. Both of these models continued unaltered into the Superfast era until the tractor was deleted from the range in 1973. The hay trailer had a number of minor casting changes as well as a modification such that the raves could not be removed. During the 1970s and 1980s it was re-released several times in different Twin Packs so that it can be found in blue again, red, tan, dark yellow and light yellow. The tan variation is usually considered to be the rarest of the hay trailers.

The GMC Refrigerator Truck (44c) released in June made a change from the Dodge and Ford trucks, which had previously featured in the range. It was a realistic replica of this marque of truck. It had a red body and chassis with a turquoise container which included a rear opening grey plastic door. No major variation occurred with this model.

New models to the range in August were the Mercedes Truck and Trailer (1d and 2d) bringing to an end fourteen years of the road roller and dumper as numbers 1 and 2. The truck was a forward-control type and the body and trailer were both representative of drop-side vehicles. Both were finished in light green with an orange plastic canopy. When the models were adapted for Superfast wheels in 1970, several colour changes took place, but only the one version was available with regular wheels.

Also in August a Volkswagen 1600TL (67b) joined the range. Early models were in red with silver hubs on black wheels, cream interior and clear plastic windows. Soon black tyres over silver wheels appeared and in the G4 Gift Set Race 'n' Rally, the red Volkswagen was fitted with a maroon plastic roof rack with luggage. A very short run that seems to have been sold mainly in Canada saw the 1600TL in metallic purple with regular wheels. This colour was usually associated with the changeover to Superfast, which for this model occurred in 1969.

The fourth model of the month was a Claas Combine Harvester (65c) which had a red body and yellow plastic blades. The cutters rotated as the model was pushed along. It continued as a regular

wheel model until 1972 and may be found with either a four or a five line base.

The Honda Motor Cycle and Trailer (38c) released in September 1967, was something of a departure from the norm for Lesney. The trailer, which had several base casting variations, was originally orange but later changed to yellow when a decal or a label in two sizes was added. "The Motor Cycle came in metallic blue-green with wire wheels. At the time this model was not well received by some of the toy trade press. *Miniature Auto* 1967: 'The bike purports to be a racing machine yet it does not resemble the real grand prix type of machine which for many years now have had at least four cylinders, apart from the 50cc which is a twin and this model certainly is not one of that particular machine. It looks like one of the twin cylinder road models stripped down for the job but any self-respecting machine prepared for racing would have at least streamlining and would not carry the toolboxes that this one seems to. Possibly the best part of the model are the wheels which give a very real semblance of being spoked but immediately the appearance of the wheels is spoilt by the tyres which are bald. The trailer looks like a Roman chariot!" Possibly the magazine reviewer forgot that this was a toy for children priced at 2 shillings (10p) and not intended as a collector's authentic model. On the other hand, perhaps this was fair comment when judged by the high standards achieved by Lesney a few years before.

In September the first Matchbox Carry Case appeared with accommodation for forty eight models. At a price of 15s. 11d. (80p) it was good value.

The final model for the year was a Mercedes Benz Binz Ambulance (3c) which was based on the standard Mercedes 220 saloon. It

had an estate car type of body and the tailgate opened so that a white plastic man on a stretcher could be removed. Coloured in cream or off white with blue windows and roof light with either decals or labels representing the Red Cross, the model was an interesting choice of ambulance.

1967 – New Models in their usual colour scheme:

7c Refuse Truck with orange cab and grey container
34c Volkswagen Camper in silver
49b Unimog with tan body and light green base
24c Rolls Royce Silver Shadow in metallic red
39c Ford Tractor
40c Hay Trailer
44c Refrigerator Truck
1e Mercedes Truck in light green with orange canopy
2d Mercedes Trailer in light green with orange canopy
67b Volkswagen 1600TL in red
65c Claas Combine Harvester in red
38c Honda Motor Cycle in metallic blue-green and Trailer in orange
3c Mercedes Ambulance in cream

1968

The innovation created by Lesney for 1968 was 'Autosteer'. The feature appeared on the first vehicle midway through the year and was hailed as a breakthrough, for no other toy manufacturer had been able to perfect a steering system for miniatures of this size. The 1969 *Pocket Catalogue*: "Another Matchbox first – Matchbox are the only small scale models to have steering. This unique device, developed by the Matchbox design team, turns the model in either direction by simple pressure. Look out for it on the latest Matchbox releases."

The first release of the year, the Ford Zodiac Mark IV (53c) was priced at 2s. 2d. (11p). This model featured an opening bonnet which included a spare wheel next to the engine. The body was in a light metallic blue with a cream interior. A tiny rear view mirror had been moulded into the plastic windscreen for the first time. A rare version of this Zodiac with regular wheels is to be found in metallic light green, a crossover with the Superfast colour change.

February saw the arrival of an Iso Grifo two-seater fastback (14d) in dark metallic blue with a light blue interior. It was one of the first models to be converted to Superfast wheels in 1969, because it was then a best seller, and is still available in 1988 in the Super GT series, but without the opening doors of the original Iso Grifo. A fair number of model cars at this time represented exotic creations, often from Italy, which in fact were built in very small numbers. The Iso as a real car was available for nine years from 1965 until 1974. The Matchbox model is still being produced twenty years after its introduction as a miniature. A colour trial model is known to exist in metallic green.

In the same month an 8 wheel Leyland Petrol Tanker (32c) joined the range. It was finished in the B.P. colours of green body and chassis and white tank; the truck had blue tinted windows and B.P. labels on the sides and rear of the tank. A short run saw the normal chrome plastic grille and base replaced by white plastic. As with the Bedford Petrol Tanker (25c) an Aral version became available for the European market which had a blue instead of a green body and chassis. Aral labels in blue and white were fitted in place of the BP labels.

In March a two-door Mercedes, a G.M.C. Tipper and a Pony Trailer joined the range. The

Mercedes 300 SE coupe (46c) was not totally accurate as the actual car did not have door pillars. Obviously these were required in the model for strengthening purposes. The car was coloured in vivid green with a white interior and boasted both opening

issued in yellow with clear windows and a light brown base. Two white plastic horses were able to approach their box by means of a dark or light grey plastic ramp. By the end of the year the base had been changed to dark green. This trailer, after

(21d), took its place. As the truck was pushed along a drive gear, connected to one pair of rear wheels, turned the barrel. This 8-wheeler had a yellow cab and barrel assembly, green tinted windows and a red chassis and base. There were several minor

a turquoise body and a yellow container with a grey roof. This was soon changed to a silver body and eventually the grey roof gave way to a silver one. All variants had green windows and a red grille and base.

In the same month a Mercury

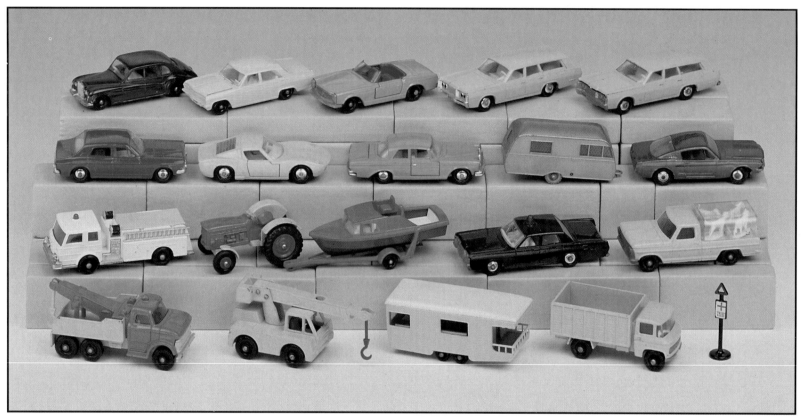

Pre-production or colour trial models provide an insight into what might have been. Most of these models were produced after 1966.

doors and an opening boot. Vacuum plating was used on the bumpers, base, headlights and grille which was completed with a tiny three pointed star. Although the box illustrated hubcaps, the model only had solid black wheels.

The G.M.C. Tipper (26c) had a red cab with green tinted windows which could be tipped forward to reveal an engine which was formed as part of the green chassis and base. The silver tipper had an operating tailgate. There are no known variations on this model.

The Pony Trailer (43c) was

deletion from the "Matchbox" Series, appeared in Twin Pack form in various colours and was still being manufactured in 1988.

April saw the arrival of a Daf Girder Truck, (58c). A pale cream or white truck with green tinted windows and a red grille and base carried a load of twelve red plastic girders which could be interconnected to form a scaffold framework.

Almost as soon as the 6-wheel Foden Concrete Truck, 26b, had been replaced by the G.M.C. Tipper (26c) in March, an updated Concrete Truck, also a Foden,

casting variations before this truck was converted to Superfast wheels.

A Mark II Ford Cortina (25d) was the first model to be fitted with the Autosteer facility. It was finished in metallic light brown with clear windows and a cream interior. Opening doors and a tow hook boosted the play value and a yellow plastic roof rack, similar to the one fitted to 67b, VW 1600TL, was included in the same G4 Gift Set in 1968.

The Daf Tipper Container Truck joined the range as (47c) in June. An early run saw the model with

Cougar (62c) became available. A cream body was shown on the first box and this was generally presumed to be a trial colour model, for so few of these models are known to collectors. Mr Wolfie Ginsberg (the author of Chapter Nine) clearly remembers the cream Mercury Cougar with white interior being the standard issue when it was released in South Africa. The common colour found in the rest of the world was metallic lime green with a red interior. Autosteer, opening doors and silver hub caps were the main features of this popular American car.

Another American vehicle

followed in August. This time it was the heavy duty Mack Dump Truck, (28d). Its colour scheme of bright orange with large black tyres on either red or yellow hubs gave the model something of a garish appearance and perhaps the all blue colour trial model on permanent show at the Chester Toy Museum might have been more realistic. Another colour trial version had a blue body and silver dump. The red wheels on this model soon faded to pink if left in the sunlight.

Lesney's first Lamborghini, a Miura (33c) also became available in August with Autosteer. Its yellow body with opening doors initially revealed a red interior which later changed to cream. Just before this model became one of the first Superfast adaptations it changed colour to gold and this variation is hard to find. All engine cover panels to this point had been in the same clear plastic as the windows but one variant on the gold model had a frosted engine cover to hide the fact that the engine was no longer fitted.

September brought a Ford Pick-up (6d) into the range. It had a red body, cream interior and a white plastic canopy. The first releases had a white plastic grille but this was soon changed to chrome before Superfast wheels replaced the black plastic originals. This Pick-up also included the Autosteer facility. The Dodge Crane Truck (63c) had an all-yellow body and crane, a black grille and base and a red plastic hook and either a single or double cable. Eventually the colour of the hook changed from red to yellow.

A Ford Heavy Wreck Truck (71c) was released in October. It had a red cab and crane with a white crane bed and chassis. The hook was usually red, but yellow hooks were affixed and the windows usually had a green tint. However, amber windows were fitted to the earliest models and

these models are now quite rare. The crane base had either a smooth or ribbed finish and the labels could be found in a larger, or later, a smaller form.

The second release for the month was a Mercury Commuter Station Wagon (73c) which was coloured in metallic lime green with a cream interior. The base came with either '1968 Mercury' on a flat base or 'Mercury' on a raised block. The change of description occurred because originally the Police Chief's Car shared the same baseplate. A pre-production model has been found in mustard yellow. Black tyres on silver wheels were always fitted to this model.

A third Police Car (55d) was also released, but instead of the previous two Fords, this model was a Mercury. It shared the same base as the Mercury Commuter Station Wagon and the base lettering can be found on a flat base or on a raised platform. The Police Car was painted white with a cream plastic interior and always had door labels depicting a Police badge. The bonnet badge initially came in decal form before being changed to a label. Both versions are known with either a rarer red or a more common blue roof light. Black tyres were fitted to silver wheels.

The final model issued in November was the Volkswagen 1500 saloon, (15d). Either decals or labels were applied to the off-white body, which had a cream interior. The doors had a number '137' decal and there was a large metal sign fixed to the front bumper which had a decal with '137 1968' and 'Rally Monte Carlo'. This was another car to have Autosteer and black tyres fitted to solid silver wheels.

1968 – New models and their usual colour scheme:

53c Ford Zodiac in light metallic blue
14d Iso Grifo in metallic blue

32c Leyland Petrol Tanker in green and white
46c Mercedes 300 SK in green or metallic blue
26c G.M.C. Tipper with red cab, green chassis and silver tipper
43c Pony Trailer in yellow with light brown base
58c Daf Girder Truck in white
21d Foden Concrete Truck in yellow and red
25d Ford Cortina in metallic brown
47c Daf Tipper Container Truck in silver and yellow
62c Mercury Cougar in metallic green
28d Mack Dump Truck in orange
33c Lamborghini Miura in yellow
6d Ford Pick-up in red and white
63c Dodge Crane Truck in yellow
71c Ford Heavy Wreck Truck in red and white
73c Mercury Commuter Station Wagon in metallic green
15d Volkswagen 1500 in off-white
55d Mercury Police Car in white

1969

At the beginning of 1969, the price of the range was increased to 2s. 4d. (12p). A retailer, however, could buy a gross of models for nine pounds. Almost half of the profit from any one model was, therefore, going to the retailer! It appeared that the company was going from strength to strength as Lesney won the coveted Boy's Toy of the Year Award, with the Matchbox Motorway, which enabled any model in the miniature range to be placed on a moving wire which could be moved along a road, thereby simulating a busy urban scene.

The Queen's Award to Industry

was given to Lesney for the third time following the successes of 1966 and 1968 and even the Highway Code gave Lesney free publicity when they featured some models in their 1969 edition. By now 85% of Lesney produced goods were being exported. Even countries such as Hungary and Yugoslavia in May 1969 received 750 gross each. The Board of Trade figures for total British Toy Exports noted that Lesney had 93.8% of the Mexican exports and 86.7% of the Spanish exports. Perhaps the most interesting export order came when eighteen dozen gift sets were ordered for the Afghan Royal family.

New models continued to flow from the Lesney design team. In January an A.E.C. 8-wheel Tipper Truck (51c) appeared with an orange body and a silver tipper with a white but later a chrome plastic grille and base. The sides of the tipper carried advertisements for 'Douglas'. Before the model was converted to Superfast wheels, the body colour was altered to yellow but the silver tipper was retained. The Douglas advertisements remained briefly on the yellow models until they were replaced by 'Pointer'.

A Case Bulldozer (16d) joined the range in February. It had a red body and yellow blade, engine and base. In addition it had a yellow plastic removable cab and green rubber tracks. There are a number of casting changes with this model, mainly affecting the body and base, indicating that at least three different moulds were used. This model was understandably never converted to Superfast and continued in the range until its deletion in 1974 though it did make another brief reappearance in Twin Pack TP16 without the cab as part of a military Twin Pack in new colours of military green body and black blade and chassis.

In March three other vehicles

became available. Another A.E.C. Truck took the form of a Horse Box, (17e). It had a red body, a dark green plastic box with an opening grey side door and two white plastic horses. It was also fitted with green plastic windows and a chrome plastic grille and base. It was not modified to Superfast wheels until 1970.

The Case Bulldozer had been introduced because the long running Bulldozer which had occupied the No. 18 position since 1955 was due for replacement. The new model was a yellow bodied Field Car (18c) with a light brown roof, cream interior and a black base and grille. The black base was quickly replaced by an unpainted version and the black tyres on red wheels normally associated with this model were changed to green wheels for a very brief period prior to Superfast conversion in 1970. Autosteer was also a feature with this model.

A Ford Kennel Truck (50c) was the third interesting March release and was based upon the same Ford Pick-up (6d) which had been released in 1968. The Kennel Truck had a metallic green body with green tinted windows and a white grille. The canopy was usually tinted blue, but the first models were fitted with clear canopies. Four white plastic dogs formed the load and these had to be separated from a sprue to fit into the four compartments. The floor of the truck could be either smooth or textured. This model also had the feature of Autosteer, which enabled the vehicle to turn when pressure was applied to one side of the body or the other. This feature was deleted when the model was adapted to take the Superfast wheels in the following year. A colour trial model is known to exist in orange.

The last truck issued with regular wheels was the Mercedes Scaffolding Truck, (11d). The pre-

production colour was yellow but the released model appeared in silver with a red plastic grille and base. Green plastic windows and a white on red 'Builders Supply Company' label enhanced the model. It was completed by six pieces of yellow plastic scaffolding, which could be interlocked to form a scaffold platform.

The final regular wheel model was the Iron Fairy Crane (42c) first available in August. By this time the new Superfast models were being manufactured, but at this time the Crane was not considered for modification, although eventually it was converted in 1971. It had a red body but the rest of the vehicle was yellow with the jib being metal and other parts plastic. The colour trial version for this model was all over yellow.

Other models were intended to have regular wheels and they reached pre-production stage but a change of mind saw the issued models with the new wheels. A silver Merryweather Fire Engine (35c) with regular wheels is on permanent display at the Chester Toy Musuem. Another regular wheel pre-production model known to exist is the Trailer Caravan, (57d). Other models exist with regular wheel boxes but they only appeared in the range with Superfast wheels.

The competition to the "Matchbox" Series was never very great until the formidable Hot Wheels range distributed in the U.S.A. commenced in 1968. Perhaps because of the success of Matchbox in America, particularly with Matchbox winning the 1968 Toy of the Year award in the U.S.A., Mattel realised the potential for their own range of miniatures. *Odell:* "America was our biggest market. We used to fill 20 forty foot containers a week. The U.S.A. market received 60% of Lesney's total production and so it was far larger than the U.K. market. Things were gong so well in America that we were expanding.

We took over a much bigger warehouse, installed larger computers and took on another sales force for the next year. Our sales for the next year were predicted to be $28 million, wholesale price."

Jack Odell now believes that the Toy of the Year Award going to a company outside the U.S.A. for the first time triggered the American Toy Industry into action. *Odell:* "They got worried; nobody had ever won the Award outsdide the U.S.; they got together and decided that they would have to kill off the enormous Matchbox sales. The product was not as good, they did it with money. They launched their range with U.S. $10 million worth of advertising. They brainwashed the kids. Every fifteen minutes on American television it was Hot Wheels, Hot Wheels, Hot Wheels." As a result, Lesney's sales in the U.S. fell from U.S. $28 million to only U.S. $6 million.

The Hot Wheels range was Mattel's answer to Matchbox. They had sought to find a distinctive feature which would appeal to children more than anything so far produced by Matchbox. Sales in the mid and late 1960s had increased enormously and the thin low friction axle hit Lesney like a bombshell. Although there had been whispers of a U.S. innovation, the fast wheel concept had not been considered at Hackney. Even when the concept surfaced Lesney were not as quick as they might have been in realising the play potential of these thin axles. The new axles did not appear to be sturdy enough to cope with the play they might be subjected to.

Jack Odell was not convinced of the need for change. He maintained that it was wrong to adapt the King Size range to Superfast wheels. When a toy was bought for a child, the desire was for something to last, not for a thin axle which could easily break. Odell insisted that the U.S. market was essentially a lost cause and

Lesney should seek to develop their superior quality models even further with other markets. However, he could not win. *Odell:* "The management, the marketing and sales personnel were all clamouring for the same feature as Hot Wheels, namely, the thinner axle. The changeover cost many millions of pounds in lost production, new machinery involved with wire welding, hot stamping and new moulds. More importantly, it put Lesney two years behind where it had been, as all research and development was now being targetted towards Superfast wheel conversions". Odell's problems until this time had been involved with fulfilling demand and finding ways of how to spend the Company's money. This revolutionary upheaval created problems that many of the Lesney's management team were ill-equipped to handle.

It took Lesney longer than expected to produce the equipment to make the thin axle. Despite seven days a week working for many employees, overheads had to be cut to accommodate the change. For the first time Lesney made an operating loss and a bridging loan of £1.5 million was necessary. Many of the bases and wheel arches had to be modified and within a short time the end of an era had dramatically arrived.

The regular wheel was quickly overtaken by the speedier Superfast wheel and so another chapter in the history of Matchbox came to an end. This did not prevent a royal visit on 12 November 1969 and Christmas presents from Lesney for Prince Edward and Prince Andrew. Perhaps they have kept them for a future generation!

1969 – New models and their usual colour scheme:

51c A.E.C. Tipper with orange or yellow body and silver tipper

16d Case Bulldozer with red body and yellow blade and cab

17e Horsebox with red body and dark green box

18e Field Car in yellow with light brown roof

50c Ford Kennel Truck in metallic green

11d Scaffolding Truck in silver

42c Iron Fairy Crane in red with yellow jib and crane

CONCLUSION: THE RAREST MODELS

The reader may wonder why some pre-production models have been described in the text. It should be remembered that there was no real concern at Lesney if models not scheduled for general release were packaged and distributed. Interesting variations have been

The rarest regulars.

known to appear boxed along with far more common models. It was not long ago that a red Vauxhall Victor (45a) a tan Morris Minor (48a) or a cream Mercury Cougar (62b), would have been dismissed as repaints or colour trial models. Now that all of these are known to have been found in shops, for example, the Mercury in large quantities in South Africa. It is not beyond the bounds of possibility that some of those models described in this chapter as being pre-production could have been issued in a country where collectors do not abound and are waiting to be found.

The scarcity of a model is often governed by the number of collectors who would like to include that model in their collections. Some collectors go to great lengths to count the treads on a partic ular wheel pattern. The knobby wheel pattern on the Tippax Refuse Collector (15c), for

example, with twenty four instead of the more usual thirty six or forty five treads is a rare variation. Not all collectors would be interested in this difference but the variation is nevertheless rare.

Some collectors only collect certain types of vehicles. Bus collectors are probably the largest thematic group, whilst others are only interested in models issued before a certain time. New collectors may satisfy themselves initially with an example of each of the 236 basic models produced with regular wheels. They may then discover that the larger Bedford Low Loader (27b) and the second issue Caterpillar Tractor (8b) and Bulldozer, (18b) are difficult to find.

Many collectors will be interested to know what others consider to be the rarest colour variations and so three lists have been compiled based on the comments of several experts. Nevertheless, the list is, of course,

subjective and other models may easily be argued for inclusion. No consideration in the listings has been given to wheel or casting variations.

VERY RARE MODELS

15a Prime Mover in yellow

22b Vauxhall Cresta in cream and turquoise

23b Berkeley Cavalier Caravan in metallic lime green

30b Magirus Deutz Crane Truck in tan with orange or red jib

33a Ford Zodiac in dark blue

45a Vauxhall Victor in red

46a Morris Minor in pale brown

62b Mercury Cougar in cream

RARE MODELS

11a Tanker in green

23c Bluebird Dauphine Caravan in metallic green

More rare regulars

26b Foden Cement Mixer
with grey barrel
27a Bedford Low Loader
in two-tone blue
27c Cadillac in metallic
green and cream

30a Ford Prefect in light blue
38a Refuse Truck in grey/
brown
30a Ford Zodiac Convertible
with tan interior
43a Hillman Minx in green
43b Tractor Shovel in all
over yellow

50a Commer Pick-up in red and
white
55b Fairlane Police Chief in
non-metallic blue
56a Trolley Bus with black
poles
74a Mobile Canteen
in pink

HARD TO FIND MODELS

17a Bedford Removals Van in
maroon
31b American Ford Fairlane
Station Wagon in yellow
32a Jaguar XK140 in red
41c Ford GT in yellow

47b Nestle's Ice Cream Van in metallic blue
50a Commer Pick-up in red and grey
53a Aston Martin in metallic red
59a Singer Van in dark green
65a Jaguar in metallic blue
74a Mobile Canteen in white or cream
46a Morris Minor in blue
43b Tractor Shovel with red shovel and driver

MATCHBOX 1-75 SERIES MINIATURES (1953-1988 BASIC LISTING)

Throughout this book when a reference is made to a miniature, the following numbers have been used. The following notes should also be of help:

a) Models are listed under the first number that they were issued. Sometimes a model may have started as a U.S.A. only issue, and then later released in the R.O.W. (Rest of the World) range with a different number. These models have not been listed under both numbers.

b) Core issue models have been listed under their R.O.W. number.

c) Many models were converted from regular wheels to Superfast wheels in 1969/1970, these have not been re-numbered.

d) Throughout the years many models have been sold in the U.S.A. and Japanese markets with different numbers. As these are only variations of existing models these have not been listed.

1A	Road Roller
1B	Road Roller
1C	Road Roller
1D	Road Roller
1E	Mercedes Truck
1F	Mod Rod
1G	Dodge Challenger
1H	Dodge Challenger
1I	Jaguar XJ6
2A	Site Dumper
2B	Site Dumper
2C	Muir Hill Dumper
2D	Mercedes Trailer
2E	Jeep Hot Rod
2F	Hovercraft
2G	S2 Jet
2H	Pontiac Fiero
2I	Rover Sterling
3A	Cement Mixer
3B	Bedford Tipper
3C	Mercedes Ambulance
3D	Monteverdi Hai
3E	Porsche Turbo
4A	Farm Tractor
4B	Farm Tractor
4C	Triumph Motor Cycle
4D	Stake Truck
4E	Gruesome Twosome
4F	Pontiac Firebird
4G	1957 Chevrolet
4H	FX4R Taxi
5A	Double Decker Bus
5B	Double Decker Bus
5C	Routemaster Bus
5D	Routemaster Bus
5E	Lotus Europa
5F	Seafire Boat
5G	U.S. Mail Jeep
5H	4x4 Jeep/Roll Bar
6A	Quarry Truck
6B	Quarry Truck
6C	Euclid Dumper
6D	Ford Pick-Up
6E	Mercedes 350SL
6F	F1 Racer
7A	Horse Drawn Milk Float
7B	Ford Anglia
7C	Refuse Truck
7D	Hairy Hustler
7E	V.W. Golf
7F	Romping Rabbit
7G	Imsa Mazda
7H	Porsche 959
8A	Caterpillar Tractor
8B	Caterpillar Tractor
8C	Caterpillar Tractor
8D	Caterpillar Tractor
8E	Ford Mustang
8F	Wildcat Dragster
8G	De Tomaso Pantera
8H	Rover 3500
8I	Rover 3500 Police
8J	Astra GTE Police
9A	Fire Engine
9B	Fire Engine
9C	M/W Fire Engine
9D	Boat & Trailer
9E	Amx Javelin
9F	Ford Escort
9G	Amx Javelin
10A	Mechanical Horse & Trailer
10B	Mechanical Horse & Trailer
10C	Sugar Container
10D	Pipe Truck
10E	Piston Popper
10F	Plymouth Police Car
10G	Buick Le Sabre
11A	Petrol Tanker
11B	Petrol Tanker
11C	Jumbo Crane
11D	Scaffold Truck
11E	Flying Bug
11F	Car Transporter
11G	Lamborghini Countach
12A	Land Rover
12B	Land Rover
12C	Safari Land Rover
12D	Setra Coach
12E	Big Bull
12F	Citroen CX
12G	Citroen CX Ambulance
12H	Firebird Racer
12I	Modified Racer
13A	Wreck Truck
13B	Wreck Truck
13C	Ford Wreck Truck
13D	Dodge Wreck Truck
13E	Baja Buggy
13F	Fire Engine
13G	Snorkel
14A	Daimler Ambulance
14B	Daimler Ambulance
14C	London Ambulance
14D	Iso Grifo
14E	Mini Ha-Ha
14F	Articulated Tanker
14G	Grand Prix Racing Car
15A	Prime Mover
15B	Atlantic Tractor
15C	Refuse Container
15D	Volkswagen 1500
15E	Fork Lift Truck
15F	Peugeot 205
16A	Low Loader Trailer
16B	Atlantic Trailer
16C	Snow Plough
16D	Case Tractor
16E	Badger
16F	Pontiac
16G	Land Rover Ninety
17A	Removal Van
17B	Removal Van
17C	Austin Taxi
17D	Hoveringham Tipper
17E	Horse Box
17F	Londoner Bus
17G	London Bus (Titan)
17H	Dodge Dakota
18A	Caterpillar Bulldozer
18B	Caterpillar Bulldozer
18C	Caterpillar Bulldozer
18D	Caterpillar Bulldozer
18E	Field Car
18F	Hondarora Motor Cycle
18G	Fire Engine
19A	MG TD Sports Car
19B	MGA Sports Car
19C	Aston Martin DBR5
19D	Lotus Mk33
19E	Road Dragster
19F	Cement Truck
19G	Peterbilt Cement
20A	ERF Heavy Lorry
20B	ERF 686 Truck
20C	Chevrolet Taxi
20D	Lamborghini Marzal
20E	Police Patrol
20F	4x4 Jeep/Roof
20G	Volvo Container
20H	V.W. Transporter
21A	Luxury Coach
21B	Luxury Coach
21C	Bottle Float
21D	Concrete Truck
21E	Rod Roller
21F	Renault 5TL

21G Chevy Breakdown
21H G.M.C. Wrecker

22A Vauxhall Cresta
22B 1958 Vauxhall Cresta
22C Pontiac GP Coupe
22D Freeman Commuter
22E Blaze Buster
22F Mini Pick-Up/Roof
22G Jaguar XK120
22H Saab 9000 Turbo

23A Berkeley Caravan
23B Berkeley Caravan
23C Bluebird Caravan
23D Trailer Caravan
23E Volkswagen Camper
23F Atlas Dumper
23G Honda ATC 250R

24A WH Excavator
24B WH Excavator
24C Rolls Royce Silver Shadow
24D Team Matchbox
24E Diesel Shunter
24EX Side Tipper
24F Datsun 280ZX
24G Datsun 280ZX
24H Nissan 300ZX

25A Bedford Van
25B Volkswagen 1200
25C Petrol Tanker
25D Ford Cortina
25E Mod Tractor
25F Railway Flat Car
26G Toyota Celica GT
25H Audi Quattro

26A Concrete Truck
26B Foden Cement Mixer
26C G.M.C. Tipper Truck
26D Big Banger
26E Site Dumper
26F Volvo Cable Truck
26E Volvo Tilt

27A Bedford Low Loader
27B Bedford Low Loader
27C Cadillac Sixty
27D Mercedes 230SL
27E Lamborghini Countach
27F Swing Wing Jet
27G Jeep Cherokee

28A Compressor Truck
28B Compressor Truck
28C Jaguar Mk 10
28D Mack Dump Truck
28E Stoat Scout Car
28F Lincoln Continental
28G Formula 5000
28H Dodge Daytona

29A Milk Delivery Van
29B Austin A55
29C Fire Pumper Truck
29D Racing Mini
29E Tractor Shovel

30A Ford Prefect
30B R B Crane Truck
30C 8 Wheel Crane
30D Beach Buggy
30E Swamp Rat
30F Articulated Truck
30G Peterbilt Tipper
30H Mercedes-Benz 280GE

31A Ford Station Wagon
31B Ford Station Wagon
31C Lincoln Continental
31D Volks-dragon
31E Caravan
31F Mazda RX7
31G Mazda RX7
31H Rolls Royce Silver Cloud II

32A Jaguar XK140
32B E Type Jaguar
32C Petrol Tanker
32D Maserati Bora
32E Field Gun
32F Atlas Excavator

33A Ford Zodiac
33B Ford Zephyr
33C Lamborghini Miura
33D Datsun 126X
33E Police Motor Cycle
33F Renault 11

34A Volkswagen Van
34B V.W. Caravette
34C V.W. Camper
34D Formula 1 Racing Car
34E Vantastic
34F Chevy Pro-Stocker
34G Chevy Pro-Stocker
34H Ford RS 200

35A Horse Box
35B Snow Trac
35C Merryweather Fire Engine
35D Fandango
35E Volvo Zoo Truck
35F Pontiac T-Roof

36A Austin A50
36B Lambretta Scooter
36C Opel Diplomat
36D Hot Rod Draguar
36E Formula 5000
36F Refuse Truck

37A Coca Cola Truck
37B Coca Cola Truck
37C Cattle Truck
37D Soopa Coopa
37E Skip Truck
37F Matra Rancho
37FX Dingy & Trailer
57G Jeep 4x4
37H Ford Escort XR3i

38A Refuse Collector
38B Vauxhall Estate
38C Honda Motor Cycle & Trailer
38D Stingeroo Chopper
38E Jeep
38EX Glider Transporter
38F Ford Camper
38G Model 'A' Ford Van

39A Zodiac Convertible
39B Pontiac Convertible
39C Ford Tractor
39D Clipper
39E Rolls Royce Silver Shadow
39F B.M.W. 323i
39G Ford Bronco 11

40A Bedford Tipper
40B Royal Tiger Coach
40C Hay Trailer
40D Vauxhall Guildsman
40E Horse Box
40F Corvette T-Roof
40G Rocket Transporter
41A D Type Jaguar
41B D Type Jaguar
41C Ford GT
41D Siva Spyder
41E Chevy Ambulance

41F Kenworth Conventional
41G Racing Porsche 935

42A Evening News Van
42B Studebaker Lark
42C Iron Fairy Crane
42D Tyre Fryer
42E Container Truck
42F 1957 Thunderbird
42G Mobile Crane

43A Hillman Minx
43B Aveling Barford Tractor Shovel
43C Pony Trailer
43D Dragon Wheels
43E 0-4-0 Steam Loco
43F Peterbilt Conventional
43G Mercedes-Benz 500SEC

44A Rolls Royce Silver Cloud
44B Rolls Royce Phantom V
44C Refrigerator Truck
44D Boss Mustang
44E Passenger Coach
44F Citroen 15 CV
44G 4x4 Chevy Van
44H Datsun 280ZX/Police
44I Skoda 130LR

45A Vauxhall Victor
45B Ford Corsair
45C Ford Group 6
45B B.M.W. 3.0 CSL
45E Kenworth C.O.A.
45F Ford Skip Truck

46A Morris Minor 1000
46B Removal Van
46C Mercedes 300SE
46D Stretcha Fetcha
46E Ford Tractor
46F Group C Racer

47A Brooke Bond Van
47B Ice Cream Van
47C Tipper Container
47D Beach Hopper
47E Pannier Tank Loco
47F Jaguar SS100
47G School Bus
48A Boat & Trailer
48B Boat & Trailer
48C Dumper Truck
48D Pi-Eyed Piper
48E Sambron Jacklift

48F	Unimog	55B	Ford Cortina	62E	Renault 17TL	69D	Turbo Fury
48G	Vauxhall Astra GTE	55H	Ford Sierra XR4i	62F	Chevy Corvette	69E	Armoured Truck
		55I	Mercury Sable Wagon	62B	Volvo 760	68F	1933 Willys Rod
49A	Army Half Track					69G	1983 Corvette
49B	Mercedes Unimog	56A	London Trolley Bus	63A	Service Ambulance	69H	Volvo 480ES
49C	Chop Suey Chopper	56B	Fiat 1500	63B	Crash Tender		
49D	Crane Truck	56C	B.M.C. 1800 Pininfarina	63C	Dodge Crane Truck	70A	Thames Estate
49E	Sand Digger	56D	Hi-Tailer	63D	Freeway Gas Tanker	70B	Grit Spreader
49F	Peugeot Quasar	56E	Mercedes 450SEL	63DX	Tanker Trailer	70C	Dodge Dragster
		56F	Mercedes 450SEL	63E	Dodge Challendger	70D	Self Propelled Gun
50A	Commer Pick-Up		Police	63F	4x4 Open Back	70E	Ferrari 308 GTB
50B	John Deere Tractor	56G	Peterbilt Tanker		Truck		
50C	Kennel Truck	56H	V.W. Golf GT1			71A	Aray Water Truck
50D	Articulated Truck			64A	Breakdown Truck	71B	Jeep Gladiator
50DX	Articulated Trailer	57A	Wolseley 1500	64B	MG 1100	71C	Ford Wreck Truck
50E	Harley Davidson	57B	Chevrolet Impala	64C	Slingshot Dragster	71D	Jumbo Jet Chopper
	Motor Cycle	57C	Land Rover Fire	64D	Fire Chief Car	71E	Cattle Truck
50F	Chevy Blazer		Truck	64E	Caterpillar D9 Tractor	71EX	Cattle Trailer
		57D	Trailer Caravan	64F	Dodge Caravan	71F	'62 Corvette
51A	Cement Lorry	57E	Wild Life Truck			71G	Scania T142
51B	Tipping Trailer	57F	Carmichael	65A	Jaguar 3.4 Litre		
51C	8 Wheel Tipper	57G	Mini Pick-Up/Roll Bar	65B	Jaguar 3.4 Litre	72A	Fordson Tractor
51D	Citroen SM	57H	Mission Helicopter	65C	Combine Harvester	72B	Jeep
51DX	Motor Cycle Trailer			65D	Saab Sonnett III	72C	SRN6 Hovercraft
51E	Combine Harvester	58A	B.E.A. Coach	65E	Airport Coach	72D	Bomag Road Roller
51F	Pontiac Firebird	58B	Drott Excavator	65F	Plane Transporter	72E	Dodge Commando
51G	Ford LTD Police	58C	Girder Truck	65G	Cadillac Allante	72F	Sand Racer
		58D	Woosh-N-Push			72G	Ford Supervan II
52A	Maserati 4CLT	58E	Faun Dump Truck	66A	Citroen DS19		
52B	B.R.M. Racing Car	58F	Ruff Trek	66B	Harley Davidson Motor	73A	R.A.F. Refueler
52C	Dodge Charger Mk III	58G	Mercedes-Benz 300E		Cycle	73B	F1 Ferrari
52D	Police Launch			66C	Greyhound Coach	73C	Mercury Commuter
52E	B.M.W. M1	59A	Ford Thames Van	66D	Mazda RX500	73D	Weasel Armoured Car
52F	B.M.W. M1	59B	Fairlane Fire Car	66E	Ford Transit Pick-Up	73E	Model 'A' Ford
		59C	Galaxie Fire Car	66F	Tyrone Malone		Saloon
53A	Aston Martin	59D	Mercury Fire Car	66G	Rolls Royce Silver		
53B	Mercedes 220SE	59E	Planet Scout		Spirit	74A	Mobile Canteen
53C	Ford Zodiac Mk IV	59F	Porsche 92B			74B	Daimler Bus
53D	Tanzara	59G	Porsche 944 Turbo	67A	Saladin Armoured	74C	Toe Joe Breakdown
53E	Jeep CJ6				Car		Truck
53F	Flareside Pick-Up	60A	Morris J2 Pick-Up	67B	Volkswagen 1600TL	74D	Cougar Villager
		60B	Site Hut Truck	67C	Hot Rocker	74E	Fiat Abarth
54A	Saracen Personnel	60C	Lotus Super Seven	67D	Datsun 260Z 2+2	74F	Mustang GT
	Carrier	60D	Holden Pick-Up	67E	Imsa Mustang	74G	Toyota MR2
54B	Cadillac Ambulance	60E	Toyota Supra	67F	Ikarus Coach		
54C	Ford Capri	60F	Ford Transit			75A	Ford Thunderbird
54D	Personnel Carrier			68A	Army Radio Truck	75B	Ferrari Berlinetta
54E	Mobile Home	61A	Ferret Scout Car	68B	Mercedes Coach	75C	Alfa Carabo
54F	NASA Tracking Vehicle	61B	Alvis Stalwart	68C	Porsche 910	75D	Seasprite Helicopter
54G	Command Vehicle	61C	Blue Shark	68D	Cosmobile	75E	MB Helicopter
		61D	Wreck Truck	68E	Chevy Van	75F	Ferrari Testarossa
55A	DUKW Amphibian	61E	Peterbilt Wrecker	68F	Camaro IROC Z28		
55B	Fairlane Police Car	61F	T-Bird Turbo Coupe			J2	Mazda RX7
55C	Galaxie Police Car	62A	General Service Lorry	69A	Nestle Van	J5	Nissan Fairlady Z
55D	Mercury Police Car	62B	T.V. Service Van	69B	Tractor Shovel	J21	Toyota Celica
55E	Mercury Police S/Wagon	62C	Mercury Cougar	69C	Rolls Royce Silver	J22	Galant Eterna
55F	Hellraiser	62D	Cougar Dragster		Shadow		

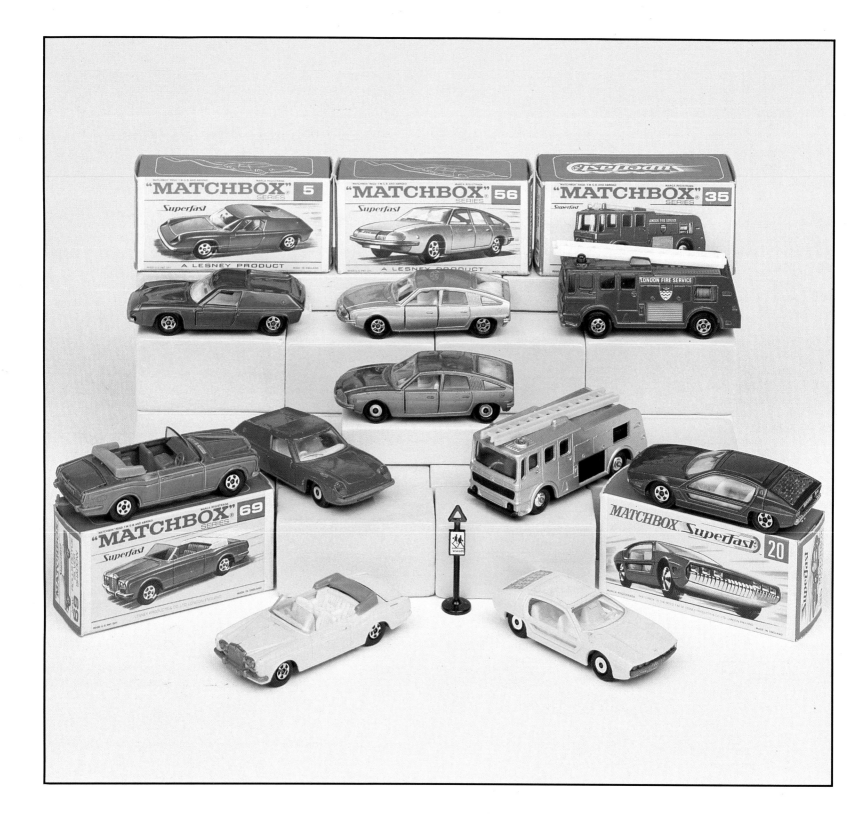

The Superfast Range

6

THE NEW ERA 1969 TO 1988

◄ *Some early Superfast issues with their pre-production versions, the Merryweather Fire Engine was a regular wheel model in the pre-production form.*

INTRODUCTION

This range of models is by far the biggest in terms of numbers and associated versions. It is quite beyond the scope of this book to cover every single model and all of their variations in complete detail. This would necessitate a chapter equal in size to this book alone.

The decision to change from regular wheels miniatures to Superfast models was undoubtedly controversial and this chapter outlines the reasons why it was undertaken and the sequence of Superfast models. During the course of research into these models much previously unreleased information has come to light and this has been reproduced here.

Section 1. The background to the range, the competitors' challenge and the adaption of the existing regular series.

In the 1960s Lesney had enjoyed a huge wave of success with its range of "Matchbox" Series all over the world, but particularly in the U.S.A. *Odell:* "America was our biggest market. We used to fill 20 forty foot containers a week, we were making five million toys a week. The U.S.A. market received 60% of our total production and so it was far larger than the U.K. market. Things were going so well in America that we were always expanding. We took over a bigger warehouse, installed larger computers and took on another sales force. Our sales for the next year (1969) were predicted to be US \$28 m at wholesale price." This kind of success did not go unnoticed by the American toy manufacturers, some of whom started to make diecast miniatures. In 1967 the Aurora Plastics Corporation released a series of models called Cigar Box. These models had finely detailed plastic bodies with zinc bases and were packaged in cardboard facsimilies of cigar boxes. Most of these competitors toys could not duplicate the quality and realism of Matchbox and so did not pose a real threat to Lesney's sales. Mattel, the giant American company, had also seen the sales potential of diecast miniatures. They were and still are one of the largest toy manufactureres in the world and in the 1960s had success with products such as the Barbie Doll, which has sold consistently for over thirty years. The Mattel company decided that they wanted a share of the diecast market and that they would not make a half-hearted attempt at getting into it. They entered into a com-

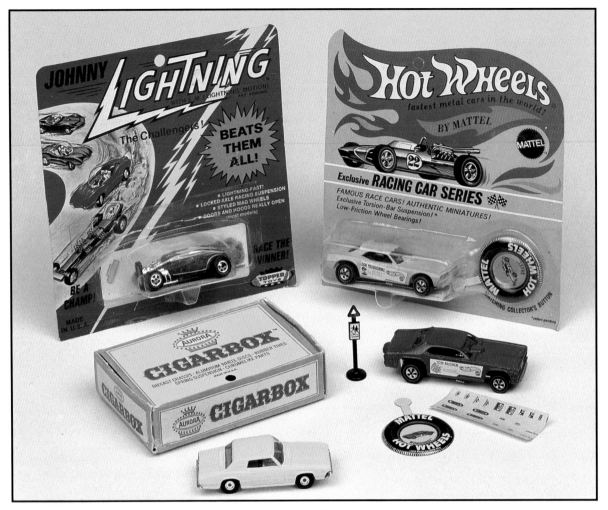

Competitors models from the sixties, Johnny Lightning and Hot Wheels models both featured fast wheels. Mattel Inc. filed a law suit in 1966 to determine whether it had the right to use the terms "Matchbox" or "Matchbox Series" on their carrying cases. They were refused.

prehensive development programme to design and manufacture a range of models that would capture the imagination of American children. The range of sixteen vehicles that emerged in 1968 captured all the excitement of the Hot Rod car with features such as metallic paint, chrome engines and large tyres on chrome wheels.

The key selling point of the cars, however, was their low friction, high speed running wheels. On a smooth floor or surface these cars would run much further than conventionally axled model cars, with only a gentle push. Track sets were available which had features such as 360 degree loop the loops, jump ramps and twin

tracks that could be set up for racing.

Jack Odell felt that the Toy of the Year award going outside the U.S.A. for the first time triggered the American toy industry into action. *Odell:* "They got worried: nobody had ever won the award outside the U.S. They got together and decided that they would have to kill off the enormous Matchbox sales. Their product was not that good, they did it with money. They launched their range with U.S.

$10m worth of advertising. They brainwashed the kids. Every fifteen minutes on American television it was Hot Wheels, Hot Wheels, Hot Wheels."

The Mattel campaign had a dramatic affect on Lesney, whose sales dropped to U.S. $6m. Demand for Matchbox models dropped to only 10% of the Lesney production output, compared with the previous 60%.

Another American company entered into the fast wheel race with the 'Johnny Lightning' range of vehicles from the Topper Toys Company. This consisted of a range of hot rods with the same features as Hot Wheels and with a 50% increase in sales during 1969 they spent U.S. $5m in 1970 on advertising. Competition was fierce

and Mattel replied by flooding the market with Hot Wheel models manufactured in Hong Kong. The competition was too much for Topper Toys, whose vehicles were made in the U.S.A. and, therefore, more expensive. They went bankrupt at the end of 1971.

With the launch of Hot Wheels into Europe and the rest of the world, Lesney had to take immediate action if they were not to go out of business. With the backing of their bankers they started a huge programme of redesign and re-tooling. *Odell:* "We got a bridging loan of £1.5 million. The changeover cost many millions of pounds in lost production, new machinery involved with wire welding, hot stamping and new moulds." This involved the mould making toolrooms having to work extra evenings and at weekends. Not only did many new models have to be designed, there were new production methods to be developed and perfected such as wheel and axle assembly, plus all the packaging and advertising material that had to be updated. *Odell:* "For the first time we made an operating loss, the change over put us two years behind where we had been, all our research and development had to be put into Superfast." Odell felt at the time that the Hot Wheel models would be a passing phase and that Matchbox models should continue as they were. He maintained that the decision to convert King Size to Superfast wheels was unsound. *Odell:* "When a toy was bought for a child, the desire was for something to last, not for a thin axle which could easily break." Odell insisted that the U.S. market was essentially a lost cause and that Lesney should develop their superior quality models even further for other markets. However, he could not win. *Odell:* "The management, the marketing and sales personnel were all clamouring for the same feature as Hot Wheels, namely the thinner axle."

The ways in which Regular wheel and Superfast models had their wheels and axles produced were very different. Regular wheel models had strong steel axles of 1.6 mm in diameter and a variety of wheel types which included combined wheels and tyres, chrome or plastic hubs with separate tyres and small rollers with rubber tracks. These wheels were held in place by axles which were pushed by hand or machine through the wheels and then through holes in the models body or base casting. The axle heads were then burred over to keep the wheels in place. These models when pushed did not run very far because of the amount of friction which took place between the wheels and axles.

The way to make Matchbox models run as fast as Hot Wheels was to have new axles of only 0.6 mm in diameter and very much thinner wheels. The new axles were manufactured from steel wire and the wheels from a new grade of plastic which made them run more smoothly. These wheels were assembled as pairs by machine onto a wire axle, which had its ends burred over by electrodes; these were called wheel sets.

The next stage was to take two wheel sets and clip them into a plastic suspension strip which would then be riveted to the model's diecast base. Each model required its own unique strip because of the difference in wheel centres and body widths. On many of the commercial vehicles in the range it was not possible to have suspension strips, and so the wheel sets had to be located by the body or base casting and then held in place by a plastic axle cover. These were usually black and had the word 'Superfast' moulded on. As these can also be easily removed, it is possible to repair models with bent axles. One of the problems that arose with thin axles was

they bent easily if a model was dropped or trodden on, and if a wheel became detached the axle head was fairly sharp and dangerous.

From the range of seventy five regular wheel models that appeared in the 1969 range, sixty were eventually converted to Superfast. Five kept their regular wheels and continued in the Matchbox range into the seventies, these were:

16D Case Tractor
39C Ford Tractor
40C Hay Trailer
61B Alvis Stalwart
65C Class Combine Harvester

Ten models were not converted to Superfast and these were deleted from the range by late 1969/early 1970. Some were unsuitable in Superfast for technical reasons such as the 5D Routemaster Bus which had small wheel arches and the 35B Snow Trac which had rubber tracks. The ten models were:

5D Routemaster Bus
20C Chevrolet Taxi
23D Trailer Caravan
34C Volkswagen Camper
35B Snow-Trac
45B Ford Corsair
52B B.R.M. Racing Car
56B Fiat 1500
68B Mercedes Coach
69B Tractor Shovel

The majority of the regulars were converted to Superfast during 1970, but five were converted during 1969. These were the 11D Scaffold Truck, 14D Iso Grifo, 15D Volkswagen 1500, 33C Lamborghini Miura and 41C Ford GT. These first models to be converted were amongst the best sellers at the time.

Some of the models that were converted to Superfast kept the same colour scheme for all of their life in the range. Many models kept their regular wheel colour for only a short space of time before being changed to a metallic or bright colour. Some of these interim models are hard to find, while some are amongst the rarest of any Matchbox model. This list outlines the fifty five Superfast models, which were produced in their regular wheel colours and their availability today to collectors.

Generally available:
3C, 4D, 6D, 7C, 9D, 11D, 13D, 14D, 15D, 18E, 21D, 24D, 26C, 29C, 32C, 36C, 37C, 38C, 41C, 43C, 47C, 50C, 51C, 54B, 55D, 59C, 60B, 62C, 63C, 66C, 70B, 71C, 72B, 74B.

Hard to find:
10D Pipe Truck (Red)
17E Horse Box (Red and green)
25D Ford Cortina (Metallic light brown)
27D Mercedes 230SL (Off white)
33C Lamborghini Miura (Yellow)
44C Refrigerator Truck (Red and green)
46C Mercedes 300SE (Metallic blue)
49B Mercedes Unimog (Blue and red)
57C Land Rover Fire Truck (Red)
58C Daf Girder Truck (Off white)
64BMC 1100 (Green)
67B Volkswagen 1600TL (Red)
73C Mercury Commuter (Metallic green)

Fairly rare:
8E Ford Mustang (White)
30C 8 Wheel Crane (Green and red)
42D Iron Fairy Crane (Red and yellow)
75B Ferrari Berlinetta (Metallic green)

This monochrome photograph illustrates the difference in construction of the base of a Superfast model, with its regular wheel equivalent shown below it.

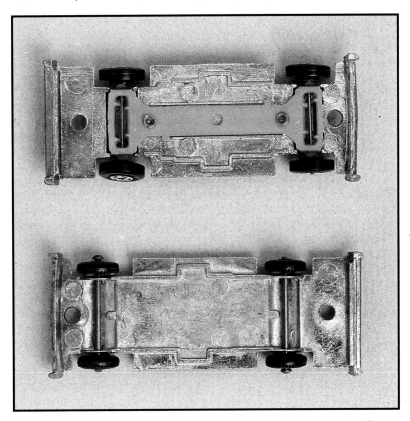

12C   Land Rover Safari (Blue)
22C   Pontiac GP Coupe (Red)
31C   Lincoln Continental
      (Sea green)
53C   Ford Zodiac Mk IV
      (Metallic light blue)

Some models did not stay in the Superfast range for very long and this adds to their rarity; the 57C Land Rover Fire Truck was only produced in red and was only in the range for a year. This model is very hard to find with its Superfast box.

Some models were not produced with Superfast wheels in their regular wheel colour scheme but went straight into a metallic paint finish, they were the 1E Mercedes Truck and 2D Mercedes Trailer, 19D Lotus Mk. 33, 28D Mack Dump Truck, 48C Dumper Truck.

Towards the end of 1969 five all new Superfast models were released:

5E   Lotus Europa
20D   Lamborghini Marzal
35C   Merryweather Fire
      Engine
56C   BMC 1800 Pininfarina
69C   Rolls Royce Silver
      Shadow Coupe

Pre-production samples of some early Superfast models have wheels with silver hubs. These were early trial sample wheels which were solid plastic. Later on the design was changed to a wheel that was hollowed out on the back. When the Superfast conversion started, there were several new models already being developed, some of these almost became Regular wheel models. This is, in fact, because the Superfast boxes that they were initially released in, were in the style of the last regular wheel type box. Examples found are: 5E, 20D, 45C, 56C and 69C. Two Superfast issue models exist in pre-production form with

The Matchbox stand at the Brighton Toy Fair 1969.

regular wheels: 35C Merryweather Fire Engine and 57D Trailer Caravan.

Generally many of the harder to find models are more commonly found in the U.S.A. There are a number of reasons to explain this. The first batch of a models production run was supplied to the U.S.A. to meet the initial demand. These early models are quite rare, for example, the 25D Ford Cortina in metallic brown. There was always a larger market for Matchbox models in the U.S.A. and also a larger following of collectors. The earliest Matchbox collectors clubs were started in the U.S.A. and thus these collectors were more aware of models available and were able to obtain them.

1970

Section 2 - *The growth of Hot Rods, prototypes, Rola-matics and Scorpions.*

This year witnessed the trend of introducing weird styling and hot rodded or customised models. This was to prove unacceptable to most of the collectors of the regular wheel models who

preferred realism to fantasy vehicles. Sales, however, were high to the general public and it looked as if the huge investment of the last two years was starting to pay off.

A range of track sets were an additional help to sales and Lesney could only just supply the demand. The new models were:

19E   Road Dragster
22D   Freeman Inter-City
      Commuter
23E   Volkswagen Camper
29D   Racing Mini
30D   Beach Buggy
36D   Hot Rod Draguar
45C   Ford Group 6
52C   Dodge Charger Mk III
57D   Trailer Caravan
62D   Cougar Dragster
68C   Porsche 910

Recolours: 5E, 15D, 33C, 45C, 46C, 49B, 62C.

Some of the new models had early casting variations which are of interest. The 23E Volkswagen Camper had a petrol filler cap detailed outline cast on the left-hand side of the rear body. This detail was removed from the

mould because it interferred with the 'Sailboat' label that was applied to the vehicle in that area. Originally with a blue body and orange interior it was changed in 1974 to orange body with a white interior. Some models were made with the orange body and orange interior which is quite hard to find. The model featured a plastic roof that hinged upwards. When the model was used in the military Two-Pack range in 1977 the roof was removed and the body casting modified. The base was changed to read 'Dormobile'. In 1987 the model was manufactured in Hungary under licence. Once more the moulds were modified, this time to put the opening roof back on!

The 29D Racing Mini had door outlines cast on the body which were also found to be a problem in production when the model had labels applied. This variation is now very rare. One of the few variations to appear on the 30D Beach Buggy was the interior being moulded in white on early issues rather than yellow as on all later issues. This model was sprayed a light metallic purple with yellow paint applied afterwards in a random spotted effect. This varies from only a few dots, to almost a complete coverage of yellow. A chrome finish foil label was applied to the boot lid of the 36D Hot Rod Draguar during its first year of production. This model was Lesney's view of how an 'E' Type Jaguar could be customised. Many variations exist in various combinations including clear or amber window and white, cream or orange interior.

The first issue of the 45C Ford Group 6 is now quite scarce. It had a non-metallic green body which was soon changed to dark metallic green and a few years later to metallic lime green. Many variations also exist of base colours and labels.

The G3 Racing Specials Superset contained six Matchbox models with some labels already applied and a sheet of labels for the customer to apply. The box gave details of where to apply the different labels, although the labels could be applied to any model. They should have been as follows: (the labels from the label sheet are listed in brackets)

5E Lotus Europa, both the metallic blue or metallic pink version exist with a combined stripe and number 20 label on the bonnet with 20, (Lotus, STP and BP) labels on the sides.

20D Lamborghini Marzal, the pink or metallic red body versions were used with a number 2 label on the bonnet and Avon (Lamborghini and STP) labels on the sides.

45C Ford Group 6, the dark metallic green body version was used with number 7 label (and stripes) on the top of the car, with Burmah, (STP and Ford) labels on the sides.

52C Dodge Charger MKIII, the metallic red body version was used with a number 5 label (and stripes) on the top and number 5 (STP, Shell and Dodge) labels on the sides.

56C BMC 1800 Pininfarina, two body colours exist, gold or orange with a Gulf label on the bonnet

The G-3 Superset with its label sheet and colour variants.

(chequered label on the roof) and on the sides had number 17 (Ferodo, Champion and STP) labels.

68C Porsche 910, the standard metallic red body was used with a number 68 (and striped yellow and black labels) on the top. On the sides there were number 68 (Goodyear, STP, Shell and Porsche) labels.

1971

This year saw nineteen new models three of these were based on vehicles that had been made by car manufacturers as styling exercises. These cars have always proved to be crowd pullers at motor shows around the world even though they are usually made as one off prototypes which cannot be driven! The cars that Lesney copied were the Vauxhall Guildsman, Mazda RX500 and the Alfa Romeo Carabo.

The full list of new models was as follows:

1F	Mod Rod
2E	Jeep Hot Rod
4E	Gruesome Twosome
7D	Hairy Hustler
8F	Wildcat Dragster
12D	Setra Coach
13E	Baja Buggy
31D	Volks-dragon
34D	Formula 1 Racing Car
40D	Vauxhall Guildsman
54C	Ford Capri
55E	Mercury Police Station Wagon
59D	Mercury Fire Car
60C	Lotus Super Seven
61C	Blue Shark
64C	Slingshot Dragster
66D	Mazda RX500
70C	Dodge Dragster
75C	Alfa Carabo

Recolours of existing models: 14D, 17E, 20D, 22D, 27D, 35C, 37C, 45C, 49B, 52C, 56C, 67B, 69C.

are the orange body and blue body versions used in gift sets.

The base of 60C reads 'Lotus Super Seven No 60' on a raised panel. This raised panel was added to the base mould to erase the original wording which was 'Lotus Seven No 60'. The 64C Slingshot Dragster is now rare in orange rather than its usual metallic light blue or pink.

As the Hot Rods produced by Lesney became more outrageous in appearance, they made the early existing Superfasts look rather tame by comparison, and so Lesney set about enhancing their appearance. The re-coloured models had new brighter body colours and were modified by having larger and wider wheels. This meant that wheel arches had to be enlarged. During the change over period in production, some models were assembled with the new bigger wheels fitted to the old bodies and also the older thin wheels were fitted to new bodies which had the large wheel arches.

These following models were all modifed to take larger wheels: 3C, 5E, 20D, 27D, 31C, 33C, 41C, 53C, 56C, 67B, 69C and 73C.

1972

This year saw eighteen new models, one of them being the 17E Londoner Bus which came to be used extensively in promotional issues. This will be described in more depth in Chapter Ten. The full list of new models were:

9E	AMX Javelin
11E	Flying Bug
15E	Fork Lift Truck
17E	Londoner Bus
25E	Mod Tractor
26D	Big Banger
37D	Soopa Coopa
41D	Siva Spyder
42D	Tyre Fryer
43D	Dragon Wheels

Most of these models had interesting variations. The 1F Mod Rod had red wheels on early issues, a novel feature that did not occur on any other model. Mod Rods with red interiors or Scorpion labels are hard to find today. The 2E Jeep Hot Rod exists with many combinations of body, base and seats. Over the years the body has been modified many times and issued under different MB numbers as well as in other ranges:

1977 MB-38E Army Jeep
1977 MB-38E Army Jeep
     with gun
1977 TP-7 Jeep & Glider Trailer
1978 MB-5G U.S. Mail Jeep
1982 MB-5H 4x4 Jeep with
    roll bar

The new models for 1971 were typical of the Superfast range during the seventies.

1982 MB-20F 4x4 Jeep with
    roof
1986 SC-8 Hawk (Super
    Truck)
1987 Parasite (Road Blaster)
1988 SC-14 Mud Monster
    (Mud Racer)

The 8F Mustang Dragster was a modified 8E with larger rear wheels and a chrome engine fitted in a bonnet recess. The body colour is normally a bright orange which is easily affected by strong sunlight. Many shades of orange and pink bodies can be found but check that the colour is the same all over. If a model has been in direct sunlight it maybe pale pink on one side and bright orange on the other! Two styles of 'Wild Cat'

label were used on the sides but the rarest label to be found is the 'Sailboat' type from the 23E Volkswagen Camper.

The 13E Baja Buggy can be found in various shades of green with its 'Flower' label on the bonnet and also with a 'Sun' label from the 47D or a 'Police Shield' label from the door of 55E. The interior was normally orange, so the red issue is rarer, but some models exist fitted with the interior from the 47D. This interior has two large front seats instead of small front and rear seats.

The 34D Formula 1 Racing Car was first issued in metallic light purple and then later in yellow. Many variations exist from the different combinations of labels and window and base colours. Two versions that are hard to find

The original Jeep Hot Rod has been modified many times.

44D Boss Mustang
46D Stretcha Fetcha
48D Pi-Eyed Piper
51D Citroen SM
53D Tanzara
58D Whoosh-N-Push
72C SRN6 Hovercraft
74C Toe Joe

Recolours:
12D, 23E, 29D, 34D, 39C, 42C, 53C, 54C, 57D.

The 9E AMX Javelin when first issued had a chrome bonnet scoop and dashboard. Yellow interiors were normally fitted but orange or white ones can be found, or the very much rarer blue version. Later the model was used in the Two Pack range and the body casting was modified to include doors cast closed. The first issue of the 11E Flying Bug had a triangular shaped label that was changed to a heart shape, the window was usually silver but blue versions can also be found.

The 25E Mod Tractor was designed by Odell. *Odell:* "We could never make enough of them, we had two sets of moulds for the body, they were being run on a double shift, in fact one of them ran continuously for a year." Early issues of the tractor had headlight shapes cast on the top of the rear wheel arches, but these were found to cause problems in moulding and were removed from the mould. Models with the headlamps are not too hard to find but models fitted with red seats are rarer.

The 26D Big Banger and 48D Pi-Eyed Piper share the same body and window parts, but the engines and bases are different. Some of the Big Bangers were issued with the base from the Pi-Eyed Piper, whose exhaust pipes cover up the labels on the sides of the body. Both the 37D Soopa Coopa and the 42D Tyre Fryer can be found with light or dark metallic blue bodies, and both models were issued with orange bodies during 1977 for a Jaffa promotion.

The 72C SRN6 Hovercraft was shown in the catalogue with a chrome roof bar and propeller but was never issued like this. Not many variations of the 74C Toe Joe were to be found until it was used in the Two Pack range in 1976. A hard to find model is the one with a yellow body and 'Hitch Hiker' labels. The red body is also very hard to find. The Toe Joe had 'Tool box' door detail on the sides, made up of a recessed outline and upstanding hinge detail ribs. Two variants exist on the 'Hitch Hiker' model. On the first issue the labels were applied over the tool box detail, and were found to lift off. The

detail was removed from the mould to give the body a smooth surface for the labels to stick to.

The 74D Daimler bus can be found with its body in various shades of red paint, as well as a bright pink shade. Combinations exist of the body and base components in red and pink. Before the deletion of the Daimler, two promotional versions were produced for London restaurants, the 'Inn on the Park' and the 'Baron of Beef'. Another promotional 74B that was well publicised in collectors magazines was the Taylors 'Big T' Scotch whisky model. This was packaged with a bottle of whisky and although attractive, was not a Lesney produced model.

The Wynns oil company in Europe had two models produced for a promotion, the 19E Road Dragster and 34D Formula 1 Racing Car. Both models had 'Wynns' labels applied to their normal colour bodies, the 19E came with a large or small sized label, while the 34D only came with the large label. Blister packed models were found on general sale in the U.K. after the promotion had finished.

The National Association of Matchbox Collectors (N.A.M.C.) was a club that ran from 1970 to 1973. During 1972 they had two promotional models produced using the 32C Petrol Tanker. There has always been some doubt surrounding these models, although they were undoubtedly sprayed and assembled at the Lesney factory there is doubt as to whether they were made officially or even labelled by Lesney. (In fact the models had clear vinyl labels, a type of label which was not used by Lesney at the time). Both models are rare, one has a purple body and silver tank and the other, which is even rarer, has a red body with white tank.

The 32C Tanker was produced for the German market in the Aral

The Daimler Bus in its various shades of red or pink. The 'Inn on the Park' and 'Baron of Beef' were promotional issues.

livery with a special Aral box, in the same way as the regular wheel issue during the sixties.

Another novel feature during 1972 was the Brroom Stick. This was a Matchbox car sold on a blister card with a plastic handle, a piece of elastic and a label that was used to stick the elastic to the bonnet of the car. Many different cars were used in this pack, but there were two models produced in different colours from their normal issue: the 20D Lamborghini in yellow and the 68C Porsche in white. In the U.S.A. this toy was called the Zingomatic. The Brroom Stick model was only available for about a year, because sales were poor. It had a retail price in the U.K. of 25 pence compared to only 16 pence for a Superfast model.

Stage two drawings of the Daimler Fleetline Bus circa 1968.

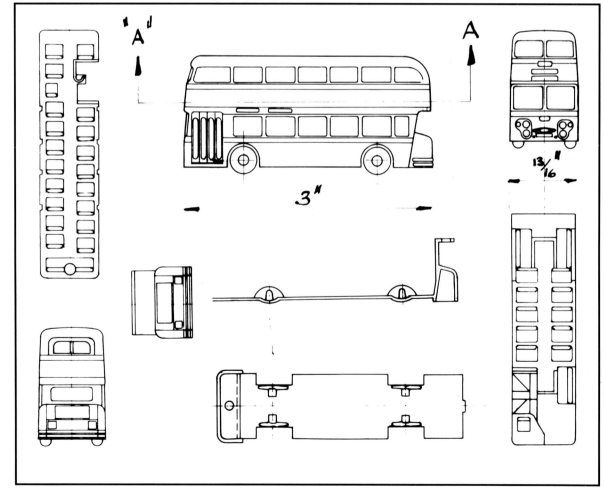

1973

This year saw the release of seven Rola-Matic models. These were vehicles with moving parts which moved when a model was rolled along. The models had slightly modified Superfast wheels, which had pegs moulded to their inner face in order to rotate gears inside them. The seven were:

10E Piston Popper
28E Stoat
39D Clipper
47D Beach Hopper
57E Wild Life Truck
67C Hot Rocker
69D Turbo Fury

The 'Brroom Stick' and 'Zingomatic' packs provide some sought after colour variations.

This years other new models were:

3D	Monteverdi Hai
21E	Rod Roller
24D	Team Matchbox
27E	Lamborghini Countach
32D	Maserati Bora
33D	Datsun 126X
38D	Stingeroo Chopper
49C	Chop Suey
50D	Articulated Truck
63D	Freeway Gas Tanker
65D	Saab Sonett III
71D	Jumbo Jet

Recolours:
12D, 24D, 36D, 45C, 64C.

Rola-matic models were used by the Terry's of York confectionery company who packed individual models into specially boxed chocolate Easter eggs. Terrys had

used Matchbox models in previous years and later used models from the Disney Series (For further information see Chapter Eleven).

Rola-matic models were used in the Superfast range for twelve years. The two models shown on the top row were prototypes that never made it to the drawing board.

Lesney released three different styles of Chopper motor cycles shown here with their colour variations and handlebars. Only two were issued with chrome forks and are quite rare.

Lesney had originally planned to issue six chopper style custom bikes but only released three. When first shown in the catalogue they all had chrome-plated handlebars but only two were issued like this, the Stingeroo and the Chop Suey. These models also came with various colours of handlebars. Black is hard to find and the rare ones are light blue on the Stingeroo, orange on the Chop Suey and light blue on the Jumbo Jet. First issues of the 21E Rod Roller had metallic red or bright red wheel hubs, later issues were plain black. The plastic base was usually green but the black version is harder to find.

Pre-production castings of the 24D Team Matchbox had an air scoop cast on the front panel in the form of a slot. When it was decided to apply a large label to this panel in production the slot was no longer required and was deleted from the mould.

The first issues of the 24D were in yellow with either a number '4' or number '8' label. This colour scheme was always shown on the box illustration although the yellow body is now quite hard to find. The body colour changed to metallic red with a number '8' label for the rest of its release before becoming a Two Pack model in 1978. The yellow body version was also packed in the G4 Team Matchbox Superfast Champions gift set. This comprised a Superking K7 Racing Car Transporter with four Team Matchbox models in yellow, blue, green and red. The blue body model is now quite hard to find. It usually had a number '5' label but a number '1' label is the rarer version. The G4 also came with the 34D Formula 1 Racing Car in orange or blue.

Early issues of the 50D Articulated Truck had labels applied to the sides

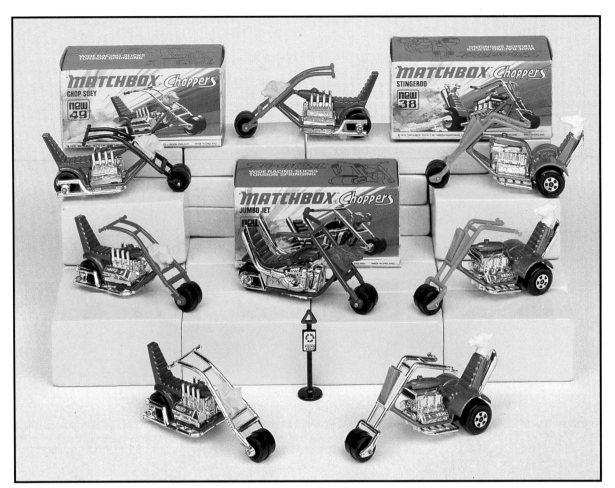

The colourful range of issues of the 24d and earlier 34d racing cars.

of the tipper and the 63D Freeway Gas Tanker had 'Castrol' labels instead of the usual 'Burmah'. These Castrol labels were in fact normally found on the A1 Service Ramp. Both models shared the same cab components.

1974

Only six new models were released, two of them were Rola-matics the 16E and 73D:

6E	Mercedes 350SL
16E	Badger
18F	Hondarora
56D	Hi-Tailer
62E	Renault 17TL
73D	Weasel

First issues of the 16E Badger had a chrome radar antenna which could also be found in white, cream or black. The first issues of the 18F Hondarora had chrome forks; the fixing of these to the frame was modified to ease assembly and they were also changed to black. The spoked zinc wheel was a copy of that used on the Y13 1911 Daimler. In 1976 the Honda was produced in orange and used in the K6 Motorcycle Transporter.

During 1973 and 1974 Britain had suffered from industrial unrest, the worst instance being the national strike of coal miners. This led to power shortages which meant many companies could only use electricity for three days a week. There was also severe shortages of crude oil which almost forced the British Government to impose petrol rationing. These incidents not only affected Lesney's production, but also supplies to them of materials such as paint and labels. To overcome these shortages many labels were used on the wrong models such as the 70C Dodge Dragster. This model normally had long labels on the sides of a snake, but other labels

fitted were the 'Wildcat' labels from the 8F, the 'Rat Rod' labels from the 62D and also the 'Star & Flame' label from the 64C applied to the bonnet.

Possibly the hardest models to find today are the ones that had 'Scorpion' labels applied. The Scorpion label is ten millimetres in diameter and shows a red Scorpion in a white circle with a black border. During 1971 Lesney released the Scorpion range, which consisted of Matchbox size cars that had electric motors and rechargeable batteries. These cars could be used on the Superfast track sets with the necessary charger unit. The vehicles had painted plastic bodies with black windows and bases. Two vehicles were made, each in two colours with the Scorpion label on them. This label was used on the electric powered models made during 1971 and 1972. The models found with these labels are 1F, 7D, 19E, 62C and 69D.

Many models which had enclosed bases that were not visible from the sides and which did not have bumpers cast on

The Scorpion models in the background with their original packaging. The six Superfast models in the foreground were all issued with the Scorpion labels in place of their normal labels.

them, had black painted bases. Lesney used models like these to use up their stocks of old or unpopular paints. Vehicles like the 24C Rolls Royce Silver Shadow, which normally had a black base appeared with pink, metallic green, grey or silver bases. Other models that had a variety of base colours were 7D, 8F, 33C, 45C, 50C, 66C, 69C and 70C.

Some models that normally had unpainted bases were made with silver painted bases instead, they were: 3D, 5E, 10E, 14D, 19E, 20D, 22D, 25D, 29D, 31D, 37D, 40D, 51D, 54C, 55E, 61C, 67C, 73C and 74C.

1975

Section 3 - The era of boats, the influence of space travel, the

introduction of tampo printing, the twin pack range, military models, innovations and toy legislation.

This year saw the gradual decline of the Hot Rod era. Only a few of the new models had big wheels and chrome engines. Two more Rola-matic models were issued, the 20E and the 35D bringing the total of Rola-matic models produced to eleven. Rola-matic models were slowly deleted from the range over the next decade until the 20E Police Patrol was the last one to leave in 1985. The new issues were:

4F	Pontiac Firebird
5F	Seafire Boat
8G	De Tomaso Pantera
12E	Big Bull
14E	Mini Ha-Ha
20E	Police Patrol
22E	Blaze Buster
23F	Atlas Dumper
34E	Vantastic
35D	Fandango
36E	Formula 5000
55F	Hellraiser
59E	Planet Scout
68D	Cosmobile

Recolours:
2E, 4E, 7D, 19E, 27E, 33D, 40D, 41D, 51D, 53D, 60C, 66D, 67C, 75C.

The 5F Seafire boat was loosely based on the design of an off-shore power boat, and had a large chrome engine and separate exhaust pipes. These exhaust pipes tended to break off quite easily and it was not unusual to find models in blister packs with the broken loose exhaust pipes inside. Many colours and combinations of parts existed on the Seafire because of colour changes to the body, base and driver. The rarest variants are a white deck with a brown hull and the red deck with blue hull.

Few variations exist on the 12E Big Bull apart from the plastic rollers being black instead of orange. Also the dial gauge design on the right hand side of the body points to eleven or twelve!

Pre-production samples of the 14E Mini Ha-Ha have the number '45' cast on the base. The 20F Police Patrol was produced in many different colours through the years for various markets and special issues. It was based on the Range Rover vehicle and because it was a Rolamatic model with a revolving roof light it had a frosted window and no interior seat detail. This did not seem to affect the popularity of the model because it stayed in the range for over ten years. *Hickmore:* "Originally we intended to hot foil in chrome the flat face of the rotating light. This idea was dropped at the pre-production stage." The 22E Blaze Buster Fire Engine usually had a yellow ladder, but some have been found with black or even a much rarer white ladder. The white ladder was used on the pre-production models. *Hickmore:* "When the model

entered production the white plastic was changed to yellow because it was not a normal stock held colour of nylon material".

The 34E Vantastic was based on a Ford Mustang. When first released it had a large chrome engine on the bonnet. This was removed in 1978 and a rectangular label was applied to the bonnet instead. Some models can also be found with the 'Sun' label from the 47D.

The 59E Planet Scout and the 68D Cosmobile were designed as vehicles from the future. In 1979 they were issued with the 2F Hovercraft in gift sets under the name of Adventure 2000 with some Superking models and plastic figures. The models were painted in a metallic light green which became known to collectors as avocado green. These sets were not very successful in these colours and so in 1980 Lesney decided to change them to a dark metallic blue. Although more attractive,

The adoption of tampo printing by Lesney was a turning point in their production process. The Streakers were the first models to use the process.

this colour change came too late and none of the sets were issued. Many of the miniatures were found on sale in Tesco stores, although the Hovercraft was never produced in blue. Only one of the Superking models was made in blue, the K-2006 Shuttle Launcher.

1975 also saw the release of Streakers. These were models in the miniature range which had decoration printed on them instead of having separate labels applied. This printed decoration was applied directly to the painted body casting by a process known as Tampo printing. This process was produced by a machine that transfered the desired coloured design in ink, from a plate, onto the body using a rubber pad. This process is also known as pad or transfer printing. The

Streaker models had two colour printing applied on the top surface of their bodies and some variations exist on the early models. There were ten models used:

7D Hairy Hustler
27E Lamborghini Countach
33D Datsun 126X
40D Vauxhall Guildsman
41D Siva Spyder
51D Citroen SM
53D Tanzara
60C Lotus Super Seven
66D Mazda RX500
75C Alfa Carabo

Most of the models had new body colours and some of these appeared without the new tampo print. The 27E was produced with black and green printing, the green can be found in two distinct shades with dark green being the least common. The 33D had a red and orange flame design and the orange was changed to black, the 40D body colour was changed from its previous pink to red for Streakers. The pink body exists with tampo print instead of its usual label and is hard to find. The 51D had a red and white stripe design that went over the centre of the body ending on the boot lid. This design was changed to a fish tail shape on the boot lid because it was found that when the body was riveted to the base the tampo print became marked. The 53D was another model that had its ink colours changed from orange and black to red and black. The benefits of using tampo print instead of labels were many. A model like the 51D Citroen SM could have decoration applied to its bonnet, roof and boot lid in one operation instead of perhaps using three labels. This meant that a higher level of decoration could be applied to a model at less cost to Lesney. As the process was developed over the years it was possible to print up to four colours on the body and also in areas where labels could not easily be applied such as around wheel arches.

A promotional model was produced in 1975 using the 35C

Merryweather Fire Engine with 'Flame proof wool' labels on the sides instead of the usual 'London Fire Service'. This model came in a special box and although it is quite sought after by collectors it is a Code 3 model.

1976

Seventeen new models were released this year and only one re-colour, the 58D. The 71E Cattle Truck was a re-issue of the 4D Stake Truck which was identical to the original except that the pair of wheels were deleted. This was the first of a number of re-issued models that Lesney were to release. This practice saved money in tooling and meant that more models could be released. This years new models were the beginning of a trend into military and construction vehicles:

1G   Dodge Challenger
2F   Hovercraft

7E	V.W. Golf
19F	Cement Mixer
26E	Site Dumper
29E	Tractor Shovel
30E	Swamp Rat
37E	Skip Truck
38E	Jeep
45D	B.M.W. 3.0 CSL
49D	Crane Truck
52D	Police Launch
54D	Personnel Carrier
58E	Faun Dump Truck
64D	Fire Chief
70D	S.P. Gun
71E	Cattle Truck

The 7E V.W. Golf featured a roof rack with surf boards which were later removed. The first release of green can be found in two distinct shades before it changed to yellow and then silver. The cab of the 19E Cement Mixer was the same design as the earlier 16E Badger and they shared the same window.

The very first issues of the body casting had the ladder detail on the side of the cab extending to the bottom edge of

the body. Although the cement barrel was usually yellow with red or black stripes, lemon and also grey barrels were also produced.

The 29E Tractor shovel has the same basic colour scheme of yellow throughout its life in the range. It was not until 1988 that it was used for its first promotional issue. It was used in Germany to promote a drug called 'Thomas Mucosolvan' which was tampo printed on the roof of the standard yellow coloured model.

The 37E Skip Truck had the same design of cab as the 23F Atlas Dumper and shared the same window and interior parts. These were originally a chrome seat and amber window which were changed to grey with a clear window. During the change-over, models were found with a combination of these parts as well as black or orange seats. The Skip Truck was also released with a blue skip which is now hard to find.

The 64D Fire Chief was to be released as a police car, as pre-production base castings show.

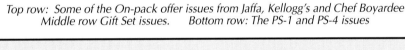

Top row: Some of the On-pack offer issues from Jaffa, Kellogg's and Chef Boyardee Middle row Gift Set issues.   Bottom row: The PS-1 and PS-4 issues

The only major variation to be found is the body in orange instead of red, although there are small variations in the printing of the labels.

The 70D SP Gun (self propelled gun) was consistently olive green. Some models were produced with black rubber tracks instead of the usual light brown. The black tracks were in fact normally to be found on the 12E Big Bull bulldozer.

This year saw the release of some attractive gift sets which had models in different colours from normal. These models were often found packed separately. The G12 Rescue Set contained six models, one of them the 62E Renault 17TL had a red body with 'Fire' labels on the doors. The G13 Construction Set had five models and a plastic 'Load-A-Vator' hopper which could drop plastic granules into a tipper truck. The 20E Police Patrol was to be found in this set with an orange body and 'Site Engineer' labels. These orange bodies were also found with 'Police' labels and a still rarer issue is the normal white body fitted with 'Site Engineer' labels.

New this year were the Two Pack range which consisted of pairs of vehicles that go together in a play theme. There were eight different packs using nine current models and seven old issues, ten of the models were in new colours, many of these for the first time.

TP1 was a re-issue of the 1E and 2D Mercedes Truck and Trailer in red with yellow canopies. The canopies had labels on the sides for the first time, and were to be found in different shades of yellow plastic. The TP2 had the 25E Mod Tractor in red with the 40C Hay Trailer in yellow which no longer had the clip in end panels. TP3 had the 9E Javelin now in blue and the 43C Pony

Trailer in orange with small labels on the side for the first time. TP4 had the 54C Ford Capri and the 57D Trailer Caravan, the caravan usually had a combined stripe and flower label, but labels were also used from two other models, the 'Seagull' label from the 31E Caravan and the '20 dots' label from the K27 Camping Cruiser. TP5 had the 40D Guildsman towing the 9D Boat and Trailer. The TP-6 had the 74C Toe Joe in yellow and the 29D Racing Mini in red. The TP7 and 8 contained the normal issues of 46D Stretcha Fetcha with 59D Mercury Police Car and the 17F Londoner Bus with the 72C SRN 6 Hovercraft. They were all packaged in large blister packs measuring 200 x 150 mm. Two Packs were often found to contain odd variations of foreign issues.

There was also a range of six military Two Packs which consisted of six obsolete and six current models. When first issued the models were in a very dark shade of olive green which became known to collectors as olive drab. This dark green colour was not very popular with retailers or consumers and so the colour was changed to a lighter shade of olive green. Most of the first issues of military Two Packs were issued in Eastern Europe and some are now quite hard to find, especially the TP13 with the 28E Stoat and 73D Weasel. The 63D Freeway Gas Tanker was used in TP14 and the olive drab versions had small labels normally found in the Sky-Buster range. The labels were the French flag from SB15 or the Canadian flag from SB5 which is the harder one to find.

Through the years the Two Packs have always been a good source of models for the collector, as often they were used by the factory to clear stocks of old or foreign issues.

Late in 1976 a new style of picture box was phased in which

was to become the last type of box used without a window. Although the 70C Dodge Dragster was deleted during 1976, it appeared in this last style of box.

1977

11F	Car Transporter
31E	Caravan
32E	Field Gun
33E	Police Motorcycle
38EX	Glider Transporter
40E	Horsebox
42E	Mercedes Container Truck
48E	Sambron Jacklift
53E	Jeep CJ6
60D	Holden Pick-up
65E	Airport Coach
66E	Ford Transit Pick-up
75D	Seasprite Helicopter

A total of twelve new models were released with three recolours: 35D, 36E and 55F. The 32E Field Gun was of interest because it came with a plastic diorama, which was a tight fit in its box. The diorama had two military figures moulded on it and also four plastic shells, which could be snapped off and fired from the gun. This model proved to be a poor seller over the years and very few variations exist, mostly concerning the shades of plastic used for the diorama.

The 42E Mercedes Container Truck has been made in various liveries through the years including special issues for the U.S.A. and Germany. These variants multiply when the base colours, window and container shades and labels are taken into account. Some of the first 48E Sambron Jacklift models produced were made for the English division of the French company of Sambron. These models had the word 'Sambron' tampo printed in a red rectangle on the side of the driver's door. Most of the models were sent to France,

although some were found on general sale in the U.K. They are now quite rare.

The 60D Holden Pick-up was initially metallic red which later changed to red and then cream. The red body can be found with various labels on the bonnet apart from the usual '500' type. Harder to find is the 'Sun' label from 47D (which had a red interior and green bikes) and the 'Shield' label from the Adventure 2000 series (which had a cream interior and yellow bikes). The cream body version usually came with 'Superbike' labels on the sides (with red or beige interior) but some models also exist with the 'Honda' label from 38C.

The 65E Airport Coach was released with three types of label for different markets. 'American Airlines' for the U.S.A., 'Lufthansa' for Germany and 'British Airways' for the rest of the world, although the various models were known to turn up in the wrong countries. These three issues normally had amber windows, models can also be found with clear windows. Not long after being released, the assembly of the model was modified so that the front grille became part of the base, instead of being a separate component. At this time two models appeared using the blue and white bodies which had labels not applied by Lesney, these were 'Fly Concorde' and 'T.W.A. World Airways'. 'T.W.A.' and 'Qantas' were then used on red and white bodies and a revised 'British Airway's' label was issued. The last version to be made in the U.K. was the all white 'Alitalia' which was later made in Macau with tampo printed decoration instead of labels. The following have been made in Macau: 'Pan Am', 'Lufthansa', 'Stork SB', 'Girobank' (labelled), 'Australian' and 'Virgin'. The 74D Seasprite Helicopter was the first helicopter in the range. Lesney had tried to design the model to scale but this made the model look too small. The window provided the only variations to be found; the normal colour was a blue tint but purple, red and green have been found.

At this time major changes were about to take place in the legislation covering toy safety. The main affect these new regulations had on Matchbox models concerned sharp projections and also the strength of small parts when subjected to a pull test such as pulling a wheel from its axle. The wire axles used by Lesney were of 0.6 and 0.8 mm diameter depending on the size of the wheel. It was found that with this size of axle, wheels could be pulled from their axles using the new pull test and expose a fairly sharp point. The diameter of the axles was increased to 1.0 and 1.2 mm, this meant that a new range of wheels had to be used and so the method of holding the wheel sets in the toy was also changed. The previous method of using a plastic suspension strip riveted to the base was changed to a system where the wheel set was secured directly to the base by a method known as clench fixing. The base had two ribs cast on where the axle rested and then these ribs were pinched together. From 1977 most new models had the new wheels and clench fixing and some existing models were converted such as the 34E Vantastic and 32D Maserati Bora. The underside of the base castings was changed from a curved to a flat surface under the axle areas. The 55F Hellraiser had its gear stick thickened so that it was no longer so sharp to the touch.

Lesney were always looking for new markets for their toys and one such market was Brazil. Although there was a demand for Matchbox models, the government in Brazil at the time was restricting imports After lengthy negotiations Lesney agreed to ship components to Brazil to be sprayed and

These are some of the Brazilian issues from 1977 which are now amongst the rarest of any Superfast models.

assembled there by a company called Roly Toys. *Smith:* "This proved to be a nightmare for the management in the U.K., who had the task of shipping the parts to Brazil and keeping accurate records of what had gone and when. We knew we did not stand to make much money out of the project, but we felt that it was better for us to do it than one of our competitors. There was always the chance that something bigger could develop in the future." Most of the range was made in Brazil, some in their normal colours and many others in new or different colour schemes. Most of the models had a plastic strip or label fixed to the base which read 'FAB ZF MANAUS' i.e. Made in Manaus. Manaus being the name of the town where the factory was located. Some of the models with plastic bases, had the words 'Made In England' scraped off. A full list of the models made and their colours has never been possible to compile.

The picture type of boxes that the models were issued in are of

interest. There were five different models illustrated: 1G, 4F, 36E, 41D and 58E. The model number was either printed or labelled onto the end of the box and later issues were put in the new style of blue window boxes.

The Two Pack range had a new TP7 containing the 38E Jeep and also a new item, the 38EX Glider Transporter. Although shown in the catalogue in silvers they were not made in this colour but were released in yellow. Later on a small run were made in red which were mostly available in Holland, these are now quite rare. The new TP8 contained a 18E Field Car towing a 38C, both in orange, some of the Field cars did appear with white bodies and are now quite sought after. In the Military Two Pack TP12, 20E was replaced with a Volkswagen Ambulance which was a modified casting of the 23E Volkswagen Camper, which no longer had its interior or opening roof panel.

New in 1977 was the Playset range, consisting of the PS1 Container Port and the PS3 Seakings Harbour. These sets consisted of printed cardboard mats, plastic accessories and some Matchbox vehicles which are of interest. The PS1 contained an all plastic Diesel Shunter (which the 24E was copied from in 1978) a 42E Container Truck with extra cardboard containers, a 15E Fork Lift Truck and an articulated truck and trailer which used the yellow cab from the 50D (red and blue cabs were also used later). There were also some plastic containers included which were different to that used on 42E, these had a separate black plastic base and no opening doors. Three types were used, red with 'NYK' labels, orange with 'OCL' and blue with 'United States Lines'.

The PS3 Seakings Harbour contained the 72C SRN6 Hovercraft, a Seaking Frigate, plastic harbour and dock accessories.

The PS2 Beach Head Assault was released in 1978 and contained three normal issue military models as well as plastic landing craft, buildings and accessories.

In the PS4 Railway Goods Yard, issued in 1979, more items of interest were to be found. Apart from cardboard containers and the normal 15E and 58E models, there was the 24EX Side Tipper with a black tipper. The 42E Container Truck had a plastic skip that fitted on the back, instead of its usual plastic container.

During 1977 Germany had a number of special issue models. The first set consisted of three blister packed models which were held together in a folded piece of card that had three windows in it. This set was called PS 1000 which meant 1000 Horsepower and the three models were all recoloured construction vehicles. The 29E Tractor Shovel in lime green, 37E Skip Truck in orange and 49D Crane Truck in red. These sets were limited in their availability and are now quite sought after, especially in their original packaging. The other special models were 6E 'Rennservice', 7E 'ADAC', 42E 'Deutsche Bundespost', 45D 'Polizei', 46D 'Unfall Rettung' and 63D 'Aral'.

In Austria a model was released for the fan club of a racing driver who was known as S. Manhalter. The model used was the 45D BMW 3.0 CSL in white. It had its usual 'B.M.W.' label on the bonnet and a label on the boot which had the signature of S. Manhalter. Although 50,000 were supposedly made of this model it has become quite hard to find.

In the U.K. the McVities biscuit company ran a promotion on packets of its Jaffa Orange Cake biscuits. The consumer sent in four wrappers together with ten pence for postage to receive a free model. Initially the 37D Soopa Coopa was used which had an orange painted body and a 'Jaffa Mobile' label on its roof. Demand

120 *The Superfast Range*

for the model was so great that Lesney were asked to produce more models. Unfortunately, the 37D had been replaced by the new 37E Skip Truck. This model was not suited to the colour scheme, so the 42D Tyre Fryer was used instead.

At this time Lesney considered manufacturing their diecast toys in the Far East. *Smith:* "I put the idea to the board of directors but they were totally against it, so I decided to undertake a small project myself". At the time Japan was a market in which Lesney were looking to expand their sales. A special range of models were produced, packaged in attractive black boxes numbered J1 to J9. The models were mostly obsolete items in new colours, they were:

The first release of nine special models for Japan in 1977 were in attractive black boxes.

5E	Lotus Europa
14D	Iso Grifo
15D	Volkswagen 1500
24D	Rolls Royce Silver Shadow
27E	Lamborghini Countach
33C	Lamborghini Miura
41C	Ford GT
52C	Dodge Charger Mk III
75C	Alfa Carabo

Les Smith went on to get four new models made of Japanese vehicles for release during 1978/79. These models were designed, tooled and manufactured in Japan at half the cost and in less time than in the U.K.

As production continued on these models the tooling proved to be poor quality. Lesney did not have any more tools made in the Far East for the miniature range.

1978

Four of this years new models were railway items and two were farm vehicles. The 63DX was a trailer used with the 63D tanker in the Two Pack series. The full list of new models were:

3E	Porsche Turbo
5G	U.S. Mail Jeep
9F	Ford Escort RS 2000
13F	Snorkel Fire Engine
21F	Renault 5TL

24E	Diesel Shunter
25F	Railway Flat Car
41E	Ambulance
43E	0-4-0 Steam Loco
44E	Passenger Coach
46E	Ford Tractor
51E	Combine Harvester
61D	Wreck Truck
67D	Datsun 260Z 2+2
69E	Armoured Truck
74D	Cougar Villager
J21	Toyota Celica
J22	Galant Eterna

Models that were re-coloured were 2F, 21F in yellow for the U.S.A., 36E, 59E, 63D and 68D.

The 3E Porsche Turbo has been one of the top selling models in the range since its release. The body colour has seen many colour changes through the years and early models could be found with many combinations of base and interior colours, although none of these variants have yet gained any rarity.

The 9F Ford Escort RS2000 kept the same colour and labels for most of its life in the range although it appeared in the Two Pack range in blue with 'Phantom' labels and then green with 'Seagull' labels. The model did go through a period where there was a mixture of interiors used as well as clear, grey or amber windows and black, grey, brown or silver bases. The rarest models to come from this mix-up were ones with red interiors. In the 1981 catalogue the model was shown with 'Castrol' labels, but this was never put into production.

The 21F Renault 5TL is another model that exists with many combinations of component colours, most are not too hard to find. The rarest variant is the silver body with tan interior. The Renault was shown in the Two Pack range in 1984 with a black

The four models on the back row were designed and tooled in Japan for the Japanese market. These models were later used in other markets in new colours before being retooled in Hong Kong.

body of which only a few samples were made and never released. The first issue of the 24E Diesel Shunter in green had a 'Rail Freight' label which was soon changed to 'D 1496-RF' to give it an international appeal. In later years cost reduction exercises first removed the interior control panel and then the zinc base was changed to plastic. The 25F Railway Flat Car used the plastic container from the 42E Mercedes. The first release of the 43E 0-4-0 Loco and 44E Passenger coach had labels with the numbers '4345' that were quite small. These were enlarged on later issues. After being used in various Two Packs the model was deleted in 1983. The train reappeared in 1988 when it was used for a U.K. promotional to celebrate 'Forty Years of British Rail'. For the first time the model was made in Macau.

The 61D Ford Wreck Truck used the jib arms from the 74C Toe Joe. The circle detail on the jib was changed to a ribbed design. The window was normally amber, although some were produced in blue. The body colour was first in red, then it was changed to yellow, of which various shades exist.

The 67D Datsun 260Z was first released in metallic red and then silver with tampo print added later. It was also used in the Two Pack range in metallic blue. When it was deleted from the range in 1983 the body was modified so that the doors were cast shut and then used in Two Pack and also the Streak Racing sets with a glow window. Finally, the moulds were shipped to China where it was used as a Chinese only issue along with the 55G Ford Cortina.

The 69E Security Truck kept the same livery throughout its release with one small change to the telephone number printed on the front wing. The number was found to be that of a private address and so was changed to one style that could not be dialed! This model was used on two occasions as a promotional model for the Dresdner Bank in Germany. The green and white model was first made in England in 1981 and then in 1987 another run was produced in Macau, even though the model had been deleted in 1983. The Macau version was a slightly darker green and is much more difficult to find.

In late 1978 the first two of four special models were issued in Japan. These were of Japanese vehicles that had been designed, tooled and manufactured for Lesney in Japan. The other two models were released in early 1979. Each were initially produced in two different colours. The moulds for these models proved to be of poor quality and were later re-made. The four models were then produced in Hong Kong and were later issued in the U.S.A. and Australia. These new models and the other

special Japanese recolours first issued in 1977 were now issued in boxes with colour illustrations. Also in the range were two of the 1977 German specials, the 6E 'Rennservise' and 7E 'ADAC'.

Late in 1978 the Two Pack range was re-named the 900 series because of the new large trucks and trailers that were to be added to the range in 1979. The new TP9 featured the 18E towing a 24D using a new plastic trailer and the TP10 consisted of the old 3C and

IV Flying Beetle(11E Flying Bug)
V Hot Smoker(70C Dodge Dragster)
VI Lady Bug (31D Volks dragon)
VII Brown Sugar 26D Big Banger)
VIII Black Widow (41D Siva Spyder)
IX Flamin Manta (7D Hairy Hustler)
X Golden (33 D Datsun 126X)

German Police set with the K7 Porsche Turbo, this time the rider and seat were in green plastic with 'Polizei' labels and the cycle frame was in cream.

The 63D Freeway Gas Tanker was used for a promotion by the Sellotape company. Most people are familiar with the clear adhesive tape made by sellotape but perhaps not aware of their other products: for many years they manufactured adhesive labels for Lesney as well as labels

47E	Pannier Tank Loco
51DX	Motor Cycle Trailer
55G	Ford Cortina
56E	Mercedes 450 SEL
62F	Chevrolet Corvette
63DX	Tanker Trailer
64E	Caterpillar D9 Tractor
68E	Chevy Van
71EX	Cattle Trailer
72D	Bomag Road Roller
73E	Model 'A' Ford Saloon
J-2	Mazda RX7
J-5	Nissan Fairlady Z

Recolours: 3E, 6E, 19E, 24E, 63D.

Back Row The U.S.A. Roman Numeral set of ten models for1977.
Front row The ten models released in 1980 as a U.S.A. Limited Edition.

59D. The only change in the military series was in TP13, where the 28E was replaced by the 49B Unimog. This came with a square 'A' label or the harder to find circular 'Star' label.

The U.S.A. had a special set of ten models produced which was known as the Roman Numeral set. They were in new colour schemes with new bases in blister packs. The bases were numbered from one to ten using the Roman Numeral system and all the models had new names as follows: (previous name and number in brackets)

I Silver Streak (1F Mod Rod)
II Sleet-N-Snow (5G U.S. Mail Jeep)
III White Lightening (48D Pi-Eyed Piper)

122 *The Superfast Range*

Some trial run models were produced to test the feasibility of chrome-plating body castings and then applying labels or tampo print. One of the models used was the 27E Lamborghini Countach which had a chrome body with black and green tampo. Also the 20E Police Patrol was made with chrome and also gold plated bodies with 'Police' labels. In the Roman Numeral range the Silver Streak was issued with silver body and the Golden with a gold body.

In the Superking range the K66 Police Set contained a Jaguar XJ6 Police Car and two 33E Police Motorcycles with riders. These riders had painted faces, gloves and helmets which the usual model did not have. During 1979 the 33E was used in the K71

used in other industries. To promote their labels, D.R.G. Sellotape Products approached Lesney to produce 500 models, but as there was only a short time available to produce them, only 288 were made, by stripping models with 'Burmah' labels and putting on the new labels by hand on the rear and sides. Most of these were then given away at a trade fair called Interflow 78.

1979

10F	Plymouth Police Car
12F	Citroen CX
24EX	Side Tipper
28F	Lincoln Continental Mk V
39E	Rolls Royce Silver Shadow

Many of the new models designed from 1979 onwards featured spring steel suspension strips, the first vehicles being: 10F, 12F, 39E and 62F. The 10F Plymouth Police car had a separate roof light and window which could be found with a blue tint or in solid blue. Later on the windows were combined as one component in blue, although some were made in purple. During 1982 the tool for the body was re-made and in order to supply orders taken for the Plymouth, the old 59D Mercury Police Car was used with the same tampo print from the Plymouth. There were also plans to release the Plymouth as an American yellow taxi numbered MB70 but this project was cancelled.

The 47E Pannier Loco was the last new train to be released, and the 24EX Side Tipper was used in the Two Pack range and PS4 Set. The 55G Ford Cortina saw many colour changes and variants during its release. First base castings did not have the patent number for the door design cast on the rear. Later the model was used in the Two Pack range, where the body casting was modified to include fixed doors. One of the rarest variants was that with a black base. Glow windows were later used for Streak Set issues and finally the moulds were shipped to Shanghai to produce models for sale in China only.

to have opening rear doors and an interior." The first model issued with an orange body had tampo printed stripes on the sides. On the first issue, the middle stripe in blue continued ahead of the front wheel arch. This was later left off because of problems in printing.

The 73E Model 'A' Ford Saloon was a model that Jack Odell had

Top Row: The 42e 'Kardstadt' truck and the five special models produced for Germany in 1981. Also shown is the 46d B.M.W. 'Manhalter' model for 1977.

were often left out of the assembly.

The new items in the 900 series were the TP2 containing the 35C Merryweather Fire Engine and the 59D Mercury Police Car, TP11 which had a 46E Tractor and 40C Hay Trailer (now with plastic end panels), TP13 which had a 49B Unimog containing an ammunition box and a 32E Field Gun without its diorama. Samples of the TP13 found today, still in its blister pack, usually have the lid of the ammunition box loose inside where it has broken away.

models and so a new pack was designed called the Multi Pack MP1 which contained a thin plastic tray that held five models. These MP packs first appeared in Singapore and later in the U.K. and Europe, the contents of which were of great interest to collectors. Many foreign issues were to be found in these packs as well as new variations.

Perhaps the rarest model ever to appear was the 41C Ford GT with a yellow body which was found in Italy. Other items that have since become rare include the 10E Piston Popper and 65D Saab Sonnet, both in white. These models had both been deleted from the range and previously had metallic blue bodies. Large stocks of many unwanted parts had remained in storage and it was decided to use these up quickly to fulfill orders for the Multi Packs. The bodies were put through the spray shop and painted with whichever paint was in use that day.

In the Superking range the K7 Racing Car Transporter was changed to a 'Martini' livery in white with a 56D Hi-Tailer in the back, which came with a yellow or blue driver. (These two models were also available in the G3 Gift Set). In the K34 Pallet Truck Set contained a 15F Fork Lift Truck which had a new design of plastic forks that sprung upwards by means of an elastic band.

There were two models in the K36 Construction Transporter Set: the 29E Tractor Shovel and the 26E Site Dumper which had a red tipper instead of yellow. This was later used on all issues of the 26E The 58E Dump Truck was used in the G5 Construction Gift Set and had a red tipper which is not common today.

Lesney were experiencing staff shortages in the assembly areas which they had overcome previously by changing the working hours of part-time staff, as well as supplying staff

The 56E Mercedes 450SEL was also due for release as a taxi as MB54 as well as the saloon version but this project was cancelled. The only major variation to appear on this model was a red interior instead of tan. In 1981 it was decided to change it into a taxi after all. The body was modified to take a red plastic taxi sign on the roof, whilst the body colour was changed to beige in the style of a German taxi.

First castings of the 62F Chevrolet Corvette body did not have a front and rear licence plate or the word 'Corvette' cast on the rear panel, these were added later. The 68E Chevy Van was a rather basic model without an interior or other feature. *Hickmore:* "When the model was first designed it was

Centre row: The first German specials were released in 1977. Front row: Three models were issued in France for the Paris-Dakar rally. They were marketed in a blister pack unique to the French market.

always wanted to produce, possibly in the Yesteryear range and indeed the miniature would not have looked out of scale in the first series Yesteryear range.

The first casting had a spare wheel cover cast on the left hand running board which was hollowed out. Some damage occurred on the mould causing this detail to become solid zinc which led to problems with the running of the mould and so the whole of the spare wheel was removed from the base. Some early bodies were sprayed white instead of cream and windows

The TP18 had a 7E VW Golf in red, towing a plastic trailer with a 5F Seafire attached. The TP17 had a tanker and trailer using the 63D and 63DX while the TP19 was a cattle truck and trailer using the 71E and 71EX. The TP21 was a 51D Citroen SM with the new 51DX Motorcycle trailer.

Four new trucks and trailers known as the Long Haul models were issued with numbers TP22, 23, 24 and 25 and these are discussed in Chapter ten.

Some of the existing 900 sets had new vehicles, TP4 had a 32D Maserati Bora in gold instead of the 40D Guildsman, and the TP6 now had the 61D Wreck Truck instead of the 74C Toe Joe.

Lesney found that they had a large stock of old and obsolete transport in the form of ex-London Transport buses. Lesney were approached by Universal with the offer of manufacturing Matchbox miniatures in the Far East. *Smith:* "I went to Hong Kong to inspect their factory but felt that the quality would not be good enough".

1980

Section 4. *Splitting the range by market, toy legislation, the growth of special models and the transfer of production to Macau.*

Towards the end of 1980 many of the military toys were phased out due to poor sales, particularly in Germany. A decision was also made to stop putting the word Superfast on the bases of new models. This was first omitted from the 54E Mobile Home in 1980 and then from all of the new models from 1981:

4G	1957 Chevy
16F	Pontiac Firebird
36F	Refuse Truck
38F	Ford Camper
50DX	Articulated Trailer
50E	Harley Davidson Motor Cycle
54E	Mobile Home
59F	Porsche 928

Recolours: 1G, 3E, 11F, 40E, 63D, 73E.

The 4G 1957 Chevy proved to be a difficult model for the factory to assemble and the fixing of the bonnet had to be modified at the pre-production stage. Because of the number of parts it was also expensive to make but it has become one of the best selling models in the U.S.A. The 16F Pontiac Firebird was an updated version of the older 4F Pontiac using modified moulds, with only the window staying unchanged. The 36F Refuse Truck had the

word 'Collectomatic' added to the front of the plastic refuse section after its initial release. Collectomatic was the name of the company that built the rear sections for refuse trucks that crush and compact rubbish, and these are made to fit many types of truck and chassis. Matchbox had copied the design of a Collectomatic vehicle and the end result was so good that Collectomatic paid for the wording to be added to the 36F.

The first release of the 38F Ford Camper came with an amber window in the camper section and also the number '35' cast on the base, and most of these were released in the U.S.A. The window was removed to save costs and the number was changed to '38'. Few variants exist on this model apart from different shades of body colours and the rear camper. The model was only made for a short time because it was modified into the 63F in 1982.

The 50E Harley Davidson Motorcycle was another model that did not have Superfast on its base, mainly due to the fact that there was not enough space for it! The wheel and tyre had been previously used on the Y15 Packard Victoria. Although shown in metallic purple in the 1983 catalogue, it was only ever produced in various shades of metallic brown. The 59F Porsche 928 has had many body colours as well as many combinations of base colours and window shades. The first interior colour was a pale primrose that was soon changed to light brown.

Because of poor sales of the Adventure 2000 series, large stocks of purple tinted plastic were in stock, and this was mostly used up on models where it would not look too unsightly such as the 11F Car Transporter and 19F Cement Truck which had small windows. Other models that had purple windows were

35D, 40E, 42E, 49D, 59D, 63D and 71E. Many models were also used to clear stocks of brown paint, probably made from a mixture of different coloured paints that were in storage. The models used mostly had bases that were only visible when turned over and so the brown base would not affect the models appearance. They were: 3E, 17F, 26E, 27E, 37E, 47E and 59F.

In the 900 series, there were some new items. The TP1 was recoloured in a blue and yellow 'IMS' livery, TP5 now had the 9F Ford Escort with 'Phantom' labels, TP11 now had a red Hay Trailer and TP16 was a new combination of a 50D Articulated Truck with the new 50DX Trailer. Although this was shown in two-tone green it was not issued. In fact it was released in its usual colours of blue and yellow as well as the harder to find red and silver verison. TP17 was changed to a 'Shell' livery.

Around the world there were a number of special models produced. In the U.K. a Matchbox Collectors' Club was formed by Lesney for children. It was advertised at the time mostly in children's comics and for a payment of £2.15 children were sent a cardboard tube containing a club model, a poster, identity card, badge, certificate and a set of stickers in bright colours. The model was a 68E Chevy Van in its usual orange colour but with side labels instead of tampo printed stripes. The club was not a success and did not last very long. Some club models were later found on general release without labels or tampo.

In France there was a release of three models to celebrate the Paris to Dakar rally, notable because it coveres rough desert terrain. The models were the 20E Police Patrol and 60D Holden Pick-up in blue and the 41E Ambulance in silver. They were all packaged in separate small blister packs that

were only ever issued in France. The Ambulance had silver plastic rear doors but some were made with the white doors from the normal white models. Some of the Police Patrol models had a yellow roof lamp instead of orange.

The four models that had been produced in Japan: numbers J-2, 5, 21 and 22 were moved to production in Hong Kong. The moulds were remade, with only a few slight differences to be found on the new body castings. They were then released in the U.S.A. in a blister packed set called the Supersticks Customising Kit. They were in new colours without any tampo print. Included in the pack was a sheet of labels that could be applied to the cars in any design that the consumer wanted. The models were later introduced into the U.S.A. range with tampo printed bodies as numbers 24F, 25G, 31F and 63E, but they were also available in a ten piece limited edition set. The other six models were all obsolete vehicles in new colours, which also had tampo printing for the first time. Advertising material for the models and their blister packs gave the models new names which did not appear on the bases, they were:

9E	AMX Javelin Cam Cracker
10E	Piston Popper Hot Popper
18E	Field Car Bushwacker
23E	Volkswagen Camper Pizza Van
46D	Stretcha Fetcha Viper Van
44D	Boss Mustang Cobra

The four Japanese vehicles numbered J2, 5, 21 and 22, were released in Australia in new picture boxes that were numbered MB76, 77, 78 and 79. Matchbox had not issued any miniatures with these numbers before and have not done so since.

1981

For the first time the range was split into two parts to suit two different markets, the U.S.A. range and the R.O.W. range (rest of the world). During the rest of this chapter reference will be made to the R.O.W. and U.S.A. ranges and also CORE models, these are models issued in both markets.

While the trend in Europe was to move away from Hot Rod vehicles, they were still popular in the U.S.A., and so the U.S.A. range now included sixteen models that were re-issues of obsolete Hot Rods in new colours.

New models were:

CORE

2G	S2 Jet
27F	Swing Wing Jet
28G	Formula 5000
30F	Articulated Truck
32F	Atlas Excavator
34F	Chevy Pro-Stocker
52E	B.M.W. M1
70E	Ferrari 308 GTB

R.O.W.

8H	Rover 3500

U.S.A.

(re-issues in new colours, old number in brackets)

8	De Tomaso Pantera	(8G)
14	Rallye Royalle	(3D)
15	Hi Ho Silver	(31D)
23	GT 350	(8F)
24	Datsun 280 ZX	(J5)
25	Celica GT	(J21)
26	Cosmic Blues	(26D)
31	Mazda RX7	(J2)
37	Sunburner	(32D)
46	Hot Chocolate	(43D)
48	Red Rider	(48D)
51	Midnight Magic	(53D)
63	Dodge Challenger	(J22)
66	Mazda RX 500	(66D)
72	Maxi Taxi	(67C)
74	Orange Peel	(70D)

Recolours:
CORE
6E, 7E, 21F, 29E, 39E, 54E, 57E, 59F, 60D, 62F.

R.O.W.
23F, 26F, 31E label, 37E, 42E, 46E, 54E, 56E, 57E, 59E, 61D, 63D, 65E, 68D blue, 74D.U.S.A.
20E, 42E, 53E, 61D, 68E.

The two aircraft introduced into the range were both based on real jets, the 2G was a Buccaneer S2 and the 27F a Tomcat F14A, both of which were already available in the Matchbox range of plastic construction kits. They featured wheel assemblies from the SkyBuster range of models and had moveable wings, which was a feature not even found on the more expensive SkyBuster models!

Early issues of the 30F Articulated Truck did not have the word 'Leyland' cast on the front of the cab. Pre-production issues had panels cast on the sides of the dumper so that labels could be applied. It was decided not to label the dumper and so the panels were removed from the mould, but later on in 1983 the panels were reinstated to the mould so that 'International' could be tampo printed.

The Pauls Agriculture Company in the U.K. had a promotional model made as a Christmas gift for their employees. Some of these models were also used to promote their animal feed business. The Articulated Truck was used in blue with the 'Pauls' logo tampo printed on the sides, and packed in a special blister card. Only 900 models were produced and they cost Pauls twice the normal price of a miniature.

The 34F Chevy Pro-Stocker was due to go into production with a green and red 'Gatorade-Thirst Quencher' orange drink livery that also had number '88' on the roof and sides. This livery had been copied from an American racing car. In fact, the Ertl toy company had already produced a model with this livery and with the full permission of Gatorade. Lesney changed the bonnet design of the model to 'Lightening' and some boxes were

also proof printed with this colour scheme. Gatorade still felt that the Lesney model was to similar to the Ertl version and so Lesney changed the design again. The green print was changed to blue and the '88' was changed to '34'. New boxes were also put into production. Pre-production models had the name 'Chevy Nascar' on the base as well as a recessed filler cap detail on the side of the body. The model was later revamped in 1983.

Not many variants exist on the 52E B.M.W. M1. Some early issues were without the black tampo print on the side, but the hardest models to find are those with green or amber windows.

The 70E Ferrari 308 GTB featued a black interior that also formed a black stripe down the car. This meant that the base curved upwards to form the lower half of the body shape. Due to the body and base castings being sprayed at different times it was found that the difference in colour of the two castings was at times quite noticeable. This was overcome by changing the colour of the base to silver! In 1988 the Ferrari was used by a company in Canada called Data East which manufactured arcade games. One of their new pin ball machines featured a game called 'Secret Service' based on a spy thriller theme, and models with special tampo print were fixed inside the machine with a screw. Although most of the models were used this way, some were made available for collectors.

Pre-production samples of the 70E Ferrari had number '8' cast on the base, while pre-production samples of the 8H Rover had number '70'.

The 8H Rover 3500 featured a sliding plastic sunroof and also a plastic base. These two factors made the model very light and some critics thought this was possibly a deliberate move by Lesney to downgrade the range, and so many lessons were learnt from this model. The pre-production trial run of the

Rover was in yellow and apart from being shown in the 1983 catalogue in this colour, some models were found packed in the G1 Car Transporter Gift Set.

The 8H, 52E and 70E all featured authentic base detail showing the engine, transmission and exhaust detail, as well as the model scale. This level of detail is still continued by Matchbox today.

Lesney were faced with rising costs and also a decline in sales, and every model was examined to see if a cost saving could be made. These included the base of the 17F Londoner bus changing from zinc to plastic. The 44E Passenger Coach first had its window removed and then its interior changed. When first issued it had three seat backs inside that were cast on the zinc body, two of these were removed and became part of the plastic interior. The 18F and 33E Honda Motorcycles had a new one piece black plastic wheel and tyre. This new wheel was also going to have a chrome rim printed on it, but this was left off. The 24E Diesel Shunter first had its interior removed and later its base was changed from zinc to plastic. The base of the 51E Combine Harvester was removed which meant that the wheels and axles had to be fixed to the body through holes in the sides using the Lesney pin firing method. The 52D Police Launch had its silver horn removed from its roof and replaced with cast detail.

Due to the latest toy safety standards models with opening doors had to pass various tests, that envolved twisting and pulling of the doors to check that they did not work loose. Lesney designed a new type of door hinge standard to meet these tests. This hinge is still used today and has also been copied by other toy companies even though it was patented. The doors of the 45D B.M.W. 3.0 CSL were converted to the new design which featured two large ribs cast on the inside of the door to provide strength and to guide the door spring.

The German market released five special models, all in German liveries. The 41E Ambulance in red 'Notartz', 42E Container Truck, 'Confern Mobeltraansportetriebe', 65E Airport Coach in orange 'Schulbus', 68E Chevy Van in white 'Addidas' and the 69E Security Truck in green 'Dresdner Bank'. The 42E Container Truck was also issued in blue for the 'Kardstadt' chain of stores. The whole German range of models could be found in boxes which had a large rear card, that contained information about the vehicle which the child cut out and kept.

The U.S.A. had a range of models produced to coincide with an A.B.C. television series called Code Red which followed the actions of an emergency team in Los Angeles. Eight models were released each on a large blister pack. They were: 33E Police Motorcycle, 41E Ambulance, 52D Police Launch, 59D Mercury in two versions as police and fire chief, a SB25 Helicopter from the Skybuster range and also two old models that were updated with new parts, the 29C Fire Pumper and 35C Merryweather.

Tesco stores in the U.K. sold special packs that contained three blister packed miniatures in an outer sleeve, at the discount price of 99 pence. Many of the models found were of great interest to collectors, including the 42E Kardstadt model, as well as other foreign issues. Possibly the rarest models to be found were the 71C Wreck Truck in blue and the 46C Mercedes 300SE in silver. Both were made using castings intended for the military Two Pack range, sales of which had been disappointing and so these models were sprayed in other colours for the Tesco packs.

In 1982 Tesco again had an exclusive triple pack, called the Tesco Value Pack. This time it

A set of eight models were produced to coincide with the American television series Code Red in 1981. All were issued in large blister packs.

was in a similar style to the MP1 Multi Pack issued by Lesney in 1979. It contained three models for 99 pence in a box that converted into a garage. A similar pack was used again in 1983 for the same price. These packs were also of great interest to collectors because they contained many of the 1982 American issues as well as variations not even found in the U.S.A.

In the 900 Series TP27 was new, containing the 43E 0-4-0 Loco with the 44E Passenger Coach in a green livery. The 44E had a new roof with upper windows and was called a Caboose. The re-coloured items in 1982 were the TP7 in red, the Jeep and Glider Trailer, the

TP9 in orange, the Field Car and Team Matchbox, the TP11 had a green Tractor and a beige Hay Trailer, which is now quite sought after. Very few of the TP7 sets were found in red, because it was eventually decided not to change it to red. Although some were released, these may have beeen a trial run. The TP4 was shown with a blue 32D Maserati Bora, but this was not produced. The TP2 and 27 had the new Leyland cab, these are featured in Chapter Ten.

Following the release of models with brown bases in 1980, this

year saw models that normally had black bases being made with grey painted bases. Once again stocks of old paint were mixed so that they could be used up. This time vehicles were used which had grilles and bumpers cast on the base. The shades of grey do vary but most have a blueish tint. Models to be found include: 3E, 7E, 9F, 21F, 22E, 27E, 47E, 54E, 59E, 61 and 67D.

1982

This year saw the biggest changes in the range since the introduction of Superfast. The

R.O.W. and U.S.A. ranges continued to be divided further with the introduction of more regional issue models and re-colours. This started to cause confusion in areas such as marketing, production and shipping, and so it was decided to change the way in which models were numbered. Miniatures had had model numbers on their bases since the mid 1950s, but now, because some models had different numbers in the two ranges this was no longer practical. It was decided not to put model numbers on the base, but instead the numbering would be shown on the packaging and catalogues for each market.

In order for production to identify components a new system of manufacturing numbers was adopted on each new model/casting. This commenced from number seventy five. Generally the number is only visible on the inside face of a component, but there are many places where these can be seen, such as on the jibs of the 61E Peterbilt Wrecker. *Hickmore:* "It's not something that Matchbox has ever tried to keep secret! This system continues today and is currently into the two hundreds. Most bases now had transmission and exhaust detail as well as the models scale, although the word Superfast was no longer used.

Packaging also underwent a major change, the blue window box being phased into Europe, first on the continent and later into Britain. This was a major blow to collectors as it marked the end of the picture box. The new blue window box was well received by the retailer because they no longer needed the special Matchbox display cabinets to display models out of their boxes. The new box could be displayed in many more ways on existing racking in supermarkets, on shelves or even pinned to a wall. The new models were:

CORE

1H	Dodge Challenger
5H	4x4 Jeep/Roll Bar
19G	Peterbilt Cement truck
25G	Audi Quattro
38G	Model 'A' Ford Van
42F	1957 Thunderbird
45E	Kenworth Cabover
51F	Pontiac Firebird SE
53F	Flareside Pick-up
61E	Peterbilt Wrecker
63E	4x4 Open Back Truck
66F	Tyrone Malone (Superboss)
74E	Fiat Abarth
75E	Helicopter

R.O.W.

14F	Articulated Tanker
17G	Titan London Bus
26F	Volvo Cable Truck
35E	Volvo Zoo Truck
37F	Matra Rancho
57F	Carmichael Commando
72E	Dodge Commando

U.S.A.

7F	Romping Rabbit
10E	Piston Popper
20G	4x4 Jeep/roof
22F	Mini Pick-up/roof
25G	Celica GT
30G	Peterbilt Tipper
35F	Pontiac T Roof
40F	Corvette T Roof
41F	Kenworth Conventional
43F	Peterbilt Conventional
44D	Boss Mustang
44G	Chevy Van 4x4
56F	Peterbilt Tanker
57G	Mini Pick-up/Roll Bar
63E	Dodge Challenger
66F	Tyrone Malone (Bandag Bandit)
69F	'33 Willys Street Rod
71F	'62 Corvette

Recolours:
CORE

1G, 2G, 3E, 4G, 6E, 16F, 18F, 21F, 29E, 32F, 36F, 49D, 54E, 55G, 58E, 59F, 67D, 68E, 73E.

R.O.W.
7E, 9F, 12F, 15E.

U.S.A
31F

Matchbox had invested a huge amount of money into the tooling for all these new models. Many of them shared the same components and some consisted of older models that had been revamped into new models. Many of the U.S.A. models had large wheels that were out of scale. These wheels had previously been used on some of the construction vehicles.

The 1H Dodge Challenger was a modified 1G with an air scoop cast on the bonnet and exhaust pipes on the side of the base. Most collectors refer to them as the Revin Rebel which was the name printed on the sides. The colour scheme and decoration was on very similar lines to the General Lee Dodge Charger car from the television series Dukes of Hazard.

Some models were found without tampo print and a white roof instead of blue, and are now getting hard to find. The Dodge was modified again in 1983 when the bonnet scoop was changed to become part of the interior and protruded through the bonnet.

The 5H and 20G 4x4 Jeeps were revamps of the faithful old 5G and 38E Jeep, although some models have been found with the roof or roll bar on the wrong models. The 22F and 57G Mini Pick-up were revamps of the 57E Wildlife Truck. The roof of the camper was later enlarged so that it no longer had a middle window and could also be found fitted with the roll bar from the 57G. In 1988 the 22F Camper was produced as a promotional model for a company in the U.K. called S.L.D. Pumps.

The 38G Model 'A' Van has proved to be very popular with collectors, and this will be reviewed in detail in Chapter Ten.

The 51F Pontiac Firebird SE was the same vehicle featured in the American television series Knight Rider. Matchbox did not produce the model in this livery because of the royalty fee required. The first red body issues had variations of window and interior colours, however, after production was moved to Macau the body colour was changed to black. The black body was later used with a glow window in Streak Sets.

In 1987 the Maaco company in the U.S.A. had 20,000 red pontiacs produced by Matchbox featuring their name. The logo proved difficult to tampo print and so clear vinyl labels were applied to the bonnet and doors. These models were given away free to customers who asked for an estimate for car body repairs and spraying.

A new wheel was designed for the Peterbilt and Kenworth models which has since been used on many more vehicles. It was named the 500 Concave Heavy Tread wheel because of its heavy ribbed design on the outside and the concave nature of the chrome hub. The application of chrome foil in production was a major break through and gave the wheel a sparkle when viewed. The development of this wheel led to the introduction in 1983 of the 440 Concave wheel used on saloon vehicles. This wheel features a concave eight hole design.

The four Peterbilt models shared many common parts, the 56F Tanker and 61E Wrecker had the same body and base while the 19G Cement Truck and the 30G Tipper shared the same body and base. Common to all four was the same window and interior but each had a different load on the rear. Many small variations exist in tampo print, base castings and window shades. During 1984 some of the Tipper Truck bodies were assembled with the cradle and cement barrel from the Cement Truck.

The 28G Formula 5000 was a revamped version of the 36E,

The Superfast range was reborn in 1982 with a range of Peterbilt and Kenworth vehicles. The tractor units were used in the new Convoy range of articulated trucks and trailers.

with the only difference being a much larger chrome engine on the back. Although it was shown in green in some trade catalogues, this was merely due to a printing error. The only major variants that exist were the base in black or unpainted.

Some early issues of the 74E Fiat Abarth were found with black interiors instead of red and these are now quite rare. Pre-production samples of the 74E had black interiors so it was possible that there was a quantity used up in produciton. In 1984 the Fiat was re-coloured in an authentic 'Alitalia' rally car livery. In production the tampo print on the boot lid was difficult to apply because of the two recessed panels, and so these were removed from the mould to give a smooth surface for printing. In the course

of production four variations appeared, with both types of boot lid appearing on both the 'Alitalia' and the previous 'Matchbox' livery.

The design of the 75E Helicopter was not copied from a real helicopter but designed to be as large as would fit in the box. The previous number 75 Helicopter had been criticized by collectors as being too small. As the 75E was used through the years in different liveries, many combinations of its window, interior and base parts have been found.

The 14F Articulated Tanker used the same cab as the 30F Truck and first appeared with 'Elf' labels which were later changed to

tampo printing. It was later produced in a 'Shell' livery for Japan on a yellow and white model, but some red and white models were made with the 'Shell' tampo print. The 26F and 35E Volvo trucks shared the same body, base and window parts with different loads. Not many variants exist, apart from the strange use of red plastic for the base instead of black!

The 72E Dodge Commando has appeared in a variety of liveries: 'Pepsi', 'Kelloggs', 'Hertz', 'Royal Mail', 'Streets', 'Jetspress', 'Risi' and 'Mitre Ten'.

The Dodge was used in an on-pack offer in the U.K. for 'Smiths Square Crisps' by Smiths Food Limited in 1984. The model cost 70 pence plus five wrappers, and a total of 80,000 models were sent out. The standard red and white model was used with new labels. These were applied with the

packet design to the rear but some exist with the packet at the front. In 1986 the Kellogg's company in Germany used the van for an on-pack offer in Switzerland. The model had the Kellogg's livery on one side and a 'Milch Lait Latte' livery on the other. The demand was greater than expected and supplies of the 72E were soon exhausted.

The 35E Pontiac T Roof used the base and interior parts from the 16G Pontiac but with a new body and window. The same idea was used to produce the 40F Corvette T roof. The design of the 71F '62 Corvette incorporated the seats being moulded with the bumpers. The bumpers needed to be chrome while the seat had to be in blue, so a method was needed to only vacuum-plate the bumpers. *Hickmore:* "A jig was designed that consisted of two strips of metal three feet long, that clipped together over the interiors and masked the seats from the plating process. The system worked well but the metal strips proved to be heavy work for the girls in production and so the idea was scrapped."

Due to the large amount of new models and tools, most of the models were not due for release until well into 1982. Sample models had to be made for catalogue photography and the toy trade fairs. For the first time duplicate models were produced using clear resin cast from rubber moulds. The moulded bodies were hand sprayed and then decorated using decals.

In Australia a Matchbox Club was started for children, similar to the previous British one. Once again the 68E Chevy Van in yellow was used for the club model, but this time it was tampo printed and featured a kangaroo. These vans were later on general release in Australia. For AUS $6 members obtained the van, a small Collector Showcase to display twenty four models, a wall poster, a catalogue and a collectors log book. The Chevy van was later sold on its own in the Limited Edition window box.

In Superkings the new K91 Motorcycle Racing Set featured the 33E Honda Motorcycle fitted with a new longer plastic seat and red plastic fairing. On the sides of the fairing were two number three labels.

In the Two Pack range the TP7 now had a 9F Ford Escort with the Glider Trailer in a new colour scheme of green with 'Seagull Gliding Club' labels. The first models were issued in metallic green and later issues were in a non metallic dark green. The Ford Escort was generally available separately in these colours. TP28 was issued and had the 55G Ford Cortina towing the 57D Trailer Caravan, both now with a tampo printed livery. The new TP29 was made up of the 53F Flareside Pick-up and the 9D Boat and Trailer both in colour schemes previously used. The new TP30 had the 5F Seafire Boat in a new black and yellow livery with the general issue 67D Datsun 260Z in silver. The new TP31 had the 12F Citroen CX in yellow with 'Team Matchbox' tampo printed on the bonnet, the word 'Team' was in the shape of a motorcycle and could be found in blue or black ink. The Motorcycle Trailer was also in yellow with red bikes and was later found packed singly in blue window boxes.

The new TP32 produced one of the rarest Two Pack models, the 74C Tow Joe Breakdown Truck in yellow with 'Hitch Hiker' labels. This model has since proved hard to find as there were not many on sale at the time. Recently a casting variation was found. The 'Hitch Hiker' labels were applied to the sides on the recessed tool box door outline. It was found that the labels did not stick down very well because of the upstanding hinge detail. The body mould was modified so that later issues had smooth sides.

1983

New models:
CORE
7G   Imsa Mazda
9G   AMX Javelin
13G   Snorkel
24G   Datsun 280ZX
28H   Ddoge Daytona
31F   Mazda RX7
34G   Chevy Pro-Stocker
41G   Racing Porsche 935
49E   Sand Digger
52F   B.M.W. M-1
55R   Ford Sierra XR4i
58F   Ruff Trek
60E   Toyota Supra
64F   Dodge Caravan
67E   Imsa Mustang
69G   1983 Corvette

R.O.W.
8I   Rover 3500 Police
12G   Citroen CX Ambulance
44F   Citroen CV15
48F   Unimog

Recolours:
CORE
1G, 4G, 53F, 61E.

R.O.W.
6E, 11F, 20E, 30F, 35E, 37F, 39E, 40E, 56E, 65E.

U.S.A.
7F, 10E, 8G, 14G, 42F, 44G, 43D, 48D, 56F, 57G, 69F, 71F.

The body of the 7G Imsa Mazda was based on the 31G Mazda RX7 with wider wheel arches and without opening doors. The same window and interior parts were used. Some models were shown in catalogues with opening doors, but these were in fact prototype models that had been made from the 31G body castings.

More revamped models were amongst the new issues. The 9G AMX Javelin was a heavily modified version of the previous 9F model and due to the extra body and spoiler detail, was

almost twice the weight. In 1986 its colour changed from silver to a maroon 'Dr Pepper' livery and at the same time the base was changed from zinc to black plastic, obviously as a cost reduction.

The 13G Snorkel Fire Engine was first issued in 1981 in the Code Red Series in the U.S.A. Although it was a re-issue of the 35C Merryweather Fire Engine, it also had the jib arm from the previous 13E Snorkel and an interior copied from the 22E Blaze Buster Fire Engine. The 24G Datsun 280ZX was designed and tooled in England to replace the 24F Datsun which had been tooled in Hong Kong and whose moulds were worn out. The 31F Mazda RX7 was produced for the same reasons and both models were an improvement. The 60E Toyota Supra was a

replacement for the 25G Toyota Celica GT, just as the real car had also been updated. The 34G Chevy Pro-Stocker was a revamp of the 34F with only a few modifications to the body and base. The car was well suited to racing liveries and had been issued in various colours. Two versions which are now hard to find were made with the wrong coloured interiors, the white 'Pepsi' issue and the white '7-Up' came with black seats instead of red.

The 41F Racing Porsche 935 was the first model to be tooled and manufactured in Macau under the new ownership of Universal.

The 52E BMW M-1 was modified so that it no longer had an opening bonnet, but it did keep its separate rear light strip. The 58F Ruff Trek was a very

Matchbox only produced 5,000 of each of the two Dodge models shown on the left, with their boxes. Opening features were later added to the models for general release. The blister pack was used in the U.S.A. and featured a competition.

modified version of the 60D Holden Pick-up, with only the window being unaltered. The interior now had a large roll bar and the rear load featured a spare wheel to match the new heavy tread wheels used. The 67E IMSA Mustang was based on the 44D Boss Mustang with the addition of some wheel arches that again increased the weight although it still retained its opening bonnet.

The 55H Ford Sierra XR4i was released at the same time as the real car with the co-operation of the Ford Motor Company. They had provided photographs and information the previous year for the development work. The first release of the model was in a special box that had been designed by Ford. To launch the model in the U.K., Matchbox had a competition where the first prize was the real Sierra XR4i. The winner of the competition was Nigel Cooper, the author of Chapter Five. He took delivery of the metallic blue car in December 1983.

Two other models were also issued in this year with the co-operation of a motor company. The Chrysler Motor Corporation of Detroit U.S.A. approached Matchbox to produce two diecast models to be issued at the official launch of their vehicles in Las Vegas. The two models were the 28H Dodge Daytona Turbo Z and the 64F Dodge Caravan. In only three months Matchbox designed, tooled and manufactured 5000 of each of these models. 500 of each of the models were fixed onto plinths by Chrysler and given away at the launch, the rest of the models were distributed to the car showrooms. This first batch of models was different to later issues in two ways: apart from the model name the bases had the wording:

The vehicles did not have opening features, but after the first batch of 5000 models the tools were modified so that the Daytona had an opening bonnet and the Caravan had an opening side door. These second issue models were available in the same colour scheme and were also packaged together on a large blister card. The two models were only on sale in the U.S.A. during 1983. In 1984 they became core issues with the colour of the caravan changed to black. Towards the end of 1983 some of the caravans were issued in silver by mistake and were generally available.

The 8I Rover 3500 Police Car was a revamped 8H Rover, with a modified roof panel to take a clip-in siren and also two lights that came through from the window. The siren was also used on the 56F Mercedes 450 SEL Police Car and at first was vacuum-plated chrome.

The 48F Unimog had been due for release a few years earlier but was stopped just as work started on the moulds. *Hickmore:* "The Chingford toolroom that were making the moulds had just taken on some new apprentice toolmakers following a one year training course. They were given the project of finishing the moulds. When the first castings were produced it was decided to issue the model after all, as the tooling had to a certain extent been subsidised."

Pre-production castings of the 69G 1983 Corvette had air intake holes cast on the front of the base. These made the casting weak in fettling and were filled in before production started. They can be spotted in some Matchbox catalogue photographs. When the model was recoloured in 1984 the base lettering was modified to read '1984'. In 1988 the body casting was altered so that there was a larger boot and no roof bar. The

base was again altered, this time to '1987'.

Two of this year's new models were produced in white metal for toy fair prototypes. The 44F Citroen 15CV and the 55H Ford Sierra SR4i were made for Matchbox by the well known company of Western Models, who produce 1:43 scale collectors models. These prototypes had modified interiors from other toys, e.g. the Sierra used the interior from the 25H Audi Quattro, sprayed in red.

In the U.K. two track sets were released under the name of Streak Racing which featured Superfast track that glowed in the dark and also vehicles with luminous windows. The S250 contained one car and the S450 had two cars. Over the years different cars were used in their standard colours with minor variations. They were the 3E Porsche Turbo and 62F Chevrolet Corvette, 55G Ford Cortina and 67D Datsun 260Z. These were all made in England.

Most of these could also be found on general release in their usual blue window box. Many variants exist on the 67D with the silver body. Some were also made in black.

In 1984 the two models packed in the Streak Sets were from Macau and were both standard issue black models, i.e. the 51F Pontiac Firebird and the U.S.A. issue 62F Chevrolet Corvette.

Towards the end of 1982 and the beginning of 1983 as many models were about to cease production, another crop of base variations were produced. Models that had previously had an unpainted or plated base were being sprayed with silver paint instead. *Hickmore:* "At the time, there was not always enough capacity in the factory to plate castings. So rather than put plating work out to another company, it was decided to paint them. It was cheaper to spray them using spare capacity in the factory."

The models affected were: 1G, 4G, 6E, 10F, 11F, 12F, 13F, 15E, 16F,

22F, 31E, 34F, 35E, 39E, 40E, 40F, 42F, 46E, 55G, 56E, 57G, 59F, 62F, 63F, 68E and 69F.

By the middle of 1983 most of the production of Miniatures had been transferred to Macau with only the R.O.W. issues being made in England. Production at the Lee Conservancy Road factory was phased out and transferred to the Rochford factory in Essex.

The 900 range was renamed Twin Pack although the range was not shown in any catalogues, it still continued to be produced for sale in Germany and France. Some interesting variants were to be found, such as the TP27 0-4-0 Loco and Passenger Coach in red with labels that had a green background instead of red.

In the U.S.A. a Christmas Stocking pack was issued containing two blister packed models held in an outer sleeve, most of the vehicles were R.O.W. issues and were of great interest to the American collectors.

1984

New models:
CORE
6F	F1 Racer
18G	Fire Engine
43G	Mercedes 500 SEC
46F	Group C Racer
50F	Chevy Blazer
54F	Command Vehicle (Foam Pumper)

R.O.W.
15F	Peugeot 205 Turbo 16
22G	Jaguar XK120
26G	Volvo Tolt Truck
37FX	Dingy and Trailer
42G	Mobile Crane

U.S.A.
37H	Jeep 4x4
72F	Sand Racer
74F	Mustang GT

JAPAN
44H	Datsun 280ZX Police Car

Recolours:
CORE
3E, 10F, 24F, 25G, 33E, 34F, 38G, 45E, 51F, 55H, 59F, 65E, 69G, 72E, 74E, 75E.

R.O.W.
21F, 65E, 72E

U.S.A.
5H, 41E, 41F, 56F, 62F

The 6F F1 Racer was issued as number 6 in the R.O.W. range and number 16 in the U.S.A. range in a red livery based on a Ferrari. From 1984 it was also available in the U.S.A. range as number 65, with the catalogue name of 'Indy Racer' in a blue STP livery. The number 16 model in red was dropped from the range in 1987 but the number 65 Indy Racer stayed and was later re-coloured in yellow, this appeared in the R.O.W. range as a re-colour in 1988.

A promotional model in a special box was issued in November 1987 at the Macau Grand Prix. It was based on a Formula Three car sponsored by the Sunkist drinks company and featured the 'Mr Juicy' orange drink livery. Models were given away at the race, which was won by the Mr Juicy car.

The 15F Peugeot 205 Turbo 16 was a good model of the real car and had a hinged rear body section as with the full sized vehicle, and for many years became the top selling miniature in Europe. Only two hundred examples of the real car were actually made, many of which were used in rally driving. The Peugeot team won the group B Section of the World Rally Championship in 1985 and 1986.

The 22G Jaguar XK120 was the last of the classic cars produced in miniatures and after being postponed several times. When it was decided to include it in the range it was found that part of the body mould had gone missing when one of the Lesney toolrooms was closed.

The 26G Volvo Tilt Truck was a revamp of the previous Cable Truck. Some people have been confused by the name Tilt thinking that the vehicle was a tipper, but the word tilt is the name given to the rear canopy. The 42G Mobile Crane was another revamped model that used the cab of 58E Faun Dump Truck and the rear crane section of the 49D Crane Truck. Some people felt that two good models had been turned into one very bad one! The person who actually thought of the revamp was John Reynods the director of the R & D Department at the time and hence, the model was decorated with the livery 'Reynolds Crane Hire'.

The 46F Group C Racer is actually one of the longest and widest Superfast models ever made, which can cause problems if you store models in the plastic trays found in Matchbox carry cases. The model has been issued in various liveries around the world. In 1986 the model was used in a twenty inch high plastic robot called the Cargantua. It held ten cars and also featured car launchers in its feet and hands. The model was in a black colour scheme and also had Superfast wheels. It was held in the head of the robot and was called the Brain Car. This model was only available in the Cargantua Robot. In 1987 a promotional model was made for a building block company in Switzerland called Bisotherm.

Four of the new models in 1988 were produced from moulds obtained by Universal from the Kenner toy company. The Kenner models had previously been sold as Fast Ones which had been manufactured for Kenner by Universal. After a few modifications to the moulds (particularly the bases) Matchbox manufactured these four new Hot Rods. The 50F was a CORE release whilst the other three

were all U.S.A. only issues. This list shows their previous names:

50F	Chevy Blazer Mighty Mule
37H	Jeep 4x4 Gravel Grinder
72F	Sand Racer Dirt Digger
74F	Mustang GT King Cobra

The Sand Racer did not stay in the range for long as the moulds soon wore out and Matchbox decided not to re-make them. The Chevy Blazer was shown in some catalogues with blue and red roof lights, but it was only ever issued with blue lights moulded as part of the window.

Matchbox Australia released three re-coloured models in a new style of box that read Limited Edition and Special Collectors Model. These were aimed at the collectors market and more issues have since been produced:

1984
38G	Model 'A' Van Arnotts Biscuits
44G	Chevy 4x4 Van Castro GTX

1985
38G	Model 'A' Van Australian
56G	Peterbilt Tanker Ampol
63F	Open Back Truck Bob Jane T Mart
72E	Dodge Commando Streets Ice Cream

1986
38G	Model 'A' Van Weet-bix
38G	Model 'A' Van Smiths Crisps
65E	Airport Coach Stork SB
72E	Dodge Commando Jetspress

1987
38G	Model 'A' Van John West
38G	Model 'A' Van Chesty Bonds
60F	Ford Transit Australia Post
65E	Airport Coach Australian
72E	Dodge Commando Minties

1988
4H	Taxi FX4R London to Sydney

38G	Model 'A' Van PMG
38G	Model 'A' Van Powerhouse Museum
38G	Model 'A' Van Big Sister
60F	Ford Transit We Deliver
72E	Dodge Commando Chokito
72E	Dodge Commando Mitre 10

In Japan the range was increased to one hundred models, made up of models from the other ranges as well as sixteen re-colours for Japan only. The range was numbered from one to one hundred and a new yellow window box was used. One new model, the 44G Datsun Police Car was made using the body of the 24G Datsun with a new plastic light bar riveted onto the roof. The re-colours were: 3E, 7E, 14F, 17F, 18F, 20E, 21F, 24G, 33E, 35F, 58F, 59F, 60E, 71F, (R.O.W. numbers). The 3E was re-coloured twice with two numbers.

Also for Japan eight models were issued in a Tokyo Giants baseball team set, the 44G Chevy 4x4 Van was used in white which was tampo printed as well as having labels on the sides shaped like a baseball shirt. Each shirt had a different players name and number on it. The vans were not packed in separate boxes, but were sold loosely in an attractive counter display pack. This held twenty four models, a total of three sets.

In the U.K. a set of U.S.A. Editions was released. These were twelve models from the U.S.A. range, all packed in a colourful stars and stripes style window box. They were mostly of the Hot Rod type of vehicle and were: 7F, 22F, 32D, 43D, 48D, 53D, 57G, 66F, 67C, 70C and 71F.

This idea was repeated in the U.K. in 1987 with a different selection of models: 23G, 26D, 37G, 41E, 42F, 48D, 67E, 69F, 74.

France also had a release of U.S.A. models in 1985 which were blister packs decorated in a stars and stripes style package: 7F, 8G, 10E, 22F, 26D, 37G, 48D, 54G, 57G, 62F, 66F, 67E.

The Japanese recoloured models for 1984 with the new style of window box.

The Matchmates range was introduced into Europe which consisted of two miniatures and a plastic badge on a blister card. Six different sets were available. Each Matchmate featured two vehicles from the same motor company with a plastic copy of the company's logo. The sets were not of any great interest to collectors because the models were all in their standard issue colours. Although Matchbox achieved large sales of the range it was never enlarged or updated.

In the U.K. many shops gave away a free wall chart/poster provided by Matchbox to promote miniatures. Apart from showing the 1-75 range and new issues, collectors could send away for free gifts by collecting and sending to Matchbox the header card strips from the blue window boxes. The gifts included models from the 1-75 range, Superkings, carry cases and even a torch which, unfortunately for collectors, didn't bear the Matchbox name. Some of the miniatures were U.S.A. only

The counter display pack for the Tokyo Giants vans held 24 models.

issues, the 22F Mini Pick-up 'Big Foot', 32D Maserati Bora 'Sunburner', 48D Pi-eyed Piper 'Red Rider' and the 56G Peterbilt Tanker in its blue and white 'Fresh Milk' colour scheme.

Twin Packs were relaunched in the R.O.W. catalogues with new numbers, which had now jumped into the hundreds. Some of these were only re-issues of previous sets while most were new

combinations. TP106 was the Motorcycle Trailer with the 21F Renault 5TL, although shown with a black body, only a few of these were made for trade fair samples before being changed to white in production. The TP107 had a 67D Datsun 260Z in silver and the 31E Caravan, both now with tampo printed designs. TP109 had the 12G Citroen CX Ambulance in a 'Marine Police' livery, and the 9D Boat and Trailer in blue and white 'Police' livery, some boats were made in all white and are hard to find. TP110 had the 37F Matra Rancho pulling a plastic moulded Inflatable Dingy on the trailer used to carry the 24D Team Matchbox in TP9 and the 5F Seafire in TP18 and 30. Although the Dingy had not been issued by Matchbox before, the moulds were in fact a few years old. When the K118 Battle King Army Helicopter was being developed it was also planned to be released in the Superking range as a rescue helicopter with the inflatable dingy. Apart from the Battle King release from 1978, the Helicopter was not issued in Superkings until 1982 in the K92 Transporter Set. Both issues were without the dingy. The TP112 had the 48F Unimog pulling the 2D Mercedes Trailer, both in an 'Alpine Rescue' livery. Some of these packs later went into production in Macau, where tampo print was used instead of labels.

The Export Sales division of Matchbox, based in Enfield, had previously been approached many times by Eastern block countries to produce Matchbox toys locally. This had always been refused as difficulties in maintaining quality control were thought to be insurmountable. Due to the previous few years of poor sales, Matchbox were keen for extra business. In 1983, however, an agreement was made with the Mladost Raznoisnos agencies to manufacture toys in the Mir factory in Razgrad, Bulgaria. It was agreed to lease the moulds on a yearly contract, with Matchbox supplying wheel sets, suspension strips and door springs. This way the agreed quantity could be monitored. As usual, there was no shortage of models to choose from the stocks of moulds that Matchbox had kept in storage. The five models chosen were all older, obsolete

find various ways to obtain them.

In 1985 a new range of models were produced using:

24C Rolls Royce Silver
     Shadow
25D Ford Cortina
40D Vauxhall Guildsman

and door springs were supplied from the production facility in Macau.

In 1986 the range was replaced with only two miniatures:

22E Blaze Buster
75D Seasprite Helicopter

20E Police Patrol
23E Volkswagen Camper
25D Ford Cortina
27D Mercedes 230 SL
39E Rolls Royce Silver
     Shadow II
41C Ford GT, 45D BMW 3.0
     CSL
51D Citroen SM
53E Jeep CJ6
    As with the Bulgarian models

Top row: The first five models produced in Bulgaria during 1983, numbers 5e, 5d, 39d, 51d and 74d. Also shown are the two models made in Bulgaria during 1986, numbers 22e and 75d.

Centre row: Seven models were produced in Bulgaria during 1985, numbers 24c, 25d, 33c, 40d, 45d, 46c and 66d.
Bottom row: During 1987 ten models were produced in Hungary, numbers 9e, 20e, 23e, 25d, 127d, 39e, 41c, 45d, 51d and 53e.

items:

5E   Lotus Europa
7D   Hairy Hustler
39D Clipper
51D Citroen SM
74D Cougar Villager

Some minor modifications were made to the moulds in the U.K. before they were sent to Bulgaria. The bases were changed to read 'Made in Bulgaria'.

The models were produced in an enormous range of body, base, interior and window colours with tampo printing being used. They were then sold in blister packs. Although the agreement did not cover the export of the toys, collectors around the world did

45D B.M.W. 3.0 CSL
46C Mercedes 300SE
66D Mazda RX500

The 33C Lamborghini Miura was also made for a short time before problems with the body mould halted any further production. This model is now one of the hardest issues to find. Two Superking models were also produced:

K56 Maserati Bora
K59 Ford Capri

The wheels, suspension strips

Three Superking models were also produced:

K30 Mercedes C11
K33 Citroen SM
K69 Jaguar XJ6

In 1987 an agreement was made with the Konsumex Foreign Trade Organisation in Budapest to produce Miniatures in Hungary. The models were manufactured by a local toy company called Metalbox. Ten models were used, some of which had previously been used in Bulgaria. They were:

9E   AMX Javelin

blister packs were used and many colour variations are to be found.

In 1988 further production took place in Bulgaria, this time with three miniatures:

28F Lincoln Continental
53D Tanzara
59E Planet Scout

Two Superkings were also used:

K52 Datsun 260Z
K72 Brabham Formula 1

Seven models are due for 1989 production:

6E   Mercedes 350SL
9E   AMX Javelin

27D Mercedes 230 SL
41C Ford GT
56E Mercedes 450 SEL
67D Datsun 260Z
74E Fiat Abarth.

1985

Section 5 - The introduction of Super GT, large consumer promotions and production in China.

New models:
CORE
2H   Pontiac Fiero
11G Lamborghini Countach
12G Firebird Racer
21G Chevy Breakdown
22F Mini Pick-up/roof
37H Ford Escort XR3i Cabriolet
39F B.M.W. 323i Cabriolet
56G V.W. Golf GTi
57H Mission Helicopter
65F Plane Transporter
71G Scania T412

R.O.W.
20G Volvo Container Truck
30G Mercedes Benz 280GE
31H Rolls Royce Silver Cloud II
33F Renault 11
40F Rocket Transporter

U.S.A.
23G Honda ATC 250R
47G School Bus

Recolours:
CORE
5H, 9G, 16F, 17G, 19G, 28H, 30G, 43G, 49E, 52F, 54G, 58F, 60E, 40F, 64F, 70E, 73E.

U.S.A.
6F

The 11G Lamborghini Countach was a much improved model compared to the older 27E Lamborghini. The design of the 12G Firebird Racer was based on the 61F Pontiac Firebird while the 21H Chevy Breakdown Truck was

based on the 68E Chevy Van. Some early body castings of the 39F B.M.W. 323i Cabriolet did not have the badge detail on the front edge of the bonnet.

The 57H Mission Helicopter was based on the helicopter used in the television series Blue Thunder. The series proved not to be as popular as the other combat helicopter TV series of the time Air Wolf. To get the model to fit the box it had rotors that folded (from the 75E Helicopter) and also a tail section that pushed into the rear of the body. Not many people realised that the model had a tail, but it proved to be the only way to get the model in the box. In 1987 the Skybuster range was relaunched in the U.S.A. and the Mission Helicopter was used in an army livery. As the model was packaged in a blister pack with its tail and rotors extended it did not look out of place in the range. In fact it was sold at twice the price of its normal issue livery.

The 40F Rocket Transporter and 65F Plane Transporter share the same vehicle but have different loads. The rocket was made up of three parts, which was changed to two parts when production moved from Macau to China. The nose cone became moulded as part of the upper section.

The 20F Volvo Container Truck was the 35F Zoo Truck with a new load. The first livery used was to have been 'Addidas', which was just about to go into production when permission was refused by Addidas. A new livery was quickly designed, the fictional 'Cold Fresh'. In 1987 a special model was produced for the trade toy fairs, using the Cold Fresh model, 5000 models were re-labelled at the Enfield warehouse with the 'No. 1 Best Selling Toy in the U.K. 1986' label. During 1986 the 72E Dodge Commando Truck was produced in a special livery for

Kellogg's in Germany as an on-pack offer in Switzerland. Supplies of the Dodge ran out (towards the end of the offer) and as it would have taken several months to obtain more models from Macau, Matchbox used up existing stocks of the Volvo Container Truck and had them re-labelled. These labels were applied over the top of the 'Coldfresh' panel on blue body Volvos and also over the top of the 'Federal Express' label on white Volvos. The labels were not as colourful as the original tampo printed Dodge and the design was slightly different.

The first body castings of the new 30H Mercedes Benz 280GE did not have the Mercedes badge on the front grille, and the smooth plastic base was changed to a textured finish. The Mercedes has since been produced in other liveries including 'Polizei', 'Lufthansa' and 'Fire Rescue'. Some of the first production samples of the 56H Golf GTi did not have the 'V.W.' and 'GTi' badges moulded on the front grille. The model was also used in a U.K. promotion in 1987 to promote spare parts sold by Volkswagen. The car was decorated in the racing livery of 'Quantum'.

In 1985 two models were made to coincide with the James Bond movie A View to a Kill, the 31H Rolls Royce Silver Cloud II in silver and the 33F Renault 11 in blue with a taxi sign on the roof. The Renault had the same number plate as the car in the film (359 ETD 75). Both models were in special boxes before being released as part of the range in 1986 in new colours. The Renault changed to black with a beige interior and some were also made with the grey interior from the Taxi version. The Rolls Royce changed to cream and later both models moved from production in England to Macau. *Hickmore:* "Two of us drove to

Lincolnshire to photograph and take measurements of a Silver Cloud owned by a car dealer. The car was stored in an old barn and the owner drove it outside for us to photograph. Once we had finished he put the car back in the barn for us to take our measurements, it was winter and very cold. He didn't leave us the keys and when we tried to push it towards a wall to measure from, it was so heavy that we gave up! We have a saying: 'We have pushed some of the best cars in the world'."

The moulds for the two models were made by an engineering company in Spain. The tool room was not equipped with diecasting machines and so the first shots of the toys were moulded in plastic. A gift set was also planned to be released containing the Rolls Royce Silver Cloud, Renault 11 and two other models. Although production samples were made of the 10F Plymouth Police Car in a 'San Francisco Police Department' livery and the 75E Helicopter in a Russian livery, they were not released.

The 23G Honda ATC 250R was to be released with the plastic rider from the Hondarora, in a new style of blister pack. This idea was dropped because the cycle and rider would have been difficult to pack in the normal American issue yellow boxes. Sales of the Honda proved to be poor and it was deleted from the range after only two years.

The 47G School Bus was a model requested by Matchbox Toys U.S.A. for many years. In 1987 it went from a U.S.A. only issue to a CORE issue. Problems with the body mould led to the shape of the rear door windows being changed. The lower window was filled in and a black window tampo printed instead. In 1988 it was used for two promotional models in the U.S.A., first in dark olive green as an army coach and then as an on-pack offer on cans of pasta products from the Chef Boyardee company.

A new range called Team Matchbox was also introduced, made up of the Convoy CY10 Kenworth Transporter and two miniatures, all in a common racing theme. The range has continued through the years with new and replacement issues:

1985
TM1 Pepsi with MB34G and 68E
TM2 Superstar with MB34G and 58F
TM3 Dr Pepper with MB9G and 68F
TM4 Brut with MB58F and 62F

1986
TM5 Seven Up with MB34G and 58F

1987
TM6 Duckhams with MB55H and 72G

In 1988 the range was renamed Team Convoy and some re-numbering took place:

1988
TC10 Fuji Films with MB24H and 72G

Some interesting variations exist on these sets. The 34G Chevy Pro-Stockers used in TM1 and TM5 usually came with red interiors. Both models were also made with black interiors and are hard to find. The 1985 catalogue shows the TM2 Superstar set with the words 'Super Boss' used on the vehicles. Some production samples were made, but never issued. The 58F Ruff Trek used in TM3 usually had a black interior. Some were made with red interior and are also hard to find.

In the U.S.A. two racing sets were issued not available

elsewhere. Both were decorated in an 'STP' livery. A blue 'Indy' set with the 68E Chevy and 12H Pontiac and a 'Son of a Gun' set with the 58F Ruff Trek and 6F F1 Racer. These two American sets proved to be popular with race fans as well as Matchbox collectors. As Matchbox Toys had paid a licence fee to use the STP trade marks, they were only made during 1985. These sets are now very hard to find, especially in their original blister packs.

Convoy Action Packs were also new. These were made up of one Convoy truck and two Miniatures with a common theme:

1985
CY201 Fire Set
CY13 Fire Engine
MB54G Foam Pumper
MB74E Helicopter
CY202 Police Set
CY11 Helicopter Transporter
MB10F Plymouth Police Car
MB61E Peterbilt Wrecker
CY203 Construction Set
MB43F Long Haul Peterbilt with low loader trailer
MB29E Tractor Shovel
MB30G Peterbilt Tipper
MB32F Excavator

1986
CY204 NASA Set
CY2 Rocket Transporter
MB54G Command Vehicle
MB75E Helicopter

1987
CY205 Farm Set
CY29 Kenworth Tipper
MB46E Ford Tractor
MB51E Combine Harvester
CY206 British Telecom Set
CY15 Peterbilt Tracking Vehicle
MB48 Vauxhall Astra GTE
MB60 Ford Transit

All of the models were already in the range and each set had at least one new re-coloured model. The 54G Command Vehicle used in CY204 had a radar antenna on

the roof instead of the usual foam pumper nozzle. The CY206 Telecom set was not shown in any Matchbox catalogues. The range was replaced by 'Motor City Gift Sets' in 1988.

In the U.K. Tesco stores sold a gift set containing twenty five models (known as the G50). It contained many models that were old and unwanted stocks from the factory. Five models are of interest as they are now hard to find:

5H 4x4 Jeep. The brown body version that usually had a roll bar was found with a red roof from 20G.
14F Articulated Tanker, red and white body used for the 'ELF' livery but with 'Shell' tampo print.
20G 4x4 Jeep with roof, white body without tampo print.
54F NASA Tracking Vehicle, without tampo print.
56G Peterbilt Milk Tanker, without tampo print

Kellogg's in the U.K. carried an on-pack offer on packets of Frosties, whereby children could send for the Tony the Tiger, 3 in 1 offer. After sending four tokens from the packs, the applicant received a supporters club magazine, membership card with number and also a model. The model used was the 35E Pontiac T Roof in black, which came with orange stripes on it. The initial demand was greater than expected and more models were supplied to Kellogg's. A total of 750,000 models were eventually sent out.

The Chef Boyardee food company in the U.S.A. ran an on-pack offer on cans of their pasta products. For 50 cents and ten labels the applicant received a poster and a 45E Kenworth Cabover in white with 'Chef' labels on the doors and roof. Production trials were undertaken to tampo print the

model, but proved to be of an unacceptable quality. Chef Boyardee produced further offers in 1987 and 1988. In 1987 they offered the SF13 1983 Corvette in its usual colour scheme but with a label applied over the number seven on the bonnet, which was without its usual orange tampo print. To obtain the model ten proofs of purchase and 25 cents were required. In 1988 the 47G School Bus was adopted in its standard yellow livery, also with a 'Chef' label on the bonnet. This cost $1 with five proofs of purchase.

To celebrate one hundred years of the motor car, Matchbox in the U.K. produced two re-coloured Porsches. The whole Miniature and Convoy range were available in special gold boxes with a coupon on the rear. By sending in the correct amount of header cards from either Miniatures, Convoy or Superking boxes a free model could be claimed. The two models used were the 3E Porsche Turbo in 'Wrangler' livery and the 41G Racing Porsche in 'Buttons' livery. Over 100,000 of these Porsches were distributed.

Australia had another Collectors' Club promotion. This time the 46F Group C Racer was used in white for the special club model. For AUS $11 the applicant received the model plus a T Shirt, cap, newsletter, cloth badge, membership card, certificate and a Matchbox catalogue.

1986

New models:

CORE
7H Porsche 959
24H Nissan 300ZX
27G Jeep Cherokee
49F Peugeot Quasar
68F Camaro IROC-Z28

72G Ford Supervan II
75F Ferrari Testarossa
64E Caterpillar D9 Tractor
(re-introduction)

R.O.W.
48G Vauxhall Astra GTE
60F Ford Transit
62G Volvo 760
Recolours:

CORE
5H, 10F, 11G, 20G, 25H, 38G, 39F, 41G, 45E, 46F, 52F, 53F, 55H, 56H, 63F, 73E.

R.O.W.
8I, 17F, 22G, 26G, 44F, 47F.

U.S.A.
31G, 41F, 42F, 43F, 67E, 71F, 74F.

Development of the 7G Porsche 959 took place at the same time as the Superking model and the same master pattern was used.

The 46F Peugeot Quasar was a vehicle produced for display at motor shows and only one real vehicle was ever made. In fact close examination of the car shows that it did not have steering and could not be driven! The 68F Camaro IROC-Z was released in green for the R.O.W. market and blue for the U.S.A. The blue version later became a worldwide release with a new tampo print design, before being changed to yellow in 1988. The 72G Ford Supervan II was also based on a real prototype vehicle. It was built by Ford to revive the interest in its Ford Transit range that was soon to undergo changes. The Supervan was capable of speeds of up to 200 MPH, and the rear wing was added to provide more stability at high speed. Early body castings had two small holes cast in the lower front spoiler representing air intakes, but as the mould wore these were

filled in. The blue tampo print on the first issue white body, varied from light to dark blue.

The 48G Vauxhall Astra GTE had not been out long before its base lettering was modified to include the words 'Opel Kadett GSi'. The 60F Ford Transit was designed with the co-operation of Ford in the U.K. who provided photographs and information well before the vehicle was in production. In fact, the first production run by Matchbox of 8,600 models was made for Ford. These were in red, without tampo print and had right-hand drive interiors. A second run of 23,000 models with left-hand drive interiors was made for Ford to use in the rest of Europe. All of these models were packed in a special window box that Ford had designed. The first release of the Transit to the toy trade were also in the Ford box but the model had 'Motorsport' tampo printed on the sides, a design was provided by Ford. In 1988 Ford again ordered the Transit Van, but this time produced for Ford of Holland. The Ford style of box was used again and the van appeared in lime green without any tampo print. The transit has been produced in a variety of liveries, some of which are of interest. In 1987 the 'Unichem' company ordered a promotional model based on their own Transit vans. These deliver medical goods to chemists. The model was packaged in a special blister card and had a right-hand drive interior. These were available from chemists.

In 1988 the Transit was re-coloured from an Ambulance livery into the 'XP Express Parcel Systems' livery. The XP company were so pleased with the model that they ordered a promotional run of the van. It featured the right hand drive interior and also an attractive window box in the XP colour scheme of white, green and yellow.

The 67F Ikarus Coach was chosen for its possible sales appeal in Eastern Block markets. As the seats were cast as part of the lower body, it was quite a heavy model. Apart from the two standard issue liveries, three promotion models have been produced 'Ikarus' in cream, 'Gibraltar' in red and white and also 'I Love Canary Island' in white.

The 64E Caterpillar D9 Tractor was re-issued into the R.O.W. range as number 9, after an absence of two years although it had been available in the U.S.A. range.

Supertrucks was a new range of eight vehicles that had huge wheels and tyres, also called Superchargers in the U.S.A. Many of the designs were of real monster trucks from the U.S.A. They were based on existing miniatures, using the same body castings but with new chrome plated bases. Early models had 'Made in Macau' cast on the base, which was later tampo printed. The models were (MB numbers in brackets):

1986
SC1 Bigfoot (57G)
SC2 U.S.A.-1 (57G)
SC3 Taurus (57G)
SC4 Rollin' Thunder (68E)
SC5 Flyin' High (63F)
SC6 Awesome Kong II (53F)
SC7 Mad Dog II (50F)
SC8 Hawk (5H)

1987
SC3 So High (38G)
SC8 Toad (61E)

1988
SC15 Doc Crush (73E)
SC16 Big Pete (30G)

In the U.S.A. the Super Chargers range was expanded to include Mud Racers. These also had large wheels with a new style of tyre. Models from the range were used with chrome engines fixed to their bonnets. Four

models were released in 1987 with two more in 1988. They were:

1987
SC11 Mud Ruler (69G)
SC1 Bog Buster (58F)
SC1 Hog (34G)
SC1 Mud Monster (4G)

1988
SC17 Mud Slinger (39G)
SC18 1957 Chevy (4G)

The SC1 was used in the U.K. in 1987 for an on-pack offer from Burtons Biscuits Ltd. They used it to promote their Wagon Wheels chocolate biscuits. Almost 90,000 models in the Wagon Wheels colour scheme were given away to consumers who sent thirty pence and five tokens from multi-pack wrappers. Four million of these special wrappers were used during the promotion.

Two new gift sets were issued in Europe, each containing four miniatures and one Sky-Buster. The G10 'Pan Am' set had the 64F Dodge Caravan and 65E Airport Coach re-coloured in a Pan Am livery. Also in the set were standard issues of the 10F Police Car, 54G Foam Pumper and SB10 Boeing 747.

The G11 'Lufthansa' set had the 30H Mercedes Benz 280 GE, 59F Porsche 928 and the 65E Airport Coach all re-coloured in the Lufthansa livery. Standard issues of the 54G Foam Pumper and SB28 A300B Airbus were also included, although neither of these sets were shown in any catalogues.

In the U.S.A. a new range of twenty four models were released called Superfast. They were all existing models but in new colours and new decoration:

SF1 Mercury Police
SF13 1983 Corvette
SF2 Pontiac Firebird
SF14 B.M.W. 323I Cabriolet

The Super GT range of forty models was made to compete against cheap imported toys. Many varations exist of body and tampo print colours.

SF3   Porsche 928
SF15 Escort XR3i Cabriolet
SF4   Dodge Daytona
SF16 Group C Racer
SF5   Mercedes 5000SEC
SF17 Lamborghini Countach

SF6   Racing Porsche
SF18 Pontiac Firebird Racer
SF7   Ford Sierra XR4i
SF19 Pontiac Fiero

SF8   1962 Corvette
SF21 Nissan 300ZX
SF9   Datsun 280ZX
SF22 Camaro IROC Z28

SF10 Chevrolet Corvette
SF23 Toyota MR2
SF11 Ferrari 308 GTB
SF24 Ferrari Testarossa
SF12 Chevy Pro-Stocker
SF25 Peugeot Quasar

Although numbered from 1 to 25, only twenty four were released. Number 20 was to have been the 56H VW Golf GTi but this was not issued in Superfast. The key selling point of the range was the new Superfast wheel. The Research & Development Department at Enfield was given the task of developing a wheel and axle that was better than the competition and also met the necessary safety standards. The range was launched in the U.S.A., blister packed as singles and also in a triple pack. In the triple pack there was one of three special models in black with 'Halley's Comet' tampo printed. The three models used were the SF1, SF2 and SF12. The new wheel had a multi spoke design and a longer internal boss. As the Superfast series used existing models, the base castings had to be modified to accept the longer wheel boss. (Many small variations can be found on the modified bases). This also meant that standard wheels already used in production had to have their bosses lengthened. The factory was faced with the task of fitting the correct wheels on the right base. To help production staff identify standard wheels with the new boss, the hubs were foiled gold instead of silver. Almost every model in production appeared with the gold hubs although some models were not affected, such as those with the heavy treaded wheel.

Gold wheels had been seen before in the range, but for a different reason. In 1983 a range of vehicles were released in the U.S.A. called Mega Blasters. These were diecast cars which were able to fire caps. They all had body castings that were similar to models in the range but slightly larger. The wheels used on Mega Blasters had gold foil on their hubs which were made in

England and shipped to Macau for assembly. These wheels with silver hubs were normally used on the 37F Matra Rancho and the 72E Dodge Commando which were made in England. Both models were also to be found with gold hubs.

A new factory was built in the Minhang development area of Shanghai in China with the company of Shanghai Universal Toys Co. Ltd being set up to run it. Initially production was of miniatures and later Superkings but other diecast toys were also produced. To celebrate the opening of the factory on 18 November 1986, a gift set containing ten miniatures was produced and given away at the opening. The models were all normal issues that had been made in the Macau factory. Many of the models first manufactured in Shanghai were U.S.A. only issues. Some of these were packed in blister packs for sale only in China.

Also produced for China release only were two obsolete models, the 55G Ford Cortina and the 67D Datsun 260Z. These had last been used in England for Streak Sets and Twin Pack. They were both made in colours issued before, but also had tampo print. The Datsun had a blue and green striped design which had not been used previously. The Cortina had a flame design also not seen before.

The Collection Card scheme was launched in 1986 in the U.K. on special blue window boxes. Each box contained a free picture card measuring 66 x 33 mm, of a current miniature. Each card contained information about the real car, and collectors card albums were available to hold them. It was not easy to collect a complete set because the cards were packed at random into the boxes. Free models were also available by sending in completed albums for checking.

A similar scheme was launched in Germany, where they celebrated one hundred years of the motor car. The cards measured 78 x 58 mm and there were twenty four to collect. Each one showed a popular German car such as the Volkswagen Beetle and Audi Quattro.

The Super GT range was introduced by Matchbox in Europe to compete with the ever growing amount of cheap diecast cars available from manufacturers in the Far East. A range of forty models were planned, made up of twenty different models each one in two different colour schemes. They were all re-issues of obsolete models from the seventies. Lesney had taken care to preserve and store obsolete tooling, so it was not too difficult to find enough moulds to produce twenty different models.

In order to produce a low cost miniature, the moulds were modified so that the models no longer had opening features, such as opening doors, bonnets or chrome engines. The windows were also moulded in black and interiors were not fitted. The models were packed on blister cards as singles and also in various multiples, some with plastic launchers.

While the moulds were being modified and new decorations being designed, the range was known as the Budget Range. This name was later changed to Super GT. Model names and numbers were not shown on packaging or on the bases although the bases did have B.R. numbers for factory identification.

When production commenced in England, only 32 of the 40 types were produced. As the range was aimed at the low price market, little attention was paid by the factory to manufacture them to the same colour specifications. Many models were found in the wrong colours

as well as an almost endless variety of tampo print colours.

It was not until late in 1987 when production was transferred to China that the eight previously unreleased models were made and issued. The whole range was now about to be re-coloured for 1988, although these did not appear until September. In the meantime twenty eight different models were produced in the colour schemes prviously made in England. These were to be found packed with Superking models in special offer packs. This made it fairly expensive and also difficult to get a full set. The Super GT range proved to be a great success with large sales in France and Germany. They have been used in a variety of sets including the G2 Gift Set, Gargantua, Motor City Garage packs as well as Streak Sets. Four different models were used in these sets, which all came with glow plastic windows. The full list is: (MB numbers in brackets)

BR1/2	Iso Grifo (14D)
BR 3/4	Gruesome Two some (4E)
BR 5/6	Datsun 126X (33D)
BR 7/8	Siva Spyder (41D)
BR9/10	Lotus Europa (5E)
BR11/12	Saab Sonett (65D)
BR13/14	Hairy Hustler (7D)
BR15/16	Monteverdi Hai (3D)
BR17/18	Fire Chief (64D)
BR19/20	Ford Group 6 (45C)
BR21/22	Alfa Carabo (75C)
BR23/24	Vantastic (34E)
BR25/26	Ford Escort (9F)
BR27/28	Lamborghini Marzal (20D)
BR29/30	Maserati Bora (32D)
BR31/32	Fandango (35D)
BR33/34	Hi-Tailer(56D)
BR35/36	Porsche 910 (68C)
BR37/38	Hot Rocker)
BR39/40	De Tomaso Pantera (8G)

Late in 1987 Super GT models were given away in packets of

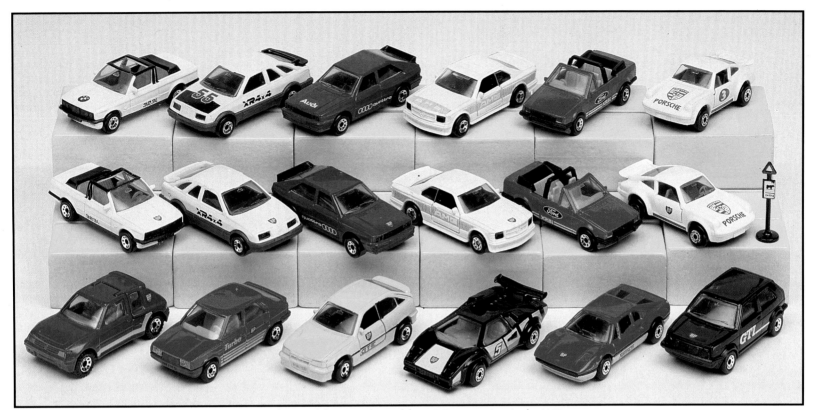

Twelve models were planned for a B.P. promotion in the U.K.
Centre row: Six models went into production before the project was stopped.
Top row: These were then over printed and issued in normal stock.
Bottom row: Six models never made it to production, although factory samples were made.

frozen sausage rolls. Kraft Foods in the U.K. used blister packed models in packets of its 50 Party Size sausage rolls. These were only available through the Bejam chain of frozen food stores.

The Super GT range was not sold by Matchbox Toys in the U.S.A. until 1988. Early that year the MacDonalds chain of hamburger restaurants ran a promotion using the Super GT range. When you purchased a Happy Meal it came in a box containing a Super GT model. Printed on the box were various games as well as a speed ramp.

In January 1986 Matchbox Toys were approached by the British Petroleum company, who were planning a big U.K. promotion for 1987. The offer was for motorists buying petrol from B.P. stations to receive tokens that could be traded for Matchbox models. Twelve models were to be used from the range in new colours. The project reached an advanced stage before B.P. pulled out. B.P.

had recently closed a large oil refinery based in Wales and they felt that they should give the order to a British company. At this stage, production samples of all twelve models had been produced for final customer approval.

With the huge number of models being required at such short notice the production department were placed in a difficult position. To ensure that delivery could be met, production had to start manufacturing toys before an official order had been placed. When the promotion was cancelled, six of the twelve models had already entered into production. They were:

3E   Porsche Turbo
39F BMW 323i Cabriolet

25H Audi Quattro
43G Mercedes 500SEC
37H Ford Escort XR3i
55H Ford Sierra XR4i

The six models not released were:

11G Lamborghini Countach
48G Vauxhall Astra GTE
15F Peugeot 205 Turbo 16
56H VW Golf GTi
33F Renault 11
70E Ferrari 308GTB

Rather than scrap the models it was decided to release them with additional tampo printing. This was applied over the top of the already applied B.P. logos. On some models it is possible to see the faint outline of the B.P. logo underneath this extra tampo print. Five of the models were to be found on sale in the U.S.A.,

blister packed in assorted sets of three. The sixth model, the B.M.W. Cabriolet was available in Europe in normal blue window boxes.

1987

New models:
CORE

1I	Jaguar XJ6
10G	Buick Le Sabre
34H	Ford RS200
51G	Ford LTD Police
58G	Mercedes Benz 300E
65G	Cadillac Allante

R.O.W.

4H	FX4R Taxi
8J	Astra Police Car
16G	Land Rover Ninety
44I	Skoda 130LR
45F	Ford Skip Truck
55G	Rolls Royce Silver Spirit

U.S.A.

| 17H | Dodge Dakota |

21H GMC Wrecker
39G Ford Bronco II

Recolours:
CORE
2H, 3E, 12H, 13G, 18G, 20F, 24H, 36H, 43G, 57H, 64F, 68F and 71G.

R.O.W.
48G, 60F

U.S.A.
6F, 37G and 40F.

The new Jaguar XJ6 was to have been released in 1984. Matchbox had developed the model with the assistance of Jaguar Cars Ltd., who had provided drawings and photographs of their prototype the XJ40. The launch of the real vehicle was delayed and Matchbox had to put the finished moulds into storage for almost three years. Woolworth stores in the U.K. featured the model free when consumers sent in three header cards from Miniatures boxes. In 1988 the Jaguar was used by the Whyte and Macckay Scotch Whisky Distillers to promote their whisky in England. The model had a black body with gold tampo print on the bonnet. Almost 10,000 models were mailed to people in the retail trade to promote a competition to win a real Jaguar. The retailer could also win a holiday in Florida.

The 34H Ford RS200 was based on the real vehicle of which only 200 were made to qualify for the Group B section of the World Rally Series. Due to a number of accidents involving different Group B cars, the Group B section was halted. Ford then decided to develop the RS200 further, so that it could be sold as a road going supercar. The first issues of the 58G Mercedes Benz 300E model appeared wthout the Mercedes badge on top of the radiator grille.

The famous black cab had been on London streets for almost

twenty eight years before Matchbox made it in miniature - the 4H FX4R Taxi. *Hickmore:* "So that the model could have opening doors it involved moving the rear wheels and wheel arch back by 3 mm. Not that many people would notice the difference because the model still looks perfect. It was not until we saw production samples, that we realised the exhaust system cast on the base had been put on the wrong side." In 1988 a special model was issued in Australia to commemorate the 'Great Taxi Ride, London to Sydney'. The normal black body was used with white tampo printing on the front doors.

The 8J Astra Police car used the same base and interior as the 48G Astra GTE, but a new body casting was made without opening doors. A new window was made to include the two roof lights. A Bentley Mulsane Turbo had been designed as a new model but the 66G Rolls Royce Silver Spirit was made instead. In fact, the change in design only affected the radiator grille. Soon after the initial release of the 21H G.M.C. Wrecker, a promotional model was produced for 'Accessory Wholesaler Inc' in the U.S.A.

The Superfast Lasers series was developed from the U.S.A. Superfast series. The main feature of the Lasers were the holographic foil applied to the wheels, which had smooth outer wheel hubs. Many of the models also had metallic paint and used the same tampo print design as the Superfast issues. They also shared similar model numbers. The Laser range was available in the U.S.A. as well as the Superfast range. In 1988 there were three re-colours, numbers 8, 9 and 23 plus six new models:

LW25   Buick Le Sabre
LW26   Cadillac Allante
LW27   Saab 9000 Turbo
LW28   Rover Sterling
LW29   T-Bird Turbo Coupe
LW30   Volvo 480ES

The Buick Le Sabre used in Laser Wheels had a modified body from the normal Matchbox issue. It featured a zinc air scoop that was riveted to the bonnet of the standard body casting.

Two gift sets issued in Europe followed the theme used in the previous G10 and G11 sets. The G5 Federal Express set contained an SB1 Lear Jet with the 20F Volvo Container Truck, 26G Volvo Tilt, 56H Golf GTi and the 60F Ford Transit all in the Federal Express livery.

The G6 Virgin Airways set contained the SB10 Boeing 747 with the 55H Ford Sierra, 64F Dodge Caravan, 65E Airport Coach and the 75E Helicopter all in the Virgin Airways livery.

Road Blasters were first released in the U.S.A. in 1987 and then in Europe in 1988. They were released in Europe in slightly different blister packs. They consisted of existing models from the range with new body colours and tampo print. Most models also had new windows or interiors. Included in the blister packs were plastic clip-on guns and armoured panels. Sixteen different models were available in two teams, the Turbo Force and the Motor Lords. (The names were printed on the blister packs but did not appear on the models).

TURBO FORCE

Streaker 28H Dodge Daytona
Road Razor 29E Tractor Shovel
Road Raider 48F Unimog
Car Pow 58F Ruff Trek
Barrel Bomber 66F Tyrone Malone
Thunder Gunner 69G1984 Corvette
Street Eater 72G Ford Supervan
Speed King 75F Ferrari Testarossa

MOTOR LORDS

Parasite 5H 4x4 Jeep
Killer Zee 24G Nissan 300ZX
Rampager 46F Group C Racer
Motor Master 49F Peugeot Quasar
Back Stabber 50F Chevy Blazer
Stick-Up Pick-Up 53F Flareside Pick-Up
Turbo Special 59D Mercury Police
Tow Nailer 61E Peterbilt Wrecker

The J.C. Bamford company in the U.K. had a gift set produced by Matchbox. It contained a Sky-Buster and three miniatures in a special box. They were all in a 'J.C.B.' livery: SB1 Lear Jet, 32F Atlas Excavator, 60F Ford Transit and 75E Helicopter. Although it was not available in retail shops, it was generally available to collectors.

With the acquisition of the Dinky brand name, Matchbox were eager to quickly produce products with the new name. To have waited for a year or two for a new range to be tooled could have enabled a competitor to register the name. Matchbox did not want people to think that they had bought the name merely to sit on it. The quickest way to market the Dinky name was to use existing tooling. Six miniatures were chosen, four of which were no longer in the range. They were all blister packed on cards featuring the Dinky Toys logo and each model was in a new colour scheme. No model names or numbers were on the packaging and the bases still had the Matchbox logo. (See Chapter Eleven).

The British Petroleum Oil Company in Holland issued a range of five models sold in their petrol stations. They were individually blister packed and all were in new colour schemes, featuring the B.P. logo.They were:

3E Porsche Turbo
11G Lamborghini Countach
24H Nissan 300ZX
43G Mercedes 5000SEC
64F Dodge Caravan

The blister packs were in a yellow and green colour scheme that were almost ruined when opened and so were not that popular with collectors. In 1988 B.P. had produced another five models, this time a window box was used in a similar yellow and green colour scheme. This box was preferred by collectors who could open it without damaging it. The models were:

27G Jeep Cherokee
39F BMW 323i Cabriolet
48G Vauxhall Astra GTE
68F Camaro IROC-Z28
72G Ford Supervan II

Two gift sets were produced for Japan containing models in Japanese liveries. The C6 set contained four miniatures in a rescue theme. The 13G Snorkel and 18G Fire Engines in a 'Tokyo Fire Service Bureau' livery and the 44H Datsun 280Z and 75E Helicopter in a 'Police Bureau' livery. The larger G11 set was in an airport theme with a vinyl play mat, two miniatures and two Skybusters. The 54G Foam Pumper was in an 'Aviation Bureau' livery and the 67F Ikarus Coach in an 'Airport Limousine' livery.

1988

New models:
CORE
2I Rover Sterling
12I Modified Racer
14G Grand Prix Racing Car
22B Saab 9000 Turbo
59G Porsche 944 Turbo
61F T-Bird Turbo Coupe

R.O.W.
20H VW Transporter
69H Volvo 480ES

U.S.A.
55I Mercury Sable Wagon

Recolours:
CORE
7H, 11G, 28H, 49F, 52F, 68F, 72G.

R.O.W.
6F, 27G, 30H, 37H, 56G, 60F, 62G, 67F.

U.S.A.
27G, 69G.

First issues of the 12I Modified Racer had a smooth plastic base that was changed to a textured finish. The 14G Grand Prix Racing Car was to have been based on the Williams Honda Formula One car that won the 1987 championship. To copy the authentic livery would have proved too expensive an exercise. As well as this a royalty would have to have been paid to Williams, and the retail price of the model would have been double the normal price. The finished model was still good, and featured a new plastic racing wheel with 'Goodyear' printed on the side of the tyre. Both the 2I Rover Sterling and the 61F T-Bird Turbo Coupe featured push in separate rear light strips.

In Europe a large number of new sets were introduced in Team Convoy and Motorcity. Theme packs contained three Miniatures, some in new colours only found in these sets:

MP-101 Emergency Set MB-8J, 21G, 60F
MP-102 Construction Set MB-19G, 45F, 64E
MP-103 Airport Fire Set MB-18G, 54G, 75E
MP-104 4x4 Set MB-5H, 20G, 37G
MP-105 Dragster Set MB-26D, 48D, 69F

MP-106 Porsche Set MB-3E, 7H, 41G

Team Convoy sets contained a Convoy vehicle and a miniature with a common theme, some in colours not available in any other sets:

TC-1 Fire Set CY-13 and MB-54C
TC-2 Tanker Set CY-17 and MB-56G
TC-3 Construction Set CY-20 and MB-29F
TC-4 Cargo Set CY-25 and MB-20F
TC-5 NASA Set CY-2 and MB-54G
TC-6 Rescue Set CY-22 and MB-75E

Five new gift sets were issued under the name of Motorcity. Two of the sets were large with a Convoy model and seven miniatures in each. The MC-7 Farm Set was mostly made up of models from the Two Pack series:

CY-20 Kenworth Tipper, green and yellow, 'Eurobran'
TP-103 Cattle Truck and Trailer, green and yellow
TP-103 Tractor and Hay Trailer, green and yellow
MB-16G Land Rover, green
MB-43C Pony Trailer, white
MB-51E Combine Harvester, yellow

The MC-8 Construction Set contained the Peterbilt cab and Low Loader Trailer used in the CY-203 set with seven miniatures. Although the models were all in standard issue colours, three were slightly different:

19F Peterbilt Cement Truck, with silver barrel
42G Mobile Crane, without tampo print
64E Caterpillar D9 Tractor, with silver shovel

The other four models were the 29E, 30G, 32F and 45F.

The three other sets were made up of two miniatures with a Convoy model. MC-11 had standard issue models, the MC-12 were all re-colours. The MC-13 was a re-release of the previous CY-202.

MC-11 Car Transporter Set.
CY-1 Kenworth Car Transporter
MB37H Escort XR3i Cabriolet
MB39F BMW 323i Cabriolet

MC-12 Aerobatic Team Set
CY-21 Daf Aircraft Transporter
MB57H Mission Helicopter
MB75E Helicopter

Two Superking sets provided re-coloured miniatures. The K159 Racing Car Transporter in a 'Porsche' livery, contained two 7H Porsche 959 models in a white livery not issued elsewhere. The K160 Racing Car Transporter in a 'Matchbox' livery had two 6F F1 Racing Cars in blue and white, only found in this set.

In the U.K. there was a Royal Mail triple pack produced by Matchbox for Promod. It contained three models in 'Royal Mail' liveries, the 38G, 46F and 60F on a blister pack.

Matchbox in Hong Kong issued a set of twelve models to celebrate the Year of the Dragon. Each model was decorated to represent one of the animals from the twelve astrological signs. Each came in an attractive red box with the heading 'Dragon Racing Team – The Worlds Greatest Racing Team'. The twelve models were all existing miniatures:

2H Pontiac Fiero Dog
3E Porsche Turbo Dragon
11G Lamborghini Tiger
12H Firebird Racer Horse
16F Pontiac Rooster
24H Nissan 300ZX Monkey

28H Dodge Daytona Goat
41G Racing Porsche Ox
43G Mercedes 500 SEC Pig
70E Ferrari 308 GTB Rat
75F Ferrari Testarossa Rabbit

Four re-coloured models were produced for a drug company in Hong Kong to promote their Redoxon Vitamin C Tablets. They were each in a special white

window box. The four models were: 1I Jaguar XJ6 in green, 7H Porsche 959 in white, 43G Mercedes 500 SEC in black and the 75F Ferrari Testarossa in red. All the models had the 'Redoxon'

logo tampo printed on them as well as Chinese writing.

Two ranges of models were released that had not been shown at trade fairs or in catalogues. First there was a worldwide release of

Super Colour Changers. These were miniatures sprayed with special paints that changed colour. Depending on the temperature of the model the body casting would change to one of three colours. This could be achieved by dipping the model in water. Because of this, plastic suspension strips were used instead of spring steel. A range of twelve models were planned, but a total of thirteen were made. As the 1987 Corvette was having a new body mould made, the Pontiac Firebird Racer was substituted for a short time.

4G   1957 Chevy
6F   F-1 Racer
7H   Porsche 959
10G Buick Le Sabre
12H Firebird Racer
12I Modified Racer
27G Jeep Cherokee
39G Ford Bronco II
51F Pontiac Firebird
51G Ford LTD Police
61F T-Bird Turbo Coupe
69G 1987 Corvette
75F Ferrari testarossa

Tesco stores in the U.K. had a range of gift sets containing two miniatures and a Sky-Buster in a common theme. They were all blister packed and numbered SB150. Many of the models were in existing liveries while some were re-colours.

A. NASA set had an SB3 Space Shuttle with the 40G Rocket Transporter and 54G Command Vehicle in their NASA liveries.

B. Virgin Airways Set contained three models previously found in the G6 set, the SB10 Boeing 747, 55H Ford Sierra and the 65E Airport Coach.

C. Federal Express Set contained three models first issued in the G5 set, the SB1 Lear Jet, 26G Volvo Tilt Truck and the 60F Ford Transit.

D. Fire Rescue Set had n SB26 Cessna with two re-coloured models, the 30H Mercedes Benz 280GE and 75E Helicopter both in a rescue livery.

E. Royal Navy Set had the SB27 Harrier in a different blue colour with two re-coloured models the 16F Land Rover Ninety and 57H Mission Helicopter both in a navy rescue livery.

F. XP Express Parcels Set has the previously released SB19 Piper Commanche MB60F Ford Transit with a recoloured 20F Volvo Container Truck.

The MC250 Motor City Play Track issued in Europe contained plastic railway track and buildings as well as re-issues of some of the Matchbox miniature trains. Four models were used in their original colour schemes, all now manufactured in Macau, some for the first. They were the 24E Diesel Shunter and 24EX Side Tipper in yellow with the 43E 0-4-0 Steam Loco and 44E Passenger Coach in red. Woolworth stores in the U.K. had one extra model in the sets, the 0-4-0 Steam Loco in green.

RARE SUPERFAST LIST

Collectors often discuss the rare models they have found or that they are looking for to complete their collections. What makes a model rare? Many things can make a model a rarity such as body colours, labels or a limited release in a foreign country. There are many, minor casting variations that are hard to find because only limited quantities were made and these could easily be listed as rarities. Due to the specialised nature of these variations they are ignored by the majority of collectors.

This list outlines possibly the fifty rarest Superfast models, which are divided into the top ten and the remaining forty. They are not in order of rarity but in number order. It should be remembered that regional differences occur in the availability of these models. Not listed here are models manufactured in Brazil as these are all fairly rare with around fifty variations known to exist.

No.	MODEL	VARIATION
12C	Land Rover Safari	Blue body
22C	Pontiac G.P. Coupe	Red body
24D	Team Matchbox	Yellow body
30C	8 Wheel Crane	Red and green
31C	Lincoln Continental	Sea-green body
38D	Stingeroo	Chrome Forks
38G	Model 'A' Ford Van	Ben Franklin
41C	Ford G.T.	Yellow body
49C	Chop Suey	Chrome Forks
53C	Ford Zodiac Mk IV	Metallic light blue
5F	Seafire Boat	Red deck, blue hull
8E	Ford Mustang	White body
8H	Rover	Yellow body
10E	Piston Popper	White body
17F	Londoner Bus	Borregaard Paper
		I.C.P. Interchemicals & Plastics
		Sellotape Selbstklebebander
		Sellotape International Operations
		C Amcel takes you places
		Sellotape Packaging Systems
		Sellotape Electrical Tapes
		Chrome or gold body
17G	Titan Bus	M.I.C.A. Convention 1986
17G	Titan Bus	Matchbox Valencia
18E	Field Car	White body
22E	Blaze Buster	White ladder
24D	Team Matchbox	Blue body
28H	Dodge Daytona	Las Vegas base
29D	Racing Mini	Metallic red with door detail
29E	Tractor Shovel	Lime green body
32C	Petrol Tanker	Red or purple body, N.A.M.C. labels
37D	Soopa Coopa	Orange body, Jaffa label
37E	Skip Truck	Red body, blue skip
37E	Skip Truck	Orange body, orange skip
38E	Jeep	Red body
38EX	Glider Trailer	Red body
38G	Model 'A' Ford Van	M.I.C.A. Convention 1987
42C	Iron Fairy Crane	Red and yellow body
42D	Tyre Fryer	Orange body, Jaffa label
45D	B.M.W. 3.0 C.S.L.	Red body
45C	Ford Group 6	Non metallic green body
48E	Sambron Jacklift	Sambron tampo printed on the side
49D	Crane Truck	Red body
64C	Slingshot	Orange body
64F	Dodge Caravan	Las Vegas base
65D	Saab Sonett III	White body
71C	Ford Wreck Truck	Blue body
74C	Toe Joe	Red body
74E	Fiat Abarth	Black interior
75B	Ferrari Berlinetta	Metallic green body

7 The Major Packs Range

LARGER ROAD-GOING VEHICLES 1957 TO 1967

Jack Odell was fascinated by the types of specialised machinery much in evidence after the war employed in the nation's agricultural, industrial and road expansion programme. Such machinery had been overlooked by other toy manufacturers, perhaps with the exception of Meccano. Furthermore, one or two models were natural subjects for Lesney to make, but could not be reproduced for reasons of scale in the "Matchbox" Series. For instance the Diamond T Prime Mover had had to be split into two models and sold separately from its trailer (MB15a and MB16a). Thus it seemed logical to produce a range one step up in size from the already successful 1-75s whilst still retaining the spirit of that range.

The first Major Pack was issued in 1957 and was the M1-1 Caterpillar DW20 Earth Scraper. It was quite evident that Lesney had had technical drawings from the Caterpillar Tractor Company as, not only did the model feature the abbreviation 'CAT' and the reference DW20, but also the box had printed on the inside flap 'Made by Lesney Products & Co Ltd and sold under permission from Caterpillar Tractor Company'. Shades of yellow are known ranging from bright yellow to a paler yellow, the paler being associated with the first released models. *Odell:* "About this time we had to change to completely lead-free paint — a good yellow was almost impossible."

The castings contain slight variations. The most obvious difference between early and later tractor castings applied to the steering wheel assembly. Due to progressive wear in the tool, the column began to break in the fettling process and it is common to find this component missing but with the resultant flaw sprayed over. The baseplate featured the inscription 'MADE IN ENGLAND NO 1 BY LESNEY'. Rear scraper castings displayed an opening underneath the jib that operated the scraper mechanism, but this tended to flash over on later examples. All models had the words 'LESNEY ENGLAND' on the upper surface of the scraper bucket. The model was advertised together with M2.1 in *Games & Toys* magazine in September 1958.

This model saw the arrival of a new more realistic type of tyre which was detachable from a simple cast hub. The new type was still accompanied by crimped axles on early models, but by 1958 these had changed to riveted ends. This move, incidentally, was more as a precaution against possible damage to playful fingers than for realism! These new tyres also had the word 'Lesney' moulded into each side, and can be found fitted either way round. When the model was launched, the marketing and distribution was undertaken by the Moko organisation – J. Kohnstam & Co. Ltd. The Moko involvement was clearly reflected on the earliest boxes. There are four known box types, all of which showed a line drawing of the model. The fourth box type described the model as 'A LESNEY'.

Unusually for Lesney, the M1-2 B.P. Autotanker model was copied from a prototype vehicle of which only one example was ever built. The real vehicle was built by Thompson Bros. on a 'Leyland Dromedary' chassis in 1958, and the Major Pack version was introduced to the range in April 1962. The model made an attractive addition to the now successful Major Pack series. If the vehicle was not instantly recognisable, certainly the B.P. logo and the B.P. corporate colours were, and it fitted in well with the MG1.2 B.P. Service Station, and the A1.2 B.P. Garage Pumps & Forecourt Signs. (See Chapter Eleven).

The model was painted in a combination of two colours – lemon yellow and mid-green. Early models had a much brighter yellow than later issues, and although all models had their headlights picked out in silver, only the earlier models had the rear bumpers in silver. All of the models had white transfers affixed to either side of the tank featuring the B.P. logo. There were two further transfers, one on the radiator area and the other on the rear of the tank. The cab window was made of a transparent green tinted plastic.

The model was a one piece body casting with a separate baseplate underneath. The baseplate, fixed to the body by a front tongue and a rear rivet, featured the words 'B.P. AUTO TANKER MAJOR PACK No 1 MADE IN ENGLAND BY LESNEY'. There was only one

An advertisement from the Railway Modeller *1962.*

small casting variation to be found on later models — a small casting hole can be found underneath the front transfer directly above the front baseplate tongue. On earlier models the non-slip walkway was well detailed and clearly visible, but as the dies wore during the model's production life this detail tended to become less apparent. This may also have been caused by the thickness of the paint applied during different production runs. All the axles were of the riveted type. There are, however, two different types of black plastic wheel — coarse tread or a very fine tread. In general later models

were fitted with the finer tread.

By 1962 the arrangements with J. Kohnstam & Co. Ltd were over and so the boxes were simply marked 'A LESNEY'. There are four known box types, the first one showing a line drawing of the model on the box, and the others being picture type boxes. The model was phased out in 1966 and was not considered by Lesney as being a suitable candidate for the King Size Range. The B.P. Auto Tanker was also released in a number of gift packs such as the G-4 Grand Prix Set of 1963 and 1964, and the G-9 Major Pack Gift Set of 1962 and 1963.

The M2 — 1 Bedford Articu-

lated 'Wall's Ice Cream' Truck, which was issued in late 1957 or early 1958, came in two parts.

The Bedford Cab featured an open split windscreen and open side windows. The container was a one piece casting with simulated cast-in doors at the rear and compartments at the sides. The black baseplate had a flange at the rear under the doors and at the front of the container directly above the swivel attachment for the Bedford cab. The baseplate inscription read 'BEDFORD ARTICULATED No 2 MATCH-BOX SERIES MAJOR PACKS MADE IN ENGLAND BY LESNEY'. There was no lettering on the underneath of the hollow cab.

The cab featured a pair of axles and four wheels. The container had one axle and a pair of wheels at the rear. Early models were produced with unpainted metal wheels on crimped axles. This later changed to grey plastic wheels and either a crimped or a riveted axle. There are slight colour variations in the shades of grey. The basic colour scheme of a mid-blue cab and cream container continued throughout its four years of production. In 1957 there was a significant colour change from cream to off-white. All the cabs had detailing in silver applied to the headlights and radiator grille. Very early models had cab bumpers also picked out in silver, but this 'glitter' was reduced as part of Lesney's continuing cost saving exercises and the introduction of mask-spraying. Every container was given a decal displaying the name of the 'Wall's Ice Cream Company', a well-known British company. Both sides of the container featured these decals in red and blue; the decals can be found placed either way round. However, the most common version had the line pointing to the rear on both sides.

On the underneath of the rear

change of body colours to 'Lep INTERNATIONAL TRANSPORT' but the decal on the front of the trailer remained unchanged.

The tractor had two axles and six wheels. The trailer had one axle and four wheels at the rear. Early models were produced with grey knobby plastic wheels and riveted axles. A short run was also produced with fine grey treads; these were later replaced by black plastic wheels, which in time appeared with a finer tread pattern.

There are three known box types. The first was a line drawing of the Davies Tyre Truck and described the model as 'A LESNEY'. The second and third were picture type boxes; the second showed the Davies Tyre Truck and the third the Lep International Transport Truck. The model was discontinued in 1966.

There are three basic parts to the large M3-1 Tank Transporter and Centurion Tank Mark III which was first issued in July 1959: the Thornycroft Antar, the Sankey 50 ton Transporter and the Centurion Mark III Tank. The tractor measured just over 6.5 cms (2.31"). There was much detail including a split front windscreen cab window and headlights. Realism also included an impressive front grille that featured the word 'ANTAR'. The baseplate was secured by two rivets, one at the front and one towards the rear. The baseplate inscription read "THORNEYCROFT (a Lesney error) 'ANTAR' MADE IN ENGLAND BY LESNEY". The Sankey trailer measured 11.3 cms (4.44") and was a one piece casting. It was permanently fixed to the tractor by means of a cast in pillar and rivet, which enabled the trailer to turn. The trailer baseplate inscription read 'MAJOR PACK No 3 SANKEY 50 TON TANK TRANSPORTER'. The Centurion Tank with its revolving turret and barrel measured 6.4 cms (2.5"). The baseplate was secured by two rivets and the baseplate

part of the cab, just above the rear axle area, all early models had a thin casting step which was filled in on later models to provide a much thicker casting.

J. Kohnstam & Co. Ltd., was given the sole rights to the domestic market, or 'Home Trade' as it was described in the advertisements placed in the trade press; so the trademark 'Moko' was featured on the box panel. There are three known box types, and all three illustrate line drawings of the model.

The M2-2 Bedford Tractor and York Trailer was first issued in September 1961 and, like the M2-1 Bedford, came in two parts. The Bedford tractor cab featured a closed-in transparent plastic windscreen which included the side windows. The rear of the tractor featured a swivel attachment to house the trailer.

The legend 'BEDFORD' was on the front of the cab. The black half baseplate was attached to the front of the cab by a small flange and directly behind the cab by means of a rivet. The baseplate in-scription read 'MAJOR PACK No 2 BEDFORD TRACTOR MADE IN ENGLAND BY LESNEY'. The trailer featured two opening rear doors and the sides featured thirteen horizontal ridge lines. There were a further seven ridges on the baseplate which was kept in place by a rear flange and a forward rivet. The trailer baseplate legend read 'MAJOR PACK No 2 MADE IN ENGLAND BY LESNEY YORK FREIGHTMASTER TRAILER'.

For the majority of its five years production, the cab was painted in bright orange, which matched

the underneath and the rear doors of the trailer. The trailer was sprayed matt silver. Early tractor cabs had the usual highlighting in silver, i.e. the headlights, grille and front bumper, but as usual the degree of trim was minimised in line with cost-saving exercises. Towards the end of this model's production life it received a new livery. The cab changed to silver and the trailer was released in a dark red colour with either matching rear doors, or with the doors in black. There were two different decals associated with these two colour changes. The earlier model in orange and silver featured two paired decals on the sides of the trailer — 'DAVIES TYRES — the best by miles'. A further decal was positioned at the front of the trailer – 'YORK FREIGHT-MASTER'. The former decals were altered with the inscription read 'CENTURION TANK MARK III MADE IN ENGLAND BY LESNEY'. The M3-1 formed part of the No. 5 Presentation Set, advertised in *Games & Toys* for September 1959 at 12s.11d. (64.5p) as part of the Lesney Christmas 1959 advertising campaign.

For obvious reasons there is only one colour – Army olive green. Early models had the front bumper and headlights highlighted in silver, but this detailing was later discontinued. Although the baseplate of the Antar was the same olive green, the baseplate of the tank was always black. The Antar featured three axles and six

wheels. Early models had smaller black plastic wheels with knobby treads fixed initially by being crimped and later riveted. These early wheels were later replaced by larger ones which were much finer in tread. The Sankey Transporter featured two axles at the rear but with four wheels much smaller than those found on the Antar. Again, early axles were crimped and with time the treads became finer and more detailed. The Centurion Tank featured eight rollers to assist the grey rubber tracks. *Odell:* "The tank was made first of all to put into the "Matchbox"

Series, but the rubber treads were so expensive, it was decided that the only way we could sell it was as a trailer load in the Major Packs." Early models were fitted with unpainted metal rollers. These later changed to grey plastic and finally to black plastic.

There are six known box types. The first three showed line drawings of the transporter and tank, the first two describing the model as 'A MOKO LESNEY' and the third describing it as 'A LESNEY'. The other three boxes were all different colour picture type boxes.

Smith: "This was a good seller, but at all times it must be remembered that the Toy Trade is a Fashion Trade . . . too many of the same product and it loses its appeal. I can remember, shortly after moving into our new factory at Eastway, you had to walk past vast stocks of the MP-3. Military was no longer in fashion and it was like trying to sell Easter eggs after Easter. The Gift Set was only one idea . . . I flew to America and saw Fred Bronner. I did a deal and the bulk were shipped to the U.S.A. . . . they were still military minded. Our success was always based upon the international trade which I had developed."

M3-1 Tank Transporter and M4-1 Ruston Bucyrus 22-RB.

M4-2 Fruehauf Hopper Train, M6-2 Racing Car Transporter and M8-2 Guy Warrior Car Transporter.

The M4-1 Ruston Bucyrus Power Shovel (or 22-RB Excavator) was probably suggested to Lesney by Richard Kohnstam as being an ideal addition to the range. Under the Moko trademark, Kohnstam had distributed two Ruston Bucyrus Power Shovels in large and small scales. Either of these models may have been developed further by Benbros who produced a Ruston Bucyrus Power Shovel in the late 1950s and early 1960s. *Odell:* "We made a few classics that really made the money . . . the little Ruston Bucyrus ran for about five years and we sold a million!" It was first issued in April 1959 and was described in an advertisement in the *Eagle* comic of 11 April 1959 as 'one of this month's TERRIFIC TRIO!'

The model comprised four main castings: a caterpillar base, a flat turntable platform and main jib, a cab body and a secondary jib including the bucket. The model was able to rotate and the bucket could elevate, but that was the extent of its working features and the model had fewer movable parts than the Benbros version. The baseplate featured the words 'RUSTON — BUCYRUS MADE IN ENGLAND BY LESNEY'. Underneath the jib were the words 'MAJOR PACK No 4'. The platform base was secured to the cab floor by means of a large rivet that enabled the cab and jib to fully rotate.

There was only one casting variation, where the rear of the cab was connected to the platform base by either a spread rivet secured by way of a rectangular slit or by a normal round rivet similar to the rivet found underneath the turntable base. All models were fitted with four unpainted metal rollers on two axles.

A short run had grey tracks taken from the M3 Personnel

Carrier (49a). The vast majority of models featured green rubber tracks. The cab was always finished in maroon, whilst the platform and jibs were in bright yellow. The tracked platform was painted black as were the simulated rollers between the axles. The decals were placed on the sides and rear of the cab. Early models featured '= 22 — RB =' in red underneath a black and white Ruston-Bucyrus transfer, but this was quickly changed as it was not easily legible. The transfer was then changed to an orangey-yellow colour. At the same time a further decal was added to the rear of the cab, 'TAYLOR WOODROW' in white and four silhouettes of men which signified the Taylor Woodrow motto 'All pull together'. There were two different sizes of these men — the larger type being associated with later models.

There are five known types of box. The first two boxes featured a line drawing of the model which was described as 'A MOKO LESNEY', and the third box also featured a line drawing and described the model as 'A LESNEY'. The last two boxes were colour picture types.

The large M4-2 GMC Tractor and Fruehauf Hopper Train, which was first issued in March 1965, consisted of a red cab with silver painted headlamps and front bumper, and green tinted plastic windows. This model was made to a much larger scale than anything which preceded it and signified the beginning of the end of the Major Pack series. Attached to the rear of the cab were two hopper trailers painted in silver. The first trailer was permanently coupled to the rear of the cab by a silver plated rivet. All later models had the same rivet but the colour was changed to a matt silver-grey. The second trailer was free to be uncoupled as required.

Two major variations affected the cab section. The first concerned the column fitted on the chassis to the rear of the cab which housed the permanent rivet joining the front trailer to the cab. Early models featured a round column, whereas later models had an added rectangular platform to support the column. The second casting variation concerns the faces of the toolboxes located behind the front wings and below the cab doors. Early models had a smooth surface, whereas later models featured a small vertical stiffening brace. The black base-plate of the cab featured the words 'MATCHBOX MAJOR PACK No M4 FRUEHAUF HOPPER MADE IN ENGLAND BY LESNEY'.

The hopper trailers featured the words 'MADE IN ENGLAND BY LESNEY' while the rivet mechanism attached to the rear trailer featured the legend 'MATCHBOX' No M4'. Once again there were two castings associated with the trailers. During the last runs of the model as a Major Pack and just as it was being introduced as a King Size in 1966, the area to the right of the rear rivet column, i.e. the area under the sloping area found on each side of the hopper container, was modified by extending right down to the baseplate. At the same time extra strengthening braces were added underneath the area where the sloping areas met the hopper container area. Each trailer featured a 'FRUEHAUF' label in white and red on either side. All wheels were red plastic and the black tyres were embossed with 'LESNEY ENGLAND' on either side.

The standard box featured a colourful picture of the model on the front and rear panels.

The complex M5-1 Massey Ferguson '780' Special Combine Harvester was in production for some seven years after its issue in July 1959 and is known to have had many casting variations. Early models had cylindrical rear axle housings, but as the model progressed in age these were strengthened eventually to include a thick web above each of the axle housings. At the same time the rear axle cross member was strengthened and thickened. A further strengthening modification was made to the triangular brace above the front left axle holding it directly below the driver. Further strengthening modifications included the square step area immediately in front of the rear rivet on the baseplate; the steering wheel column, which originally began as a straight upright column, eventually evolved into a chunky 'cooling tower' shape and finally the driver's platform for his seat, which originally had just two outer corners rounded off, ended up with the front corner rounded off as well. Very early models featured a well-defined lower sprocket wheel below the chain-drive detail on the right hand side of the model. This detail was quickly deleted to be replaced by a casting circle only. Other strengthening modifications to the upper body were carried out to enable the model to withstand the rigours of mass production. *Odell:* "The Harvester was ahead of its time . . . engineering wise."

The overall colour of the model was red. The paddle wheel varied in colour from bright rich yellow to a pale yellow and in some instances due to fading to a pale tan colour to match the driver. *Odell:* "A lot of people would have difficulty even today designing that paddle wheel!" The steering wheel on early models was red. This was followed by a silver unpainted wheel and finally by yellow plastic. All axles were riveted. Early front large wheels were in silver plastic with black plastic tyres; these were followed by

orange and finally by yellow. It should be noted that very early models had finer treads on their tyres and no lettering, whereas later models had much heavier treads and the words 'LESNEY ENGLAND' embossed on either side. The black rear wheels, which were considerably smaller originally had all black tyres. The wheels changed to orange and finally to yellow.

There are six known types of box. The first three showed line drawings of the model, the first and second boxes describing it as 'A MOKO-LESNEY' and the third as 'A LESNEY'. The last three boxes were colour picture type boxes.

The very long M6-1 Pickfords 200 Ton Transporter, which was first issued in September 1959, comprised a small tractor unit and a long low loader trailer. The tractor featured a split wind-screen, a simulated spare tyre on the rear behind the cab and a coupling device at the back. The black baseplate was riveted to the body between the two rear axles and clipped itself secure at both the front and rear. The baseplate bore the legend 'Scammell 6 X 6 TRACTOR MADE IN ENGLAND BY LESNEY' (The word Scammell was spelt incorrectly by Lesney). The low loader featured two dollies either end. The front dolly was riveted to the loader with just one rivet, thus enabling it to rotate and had a wire hook attaching it to the Scammell Tractor. The rear dolly was a different casting featuring an extended platform at its rear with an extra rivet to restrict rotation. The underneath surface of the trailer featured the legend 'CRANE 200 TON TRANS-PORTER MADE IN ENGLAND BY LESNEY MAJOR PACK No 6'.

The Scammell Tractor and the two dollies were painted in dark blue, but later models were changed to a much brighter shade.

Each dolly had three axles and similar wheels.

There are five known boxes. The first two boxes designated the toy as being 'A MOKO-LESNEY' and showed line drawings of the model. The third box also showed a line drawing but described the model as 'A LESNEY'. The fourth and fifth boxes were of the colour picture type.

As an attempt to make the Major Pack series more attractive to youngsters Lesney dramatically enlarged the size of the toys. The scale was increased so that the toys began to look like better value for money. *Odell:* "By this time we found we were getting through so much metal we could afford to offer larger models at not much more cost — more of a box full for the same money."

The extension into the King Size Range, however, became inevitable and so the M6-2 Racing Car Transporter, which had been issued either late in 1965 or in January 1966, was moved across to be the new K5-2 for 1967. As a Major Pack the Racing Car Transporter looked out of place (as did the M4-2 GMC Tractor) — rather too large and totally out of scale. Much of the charm created by their simplicity was lost.

The transporter body was attached to the baseplate by means of two rivets at the front and flange rivets at the rear. The baseplate featured the words 'RACING CAR TRANSPORTER MATCHBOX MAJOR PACK No M6 MADE IN ENGLAND BY LESNEY'. Early models featured a thin body cross-frame at the rear beneath the hinged tailgate and this was quickly modified to become thicker. The transporter could carry two cars, one on each level, as a mid-deck platform could be pulled to the rear against the pressure of a clear plastic lever fitted behind the rear cab window. Early models featured a short 'pull' tab and

M5-1 Combine Harvester and M6-1 200 Ton Transporter.

The low loader was finished originally in maroon and later in dark red. Pickfords decals were applied to either side of the tractor and on each side of the two dollies. The wire hooking device was painted originally in dark blue, then black and eventually on the last run of models was left unpainted. The tractor unit had three axles and six wheels, originally with knobbly treaded tyres and later a fine tread.

this was increased in length for later models. A further casting variation affected the tailgate; early models were solid but later models featured a slot in the tailgate to accommodate the extended 'pull' tab. The overall colour of the transporter was mid-green.

The baseplate, rear decks and tailgate were painted silver, and the interior was an off-white plastic. Clear perspex panels simulated the windows, cab sunroof and rear roof area. Two separate decals were fitted to each side of the model. The upper decal featured a black and white racing car and was fitted either way round. The lower decal listed the race tracks of Le Mans, Sebring, Silverstone and Nurburgring and showed the 'B.P.' logo against a chequered flag in its traditional black and white. *Ward:* "Pre-production models and boxes listed the following circuits: Monza, Le Mans, Sebring and Nurburgring . . . I just wonder if any of these decals were applied to any production releases?" All models were fitted with red plastic wheels and black plastic tyres on which the words 'LESNEY ENGLAND' appeared on both sides. All axles were riveted.

The model was packaged in a large picture type box.

The M7-1 Jennings Cattle Truck, which was first issued in June 1960, like the M2-2 Bedford came in two parts. The Thames Trader cab featured an open windscreen and side windows. The rear of the cab featured a swivel attachment to locate the trailer section. The baseplate was riveted towards the front of the cab and in the midway area to the rear of the front axle. The baseplate inscription read 'THAMES TRADER No 7 MADE IN ENGLAND BY LESNEY'. There is only one major variation

M7-1 Jenning's Cattle Truck and M8-1 Petrol Tanker.

in relation to the cab. On the inside of the cab the vertical internal stiffener was in the shape of a rectangle; on early models it was quite shallow and did not touch the cab roof — on later models it did and had been doubled in thickness.

The trailer body was well detailed, particularly at its sides, and included four ventilation slots and a rear door fixed on hinges. All early models featured a casting seam along the trailer roof – this was later removed. As the model

aged the internal stiffeners were changed from a curved shape to a square shape. The baseplate was fixed in position by a spread rivet at the front and by means of a tongue cast to the baseplate rear. The cross frame member of the trailer into which the tongue fitted existed in three different states, with early models having a slightly larger opening than later models. The baseplate inscription on the trailer read 'JENNINGS CATTLE

TRUCK MAJOR PACK No. 7 MADE IN ENGLAND BY LESNEY.'

The cab and both baseplates were painted in red. *Ward:* "I can also confirm that this model exists with a pale blue cab, baseplate, trailer baseplate and rear door, the trailer is in a bronze colour . . . all with grey plastic wheels. It was purchased in a store many years ago . . . and obviously now very rare indeed." The cabs had silver grilles, bumper and headlamps but can also be found with trim missing. Early trailers were painted in a light brown colour with matching rear door but these were later changed to a rich tan colour with a red rear door. Early models featured dark grey plastic knobbly wheels. The grey was later lightened in shade. With time the tyre tread was modified to produce both fine grey and black knobbly treads. The last models were released with black plastic fine tread wheels. All three axles were riveted.

The model was issued in three different types of box. The first showed a line drawing describing the model as 'A MOKO-LESNEY'. The second also showed a line drawing but described the model as 'A LESNEY'. The third box was a colour picture type box.

The M8-1 Mobilgas Petrol Tanker, which was first issued in August 1960, featured a Thornycroft Tractor. The baseplate featured the words 'MAJOR PACK No 8 THORNYCROFT TRACTOR MADE IN ENGLAND BY LESNEY'. There was only one casting variation in relation to the tractor unit. The reinforcing bracing column inside the rear wall of the cab extended down to form the rivet which joined the cab to the base-plate. There were two types of column. Early models featured a rectangular column that joined the baseplate in a rectangular slot. Later models featured a much thicker and more rounded column which consequently increased the size and shape of the baseplate slot. The tanker trailer featured a hole in its baseplate to secure it to the rear of the tractor unit. The baseplate was secured to the tanker by front and rear rectangular rivets. The baseplate featured the legend 'MAJOR PACK No 8 — THORNYCROFT 2400 GALLON TRAILER TANKER MADE IN ENGLAND BY LESNEY'.

Both the tractor and tanker were painted in dark red.

Major Packs were seldom advertised in their own right and were normally coupled to other Matchbox ranges.

Mobilgas decals were located on both sides of the tanker and on the rear, which incorporated the Mobilgas motif. The lettering was always in dark blue but can be found on either cream or white backgrounds, or even a combination of cream and white. Early models were released with a full complement of silver trim on the radiator grille, headlights and front bumper; later models were released with less trim. The tractor unit featured two riveted axles and four small dark grey plastic knobby treaded wheels, whereas the tanker featured just one axle and two wheels matching those of the tractor. Gradually the shade of grey changed to a much paler colour. Later models were released with black wheels featuring either fine or knobby treads.

The artwork for the box had been designed and printed in 1960 as the Moko — Lesney co-operation was coming to an end. So early models were released with the model being credited as 'A MOKO-LESNEY'. Thereafter, the boxes were changed to 'A LESNEY' only. Both boxes showed line drawings of the model. *Odell:* "A poor seller."

As the M8-2 Guy Warrior Car Transporter was brought into the Major Pack Range in May 1964 just three years before the whole range ceased, it eventually moved across to become K8-2 in 1967. *Odell:* "That model just sold and sold; we never really knew why; so we just kept knocking them out — it was a very good model in engineering terms. I had a hand in that one."

The cab section was fitted with closed-in plastic windows, which were tinted green. The baseplate was secured in place by a rear rivet and a front baseplate tongue which fitted into the front bumper. The baseplate featured the words 'GUY WARRIOR TRACTOR MAJOR PACK No 8 MADE IN ENGLAND BY LESNEY'. There were two different castings of the cab. Later models featured two strengthening triangular wedges at the bottom rear of the cab, and at the same time a strengthening cross-member was incorporated between the two rear wheel arches directly behind the trailer pivot and connecting boss.

The upper deck platform of the transporter trailer was hinged at the front and at the rear. Two extension arms, the lower halves being joined to an axle at the rear which also retained the extension ramp, extended up to join the upper deck. Two simple slots in the upper deck casting enabled the upper deck to be raised or lowered onto the lower deck area. The arms on later models were increased in width to make them stronger. The upper deck had a triangular brace underneath towards the rear. Small modifications were made to this brace. An extra strengthening cross member was placed outside the axle holding the rear tail gate on later models and at the same time extra strengthening ribs were added to each axle housing. The baseplate featured the legend 'GUY WARRIOR CAR TRANSPORTER MAJOR PACK No 8 MADE IN

ENGLAND BY LESNEY'. Early models featured a tailgate which was totally smooth underneath. This surface was modified later to include two strengthening ridges either side of the securing slot.

The tractor unit was painted in a blue-green shade and this varied from turquoise to a near metallic blue-green. The cab had silver trim applied to the front bumper, headlights and part of the grille. The baseplate was finished in black. Each side of the trailer carried a two-line decal; the first line read 'FARNBOROUGH MEASHAM' on either side of the motif or logo of 'Southern Counties Car Auctions Limited', and was placed along the upper deck. The second line read 'CAR AUCTION COLLECTION' and was placed along the lower deck. The trailer was painted in orange.

There were two different versions of the decal. Early models had letters in black with white shading, whereas later models had white letters with a black outline.

All axles were of the riveted type and all wheels were in orange plastic. Early models had grey tyres whereas later models had black. Both types were embossed 'LESNEY ENGLAND' on either side. A spring suspension was provided on the cab and trailer, by way of a flexible plastic spring.

The model was packaged in a colour picture type box. *Ward:* "Pre-production Guy Warriors had a painted orange trailer, a blue cab and rear ramp . . . metal hubs and black tyres."

The M9-1 Inter-State Double Freighter was first issued in May 1962 and comprised three separate units. The Hendrickson Tractor was fitted with pale green tinted windows and featured gold plated horns on the cab roof.

Early horns had a very deep recess and tapered front ends, whilst later horns were much shallower and had flared front ends. The black base plate was riveted to the cab at the rear and held by a tongue at the front. The baseplate featured the legend 'HENDRICKSON TRACTOR MAJOR PACK No 9 MADE IN ENGLAND BY LESNEY'. Very

*M9-1 Inter-State
Double Freighter and
M10-1 Whitlock Dinkum Rear
Dumper.*

early models featured the name Hendrickson in inverted commas.

There were two types of trailer body. Early trailers were devoid of internal features except for four semi-circular columns on the sides of the trailer. Later models included these columns, but also had a similar column at the very front of the trailer and four triangular strengthening braces midway along the bottom of the trailer sides. The trailer featured small longitudinal strengthening ribs along the surface of the baseplate. There were two trailer variations. Early baseplates were joined to the trailer by means of a tongue at the front. The legend 'MADE IN ENGLAND BY LESNEY INTER-STATE DOUBLE FREIGHTER MAJOR PACK No 9' was written parallel to the connecting slot. The second type of baseplate featured a new rivet, forward of the connecting slot. The tongue was removed and the gap filled in. The layout of the description was altered to accommodate the extra space taken up by the rivet and included the word "MATCH-BOX" and quoted the model number as "M-9". The connecting slot was either straight or at a slight angle. The connecting dolly is not known to have had any variations.

The cab bodies were painted in dark blue. Silver paint was generally applied to the grille and headlamps but examples do exist with only the grille or the headlamps detailed in silver. Early models and very late models had trailers and their baseplates painted in silver, whereas a shade of grey was used on trailers issued midway through the model's life. The trailer doors were painted in either blue or silver on silver trailers and grey on grey trailers. The connecting dollies were either painted blue or left unfinished in bright metal.

Two different decals were used. The more common label featured a yellow or orange/yellow background and lettering 'COOPER-JARRETTINC' in blue. The other type featured an orange/brown background, white lettering 'COOPER-JARRETT INTERNATIONAL' and a black and white Cooper-Jarrett logo. These decals were applied to both sides with matching decals on the fronts of both containers. The tractor was fitted with three riveted axles and featured two wheels on the front and four wheels on each rear axle. The connecting bogies featured a pair of axles and a further eight wheels.

There were three different types of wheel. All were in black plastic. Early models had wheels featuring a hub cap and with the letters LESNEY ENGLAND embossed on the outer face fitted to the front axle of the cab. The other axles had double wheels i.e. two wheels joined together with the outer wheel recessed deep and with no hub cap. The words 'LESNEY ENGLAND' were again featured on the outer surface. The third type was a standard fine tread wheel and was fitted to all axles on later models.

There were three different packaging variations, all based on the colour picture type box. Unlike all the other models in the Major Packs Range, M9-1 continued to be shown in the 1967 catalogue.

The M10-1 Whitlock Dinkum Rear Dumper, which was first issued in July 1962, was a two piece model and was permanently joined together by a long rivet which also doubled up as a traversing pivot for the model. The tractor baseplate was riveted to the main body both at the front and underneath the seat area. The baseplate featured the words 'DINKUM DUMPER MAJOR PACK No 10 MADE IN ENGLAND BY LESNEY'. A red plastic steering wheel was fitted to the tractor unit. The model was painted in yellow. Two identical decals in black and white showing 'D-D 70' were placed on either side of the rear dumper. Both axles were riveted. Early wheels were of bright unpainted metal, but later on these were replaced by red plastic wheels. All tyres were in black with the words 'LESNEY ENGLAND' embossed on each side.

There were two picture type boxes. The first boxes featured a simple picture of the model. The boxes were printed by the Pembroke-Abbey printing company. Later boxes featured a more colourful front and rear panel with the added detail of a background for the model.

It should be noted that the 1965 catalogue showed a Dodge Tractor with Tipper Train as M7. This was never released as a Major Pack, but instead was issued as K-16 in the King Size Range.

The Major Packs Range form a small and collectable range of Matchbox products. At the time of writing they are beginning to become more and more popular, and so the prices asked for mint and boxed models are reasonable although they are hard to find in perfect condition.

SERIAL	TITLE	YEAR	SCALE	LENGTH (CMS)	U.K. PRICE WHEN NEW
M1-1	CATERPILLAR EARTHMOVER	1957	1:125	11.5 (4.5")	2s. 6d (12.5p)
M1-2	B.P. AUTOTANKER	1962	1:89	10.2 (4")	2s. 6d (12.5p)
M2-1	BEDFORD ARTICULATED TRUCK	1957/8	1:95	10.1 (4")	2s. 6d (12.5p)
M2-2	BEDFORD TRACTOR AND YORK TRAILER	1961	1:77	11.6 (4.56")	3s. 6d (17.5p)
M3-1	TANK TRANSPORTER AND CENTURION TANK MARK III	1959	1:125	15.5 (6.13")	3s. 11d (19.5p)
M4-1	RUSTON BUCYRUS POWER SHOVEL	1959	1:92	9.8 (3.13")	2s. 6d (12.5p)
M4-2	GMC TRACTOR AND FRUEHAUF HOPPER TRAIN	1965	1:67	28.5 (1.5")	9s. 11d (49.5p)
M5-1	MASSEY FERGUSON COMBINE HARVESTER	1959	1:58	11.8 (4.13")	3s. 11d (19.5p)
M6-1	PICKFORDS 200 TON TRANSPORTER	1959	1:116	28.0 (11")	3s. 11d (19.5p)
M6-2	RACING CAR TRANSPORTER	1965/6	1:54	13.0 (5.13")	6s. 11d (34.5p)
M7-1	JENNINGS CATTLE TRUCK	1960	1:81	12.1 (4.75")	2s. 6d (12.5p)
M8-1	MOBILGAS PETROL TANKER	1960	1:91	9.6 (3.5")	2s. 6d (12.5p)
M8-2	GUY WARRIOR CAR TRANSPORTER	1964	1:73	20.9 (8.25")	7s. 6d (38.5p)
M9-1	INTER-STATE DOUBLE FREIGHTER	1962	1:100	28.8 (11.38")	6s. 11d (34.5p)
M10-1	WHITLOCK DINKUM REAR DUMPER	1962	1:70	10.6 (4.19")	3s. 11d (19.5p)

The Models of Yesteryear
8 Range

THE FLAGSHIP RANGE 1956 TO 1988

Before commencing the analysis of the Yesteryear range there are several comments that need to be made which will go some way to explaining the inconsistencies of the series. As has already been written, the inspiration for the range came from Jack Odell, but the models were conceived to appeal to the adult as an impulse purchase or a small gift ideal for birthdays and Christmas. It should always be remembered that the models were without precedence and without any competition from the Dinky range of toys or Mettoy's new Corgi range. In short, they were a secondary range to the "Matchbox" Series aimed at an older age group. The first series, therefore, bear the influence of that group and one of the strongest influences is that of scale.

No attempt at a consistency of scale was ever made by Lesney; rather they were all built to a certain size irrespective of their subject, and thus a Morris Bullnose was made to appear larger than a 7 Ton Leyland Lorry! The introduction of the first selection of replacement vehicles or second series models was slightly more consistent and much larger than the first which revealed a decrease of the "Matchbox" Series influence as well, perhaps, as an assertion of Odell's desire to produce detailed models. The only competition Yesteryears had even in 1964 was a range of models by Rio. Yesteryears were undoubtedly not as detailed as this brand, but they were far cheaper and far more readily distributed.

A further aspect of Yesteryear collecting and one which infuriated the collectors of the 1960s and 1970s were the unusual and totally unrealistic paint finishes that appeared on Yesteryears. The first series were all quite accurately finished, but with the appearance of the second series metallic paint became very evident. This factor is really quite revealing because it uncovers a duality of approach. On one hand is the brilliance of the casting which by today's standards cannot be equalled at the then price, and the other is the perceived belief by Lesney that they were toy makers responding to the needs of the market. When metallic paint finishes were brought in by Ford and British Leyland for their current products, Lesney merely followed suit.

The early 1970s nearly saw the demise of the range altogether as the Company directed all its resources into the adaptation of the "Matchbox" Series to produce the Superfast range. By this time the need to streamline production was a very real necessity, so 1973/1974 saw the Yesteryear range re-emerge but with common components such as a standard plastic twelve and twenty-four spoked wheel.

This wheel was an attempt to rationalise, which suited very few of the models then in production. A further irritation to collectors seeking authenticity came in the form of whitewall tyres. The wheel standardisation inevitably led to the fitting of these tyres on models which should not have worn them.

In recent years these irritations have become a thing of the past and much greater realism is applied to new issues with very often new wheels being moulded especially for individual models. Models of Yesteryear now have a stronger identity and their understanding of the market is greater than it appears to have been through the previous two decades. Much of the very real pleasure that collectors derive from the series is an understanding of fashions, quirks, mistakes and triumphs that the range has witnessed in over thirty years of production.

This chapter has been subdivided to make reference easier:

Steam Driven Vehicles
Public Transport Vehicles
Public Service Vehicles
Sports and Racing Cars
Passenger Cars
Commercial Vehicles
Code 2 Models

STEAM DRIVEN VEHICLES

It is well known that the inspiration and moving force behind the inclusion of steam driven vehicles was Jack Odell. His enthusiasm for old, well-engineered vehicles was undoubtedly matched by his genius in the art of diecasting and the manufacture of a range of vintage vehicles gave expression to both. The prospect of developing the

Models of Yesteryear range was not quite so enthusiastically shared by Leslie Smith who was concerned that the range would not have quite such a wide appeal as the successful "Matchbox" Series. Other factors included the relative complexity of the models and the amount of hand finishing which was required to apply items of gold and silver trim, not forgetting the intricate waterslide transfers required for many of the originals. Clearly much of Lesney's success was in the economies of scale that the miniatures allowed.

It was believed in popular mythology that the first model, an Allchin Traction Engine, was originally to be a miniature. The story goes that Jack Odell was about to go on holiday and left the instructions for the plans of the model with the drawing office. They executed the plans correctly, but the tools were made to the wrong scale. Pleasant as this story is, it is not true! The model was designed to be small enough not to depart too far from the successful formula of the "Matchbox" Series, but large enough to set it apart as one of a distinct range and large enough to incorporate sufficient detail.

The **Y1/1 7 N.H.P. Allchin Traction Engine,** introduced in 1956 as the first ever Model of Yesteryear it is justifiably famous as it is also probably the first ever diecast miniature of a steam driven road-going vehicle. *Smith:* "There was no clear rationale for the choice – we bought books on old vehicles. . ." The model appeared in a mid-green livery with red wheels, but with a black six-spoked flywheel. Several parts of the casting were picked out in gold paint and the first production run featured gold trim applied to the chimney top, the valve gear, the piston housing transmission cover, the steering boss and the lower chimney ring. The boiler door was highlighted in plated copper. These very early models had the

treads cast straight across the rear wheels. This feature was changed to produce treads of a diagonal pattern which enhanced the appearance of this delightful model still further.

Early Yesteryears such as the Allchin did not appear to have strict specifications applied to the detailing of the finish, and over the seven years production life of this model it is generally true that the later the model the less gold trim was applied. It is even possible to find an example with all of this trim missing. Other variations include models with all of the rear wheels and outer faces in red. In 1963 a small batch of Allchins were produced using the smooth faced rear wheels from the Y11 Steam Roller. It has always been thought that this was because the moulds for the rear wheels had worn out. *Odell:* "These were put on in error." One last area of difference concerns the boiler doors. These have been found with gold and silver plating and in very rare cases even green paint.

The **Y4/1 Sentinel Steam Wagon,** a most unusual but attractive model, had a production life of only five years from 1956 to 1961. Its withdrawal, however, was not due entirely to poor sales, but also to the disintegration of the diecasting tools. The model was only ever produced in deep blue with water-slide transfers applied to both body sides and its front and rear. *Smith:* "I remember quite clearly that there was a baker in Enfield town who was regularly called upon by a Sentinel lorry delivering flour. I can see it in my mind now, the ashes falling and the smoke pumping out of the funnel – we thought to ourselves now there's a bit of nostalgia."

In common with all early Yesteryears, the first versions of this model had crude axles which were crimped at one end to retain the wheels. The wheels were grenodised, i.e. a chemical solution

was applied to the wheels to turn them to a grey colour. To comply with safety regulations the method of securing the axles was soon replaced by a single headed axle which had the other end spun over on assembly. One rare variation of this model concerns the wheels. In 1960 the dies for the cast wheels were found to be worn out, so black plastic wheels, already in production for the miniature range, were substituted. For today's collectors this variant is by far the most valuable. Before the application of extra trim became too expensive, Lesney were advised by the trade to make the model somewhat more attractive and more like a toy. *Smith:* "People would say about the Sentinel . . . very nice, lovely but put a bit more gold on the funnel . . . anything to make it glitter and have more interest." The gold trim, applied initially to the chimney rim and a box on the chassis, can be missing on later issues.

Lesney was never entirely satisfied with the Y4 Sentinel. *Smith:* "We probably made it a little too small, which didn't add to its attraction – it's a bit like in the "Matchbox" Series where we made the early models too small and then as time went on we made them bigger so that visually they looked right."

The **Y9/1 1924 Fowler 'Big Lion' Showman's Engine** has come to be regarded as a masterpiece of miniature diecasting and one which, in relation to its size and price, is unlikely ever to be equalled. The public thought so too, and the model had a ten year life span between 1957 and 1967 during which time hundreds of thousands were sold. *Odell:* "Yes, although the export market found it impossible to sell." The model was also unique in that such an engine had never been modelled by a commercial manufacturer before.

The most visible difference between early and late issue

from copper to gold and finally to silver plating.

The model ceased production in 1967 more as a result of worn out tooling than from lack of demand. The intricacy of the many components involved in the assembly have given rise to countless variations and combinations of plated parts, colour schemes and levels of trim. Close inspection of an example, however, will soon persuade the collector that its classic status is well-earned.

The steam driven **Y11/1 Aveling & Porter Road Roller**, is simply a further example of Odell's love of road-making machinery. At its time of introduction in 1958 there were still numerous examples working for their living on the roads of Britain. The model had a short production life of five years, and perhaps was overshadowed by the sales of the Showman's Engine. The model was only ever produced in an authentic mid-green colour with some gold trim applied to the chimney rim, the steering gear and the piston gearbox housing. The only striking variation on this model concerns the three canopy supports which were green on the early versions but black on later types. Many batches of these supports were of different lengths and this led to models with higher or lower roof-lines.

A full sixteen years were to pass before a steam driven vehicle was next to appear in the range. The intervening years had been largely taken up with cars and latterly petrol-driven vans. The van series had proved to be immensely popular and had stimulated a new market mainly interested in collecting the liveries periodically introduced by the company. The appeal of these vans began to pall somewhat, and this coincided with a shift of responsibility for the initial selection and prototyping of subjects to the Research & Development Department, which had moved

Y27 1922 Foden Steam Lorries
Top row: Left, With tow hook.
Centre, Early pre-production model.
Second row: Right, Original model
maker's suggestion.

models is the colour. The early issues were of a very dark maroon brown colour, but as the years went on the colour lightened to mid-maroon and red, ending with a final run in an almost crimson shade. Similarly the canopy started life in cream, but by the time the red versions appeared they were in white. As with the

Allchin, the amount of gold trim declined over the years; early issues had the cylinder block, chimney rim and other details in gold, whilst on some red versions

a section of the baseplate was painted black. The boiler door and roof supports were plated in brass originally, but as the years progressed the supports altered to painted gold and later became silver. On red versions these supports can be found in silver plating or even left unfinished. The boiler door similarly changed from its base in Chingford to new offices in Enfield in July 1983. *Tekerian:* "We knew that the trend had been set in the market; commercial vehicles were the ones that were the high sellers. Entering into the steam market was thought at the time to be fairly controversial . . . Is it an unknown area? We thought, no! What we are doing is reproducing models that are truly representative of all vehicles as we had already done way back in the 1950s. It has been very successful and has set us on the steam trail again."

The first production model to appear, in 1984, was the **Y27/1 1922 Foden Steam Lorry.** Any family resemblance to that of the earlier Sentinel was virtually non-existent as this was a much larger and consequently more detailed miniature. The model was produced in the authentic red and blue livery of the *Pickfords Removal Company.* The Pickfords head-quarters were situated some five hundred yards away from Burleigh House, the main office of Matchbox Toys, U.K.

The model was enthusiastically received by the ever-burgeoning collector fraternity, and it is surprising to note that none of the Matchbox competitors had anything like it on the market. Two variations in the castings are perhaps of more interest to the avid collector than the general enthusiast. During initial production, a weakness in the casting between the cab and the body became apparent. The solution was to alter the tools by inserting a brace at the weak point. The exact location of this brace was misinterpreted, however, and the tool was reinstated to production before the mistake was discovered. *Grundy:* "By the time the mistake was noticed, two hours had elapsed and about five hundred or so were made; the mould had been altered late the previous evening and put up at six o'clock in the morning and

I stopped it at ten past eight as the toolroom had not done the modification in the way that I had requested. Two skips had been filled and I let them through the system. Consequently, in a period of less than three full working days, there were three casting variations on this model." It is precisely this type of unintentional error that the enthusiast holds so dear.

Y18 1918 Atkinson Steam Wagons. *Second row: Left, A pre-production version.*
Third row: Right, An undecorated pre-production model.
Fourth row: A pre-production colour trial. Right: A pre-production colour trial.

The Pickfords livery was changed in 1985 to that of the *Hovis* livery and this model reflects the growing pre-occupation of the company to reproduce accurate liveries on their commercial vehicles. Interestingly, the livery of this particular company was thought to be too sparse and so authentic advertisements culled from other contemporary Hovis vehicles were added. The only variation of note with this particular model is that some of the canopies and wheels are noticeably lighter in colour than others. This model was marketed as a Limited Edition and 100,000 were produced worldwide.

The *Tate & Lyle* sugar refining company was chosen as the next livery and this became the standard issue for 1986. This particular logo design ran foul of the detail cast into the body sides and tended to cause the tampo inks to smudge during application. The mould was quickly altered to reduce the height of the raised centre rib thus giving consistent, accurate printing.

In 1986 the copyright date on the Foden chassis was changed from 1984 to 1986, and models with shallow side panels can be found with either copyright date. For Christmas 1986 a unique version of the standard model was produced by fitting a tow hook to the chassis and introducing a trailer. The model was decorated in the attractive red, green and white livery of the *Frasers* removal company using archive materials uncovered by the Research and Development Department.

Production of the Pickfords livery continued after the Frasers version and a few examples appeared with the tow hook still attached. This subsequent run of Pickfords all had the 1986 copyright date chassis with or without hooks, and all with shallow side panels. In 1987 immediately before the move to Macau the last U.K. version of the Foden was produced containing a simulated load of plastic sacks and in the livery of *Spillers* grain. For the Frasers, the chassis mould had to be modified so that a cast rivet appeared on the X bracing at the rear of the chassis. Some of these rivets were found by quality control to be too short for the attachment of the hook and could not be used for the Frasers. These chassis castings were utilised during production of the Spillers version and so models were

produced with or without a cast rivet on the chassis. A final run of Spillers in late 1987 was made using a much lighter shade of green on the tampo decorations. By this time, however, all the Frasers' type chassis had long been used up.

One year after the introduction of the Foden and pleased with the public reaction to it, the company launched a sister model – the **Y18/2 1918 Atkinson Steam Wagon.** *Smith:* "It is interesting to see that even today Matchbox are going back to some of the early models like the Sentinel." The company chose to release the model as a Special Limited Edition which at that time meant a total production run of only 65,000 models worldwide. A premium price of £6.99 was charged for the model, which was a reflection of the need to recoup the estimated £85,000 then required to pay for the tooling with just one sales drive. The model bore the livery of the *Lake Goldsmith* quarry company, and the only notable variation was that the plastic front mudguards were squared off on later issues.

The next version of the Atkinson Steam Wagon was subject to considerable modification before its release in August 1986. This issue had the water tank moved from behind the cab to under the rear chassis, which considerably lengthened the available load area. The model appeared in the livery of *Blue Circle Portland Cement* as a standard range model. The first 5,000 produced had a pale yellow finish but succeeding examples bore a deeper shade by being sprayed twice. Early issues displayed a wider gap where the front cab coachlines met the sides caused by difficulties in the tampo printing process, i.e. the cab was of such a severe curve that the tampo pads did not make a complete contact; a slight increase in pressure to the tampo plates resolved this problem.

A Special Limited Edition version of the Atkinson in the livery of *Bass,* the brewing company, was issued in December 1987. This livery and subject was conceived and developed by Brian Bailey of the Research & Development Department, whose hobby is collecting brewery memorabilia. This version was another Special Limited Edition and featured a flat body bearing beer casks retained by posts linked by a chain. It had a production run of only 60,000 and was virtually sold out before a single model had been produced.

In 1988 the Atkinson appeared carrying a simulated load of sacks and was dressed in the colours of *Burghfield Mills,* a company of flour millers. The model attracted some criticism on its release as the load was not a particularly good fit to the body and the colour of the plastic used for the load of sacks was not very realistic. There was also a transfer on the cab front panel instead of the more usual tampo application.

In August 1987 the company produced a third steam driven lorry, the **Y8/5 1917 Yorkshire Type W/A Wagon.** This unusual model first appeared in the livery of *Johnnie Walker Whisky* and was the first steam vehicle in the series to come from Macau. The model was chosen with a view to its adaptability; the Yorkshire, for example, was also widely used as a brewer's dray and even a dust cart! The model was nominated to be part of the Framed Cabinet offer for 1989, in a green and white colour scheme with *Samuel Smith Victoria Corn Mills, Sheffield* livery.

In December 1986 Matchbox released an all-new version of a **Showman's Engine – the Y19/2 Fowler B6.** Although the actual model on which it was based was not that used for the Y9/1, the two models were nearly identical, but as with its predecessor this model met with almost universal acclaim. Its very intricate construction called for nineteen individual components and, indeed, the reject

MODELS OF YESTERYEAR
1956 - 1988
STEAM DRIVEN VEHICLES

Ref Number	Date of Issue	Model	First Livery	Scale
Y1-1	1956	Allchin Traction Engine	Green	1:80
Y4-1	1956	Sentinel Steam Wagon	Blue	1:100
Y8-5	1987	Yorkshire Steam Wagon	Red	1:61
Y9-1	1958	Fowler Showman's Engine	Maroon	1:80
Y11-1	1958	1920 Aveling & Porter Road Roller	Green	1:80
Y12-4	1987	1829 Stephenson's Rocket	Yellow	1:64
Y13-1	1959	1862 Santa Fe Locomotive	Green	1:112
Y14-1	1959	1903 Duke of Connaught	Green	1:130
Y18-2	1985	1918 Atkinsons Steam Wagon	Lake Goldsmith	1:60
Y18-2	1986	1918 Atkinsons Steam Wagon	Blue Circle Cement	1:60
Y18-2	1987	1918 Atkinsons Steam Wagon	Bass	1:60
Y18-2	1988	1918 Atkinsons Steam Wagon	Burghfield Mills	1:60
Y19-2	1986	Fowler Showman's Engine	Blue	1:68
Y21-3	1987	Aveling & Porter Steam Roller	Green	1:60
Y27-1	1984	1922 Foden Steam Lorry	Pickfords	1:72
Y27-1	1985	1922 Foden Steam Lorry	Hovis	1:72
Y27-1	1986	1922 Foden Steam Lorry	Tate & Lyle	1:72
Y27-1	1986	1922 Foden Steam Lorry	Frasers	1:72
Y27-1	1987	1922 Foden Steam Lorry	Spillers	1:72

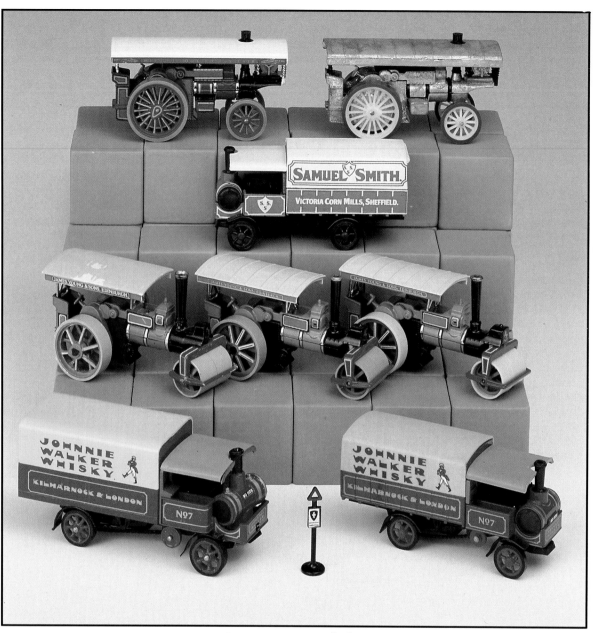

coachlining and decoration for absolute authenticity. In spite of this the model, a Special Limited Edition, was deservedly popular and, as with the Showman's, the model was a sell-out even before the production of 60,000 commenced. A small number of these models have been found without the cast inscription on the underside of the canopy. These were 'early shot' canopies which became mixed up with those cast during the normal production run.

The final section of this division of the chapter concerns steam locomotives. To date only three have been included in the range, and there is a gap of some twenty years between the demise of the second and the introduction of the third. The **Y13/1 Santa Fe Loco**, although an attractive model, was produced to an amazingly small scale and it fits most uncomfortably with the rest of the original range. The first production issues featured the most gold trim, in particular on the walkways to either side of the boiler as well as on the condensers, smoke-stack and headlight lens. As time went on, however, all but the gold trim on the smoke-stack tended to be left off, whilst the headlight lens appeared in silver. The final short run of these models was finished in a much lighter shade of green and it is this variation which is the most sought after.

The **Y14/1 Duke of Connaught** locomotive was scaled down to an equally small size as its American counterpart and joined the range in 1959. Although there were no significant colour variations, the gold trim which highlighted the walkway boxes was deleted from all but the first issues. The walkway boxes were later recast to join with the main wheel covers. The boiler door, which was originally in a gold plated finish, eventually became silver in the final issues of 1964. *Simmons:* "One of the main reasons for sales resistance to these two models, was the fact that they

---

rate during assembly was as high as 50%. Prototype models of the engine had actually been built in previous years, but the costs of production had hitherto prevented its appearance. The model was marketed as a Special Limited Edition and came in a deluxe hinged presentation box complete with a descriptive card text stating that the model would not be repeated. At a cost of

Recent Issue Steam Vehicles.
Top row Right, A pre- production Y19 Showman's Engine.
Second row: The Y8 Yorkshire in Samuel Smiths livery.
Third row: Left, A pre-production Y21 Steam Roller with two general release models.
Fourth row: Left, The original oversized model maker's suggestion, which was reduced in size for production.

£18.00 it was the most expensive single Yesteryear produced. At one time the roof was to be made in plastic but a late decision ensured

that the roof component was diecast metal.

One year later a new version of a steam roller made its appearance. The **Y21/3 Aveling & Porter Steam Road Roller**. At first glance it appeared to use many of the components of the Showman's Engine, but in fact was quite different. The model featured a half-length canopy. Whilst the colours were close to those of the original vehicle, their shades were rather too bright with too much

19th Century Locomotives.
Second row: Left, The very rare Y13 Santa Fe Loco on light green.

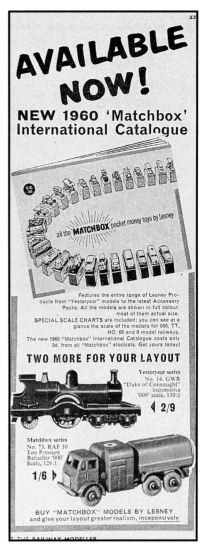

A contemporary advertisement from the Railway Modeller *in 1960.*

were issued without tenders, leading many possible purchasers to feel that they were incomplete." *Railway Modeller* November 1959: "It would also be nice to have the beautiful G.W. 2,500 gal. tender to complete the picture."

In 1987 Matchbox ventured into the world of railway miniatures for a third time and made a limited edition of the **Stephenson's Rocket**, the new Y19. This model became the earliest of all the subjects

covered in the range. The total production run was only 60,000 units worldwide and the model came in a specially packaged deluxe carton. *Tekerian:* "The whole idea of narrowing the range just to cars and vans is too short-sighted. We have to give the range a wide and interesting perspective. The Stephenson's Rocket was felt to be a

model we had to do . . . you've got to keep that wide appeal, it creates discussion . . . Look what Matchbox have come along with now!"

PUBLIC TRANSPORT VEHICLES

The **1911 'B' Type London Bus** was introduced into the range as the Y2/1 in 1956. The subject matter

was chosen quite simply because Jack Odell's father had driven similar buses in London. The casting had four windows over the four main side windows, but it was soon discovered by Lesney that the struts broke too readily in the fettling process. The tool was modified and new extra window struts were incorporated. The colour of the driver, throughout production, was either black or blue. As with other early Yesteryears there was a tendency to reduce the amount of extra paint trim applied. Later models were fitted with riveted axles, and

Public Transport Vehicles from the first series.

whereas earlier models featured unpainted metal wheels, later models had black metal wheels. *Smith:* "It was a touch of nostalgia – Jack's father had been a bus driver and probably his father had said that a bus would be a good idea and Jack agreed."

To establish a more definite public transport theme the third Models of Yesteryear chosen was a **London 'E' Class Tramcar**, the Y3/1, and it too was released in 1956. The earliest castings featured a realistic cut out under the stairs forming a triangular shaped area. Unfortunately this area tended to fill up with excess metal known as flashing and was often not removed during the tumbling

A competition which appeared in a comic as part of an on pack promotion in 1959.

Despite Lesney's growth, and modern methods employed "Matchbox" models still receive a special finishing touch, by hand.

process. The tool was modified and this area was cast in. The very earliest models featured a thin cow catcher at the front; this proved to be fragile and was strengthened by doubling up its dimensions on all later models. Wheels were either unpainted or black. Baseplates were black but one short run towards the end of the model's life were finished in a light grey. By 1964, when the tooling was virtually worn out, the hole that simulated access into the top deck was closed in. *Smith:* "It created a regional demand but not an international demand . . . I suppose there was a little bit of frustration because it was well made, but why didn't it sell better?"

1959 saw the introduction of the **Y12/1 London Horse-Drawn Bus**. This was conceived entirely by Jack Odell as he had a nostalgic weakness for horse-drawn vehicles of any description. *Smith:* "The range could have got too horsey . . . there was no demand as it was going too far back in history." The London Transport Bus, in various shades of red, always featured *Lipton's Tea* advertisements. Earlier models had two horses

(smaller than the Shand Mason Fire Engine horses) in light brown, which became progressively darker throughout their production life. The only significant casting variation related to the method of joining the horse-bar to the underside of the bus. This was initially fixed by a single rivet but on later models an additional plate with two rivets was used to afford extra strength to this fragile casting. The bus was withdrawn in 1966 and was replaced by the Y12 1909 Thomas Flyabout.

The **Y23/1 1922 A.E.C. Omnibus** was added to the range in 1983. The bus had been researched and developed at the Hackney factory, Waterden Road, in 1975. Delays in development occurred inter alia because the Research & Development Department had moved to Hall Lane in Chingford in 1981. The earliest pre-production castings did not feature the toolbox to be found underneath the stairs, and there were no supporting brackets under the driver's canopy. Many tests were made of the upper plastic body and the top handrail, in particular, was thickened to provide greater strength. The

original designer's model bore the livery of Black & White Scotch whisky. This livery was shown at the trade shows and was reproduced in an artist's drawing in the 1983 catalogue. Matchbox never intended to reproduce this livery and did not obtain per-mission to use it. Delays occurred before the paper labels arrived from the printers with the nominated livery of *Schweppes*. When the factory began applying the original white paper labels it was noticed that the red ink printing was bleeding into the model and so the application of the labels was stopped and the ink for the labels was changed to black. However, some of the buses with the original labels were packaged and sold in Hamley's Toy Shop in London, but soon fake red labels were flooding the market. Events became more complicated when Schweppes objected to the artwork on the label, primarily because there was no registered copyright sign and the style of lettering was not relevant to Schweppes. A new yellow label was subsequently designed and approved by Schweppes. Consequently, the casting of the upper deck was modified by filling in the lower gaps which resulted in a

broader side hoarding with just a single top hand-rail. The red Schweppes bus with black and white labels was issued with three distinct shades of brown seats — dark, medium and a mushroom brown. Seats and side guard-rails can be of any of these combinations. The buses with yellow labels can also be found with the radiator castings either chrome plated or in bare metal.

In 1984 the Schweppes label was replaced by an *R.A.C.* label and was based on a bus displayed at the National Motor Museum, Beaulieu. This was changed in 1985 to *Maples.* This livery was released as part of a three model set to coincide with Fathers' Day, and total production was limited to 40,000 buses worldwide. In 1986 the bus received a new colour scheme, dark brown and cream, and featured a *Haig* advertisement. In 1987 Kellogg's commissioned Matchbox Toys to produce a Y23 Omnibus with a *Kellogg's* advertisement to celebrate 60 years of Rice Krispies. The model was part of an on-pack offer together with the MB38 Rice Krispies van. However, enough models were made available worldwide through retail shops to

Ref Number	Date of Issue	Model	First Livery	Scale
Y2-11	956	1911 'B' Type London Bus	Red	1:100
Y3-11	956	1907 London 'E' Class Tramcar	Red	1:130
Y10-5	1988	Diddler Trolley Bus	Ronuk/Jeyes	1:76
Y12-1	1959	London Horse Drawn Bus	Red	1:100
Y15-3	1987	1920 Preston Tram	Swan Vesta	1:87
Y15-3	1988	1920 Preston Tram	Swan Soap	1:87
Y16-4	1988	Scania Vabis Post Bus	Yellow	1:49
Y23-1	1983	1922 AEC Omnibus	Schweppes	1:72
Y23-1	1985	1922 AEC Omnibus	RAC	1:72
Y23-1	1985	1922 AEC Omnibus	Maples	1:72
Y23-1	1986	1922 AEC Omnibus	Haig	1:72
Y27-1	1988	1922 AEC Omnibus	Kelloggs	1:72
Y28-1	1984	1907 Unic Taxi	Red	1:42

MODELS OF YESTERYEAR
1956 - 1988
PUBLIC TRANSPORT VEHICLES

on a 1907 Unic. The **Y28/1 1907 Unic Taxi** was modelled on an original taxi owned by the London Taxis' Preservation Society in Brixton, London. The colour scheme was taken from a similar vehicle on display at the Beaulieu National Motor Museum, bright red with a cream hood. A combination of the two actual taxis led Matchbox to issue a dark red taxi with black hood. Originally Matchbox intended to cast the windscreen and weather-guard assembly in metal, but tests revealed that they would not stand up to the fettling process. These components were then made in plastic and the tools were modified to add braces to the windscreen pillars to prevent the weather-screen bending. A raised lug was incorporated behind the dashboard to ensure that the windscreen component and the floor remained intact. As the meter was moulded with the windscreen component, (in the same mould), it too was changed from metal to plastic. The baseplate of the Y28 Unic Taxi and its front seats were modified from the tools originally designed for the defunct Y5 Peugeot. The taxi was designed by Mr Victor Lewis at the Research & Development Department in Enfield. As was common practice with the designers, if they were given an opportunity to personalise their own models they invariably placed on the model an obscure recognition mark. In the case of the taxi this is to be found on the number plate VL 5392 (Victor Lewis, his date of birth and the ninety second model designed by him). When the model was launched, small variations in the tampo print immediately appeared. Often the very fine wood window framing was missing along with the tiny lettering on the doors. Equally as common were hoods with or without silver hood tensioning arms. Modifications were made to the tools to correct production problems. First, the rear lights were

cater for collectors. The Rice Krispies bus was issued in late January 1988, once again in overall red and black. *Tekerian:* "Our best selling Yesteryear in 1988 was the Rice Krispies Bus. When we first launched the omnibus, it was very successful. Then we changed the

Y23 A.E.C. Omnibus and
Y28 Unic Taxi.
Top row: Left, A pre-production model.
Centre: The rarer red labelled version.

livery from the first Schweppes logo to the second Schweppes logo, but when the trade saw the R.A.C. they said 'Oh no! Not another red bus, why don't you do

a brown or blue one?' Basically, they said it was the same model with a new label . . . We took them up on this and so the next one was the brown Haig Bus – but when Kellogg's came along and ordered thousands of red buses, we had to do it!"

In 1984 Matchbox introduced their first taxi into the range, based strengthened by webbing out the mould and so providing a stronger attachment. Secondly, the poorly fitting hood was cured by incorporating pins on either side of the body to hold down the hood more permanently. In 1986 the plastic meter was changed back to diecast metal as the production line complained of finding too many of the plastic components fitting badly or breaking loose. The livery was changed to a dark blue in 1987. Transitional variations occurred, and it is common to find blue taxis without body pins. The tampo printing of the window frames and the lettering on the cab doors was not applied to the dark blue taxis.

In 1987 Matchbox introduced the **Y15/3 Preston Tram**, similar in design to the earlier Y3 London Tram, but on a much larger scale. The components were a mixture of diecast metal and plastic but with a greater emphasis on metal. The first livery was in overall red and incorporated a *Swan Vesta* advertisement. This was only the second model to be made at the Macau factory, and collectors were pleasantly surprised at the quality. Quality Assurance at Rochford, however, did random quality assessments and found some trams to have defects in the casting on the upper deck. Production at Macau ceased until the tools were modified. At the same time the resistor box, located at one end of the lower deck, was modified to improve the flow of metal in the mould and to prevent pitting of the metal on the outside of the casting. The components of the tram were presented in a framed cabinet and made available primarily to collectors within the United Kingdom and the Republic of Ireland as an incentive to purchase Yesteryears from officially appointed retail shops. Later the Framed Cabinet was made available to overseas markets.

In 1988 the Y15 Tram was re-liveried in overall blue and white, with *Swan Soap* advertisements.

Classified as a Special Limited Edition, the **Y10/5 1931 Diddler Trolley Bus** was launched in late 1988. Its higher than normal selling price was justified by the model having over twenty separate castings – with the majority being in diecast metal. This particular model was eagerly purchased by collectors. Limited to only 60,000 models worldwide it was sold out within days. It was immediately acclaimed as one of the finest models ever produced by Matchbox. The model was based on the vehicle housed in the London Transport Museum.

This was quickly followed by a further Special Limited Edition model, the **Y16/4 1923 Scania Vabis Post Bus** in yellow. As with the Diddler the Scania was specially packaged and limited to 60,000 models worldwide.

Y15 Tram, Y10 Trolley Bus and Y16 Scania Post Bus.
The Y16 was actually produced with gold spoked wheels.

PUBLIC SERVICE VEHICLES

The **Y4/2 Shand Mason Fire Engine** was shown in the 1960 Catalogue in an outline sketch as the proposed Y16 model. It did appear in 1961, but as a new Y4 to replace the Sentinel. *Smith:* "Again a touch of nostalgia – especially with the horses." A colour picture drawing was featured in the 1961 Cata-

The Y4 Shand Mason was originally destined to be the No. Y16 and was also described as being a Merryweather!

logue showing as the new Y4 model the Shand Mason Hythe fire engine, but the model was never released under the Hythe branch of the fire services. *Railway Modeller* July 1961: "The Yesteryear series Merryweather fire engine by Lesney . . . once again every significant detail is included and the parts are all correctly coloured. The scale is 63/1, and the model is, therefore, just a little too large for OO, and yet too small for O. This is a pity since it would undoubtedly add interest to any period model layout. It costs 3s. 11d .(19.5p)."

In 1960, the year that Lesney went public, it was thought to be the right time to put some rationale into the Yesteryear range. Up until then, Lesney had been adding models to the range with little or no strategy. To contain the Yester-year range, Lesney decided to stop the numbering at Y16. This policy was to continue until 1975. *Smith:* "People were saying to us, 'we can't keep having all this stuff'; so we thought 'chuck the old ones out and go back and do the same thing as we were doing with the "Matchbox" Series – and then up-date it in a limited range' . . . We didn't realise just how clever an idea that was. This was directly

opposite to what Dinky were doing as they just kept adding to their range and numbering them accordingly leaving vacant numbers in the range. Dinky went 1, 2, 3, 4, 5, 6 . . . at least up to 999."

The Shand Mason was initially issued with white horses and Kent Fire Brigade decals. The decals later changed to those of the London Fire Brigade, first with a double black line border and later

with a single gold line. The London liveries had black horses, but a short run of cross-overs exist, i.e. London Fire Brigade markings, but with white horses.

The boiler assembly can be found plated in gold or in some cases with the rear section un-plated. *Smith:* "It was a delicate casting and the back end was a bad assembly, as it was only one fixing . . . It's always a mistake to

have one fixing as there should always have been two." As the model progressed the number of slats at the rear of the boiler plat-form reduced from a maximum of eleven down to six. *Odell:* "The mould broke down and we had to fill it in because we couldn't put the detail back in." When the model changed from the Kent to the London version the tool was modified to remove the raised ribs which located the Kent decal. The Y4 Shand Mason was always a good seller and with the upsurge in popularity of early Yesteryears a fire engine was a natural choice. The Shand Mason, in fact, was thought by many collectors to be the most attractive of the early issues and it certainly became the most sought after. Each Shand Mason was issued with three plastic firemen, one of which was a driver. Firemen often came at-tached to a plastic sprue and usually in a plain brown paper bag. Very early firemen featured painted helmets and breast plates. *Smith:* "We used black plastic as it was cheap and put on a bit of gold to give some relief."

A Lesney advertisement from the Railway Modeller

Four variants of the much sought after Y4 Shand Mason Fire Engine.

Much interest was aroused by the initial model of the **Y6-4 Rolls Royce Fire Engine** introduced in 1977. *Simmons:* "The new model was based on one of two models produced by myself at the R. & D. Department for my own pleasure. A fire engine was required for the Yesteryear range in a hurry and the Rolls Royce was chosen to be produced but without the trailer pump. The ladder was taken from the MB35 Fire Engine with the side lugs removed. However, produc-

MODELS OF YESTERYEAR
1956 - 1988
PUBLIC SERVICE VEHICLES

Ref Number	Date of Issue	Model	First Livery	Scale
	1960	1905 Shand Mason Fire Engine	Y4-2 Red	1:63
Y6-4	1977	1920 Rolls Royce Fire Engine	Red	1:48
Y7-4	1985	1930 Ford Breakdown Truck	Orange	1:40
Y7-4	1988	1930 Ford Breakdown Truck	Yellow	1:40

tion versions left these in place and the lugs at the end added. A further modified version of this ladder was used in the MB22 Blazebuster. The original version of the ladder was to have been brown with no lugs." The first run of fire engines had white ladders which were soon replaced by brown versions. *Lister:* "Due to capacity difficulties this model was one that was assembled by a sub-contractor based in Waterlooville outside Portsmouth." These early models also had Y7

Y6 Fire Engine and Y7
Breakdown Truck.
Both of these models used parts
originally from other models in the
Yesteryear range.

cast into their chassis as the component was identical to the then current Silver Ghost. This was soon modified to read No Y-6 + 7. White ladders were re-introduced in 1983. A few models with brown ladders were also issued with a bright red driver's seat and this variation is most sought after. In 1984 the model appeared with black wings and running boards and was eventually withdrawn from the range in 1988.

The **Y7-4 1930 Ford Break-down Truck** in orange and featuring the livery *Barlow Motor Sales Quality Cars* was issued in 1985. The Research and Development Department used the then current Y21 Model 'A' Ford as the basis. They modified the cab, fitted a canopy in place of the cab roof and

opened up the rear to hold a plastic crane jib and hook. *Tekerian:* "That actual livery was featured in a photograph in Automotive Quarterly from America. The telephone number was also shown and so we dialled the number. The same family still own the vehicle . . . we told them that we were doing the livery. They were not too sure about letting us do it, so we told them we would send them some free models, to which they agreed." The tools for the breakdown truck were moved to Macau in 1986 and the last run of the truck featured a Macau baseplate. A new all yellow livery featuring *Shell* was introduced in early 1988.

SPORTS CARS

In 1956 when the Models of Yesteryear range was introduced, Smith and Odell had agreed not to involve J. Kohnstam & Co. Ltd. *Smith:* "We said no . . . listen now, we've got money to spend on this range and we've got to start getting our own little camp in order". Lesney realised the need to exploit the American market with their new range. At this time Richard Kohnstam had three importers in the U.S.A. This arrangement probably suited Moko with all the ramifications of supply and price cutting. The main figure of the three was Fred Bronner and Lesney gave him the sole right to distribute Models of Yesteryear in the U.S.A. The first thing Bronner asked for was a Model of Yesteryear of an American car. The Y13 Santa Fe had been popular with the

Americans, but being a railway locomotive it did not appeal to everyone, and so the **Y7/2 1913 Mercer Raceabout Sports Car** was introduced in 1961. It was also shown as a line drawing in the 1961 Pocket Catalogue. Originally it had been planned to replace the Y6/1 A.E.C. but the eventual collapse of the Y7/1 tools necessitated a quick change of plan. Known as a second series model, it, like the second series Y5 Bentley, featured a plastic component, black seating. The first livery was a metallic lilac purple shade with either brass or silver detailing. In 1964 the tool was found to be wearing and so the running boards on the model were filled in to strengthen the casting. This modification was further extended in 1965 and at the same time the model was recoloured in bright yellow. The original selling price was 3s. 11d. (19.5p).

Leslie Smith recalls how the years 1959 and 1960 were critical ones for Lesney. They had bought out Richard Kohnstam and they had gone public. They looked to their overseas market for expansion. *Smith:* "Our market in Germany wasn't very strong, and we thought to ourselves 'well this is not right', a great market of 50 million people. We had at this time an importer in Holland called Edor who had a brother-in-law called Jap Prins, who had just left the Dutch East Indies Company and was looking for something to do". Smith met Prins at the Harrogate Toy Fair, where he suggested to Prins that he start up a warehouse in Germany and continue trading under the name Edor. *Smith:* "In fact, he did, just the other side of the Dutch border in an old farm barn." Prins commuted each day from his home in Holland to his new warehouse in Bienen in Northern Germany. The policy on prices was agreed. *Smith:* "We have all got to try and make this a real goer and if we work closer together, let's go for a 1 D.M. Matchbox toy."

Y3 Riley M.P.H., Y7 Mercer and Y10 Mercedes Benz.
Top row: Left, A pre-production Riley originally designed with pre-standardised wheels.
Second row:
Left, A pre-production Mercer.
Third row: Right, A Mercedes with grey plastic seats.

By working on low margins and keeping expenses low Prins soon turned the German market into one of Lesney's biggest. By dealing closely with the new team in Germany, Lesney learned quickly of their needs. *Smith:* "They must have a better German car if we want them to sell more Yesteryears. They need a lead-in . . . something with nostalgia like the Rolls Royce."

The **Y10/2 1928 Mercedes Benz 36 – 220** was deemed a great success, especially with German collectors, as it was a famous

example and unlike the Y10 Mercedes G.P. it was instantly recognisable to most enthusiasts. It was first shown at the 1961 Harrogate Toy Fair and was eventually introduced into the range in 1963. *Smith:* "It was our first big order from Germany, a thousand gross order from the Kaufhalle chain of German departmental stores. From there we never looked back in Germany and just went from strength to strength."

The Mercer was announced to the public in this advertisement from the Railway Modeller.

The first runs of the new model were fitted, not only with two spare wheels on the rear of the car, but also with either black or grey plastic seats. Almost immediately the colour of plastic was changed to a bright red. For no other reason than a saving in costs, the model was later issued with only one spare wheel. This model was issued in a plated guise, and so the painted model can be found with baseplate holes fitted to earlier models but none on later issues.

In 1973 Edor became a subsidiary of Lesney and Prins became the Geschafts Fuhrer (Managing Director) of Lesney Spielwarren, Prins eventually retired in 1977. Lesney adopted the same policy in Australia with their importer George Leeman. *Smith:* "The reason why I liked Australia from the beginning was I knew George Leeman there very well . . . He sold our first toys and when his sons John and David got older they took over the business for him. We then bought them out and they carried on working for us." *Odell:* "Australia was another wonderful market for us. We sold more per head of the population in Australia than we did anywhere else in the world. There were only ten or twelve million people, but the quantity they bought was staggering . . . our aim was to bring as much foreign currency to England as we possible could."

The **Y3/3 1934 Riley MPH** was first shown to the toy trade in early 1973 at the Harrogate, Brighton and Nüremberg Toy Fairs. The trade were informed by Lesney that the new theme for Models of Yesteryear would be classic styled cars of the 1930s. *Smith:* "The hardest part often was to ask ourselves what are we going to make now – something new . . . Do we jump an era and go for, let's say, 1930s vehicles, as there are more dads alive now than there were with Packard Landaulets? . . . Has the nostalgia factor gone and burnt itself out?". The Riley went into production in September 1973 and the first small quantity were exported to Germany. However, with the recession and the introduction of the three day week, Lesney could not afford to package and distribute the already assembled models. The demand for the Superfast range was considerably higher and it was decided that the Models of Yesteryear range had to take a less prominent priority. It was not until late 1974 that the Y3 Riley eventually turned up in British shops, in newly designed packaging commonly referred to as Woodgrain boxes. A much increased influence of plastic was evident in the radiator seats, wheels, windscreen, horns and lights. Many shades of red are associated with this model varying from dark red through to a metallic reddish purple. The price in 1974 was 60 pence. In 1979 Lesney recoloured the Riley to a light blue body with a decal, usually No. 6 but sometimes No. 3. The Riley was taken out of the range in 1980.

The **Y14/3 1931 Stutz Bearcat** was another model that was first shown in early 1973 at the major toy fairs, but was not

*Y8 MG TC, Y19 Auburn and Y14
Stutz Bearcat.
Second row:
Left, A pre-production MG TC.*

finally issued until 1974. The baseplate was inscribed 1973 but because of the delay it was later changed to 1974. Early modifications to the two-tone green liveried model included a filling in of the original open rear bumper. Some models with the 1974 baseplate were issued with a dark red seat as opposed to the standard bright red; these are now rare. In 1979 Lesney changed the livery to cream and red. The paint sprayers encountered difficulties with the boat tail as the paint spread out of the designated pattern area. The tool was modified so that the boat tail featured a raised edge and this stopped the paint spreading. In 1981 the livery changed to an emerald green and cream and finally in 1985 to a mid-blue and grey. The Stutz Bearcat was

withdrawn from the range in 1986.

In 1978 Lesney introduced their first ever post-war classic, the **Y8/4 1945 M.G. T.C.** in dark green which also sported a No. 3 decal. The seat was normally red plastic, but a very early short run with tan seats were released. Further recolours were carried out until the model's demise in 1987 – 1981 bright red, 1983 mid-blue and 1984 cream and dark brown.

A further example of these 1930s classics was the **Y19/1 1936 Auburn Speedster** introduced into the range in 1979 and shown as a new model in the 1980 Trade Brochure. The brochure also extolled the

virtues of the range: 'This range is the collectors' dream. A series of faithfully reproduced vintage and veteran cars all with a history of excellence. The cars are all in authentic livery and come in a newly designed presentation (straw) box. This highly sought after range is updated by one or two models every year and collectors have been known to pay very high prices for discontinued models.'

The first livery of the Auburn was a three colour scheme – fawn brown bonnet and tail, creamy brown sides and a dark brown chassis. Various colour trials of the seat were produced and released and these include yellow, black, green and pink. The colour of the standard seat was eventually to be orange-red. In 1983 the colour scheme was changed to an off-white body with black chassis. The colour was changed once again in 1985 to a brilliant white with bright blue panels, seat and plastic wheel spokes and issued as a Limited Edition. The model was then withdrawn from the range.

With the demise of the Y1 Model 'T' Ford in 1976 Lesney decided to incorporate into the Models of Yesteryear range an all time British classic, the **Y1/3 1936 S.S. 100 Jaguar.** Simmons: "This model was also the first to be made to scale without any extra being added to the width." The model was introduced into the range in 1977, but almost immediately a modification was made to the side lights on the front wings. The early casting revealed two small protrusions which did not really look like side lights. They were also rather sharp and potentially dangerous to youngsters and so the tools were modified to enlarge the size and detail of the lights. Small ridges were added to the underside

of the running boards as models had been sticking to the conveyor belt during painting; these ridges reduced the contact area. Further the rib which supported the registration plate was strengthened. In 1978 after only one year in white the livery was changed to a metallic grey colour, which was quickly followed by a steel blue.

1981 saw the Jaguar issued in dark green and this colour lasted for five years. It had been decided by the Marketing Department to change the colour to yellow in 1986, but at the last minute the green livery was retained. The Rochford factory did not immediately follow the marketing instruction to postpone the change of colour and they sprayed five thousand Jaguars in yellow. When

Y1 Jaguar SS100 and
Y20 Mercedes 540K
Third row:Left, A preproduction
colour trial Mercedes.
Centre, A pre-production colour trial
Mercedes.

Ref Number	Date of Issue	Model	First Livery	Scale
MODELS OF YESTERYEAR 1956 –1988 SPORTS CARS				
Y1-3	1977	1936 SS 100 Jaguar	White	1:38
Y3-3	1973	1934 Riley MPH	Red	1:35
Y7-2	1961	1913 Mercer Raceabout	Lilac	1:46
Y8-4	1978	1945 MG TC	Green	1:35
Y10-2	1963	1928 Mercedes Benz 36-220	White	1:52
Y14-3	1974	1931 Stutz Bearcat	Green	1:44
Y19-1	1979	1936 Auburn Speedster	Brown	1:42
Y20-1	1981	1937 Mercedes Benz 540K	Silver	1:45

the Marketing Department discovered this they told the factory to repaint the majority of the unassembled models in green – these models were subsequently released and have a definite yellow hue. However, two thousand yellow models had already been assembled and these were exported to East Germany and the U.S.A., although it is known that one hundred models were stolen from

the factory and some even ended up in local retail shops. In 1987, with the move to Macau complete, the Jaguar colour was finally and officially changed from green to yellow. The model was issued in what the manufacturers refer to as Sunrise Yellow as opposed to the previous yellow which is known as Talbot Yellow. The new model was issued with a Macau baseplate and was packaged with a diorama.

In 1981 Lesney extended the range by producing the **Y20/1 1937 Mercedes Benz 540K**. The 1981 Trade Brochure showed the car with tan coloured seats. Trials had been carried out and various colour schemes such as metallic red and even metallic blue and silver were examined and rejected. Instead the first livery was metallic silver with black chassis. The model featured an opening dickey seat. Problems were encountered with the plastic mouldings and unsightly gaps appeared on either side of the red seat. The moulds were modified and the seat increased in width. Shades of red in the front seats vary. In 1985 the livery was changed to a brilliant white with contrasting red body stripes.

RACING CARS

There is something of an indistinct line to be drawn between racing cars and sports cars and racing cars

The 4.5 Litre Bentley has always been a popular choice for manufacturers and collectors alike.

are a category which Models of Yesteryear have not seen fit to model in great numbers. The first of nine such Yesteryears to be produced was the **Y5/1 1929 Le Mans Bentley.**

Introduced in 1956 early versions of this model had hand-painted detailing added to them to afford greater realism. Early models had silver radiator surrounds with grey tonneau covers but as time

progressed some of these details were omitted. The standard model had a gold radiator with no grey tonneau and a very small run was produced with the silver-plated steering wheel omitted in favour of a green painted version. In 1959, in common with the rest of the range, the pinched axles gave way to riveted versions. *Smith:* "The Bentley was, well, nostalgia comes into it . . . it was a car everyone

wanted to have. We made it a bit on the small side – it sold quite well."

The first version proved to be a reasonable seller and when the dies had worn-out it was replaced in 1962 with a larger and altogether more sophisticated model of the same car, the **Y5-2 1929 4.5 Litre Bentley.** *Smith:* "We had begun to realise as time went on that the Yesteryears ought to be bigger and

really give more value . . . OK, the first Bentley had sold quite well, it was worth investing in another . . . if we made it bigger it should be better." The first run of these models were painted in a rather unrealistic metallic apple-green shade and these models, which are now rare, were quickly replaced by a more accurate British Racing Green shade. Both colour schemes could be found with dark red and green plastic seats and tonneaus but by 1964 bright red tonneaus became standard. Early versions of this second casting looked realistic but the radiator shells were painted green. To alter this rather dull appearance the casting was changed to allow the radiator shell to be cast separately, hence avoiding the need to mask it separately. This improved appearance coincided with the introduction of the standard bright red tonneau. Two further variations appeared towards the end of the model's life a No. 6 in red, and a No. 3 in black were used instead of the No. 5. The Bentley was a popular model produced in great quantities and was not phased out until 1968.

The **Y2/4 1930 4.5 Litre Bentley** was introduced by the company sixteen years after the demise of the Y5 version. This completely new model designated Y2 was far larger than the old version, but featured a higher degree of plastic in its manufacture. A sub-contractor (Rayleigh Technical Design) in Essex made the moulds. This firm did not have diecasting machines and consequently the first shots were all in plastic. Production in diecast and plastic took place at the Rochford factory, once these moulds had been passed. The use of plastic has long been an issue between the company and its fervent following of collectors. The company favour plastic to reproduce accurately, fine detail such as the mudguard stays on the Bentley, which they felt would be of necessity thicker and more fragile if produced in metal. Collectors have always preferred diecast metal as they believe it gives a more solid feel to the model.

The Bentley has been reported with these plastic components in a darker shade than those of the body, due to a slight mis-match of the plastic colour compound. The Bentley, originally made at the Rochford factory, was continued in 1987 from Macau. *Tekerian:* "We should continue to look at re-introducing more cars of this era . . . one of the best cars we have ever done is the Bentley . . . still a good seller, it outsells all the other cars."

Vintage car enthusiasts must have been delighted with the introduction of the **Y6/2 1923 Type 35 Bugatti** in 1961. A drawing of the car was first shown in the 1961 Pocket Catalogue. Lesney had managed to capture the lines of the car perfectly, lines which are thought by many to be the purest of any pre-war racing car. *Railway Modeller News Special* November 1961: "The latest release in the Yesteryear series is the attractive Bugatti racing car, retailing at only 2s.11d. It is a model of the Type 3.5 and has been finished in the colours of one of these fine machines now privately owned in South Africa." The wheels, for which these Bugattis were famous, were of an ultra-sophisticated aluminium eight spoke variety and

were beautifully modelled. The only main casting change to the Bugatti actually occurred not to the body, but to the wheels. Very early production models featured grey tyres but these soon gave way to black heavily treaded versions. These in turn became much finer and this coincided with a thinning out of the wheel rims, no doubt to aid assembly. The very last run of the Bugatti in its original and authentic French racing blue featured the floor and dashboard in white, a component which was standard on the second livery of bright red.

There are only two variations of this model in its revised red livery. It is common to find the model with the radiator shell in gold or even completely untouched. Much rarer though is the existence of a red model with black dashboard and floor as opposed to the normal white.

In the first series of Yesteryears

Y6 Bugatti and Y10 Mercedes GP.

the only German vehicle was an early racing car, the **Y10/1 1908 Grand Prix Mercedes**. Although very well modelled for its size it fitted very uncomfortably into the range and stood rather on its own. It was badly out of scale with the other vehicles, yet its small overall size belied the fact that the original was actually an enor-mous vehicle with a twelve litre engine. Very few variations exist of this model except for minor casting changes. Later releases had a much darker green seat than before and a very few models appeared in pure white as opposed to the normal cream variety.

In the 1980s the emphasis for the choice of subject matter is clearly centred on commercial vehicles so it came as quite a surprise to collectors to see the release of four famous racing cars in 1986. The introduction of these cars was not entirely welcomed by collectors but the story behind their introduction has never before been fully related.

Senior management had decided that the huge growth in popularity of classic car racing would provide an opportunity for them to launch a small series of racing cars which could be linked by company sponsorship to a historic car racing event. These races were to be international and Matchbox would follow the Formula One events around Europe. In order to co-ordinate the dates for such an event the company had to commission the tooling some eighteen months before the actual races.

The true costs of this bold move did not emerge until work was well progressed on the models and in the event Matchbox realised that the finance and organisation involved were completely impractical. The idea was eventually shelved but as the models were at an advanced stage and are, incidentally, extremely accurate replicas, it was decided to release them as normal issues in specially designed Grand Prix boxes.

The first model released was the **Y10/4 1957 Maserati 250F** and the first 30,000 examples were produced without the full copyright description on the base. Later production bases were over-sprayed red, to match the bodies more closely, problems having been encountered with the colour of the plastic employed. The plastic moulded rear suspension units were also modified to reduce the amount of rear axle float evident on early releases.

A **Y11/4 1932 Bugatti Type 51** then followed. Once again, minor casting variations had to be made to the dashboard to correct the location of the dashboard and the body was marginally widened to reduce rear end axle float.

The third model of the series was undoubtedly the most interesting as this subject had never been commercially modelled before but was indeed a famous marque, the **Y14/4 1936 E.R.A.** The original model was to have been in blue and yellow but the death of its owner left the car's future ownership uncertain and so the colour scheme was altered to black.

The E.R.A. sold better than the other three and, in fact, was re-run in August 1988 in the original colours of blue and yellow. The plastic chassis was replaced by a diecast version, a move the Company recognised as being

Yesteryear Racing Cars.
Y11 Bugatti, Y14 ERA., Y16 Ferrari and Y10 Maserati.

Three first series passenger cars. Y8 Morris, Y15 Silver Ghost and Y16 Spyker.

beneficial to the model and appealing to collectors.

Last in this group came a **Y16/3 1960 Ferrari Dino 246/V-12**. As with the Maserati the brake drums were slightly enlarged to reduce rear end wheel float on the model.

PASSENGER CARS

The first passenger car was made in 1958, the **Y8/1 1926 Morris Cowley 'Bullnose'**. Until recently it was believed that originally the model was to have been issued with a towing hook, but this idea was shelved before the model was issued. *Simmons:* "The purported tow-hook is, in fact, an over-flow that allows the mould to fill completely; for some unknown reason it was not removed in

fettling. If an inspection is made of a chassis without this piece, it will be seen that the edge of the chassis casting is slightly rough in the central area where this over-flow piece has been broken off." The colour of tan varied slightly; early models had a lighter finish. As the model was in production until 1962 the two main types of axles are to be found, with later models always having riveted axles. *Smith:* "That one showed a lift in sales . . . There was a greater demand for that model than many of the others in that series."

During the months before going public Lesney thought that one way in which to attract some good publicity would be to include a Rolls Royce in the Yesteryear range. *Smith:* "Our first Marketing Manager, Peter Webb, made contact

with Lord Montagu and arranged for the Rolls Royce Silver Ghost to be put on display to get us some good publicity." The actual Rolls Royce was, of course, in silver, but Lesney at the time did not have a paint supplier capable of producing a suitable metallic silver. A compromise had to be reached with the paint suppliers, and so the **Y15/1 Rolls Royce Silver Ghost** was produced in a metallic green, and released in September 1960 to coincide with the flotation of Lesney Products & Co. Ltd. when Lesney went public on the 29 September 1960. Not only was it the first Model of Yesteryear to have a metallic finish, but it was also the first to feature plastic components other than plastic tyres already featured on the Y8/1 Cowley, the Y5/1 Bentley and the

Y10/1 Mercedes. The earliest models featured grey tyres and rear lights highlighted in red. As the model's life extended, the tyres changed to black and the highlights reduced. With time the tooling deteriorated, so the model was strengthened, most notably around the wheel braces. A short run of dark green plastic seats also associated with the silver plated giftware series occurred in the mid-1960s and the model eventually left the range in 1968. This model demonstrated to Lesney that there was a need for famous and recognisable marques within the range, and that rather obscure subjects such as Showman's Engines had limited international appeal. Lesney began to face up to the fact that consumers were more interested in saloons than commercials, or steam-driven vehicles.

AX 201 – The most famous Rolls-
Royce of all, being measured by
Lesney's Fred Rix and Ken Wetton
in 1965.

Amazing value indeed.

Smith: "When we produced the
Y15 Rolls Royce it told us that
there was a greater international
interest in cars than any other
Yesteryear model. The Y15 sold so
well because of its much bigger size
. . . This was the size to establish
for Yesteryears, and the market
recognised that it looked a handful,
and it looked right . . . The other
smaller ones in contrast were
almost too precious."

The only Dutch car ever to be
modelled in the range was the
**Y16/1 1904 Spyker Veteran
Automobile** and a drawing of the
car was first shown in the 1961
Pocket Catalogue. Originally it was
to have been issued in a two-tone
green livery. This colour scheme
was shown in the 1962 Pocket
Catalogue. It was advertised in the

AMAZING "MATCHBOX" VALUE!

See these all-star features for yourself

NEW AT ONLY 1'9

1 Double coat, lead-
   free, stove enamelled
   finish.
2 Flush-fitted windows.
3 Tinted roof-window.
4 Fully hinged and
   opening doors.
5 Dining table.
6 Seats.
7 Washbasins, etc.,
   modelled in relief.
8 Unbreakable plastic wheels.
9 Super-detailed, fine diecast
   exterior fittings.

New "Matchbox" Series No. 34, Volkswagen Caravette camping car. OO scale,
2½ inches long. Price 1/9.

"Models of Yesteryear" No.
Y-16, 1904 Spyker veteran car.
Brass-plated fittings, O scale,
over 3 inches long.
Price 4/-.

1962 catalogue now avail-
able at your "Matchbox"
store.
In case of difficulty
write direct sending
3d. stamp to Dept.
RM3, Lesney Products
& Co. Ltd., Eastway,
London, E.9.

NEW

Railway Modeller in July 1962. It
first appeared in a very creamy-
yellow colour, and soon after in a
more standard pale yellow. All
early models were given an
abundance of gold trim, all by
hand. There was a deviation from
the yellow livery in 1965; a small
batch were painted in a maroon
colour, identical in colour to the
then current Y13 Santa Fe. The
maroon model is extremely rare
and has been seen with or without
full gold trim and in a few cases
with wheels taken from the then
current Y6 Bugatti. Towards the
end of its production, the shade of
yellow was considerably darkened
and much of the gold trim was
deleted.

During the late 1950s Lesney
began to increase the international
flavour and distribution of the
Yesteryear range. Smith, who co-
ordinated distribution, was not
happy with their French importer
who had been originally
introduced to Lesney by Richard
Kohnstam. Lesney's trade in
Yesteryears in France was poor,
and when there was an order, the
models had to be packed up in tea
chests and shipped across from
England direct to the importer.

A meeting took place in France
with the importer who volunteered
to give up his rights to distribute
Lesney products. Smith asked him
if he knew of anyone who might be
prepared to undertake the now
vacant position. *Smith:* "I was told
by the importer 'I think I've got the
man for you, he knows the toy
trade'." His name was Georges
Bieber. His English wasn't good
and neither was Smith's French,
but they immediately struck up a
good relationship using a form of
sign language. Smith and Bieber
came up with a marketing strategy
that they termed 'Our Franco-
Domicile'. Bieber had worked for
thirty-one years with the well-
known French toy manu-
facturing company, Compagnie
Industrielle du Jouet (C.I.J.). When
he met Leslie Smith in 1961,

he was the Commercial Director of C.I.J.

Bieber began to visit wholesalers, show them the Matchbox range and take their orders. *Smith:* "The orders would be collected by Bieber and sent to Lesney U.K. who packed up the orders and sent the total consignment to a forwarding agent in Paris, who in turn distributed the individual orders throughout France. Bieber would invoice the wholesaler from his French office. Georges would

Georges Bieber on the occasion of his retirement in 1978.

do all the talking to the wholesalers. Any troubles with his wholesalers – they could ring up Georges . . . it made the wholesalers feel that the whole operation was French!" Bieber wanted to increase the appeal of

Y1 Ford 'T' and Y2 Renault – two cars to reflect the growing international flavour of the range in the 1960s.

the range to the French and pleaded with Smith. *Smith:* "He asked for years for a Renault . . . I must have a Renault – I must have a French car."

By 1962 Bieber had established himself as the exclusive agent for Lesney. In 1972 this agency became Lesney France and Bieber became the Managing Director, He eventually retired from Lesney in 1978.

The **Y2/2 1911 Renault Two Seater** was eventually introduced

in mid-1963 and was shown in drawing format in the 1963 Pocket Catalogue as a new Model of Yesteryear. The drawing was a much more accurate representation of the actual 1911 Renault and included a rear folded-down hood. Lesney had anticipated that the livery was going to be a metallic silver, but due to the poor quality of silver metallic paints from their paint suppliers, the scheme colour was changed to green. Early models were fitted with a four-pronged spare tyre carrier. This was changed later to one with three prongs. As with many of these second series models, the metal steering wheel and column were later replaced by an all black plastic component. The Renault was deleted from the range in 1969, but in the same year the Y5 1907 Peugeot was introduced so ensuring a continued French representation.

The **Y1/2 Ford Model 'T'** was introduced in 1964 at the request of the U.S.A. exclusive distributor of Matchbox, Fred Bronner. Odell made the tools quickly and the 1964 Collectors' Catalogue revealed the 'T' Ford as being a 'new' model shown in a bottle green livery with black running boards. The accurate colour should, of course, have been black, but although trial models were made in black, it was thought to be too sombre and so a brighter colour was chosen, dark red! *Smith:* "It just looked better in red." The first production issues of the model featured a finely cast twin-levered handbrake which was almost immediately changed to a single less detailed version. The model continued until 1970, but two other noticeable variations were the change from metal to black plastic steering wheels and in 1968 a few examples were produced featuring a black textured roof. Both the first and last types of models are rare and valuable.

The first ever Collectors' Club model to be based on a Yesteryear.

Following the relaunch of the range in 1974 the model appeared with a cream body and red chassis together with a red textured roof, red upholstery and the larger style wheels. A very few also appeared with this textured roof in black. In 1976 the Matchbox Collectors' Club ordered a 'limited' amount of all black Y1 Model 'T's'. These were sold at U.S. $5.50 each including postage and packaging exclusively to the members. This particular variation has since been classified as a Code 2 model. (For further information see the Code 2 sub-section). In 1984 Matchbox International refurbished the old tools of the Y1 Model 'T' Ford, and relaunched the model with five

other models in what was known as the Connoisseur's Set. The Y1 was painted in black and the textured black roof was stamped 'Limited Edition' to differentiate it from the earlier and much sought after earlier black model and roof.

In the same year, 1964, to complement the Y1 Ford Model 'T' in the range, Lesney decided to replace the Y11 Steam Roller with another American car, this time the **Y11/2 1912 Packard Landaulet**. The colour of the red body can vary with later models having a more orange shade of red. With the need to save on expenses, and just like the Model 'T' Ford, metal steering wheels were eventually replaced with black plastic steering

wheels. The finish to the metal plating also varied, some with a silver finish, others with brass. In 1972 the Y11 Packard was withdrawn, but in 1984 it was relaunched again, this time in a two-tone brown livery in the Connoisseur's Set.

In 1959, with the amalgamation of Moko into Lesney, Les Smith found that there was now greater direct liaison between Lesney and their overseas distributors. The German market, under Prins, had enjoyed increased success with the range after the introduction of the Y10 1928 Mercedes Benz 36 220E in 1963. They asked for more German cars, and were rewarded for their persistence in 1965 with the inclusion of the **Y3/2 1910 Benz Limousine**. *Smith:* "They, like the Americans, began to demand their own models like the Benz." *Miniature Autoworld* April 1966: "The Matchbox Yesteryear replica was produced with the co-operation of Daimler-Benz and is modelled on an actual car in their famous museum at Stuttgart." The first livery was in all over cream with dark green roof, grille and seats. Alternative red seats and grille were also produced, and any combination can be found. A brighter and more attractive scheme was introduced in 1969, and obvious mismatching of coloured components occurred so that examples of the cream model have been found with the lemon roofs of the light green 1969 model. Metal steering wheels were phased out in 1969 and were replaced with black plastic components. 1970 saw the model colour change to a dull dark green with black roof and a continuation of red seats. As with

Y3 Benz, Y14 Maxwell and Y11 Packard.
Top row: Centre, The American style of blister packs.
Second row: Centre, A proposed two-tone colour scheme - unissued.

the Y1 Model 'T' Ford, the Y3 Benz was relaunched in 1984 as part of the Connoisseur's Set, this time in black and blue.

A further American car was the **Y14/2 1911 Maxwell Roadster** which was added to the range in 1965. It was, however, first shown in the 1964 Collector's Catalogue in overall gold with dark red seat, black hood and green spoked wheels. The scale of the intended model was to be 1/43 and the length 79 mm (3.13"). Changes were considered and the 1965 Catalogue showed the Maxwell in a blue livery and with a very different hood that featured straps attached to the car body. The length of the model was also increased to 82 mm (3.25") and the scale altered to 1/49. However, neither of these two liveries ever appeared on the released Maxwell. The hood supports were discarded as being too expensive to produce. The Maxwell was issued in a turquoise livery and was usually fitted with a red seat and a black smooth or textured roof. Both the Y1 Model 'T' Ford and the Maxwell were regarded as being a further step forward. *Smith:* "We grabbed for a tourer because it gave us another little shape with a canopy on top . . . it made for variety and so the range just didn't look like the style of the Spyker." One early variation of note is the Maxwell fitted with a gold finished rear petrol tank. The standard finish was copper. Although the Maxwell was withdrawn in 1973, it was re-introduced into the range in 1984 in a dark green and cream livery in the Connoisseur's Set.

1966 is regarded by some

Y4 Opel and Y13 Daimler – two second series cars.

Y6 Cadillac and Y12 Thomas Flyabout.
Top row: Left, A pre-production Cadillac.
Second row: Centre. The much sought after Thomas with yellow seats.

collectors as being the technical peak of perfection for Models of Yesteryear under Lesney. The **Y13/2 1911 Daimler** was introduced in a bright yellow with sharply contrasting seats in black plastic. Early models featured a two-line inscription on the base-plate, and the spare wheel was closed in on the running board. To brighten up the model the colour of seats was changed to a dark red, and soon after the mould was altered to open up the spare wheel. Early details such as brake and clutch pedals were later aban-

doned in the interest of cost. Towards the very end of its production life the baseplate was modified and the two line inscription was extended to three lines. Although production of the Daimler had ceased by 1973 it was included in the 1984 Connoisseur's Set in a two-tone blue livery.

The steadily increasing influence of the German market resulted in the introduction of the **Y4/3 1909 Opel Coupe** in 1967. There are

three distinct colours found on what was known as the 'doctor's car'. The model was initially issued in white with a tan coloured hood, which was attached to the body by two small cast-in body pegs found on either side, near the dark red seat. Not only did the colour of the seat change to a brighter red, but the tool was changed to delete the body pegs from the sides of the body, but still retaining the rear ones. The seat

was then moulded with these pegs to secure the hood. The roof too had many variations, the standard finish being smooth and tan, but examples of roofs with a textured finish are known. The roof was redesigned for the 1974 recoloured model (orange) with a rear window. However, the last run of white models was fitted with tan roofs featuring this window in an attempt to complete the last batches of the white version. The orange model only lasted two years before being replaced by the Y4-4 Duesenberg. In 1984 the

Connoisseur's Set was issued containing the Y4 Opel in bright and dark red livery with a tan roof.

In 1967 the **Y12/2 1909 Thomas Flyabout** was introduced as a new model. The model was shown in the 1967 Collector's Catalogue in a rich red livery, black seats and roof. The model was released, however, in a deep metallic sea-blue livery, tan roof and bright yellow plastic

secured to the body via metal body pins to the more common practice of being secured to the seats. In 1974 the model was relaunched in a metallic purple with black roof, white seats and larger size wheels. It was withdrawn in 1979.

1968 saw the inclusion of the **Y6/3 1913 Cadillac** in gold with a

with many differently coloured seats as opposed to the standard colour of yellow. There had been complaints from the trade that models such as the Y6 Cadillac, which had been sitting in their see-through boxes, often under fierce display lights deteriorated: the radiator grilles shrank and fell out,

alongside normal issues. In fact, Lesney never found a completely non-shrink plastic, instead they had to rely on improved pins, pegs and lugs to secure grilles, hoods and seats. The issue of melting tyres was resolved by changing from rubber to a material called Polyfleet and then to a compound known as E.V.A. *Lister:* "We also had a fire at Rochford at this time

Y7 Rolls Royce and Y9 Simplex.
Third row: Left, A pre-production Simplex.

seats and grille. This model was based on the actual Thomas Flyabout situated at the Harrah's Automobile Collection, Reno, U.S.A. The yellow plastic seats were a very short run and were quickly replaced by a dark red colour. The plastic roofs were produced in either a smooth or a textured finish. One rare variation has the '1909 THOMAS FLY-ABOUT' inscription on the base-plate reversed. After several years the roof was changed from being

red plastic hood and seat. The 1968 Collector's Catalogue actually featured the Cadillac in a blue livery with yellow seats and grille and a tan hood. The baseplate of the Y6 Cadillac usually read '1913', but a short run left the factory with a modification to the baseplate, '913' instead of '1913'. Various shades of gold exist with the lighter shades being associated with models made in the late 1960s, and darker gold between 1970 and 1973. In 1974 the colour of this model was changed to green. This model can be found

the seats contracted and became loose and the tyres became flat and lumpy. As a result Lesney put out tenders for a non-shrinking plastic. Samples arrived and it was not practical to have them colour matched to the current colours being used, such as yellow for the Y6 Cadillac. The plastic components were moulded in various colours of no consequence – blues, greens, reds, purples and whites – and some of them were removed from the production line for testing. The balance were assembled, packaged up and sold

which destroyed a lot of our plastic . . . a number of concessions were given so that we could maintain production." In 1981, four years after the model had been discontinued, a large batch of unboxed green models were discovered in one of the ware-houses. These were packaged in Y6 Rolls Royce Fire Engine boxes and sold through shops at £1.00.

With the imminent demise of the Y15 Rolls Royce Silver Ghost in 1968, Lesney pre-planned the event with the inclusion of the

Y7/3 1912 Rolls Royce. The first livery was that of a silver body with the roof (initially unribbed) in red matching the chassis. Lesney at this time were using paint obtained from both Berger and Porter Paints. *Smith:* "We used to keep two going and they were always fired up to get something new and different out . . . one of them at last

tooling was modified to include retaining lugs on the underneath of the roof. Batches of new lugged components were painted in red, and this red half-ribbed roof on a silver and red body became the standard issue until 1972. It was decided to revamp the livery for the relaunch in 1974. The new

half roof lasted until 1979 when the model was revamped in bright yellow and black. The baseplate was modified to include both Y6 and Y7, as the baseplate was common to both the 1912 Rolls Royce and the Y6 1920 Rolls Royce Fire Engine. The Y7 Rolls Royce was withdrawn in 1984 and

fittings was initially released. The shade of green was soon changed to a more medium green. Due to the problem of shrinkage of the plastic, the lugs retaining the roof were switched from the body to the sides of the seat. The modified mould was first used in 1970 and Lesney took the opportunity to change the colour of the model to a

Y5 Peugeot and Y8 Stutz. The Peugeot gave rise to several rare variants..

brought out a good silver paint." Shortly afterwards there followed an unribbed grey roof. A new casting was then made which changed the rear section of the roof to a ribbed pattern. This grey ribbed roof version is now rare. *Grundy:* "The modification on the roof was done to square the body sides up during assembly as the body tended to bend in during the fettling process." It was noticed that the roof, however, had a tendency to become loose. The

livery had a gold body with red chassis and larger style wheels. However, transitional models were produced and released including a run of models finished in gold and silver with a silver bonnet. Lesney took the opportunity to revise the spare tyre carrier as the new style of bigger tyres was about to be launched. Some of the pre-1974 models were fitted with this new-style spare tyre carrier. This new livery of gold and red with a red

replaced by the Y7 Breakdown Truck.

The theme of American cars was further extended in 1968 with the introduction of the **Y9/2 1912 Simplex**. It was first seen in the 1968 Collector's Catalogue on the same page that described the Models of Yesteryear range: "The 'Matchbox' – 'Models of Yesteryear' series is a wonderful collection of miniature reproductions based on the finest cars ever made." A lime-green car with tan roof and red

metallic gold and red with black roof. This was changed in 1973 to an all over bright red with yellow seats and black roof. A further change took place in 1979 – the red was darkened and the chassis was given a black finish. In 1986 the model was given one final colour change, this time to yellow with black chassis, brown seats and black roof. The model was also packaged with a contemporary looking diorama.

More American saloon cars

Y2 Vauxhall, Y10 Rolls Royce and Y15 Packard Victoria.

followed in 1969. A metallic red liveried **Y8/3 1914 Stutz** was produced with smooth tan roof, petrol tank in copper, seat in green and rear tyre retainer straps and luggage box in black. However, there are many variations known including textured tan roofs, petrol tanks in gold and seats, tyre retainer straps and rear luggage box in bright red. In 1974 the model was relaunched with larger style tyres in an all over blue. Once again several different coloured components are associated with the blue Stutz. The model was replaced by the Y8/4 M.G. T.C. in 1978.

With the demise of the Y2 Renault, Bieber suggested and Lesney agreed to produce a model of a **1907 Peugeot** to maintain the French flavour as the Y5/3 in the range. The model was shown for

the first time in the 1969 *Collectors' Catalogue* as a coloured drawing, not in yellow but in blue. The actual Peugeot used by Lesney to make their model was on display in the Bonnal Renaulau Museum and full credit was afforded to the Museum on the model's baseplate. The very early models were without a beading trim on the rear vertical edge of the front seat. The colour of the plastic windows got progressively paler, beginning with a dark amber shade and eventually ending with clear windows. These clear windowed models are now very rare and it is known that the majority of this production run went to South Africa. In 1974 the livery was dramatically changed to a gold body with a black chassis. The colour of the plastic windows went back to a pale orange shade and remained this colour for the rest of

its life. A member of the Lesney Corporation, U.S.A., who visited Lesney in 1976, requested a quick on the spot variation to create a bit of interest in the American market. It was agreed to do a short run with black roofs and these were, in the main, distributed solely in the U.S.A. There are many different shades of gold associated with this model ranging from a light gold to a much deeper orange gold. The Peugeot was withdrawn from the range in 1978.

The popularity of the Rolls Royce marque encouraged Lesney to add a further Rolls Royce to the range in 1969. The **Y10/3 1906 Rolls Royce Silver Ghost** appeared in a slightly larger scale than the Y15 Silver Ghost, but once again in a non-authentic colour, metallic lime green. After the relaunch of the Yesteryear range in 1974 it appeared in even more unrealistic

colours, overall white with either a metallic purple chassis, or dark red chassis. It was only in 1979 that Lesney finally reproduced the Silver Ghost that was indeed silver! *Lister:* "Silver is one of the most difficult paints to get. To get a good coverage you have to use a lot of paint because it tends to be very thin . . . Basically, two coats have to be put on and that is expensive." A reasonably short run of Y10 Rolls Royces were fitted with bright yellow seats in 1983. However, the standard colour of plastic components was originally black, which later changed to dark red. The Y10 Rolls Royce was withdrawn in 1985.

In 1969 a new theme emerged within the Models of Yesteryear range – 'classic cars of the thirties' – which was developed further in 1974. The first subject was the **Y15/2 1930 Packard Victoria**. The initial livery was a metallic brown-gold body with a dark brown chassis. The plastic components were usually a maroon colour, but some production runs were issued with black. With the cessation of the range in 1973, the model reappeared in 1974, this time in a more golden colour and the old style tyres were replaced with standardised ones. In 1979 the livery was changed to red and black, and finally in 1984 to cream and dark brown. This colour scheme was the same as the Lesney plastic kit version of the Packard Victoria. All these liveries have been found with countless combinations of plastic components, some genuine, and some less so. The model was eventually replaced by the Y15/3 Preston Tram in 1987.

The immediate successor to the Renault was the **Y2/3 1914 Prince Henry Vauxhall**, introduced in 1970 in a colour scheme of red and silver with gold or brass trim. An extremely rare variation was produced in 1974 during the period when the model was being recoloured to blue and silver. The new coloured model was to be fitted with copper petrol tanks, and it is known that the last few red models leaving the factory were fitted with these new components as the source of brass components had been exhausted. *Simmons:* "Interestingly, the filler is horizontal. When the prototype model was made the filler was vertical, but after being dropped in the tool room and the tank breaking off it was hastily stuck back on the wrong way round, and then passed to the drawing office who faithfully copied the error." The 1975 Catalogue showed the blue model with bright red plastic seats and a black radiator grille. Two thousand of these models were manufactured solely for the East European market, and for obvious reasons are now extremely rare. When this short run was finished, the pre-1974 colour scheme of white seats was adopted. The blue

Top row: Left,
A pre-production model. Centre, A colour trial model.
Right, The rare purple colour.
Second row: Left, The standard maroon colour.
Centre, The rare pink shade.
Right, The rare dark red issue.

and silver Vauxhall with white seats was produced until 1979. In 1984 collectors expressed disappointment at being offered a newly coloured model, which rather unimaginatively was close to the basic colour of red and silver, although this time at least the chassis was finished in black. The Prince Henry Vauxhall was withdrawn at the end of 1984.

Lesney's policy of making new models is evident with the **Y11/3 1938 Lagonda Drophead Coupe** issued in 1972. It had followed on from the new size concept first started with the Y15 Packard Victoria and simultaneously expanded with the Y16 S.S. Mercedes Benz. Many collectors regard 1972 as being a major watershed in their collecting as some expressed dislike of this larger scale and the more obvious use of plastic components. Few realised that, for other reasons one year later, Lesney would have to

cease the Yesteryear production for a time, and it is clear that many collectors gave up the hobby completely during this period. This classic Lagonda was the subject of many colour experiments. The standard colour in 1972 was to be dark maroon, but it was only by trial and error that Lesney eventually achieved the issued colour scheme. Lesney had been experimenting with a new paint process whereby they gave the model a basecoat, then applied a coloured dye and finished it with a clear lacquer. *Smith:* "The paint for the second coat was like a dye and it all depended on how much was put into it . . . the lacquer was to give some glitter." While Lesney

were trying to perfect the deep maroon finish they released fully finished models in various shades beginning with purple then dark red, then pinky red and eventually maroon. Soon after the purple Lagonda was on the production line it was decided to alter the chassis. *Simmons:* "Due to the front and rear bumpers being identical, they could be put on upside down. The fixing rivets were of two sizes to prevent this, but this caused problems in production; so the rivets were made equal in size. To prevent the bumpers being put on upside down small pips were added to the underside." Many maroon models have purplish baseplates; this is not the rare early version but merely one that had a weaker application of dye.

In 1974 the model was relaunched with thicker tyres and in a rather ornate livery of orange and gold. Various combinations of

Y16 Mercedes. Top row: Left, A pre-production model.

coloured plastic components are associated with this 1974 issue. In 1979 the model was recoloured in beige and black and finally in 1985 in a deep red colour, as part of a special Fathers' Day Gift Set.

With the demise of the two Y10 Mercedes cars, it was felt essential to maintain interest in Germany by finding another German car. The **Y16/2 1928 Mercedes Benz S.S. Coupe** was agreed upon and was launched in 1972. The first run model was fitted with a differential casting on either side of the rear axle. This was soon removed. *Grundy:* "The reason for removal was so that the pin-feeding machines could be used. These were pre-production castings." At

the same time the smooth rear luggage trunk was given a textured finish. In 1974 the livery was changed from red and silver to a metallic lime-green colour. There then followed a two-tone green Mercedes. Paint being used for the Y14 Stutz Bearcat chassis was used for the Mercedes chassis. This was a reasonably short run and was undertaken at the request of the American Lesney subsidiary to stimulate interest amongst collectors in the U.S.A. The great majority of two-tone green Mercedes went to that market, and were sold as standard models. With this short run finished, the livery reverted to a single colour metallic lime-green. For a short while the Y16 Mercedes was

issued with dark green plastic components rather than the standard black plastic. In 1976 a further casting modification was made to the baseplate; the very attractive brass plated exhaust system was withdrawn and instead an exhaust system was cast into the baseplate. It was originally thought that this was another necessary cost saving exercise by Lesney. In fact, when the original exhaust pipes were cast they were put in bulk into the tumbling machine to remove excess flashing. Frequently the ends of these components became entangled with each other so that by the time they were plated many of them were unusable. *Grundy:* "Mainly it affected final assembly due to

bending which could not be picked up by the eye due to the shape of the component." They were then cut short to reduce the chances of entanglement. Additional casting detail was added to the baseplate to replace the pipe. In 1979 the livery was changed to all-over white. However, a short run did leave the factory with a black chassis. *Grundy:* "No samples were submitted by me to the R. & D. Department due to the problem of matching white paint on the body and base. The base also got marked by the card in the tins and caused scrap. The R. & D. turned it down as at that time black was not in favour." 1981 saw a further new colour, mid-blue body with grey side panels. Two things then happened in the space of a few

Y17 Hispano Suiza.
Top row: Left, A pre-production model.
Second row: Right, A colour trial model.
Third row: Right, A colour trial model.

months in 1983. First, a genuine mistake happened at the Rochford factory in that the paint line ran out of grey paint. A concession was granted to use a pale shade of blue. The production run of this two-tone blue model was only 5,000. Shortly afterwards the factory created their own 15,000 run variation by replacing the standard grey paint with fawn paint, to fit the production programme while waiting for the specified grey paint to be delivered. Once this run was finished, the standard grey was continued. In 1985 the Y16 Mercedes was issued with a modification, the erected hood was replaced with a folded down roof. The livery was also changed to bright red and silver, and was issued as a Limited Edition. The model was finally

replaced in 1986 by the Y16 1960 Ferrari.

The **Y17/1 Model 1938 Hispano Suiza** was released in 1975. *Matchbox Catalogue* 1975: "'Models of Yesteryear' are a collection of seventeen superlative models of classic early motor cars. Each model is a tastefully produced true-to-scale replica of the original car, complete with finely detailed 'chrome' trimmings, ornate grilles, and life-like upholstery." Why had it taken so long to expand the range? *Smith:* "Mainly we just could not break out of the mould. By 1975 we had beefed up our Research & Development Department, and we felt that they

should now be able to add one or two further new models each year." It had been shown as a new model in the 1973 Catalogue and the copyright date 1973 was still on the baseplate. The prototype model in silver and black, as shown in the catalogue, was made using components of the Y11 Lagonda. Preproduction models had louvres on the bonnet, rather than the small door panels found on production versions. The first production versions finally appeared in 1975 in a dark metallic red body with gloss black mudguards. In 1980, the livery changed to metallic silver and light blue. Shortly afterwards the livery

changed to silver with a black chassis. In 1986 the colour scheme changed to a dark two-tone green, and each model was packaged with a contemporary background diorama. Production of the Hispano Suiza later continued at the Macau factory.

The most famous and sought after model within the range is the white, red and yellow **Y4/4 1930 Duesenberg Model 'J' Town Car** introduced in 1976. This particular model has changed hands between dealers and collectors for prices sometimes in excess of £1,800. The reason being that the very few examples that were made have survived. For many years authoritative sources classified the model as being a preproduction model – only twelve being made – which was rejected by the directors as being too toy-like and garish. With time it has become accepted that more than twelve have been located and in a survey carried out by M.I.C.A. in 1988 from amongst 7,000 interested collector members some 15 were reported to exist. Due to its rarity this model and livery was chosen to be part of the M.I.C.A. logo in 1986 (For further information see Chapter Twelve). One hundred and forty four models are believed to have been pro-

obvious premium price being asked for genuine models, private individuals (without the permission of Matchbox International) now offer for sale at a nominal price repainted standard Duesenbergs in white, red and yellow. Collectors can spot an original genuine model by using the following checks: Red chassis and wings, white body and yellow plastic roof and seats; smaller window to the rear of the roof; the

secured by a rectangular shaped frame. Slight variations occurred, the most notable being solid or hollow fronted horns and a very short run of models with an experimental maroon coloured seat. In 1979 the livery was changed to two-tone green with a green roof and seat. The initial short run of models had a pale green rear panel. This was later changed to match the overall light green of the car. Just before the

Yesteryear range had been fairly steady, but interest was beginning to wane . . . Some new input was needed, especially the cars . . . Some new charismatic cars of the 1930s were produced to take the range out of the 1910s and 1920s. This was a deliberate attempt to make the range more up-to-date and vital." Early trials of the model were in white with red plastic components. Several of these pre-production models, none

Y4 Duesenberg.
Top row: Left, The original model maker's prototype.   Centre, The much sought after and most famous issue.
Foreground: Right, Unreleased colour trial with extended side panel decoration.

duced, boxed and distributed to countries such as Mexico and Northern Ireland.

There are known to have been several casting imperfections with this model and Lesney were not at all happy with the roof in particular. Upon seeing the quality of these early fully assembled and finished models Lesney stopped production, made basic modifications and chose a new livery. Due to the lack of available models to satisfy collectors and the

number Y4 engraved on to the plate securing the bumper; an X shaped frame underneath the roof; a larger front rivet on the baseplate and shorter pegs to secure the front bumper plate. Equally as rare is the red, white and yellow model with a black roof, again with the X shaped frame.

The all red livery was introduced in 1976 with a black hood that was

two-tone green model was phased out a short run of black plastic components were incorporated. 1983 saw the model revamped in a two-tone brown with various shades of beige-brown plastic fittings. In 1986 a run of blue and silver models were made.

1979 saw the range extended with the **Y18/1 1937 Cord 812**. *Tekerian:* "During the 1970s the

featuring the Y number on the baseplate, left the factory, but they were never officially issued. The first colour of a red body and white plastic components lasted until 1983 when the colour changed to a plum-maroon colour. The Cord was withdrawn from the range in 1985. *Matchbox Collectors' Club* 1979: "Mr Skip Marketti, Executive Director of the Auburn Cord Duesenberg Museum, had this to say to Lesney Products – 'Congratulations, you have recreated the spirit of the car. The body dimensions and appointments are accurately and faithfully re-produced'." A new model was introduced in 1983, the **Y24/1 1927 Bugatti Type 44**, at the request of the Marketing Department. It was felt that such a famous marque

Y18 Cord and Y24 Bugatti.
Top row : Left, A pre-production colour trial Cord.
Foreground: Left, A pre-production Bugatti. Right, An original Cord, built solely in white metal.

replaced mask spraying; consequently, the shade of yellow changed from a dark yellow to a pale lemon colour. This tampo process also required Matchbox to alter slightly the overall design of the model by incorporating a thin yellow line below the window on the doors. The door handle was also highlighted in black. Two further developments occurred in relation to the castings. First, the

chassis at the back of the wings was strengthened by filling the space that had existed between the rear wings and the petrol tank. Secondly, the rear window was reduced in size to improve the flow of metal into the roof space during casting. In December 1986 all the tools associated with the Bugatti were transferred to Macau. The livery was changed in 1987 to a maroon chassis and side

panels and a light grey body. These models were also issued with a French theme diorama.

One model which will not fit into the categories under which Models of Yesteryear are described is the **Y8-2 Sunbeam Motorcycle and Sidecar** and so it has been included under this passenger car section.

It is Jack Odell's opinion that in many ways this model set the standard by which others could be judged. *Odell:* "When I made that and people could see what could be made in diecast, that was it". Indeed, the fineness of casting apparent in this model was to give rise to a golden age of Yesteryears, with such models as the Y13 Daimler and the Y2 Vauxhall displaying beautifully thin cast and accurate wheels. The model was introduced in 1962, but was not that popular with collectors, mainly because of its plated finish. *Smith:* "It was plated because when it was painted it didn't look so nice. It was probably to have been green . . .

Y21 B.M.W. and Y8 Sunbeam.
Second row: Centre, Colour trials.
Foreground: More colour trials.

should always be represented in the range. In 1981 the R. & D. Department contacted Hugh Conway, the historian, who supplied Lesney with photographs and the whereabouts of a Type 44. Final trials of the model were completed in March 1982 featuring a silver chassis, red body and yellow side panels. Although the original Type 44 was dark blue with black roof and wings, Matchbox decided to launch the model in overall black with yellow side panels. These were the colours in which the original car had been resprayed following restoration. The first models appeared on the market in August 1983 and early versions featured yellow panels that were created by mask spraying. By 1984 the technique of tampo printing was so advanced that this process

maybe two colours, but it didn't look right and the .problem was to combine the colours without it looking wrong. Electro-plating (also known as vacuum coating) was becoming fashionable and when we saw it we said 'Yes, this looks good' – it brought a bit of glitter to it. We used electro-plating for the simplicity of having a uniform colour. It triggered off another dimension without realising it." Many of the variations which accompany this model are now extremely rare. These include unspecified numbers in a gold finish and others with bright green sidecar seats. The last run of all had this sidecar seat in black plastic. As the tool for the plastic seat was near to exhaustion many of the black seats show signs

of .wear. The model was also one of .several different Yesteryear models given away free by Mobil Petrol as part of a service station promotion in 1966. *Smith:* "Sales were quite good on this one."

In 1981 Lesney considered relaunching the Sunbeam Motorcycle to commemorate the twenty-fifth anniversary of Models of Yesteryear. A small batch of motor cycles were made using existing Lesney Y8 tools and painted in various liveries including blues and reds. An assortment of colour plastics were fitted. Although the motorcycle was seriously considered, it was eventually rejected and instead the then current Y12 Model 'T' Ford Van was chosen.

As this book was going to print in late 1988 a further new model .was

added to the range at the behest of the German market. Although this model, strictly speaking, should not be included in this section it has been included here for convenience – the **Y21/4 1955 B.M.W**. *Tekerian:* "When Matchbox acquired the Dinky brand this model was considered to be included in the Dinky Collection due to it being post-war. As tooling progressed we realised that the B.M.W. wouldn't be 1:43rd scale, it was decided to launch the model as a Yesteryear after all but as a Special Limited Edition."

The B.M.W. was issued with a blue body, red interior and black hood. The model was both limited and special in that a minimum number were made, i.e. only sixty thousand pieces worldwide. It was unique in that it was the first Model of Yesteryear to feature an opening bonnet.

COMMERCIAL VEHICLES

The original Models of Yesteryear range, in its first series, featured several commercial and public service vehicles, but early public and, significantly, international reaction was not entirely favourable. In particular, the American market could not identify with such thoroughly British names as Leyland, A.E.C. and Sentinel. These early commercial vehicles were also felt to be too small and too similar to the miniatures, and so these first series models, so avidly collected today, came to be withdrawn and replaced by larger passenger and sports cars. These cars came to dominate the range almost entirely for fifteen years and it was not until the introduction of the famous Y5-3 Talbot that this trend was reversed. In fact, this reversal was of enormous significance and will be discussed later.

The first lorry to appear was the **Y6-1 A.E.C. Four Ton Lorry** in the livery of *Osram Lamps*. The vehicle was discovered in one of the many reference books kept at Lesney and the G.E.C. company which made Osram Lamps was well known in the area. *Smith:* "We went through the books and said: That's it, use Osram Lamps; why think further?" This model was initially in a pale duck-egg blue colour. It is not known exactly how many were made in this shade, but it is known that free samples in this colour were given to retailers who attended the 1957 Toy Trade Show. The colour was modified to a light grey for the first two years of the model's life, and as with the other models at that time, it is common to find examples with bonnet handles and radiator surrounds which have no silver trim. In 1959 the colour was altered to a more attractive and much darker grey. These darker shades are much less common today than the preceding shade. *Smith:* "When we produced this model first of all it wasn't a good seller because the size was too precious . . . Much too small. We would do anything to try and make it a bit different. Why not blue or grey? These colours were often just personal taste. What looks best, though in my eye I liked the grey." By this time Lesney had also altered their method of securing the grenodised wheels by having their axles riveted instead of the earlier pinched end variety. Finally, the last few batches of models left the factory with black plastic wheels borrowed from models in the Major Pack Series. Very few of this type survive today and they are now highly prized models. In the case of many of these very early Yesteryear commercials, Lesney did not see the need to approach the various companies and seek permission to use their names. *Smith:* "We learnt like most things the hard way. We used a name and they would say

MODELS OF YESTERYEAR 1956 – 1988 PASSENGER CARS

Ref Number	Date of Issue	Model	First Livery	Scale
Y1-2	1964	1911 Model 'T' Ford	Red	1:42
Y2-2	1963	1911 Renault 2 Seater	Green	1:40
Y2-3	1970	1914 Prince Henry Vauxhall	Red	1:47
Y3-2	1965	1910 Benz Limousine	Cream	1:54
Y4-3	1967	1909 Opel Coupe	White	1:38
Y4-4	1976	1930 Duesenberg	White/Yellow/Red	1:43
Y5-3	1969	1907 Peugeot	Yellow	1:43
Y6-3	1968	1913 Cadillac	Gold	1:48
Y7-3	1968	1912 Rolls Royce	Red/Silver	1:48
Y8-1	1958	1926 Morris Cowley 'Bullnose'	Brown	1:50
Y8-2	1962	1914 Sunbeam Motorcycle	Plated	1:34
Y8-3	1969	1914 Stutz	Red	1:48
Y9-2	1968	1912 Simplex	Lime green	1:48
Y10-3	1969	1906 Rolls Royce Silver Ghost	Metallic lime	1:51
Y11-2	1964	1912 Packard Landaulet	Red	1:50
Y11-3	1972	1938 Lagonda Drophead Coupe	Gold/Purple	1:43
Y12-2	1967	1909 Thomas Flyabout	Blue	1:48
Y13-2	1966	1911 Daimler	Yellow	1:45
Y14-2	1965	1911 Maxwell Roadster	Turquoise	1:49
Y15-1	1960	1907 Rolls Royce Silver Ghost	Green	1:55
Y15-2	1969	1930 Packard Victoria	Brown	1:46
Y16-1	1961	1904 Spyker Veteran Automobile	Cream/Yellow	1:45
Y16-2	1972	1928 Mercedes Benz SS Coupe	Silver/Red	1:45
Y17-1	1975	1938 Hispano Suiza	Red	1:48
Y18-1	1979	1937 Cord 812	Red	1:48
Y21-4	1988	1955 B.M.W. 507	Blue	1:38
Y24-1	1983	1927 Bugatti T44	Black/Yellow	1:72

Y6 A.E.C. and Y7 Leyland.

'What are these people using our name for?' We would then apologise, as we had 200,000 vehicles in stock, and ask if we could use their name. In those early days they were always very good and helpful . . . no problem."

The **Y7-1 Four Ton Leyland** also appeared in 1957 and undoubtedly had the most striking livery of any of the early issues, that of *W & R Jacob & Co. Ltd*. The first models were produced in a rich red-brown colour with a cream roof and silver trim applied to the radiator surround only. By 1959 this had altered to a much redder shade with a whiter roof and the silver

trim was applied to the radiator grille only. In common with the A.E.C. lorry a very few models were issued with black plastic wheels, instead of the normal grenodised grey metal wheels, and again it is this rare variation that is so prized today.

There is, however, one further aspect to the story of this model. Occasionally an example appears with the centre line of the transfer missing, and it is apparent that this centre line (which states – 'By Royal Appointment to His Majesty the King') was cut from the transfer

by hand and the two halves were applied to the model separately. Various theories have been put forward to explain this mystery, but none has ever proved conclusive. One well-known collector, Mr Geoffrey Leake, found several such models in Nairobi during the early 1960s and concluded that at that time the British were very unpopular in Kenya and so the reference to the monarchy was deleted so as not to cause offence. A further model has been recently obtained from a director of W & R Jacob & Co. Ltd. in the Republic of

Ireland, who had been given it as a promotional item from Lesney in the late 1950s. Leslie Smith felt that there may have been a problem in obtaining accurate registration of the fine print and that the printer had simply deleted it. In hindsight this is unlikely as the transfer is in two pieces and a printer would most probably have simply removed the line, but retained a one piece backing. It has also been thought that the out-workers employed at that time may have removed the line and given it to railway modeller friends. At the time of writing no final confirmation has come to light and so the debate continues. The Y7 Leyland was phased out in 1961.

A further fourteen years passed before the next commercial vehicle made its appearance. *Simmons:* "In fact, two model vans were made based on the then current Model 'T' Ford car. One super livery was of Lyons Tea. These were shown at the 1972 Toy Fairs and were enthusiastically received by dealers wanting to know when it would be delivered and what would the next commercial be. Unfortunately, the company did not respond until two years later when the R.A.F. Tender, originally made

grain), completely new colour schemes often in metallic paint, and many new standardised components. The most noticeable standard components of these new 1974 models were new wheels. These were chrome plated plastic wheels with either twelve or twenty four spokes, complete with thick black tyres on either version. Undoubtedly this was a move which saved Lesney a fortune in moulds, stockholdings and production capacity, but it infuriated their small but growing army of enthusiastic collectors. The standard wheels designed to suit

but we took them off because we wanted to put a label there."

The very first run of this model had seats moulded in maroon plastic, but the most common colour was white. The canopy colour was changed in 1975, and a batch of models appeared with canopies and radiator grilles in drab olive green. *Grundy:* "This was plastic material used up from the Battle King range when they were deleted." It would appear that most of these models were shipped to the U.S.A., but it is quite common to find an olive green grille on a normal model. A

Y5 Talbot Van spurred Lesney into reissuing the Crossley in 1979 as a true commercial vehicle, initially as a coal truck in *Evans Bros Coal & Coke* livery complete with a simulated load of coal sacks moulded in plastic. This realistic model was painted red with black wings and roof, and was available with either red or chromed wheels. The marks of this hurried conversion were evident on the chassis, however, which bore the description 'R.A.F. Tender' for two years after its launch.

The model was relaunched in 1983 as a delivery vehicle in *Carlsberg* livery with a further

Y13 and Y26 Crossley. Top row: Left, A pre-production R.A.F. Tender.

by Ken Wetton for his own pleasure, was shown and accepted."

The **Y13/3 1918 Crossley R.A.F. Tender** was modelled on the vehicle at the R.A.F. Museum in Hendon. It fitted uneasily into the series as it was at this time the only commercial in the range and was launched in 1974 as part of a major revamp for the whole series. This included new style boxes (wood-

all the models in fact suited very few of them, and a comparison of a 1960s Y2 Vauxhall with its 1970s counterpart reveals a clear deterioration in authenticity. The Y13-3 Crossley had extremely unlikely chrome wheels. It also had a modified tilt canopy over the driver's compartment borrowed from the Y8-3 Stutz but moulded in textured tan plastic. *Lister:* "The very first pre-production run had all the dots along the body sides

very small run was also produced using these plastic components in black to make up for a shortfall of the normal issues. These black components were normally used on the plated version. Production of the plated version necessitated the insertion of two insets into the tool to accommodate holes for locating screws, and these insets obscured the word 'Ltd' on later issues.

The tremendous success of the

revision of the canopy. The original rear canopy component was altered by having a rectangular panel incorporated onto its side, which would accept a label. This was another clear recognition by the company of the tremendous interest of collectors in alternative liveries. The model was also available with brass effect wheels, and still further models were found with black seats and radiator grilles. This

Carlsberg livery was replaced in 1985 by that of the furniture store of *Waring's*. The label was the source of much confusion initially as it was intended to have a cream background to match its cream canopy, but the labels were found to be white and a small quantity were released with this mis-match. This was soon corrected by the interim measure of producing 5,000 canopies in white to match the labels. Subsequent production was corrected to produce cream labels with cream canopies. This model also appeared with the wheels plated in a brass effect.

The Crossley also appeared with a new number **Y26** in 1984 when it appeared as a brewer's dray for *Löwenbrau*. The load had once again been altered, this time to simulate three barrels somewhat precariously balanced over the rear wheels. The first issues of this livery had Y13 cast on to the baseplate, but this was soon altered to read Y13-26 to enable either model to be cast from one mould. The cab cover can be found in tan, light tan and very pale cream. Barrels can be found in varying shades of brown plastic.

In late 1986 a Limited Edition model was produced in the livery of the *Romford Brewery Co.* Very few variations were reported due to the single production run, except to say that a small quantity were found with ruby red seats as opposed to the normal brown.

The beverage theme of the Y26 Crossleys was continued in 1987 when the livery of *Gonzalez Byass* appeared. Matchbox were quick to realise that some of the buying public were not aware that this was a brand of sherry, and so all subsequent production after the first run had the word 'Sherry' printed onto the rear barrels. In 1988 the Crossley reappeared in a form much closer to the original Evans Bros Coal and Coke livery. The new livery was in overall yellow but of a German company advertising *Kohle & Koks.* This was

the first Crossley to be made in Macau and was designated a Y13. At the same time, a run of Talbot vans in Rose's livery was also being produced in Macau and some of the dark green wheels for the Rose's were fitted to the Kohle & Koks. However, the more common wheel was black.

The next model to be reviewed is without doubt the most significant Yesteryear commercial ever to emerge from Lesney. It is fair to assume that the **Y5/4 1927 Talbot Van** was the one which sparked off the interest in collecting Yesteryears with various company logos, and which in turn influenced Lesney, and later Matchbox, to concentrate on commercial vehicles, hence removing the domination of over a decade of passenger cars. *Tekerian:* "There was quite a lot of controversy about adding the Talbot Van into the range . . . 'Who wants a drab old van?'. . . The selection of vans was questioned. It was believed that what children and collectors were looking for was a wider selection of cars and not vans. However, it was eventually selected and included in the range, more for testing the market, I guess."

This was not a new idea and, in fact, before the war Meccano had been aware of this collecting trend and had produced similar but contemporary vans in various liveries. Their arrangements were slightly different in so far as they were able to get the featured companies to pay for the origination of the decals that were affixed to the sides. This was perhaps easier to achieve in the 1930s, as the vans and lorries modelled by Dinky in those days were a common sight on the roads, and, therefore, the miniatures made a neat and economic advertisement for various companies.

The Talbot made an inauspicious entry into the range and was not liked by the enthusiasts. It was felt that the choice of a Talbot as opposed to a Morris or a Ford was

Talbot Vans. Left, the original model of the Clement Talbot. Right, a colour trial prototype of the Y5 Talbot.

inappropriate because Talbot were famous as manufacturers of sporting saloons and even racing cars, but distinctly unknown as manufacturers of light vans. *Simmons:* "The Talbot should have been a Clement-Talbot, for the model is based on that car chassis before the Clement was dropped by the Star Newspaper who had their own design of bodywork added. It became a Talbot when a draughtsman, who thought he knew better, altered the radiator design from a Clement-Talbot to a Talbot and patterns had been made before the error was spotted." It was modelled on a real vehicle, a picture of which is to be found in *'Lorries, Trucks & Vans 1897 – 1927'* published by the Blandford Press. The livery of this new model was actually copied from an Austin 7 van well-known to bodies such as the Vintage Commercial Vehicle Society, and as the Austin 7 was a vehicle the public would have much preferred, this also detracted from the Talbot's popularity.

It is, of course, the *Lipton's Tea*

livery that was controversial, as it featured the Royal Crest on both sides. Permission in writing was sought from the Lord Chamberlain's Office as a matter of course; a reply was not forthcoming and so Lesney, assuming that everything was in order, set about production. The consternation and embarrassment that the negative decision must have caused needs no amplification. It is estimated that at least 100,000 models had been produced and distributed prior to the unwelcome news.

The information that consent to use the crest had been refused was common knowledge to the public and the toy trader alike and at one stage it was thought that all the models would have to be withdrawn. This prompted the public and the trade to purchase and hoard every model that could be found, and naturally the models started to change hands at rising prices, all of which was noted at first with amusement, and then with growing interest, by the Lesney management.

Talbot Vans. The ten liveries of this commercial van as produced by Lesney and Matchbox. Lyles Syrup was the 1989 and final livery.

The Lord Chamberlain's Office finally let Lesney off the hook, by insisting that only the design be altered, and not that the offending models be withdrawn. Lesney duly obliged, only to find that the revised version was also bought in large quantities. This model was identical except for the addition of the logo and address of the Lipton's company, which replaced the crest. Variations to the model include the colour of the wheels which can be green, olive green, chromed, twelve spoked or twenty four spoked. The early releases of both versions featured a shadowed

effect on the main wording, but this was deleted from later issues. *Smith:* "We realised what we had got – a sort of free advertising space on which to put colour."

The Talbot was also the first vehicle to have decoration applied to it by the production process known as tampo printing, the machines for which had been developed to perfection during the 1970s in West Germany. Prior to that, lettering was usually applied by transfers or labels. *Smith:* "The new process of tampo printing opened it up completely, because

with transfers or decals you had to buy so many on a print run, you had to buy half a million or even a million. Then if you had, say a dozen different transfers you would try and marry them all together and give the printer a good run and hope to goodness none got lost or wasted. But with tampo printing you could do short runs for a better finish in the end."

Although the excitement generated by the Lipton's Tea livery was noticed in Europe, European sales were low and this was attributed to the lack of awareness of Lipton's

Tea in, for example, France. To redress this balance Lesney decided to produce a livery based on a French company well known in Europe. Initially, it was not thought to be a sound proposition for the U.K. and the *Chocolat Menier* livery was, therefore, for export only. The public thought otherwise, however, and there were soon signs that a roaring trade was developing as wholesalers started buying back these models to sell to the steadily growing ranks of collectors. It was some fifteen months before Lesney released the model to the U.K., much to the disappointment of those who had already obtained one at any price

The original advertisement for the Y5 Talbot Bread Vans.

to add to their prized collection. Early France bound models often can be found with French text descriptions applied to their cartons. This model also appeared with twelve and twenty four spoked wheels. The colour of the tampo printing also varied from pale yellow to off-white. *Smith:* "We had gone to Germany and bought some of their tampo machines – simple really, like all good things are. Tampo printing opened up the market."

In May 1980 and in conjunction with the American Bakeries Company the Talbot appeared in the livery of *Taystee*. It transpired that the company owned two further brands, Langendorf and Merita Bread. These two subsidiaries were able to have their own locally-produced labels applied to painted blank vans. Such was the demand from collectors for these vans that stocks of the Taystee version from Lesney were soon exhausted. A third label, that of Taystee again but produced in the U.S.A. also appeared. All four versions were actively collected. It should be noted that the American labelled vans were not wholly produced by Lesney and are thus classified as Code 2 models.

In 1981 Lesney produced a second run of the Taystee livery, but this time the chassis, wings and running boards were painted black. Variations to both these colour schemes appeared with models featuring solid red plastic wheels and with others without the standard whitewall tyres.

Lesney continued their policy of producing decorated vans with the liveries of international companies in late 1981 with the arrival of the *Nestle's Milk* livery. A mistake in the factory led to the production of a small run of models with matt black roofs left over from the Taystee run, but this was quickly rectified and the majority were produced with a medium grey roof. This livery was actually intended for sale in the U.K. and Europe only; but such was the demand from Australia that a second run was produced for them. These second run models have a distinctly lighter grey roof and are far less common than the dark grey versions.

Lesney's policy of launching certain liveries in limited quantities attracted criticism from both the public and the ever-growing collectors market. In an attempt to rationalise the market the next livery was launched worldwide and termed a standard livery or edition. The *Chivers & Sons Ltd* livery was produced in extremely large quantities (over

150,000 units) and continued to be the standard model even after the *Wright's Original Coal Tar Soap* version had come and gone. Very few variations were apparent except for some models with and without whitewall tyres and with bright and dark red wheels.

The livery of Wright's Original Coal Tar Soap really came in two versions. It was planned to have the radiator, windscreen, wheels and headlights in brass plating but this initially failed for technical reasons. Most models are, therefore, found with silver-plated parts, but the remainder did eventually appear in brass, due to improved techniques. A mixture of both chrome and brass-plated fittings on some models can occasionally be found.

The Chivers livery was eventually replaced in late 1983 by that of *Ever Ready*, the world-wide makers of electrical batteries. Initially these models all had tan plastic seats, but later batches featured seats in black plastic. Lesney often faced criticism as a result of these minor changes and were frequently accused of manipulating the collectors market. It has to be said, though, that such a change as that described was merely the result of a lack of raw material or dye which either meant

halting the assembly line or finding a reasonable substitute to keep production moving. *Lister:* "We did consider going from opening doors to solid doors because of the rejection rate for the finished doors . . . They obviously had to match in colour, but because they were so light they used to blow off or turn over when the spray gun passed them . . . This gave us variances in the coating of spray; some were dark or some were light. We put the painted doors in bins marked left and right and tried then to match them as best we could with the body shades." During production of the Ever Ready livery with black seats the new maroon style box was introduced to replace the straw type box.

The Ever Ready livery gave way to that of *Dunlop* in 1984. The model was listed as a Limited Edition and was readily available in all the Matchbox markets. By this time the management of Matchbox was well aware of the growing interest in the Yesteryear brand and was paying close attention to the buying public. This led to accurate livery reproduction and certain criteria having to be met before a livery could be considered. Most noticeably the liveries had to be those of companies in existence at the time (1927). *Tekerian:* "Dunlop approached us . . . They asked us if we would like to use the Dunlop livery on one of our vans. The Public Relations Manager at Dunlop was quite a keen collector; he was very obliging and helpful. They also bought a quantity themselves to use for public relations." The logo was on a self-adhesive label, with the remainder of the printing applied by tampo.

The livery of *Rose's* succeeded that of Ever Ready in 1985 as a standard issue. The model was not especially well received at its time of launch as many felt it was too close in colour to that of the Chivers model. Indeed, with the demise of production of the range at the Rochford factory in 1986, old stocks of paint left over from the Chivers livery were used to fill back orders for Rose's. Earlier versions could also be found with tan seats.

In mid-1988, a run of Talbot vans were made in Macau in the livery of Rose's. The baseplates were amended to 'Made In Macau'. It has been noted that the tampo inks were of a slightly darker colouring.

A completely new marketing strategy accompanied the arrival of the **Y9/3 1920 Three Ton Leyland Lorry** in December 1985. Matchbox decided to produce a model aimed solely at collectors by producing a one off model, the dies for which would not be used again. Indeed, the dies were made in such a way that they would be obsolete once the single production run of 40,000 was complete.

Equally unusual was the way in which the toy trade was asked to order them. For every two or three other special commercials they were asked to order, they could order only one of the Leylands. This move was primarily designed to prevent hoarding, but also to ensure good distribution. The model was packed in a special presentation box which won an international packaging award and came with a numbering system comprising of a letter and four digits.

The model was actually rather ordinary in appearance but featured an authentic colour scheme of dark green with a red chassis advertising the firm of *A. Luff & Sons Ltd.*

There are, in fact, quite a few variations which have come to light on this model. Seat colours varied and even the mudguards were shortened during the run and

Y12 Ford Model 'T' Van.
The eighteen liveries of this commercial van as produced by Lesney and Matchbox. Also included is the original design in silver for the 25th Anniversary model.

several models appeared by mistake with bright red grilles and headlights. Matchbox encountered many difficulties with the production of the model as many of the castings had to be rejected and this meant that although only 40,000 were released, many more castings were made and because of the high scrap factor were destroyed. The moulds were finally chrome plated and presented to the Chester Toy Museum in 1988 where they are on display in the Matchbox Room (For further details see Chapter Twelve).

A new commercial van under consideration came into being in 1979 as a result of the success of the Talbot but one which was to eclipse it in terms of popularity. It bore none of the slightly obscure origins of the Talbot but was immediately identifiable as a **Ford Model 'T' Van** – the new Y12/3.

Without doubt it can be said that this model changed the way in which models were collected because its appearance started a whole group of collectors whose sole interest was to collect the various commercial liveries only, a trend quickly emulated by Matchbox's competitors. This idea has several advantages to the manufacturer, as much of the expensive origination costs can be spread over a longer time span.

As a general note there are three distinct types of rear doors to be found on the model and these can greatly affect the rarity, and thus the value, of some of the early issues. Initially, the doors were depicted simply as a single printed outline of each door and these were applied to the first five liveries. (Type One). Midway through production of these first five liveries a very few models appeared with a second type of door decoration. These were a more detailed type and had a keyline around the twin oval windows. (Type Two). The third door type bore no printing, this having been replaced with cast in door detailing. (Type Three).

The first livery issued was that of *Colman's*, the famous makers of English mustard. This was a standard model with a very large production run. Several variations occurred, including twelve and twenty four spoked chrome wheels, rear lights in black as opposed to red, and finally both the second type of doors and models with the 'Y12' inscription on the baseplate blanked out. Today models with the second type of doors are the most sought after.

Concurrent with the Colman's livery, production commenced of a version in the livery of *Coca-Cola.*. Coca-Cola are most protective of their famous trademark and although an agreement was secured with the company in the U.S.A. and West Germany, the agreement did not hold for the U.K. or the rest of Europe. *Tekerian:* "Coca-Cola U.K. decided that putting their name on a Model 'T' Ford was not the right image, and refused the licence." Also the European agents of Coca-Cola demanded 40p for each model sold. *Smith:* "We felt this to be quite unacceptable and we would, in fact, be losing money on every model sold. We agreed only to sell the model in the U.S.A. and so it was withdrawn very quickly." This sudden curtailment of production naturally prompted an immediate transatlantic trade with prices rocketing from £4 to £30 almost overnight. The situation was further exacerbated by the discovery of a very few models with an extra coachline added just in front of the rear wheel. Models also appeared with twelve and twenty four spoked chrome wheels in place of the normal red variety.

Following comments from some European markets that the Colman's livery was too English, and being unable to distribute Coca-Cola liveries, a third livery appeared bearing the name *Suze*. Destined for Europe only, the U.K. trade naturally demanded the model as well. This model appeared with the usual wheel, rear light and rear doors variations. A very short run with Type Two doors in red were shipped to West Germany. These are now prized by the keenest of collectors.

The livery of *Smith's Potato Crisps* was the first Y12 to be produced as a sales promotion activity. The promotion had been instigated by Smith's who earlier had given away a most attractive, but privately produced, Y12 to retailers who purchased forty eight boxes of crisps. Naturally many of these had fallen into collectors' hands, some of whom had gone to the lengths of buying forty eight boxes of crisps in an effort to obtain the model!

The Lesney produced model could be purchased for £1.95 plus five empty crisp packets, although, three months after the promotion was over, they were available through normal retail outlets. *Tekerian:* "Shortly afterwards the model was put on general release and that created a certain amount of controversy." The usual variations were also in evidence. It should be noted that all of the above models can be found with the Y12 inscription on the base as well as having the Y12 blanked out. This was removed to enable the baseplate to be used to produce a new model designated Y3 and which appeared as a petrol tanker in 1981. This model is described elsewhere in this chapter.

Something of a departure appeared in 1981 when a model was issued to celebrate *25 Years of Models of Yesteryear*. In fact, the model only just appeared in 1981 and what should, or could, have been a sure-fire success was met with a luke-warm reception by the public. This model was packaged in a special white box proclaiming the anniversary, but the model's uninspired colour scheme of grey and green with toy-like bright yellow wheels was not much admired. These too can be found with or without Y12 on the base.

The majority had Type Two rear doors, but a very short run had Type One rear doors.

The livery of *Cerebos Table Salt* followed next in the series and again this model was not particularly well received. It did, however, encompass a major variation. An accident in the factory allowed yellow roofs from the then current Bird's Custard van to be fitted to the Cerebos van instead of the standard white roof. It has been estimated that some five hundred yellow-roofed Cerebos vans were produced. Chrome, brass and red twelve spoked wheels were fitted, as were a few tan seats as opposed to the more normal black seats. The yellow roofed models are highly prized because of their rarity and more colourful appearance.

Bird's Custard Powder became the seventh in the series in 1982. Some models had a metallic blue finish, whilst others had yellow wheels left over from the 25th Anniversary model. The very last batch had the third type of doors and many of these were fitted with black seats as opposed to the normal tan variety.

The meteoric rise in value of the *Arnott's Biscuits* liveried van was particularly due to the receivers being called in to Lesney after only 18,000 models had been completed. This model was scheduled to be available world-wide but the collapse of Lesney meant that the larger run for the rest of the world did not proceed. A world-wide band of collectors quickly bought up all the available stocks and the model became the classic collector's piece, well illustrating the effects of supply and demand. At today's prices this model often sells in excess of £150.00. *Tekerian:* "The collectors market was really starting to bubble, when Lesney Australia ordered the Arnott's Biscuits. Although they had ordered it and said they wanted this livery, no other Lesney Company had said they wanted it. This was right in the middle of the receivership period, but I did say that if Australia is having it, then so should the U.K. Then we found out that Arnott's vans were coming back from Australia at really high prices, I felt that if we suddenly made a whole batch and put it into the market, it would wipe out interest. So we did not make any more even though we had planned it into the production schedule."

The famous department store of *Harrods* in London had long been a

about a millimetre border all around the models surface. Some of the Harrods vans had to have a second impression and so some are much darker than others."

Generally thought to be the most attractive livery to appear on the Model 'T's was that of *Sunlight Seife* produced in 1983 at the request of Matchbox Toys Germany. The production run of 12,000 would have been much larger, but many of the labels were lost and the

which could easily be seen by lifting one corner of the label. Original factory-produced Sunlights had their labels applied to yellow van bodies which had no tampo logos of any description.

The release of the 1983 *Royal Mail* van was rumoured to be a limited run, but in fact was produced in very large quantities. Slight variations exist within the Royal Mail transfer and second and third type doors exist. At this time

colours of *Captain Morgan*. This van originally bore a one-piece paper label which covered the small gap between the door and the body. These labels tended to split at this point in pressing operations during assembly and were replaced with a two-piece transfer. *Tekerian:* "We contacted Seagrams as a matter of course, telling them that we wanted to do the Captain Morgan livery . . . We filled in the form which agreed that we would only use the correct

The Y21 Woody Wagon and the Y22 Model 'A' van.

large retailer of Matchbox products and in 1982 an agreement was made which enabled the store to sell a model in their own livery. This issue proved to be a great seller and successive runs were produced with both Type Two and Type Three doors. Also black seats and tan seats were fitted. *Lister:* "We originally tended to make the tampo plates too big . . . We then reduced the size of the plate so that we would have

run was prematurely ceased. The model was promoted in Europe as a Limited Edition and as with the Arnott's livery the price rocketed overnight. No variations are thought to exist on this model, the only Y12-3 Ford 'T' Van to have no variations! In 1987/88 some Sunlight Soap liveried models, thought to have originated in Germany, started appearing with fake labels. These fake labels had been applied to Colman's liveried vans, the livery of

Matchbox decided to keep a much tighter control on the Yesteryear Range, i.e. no more individuals would get permission to alter the official liveries, (Code 2's), and an attempt would be made to ensure that all models were made available to all the Matchbox markets simultaneously.

In 1983, and a reflection of the realisation by Matchbox that the range was being bought primarily by adults, came a van bearing the

livery . . . No money changed hands. After launching the product we were then told by Seagrams that we did not have an agreement with them to produce the van, and they wanted us to withdraw it. We had to stop production there and then!"

In the same year Matchbox produced a model in the livery of *Hoover*. As part of the agreement between the two companies just over five hundred models were produced in blue for the directors of the company with a special certificate as opposed to the normal orange livery. This model reflected the amount of detailed research now being undertaken by the company to produce authentic and realistic models.

In 1984 Coca-Cola's main rival *Pepsi-Cola* gave their permission to use their logo on the Y12 with none of the royalty problems that had affected the Coca-Cola model. The model also appeared with red twelve and twenty four chrome spoked wheels. This model was to remain a standard issue for three years and in 1987 a batch appeared with a revised baseplate inscribed 'Matchbox International © 1985'.

The company was involved with the *Motor 100* celebrations in 1985 and brought out a commemorative model to publicise the event. The proceeds of the sale of the first 2,300 went to charity and these models had an accompanying certificate.

In November 1985 the company brought out a model with a completely new rear pick-up body cab back and roof with a limited production run of 65,000 models. This dark blue model, in the livery

of *Imbach,* was actually one of a set of four produced at that time – all classified as Special Limited Editions.

An attractive addition joined the Y12 ranks in 1986 when the model's roof was altered by the addition of a plastic gherkin located into two holes. The first 1,000 run of this model was given to *H. J. Heinz Co.* as samples for their salesforce to use. Heinz asked for some improvements to be made notably to the lettering of the word Gherkin and the size of the word Varieties. Later versions thus had these small changes evident, as well as the usual variations of black and dark green seats. *Lister:* "On a very small quantity of models the operator put the gherkin the wrong way round!"

The last variation to be produced to date was that of *Rosella,* designed primarily for the Australian market, but available world-wide. The model was also the last of the Y12's to be produced at Rochford and consequently a mixture of wheels and baseplates can be found.

Tekerian: "This model was specifically withdrawn from production . . . We issued a precise proclamation to the trade and collectors alike that the Y12 Model 'T' van would not be repeated"

In July 1988 a new van entered the range to replace the Y12. The model was the **1937 G.M.C. Van** in the livery of *Goblin Vacuum Cleaners,* a new and exciting design which was well received by collectors. Models were produced with both grey and black roofs. Originally destined to have a grey roof, problems were encountered when mask-spraying the roofs. So as not to delay production any longer, the grey roof was omitted and the models were produced in all-over gloss black. The six thousand grey-roofed models were distributed to the trade along with the standard all-black models. *Tekerian:* "The selection of the G.M.C. Van was a very deliberate one. It is pre-war, but the shape is entirely different from the square shaped Model 'A' Vans or Model 'T' Ford Vans."

The shift in emphasis towards

commercial vehicles can be most clearly seen in the metamorphosis of the **Y21/1 Ford Model 'A' Woody Wagon** originally designed before receivership. It was not well received on introduction in 1981, mainly because of its all plastic body. It was adapted, however, after two years into a panel-sided box van bearing the livery of *A & J Box.* *Tekerian:* "This model has always suffered under the shadow of the Model 'A' Van . . . maybe too much plastic." The A & J Box was replaced by a new livery in 1985 – *Carters Tested Seeds. Tekerian:* "Carters Seeds approached us with the livery and bought a quantity for their own use."

The limitations of the Y21 in both forms soon gave rise to a more suitable medium of advertising in the shape of a **Y22 Ford Model 'A' Van.** This model used many of the moulds associated with the Y21, most obviously the chassis, front bumpers, radiator and headlights. It was the first Yesteryear to have clear plastic glazed windows and windscreen. The first livery issued was that of *Oxo* stock cubes and early issues of this model had no

The Y29 Walker Electric van and the Y25 Renault van .
All the liveries produced to date.

raised detailing to the cab roof, but this was soon incorporated into succeeding issues. *Tekerian:* "We didn't get that model right initially; the casting was a one piece body and we could not mould it properly, so we had to rework the mould and make the roof of the van and body a separate piece. It couldn't be mask-sprayed properly."

Further changes arose with the issue of the *Maggis* livery in 1984. The van body had a raised ridge added to it to make the task of mask spraying easier. The wording 'Suppen & Speisen' was also enlarged to make it more legible.

Toblerone was the next company name to appear on this model and the livery appeared with black, dark brown and light brown lettering. The model also had a variation with a projecting ridge to the van roof, again in an effort to prevent problems with the mask-spraying.

The recurring problem of mask spraying was finally solved by removing the diecast roof from the van body completely and replacing it with a plastic pre-coloured version which first appeared on the *Walters' Palm Toffee* livery of 1984. The apparent mis-spelling of the word 'creemy' was a deliberate copy from an original livery. *Tekerian:* "The R. & D. Department was having real difficulty in coming up with a new livery. I remembered as a child my grandmother having a tin of Palm Toffee; and that really stuck in my mind. We had to find an example of the brand because the original company that owned it had gone out of business. We went to the Creative Department at the Museum of London and they provided everything we needed."

Late in 1984 Matchbox were asked by the Canadian Post Corporation to produce a special livery for sale – *Postes Canada Post* through their post offices as an exclusive. Mindful of the furore this would cause, this exclusivity was not agreed to by Matchbox, but instead the first batch were shipped to Canada with special packaging proclaiming that they were the first run. The rest of the run was packaged in standard maroon boxes and made available worldwide.

In 1986 a Limited Edition livery was produced of *Spratt's* dog food. By this stage Matchbox had finely tuned its sales expectations and for a Limited Edition model such as this 40,000 were produced for the UK with an identical quantity destined for abroad.

The standard issue for 1987 was that of *Lyons' Tea*, an authentic rendition of that famous company's livery.

It is easy to trace the growth of a disciplined market awareness to the international popularity of the range. The Talbot was a very British make, but the Model 'T' and 'A' box vans owed their origins to the United States markets. An archetypal **Y25/1 French Renault Type A.G.** from 1910 made its inevitable appearance in 1983, to give a truly international aspect to the range.

Introduced bearing the livery of *Perrier* Mineral Water, this model was more ornate and striking in appearance than the rather slab-sided Model 'A' Ford. The very first issues of the model are avidly collected because they featured fewer struts (only three in number) along the luggage rail on the roof. An example of an early model was shown in the 1983 Trade Brochure. These were found to be weak and caused the rail to break; so a further two were added as a corrective measure. Early models also featured a raised and detailed (driver's side) side-lamp lens, but this was soon removed to match the other side. A later batch of models appeared with red seats but it should be noted that this seat also fits the Crossley model in all its forms; so many variations exist.

The next livery, that of *James Neale & Sons,* became the cause of much controversy between Matchbox and the collectors. The Connoisseur's Collection of six models had met with some resistance from the trade and as an incentive the company offered the James Neale model free on a one to one basis for every Connoisseur's Set ordered, a simple enough arrangement on the face of it, but many traders felt unable to re-order further sets as they had fulfilled their orders for their customers. The customers naturally felt entitled to their model and so the situation developed into one of much ill-feeling. Matchbox relented and asked the public to send in their sales receipts in exchange for their free model.

In the midst of this came the unwelcome news that significant variations were occurring in the production runs of these models. Some models appeared with the hitherto open grab handles filled in, others displayed a hole in the cab floor caused by a sticking ejector pin and a final batch appeared with a much darker blue chassis than their predecessors with both the open and closed grab handles.

The James Neale model was never a standard livery and was swiftly replaced in 1985 by that of *Duckham's Oil.* This model was one of three models issued in the Fathers' Day Gift Set, which included the Y23 Bus and the Y11 Lagonda. It also could be found with closed grab handles. The total production of this model was only 40,000 units.

The livery of *The Eagle Pencil Co.* appeared in 1985 and became the standard livery for the model. It also appeared as part of a set of three to celebrate 30 years of Models of Yesteryear. Some of the later issues had a lighter eagle motif, some of which were fitted with baseplates marked 'Limited Edition' which were left over from the Renault Ambulance.

In 1986 the Renault emerged as a special Limited Edition in the guise of an Ambulance. This was achieved by the addition of a completely new body section with windows and red cross markings.

This model proved difficult to produce because the roof, which was moulded in plastic, tended to warp away from the body and many had to be withdrawn. *Simmons:* "This was due to the roof being painted and baked at too high a temperature." Some models did not bear the limited edition wording cast into the baseplate.

In 1987 the logo of the the bakery firm *T. Tunnock* was applied to the Renault and the results were most attractive. Many of the limited edition baseplates found their way on to the model; however, whilst all the Renaults have brass-plated fittings, a few of the Tunnock vans have been reported with a chrome-plated headlight/front numberplate component. Later in that year the famous French grocery company *Delhaize* celebrated their 120th Anniversary and their livery was produced on the model. Attractive though the decoration was, many collectors found, the overall colour scheme too close to that of the Perrier to be truly distinctive.

The **Y29 Walker Electric Van** stands very much on its own within the commercial van series. This is because the model was instigated by Harrods for sale from their store and followed on from successful sales of the Model 'T' Ford in their livery. The Walker Van was quite a famous sight in and around London and was, therefore, an ideal choice. Matchbox arranged a contract with *Harrods Ltd* whereby they would pay for the development costs in exchange for exclusive rights to the model for one year. The model was released through Harrods in 1985.

Immediately after the one year agreement was over, Matchbox produced the model in the colours of *Joseph Lucas Ltd.* This was a natural choice as this company had made its name as producers of electric components.

The 1988 livery was that of *His Master's Voice* gramophones. This was the most attractive of the three versions. Originally Matchbox were going to use a maroon livery but

Y3 Ford Tanker and Y12 G.M.C. van.
The many liveries of the Y3 Ford including two pre-production examples.

there was an objection from the trademark owner, who stated that the dark blue was the authentic colour.

In 1985 a faithful model of the **Y30 1920 Mack Truck** appeared in the range. *Tekerian:* "Matchbox Toys U.S.A. really needed a model to push the Yesteryear Range in their market." This was the first of the series to represent a full-size truck, as opposed to the light commercial vans such as the Talbots, Fords and Renaults. The model was initially to bear the livery of Goodyear Tyres, but this idea was dropped when it was realised that the model featured solid tyres, whereas Goodyear were famous for pneumatic tyres. First issues of the

model in *Acorn Storage Co.* livery featured dark blue mudguards and steps, but in the final days of U.K. production a batch appeared with these parts in grey. Other models featured the chassis engraved with either 'Made in England' or 'Made in Macau', depending on their country of origin.

While the Acorn model was still current, a special edition of the Mack was introduced in the livery of *Consolidated Motor Lines Ltd* and was one of a set of four trucks released in December 1985 as Special Limited Editions. The castings were radically altered to produce a deep-sided body, cab

doors and a windscreen. The location of the windscreen in relation to the cab roof proved difficult in trials. The moulds for the cab roof were altered so that a small lug could be cast onto the underside of the cab roof, thus making the location of the top of the windscreen much simpler.

After the run of Consolidated, production reverted to Acorn Storage, and thus they too had the lug cast onto the underside of the cab roof.

The baseplate for the Consolidated was produced with 'Limited Edition' and the copyright date changed from 1984 to 1985. After

the Consolidated run, 'Limited Edition', was deleted, but the copyright date of 1985 was left unchanged. The run was limited to 65,000 models worldwide.

In 1987 a completely new livery succeeded the Acorn Storage, the *Arctic Ice Cream Co.* lorry which was the first model to be made entirely in Macau. The Arctic Ice Cream livery was, in fact, a last minute choice as Matchbox had been refused permission to use their original choice.

The standard livery for 1988 was that of *Kiwi Boot Polish,* thought by many to be the most attractive livery produced to date.

The Ford Model 'T' Van formed many of the parts for a sister model introduced in 1981 as the number **Y3 Ford Model 'T' Tanker.** The model first appeared in the livery of *B.P.* Very early issues actually still had the inscription Y12 cast into the chassis, but that was soon removed to avoid confusion. The model was introduced at a time when the process of tampo printing was in its development stages, as a result of which quite a few variations occurred to the decorative lettering. The lettering was enhanced initially with a black shadow effect, but this proved difficult to register and some production runs reflected this, whilst others did not have it at all. Gold paint was applied to the filler caps on some, but not all issues, whilst matt black paint can be found on others. One final variation concerned the cab roof. This component was cast from the same mould as the plated pipes and a batch of the roofs was accidentally plated, assembled and released. The standard model was also released in a five piece Gift Set in 1982.

The second livery was produced in limited quantities (35,000) and was destined for the European market primarily. *Zerolene* petrol tankers were known to be in short supply from the outset and the prices immediately increased to reflect this. *Tekerian:* "Zerolene was decided upon by Central Marketing, but the U.K. Sales Force thought that it was such a poor livery they would be unable to sell it. At the same time Matchbox had produced a five piece Gift Set . . . 50,000 of these were made . . . Instead of making it a limited edition set with five new models, they just put in five standard models . . . It took a long time to sell them. So, to help this set, they used the Zerolene as a free incentive to the trade. We actually never sold Zerolenes – we gave them away on a trade incentive, i.e. the trade were to sell a gift set and give away a Zerolene with it." Very few variations exist of this model. Some have matt black chassis and a very few have been found with red twelve spoked plastic wheels.

Rumours of a short run of the third livery, that of *Express Dairy,* were rife in 1983 but to the disappointment of many proved to be unfounded. The only variation

Ref Number	Date of Issue	Model	First Livery	Scale	Ref Number	Date of Issue	Model	First Livery	Scale
Y3-4	1981	Ford Model 'T' Tanker	BP	1:35	Y12-3	1986	1912 Ford Model 'T' Van	H. J. Heinz Co.	1:35
Y3-4	1982	Ford Model 'T' Tanker	Zerolene	1:35	Y12-3	1987	1912 Ford Model 'T' Van	Rosella	1:35
Y3-4	1983	Ford Model 'T' Tanker	Express Dairy	1:35	Y12-5	1988	1937 G.M.C. Van	Goblin Vacuum Cleaners	1:45
Y3-4	1984	Ford Model 'T' Tanker	Carnation	1:35	Y13-3	1974	1918 Crossley	RAF	1:47
Y3-4	1985	Ford Model 'T' Tanker	Mobiloil	1:35	Y13-3	1979	1918 Crossley	Evans Bros	1:47
Y3-4	1986	Ford Model 'T' Tanker	Castrol Motor Oil	1:35	Y13-3	1983	1918 Crossley	Carlsberg	1:47
Y3-4	1986	Ford Model 'T' Tanker	Red Crown Gasoline	1:35	Y13-3	1985	1918 Crossley	Waring's	1:47
Y5-4	1978	1927 Talbot Van	Liptons Crest	1:47	Y13-3	1988	1918 Crossley	Kohle & Koks	1:47
Y5-4	1978	1927 Talbot Van	Liptons Tea	1:47	Y19-2	1987	1929 Morris Van	Brasso	1:39
Y5-4	1979	1927 Talbot Van	Chocolat Menier	1:47	Y19-3	1988	1929 Morris Van	Michelin Tyres	1:39
Y5-4	1980	1927 Talbot Van	Taystee	1:47	Y21-1	1981	Ford Model 'A' Woody Wagon	Yellow	1:40
Y5-4	1981	1927 Talbot Van	Nestle's	1:47	Y21-2	1983	Ford Model 'A' Woody Wagon	A & J Box	1:40
Y5-4	1982	1927 Talbot Van	Chivers & Sons Ltd	1:47	Y21-2	1985	Ford Model 'A' Woody Wagon	Carters Tested Seeds	1:40
Y5-4	1982	1927 Talbot Van	Wrights Original Coal Tar Soap	1:47	Y22-1	1982	1930 Ford Model 'A' Van	Oxo	1:40
Y5-4	1983	1927 Talbot Van	Ever Ready	1:47	Y22-1	1984	1930 Ford Model 'A' Van	Maggis Soup	1:40
Y5-4	1984	1927 Talbot Van	Dunlop	1:47	Y22-1	1984	1930 Ford Model 'A' Van	Toblerone	1:40
Y5-4	1985	1927 Talbot Van	Rose's	1:47	Y22-1	1984	1930 Ford Model 'A' Van	Walter's Palm Toffee	1:40
Y6-1	1957	1916 AEC 'Y' Type Lorry	Blue	1:100	Y22-1	1984	1930 Ford Model 'A' Van	Postes Canada Post	1:40
Y6-5	1988	1932 Mercedes Benz Truck	Struttgart Hofbrau	1:69	Y22-1	1986	1930 Ford Model 'A' Van	Spratt's	1:40
Y7-1	1957	Four Ton 'Leyland' Van	Brown	1:100	Y22-1	1987	1930 Ford Model 'A' Van	Lyons'	1:40
Y9-3	1985	1920 3 Ton Leyland Lorry	A. Luff & Sons Ltd	1:62	Y25-1	1983	1910 Renault Type AG Van	Perrier	1:38
Y12-3	1979	1912 Ford Model 'T' Van	Colmans	1:35	Y25-1	1985	1910 Renault Type AG Van	James Neale & Sons	1:38
Y12-3	1980	1912 Ford Model 'T' Van	Coca-Cola	1:35	Y25-1	1985	1910 Renault Type AG Van	Duckham's Oil	1:38
Y12-3	1980	1912 Ford Model 'T' Van	Suze	1:35	Y25-1	1985	1910 Renault Type AG Van	Eagle Pencil & Co	1:38
Y12-3	1981	1912 Ford Model 'T' Van	Smith's Potato Crisps	1:35	Y25-1	1986	1910 Renault Type AG Van	Ambulance	1:35
Y12-3	1981	1912 Ford Model 'T' Van	25th Anniversary	1:35	Y25-1	1987	1910 Renault Type AG Van	T. Tunnocks	1:35
Y12-3	1982	1912 Ford Model 'T' Van	Bird's Custard Powder	1:35	Y25-1	1987	1910 Renault Type AG Van	Delhaize	1:38
Y12-3	1982	1912 Ford Model 'T' Van	Cerebos Table Salt	1:35	Y26-1	1984	Crossley Delivery Truck	Löwenbrau	1:47
Y12-3	1982	1912 Ford Model 'T' Van	Arnott's Biscuits	1:35	Y26-1	1986	Crossley Delivery Truck	Romford Brewery	1:47
Y12-3	1982	1912 Ford Model 'T' Van	Harrods	1:35	Y26-1	1987	Crossley Delivery Truck	Gonzalez Byass	1:47
Y12-3	1983	1912 Ford Model 'T' Van	Sunlight Soap	1:35	Y29-1	1985	1919 Walker Electric Van	Harrods Ltd	1:51
Y12-3	1983	1912 Ford Model 'T' Van	Royal Mail	1:35	Y29-1	1986	1919 Walker Electric Van	Joseph Lucas	1:51
Y12-3	1983	1912 Ford Model 'T' Van	Captain Morgan	1:35	Y29-1	1988	1919 Walker Electric Van	His Master's Voice	1:51
Y12-3	1983	1912 Ford Model 'T' Van	Hoover	1:35	Y30-1	1985	1920 Mack Truck	Acorn Storage	1:60
Y12-3	1984	1912 Ford Model 'T' Van	Pepsi-Cola	1:35	Y30-1	1985	1920 Mack Truck	Consolidated Motor Lines Ltd	1:60
Y12-3	1985	1912 Ford Model 'T' Van	Motor 100	1:35	Y30-1	1987	1920 Mack Truck	Arctic Ice Cream	1:60
Y12-3	1985	1912 Ford Model 'T' Van	Imbach	1:35	Y30-1	1988	1920 Mack Truck	Kiwi Boot Polish	1:60

The Y30 Mack Truck, Y19 Morris and Y6 Mercedes.
Top row: Right, A pre-production Mack Truck.

of note was that a few models appeared with red twelve spoked wheels, most of which went direct to Express Dairies. *Tekerian:* "I dealt direct with Express Dairies because they bought a large quantity after we said that we could do their livery. We began to realise just how important the collectors' market was . . . We put out 25,000 questionnaires with this model to determine their likes and dislikes."

The dairy theme was repeated for the release of *Carnation* in 1984, a standard livery which bore few

A selection of models produced by Lesney and Matchbox now referred to as Code Two models.

variations except for its wheels. Models appeared with red twenty four spoked and gold twelve spoked wheels. The last run of the model had twelve spoke dark cherry red wheels, the colour being almost identical to that of the tank.

The *Mobiloil* livery of 1985 was a Limited Edition of 80,000 models; a small run was produced with black seats.

Yet another oil company appeared as the standard livery in 1986, *Castrol Motor Oil*. This model was in production during the transition period of altering the baseplates of all models from Lesney Products to Matchbox International; hence models with either description can be found. Models also appeared with chrome radiators, black seats and even gold wheels. The dull red wheels associated with the Mobiloil have also been found on this model.

As part of the set of four Special Limited Edition models in 1986 the tanker was released in the livery of *Red Crown Gasoline*. The model was substantially changed to have side tank hoardings as well as an altered side window and new cast roof. Widely accepted as the most attractive of all of the tankers, it could be found with both baseplate inscriptions and whitewall tyres. Production was limited to 70,000 units worldwide.

Late in 1987 an entirely new model joined the range, the **Y19/2 1929 Morris Van**. This van featured the livery of *Brasso* metal polish. The introduction of the model had been delayed by two other Yesteryears coming on to the market and so the Brasso version was only on sale for four months. During early casting runs, a weakness was found in two places in the roof component. This was overcome by modifying four struts on the underside of the roof component. It was replaced by the model in *Michelin Tyres* livery in May 1988. This model was unusual in that both sides of the van bore completely different designs. Once again the livery was carefully researched and completely authentic.

The **Y6/5 1932 Mercedes Truck** was introduced into the range in 1988. The idea of the Mercedes was suggested by a M.I.C.A. member living in the U.S.A. He supplied the Matchbox R. & D. Department with a black and white photograph of the truck parked outside a brewery in New York. Matchbox liked the subject and issued it with the *Gtuttgarter Hofbrau* livery. The model incorporated a fair degree of diecast components, but caused some discontent amongst collectors because of the ill-fitting rear plastic tilt.

CODE TWO MODELS

Certain rules have been established by the collectors of Matchbox models in relation to their status. These rules arose because certain models, mostly Yesteryears, began to be changed in some way from how they originally left the factory, either by collectors, model makers or entrepreneurs.

In the majority of cases the individuals in question did not approach Lesney and seek permission to alter the models. This lack of courtesy could, of course, be excused if the models were being doctored by an enthusiast and the altered models were simply going into his collection. More sinister problems would ensue if the altered models were going to be sold on the open market. Certainly by the late 1970s altered models were often passed off as genuine Yesteryears, and did not comply with the rigid quality controls adhered to by Lesney. These privately altered models are known as Code Three models.

In some cases, however, individuals did receive permission from Lesney to alter a standard Yesteryear; changes could include a new paint scheme or the addition of a new plastic component or simply the re-labelling of a model. Further, there has been over the last thirty three years, the odd occasion when the manufacturers have made a model but have only made very limited numbers and not offered it for sale through the normal outlets. An example of this policy, which has not been adopted since 1983, was the Y12/3 Hoover. Some five hundred vans in blue, as opposed to orange, with the Hoover livery, were manufactured and individually certificated by Matchbox for the directors and management of Hoover. In other words, they were not sold to retail shops. Consequently, this extremely rare model currently commands prices anywhere between £500 and £800. Either one of the reasons explained above has given rise to the second accepted category – Code Two models.

The collecting of Code Two models has been variable, as for several years the majority of collectors were unaware that they existed. When information has been supplied via collectors' periodicals and books, the desirability of these models increased dramatically. In the last two years, however, an overwhelming number of fakes and copies have found their way onto the market and this had the effect of undermining the collectability of Code Two models.

Code One models are models that have been made in their entirety by either Lesney Products or Matchbox and have been distributed for sale to the general public via retail outlets.

THE DEFINITION OF MODELS OF YESTERYEAR STATUS

CODE ONE

Models that have been manufactured in their entirety by either Lesney Products or Matchbox Toys and have been distributed for sale to the general public via retail outlets.

CODE TWO

Models that were originally of Code One status but whose livery or decorations have been altered, removed or replaced by a third party with the full agreement and acknowledgement of Lesney Products or Matchbox Toys OR where an otherwise Code One model has not been made available to the general public via retail outlets.

CODE THREE

Models that were originally of Code One status but whose livery or decorations have been altered, removed or replaced by a third party without the agreement or acknowledgement of Lesney Products or Matchbox Toys.

CODE TWO YESTERYEARS

Y No.	Model	Year Of Issue	Colour	Livery	Known Quantity Produced	Fakes Known To Exist	Certificate
Y1	Model 'T'	1976	Black	Not applicable	900	Yes	No
Y5	Talbot	1978	Green/Black	2nd A.I.M.	Unknown	No	No
Y5	Talbot	1981	Blue/Black	Crawley	Unknown	No	No
Y5	Talbot	1981	Yellow	Variety Club	300	No	No
Y5	Talbot	1980	Yellow	Merita	Unknown	Yes	No
Y5	Talbot	1980	Yellow	Langendorf	Unknown	Yes	No
Y5	Talbot	1980	Yellow	Taystee	Unknown	No	No
Y5	Talbot	1981	Yellow/Black	Ironbridge	600	No	No
Y5	Talbot	1981	Yellow/Black	Bee's	500	Yes	No
Y5	Talbot	1981	Blue	Klokkenzolder	Unknown	No	Yes
Y7	RR	1982	Yellow/Black	Duchy of Cornwall	Unknown	Yes	No
Y12	Model 'T'	1981	Red/White	B & O	750	Yes	Yes
Y12	Model 'T'	1981	Yellow	Rayleigh	600	Yes	No
Y12	Model 'T'	1982	Yellow	Cada	600	No	No
Y12	Model 'T'	1982	Yellow	Deans	1000	Yes	No
Y12	Model 'T'	1980	Yellow	Camberley	750	No	No
Y12	Model 'T'	1983	Blue	Hoover	560	Yes	Yes (1st 540)
Y13	Crossley	1979	Red/Yellow	U.K. Matchbox Club	930	No	No
Y13	Crossley	1981	Red	Surrey	Unknown	No	No
Y13	Crossley	1981	Red	Aspects & Images	Unknown	No	No

The King Size 9 Super King Range

BUILDING FOR SUCCESS 1960 TO 1988

The first seven models in the King Size range showing the wheel styles. An example of the early King Size Civil Engineering Gift Set is shown in the background.

The King Size and Super King range were Lesney's attempt to break into the standard scale (approximately 1:42) market which by the 1960s were the domains of Dinky, Corgi and Spot-On toys. In today's collector dominated world it is all too easy to dismiss this whole range as unsuccessful and not as good quality as their competitors. This would be a great mistake, as close inspection will reveal certain examples to be as good as the toys that the opposition could offer.

It is true that this range is not widely collected, but those individuals who take the opportunity to search them out may well find their endeavors rewarded. This current lack of demand certainly means that the models are inexpensive and on those grounds offer the collector excellent value for money.

Detailed in this chapter are some of the ranges which met with poor public reaction (the Big MX models being a particular case in point) but this should not deter the collector as very often in this hobby the manufacturers failures are the collectors successes

The Super King range includes some of the largest and impressive models of the heavy haulage vehicles and as these types of model from other manufacturers are avidly sought after today, it may well pay the enthusiast to examine models such as the G.M.C. Tractor (K4-2) or the Prime Mover (K8) or even the current Peterbilt (K32) in detail as they offer real value for money.

By 1960 with the Regulars, Major Packs, Yesteryears and Accessories well established, Lesney Products decided to introduce a range of slightly larger models. This range was based upon some of the already successful tractor type models in the "Matchbox" Series and was named the King Size Series. *Smith:* "We decided to use the name King Size from the standard king size cigarette packet to complement the "Matchbox" Series."

The first models to be introduced in September 1960 were:

K1-1 Weatherill Hydraulic
      Shovel
K2-1 Muir Hill Dumper
K3-1 Caterpillar Bulldozer
K4-1 McCormick
      International Tractor

All of these were larger scale examples of models which had proved successful as miniatures, but the model makers were able to take advantage of the larger scale by introducing far greater detail than they were able to in the miniatures or Major Packs.

These first two King Size models were marketed at a price of 3s.0d (15p) each, when miniature models cost about two shillings (10p). They were targeted to compete with the then highly successful Dinky range. What irony that some 27 years later we saw that famous marque being taken over by Matchbox!

In the beginning, the models were fitted with grey metal, and then later plastic wheels with removable tyres, one of the play-value features of the opposition. *Smith:* "We had been told many times that the metal wheels of our toys scratched table tops, so we had to think up a way of overcoming this. For the smaller series we introduced plastic wheels, but for the King Size we were able to produce wheels and tyres." All of the early King Size models were issued with plastic tyres on either silver metal or plastic hubs.

In 1961 the range was increased to seven models by the introduction of:

K4-1   McCormick International Tractor (red)

K5-1   Foden Tipper Truck (yellow)

K6-1   Allis-Chalmers Earth Scraper (orange)

K7-1   Curtiss-Wright Rear Dumper (yellow)

In order to overcome the problem of allowing the scraper to descend to do its work, it was decided that ordinary springs would be used. Although un-characteristically unrealistic for a Matchbox toy, these springs did not harm the popularity of this model.

The K8-1 Prime Mover and Transporter with Caterpillar Tractor, 31.8 cm (12.5 inches) which was introduced at the price of 11s. 3d. (56p) in April 1962 was the first of many construction vehicles in the series to carry the name 'John Laing', the major international construction company with headquarters in North London. A close rela-

tionship was established between Lesney and John Laing over a number of years during which they built two factories, including the large modern factory at Lee Conservancy Road in Hackney Wick. The Prime Mover was the first King Size model to be fitted with plastic windows. The Caterpillar Tractor was the K3-1 Bulldozer without the front bulldozer blade. Other models released that year were:

K9-1   Aveling-Barford Diesel Road Roller – a green roller with red metal rollers

K10-1   Aveling-Barford Tractor Shovel.

The Tractor Shovel was the first to make use of a very successful imitation hydraulic system, a feature which has remained in use throughout the history of the King Size range. The hydraulic system was based upon a split pin fitting into a plastic sleeve. By precision tooling the close fit meant that the

This model is virtually a revised version of the early Prime Mover described in Chapter Three.

The second generation of King Size models, each of which had a moving feature.

piston retained its hydraulic effect for many hours of tough play. Early models of the turquoise-green Tractor Shovel included an air filter assembly at the rear right side of the body. Later models with red plastic wheels did not have this feature.

In 1963 the blue K11-1 Fordson Super Major Farm Tractor and grey Tipper Trailer also made use of this hydraulic system. The K12-1 Heavy Breakdown Wreck Truck was issued in the green livery of 'B.P. Petrol'. This model, though out of scale at 62:1, was introduced together with the then newly re-released B.P. Garage (for further information see Chapter Eleven). The first Foden Breakdown trucks carried a seperate rivetted name-board on the roof which incorporated side lamps at either side. Later models carried name boards cast with the cab as one unit and did not feature these lamps.

The K13-1 'Ready-Mix Cement' Truck released in September 1963 was the first of many models in the King Size, and later the Super King range, to make use of the turning road wheels to power a working feature – in this case the revolving cement bucket. Ready Mixed Concrete is a large multi-national company whose orange coloured vehicles are familiar on the roads of the U.K. Collectors of the Convoy series in the U.K. were surprised to see this familiar name on the pink Australian issue Scania in 1986. The two liveries of this model carried either 'R.M.C.' or 'Readymix' on the barrel.

Gift sets on sale in 1963 included the mixed King Size and Regular G3 'Farm and Agriculture Set' which included a K3-1 Caterpillar Tractor and a K11-1 Fordson Tractor and Farm Trailer and the G8 Civil Engineering Set which contained the following models:

K1-1 Weatherill Hydraulic Shovel
K2-1 Muir Hill Dumper
K3-1 Caterpillar Bulldozer
K5-1 Foden Tipper Truck
K6-1 Allis-Chalmers Earth Scraper

The K1-2 Foden Eight Wheel Tipper Truck introduced in 1964 was the first of many models in the range to be fitted with suspension, using a system which had been successful in the miniature range. The Tipper Truck together with the MB17 carried 'Hoveringham' transfers on the sides of their tipper buckets. Hoveringham was a U.K. aggregate supplier which was later taken over by Ready Mixed Concrete.

New King Size models illustrated in the catalogue that year included the first in a long kept tradition of King Size fire engines. The K15-1 Merryweather Fire Engine released in August 1965 at a price of 6s. 11d. (34.5p) with its extending and revolving turntable ladder was an excellent model of the original. The model carried transfers and labels on its doors identifying it as an appliance of the Kent Fire Brigade. The yellow K2-2 Dump Truck was a model of a complicated articulated hydraulic dumper, and K14-1 the Taylor Jumbo Crane, a mobile crane with a revolving lifting jib. The first cranes came with a yellow weight box and feint decal; these were soon changed to red weight boxes with clearer decals.

During 1965 there was a glimpse of things to come when the Dodge Truck with Twin Tippers was illustrated in the catalogue as the future Major Pack series model M7. However, it never appeared in that series as Lesney decided to abandon Major Packs.

K3-1 Hatra Tractor Shovel. The orange tractor with its hydraulic lifting and tipping shovel bucket carried the labels Hatra on its sides.

In 1966 selected examples of the discontinued Major Pack series were re-issued in the King Size Range:

MP	No.	K No.
4-2	4-2	GMC Tractor with Hopper Train
6-2	5-2	Racing Car Transporter
8-2	8-2	Car Transporter

In each case identical models were issued but in the larger King Size boxes and with modifications to their baseplates to show their new K numbers.

The red K4-2 GMC Tractor with silver Hopper Train carried the labels Fruehauf, an internationally known trailer manufacturer.

The K5-2 Racing Car Transporter which could accommodate two miniature models was issued

in the green livery of B.P. Petrol, and bore labels listing the names of four major Formula One racing circuits.

The K8-2 Car Transporter was the first car transporter in the King Size range. The trailer carried the transfers 'Farnborough Measham'. Early models had turquoise cabs with orange trailers but this was soon changed to all yellow. F.M. was a car auction company based at these two towns which later became the well known British Car Auctions. Ever since then car transporters built to a scale which allowed them to be used to carry miniature models, have always been included in the King Size range.

The K4-2 GMC and K16-1

Dodge Trucks with their trailers were the first of the many large articulated trucks which, for years to come, would prove so popular in the King Size and Super King ranges.

Other new models released that year were:

K7-2 SD Refuse Truck. The red truck with its silver tipping dumper carried the description 'Cleansing Services' on its sides.

K17-1 Ford Tractor with Dyson Low-Loader and Case Bulldozer.

K18-1 Articulated Horse Box. The red Dodge KEW truck with its articulated beige trailer carrying four beige plastic horses had the label 'Ascot Stables' on its sides.

The green Ford Tractor was

issued both in 'John Laing' livery and then later with 'Taylor Woodrow' printed at the back of the cab with patterned transfers on the doors. Whereas all of the articulated trailers in the series up to this time had been permanently attached to their towing tractors, the Low Loader could be uncoupled from the Ford by lifting the side petrol tanks. The yellow metal roof of the red Case Bulldozer could be easily removed.

The first passenger vehicle in the range issued in June 1967 at a price of 6s. 11d. (34.5p) was the K6-2 Mercedes Benz-Binz Ambulance, a model of a typical continental ambulance of the time. It was one of many models in the King Size range which reproduced, at a larger scale a model in the regular series. *Smith:* "It was practical for the company to manufacture similar models for both series as all of the preliminary research and design work could be used for models produced to both scales. However, for models made in the larger series more features could be incorporated." This model was fitted with True-Guide directional steering, independent suspension, opening front doors and tailgate, and came complete with a patient on a stretcher covered with his own red blanket.

1967 also saw the introduction of:

K9-2 Combine Harvester. Though illustrated in the 1967 collectors catalogue as carrying transfers saying 'Matchbox', the actual Combine Harvester, when issued, carried the transfers 'Claas'. Early models had a driver but the figure was later deleted

K10-2 Scammell Pipe Truck with six interlocking pipes. The yellow tractor and dolly trailer carried six grey pipes

K19-1 Scammell Tipper Truck

K20-1 The red Ford Tractor Transporter introduced in

The demise of the Major Pack range led to the transfer of two of these articulated trucks into King Size. The Dodge was not produced as a Major Pack.

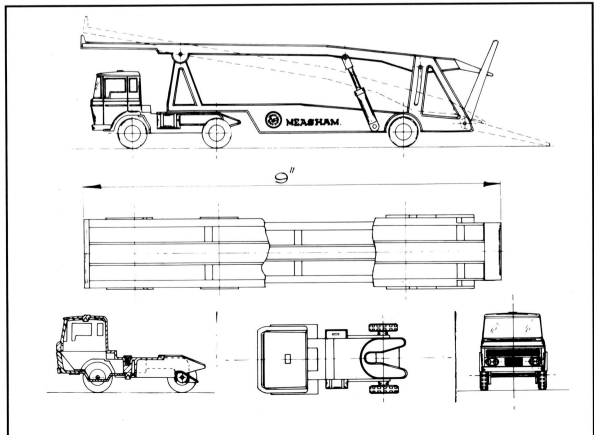

November 1967 carried three regular series models. The MB39-3 Ford Tractors, which were then being issued in yellow and blue in the regular series, were painted plain blue when first issued with the K20-1. They were attached to the flat bed trailer by a removable yellow plastic clip.

The release of the K21-1 Mercury Cougar with True Guide steering and suspension was delayed, and although illustrated in the 1967 catalogue it was only issued in October 1968. Though illustrated in the catalogue in blue this model was eventually released in gold. The interior of the Cougar was normally red but some models

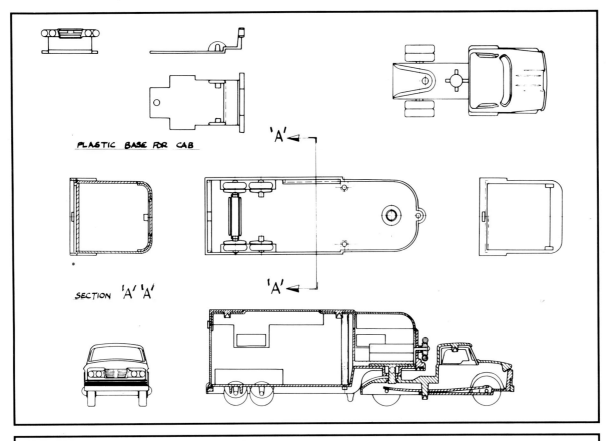

PLASTIC BASE FOR CAB

SECTION 'A' 'A'

'A'

'A'

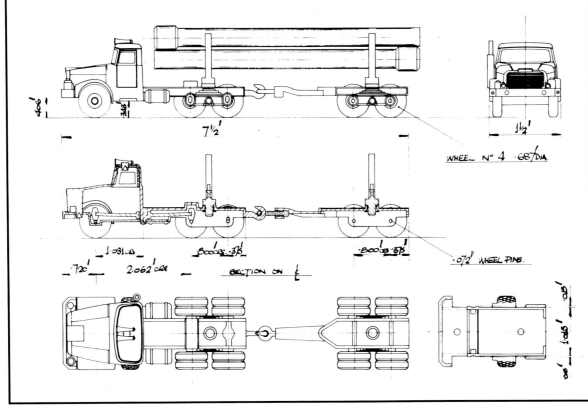

7½'

WHEEL N° 4 ·687 DIA

406

345

1½'

1·031 DIA

800 DIA ·375

800 DIA ·375

·072" WHEEL PINS.

·720'

2·062' CRS

SECTION ON ₵

with white interiors have been found.

The True-Guide steering relied on rubberised tyres on plastic hubs which turned the front wheels in the direction the car was pushed.

The K22-1 Dodge Charger in metallic blue soon followed.

Only two commercial vehicles were released in 1969, the Scammell Heavy Wreck Truck which, in white was issued in the livery of the 'Esso' petrol company and the K4-3 Leyland Tipper. The original tipper truck issued with a red cab and silver dumper carried the labels 'L.F. Transport'. They were later released in orange and green with the labels 'W. Wates'. In 1969 five hundred of these trucks were produced in all over pea-green as a thank you for permission by Mr John Wates to use his company's logo. Of the five hundred, fifty were given away in boxes signed by Mr Wates to the main clients of his company. Two cars were issued:

K23-1 Mercury Police Car with
 Highway Patrol
 'POLICE' labels
K24-1 Lamborghini Miura

Each was illustrated to have opening doors, but when issued, the Lamborghini, unlike MB33-3 didn't; its tail section tipped back to reveal the first crudely detailed engine compartment on a car in the series. Although all early Miuras were issued in bright red, later models were issued in bright blue and yellow and carried on their bonnets a label depicting a bull's head and sword.

By 1969 each of the models in the King Size range had a working feature. According to the catalogue of that year there were 'lorries that tip, cranes that lift, doors that open, mixer drums that turn and wheels that steer'.

The Mercury Cougar and the Dodge Charger with the True-Guide steering and their dragster replacements.

Only five King Size models were released with True-Guide steering between 1968 and 1971:

K6-2   Mercedes Benz – Binz Ambulance
K21-1 Mercury Cougar
K22-1 Dodge Charger
K23-1 Mercury Police Car
K24-1 Lamborghini Miura

The system was then replaced by the free-wheeling Superfast style wheels.

New models released in 1970 were:

K1-3 O & K Excavator. The red hydraulic excavator with its silver lifting arm carried the labels 'O & K' on the sides of its cab and the description 'MH6' on its arm. It had been proposed that the excavator bucket should be cast as a solid piece with the lower arm. This made the scoop action impossible. It was, therefore, decided that this bucket should be made from a separate casting with an extra hydraulic ram – an expensive re-tooling job!

K3-3 Massey Ferguson Tractor. The red tractor carried the labels 'Massey Ferguson 165' on its engine cowlings and towed a tipping four wheeled trailer. Early trailers had smooth floors,

all later models were textured.

K8-3 Caterpillar Traxcavator. First issued with and then later without a driver, this model was issued in various shades of yellow with an orange bulldozer blade.

K11-3 DAF Car Transporter. This model which carried 'DAF' labels on the sides of the tractor was issued with a metallic blue cab and gold trailer. It has been found with silver tractors.

K12-2 Scammell Crane Truck.

Issued in yellow in the livery of John Laing.

1971 saw the introduction of the Super King range and the gradual discontinuation of the King Size models. The change in name came about with the introduction of the Superfast type wheels (similar to the change in the miniature series from Regular to Superfast). The following models survived the transition over the next year – some suffering unrealistic colour changes:

K1-3 O & K Excavator
K2-3 Scammell Heavy Wreck Truck
K4-3 Leyland Tipper
K7-2 SD Refuse Truck
K10-2 Pipe Truck
K11-2 DAF Car Transporter
K12-2 Scammell Crane Truck
K15-1 Merryweather Fire Engine
K16-1 Dodge Tractor with Twin Tippers
K17-1 Ford Tractor with Case Bulldozer
K18-1 Articulated Horse Box
K19-1 Scammell Tipper Truck
K20-1 Tractor Transporter

In each case the bases of the models were modified in order to accommodate the new style wheels.

The cars became Speed Kings. The 1971 catalogue stated: "Featuring the new speed-slick tyres and extra large customised bodies they're Kings of speed on floor or table". For two models this meant only a change in wheels and axles – K23-1 and K24-1; for one it meant a change in number, the K6-2 Mercedes Benz-Binz Ambulance became the new K26-1.

With the introduction of this range the K21-1 Mercury Cougar and K22-1 Dodge Charger were converted into dragsters, the Cougar became a pink Cougar Dragster with 'Dinamite' on its

opening doors and boot, and the Dodge, a Dodge Dragster with 'Bender' on its engine. This heralded a period during which Lesney would introduce a large number of unrealistic, customised models which the company perceived the market wanted such as models of futuristic prototypes and custom car conversions. In order to meet the demands of the international market and to avoid being identified with real vehicles on the roads in different parts of the world, commercial vehicles

and tractors issued during this period suffered anonymity by not representing true vehicles.

When the Mercedes Benz-Binz Ambulance was re-released as K26-1, a GMC Cement Mixer with revolving barrel was issued as K6-3. The earlier K13-1 Ready-Mixed Concrete Truck was replaced by K13-2 a DAF Building Transporter with a pre-fabricated building. The replacement for the Jumbo Crane was K14-2, a Scammell Freight Truck with sliding side doors. Throughout its life it

carried the livery of 'LEP International Transport', the international freight forwarding company.

Other models for that year were:

K25-1 'Seaburst' Power Boat and Trailer. The plastic power boat which could float carried one outboard motor. Later examples used in some sets had twin outboards.

K27-1 Camping Cruiser. This model, with its raising sun roof and rear door, even carried a representation of a stainless steel kitchen sink

K28-1 Drag Pack comprising K21-2 the Cougar Dragster on a trailer towed by a Mercury Estate car complete with roof luggage and spare wheels.

K29-1 Miura 'Seaburst' Set. The K25-1 Power Boat towed by K24-1, the Lamborghini – not successfully, became when the trailer was attached the rear wheels of the Miura could not touch the ground!

In 1972, the K5-3 Muir-Hill Tractor and Trailer was issued with a detachable plough shovel and a tipping trailer dumper. It was reported that the two prongs of the shovel could fit neatly into certain European electricity sockets and represented a significant risk to children. The attachments were quickly redesigned and the tractor has remained in production since 1972 in its various forms. In 1987 descendants of these Muir-Hill Tractors (or were they the very aged originals?) were found loaded on transporters as K108-2.

This successful model, however, cannot match the success of the 1972 model of a London Bus. First introduced with an opening passenger door and a stop and start bell fitted at the rear which could be struck with a sprung metal lever and carrying the labels 'Carnaby Street', Lesney soon found that this popular

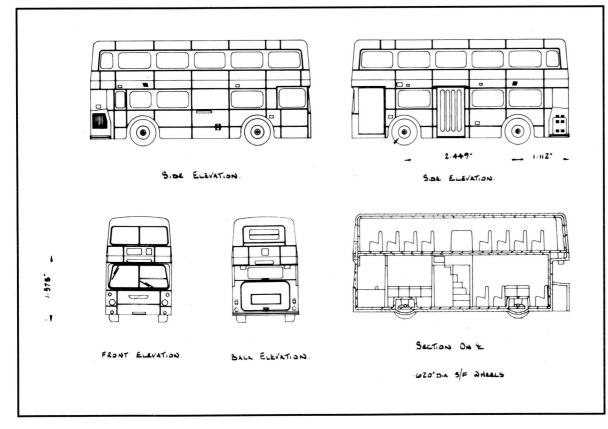

SIDE ELEVATION.

SIDE ELEVATION.

2·449"   1·112"

FRONT ELEVATION.

BACK ELEVATION.

SECTION ON ℄

·620"DIA S/F WHEELS

1·376"

Early Muir Hill Tractors had removeable plough blades which fitted into European electricity sockets. A normal release yellow tractor is illustrated together with a Hoch and Tief model only released in West Germany.

model sold successfully without the gimmick and complication of the bell. Even the opening door was eventually dispensed with. As with any typical London bus, this model was initially made in red with various advertising labels.

A silver bus was issued in 1977 to commemorate the Silver Jubilee of the Coronation of Queen Elizabeth II. Subsequent buses have been made in various colours; a second in silver commemorated the wedding of the Prince and Princess of Wales in 1981. One model, carrying the labels 'Tourist London by Bus', was mounted with screws on a small plastic plinth. One, in tan with labels 'Berlin ist eine Reise

COLOUR	OPENING DOOR	LABEL	DESTINATION
Red	Yes	Hamleys the finest toy shop in the world	Praed St, Kensington
Red	Yes	Enter a different world - Harrods - 1976 issue	Hackney
Red	Yes	Harrods for more than money can buy - 1982 issue	London Bridge
Red	No	Harrods for more than money can buy - 1984 issue	London Bridge
Blue	No	Alton Towers	
Blue/White	No	Macleans Toothpaste	Beecham House
Blue/Cream	No	Bradford Telegraph and Argus	Bingley
Yellow/Beige	No	Butterkist	
Blue/White	No	Chesterfield Parish Church	Town Centre
Red	Yes (with bell)	Swinging London Carnaby Street	Praed St Kensington
Red	Yes	Swinging London Carnaby Street	London Bridge
Silver	Yes	Silver Jubilee 1952 - 1977	1952 E R 1977
Red	Yes	Visit the London Dungeon	London Bridge
Silver	Yes	Visit the London Dungeon	London Bridge
Red	Yes	Tourist London by Bus	Hackney
Silver	Yes	The Royal Wedding 1981	St Paul's Cathedral
Red	Yes	Firestone (Similar to the label on TP23)	London Bridge
Red	No	London Wide Tour Bus	Westminster Abbey
Red	No	London Planaterium	The Planeterium
Red	No	Come to Petticoat Lane	Petticoat Lane
Red/White	No	Nestle Milky Bar	London Bridge

wert' (Berlin is worth a trip) with its direction indicator saying that it was going to the Wittenbergplatz, was released in West Berlin as a left-hand drive model to commemorate the 750th anniversary of that city, whilst another, in red with right-hand drive carried the label 'Besuchen Sie Berlin Haupstadt der DDR 1237-1987 750 Jahre' (Visit Berlin, Capital of the GDR 1237-1987 750 years).

K15-2 London Buses have been made as Code 2 promotional models for a number of customers. (For definitions of model catagories see Chapter Eight.)

The Hamleys and three Harrods buses carried labels which were identical to those carried by contemporary real buses on the streets of London.

Further K15 buses which have been on general release since 1972 include:A special K15-2 Bus that was designed as a special issue to commemorate a proposed trip by Queen Elizabeth II and Prince Phillip to the Middle East in 1979 but was never released when, because of the impending revolution in Iran, the trip was called off.

Another model released in 1972 was far less successful. Of the first 100,000 K30-1 Mercedes C111's, which carried working front headlights, nearly 85% were found to be faulty. When a baseplate lever was moved the headlamps were raised activating the tiny lamps. These were powered by a battery mounted in the boot. *Smith:* "As toys they were not robust enough!" The company quickly redesigned the model. Later K30-1's had retractable imitation headlights operated by a small lever under the body and an opening rear compartment enclosing the detailed engine, and as recently as 1987 K30-1 Mercedes C111's have been produced in Bulgaria.

Other new issues for 1972 were:

K31-1 Bertone Runabout – A prototype open sportscar with an

This photograph ilustrates the working bell to be found in early models. Left: The unreleased souvenir bus planned to celebrate the state visit to Iran. Right: The left hand drive Berlin issue.

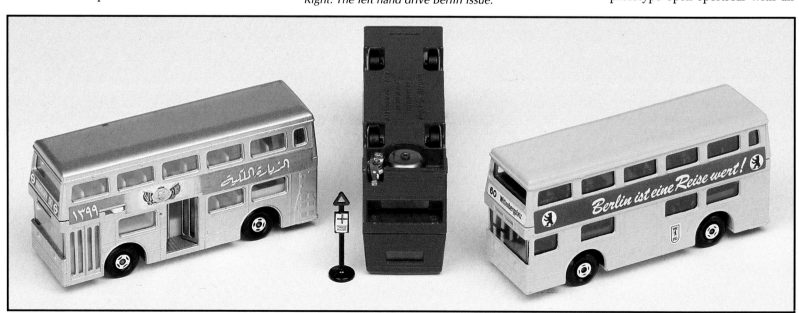

K15-2 buses including the three Harrod's versions.

redesigned and altered to incorporate these features they couldn't be used to make the standard models.

Each of these models was released in a large box which included associated working accessories, loads and buildings. The models released in this way included the following:

K7-3 BM-1 S.D. Refuse Truck with Incinerator.

K20-2 BM-2 Tractor Transporter and Tractor Plant.

K12-3 BM-3 Scammell Crane Truck and Building Site.

K4-4B M-4 Leyland Tipper and Mechanised Coal Delivery Hopper.

K8-3 BM-5 Caterpillar Traxcavator and Quarry Site.

K15-2 BM-6 Merryweather Fire Engine and Rescue Scene.

Smith: "They got too clever with too many components . . . a child in the end has his own imagination and he does not want it given to him on a plate . . . he gets the fire going in his own mind, he gets out the hosepipe . . . he doesn't need us to make him a hosepipe."

The early K7-3 yellow Racing Car Transporters issued in 1973 carried a MB34 Formula 1 Racing Car, while later white transporters carried a MB56 Hi Trailer. K20-2, the Cargo Pauler & Pallet Loader shared its box with a MB15 Fork Lift Truck. A new futuristic Fire Tender with twin rotating water cannon, revolving turntable with high lift extending ladder carrying the labels Denver Fire Dept and designated K9-3 replaced the Claas Combine Harvester. The following cars were added to the Speed King list:

K37-1 Sandcat. An orange beach buggy.

K38-1 Gus's Gulper. A dragster based upon a Ford Mustang with its V8 engine and support bars for lifting its body and crash cage.

opening detailed engine compartment and crystal-like headlights.

K32-1 Shovel Nose. A prototype sports car with a cockpit that opened to reveal its detailed interior.

K33-1 Citroen SM. A sleek example of this Citroen/Maserati joint venture in bright red with opening doors, also recently reintroduced manufactured in Bulgaria.

K34-1 Thunderclap. A racing car with chromed engine, exhausts and racing suspension first issued in yellow in the colours actually used by Team Matchbox that year, and later in black.

K35-1 Lightning (another racing car in white with a V8 engine, branched megaphone exhausts and racing suspension). The first models in white carried various racing labels of Texaco, STC and Firestone and carried the number 35.

K36-1 Bandolero. This blue prototype with its opening cockpit with detailed interior was powered by two V8 engines.

Also that year a number of the then current Super King models were issued with working components and renamed Big 'M-X' models. The working features were powered by a Power Activator gun (designated BM-A) which when plugged into a socket on the vehicle and activated the mechanisms. *Smith:* "This series incorporated the invention of Marvin Gloss, a Chicago based inventor, who also gave us many other ideas for our toys." These models were never popular. It was found that children preferred to do their own playing and shunned the activators which took away rather than added to their fun. Collectors also gave these models a thumbs down as they did not like the activator sockets which protruded from the models. As far as the company was concerned the failure was made worse by the fact that once the tools had been

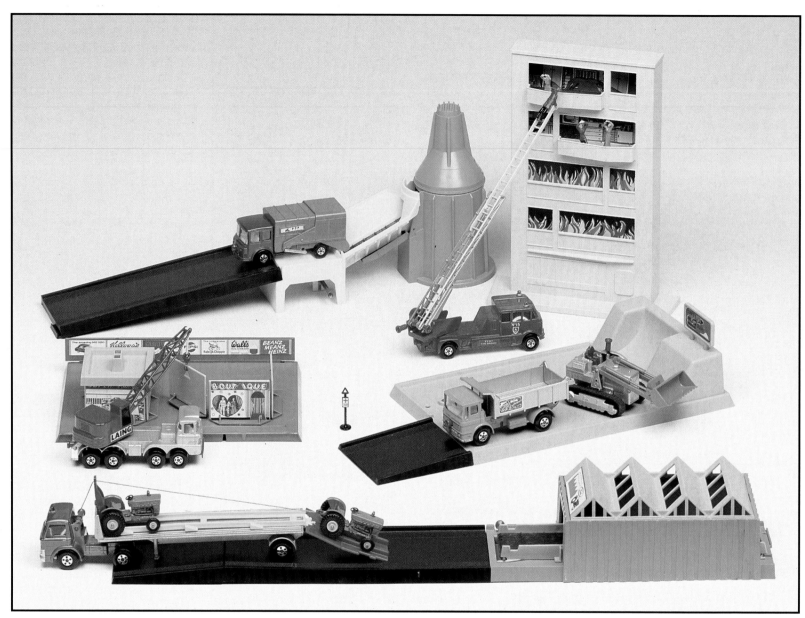

The ill-fated Big MX range could be regarded as extremely collectable.

K39-1 Milligan's Mill. Another similar dragster.

K40-1 Blaze Trailer

K32-1 Shovel Nose in red with Fire Chief markings.

K41-1 Fuzz Buggy K36-1 Bandolero in white and orange with Police markings.

K42-1 Nissan 270X. This prototype Nissan had an opening cockpit with a detailed interior. On the sides of its forward lifting cockpit

and on its bonnet it carried the number 8.

K43-1 Cambuster. A dragster displaying an enormous engine and outsize rear wheels.

K44-1 Bazooka. Another similar dragster.

K45-1 Marauder. A single seater sports car first issued in pink with the number 7 powered by a V8 rear engine, roll over bar and aerofoil stabiliser.

K46-1 Racing Car Pack. A set comprising K34-1, the Thunder-

clap racing car on a trailer towed by a Mercury Estate in yellow.

K47-1 Easy Rider. A large motor tricycle made at a scale of 20-1 when most of the Speed King cars were about 40-1. This model of a custom-built chopper had a steering front wheel and the long haired driver had moving joints in his hands, arms and legs.

K48-1 Mercedes 350 SLC. A good representation of the real car with opening bonnet and doors and detailed engine and interior.

K49-1 Ambulance in white with its opening rear door with a stretcher patient and two attendants, which was later released in Germany in red with 'Maltese Hilfdienst' labels on its sides and the number 7461 in black on its white roof.

K50-1 Street Rod. The custom hot rod based on a vintage Model T Ford body had a chrome plated V8 engine and chassis, and a rear tool box complete with a range of tools. On its sides it carried Hot T labels.

K51-1 Barracuda. A single seater

sports car first issued in blue with the racing labels of STP and the number 5. This model had an aerofoil stabilizer, V8 engine and rollover crash cage.

Another highly successful Super King model was introduced in 1974, the K16-3 Ford LTS Petrol Tanker. The bonnet of the truck tipped forward by the release of a chrome air inlet at the side. On early models the bonnet was sprung and would tip open automatically at a touch, but for later models the bonnets had to be opened by hand. The exhaust stacks on early models stuck out above the roof of the cab but on later models the straight exhaust stacks did not reach the roof. After its first success in red and white carrying 'Texaco' labels, this model was later released in the liveries of the following companies:

Ford Truck	Livery	Trailer
Red	Texaco	Red/White
White	Shell	Yellow/White
Blue	Aral*	Blue/White
White	Exxon	White
White	Total	Red/White
Blue/Yellow	Chemco	Yellow
White	BP	Yellow/White
White	Total	White

*Early Aral tankers carry labels which include clouds, on later examples the labels are plain.

In 1975 about one thousand of these tankers were produced for the Quaker State Oil Company of Canada and given away to their representatives. These green tankers carried the label 'Quaker State Peace of Mind by the Quart'.

After this promotion a number of these special green and white tankers were offered by Lesney (N.J.) U.S.A. to members of their Newsletter Club carrying the normal Texaco labels.

In 1976 the K16 tanker was packed in a blister card and sold in West Germany and South Africa in military olive drab as MM-1 carrying two label varieties 'Armored Div' (earlier seen on the .K102-1

A number of the Ford LTS Petrol Tankers including: the green Quaker State model, the green Texaco models which were made to use up the spare green and white bodies, the two military tankers released as MM models, one of the Aral Tankers and one with B.P. labels fitted to a yellow and white Shell model.

M.48 AZ carried by the K106-1 Tank Transporter) and '8' in a small square, together with MM-2 the K20-3 Cargo Hauler carrying a

SF73 Weasel and a spare engine as its cargo. Their success in military colours led to the introduction of the Battle King series later that

year. The Battle King model K115-1, another Ford LTS Tanker, carried labels stating 'Army Flammable CD34-94'.

At the same time as the K16-3 Petrol Tanker was introduced two other articulated trucks were brought on to the market, the K17-3 Scammell Articulated Container Truck and the K18-3 Articulated Tipper Truck. The Tipper Truck was towed by a Ford LTS similar to the one found towing the K16-3 Petrol Tanker. The Container truck has, on general release, carried containers with five labels — 'Gentransco', '7UP', 'P' P' Pick up a Penguin', 'DBP' (German Post Office) and 'Deutsche Bundepost'. In 1977, Lesney Products acquired the Vogue Doll Company in the U.S.A., and in promoting this new product, produced 250 K17-3 Container Trucks in special livery of 'Ginny Vogue Dolls' as a publicity exercise. The Tipper Truck, amongst others, carried the labels of 'Tarmac', 'Condor', 'United States Steel' and 'Hoch & Tief'. In 1978 a number of Super King models were released in West Germany in light and dark blue carrying the labels of 'Hoch & Tief Bauunternehmen', a German construction company. These included:

- K5-3   Muir Hill Tractor and Trailer
- K12-4   Hercules Mobile Crane
- K18-3   Articulated Tipper Truck
- K23-3   Low Loader
- K26-2   Bedford Cement Truck
- K28-2   Bedford Skip Truck

The first eight Battle Kings Military Series were introduced in 1974.

K101-1	Sherman Tank	Gold	48350 USA
K102-1	M.48 AZ Tank	Green	Green and white star
K103-1	Chieftain Tank	Green	No. 8
K104-1	King Tiger Tank	Silver	Black Cross No. 23
K105-1	Hover - Raider		The K22-2 Hovercraft in green with two silver missiles
K106-1	Tank Transporter with M.48 Tank		The articulated transporter was equipped with tank loading ramps and carried a K102-1 M.48 AZ Tank in mottled green with Armored Div labels
K107-1	155 mm Self Propelled Howitzer	Olive green	'A' in a blue and red square flag
K108-1	M3A1 Half Track Armoured Personnel Carrier	Metallic green	Green and white star

Early models of the K22-2 Hover-craft issued that year carried the labels 'SEASPEED' and 'SRN6'. Later models bore the livery of 'HOVERLLOYD' and bore labels stating Ramsgate – Calais and GH-0022. The hovercraft had a shaft-driven revolving radar scanner and propellors.

Other new models for 1974 were:

K3-4 Mod Tractor and Trailer
K4-5 Big Tipper
K21-2 Tractor Transporter
K23-2 Scammell Low Loader
        with Bulldozer

The K3-4 Mod Tractor and Trailer sported a chrome effect detailed V8 engine with a four position gear leaver and carried stars and stripes decorative labels.

The K4-5 Big Tipper was first introduced with the now familiar hydraulic pistons to hold the tipper bucket. Later, in 1976, this model together with the K110-1 Recovery Vehicle were released with a mechanical system called Press-amatic by pressing the petrol tank this caused the tipper and jib to rise. This system was not again seen in this series for about twelve years.

The first eight models in the Battle King Military series were also introduced in 1974. Although the colours of the first few tanks were inaccurate the models were popular in the selected countries in which they were marketed and after a few years as the range increased the colours became more realistic. Each of the first Battle King models was packaged with plastic military figures.

The only realistic car introduced to the Speed King range in 1974 was K52-1 the Datsun Rally Car, a well-proportioned model with a detailed engine, the bonnet being held closed by a small clip under the body. This model was first issued in yellow with the number 52 on its roof, doors and bonnet together with various Datsun, Shell and STP labels.

Since 1974 this model has been seen in many colours and in various guises and has remained popular ever since.

1975 saw the introduction of the then heaviest model in the whole Lesney range. The solid K12-3 Hercules Mobile Crane with its pivoting, lifting, extending crane with detach able grab-hook and extending chassis-jacks proved popular both in its civilian 'Laing'

livery and in K113-1 military con-figurations. The Motor Cycle trans-porter K6-4 was first introduced that year with its engine bursting from its bonnet. Later, with some clever recasting, Lesney were able to place all the machinery under the bonnet. The transporter went just as quickly but looked better! Early models carried an MB18 Hondarora but later they carried riderless MB33 Motor-cycles. The K11-4 Pickup Truck, with its drop down tailgate, swinging twin pick-up booms and hooks, was based on

the same unidentifiable truck as the Motor Cycle Transporter. In additon to the normal yellow models with either 'A.A.' or 'Shell' recovery labels, in 1977 a consignment of these in red with the labels 'Falck Zonen', a Swedish rescue organisation, were distributed by

Some of the K18-1 Articulated Tipper Trucks showing the liveries that were used in various countries where the model was issued.

Lesney U.S.A. to its club members.

In 1976 the K53-1 Hot Fire Engine with its plated engine and detachable rescue ladder and firemen carried Fire Chief labels and was based upon the same hot rod chassis as the K50-1 which had been introduced in 1974. Some models released that year used unidentifiable and rather ugly designs. These included:

K10-3 Car Transporter – An articulated five car transporter in red with Auto Transport labels and

with a hydraulically operated drop down top deck.

K13-3 Aircraft Transporter. The red transporter, with the label 'X4' on its roof, carried a white plastic Alpha jet.

K14-3 Heavy Recovery Truck. The white and red recovery had a spring loaded crane and carried 'Shell' recovery labels.

K54-1 A.M.X. Javelin. This model, first issued in metallic pink, had opening doors and a chromed grille. On its roof and bonnet it carried the number 7.

K55-1 Corvette Caper Car. A modified Chevrolet Corvette with opening doors and detailed interior. Its Californian number plates identified where it might possibly be seen.

K56-1 Maserati Bora. This Maserati was first issued in silver with a black label to represent a sun roof. On its opening bonnet and doors it carried the trident marking of Maserati

K57-1 Javelin Drag Racing Set.
K39-1 Milligan's Mill on a trailer towed by a K54-1 A.M.X.

K58-1 Corvette Power Boat Set. K25-1 Speedboat towed by K55-1 Corvette.

The new Battle Kings for the year were:

K109-1 M551 Sheridan Tank. Olive green carrying the number '7 in a blue and red triangular flag.

K110-1 Recovery Vehicle. The

released that year there were some good models:

K59-1 Ford Capri Mk2. First released in white with a black roof but later in a number of colours, this model had an opening fastback

The Motor Cycle Transporter illustrated with and without its chromed engine. The Recovery Vehicle in its box is carrying a Ford Mustang Cobra, one of the better models issued during the period of Hot-Rods and Custom Cars.

K61-1 Mercedes Police Car. Based on the 1974 K48-1 Mercedes 350 SLC this model, with its blue lights and chrome siren trumpets, was released with either white or green doors and bonnet with 'Polizei' labels in Germany or in plain white with 'Police' labels in the rest of the world. On its bonnet it carried the number '346'.

Lesney then cast their eyes out to sea! The following models of Naval ships were introduced as the Sea

K305-1 Submarine Chaser
K306-1 Convoy Escort
K307-1 Helicopter Carrier
K308-1 Guided Missile Destroyer

The 1977 red Scammell Container Truck K24-3 was released carrying removable containers with opening doors in various liveries. In France and the U.S.A. the containers were orange with 'Michelin' labels, in Germany they were white with 'Bauknecht-Komplettkuchen', while elsewhere the white containers carried 'Crewe London – Geneva' labels. These containers were interchangeable with those found on the K17-3 Articulated Container Truck.

The Digger and Plough K25-2 released later that year was based upon the K5-3 Muir-Hill Tractor carrying the digger of the K1-3 O & K Excavator.

The green K2-5 Car Recovery Vehicle was first released in 1977 carrying a K37-1 Sand Cat. In later years this model was released carrying a K59-1 Ford Capri, in Germany carrying a K48-1 Mercedes 350 in silver with labels 'Auftrag des A.D.A.C.' (A.D.A.C. stands for Allgemeine Deutscher Automobil Club), and elsewhere in white and gold with a K61-1 Ford Mustang Cobra in red.

Two single seater Formula One racing cars were brought into the range which were far better representatives than the anonymous Thunderclap and Lightning. These two models were each issued by Lesney with three different numbers:

K14-3 Heavy Recovery Tank in metallic green – 66 Repair.

K111-1 Missile Launcher. The olive green Missile Launcher had an opening missile compartment which enclosed a rotating and elevating rocket launcher. A wheel driven shaft caused the radar scanner to turn.

In addition to the various futuristic models and dragsters

rear door and detailed interior. Earlier models carried 'Capri II' labels on its doors. This is another model which has recently been produced in Bulgaria.

K60-1 Ford Mustang. The metallic blue Mustang carried the number '20' on its doors and roof and a white mustang on its sides and bonnet. On its back bumper it carried a chromed brake-parachute pack.

King range with cut-away hulls hiding small Superfast wheels. Although in most cases they sported unrealistic plastic coloured components, they had some play value as toys. The ships launched in 1976 included:

K301-1 Frigate
K302-1 Corvette
K303-1 Battleship
K304-1 Aircraft Carrier

1977	1979	1982	
Number	Number	Number	
K41-2	K72-1	KP1	Brabham F1
K44-2	K73-1	KP1	Surtees F1

The 1982 KP models were special inexpensive issues without any decals; the Surtees in gold and black and the Brabham in green. Other models included in this inexpensive range were:

Examples of the King Size Battle King range including the MM DAF Truck which carried an SF73 Weasel.

Civilian	Military	
K22-3	K105-1	Hovercraft/Hover-raider
K14-3	K110-1	Heavy Recovery Vehicle
K12-4	K113-1	Hercules Crane with labels showing a white circle on a red background and the number 85
K13-3	K114-1	Aircraft Transporter with a brown plastic Alpha jet
K16-3	K115-1	Petrol Tanker

Unlike the K14-3, the military Recovery Vehicle had a Pressamatic heavy duty lifting crane with twin towing hooks.

The models specially made for this series included:

K112-1 DAF Ambulance – olive green with red cross labels.

K116-1 Artillery Truck and Field Gun.

The truck had a detachable canvas type canopy and machine gunner. The field gun could fire small plastic projectiles. The cab carried the same flag as the K107-1 Self Propelled Gun and on the canvas canopy there was a helmet and the number '44'.

The beige and green Self Propelled Hawk Missile Launcher had an elevating rocket mounting that fired missiles. On its sides it carried 'Army U.S. 560' labels.

1977 also saw the introduction of Lesney's answer to the space onslaught. The first three space age Adventure 2000 models K2001-1 Raider Command, K2002-1 Flight Hunter and K2003-1 Crusader were introduced in metallic green. *Tekerian:* "Adventure 2000 was ahead of its time in that although space toys as a category were very popular and this was certainly seen as an answer, it did not really come into its own in the same way as Star War toys did later."

Among the Super King models illustrated for the first time in the 1978 catalogue were a few which lent themselves to livery changes. Lesney were experiencing great success with the K16-3 Petrol

K51-1 Barracuda in white, K54-1 A.M.X. Javelin in black, K55-1 Corvette Caper Car in metallic blue, K56-1 Maserati BORA in silver grey and K59-1 Ford Capri in metallic silver. These KP models did not carry any base numbers.

The K62-1 Doctor's Car which was illustrated in the 1977 catalogue was based upon the K33-1 Citreon SM which had been in the shops for some five years at the time, but in white with a yellow roof lamp and 'Emergency'

Civilian Military
K22-3 K105-1
Hovercraft/Hover Raider
K14-3 K110-1
Heavy Recovery Vehicle
K12-4 K113-1
Hercules Crane with labels showing a white circle on a red background and the number 85
K13-3 K114-1
Aircraft Transporter with a brown plastic Alpha jet
K16-3 K115-1
Petrol Tanker

and'Doctor' labels with red crosses. By 1977 the Military series had been increased to seventeen models. In addition to the following models which had been recoloured from their normal civilian liveries to military olive green, there were a number of models made specially for this series.

Cab	Box	Labels
Red	Red	Avis Truck Rental
Orange/white	Grey	U-Haul One way and local rentals
Blue	White/blue	TAA
Blue	White/blue	Bassett's Jelly Babies
Turquoise	Turquoise	75 Express 205-83-69
		Paris et Limitrophes 2
		Fois par Jour (Paris and its suburbs twice a day)
White	Light green	Mr Softy Milch - Kastlichkeiten elefanten Junge Mode

The K31-2 Peterbilt Refrigeration Trucks. The 'Dura Penta' Truck in the foreground was made by Lesney Products for distribution at a congress in Cape Town, South Africa in 1983.

City of Hackensack New Jersey badge on its bonnet. Each came with a figure carrying a loud hailer. In some cases his helmet and megaphone have been painted white. *Matchbox Collectors' Club 1978:* "On 13th May 1978 Mr Wayne Lynch, Vice President of Marketing and Mr Terry Husker, Diecast Product Manager, presented a first production model of our new K67 Fire Chief's Car to Chief Charles H. Jones of the Hackensack Fire Department."

As K69-2 this Dodge was also issued in blue towing a Europa Caravan.

Other new models for 1978 were:

K26-2 Bedford Cement Truck. (the barrel could be rotated by a plastic handle) – This model was released both with and without 'McAlpine' door labels.

K27-2 Ford Transporter and Powerboat. The power boat has carried a number of liveries – 'Embassy', the first cigarette livery in the series; 'Miss Solo'; 'Benihana'; 'Matchbox' and '506', the Ford being the same as K29-2 issued earlier that year. *Matchbox Collectors' Club* 1979: 'Off-shore powerboat racing has grown to be second in spectator attendance only to the Indy 500. The excitement of this year's Benihana (Japanese for red flower) Grand Prix was greater than ever with Rocky Aoki the first place finisher. The Matchbox Super King K-27 is modelled from Rocky Aoki's 38 foot Beltram racer.'

K28-2 Bedford Skip Truck. 'Hales' is a London based skip hire subsidiary of Ready Mixed Concrete.

K30-2 Unimog and Compressor. The Unimog carrying 'MJ' labels carried a set of cones and road signs – ready to divert the Matchbox King Size traffic.

K32-2 Farm Unimog. This model was released with a shepherd, his sheepdog and a flock of four sheep.

K33-2 Cargo Hauler (the

Tankers and the potential of the Yesteryear series commercial vehicles was only just being appreciated.

The K29-2 Ford Delivery Van had opening rear doors and a pull out loading ramp. A man with a trolley was ready with his two baskets to pick up a load. This model was issued in the above colours and liveries.

The impressive K31-2 Peterbilt Articulated Refrigeration Trucks were first released with the liveries of 'Christian Salvesen' and 'Lagnese-Iglo'. Later models carried the colours of 'Glace Gervais', 'Pepsi', 'Euro Express', 'Coca-Cola', 'Burger King', 'Dr Koch's Trink 10' and one known Code Two model specially manufactured for release at an engineers' convention in Cape Town, South Africa in 1983 with the labels 'Acorn Koue en Warmwater Pypstelsels Duro Penta' (Acorn cold and hot water piping systems).

Among the Speed King models issued in 1978 was a Jaguar XJ12 which was released in its civilian colours as K69-1 with a Europa Caravan as K66-1 in white with two Superfast model Police Motorcycles (M.B. 33). Early Jaguars were painted metallic light blue while later models included various shades of red. The caravan, with its detailed interior and opening door, was made with various mixtures of white and beige components. The first Police Cars carried a blue stripe which curved with the lines of the car and the sign 'POLICE' on the front doors. Later models had a red stripe bordered by two thin blue lines. This straight stripe, which also included the 'POLICE' sign, did not follow the shape of the car. Later issues carried a black and white chequered design and 'County Police' labels. This was another model chosen for production in Bulgaria in 1987.

K67-1 A Dodge Monaco Fire Chief Car with its opening tailgate was issued in the USA in lemon yellow and elsewhere in red.

The red version carried the labels 'County Brigade Headquarters Fire Chief Area No 3' on its sides and 'Fire Area 3 HQ' on its bonnet. The yellow version had 'Fire Chief Engine Co No 1' on its sides and a tarpaulin has carried 'MW', 'Gauntlet International' and 'United States Steel' labels).

K36-2 Construction Transporter. An open version of the K7-3 Racing Car Transporter in 'Laing' livery carrying MB29 Shovel Nose Tractor and MB26 Site Dumper.

K41-2 Martini Brabham F1 in red with the number '7' and 'Martini Racing' labels.

K63-1 The same Mercedes Benz-Binz Ambulance that was K6-2 back in 1966 and K26-1 in 1971.

K64-1 Fire Control Range Rover. The red Range Rover carrying a removable ladder and a revolving searchlight came with two fire fighting figures. One carried a plastic hose which could be attached to the truck. Some of these were also issued with Swedish 'Falck Zonen' livery.

K65-1 Plymouth Mountain Rescue Vehicle – with its patient on a stretcher. The truck was fitted with a front mounted working winch.

This model was also released in West Germany in green with 'Bergrettungswacht' labels.

The last model to join the Battle King range was to be K118-1 an Army Helicopter. The olive green Kaman Seasprite Helicopter carried 'Army 5415 HFS – 64' labels. From its sides it could fire two projectiles.

K2004-1 the Adventure 2000 Rocket Striker released in the Adventure 2000 series was identical to K111-1 the Battle King Missile Launcher.

During 1978 the colour schemes of the tanks in the Battle King series were changed to introduce camouflage colours.

Only two further models were to be added to the Sea King range before it was discontinued. These were:

K309-1 Submarine
K310-1 Anti-Aircraft Cruiser

Sea Kings - destined to sink without a trace.

By 1979 the name Speed King was dropped and all of the cars rejoined the Super King range.

In order to complement the typically British Jaguar XJ12, a Porsche Turbo was introduced to the range. K70-1 the civilian model was an excellent model of the real thing and K71-1 a Police version was issued with two Superfast MB33 Motorcycles. The doors on early models of these Porsches were opened with little door handles, but these handles were soon dispensed with. Early green K70-1 Porsches carried a small Porsche badge on their bonnets and a black label to represent a sun roof. Later models in black had much larger Porsche badges and black labels to represent cabriolet hoods. Both of these sun roof effects were unsuccessful because of the paper labels' inability to bend around the curved roof. This model consistently remained one of the best selling models in the range, and has been re-released in numerous colours.

K71-1 was painted green and white and had a blue lamp fitted above the driver's seat. It carried 'Polizei' labels on its doors and bonnet and the number '1705' on its roof. It was released with two MB33 Police Motorcycles in white and green carrying 'Polizei' labels.

The K19-3 Ford Security Truck was released with its load of gold bars carrying the livery 'Fort Knox' in the U.S.A. and the 'Group 4 Security Services' everywhere else. The rear door was locked with three combination locks. The side windows of the truck were protected by security bars to protect the precious cargo. This model was, in 1984, converted into a child's money box as K88-1.

When issued the K21-4 Ford Transcontinental, 33 cms (13 inches) with its trailer became the biggest diecast toy in the range. Amongst the liveries which this long juggernaut has carried are 'Continental', 'Polara', 'Santa Fe', 'Danzas', 'Weetabix' and 'Nichts geht uber Barenmarke'. The last version, in which the roof of the cab was modified by an aerodynamic wind deflector, and the plastic removable tarpaulins found on the earlier Transcontinentals was replaced by solid covers on the version which carried the livery 'Sunkist'. In 1985 a few Ford Transcontinentals were released in yellow as open trucks towing compressors as part of K118-2, the Road Construction Set.

The other models released in 1978 were:

K20-3 Peterbilt Wrecker (a sophisticated recovery vehicle with many working features).

K34-2 The Pallet Truck in white and blue carried the letter 'K' on its tarpaulin and in white and red the label 'IKM International'

K35-2 Massey Ferguson Tractor and Trailer. This tractor, which replaced the earlier K3-3, was a model of a 595 and carried the label 'MF 595' on its bonnet. On its two wheeled trailer it carried six bales of straw.

K37-2 Leyland Tipper (a new casting of the truck first issued as K4-5 in 1974)

	K75-1	K77-1
English	Airport Fire Tender	Highway Rescue System
German	Flughafen Feuerwehr	Strassen Service
French	Securite Aeroport	Secours Routier

K78-1 US Police Car (both in black and white and in blue and white)

K79-1 US Taxi (a typical American Yellow Cab)

The K74-1 Volvo Estate introduced in 1978 has continued to prove a most popular model. Early Volvos carried black sun roof labels and impact resistant front and rear bumpers but these were soon dispensed with. Early K74-1 Volvo boxes contained an assortment of sets of number plates, international country symbols and windscreen discs which could be used to decorate the model. The Volvo has been issued in a variety of colours, towing a Europa Caravan as K69-3, a racing Datsun as K76-1, and, as an Ambulance, as K96-1.

The K75-1 yellow Airport Fire Tender and white K77-1 Highway Rescue were issued on the continent with German and French labels.

Two special models issued during 1979 were K98-1 the Forestry Unimog in green with 'Forstamt' labels and the K99-1 Range Rover 'Polizei' set. These two German sets included a set of German labels which could be applied to various plastic sign boards.

K2005-1, the Command Force set which was made up of a K2004-1 Rocket Striker, and three SF models SF2 Hovercraft, SF59 Planet Scout and the SF68 Cosmobile in metallic green were added to the Adventure 2000 series. In 1980 it was planned that the colours of the models in this series were to be changed from metallic green to metallic blue, but because of the reasons explained in Chapter Six only some of these were issued.

That year the K38-2 Dodge Ambulance was brought onto the market. In Germany it carried the label 'Notarzt' and elsewhere 'Ambulance' printed backwards across the bonnet.

K80-1 The Dodge Custom Van which was based upon the same model carried the label 'It's only Rock 'n Roll'.

Also released in 1980 was the 20.8 cm (8.56")long K39-2 E.R.F. Snorkel Fire Engine with its Simon Snorkel Hydraulic Lifting platform. This substantial model, in typical fire engine red, carried the labels 'County Fire Department' and the number '32'. Fitted with retractable stabilisers to hold the truck steady when the platform was raised this model came complete with a team of four firemen.

The soft drink delivery truck K40-2 was issued in Germany with the livery of 'Bizzl Frolische Durstloschen' (Pleasant thirst quenching Bizzl) and elsewhere that of 'Pepsi Cola'. This was another model released together with a MB15 Fork Lift Truck.

By 1981 no mention remained of the Sea King range. All seemed to have sunk without trace! It had been planned that a container ship and a tanker would be added to the Sea King range. All the tooling was

The Adventure 2000 series includes the Shuttle Launcher.

ready for their production and a few samples had been made when the company was forced to abandon ship! In that year there was one addition to the Adventure 2000 series – the K2006-1 Shuttle launcher. This model was only released in metallic blue.

The Bedford Bulk Transporter K3-5 introduced that year was described as a grain transporter. This description was appropriate for the red and white livery 'Kellogg's the best to you each morning' and those which only carried the labels 'Kellogg's', but could not be considered correct for the German issue in green and white sporting the livery of 'Heidelberger Zement'.

The K8-4 Animal Transporter pulled by a Mercedes tractor came with a veritable herd of cattle. This large truck was dwarfed by the K44-3 Berliet Turbo truck in the Bridge Transporter Set. The bridge when fully erected stretched to nearly a meter long. This model was introduced at a retail price of £12.50 when the cheaper Super King models cost about £1.95.

Another large model introduced to the Super King range was the K41-3 JCB Excavator. This large model was out of scale to anything else in the series, and its unpopularity can be measured by the fact that it only remained in the range for two years.

K43-2 the Log Transporter, had been illustrated in blue in the 1980 catalogue as K85-1 but was never issued with that number, K85 has never been used for any model in the range. The Log Transporter was another unpopular model, which had a very short life in the range.

Three models introduced in 1981 which were definitely out of scale to the rest of the range have, in fact, proved extremely popular. These were the three motor cycles K81-1 the Suzuki, K82-1 the B.M.W. and the K83-1 the Harley Davidson. These three motor cycles have been

issued in a number of colours. Whereas the saddle bags of the early B.M.W.'s were plain, later models had the letters B.M.W. cast on their sides. Early crash helmets had tilting visors but these were dispensed with.

Other new models released in 1981 were:

K11-4 Dodge Delivery Van in the liveries of 'Frankfurte Allgemeine' and 'Suchard Express' in West Germany, 'France-Soir' in France with an advertising board positioned diagonally across the roof and 'Michelin' elsewhere.

K84-1 Peugeot 305. First issued in blue but later in white as a mud-spattered rally car.

K87-1 Massey Ferguson Tractor and Rotary Rake

By 1981 most of the models in the Super King range carried chromed windscreen frames and windscreen wipers, and a number had aerials, all of these features making the models just a little more realistic.

In 1982 the Super King range was reduced by the deletion of all unpopular models. *Smith:* "Superking just had too many parts . . . Too many parts means breakages, long assembly lines did all the rest of it . . . All the expense, and it happened at the time of high inflation. So what was going to be good value at £3 looked expensive at £6. It was just that era, and once you had started on a policy it was two years before they came through the pipeline even if the trade were telling us 'this is no good' . . . we couldn't stop them."

Out went the Battle King and Adventure 2000 series; the Super King list, which in 1981 totalled eighty-two different models, was reduced to forty-five models in 1982.

The K86-1 V.W. Golf, introduced during the year, came together with its own Shell petrol pump. First issued in black, this popular little model (one of the smallest Super King models for years) was later

released in white. Yellow VW Golfs with the labels 'A.D.A.C. Strassenwacht' (the West German equivalent of the A.A.) were marketed in West Germany.

The anonymous red K10-4 Car Transporter was withdrawn and replaced by an excellent blue and white Bedford using a similar but completely redesigned trailer as K10-5. This model carried 'Courier' labels on the wind deflector and on the sides of the trailer.

Among the other new models introduced in 1982 were:

K89-1 Range Rover Forestry Set. This set, using a Range Rover, was based upon the K98-1 German Uni-mog Forestry Set released in 1979.

K90-1 Matra Rancho. Early models were painted red and carried a 'Trans Globe Couriers' logo on the bonnet, while later models were yellow. 1988 Matra Ranchos are red with 'Fire Control Unit' labels covering the roof, bonnet and doors. The Matra featured a towing hook, plated door mirrors, alloy wheels, spring suspension, headlights, roofrack and detailed interior. These were the typical features of a model released at the time.

K91-1 Motorcycle Racing Set. A Plymouth Grand Fury in metallic silver based upon the K78-1 and K79-1 Police Car/Taxi towing a red trailer with two modified MB33 Motorcycles.

K92-1 Ford Helicopter Transporter Set. The Helicopter was fitted with floats. The yellow truck had two tall aerials mounted on the roof of the cab which had not been seen on earlier models of the Ford LTS. The white-bodied helicopter carried the markings of 'Heli-Hire International'. The helicopter was well equipped with crop spraying booms, a lifting crane and a swivelling TV camera.

K93-1 Unimog Lamp Maintenance Set. The Mercedes Benz Unimog, with the label 'Autoroute Services' on its bonnet, came with a

repair man who could be lifted in the lifting platform to reach to the top of the supplied lamp standard. Because of the lamp this model was released in a very tall box!

K94-1 Was to be used for a large Airport Fire Tender which, equipped with water tanks and electrically powered pump, was found impractical and scrapped. None of these was ever released although a number of pre-production models were con-structed by the R & D Department at Matchbox. *Smith:* "It was a beautiful Fire Engine . . . with water and a pump . . . but there we are." (For further details see Chapter Four).

K95-1 Audi Quattro. An excellent model of the rally world beater which has been released in a number of colours.

Early Audi Quattros, with their six large foglights, were metallic grey, but these were replaced by white Audi rally cars. Some carried the names of the rally drivers on their doors. While J Arthur had a navigator called D Trew Jnr, G Mills seems to have driven on his own! These were not world famous rally drivers but, in fact, managers at the Matchbox Rochford factory! 1988 models of this car are metallic blue with the four Audi rings on its bonnet and opening doors and the word Quattro neatly printed on its sides.

The Ford Sierra XR4 introduced at the same time as a miniature Sierra as K100-1, was an immediate success in 1983. The first Ford Sierras were issued in white and grey in special boxes printed in the livery of Ford. Later Sierras have been released in many different colours.

Two more Porsches were also added to the range — K98-2 a Porsche 944 and K101-2 a Racing Porsche. The same Racing Porsche on a trailer towed by a K11-4 Dodge Delivery Van became K102-2. On its roof the Dodge racing support vehicle carried a set of spares, including wheels, for the Porsche.

The other new issues for 1983 were:

K96-1 Volvo Ambulance — A white Volvo Ambulance based upon K74-1

K97-1 Range Rover Police Car. Like the K66-1 Jaguar and K71-1 Porsche, the Range Rover Police Car was issued in a set with two MB33 Motor Cycles in white with Police labels. The white Range Rover carried bright orange striped labels and the signs 'Police Accident Prevention' and a red accident sign on a roof sign board.

K99-2 Dodge Polizei Van. A white and green Dodge Van similar to K11-4 with 'Polizei' labels.

K103-2 Peterbilt Tanker Truck. The tanker with 'Comet' labels was illustrated with a chromed stainless steel tank, but, because of production difficulties, when the model reached the shops the tank was white.

K104-2 Ranch Rescue Set — The K90-1 Matra Rancho towing K25-1 the speed boat issued in 1971. The white Matra carried the labels 'COASTGUARD PATROL' and the number '370' on its roof. The blue and white speedboat with its twin outboard motors carried the number '370'.

A large Cabin Cruiser mounted on an adapted trailer towed by a Mercedes tractor became the very handsome K107-2 Power Launch Transporter released in 1984.

Two neat trucks introduced that year were the K109-2 Petrol Tanker with yellow and white 'Shell' livery and the K110-2 Fire Engine.

Other models for 1984 include:

K88-1 Ford Money Box. Matchbox re-released the K19-3 Ford Security Truck as a money box in 1984. *Sullivan:* "All that was needed was a money slot in the roof and we had a money box." In France the money box was orange and beige and carried the livery of 'Caisse d' Espargne', in Germany, 'Volksbank Raiffelsenbank' and in the rest of the world, 'Save Your Money With Me Matchbox'. More

recently, in 1986, the model has been re-issued in the 'Fort Knox' livery first seen on K19-3.

K105-2 Peterbilt Tipper. An adaptation of the Peterbilt truck.

K106-2 Aircraft Transporter . The Scammell Truck first issued as K17-2 in 1972 towing the aircraft first seen as K13-3 in 1976.

K108-2 Digger and Plough Transporter. Another use of the Peterbilt and the Muir-Hill Tractor first seen in 1972.

1985 saw the introduction of K115-2 the Mercedes-Benz 190F 2.3 16V first in white and more recently in metallic light blue and in black. The Mercedes had opening doors, opening bonnet with detailed engine, detailed dashboard, front and rear lights and sprung suspension. A number of large trucks were also issued that year. Among these were the K116-2 Racing Car Transporter with its two SF6 F1 Racing Cars, the K112-2 Fire Spotter Transporter and the K113-2 Garage Transporter in 'Shell' livery (This has proved to be the most difficult Matchbox model for a collector to put back into its box) and the K117-2 Bulldozer Transporter. In 1988 the Racing Car Transporter was re-released as K159-1 in Porsche livery and as K160-1 in 'Matchbox Racing Team' colours. The Garage Transporter was displayed at the 1986 Toy Fairs in red and white 'Texaco' livery and has long been illustrated in these colours, but has only recently been so released. The Bulldozer Transporter was towed by a Scammell Tractor, which was an excellent representation of the real Scammell heavy prime mover.

The K114-2 Mobile Crane with its five axles was even heavier and stronger than its now aged predecessor the K12-4 Hercules.

The remaining new issue for 1985 was K111-2 Peterbilt Refuse Truck. another use of the Peterbilt in orange with the labels '52nd Precinct Cart 268 Waste Beater'.

Two King Size sets were issued in 1985:

K118-1 Road Construction Set comprising:

K21-4 Ford Transcontinental flatbed truck towing the compressor last seen behind a K30-2 Unimog and K30-2 the Unimog towing the tipping trailer last seen behind a K35-2 Massey Ferguson Tractor.

K119-1 Fire Rescue Set comprising:

K110-2 Fire Engine
K30-2 Unimog and Compressor

For 1985 the large construction vehicles were released in the livery of 'Taylor Woodrow', large multinational construction group; these included the K105-2 Peterbilt Tipper, the K114-2 Mobile Crane and K117-2 Bulldozer Transporter.

1986 saw the introduction of automatic steering to all of the trucks which could accommodate a

	K110-2	K132-1
Colour	Grey Ladder	White ladder
Label	008	201 Fire
	K112-2	K134-1
Colour	Red Chassis	White Chassis
Label	Patrol Unit 23	Patrol Unit 12
Colour	Black Plastic	Brown Plastic
	Cradle	Cradle
Label	Fire Observer	Unit 23
		Unit 12
	K21-1	K121-1
Colour	Green/white	Black/white
Labels	Heavy Duty	Highway
	Recovery	Patrol
		City Police
	K103-2	K127-1
Colour	Blue/white	Red/white
Label	Comet	Total
	K119-1	K138-1
Colour	Grey Ladder	White Ladder
Label	008	201 Fire
Label	9 Foam Pump	Foam Unit 8

Pre 1986 Number	Post 1986 Number	
K21-1	K121-1	Peterbilt Wreck Truck
K103-2	K127-1	Peterbilt Tanker
K107-2	K129-1	Power Launch Transporter
K108-2	K130-1	Digger Transporter
K109-2	K131-1	Petrol Tanker
K110-2	K132-1	Fire Engine
K112-2	K134-1	Fire Spotter Transporter
K113-2	K135-1	Garage Transporter
K116-2	K136-1	Racing Car Transporter
K119-1	K138-1	Fire Rescue Set

new steering mechanism. In the case of the Peterbilt trucks the steering mechanism was operated by the silver air filter tanks on either side of the bonnet, whereas in all of the other models the steering mechanism was operated by pressing one of the two roof lamps to indicate the direction of travel. Amongst the models which were modified to incorporate automatic steering and re-released were:

Whilst the K127-1 Tankers released throughout the rest of the

world carried 'TOTAL' labels, those released in the U.S.A. had red tractor units and white trailers with red 'GETTY' labels.

In addition to the automatic steering feature the following additional differences are easily identifiable:

Some other commercial vehicles were re-introduced with new trucks which could accommodate the mechanism, many sporting new colours and liveries:

The Leyland Car Transporter was released in white with Carrier

	Pre 1986		Post 1986	
Number		Number		
K10-5	Bedford	K120-1	Leyland Car Transporter
K21-4	Ford	K122-1	DAF Road Train
K26-2	Bedford	K123-1	Leyland Cement Truck
K31-2	Peterbilt	K124-1	Mercedes Container Truck
K92-1	Ford	K126-1	DAF Helicopter Transporter
K106-2	Scammell	K128-1	DAF Aircraft Transporter
K111-2	Peterbilt	K133-1	Iveco Refuse Truck
K118-1	Ford	K137-1	DAF in the Road
			Construction Set

labels on the tractor and trailer. U.S.A. models of the K133-1 Iveco Refuse Truck were released in white with the label 'City Sanitation' on the front and sides of the cab and the 'Recycle Aluminum Paper Plastic Glass' on the sides. Elsewhere this model in red carried the labels 'Refuse City Corp'.

The K92-1 Ford Helicopter Transporter was replaced by K126-1, a royal blue DAF truck and trailer. The truck carried the letters 'RN' on its sides and Royal Navy

above its radiator grill. The dark blue Helicopter carried the labels Royal Navy Rescue and an 'Ace of Diamonds' label. Unlike the helicopter on K92-1 this one did not have any of the extra attachments.

Two different working mechanisms were introduced in 1987. The system by which the K139-1 Iveco Tipper Truck, the K140-1 Leyland Car Recovery Vehicle and the K141-1 Leyland Skip Truck lift their loads is very similar to the Pressamatic system

Some of the large Ford Transcontinental Trucks.

last seen in the mid 1970s. Whereas early K139-1 Tippers carried 'Wimpey' labels, those released in the U.S.A. in 1988 carried 'Department of Highways' labels on the front, the cab and the tipper.

The three emergency vehicles were fitted with warning signs which were activated by the revolving wheels. K142-1, the B.M.W. Police Car, was released in Germany in green and white with 'Polizei' labels. Elsewhere it was white all over and carried a 'Police' label. The K144-1 Land Rover which has been issued with names of both Heathrow Airport and Frankfurt Flughafen, had a 'Follow Me' sign on its roof and K143-1 the Emergency Van flashes 'Accident Stop'.

New issues for 1988 included:

K145-1 Iveco Tipper. An articulated truck with twin tipping trailers. This large double articulated tipper truck is similar to the K7-2 Dodge first released in 1965, but the orange Iveco Truck with 'S + G' labels does have steering front wheels.

K146-1 Jaguar XJ6. A superb model of the 1988 Jaguar XJ6 in bright red with opening doors and bonnet and a detailed Jaguar engine.

K147-1 B.M.W. 750 iL A silver B.M.W. with opening doors and detailed engine.

K148-1 Crane Truck A Mercedes flat bed truck with midmounted crane. The white and red truck is based upon the tractor of the K43.2 Log Transporter. It carries the name 'Apex' on its sides.

K149-1 Ferrari Testarossa In classic Ferrari red. The Ferrari has opening doors and rear engine compartment revealing the Ferrari engine.

K150-1 Leyland Truck The blue truck with 'SMF' labels has three separate backs; a flatbed, a slide tipper and a closed van. These backs clip onto the chassis by two lugs.

K151-1 Skip Truck A yellow Leyland skip truck.

K153-1 Jaguar XJ6 Police Car A white K146-1 in Police livery.

K154-1 B.M.W. 750 iL Police Car A green and white K147-1 B.M.W. with 'Polizei' labels.

K155-1 Ferrari Testarossa K149-1 in racing yellow.

K156-1 Porsche 911 K70-1 in red racing livery with 'Pioneer and Elf' labels and the number '18'.

K157-1 Porsche 944 K98-2 in yellow with 'Porsche Turbo' labels.

K158-1 Sierra XR4i K100-1 in white 'Total' livery with the words 'Total Pace Car' on its doors and 'Ford Motorsport' on its roof.

K159-1 Racing Car Transporter An Iveco racing car transporter in white Porsche livery carrying two MB7 Porsche 959 racing cars in white.

K160-1 Racing Car Transporter K136-1 in Matchbox livery. The same transporter, but in the colours of Matchbox carrying two MB6 racing cars in white and blue. The truck carries 'Matchbox Formula Racing Team' labels.

Four Super King models have formed the backbone of the futuristic Road Blasters series issued during 1988.

A.L.T.R.A.C., the Air Land Transport and Repair Centre, makes use of the Peterbilt truck, the trailer of the K10-4 Car Transporter and the K126-1 Helicopter. V.A.R.M.I.T, the Vehicle Armor Redesign and Modular Intelligence Transport, uses the K114-2 Crane and T.R.A.P.P.E.R., the Turbo Force Reconnaissance and Power Reserve, uses a Peter built track and the flatbed trailer of K127-1 the Tanker. M.O.R.G., the Mobile Operations Supply Gantry uses the Scania cab and the flatbed trailer of the K127-1.

SERIAL	TITLE	YEAR	LENGTH (cms)
	LISTING OF THE KING SIZE / SUPER KING RANGE 1960 - 1988		
K1-1	WEATHERILL HYDRAULIC SHOVEL	1960	9.2
K1-2	8-WHEEL TIPPER TRUCK	1964	10.8
K1-3	O & K EXCAVATOR	1970	12.4
K2-1	MUIR-HILL DUMPER	1960	7.6
K2-2	DUMP TRUCK	1964	14.3
K2-3	SCAMMELL HEAVY WRECK TRUCK	1969	11.9
K2-4	CAR RECOVERY VEHICLE	1977	12.0
K3-1	CATERPILLAR BULLDOZER	1960	8.4
K3-2	HATRA TRACTOR SHOVEL	1965	15.0
K3-3	MASSEY FERGUSON TRACTOR AND TRAILER	1970	20.3
K3-4	MOD TRACTOR AND TRAILER	1974	19.7
K3-5	GRAIN TRANSPORTER	1981	30.0
K4-1	INTERNATIONAL TRACTOR	1961	7.2
K4-2	GMC TRACTOR WITH HOPPER TRAIN	1067	28.6
K4-3	LEYLAND TIPPER	1969	11.4
K4-4	BIG TIPPER	1974	11.8
K5-1	FODEN TIPPER TRUCK	1961	10.8
K5-2	RACING CAR TRANSPORTER	1967	12.7
K5-3	MUIR-HILL TRACTOR AND TRAILER	1972	24.1
K6-1	ALLIS-CHALMERS EARTH SCRAPER	1961	14.9
K6-2	MERCEDES-BENZ BINZ AMBULANCE	1967	10.5
K6-3	CEMENT MIXER	1971	14.7
K6-4	MOTOR CYCLE TRANSPORTER	1975	12.0
K7-1	CURTISS-WRIGHT REAR DUMPER	1961	14.5
K7-2	S D REFUSE TRUCK	1966	11.7
K7-3	RACING CAR TRANSPORTER	1973	15.6
K8-1	PRIME MOVER & TRANSPORTER WITH CATERPILLAR TRACTOR	1962	31.8
K8-2	CAR TRANSPORTER	1967	20.9
K8-3	CATERPILLAR TRAXCAVATOR	1972	10.6
K8-4	ANIMAL TRANSPORTER	1981	31.0
K9-1	DIESEL ROAD ROLLER	1962	9.5
K9-2	COMBINE HARVESTER	1967	14.0
K9-3	FIRE TENDER	1973	15.6
K10-1	AVELING-BARFORD TRACTOR SHOVEL	1962	10.5
K10-2	PIPE TRUCK (WITH SIX INTERLOCKING PIPES)	1967	20.3
K10-2	CAR TRANSPORTER	1976	26.9
K10-4	BEDFORD CAR TRANSPORTER	1982	26.3
K11-1	FORDSON TRACTOR AND FARM TRAILER	1963	15.8
K11-2	DAF CAR TRANSPORTER	1970	22.8
K11-3	PICK-UP TRUCK	1976	12.7
K11-4	DODGE DELIVERY VAN	1981	13.5
K12-1	HEAVY BREAKDOWN WRECK TRUCK	1963	12.1
K12-2	SCAMMELL CRANE TRUCK	1970	15.2
K12-3	HERCULES MOBILE CRANE	1975	15.6

SERIAL	TITLE	YEAR	LENGTH (cms)
K13-1	READY-MIX CEMENT TRUCK	1963	11.4
K13-2	DAF BUILDING TRANSPORTER	1971	14.7
K13-3	AIRCRAFT TRANSPORTER	1976	20.3
K14-1	JUMBO CRANE	1963	12.5
K14-2	SCAMMELL FREIGHT LINER	1971	13.9
K14-3	HEAVY BREAKDOWN TRUCK	1977	13.1
K15-1	MERRYWEATHER FIRE ENGINE	1971	15.4
K15-2	THE LONDONER	1973	12.0
K16-1	DODGE TRACTOR WITH TWIN TIPPERS	1966	30.2
K16-2	FORD LTS PETROL TANKER	1974	22.9
K17-1	FORD TRACTOR WITH DYSON LOW-LOADER & CASE BULLDOZER	1966	24.2
K17-2	ARTICULATED CONTAINER TRUCK	1974	25.1
K18-1	ARTICULATED HORSE BOX	1966	16.6
K18-2	ARTICULATED TIPPER TRUCK	1974	20.3
K19-1	SCAMMELL TIPPER TRUCK	1967	12.1
K19-2	FORD SECURITY TRUCK	1979	13.7
K20-1	FRACTOR TRANSPORTER	1968	22.8
K20-2	CARGO HAULER AND PALLET LOADER	1973	19.0
K20-3	PETERBILT WRECKER	1979	16.3
K21-1	MERCURY COUGAR	1968	10.5
K21-2	COUGAR DRAGSTER	1971	10.5
K21-3	TRACTOR TRANSPORTER	1974	16.2
K21-4	FORD TRANSCONTINENTAL	1979	33.7
K22-1	DODGE CHARGER	1968	11.5
K22-2	DODGE DRAGSTER	1971	11.5
K22-3	SRN6 HOVERCRAFT	1974	12.7
K23-1	MERCURY POLICE CAR	1968	11.1
K23-2	LOW LOADER	1974	25.1
K24-1	LAMBORGHINI MIURA	1968	10.0
K24-2	SCAMMELL CONTAINER TRUCK	1977	13.3
K25-1	'SEABURST' POWER BOAT AND TRAILER	1971	16.2
K25-2	DIGGER AND PLOUGH	1977	12.9
K26-1	MERCEDES-BENZ BINZ AMBULANCE	1967	10.5
K26-2	BEDFORD CEMENT TRUCK	1978	10.0
K27-1	CAMPING CRUISER	1971	11.1
K27-2	POWERBOAT AND TRANSPORTER	1978	25.7
K28-1	DRAG PACK	1971	25.2
K28-2	BEDFORD SKIP TRUCK	1978	11.0
K29-1	MIURA 'SEABURST' SET	1971	25.2
K29-2	FORD DELIVERY VAN	1978	11.0
K30-1	MERCEDES C111	1972	10.2
K30-2	UNIMOG AND COMPRESSOR	1978	18.5
K31-1	BERTONE RUNABOUT	1972	10.2
K31-2	PETERBILT TRUCK	1978	30.0
K32-1	SHOVEL NOSE	1972	10.2
K32-2	FARM UNIMOG	1978	22.5
K33-1	CITROEN SM	1972	11.4
K33-2	CARGO HAULER	1978	23.0
K34-1	THUNDERCLAP	1972	10.8
K34-2	PALLET TRUCK	1979	14.2
K35-1	LIGHTNING	1972	10.8
K35-2	MASSEY FERGUSON TRACTOR AND TRAILER	1979	22.4
K36-1	BANDOLERO	1972	11.4
K36-2	CONSTRUCTION TRANSPORTER	1978	16.2
K37-1	SANDCAT	1973	8.6
K37-2	LEYLAND TIPPER	1979	11.8
K38-1	GUS'S GULPER	1973	10.8
K38-2	DODGE AMBULANCE	1980	13.5
K39-1	MILLIGANS MILL	1973	10.8
K39-2	ERF SNORKEL FIRE ENGINE	1980	20.8
K40-1	BLAZE TRAILER	1973	10.2
K40-2	FORD SOFT DRINK DELIVERY TRUCK	1980	15.1
K41-1	FUZZ BUGGY	1973	11.4
K41-2	BRABHAM F1	1978	10.9
K41-3	J C B EXCAVATOR	1981	25.0
K42-1	NISSAN 270X	1973	10.2
K42-2	TRAXCAVATOR ROAD RIPPER	1979	14.0
K43-1	CAMBUSTER	1973	11.2
K43-2	MERCEDES-BENZ LOG TRANSPORTER	1981	31.5
K44-1	BAZOOKA	1973	11.2
K44-2	SURTEES F1	1978	10.8
K44-3	BRIDGE TRANSPORTER	1981	33.5
K45-1	MARAUDER	1973	10.5
K46-1	RACING CAR PACK	1973	25.0
K47-1	EASY RIDER	1973	12.0
K48-1	MERCEDES 350 SLC	1974	10.6
K49-1	AMBULANCE	1973	11.2
K50-1	STREET ROD	1974	10.0
K51-1	BARRACUDA	1973	10.8
K52-1	DATSUN RALLY CAR	1974	10.5
K53-1	HOT FIRE ENGINE	1976	9.8
K54-1	A.M.X. JAVELIN	1976	10.8
K55-1	CORVETTE CAPER CART	1976	10.8
K56-1	MASERATI BORA	1976	10.1
K57-1	JAVELIN DRAG RACING SET	1976	24.7
K58-1	CORVETTE POWER BOAT SET	1976	25.7
K59-1	FORD CAPRI MK 2	1976	10.5
K60-1	FORD MUSTANG	1976	10.7
K61-1	MERCEDES POLICE CAR	1976	10.7
K62-1	DOCTORS CAR	1977	11.4
K63-1	MERCEDES-BENZ BINZ AMBULANCE	1978	10.5
K64-1	FIRE CONTROL RANGE ROVER	1978	10.5
K65-1	PLYMOUTH MOUNTAIN RESCUE VEHICLE	1978	11.5
K66-1	JAGUAR XJ12 POLICE SET	1978	12.0
K67-1	DODGE MONACO FIRE CHIEF	1978	11.5
K68-1	DODGE MONACO AND TRAILER	1978	21.0
K69-1	EUROPA CARAVAN AND JAGUAR XJ12	1978	27.0
K69-2	EUROPA CARAVAN AND DODGE MONACO	1978	27.5
K69-3	EUROPA CARAVAN AND VOLVO ESTATE	1980	28.8
K70-1	PORSCHE TURBO	1979	11.8
K71-1	PORSCHE POLIZEI SET	1979	11.8
K72-1	BRABHAM F1	1979	10.9
K73-1	SURTEES F1	1979	10.8
K74-1	VOLVO ESTATE	1979	13.8
K75-1	AIRPORT FIRE TENDER	1979	13.5
K76-1	RALLY SET	1979	27.0
K77-1	HIGHWAY RESCUE	1979	13.5
K78-1	U.S. POLICE	1979	13.9

SERIAL	TITLE	YEAR	LENGTH (cms)
K79-1	U.S. TAXI	1979	13.9
K80-1	DODGE CUSTOM CAN	1980	13.5
K81-1	SUZUKI MOTOR CYCLE	1981	11.0
K82-1	B.M.W. MOTOR CYCLE	1981	11.0
K83-1	HARLEY DAVIDSON	1981	12.0
K84-1	PEUGEOT 305	1981	12.8
K86-1	V.W. GOLF	1982	10.4
K87-1	TRACTOR AND ROTARY RAKE	1981	-
K88-1	MONEY BOX SECURITY VAN	1984	13.7
K89-1	FORESTRY SET	1982	23.5
K90-1	MAIRA RANCHO	1982	13.0
K91-1	MOTOR CYCLE RACING SET	1982	26.0
K92-1	HELICOPTER TRANSPORTER	1982	27.6
K93-1	LAMP MAINTENANCE SET	1982	10.8
K95-1	AUDI QUATTRO	1982	12.8
K96-1	VOLVO AMBULANCE	1983	13.8
K97-1	RANGE ROVER POLICE	1983	10.5
K98-1	FORESTRY UNIMOG SET	1979	18.5
K98-2	PORSCHE 944	1983	11.5
K99-1	RANGE ROVER POLIZEI SET	1979	10.5
K99-2	DODGE POLIZEI VAN	1983	13.5
K100-1	FORD SIERRA XR4i	1983	12.7
K101-1	SHERMAN TANK	1974	9.4
K101-2	RACING PORSCHE	1983	12.8
K102-1	M48 AZ TANK	1974	11.4
K102-2	RACE SUPPORT SET	1983	30.0
K103-1	CHIEFTAN TANK	1974	12.1
K103-2	TANKER TRUCK	1983	30.5
K104-1	KING TIGER TANK	1974	11.5
K104-2	RANCHO RESCUE SET	1983	26.0
K105-1	HOVER-RAIDER	1974	12.5
K105-2	PETERBILT TIPPER	1984	15.0
K106-1	TANK TRANSPORTER	1974	26.6
K106-2	AIRCRAFT TRANSPORTER	1984	23.8
K107-1	S.P. HOWITZER	1974	10.8
K107-2	POWER LAUNCH TRANSPORTER	1984	35.0
K108-1	M3A1 HALF TRACK A.P.C.	1974	9.8
K108-2	DIGGER TRANSPORTER	1984	28.9
K109-1	M551 SHERIDAN TANK	1976	10.5
K109-1	PETROL TANKER	1984	13.4
K110-1	RECOVERY VEHICLE	1976	13.1
K110-2	FIRE ENGINE	1984	17.0
K111-1	MISSILE LAUNCHER	1976	11.2
K111-2	PETERBILT REFUSE TRUCK	1985	15.0
K112-1	DAF AMBULANCE	1977	9.5
K112-2	PETERBILT FIRE SPOTTER PLANE TRANSPORTER	1985	28.0
K113-1	MILITARY HERCULES CRANE TRUCK	1977	15.6
K113-2	GARAGE TRANSPORTER	1985	30.6
K114-1	ARMY AIRCRAFT TRANSPORTER	1977	20.3
K114-2	MOBILE CRANE	1985	20.0
K115-1	ARMY PETROL TANKER	1977	22.9
K115-2	MERCEDES-BENZ 190E 2.3 16V	1985	13.0
K116-1	TROOP CARRIER AND HOWITZER	1977	22.6
K116-2	RACING CAR TRANSPORTER	1985	28.0
K117-1	ROCKET LAUNCHER	1977	10.5
K117-2	BULLDOZER TRANSPORTER	1985	32.0
K118-1	ARMY HELICOPTER	1978	15.0
K118-2	ROAD CONSTRUCTION SET	1985	
K119-1	FIRE RESCUE SET	1985	-
K120-1	BEDFORD CAR TRANSPORTER	1986	26.
K123-1	LEYLAND CEMENT TRUCK	1986	11.0
K124-1	MERCEDES CONTAINER TRUCK	1986	30.8
K126-1	DAF HELICOPTER TRANSPORTER	1986	27.6
K127-1	PETERBILT TANKER	1986	30.0
K128-1	DAF AIRCRAFT TRANSPORTER	1986	23.8
K129-1	MERCEDES-BENZ POWER LAUNCH TRANSPORTER	1986	35.0
K130-1	PETERBILT DIGGER TRANSPORTER	1986	28.0
K131-1	PETROL TANKER	1986	13.4
K132-1	FIRE ENGINE	1986	17.0
K133-1	REFUSE TRUCK	1986	15.0
K134-1	PETERBILT FIRE SPOTTER PLANE TRANSPORTER	1986	28.0
K135-1	MERCEDES-BENZ GARAGE TRANSPORTER	1986	30.6
K136-1	RACING CAR TRANSPORTER	1986	28.0
K137-1	ROAD CONSTRUCTION SET	1986	-
K138-1	FIRE RESCUE SET	1987	-
K139-1	IVECO TIPPER TRUCK	1987	14.1
K140-1	LEYLAND CAR RECOVERY VEHICLE	1987	14.8
K141-1	LEYLAND AUTO LOADER	1987	14.5
K142-1	B.M.W. POLICE CAR	1987	13.2
K143-1	BEDFORD EMERGENCY VAN	1987	13.6
K144-1	LAND ROVER AIRPORT RESCUE	1987	13.0
K145-1	IVECO TIPPER AND TRAILER	1988	36.5
K146-1	JAGUAR XJ6	1988	13.0
K147-1	B.M.W. 750iL	1988	
K148-1	CRANE TRUCK	1988	14.8
K149-1	FERRARI TESTAROSSA	1988	12.1
K150-1	LEYLAND TRUCK	1988	14.0
K151-1	SKIP TRUCK	1988	11.7
K152-1	AUDI QUATTRO SALOON	1988	12.8
K153-1	JAGUAR XJ6 POLICE	1988	13.0
K154-1	B.M.W. 750iL POLIZEI	1988	12.7
K155-1	FERRARI TESTAROSSA RACING	1988	12.1
K156-1	PORSCHE 911 RALLY	1988	11.0
K157-1	PORSCHE 944 RALLY	1988	11.5
K158-1	SIERRA XR4i PACE CAR	1988	12.7
K159-1	RACING CAR TRANSPORTER (PORSCHE)	1988	28.0
K160-1	RACING CAR TRANSPORTER (MATCHBOX)	1988	28.0
K301-1	FRIGATE	1976	21.9
K302-1	CORVETTE	1976	19.9
K303-1	BATTLESHIP	1976	21.8
K304-1	AIRCRAFT CARRIER	1976	22.2
K305-1	SUBMARINE CHASER	1976	21.9
K306-1	CONVOY ESCORT	1976	19.9
K307-1	HELICOPTER CARRIER	1976	21.0
K308-1	GUIDED MISSILE DESTROYER	1976	21.3
K309-1	SUBMARINE	1978	20.5
K310-1	ANTI-AIRCRAFT CARRIER	1978	20.5
K2001-1	RAIDER COMMAND	1977	16.2
K2002-1	FLIGHT HUNTER	1977	11.7
K2003-1	CRUSADER	1977	11.3
K2004-1	POCKET STRIKER	1978	11.2
K2005-1	COMMAND FORCE SET	1979	-
K2006-1	SHUTTLE LAUNCHER	1971	16.0

The Long Haul Convoy, MB17 Bus and MB38 Model 'A' Van Ranges

10

VEHICLES USED IN PROMOTIONS

The Long Haul models led the way for the Convoy range. The 'Kodak' truck has become a sought after rarity. In the foreground are two prototype models that were made to assess the feasability of updating the range.

THE LONG HAUL RANGE

These four ranges have been set apart from the Superfast chapter because they attract a specialist following of collectors whose main interest is in the pursuit of all the different colours and liveries Lesney and Matchbox have applied to them. This chapter does not describe models altered by individuals without the permission of the manufacturer.

The origins of Convoy go back to 1979 when the Two Pack range was updated. Launched in 1976, the Two Packs consisted of two models from the miniature range blister packed together in a play-theme. These had sold well, so a range of articulated trucks and trailers were introduced. This prompted the range to be renamed as the 900 Series.

The Long Haul trucks were named as such on their bases, whilst the design of the cabs was based on the American Peterbilt tractor. In order to keep costs down, Lesney decided to mould the bases in black plastic without the chrome finish normally associated with the Peterbilt radiator grille.

When Matchbox approached the owners of Peterbilt, Paccar Inc. for permission to use the name, it was refused because Paccar felt that the toys were a poor representation of their trucks. Pre-production shots of the base have the word 'Peterbilt' moulded on them, but the words 'Long Haul' on a raised panel, were then engraved in the base mould over the top of 'Peterbilt'. The licence plate number 'A789168' was also added below the front grille.

BASIC LISTING

TP-22   Long Haul Double Container Truck

TP-23   Long Haul Covered Container Truck

TP-24   Long Haul Box Container Truck

TP-25   Long Haul Pipe Truck

Standard parts were used for the series comprising of the body, base and window. The windows were always amber although pre-production issues exist with other colours. Riveted to the top of each cab was a small zinc cast horn which Lesney had used on other products. The same trailer casting was used in different colours and fitted with four types of load.

TP-22. The Double Container Truck used a plastic container similar to the one used on the MB-42E Mercedes Container Truck but without opening doors, which had first been used in the Playset range launched in 1977. The standard livery was always 'O.C.L.' although other labels were used. The colour of these plastic containers varies from cream to white although the bases are always black. The containers used in the Playsets were produced in various colours and liveries, two of these are to be found on the TP-22 and they are red containers with 'N.Y.K.' labels and blue containers with 'Sealand' labels. These both came with the red cab from TP-23 and are now fairly hard to find.

TP-23. Two designs of label were used on the Covered Container Truck, using the 'Firestone' livery. The first version had the word Firestone printed with letters that had a thin white outline. The second label had Firestone in solid white lettering and also a red 'F' enclosed in a shield on a white square.

TP-24. The Box Truck was put into production with a 'Kodak' livery, which was shown in the 1979 catalogue with a yellow cab and trailer, a yellow box and white roof and doors. At this time Kodak were approached for permission to use their name, but they refused. Rather than scrap the models Lesney considered over-labelling the trailers, but eventually the livery was changed to 'Matchbox' with a red cab and trailer and a red box with white roof and doors. The Kodak trailers were destroyed although the yellow cabs were issued with the Matchbox trailer and also the TP-25 Pipe Truck. Samples of the Kodak truck are still to be found, but attract very high prices. Also used on the Box

Truck were the second version of the 'Firestone' labels from TP-23. The only other variation to be found are models with black trailers.

TP-25. The Pipe Truck used plastic pipes from the Super-king K-10 Pipe Truck, which had been deleted in 1975. The mould was modified to shorten them although the only variations to be found are the trailer in black instead of silver and also the cab in yellow from the scrapped production run of the TP-24 Kodak trucks.

THE LEYLAND SERIES

In May 1981 two more models were added to the 900 Series:

TP-2   Petrol Tanker 'Exxon'
TP-26   Boat Transporter

These both used new Leyland cabs and two new trailers. Pre-production cabs did not have the front grille panel from the base but had two rivets holding the assembly together, i.e. one in the centre and one at the rear. The model looked very plain and so the castings were modified: a grille was added to the base which tucked into a slot in the body. This altered the assembly of the model, hence the centre rivet became redundant and was removed.

One anomaly was that the cab had the licence plate number 'SPD 118 V' while the trailer had 'SPD 118'; this was because of a tool-maker's error. On a U.K. vehicle, the last letter V indicates a vehicle registered during the period of 1 August 1979 to 31 July 1980.

It was the practice of Lesney not to engrave the full licence plate number on a casting until a release date had been decided.

The suffix letter would be added just before the moulds were ready to enter production. When the mould for the low bed trailer was made the licence plate number was copied from an early casting of the Leyland base which read 'SPD 118'. The base casting was then finished to include the letter V, but the trailer was not altered.

The TP-2 cab was in red with two different window colours, green or amber. The cab of the TP-26 was metallic blue with clear or amber windows. Some cabs were also found packed with the TP-25 Pipe Truck.

THE CONVOY SERIES

The popularity of the Long Haul trucks indicated that something more was needed, and so the Research & Development Department looked at ways of upgrading the series. Mock-ups were made using the Long Haul and Leyland cabs with chrome bases and exhaust stacks. A new wheel was also developed, the 500 Concave Heavy Tread which had a concave chrome spoked hub and a ribbed design on the outside. The idea of revamping the range was dropped, however, and it was decided to invest in a new range of trucks with completely new tooling. These were to replace the Long Haul cabs in the 900 Series with new T.P. numbers. This idea was also dropped and the range was launched in 1982 with the name Convoy. This word was a household name following the success of the feature film Convoy, based on a story of a driver determined to make his delivery without the police getting in the way!

Three new cabs/tractor units were developed which were also issued as miniatures:

MB-41F Kenworth Conventional
MB-43F Peterbilt Conventional
MB-45E Kenworth Cabover Aerodyne

Two more cabs have since been used, the Scania which was available as a miniature while the Daf has only been used in the Convoy range:

MB-71G Scania T142
Daf 3300 Space cab

The existing trailers were also used with some modifications. A new fifth wheel design was added to clip into the new cabs and the rear axle housing was modified to take the new larger Heavy Tread wheel. Legs were incorporated to support the trailers when not being pulled, these have since seen a few minor casting variations. Three new trailers were introduced, the Rocket Transporter, Car Transporter and Horsebox.

The Horsebox was to have been in the 900 Series with the Leyland cab as TP-28. Pre-production samples of the Horsebox have a brown plastic roof and are without the raised panel detail on the sides where tampo printing was later applied. The model also has the early type of trailer casting used in the 900 Series.

The Convoy range has proved popular with children as well as collectors, both existing Matchbox collectors and truck collectors in general. The range has been continually updated with new liveries and tractor units. Promotional issues have also been produced as well as some limited issues.

MODEL LISTING 1982 - 1988

The Convoy range is full of many minor variations that

These are some of the rarest Convoy issues.
Top row: The CY-3 Container Truck was found with either the 'Pepsi' or 'Smiths Crisps' labels from the MB-72E.
Second row: Two models made by Matchbox for promotional use in Hong Kong.
Third Row: The 'Edwin Shirley Trucking' model with the Kenworth cab.
Bottom row: The CY-9 'New Directions' model with roof label and the CY-9 'Midnight X-Press' model with Kenworth cab.

occur during the production life of a toy. As well as different shades of tampo print, cabs were often found with a style of printing used on a different model. It was also common to find the wrong cab packaged with the wrong trailer. Base lettering on both the cabs and trailers have seen many minor changes, with models from Macau often not having the country of manufacture shown. This list outlines the main changes in colours and liveries. The range was originally made in England but production was moved to Macau in 1983.

NOTES

CY-3. The colour of the containers of the 'Federal Express'

CY-1 Kenworth Car Transporter

CAB	TRAILER	RAMP		MADE IN
Red	Red	Cream		England
Red	Red	Beige		
Red	Red	Cream		Macau
Yellow	Blue	Yellow		

CY-2 Kenworth Rocket Transporter

CAB	TRAILER	ROCKET		MADE IN
Silver	Silver	White		England
Silver	Silver	White		Macau
White	Silver	White		

CY-3 Peterbilt Container Truck

CAB	TRAILER	CONTAINERS	LABELS	MADE IN
Red	Black	Cream	Uniroyal	England
Red	Red	Beige	Uniroyal	
Red	Red	Light brown	Uniroyal	
Red	White	Cream	Uniroyal	
Black	Black	Cream	Pepsi	
White (MB-45E)	Black	Cream	Pepsi	
White (MB-45E)	Black	Cream	Smith's Crisps	
White	Black	Cream	Federal Express	
White	Black	White	Federal Expres	Macau

CY-4 Kenworth Boat Transporter (MB-41F)

CAB	TRAILER	BOAT HULL	WINDOW	MADE IN
Light orange	Silver	Orange	Green	England
Light orange	Silver	Dark orange	Green	
Dark orange	Silver	Orange	Green	
Dark orange	Silver	Dark orange	Green	
Dark orange	Silver	Orange	Red	
Dark orange	Silver	Orange	Clear	
Light orange	Silver	Orange	Green	Macau

CY-5 Peterbilt Covered Truck

CAB	WINDOW	TRAILER	CANOPY	LABEL/TAMPO	MADE IN
White	Amber	White	Green	Interstate Trucking	England
White	Clear	White	Green	Interstate Trucking	
White	Clear	White	Green	Interstate Trucking	Macau
Yellow	Clear	Silver	Yellow	Michelin	
Orange	Clear	Silver	Grey	Walts Farm Fresh Produce	

CY-6 Kenworth Horse Box

CAB	HORSEBOX	ROOF	TAMPO	MADE IN
Green	Cream	Green	Blue Grass-Farms	England
Green	Cream	Green	Blue Grass	
Green	Cream	Green	Without	
Green	Beige	Green	Without	
Green	Cream	Green	Blue Grass-Farms	Macau

CY-7 Peterbilt Petrol Tanker

CAB	WINDOW	TRAILER	TANK	LABEL/TAMPO	MADE IN
Black	Amber	Black	Yellow	Supergas	England
Black	Clear	Black	Yellow	Supergas	
Black	Clear	Black	Yellow	Supergas	Macau
Red	Clear	Silver	Chrome	Getty	

issue, manufactured in England, should have been white. As the factory had over produced cream coloured containers of the 'Uniroyal' issue, these had to be used up.

As production was being wound down in England three interesting variations appeared. Smith's Crisps labels and also Pepsi labels from the MB-72E Dodge Delivery Truck were applied to the containers. The trailers were then packed with two types of cab, which were incorrect for the CY-3, i.e. the Peterbilt in black and the Kenworth Cabover in white. Most of these models were found in the G-4 Convoy Action Set.

CY-8. The 'Showliner' model was made as a gift to present to trade customers who visited the preview of 1986 new products. The display was inside an articulated box trailer which toured Europe as a mobile showroom. Although the Convoy model had a similar decorAtion to the real vehicle, the actual Showliner truck was white.

The models were made in the U.K. using parts sent from Macau as well as models that were taken from stock and then stripped and resprayed. Most of the work was undertaken by the Research and Development workshop, although outside model-makers were also used. Originally 400 were made but these were soon exhausted and another 200 were produced.

The 'K-Line' model was produced in 1986 for a Hong Kong subsidiary of a shipping company based in Japan called Kawasaki Ltd. Only 5,000 models were produced for the company with none being made available to the collectors market in general. A special box was produced that had no reference to Matchbox, Convoy or other information such as the country of manufacture.

The 'Linfox' truck was an Australian release as CY-3. It was shown in the Matchbox catalogue with a Peterbilt cab, but this cab was not used.

The 'This Truck Delivers' model was made using the Matchbox truck with a 1988 calendar label applied to the roof. The labels were applied in England by the R. & D. Department in Enfield. The truck was then packaged with an MB-38 Model 'A' Van with a 'This Van Delivers' livery. The models were mailed to companies in the U.K. to promote the use of Matchbox toys for promotional use.

CY-9. The first issues of the 'Midnight X-Press' were made in England with labels applied to the box. Although the labels were handed with the correct position of the wording to the rear, models were made with the labels on the wrong sides, which put the wording to the front. When production commenced in Macau, tampo print was used instead of a label. An incorrect model was copied to produce a model with the wording to the front.

One interesting variation on the 'Midnight X-Press' truck is the use of the 45E Kenworth cab instead of the Kenworth Conventional. This model could be classed as a CY-8, but the models were issued in the CY-9 box. The cabs were in the correct colour scheme of black and grey and were also sold as miniatures packed singly in the blue window box.

In 1986 the 'Stanley helps you do things right' truck was the first on-pack offer Convoy model to be used in the U.S.A. It was available for $2 plus a proof of purchase from a selection of tools.

Two more promotional models have since been produced for the U.S.A., all have been

CY-8 Kenworth Box Truck (MB-45E)

CAB	TRAILER	CONTAINER	ROOF/DOORS	LABELS/TAMPO	MADE IN
White	Red	Red	White/white	Redcap	England
White	Red	Red	White/white	Matchbox	
White	Red	Red	Black/black	Redcap	
White	Red	Red	White/black	Redcap	
White	Red	Red	Black/white	Redcap	
Silver	Silver	Silver	Silver	Showliner	
White	Black	White	White	K Line	Macau
Red	Yellow	Red	Yellow	Linfox (Australian CY-3)	
White	Blue	White	White	Matchbox	
White	White	White	White	Matchbox	
				This Truck Delivers	

CY-9 Kenworth Box Truck (MB-41F)

CAB	WINDOW	TRAILER	CONTAINER	LABELS/TAMPO	MADE IN
Black	Amber	Black	Black	Midnight X-Press	England
Black	Clear	Black	Black	Midnight X-Press	
Black	Amber	Black	Black	Midnight X-Press (MB-45)	
Black	Clear	Black	Black	Midnight X-Press	Macau
Black	Clear	Black	Yellow	Stanley	
Black	Clear	Black	Black	Moving In New Directions	
White	Clear	Black	White	Matchbox -	Macau
				Die Casting Toys Ltd	
White	Clear	Black	White	Matchbox - Universal Group	
				20th Anniversary	
White	Clear	White	White	Paul Arpin Van Lines	
White	Clear	White	White	Canadian Tire	

CY-10 Kenworth Racing Transporter (with MB-66F)

BODY	TAMPO	MB-66 WINDOW
White	Malones Transporter	Green
White	Malones Transporter	Red

CY-11 Kenworth Helicopter Transporter (with MB-75E)

			MB-75E HELICOPTER			
CAB	TRAILER	BODY	BASE	WINDOW	SKIDS	MADE IN
Silver	Silver	Silver	Orange	Amber	Silver	England
Silver	Silver	Silver	Orange	Amber	Black	
Silver	Silver	Silver	Orange	Clear	Silver	
Silver	Silver	Silver	Orange	Clear	Black	
Silver	Silver	Silver	Black	Amber	Silver	
Silver	Silver	Silver	Orange	Amber	Silver	Macau
Black	Silver	Black	Black	Amber	Silver	
Blue	Silver	White	Black	Amber	Silver (MC-13 set)	

CY-12 Kenworth Aircraft Transporter

CAB	TRAILER	CRADLE	AIRCRAFT	TAMPO	MADE IN
White	Silver	White	Blue	Darts	England
White	Silver	White	Blue	Darts	Macau

CY-13 Peterbilt Fire Engine

CAB	LIGHTS	TRAILER	TAMPO	MADE IN
Red (Peterbilt)	Without	Red	White	England
Red (Long Haul)	With	Red	White	Macau
Red		Red	White	
Red		Red	Yellow	
Red		Red	Yellow/white	

CY-14 Kenworth Boat Transporter (MB-45E)

CAB	TRAILER	CRADLE	BOAT
White	Silver	Brown	White

CY-15 Peterbilt Tracking Vehicle

CAB	TRAILER	CARAVAN		TAMPO
White	Silver	White		N.A.S.A.
Yellow	Blue	Yellow		British Telecom (CY-206 Set)

CY-16 Scania Box Truck

CAB	BASE	TRAILER	BOX	TAMPO
White	Green	Black	White	7-Up (labels)
White	Blue	White	Blue	Duckhams
Purple	Purple	Purple	White	Edwin Shirley Trucking
White	White	Black	White	Ansett (Australian CY-4)
White	Red	Red	Red	Heinz Tomato Ketchup
Red	White	White	Red	Kentucky Fried Chicken
Blue	Blue	Blue	Blue	Matey Bubble Bath
White	Black	Black	White	Wimpy Hamburgers
Yellow	White	Red	Yellow	Weetabix
White	Blue	Blue	White	Signal Toothpaste
White	Black	Black	White	Golden Wonder Crisps
White	Red	Red	White	Merchant's Tire

CY-17 Scania Petrol Tanker

CAB	BASE	TRAILER	TANK	TAMPO
White	Blue	Blue	White	Amoco
Red	Red	Red	Red	Tizer the Appetizer
White	Green	Green	White	Diet 7-Up
White	Grey	Grey	Chrome	Shell
Orange	Orange	White	Orange	Cadbury's Fudge

CY-18 Scania Container Truck

CAB	BASE	INTERIOR	TRAILER	CONTAINERS	TAMPO
Blue	Yellow	Silver	Yellow	Blue	Varta Batteries
Blue	Yellow	Black	Yellow	Blue	Varta Batteries
Red	Red	Black	Red	Red	Kit Kat
White	Blue	Black	Blue	White	Wall's Ice Cream
Orange	Brown	Black	Brown	Orange	Rowntree's Breakaway
White	Green	Black	Green	White	7-Up
Red	Black	Black	Black	Red	Beefeater Steak Houses

CY-19 Peterbilt Box Car

CAB	TRAILER	BOX	TAMPO
White	Silver	White	Ansett Wridgways

CY-20A Scania Tipper

CAB	BASE	TRAILER	TIPPER	TAMPO
Pink	Pink	Black	Pink	Ready Mix

CY-20B Kenworth Tipper

CAB	TRAILER	TIPPER	TAMPO
Yellow	Black	Yellow	Taylor Woodrow
Yellow	Black	Yellow	Motorway (TC-3)
Green	Black	Yellow	Eurobran (MC-7)

CY-21 Daf Aircraft Transporter

CAB	BASE	TRAILER	CRADLE	AIRCRAFT	TAMPO
White	Blue	Blue	Blue	Orange	Airtrainer
White	Blue	Blue	White	Red	Red Rebels

generally available to collectors: 'Paul Arpin Van Lines' and 'Canadian Tire'.

The 'Moving In New Directions' model was given away by Matchbox salesmen in Australia to promote their new system of direct supply to the retail trade. The models were factory produced with tampo printing, some also had a roof label with the name and telephone number of the salesman.

Two of the rarest Convoy models ever produced are the Macau Diecasting Toys Ltd and Matchbox-Universal Group 20th Anniversary models. The M.D.C. model was made in 1986 and given away to customers visiting the Matchbox production site in Macau. Macau Diecasting is one of the companies in the Universal group that manufactures the diecast products for Matchbox.

The Anniversary model was made to celebrate the 20th Anniversary of the Universal Group of companies which owns Matchbox Toys. These were given away to some members of staff management. Both these models were never on retail sale and are extremely rare.

CY-10. The Kenworth Racing Transporter proved expensive to produce and was deleted after only a year. In 1985 it was used in a new range called 'Team Matchbox' which consisted of the transporter and two miniatures in a racing livery. These are listed in the Superfast chapter.

CY-13. The first issue of the Fire Engine was made in England using the Peterbilt cab, which was without roof lights, but when production moved to Macau a different cab was used. It was decided to use the Long Haul cab instead because it was cheaper to produce. Many modifications were made to the moulds. The cab had two roof lights and a storage box added behind the cab. The base was modified to take the heavy treaded wheel and was chrome plated. The fifth wheel coupling also had to be altered to the new Convoy fixing.

CY-15. The mould of the CY-6 Horsebox was remade to produce the rear box of the CY-15 Tracking vehicle, although a new roof was required.

CY-16. The 'Edwin Shirley Trucking Company' (E.S.T.) is well known to most truck enthusiasts in Europe because of their distinctive purple paintwork and brightly coloured livery.

In 1984 they took delivery of three D.A.F. F.T.3300 D.K.X. tractors fitted with the 'Space Cab' option which provides overnight accommodation within the vehicle, for two people.

They approached Matchbox in late 1984 with the hope that a Convoy model could be produced with a D.A.F. space cab in their livery. Although Matchbox were at the time developing a Daf space cab model for a 1986 release in Superkings, there were no plans to produce a miniature.

The factory then produced a tampo printed sample using the MB-45 Kenworth Cabover model, this being the only model in the Convoy range that had a similar shape and flat front to the Daf. E.S.T. decided not to proceed with the minimum order required of 10,000 and so the idea was scrapped. Only a few samples of the Kenworth model were produced.

CY-19. The Peterbilt Box Car was shown in some catalogues, in a red and white 'Statewide Freight' livery. This was a one off prototype mock-up and none were made in production.

CY-22 Daf Power Launch Transporter

CAB	BASE	TRAILER	CRADLE	HULL	DECK	TAMPO
White	Blue	Blue	Grey	Red	White	Shark
White	Blue	Blue	Grey	Red	White	CG22

CY-23 Scania Covered Truck

CAB	BASE	TRAILER	BED	CANOPY	TAMPO
Yellow	Blue	Grey	Blue	Yellow	Michelin

CY-24 Daf Box Car

CAB	BASE	TRAILER	BOX	TAMPO
Red	Black	Black	Red	Ferrari
Blue	Black	Black	Blue	Pickfords Removals

CY-25 Daf Box Truck

CAB	BASE	TRAILER	BOX	TAMPO
Yellow	Yellow	Yellow	Yellow	Ipec (Australian CY-9)
BLue	Blue	Blue	Blue	Crookes Healthcare
White	Orange	Orange	White	T.N.T. Ipec (TC-4)
Red	Black	Black	red	Royal Mail Parcels
White	Black	Black	White	Unigate Fresh Milk

CY-26 Daf Container Truck

CAB	BASE	TRAILER	CONTAINERS	TAMPO
Light blue	Blue	Black	Blue	P. & O.

CY-20A. The Scania Tipper was an Australian only release. It was shown in the Matchbox catalogue with a white roof, but this version was not issued.

CY-25. The Crookes Healthcare model was produced to promote the company's new distribution service and seventy five years of business. An MB-20G Volvo Container Truck was also produced in the same colour scheme.10,000 of each model were produced, with 'Crookes Healthcare' taking half the order and Matchbox selling the rest to the collectors market.

Crookes took 4,000 of the models and packaged them as pairs in a presentation pack, which was distributed to the pharmaceutical trade. 200 special packs were produced containing the Daf Box Truck and a repainted Code Three Yesteryear Y-5 Talbot Van.

CY-26. The Daf Container Truck was a new combination produced for the 'P. & O.' shipping company. The models were sold in gift shops aboard their cross channel ferries operating between England and Europe and some models were also supplied to the collectors market.

Two more models are worth highlighting. In 1984 the CY-2 Kenworth Rocket Transporter was issued in the U.S.A. with a Matchbox Sky-Buster model. The SB-3 N.A.S.A. Space Shuttle was used on the trailer instead of the rocket. It was sold in the N.A.S.A. Countdown Gift Set packed with another Rocket Transporter and an MB-54G Command Vehicle.

In 1985 a Peterbilt Low Loader was issued in the U.K. packed in the CY-203 Construction Set. It used the Long Haul cab from the CY-13 Fire Engine in a yellow and blue livery. The set also included an MB-30G Peterbilt Tipper and an MB-32F Atlas Excavator mounted on the trailer.

MB-17F LONDONER BUS

Buses have always been a popular subject for toy collectors and Matchbox have always featured a bus in the miniature range. The release of the 17F Londoner Bus in August 1972 was to become one of the most popular models for both bus enthusiasts and Matchbox collectors.

The bus was modelled in 1:121 scale on the Daimler Fleetline D.M.S. series which were supplied to London Transport, where it was known as the Londoner. The body work was built by Metro-Cammell and Park Royal. The best way to review the model is to examine each component separately.

Body. This was divided into two parts, the upper and lower decks. These were assembled with a front tuck-in and a rear

*MB-17F The Londoner Bus – twenty promotional models,
some rare and some less so.*

rivet. As access to the rear rivet was limited, problems were always experienced in production and so models were often scrapped. Minor differences are to be found in the detail cast on the bodies due to the use of multi-impression moulds. The front tuck-in was strengthened in 1978 by being enlarged.

Being a London Bus the colour was normally red, although other colours were used and these are shown in the listing.

Base. The first base castings were without strengthening ribs over the front and rear axle areas, these ribs were added in 1973. During 1973 the bus was issued in the Lesney Gift Ware Series mounted onto a ceramic oval ashtray. The mould was modified so that two types of casting could be produced. One for the normal base and one for use on giftware. These bases had two circular bosses cast which were just long enough to hold the model with its wheels above the surface of the ashtray. Two self tapping screws were then screwed through holes in the ashtray and into the base, to secure the model.

The colour of the base was generally gloss black but other colours also exist in various shades: matt black, brown, grey and unpainted. In late 1980 the material of the base was changed to plastic to reduce costs. A textured finish was also added as well as some extra strengthening ribs over the axle areas.

Two wheel types were used, first a five spoke hub design

General Release:		
1972 - 1974	Swinging London Carnaby Street	Red
1973 - 1976	Berger Paints	Red (Cream & beige, silver or orange)
1975	Esso Extra Petrol	Red
1977	Silver Jubilee	Silver (Red)
1978	Matchbox 1953 - 1978	Red (Blue or orange)

YEAR	LABEL	BODY/ROOF
1972	Preston Guild Merchant	Red
	Barclays Bank	Red
1973	Impel 73 Trade Fair	Red
	The Baron of Beef 01-606-6961	Red
	London Hilton/Kensington Hilton	Red
	Sellotape Packaging Systems/61108-9	Red
	Sellotape Electrical Tapes/01-952-2345	Red
	Sellotape Selbstklebebander	Red
	I.C.P. Interchemicals & Plastics	Red
	Barclays Bank	Red
	Charbonnier Wine	Red
	Chambourcy Yogurt	Red
	Borregard Paper	Red
1974	Typhoo Puts the T in Britain	Red
1976	Selfridges	Red
	Aviemore Centre/Santa Claus Land	Red
	Impel 76 Trade Fair	Cream/beige (red)
	A.I.M. Building Fund 1976	Red
	The Old Country-Busch Gardens	Red
	Eduscho Kaffee	Red
	Ilford HP5 Film	Red
	C Amcel Takes You Places	Red
1977	Jacobs - The Biscuit Makers	Orange (red or silver)
	New! The Museum of London	Red
	Army & Navy	Red
1978	Aral - Deutschlands Autopartner Nr.1	Blue (red)
1980	Bisto - The Bisto Bus/You Can't Kid a Bisto Kid	Red

applied to the wrong colour of body, which in these listings are shown in brackets.

List of labels. This listing shows all the promotional label types that are generally accepted as having been produced by Lesney. Body colour variations are shown in brackets. Over the years thousands of different labels have been applied to models by collectors, charities and businesses. Many of these are of interest because they are attractive or perhaps were produced for a charitable cause. These Code Three issues are not listed here, however, as they are beyond the scope of this book. Each label type is also to be found with variations of body castings and base colours.

GIFTWARE

In 1973 the bus was used in the Lesney Gift Ware Series with a plated body in either gold or silver finish, with two different labels. All of these are now very hard to find, particularly in mint condition and with the original packaging.

Basic List:
Gold plated Berger
Gold plated Swinging London
Silver plated Berger
Silver plated Swinging London

Brazil. Possibly the rarest issues are the buses manufactured in Brazil. In 1977 Lesney had components shipped to Brazil to be manufactured by a local company. Although the normal issue 'Berger' and 'Swinging London' labels were used the colours of the models were quite unusual. 'Lufthansa' labels were also used from the 65E Airport Coach. The above are known to exist:

and then from 1976 a new wheel was used with a dot-dash design This model did not have suspension like other models in the range, because the wheels were held inside the model trapped between the base and interior.

Interior. Two plastic components make up the interior, which features a steering wheel that is moulded flat and then folded upwards in the assembly process. It is not unusualto find models without the steering wheel as it was often broken off before being assembled. The interior was always moulded in white except for the Silver

Jubilee model which had red interiors in a silver body.

Labels. The paper labels were always applied after the rest of the model had been assembled.

The first labels used had square cut corners which were later changed to a small radius.

BODY	ROOF	LABELS
Blue	Yellow	Berger
Blue	White	Berger
Red	Yellow	Berger
Red	White	Berger
Metallic red	Metallic red	Berger
Metallic red	Metallic red	Lufthansa
Red	Yellow	Swinging London

Different suppliers were used although two companies Sellotape and Dolphin produced the majority of labels used for general release. In this list the body colours used are given, and also shown in brackets arc the alternative body colours available.

Two versions exist of the 'Swinging London' label with different styles of the letter 'a' used in the word Carnaby. The 'Berger' labels exists with many variations in ink colours, early issues had square corners, later issues round corners. Handed labels (left and right hand) were often applied on the wrong sides. Labels were often

MB-17F The Londoner Bus: Many variations exist of labels and body colours. Possibly the rarest issues are those made in Brazil. They are shown here with yellow and white roofs.

MB-17G LONDON TITAN BUS

Just as the Londoner Bus was beginning to look out-moded, the original mould also started to deteriorate. The British Leyland Titan Bus had joined the London Transport fleet in 1978 and so Lesney chose this as the replacement. The model was to a scale of 1:124. Although released in the R.O.W. range as number 17 and the Japanese range as number 7, it was in the U.S.A. range from 1984 to 1985 as number 51.

Pre-production notes. The base and two body halves had been designed to be cast in zinc. Lesney were faced with rising costs at this time and it was decided to change one of the parts to plastic. Shots were taken in plastic and models assembled in various combinations of materials. The ideal cost saving was to make the upper body plastic with the lower body and base in zinc. Pre-production trials proved that the plastic and zinc bodies could be assembled satisfactorily. The only problem was the difference in the finish of the red plastic upper body and the red painted lower body. It was thus decided to make the base in plastic after all. Pre-production castings of the base exist with number 35 and also number 50.

Production notes. Because of the problems found with the rear rivet during the assembly of the Londoner Bus, a new method of fixing was designed. After spraying the body halves, the lower body, base and interior were riveted together. The upper and lower bodies were then clipped together and the labels applied. This method proved to be very satisfactory. This is one of the few models in recent years to feature a snap together assembly. Models can be found with the roof on the wrong way round, even though the underside of the casting has an arrow cast on it, pointing to the front.

The first production run of the plastic base had a smooth finish which was changed to a textured finish. The model name on the base at first was 'London Bus'. This was removed in Macau because many

General Release (all red bodies):
1982   Laker Skytrain Berger Paints

1984   Matchbox London Bus (two types)
1985   You'll Love New York. U.S.A. T.W.A.

1986   Around London Tour Bus

YEAR	LABELS	BODY/ROOF	YEAR	LABELS	BODY/ROOF
ENGLAND				Rowntree's Fruit Gums	Red
1982	Matchbox No1/Montepna Narnniaia	Blue/white		Nestle Milky Bar	Red
	Matchbox No1/Montepna Narnniaia	Red		Space For Yough	Blue/white
	Matchbox London Bus	Blue/white		Cityrama Sightseeing	Blue
	Chesterfield Transport Centenary	Green	1986	Matchbox Nurnberg 1986	Red
1984	York Festival & Mystery Plays	Red		First M.I.C.A. Convention	Red
	Rowntree's Fruit Gums	Green		Midland Bus & Transport Museum	Red and white
	Nestle Milky Bar	Blue		The National Tramway Museum	Blue
	Keddies No. 1 in Essex	Blue	**CHINA**		
	RapportMaroon		1986	Band-Aid Plasters Play Bus	Red
	35 Roakhk PA3HOK3HOC (Greek)	Red		Yokohama Takashimaya	Red
	Nice To Meet You Matchbox Japan 1984	Red	1987	M.I.C.A.	White (red seats)
				Girobank	Blue
MACAU				Matchbox Niagara Falls	Red
1984	Yokohama Matsuzakaya 198	Red		Matchbox Valencia 12 Febrero 1987	Red
	Torvale Fisher Engineering Limited	Black/white		West Midlands Travel	Blue/beige (tan seats)
1985	W.H. Smith Travel	Orange/white	1988	Denny Happy 1000th Birthday Dublin	White

MB-17G the Titan Bus, has proved as popular as the previous Londoner Bus model.

of the promotional issues produced were not actually London buses. Later the words 'Leyland Titan' were put on the base. The bus was first manufactured in England and then it was transferred to Macau in 1985 and then to China late in 1986.

Labels. The first issue was 'Laker Skytrain' which went into production just as the Laker company went bankrupt. To keep production going the 'Berger' label was brought back from retirement after many years on the Londoner.

Some of the labels of interest:

'Nestle Milky Bar' and 'Rowntree's Fruit Gums' were only available in the U.K. through a mailing offer from Matchbox. By sending in the header cards from Matchbox Miniature, Convoy and Superking packs the consumer was sent the bus of his choice, free. Demand was great with a total of 60,000 models being sent out in white cardboard boxes. These buses had been made in England with a blue body for the Milky Bar and a green body for the Rowntree's Fruit Gums. When stocks had almost run out, more buses were ordered to meet the continuing demand. Production had now moved to Macau, where another 20,000 of each were made. Due to a misunderstanding between the English and Macau factories the models were made with red bodies.

An additional model was available with 'W.H. Smith Travel' labels by sending the header cards plus a till receipt from a W.H. Smith shop. It had an orange body and white roof and was also made in Macau.

The 'Keddies No 1 in Essex' bus was only available from the

MB38 MODEL A VAN BASIC LISTING

GENERAL RELEASES

LIVERY	BODY	BASE	ROOF	RIVETS
1982				
Champion Spark Plugs (Made in England)	Dark Blue	Black	White	3
1983				
Champion Spark Plugs (Made in Macau)	Dark Blue	Black	White	3
1984				
Pepsi Cola/Come Alive	White	Blue	Red	3
Pepsi Cola	White	Blue	Red	3
Pepsi Cola	White	Blue	Red	2
1986				
Matchbox Speed Shop	Dark Blue	Black	Black	2

PROMOTIONALS

LIVERY	BODY	BASE	ROOF	METHOD OF OBTAINING
1984				
Kellogg's Cornflakes	Dark Blue	Black	White	A
Matchbox on the Move	Dark Blue	Black	White	B
Matchbox U.S.A.	White	Blue	Red	C
Ben Franklin	White	Blue	Red	C
Arnott's Biscuits	Red	Black	Black	D
Lark Lane Motor Museum	Beige	Brown	Brown	E
Tittensor First School	Grey	Red	Red	E
1985				
Bass Museum	Dark Blue	Black	Red	E
The Pocket Guide	Yellow	Green	Green	E
The Australian	White	Black	Black	D
B.B.C.	Dark Green	Black	Black	E
1986				
Weet-bix/Sanitarium	Green	Black	Green	D
H.H. Brain's Faggots	Cream	Green	Green	A
Isle of Man TT86	Light Blue	Blue	Red	E
Smith's Potato Crisps	Blue	Red	White	D
1987				
Isle of Man TT87	Black	Red	Red	E
2nd M.I.C.A. Convention	Black	Black	Black	F

W.H. Smith & Son Ltd	Red	Black	Black	G
Junior Matchbox Club	Yellow	Blue	Blue	F

LIVERY	BODY	BASE	ROOF	METHOD OF OBTAINING
Isle of Man Post/1	Red	Black	Black	E
Chesty Bonds	White	Black	Black	D
Silvo Silver Polish	Dark Blue	Black	Black	H
John West	Green	Red	Red	D
Kellogg's Cornflakes (Denmark)	Dark Blue	Black	White	A
Dewhurst Master Butcher	Red	Black	Black	E
Kellogg's Rice Krispies	Light Blue	Black	White	A
This Van Delivers (U.K.)	Dark Blue	Black	Red	I
1988				
Royal Mail	Red	Black	Red	E
3rd M.I.C.A. Convention	Yellow	Yellow	Red	F
North America M.I.C.A.	Orange	Black	Black	F
Isle of Man TT88	Yellow	Black	Red	E
Mervyn Wynn Models	Red	Black	Black	J
The Manx Cattery	Red	Black	Black	J
Isle of Man Post/2	Red	Black	Black	E
James Neale & Sons	Yellow	Blue	White	E
Barrett Sherbet Fountain	Yellow	Black	Red	A
Alex Munro Master Butcher	Red	Black	Black	E
Cobb of Knightsbridge	Brown	Black	Black	E
P.M.G.	Orange-red	Black	Black	D
W.H. Smith & Son Ltd	Yellow	Black	Black	G
This Van Delivers (H.K.)	Dark Blue	Black	Red	I
Chester Toy Museum	Light Blue	Grey	Grey	E
Chester Heraldry	Light Blue	Grey	Grey	E
Powerhouse Museum	Dark Green	Black	Black	D
Guernsey Post Office	Blue	Black	Black	E
Rayner's Crusha	Red	Black	Black	A
Rowntree's Jelly	Green	Black	Yellow	A
Big Sister	Red	Black	Black	D
Green's Cake Mix	Green	Green	Green	A
Uniroyal	Black	Red	Red	K

Keddies department store in Southend, Essex. Although only 936 models were supplied to Keddies a small quantity were later found on general sale in the U.S.A. These were part of a large amount of surplus stock sold by Matchbox to an American store.

In February 1986 Matchbox Toys in Germany produced 200 buses with the 'Matchbox Nurnberg 1986' labels. Unlabelled models were sent from Macau and the new vinyl labels were applied in Germany. These were given away to customers at the Nüremberg Toy Trade Fair in West Germany.

To celebrate the 'First M.I.C.A. Convention' in March 1986 the Matchbox Research & Development Department in Enfield produced 250 buses in special boxes. The boxes were based on the old Moko-Lesney design. Buses were taken from stock at short notice and were found to have three different base types: England, Macau and China. The existing labels were removed and the models relabelled with five separate vinyl labels.

Matchbox Toys in Spain made 2,000 models for the Valencia Toy Trade Fair in February 1987. They took existing stocks of the 'Around London Tour Bus' model and applied another label over the top with the words '26 Feria Del Juguette Valencia 12 - Febrero 1987'. The box also had a bright yellow triangular label across the bottom of the front right hand corner.

The two different 'Yokohama' issues for Japan were both labelled by Matchbox Toys in Japan for local promotions.

MB38G MODEL 'A' FORD VAN

In 1979 Lesney released the MB73E Model 'A' Ford Saloon. This was a model that Jack Odell had always wanted to produce. The model proved to be popular so the MB38G Model 'A' Ford Van was released in 1982. The zinc base, plastic sub-base, window and grille were used as common parts so new moulds were only required for the zinc body and plastic roof. Production initially took place in England. In 1983 the moulds were transferred to production in Macau.

Following the second M.I.C.A. Convention in March 1987 the interest in this model increased. A special run of only 450 models was produced for M.I.C.A. members and their guests attending the dinner. Apart from Superfast collectors, the model is also popular with Yesteryear collectors. During 1987 and 1988 its use in a number of regional on-pack offers has made the acquisition of every issue a demanding task for collectors.

THE COMPONENTS

Body. Following the huge number of models made for the Kellogg's Cornflakes promotion in 1984 the body mould was remade. Only a few slight differences can be found between the different castings.

The rear number plate lettering 'KG 6567' is slightly larger on the new body and the front window bars vary in thickness. During 1988 models were to be found with or without some of the rear door detail lines, this may be a sign that another new mould is needed!

Base. The zinc base originally had a rivet in front of the rear axle. This was used in production to assemble the base, sub-base and wheels together before final assembly to the body. Early in 1985 the method of assembly was changed, with the removal of the central rivet, the model was then assembled in one operation. The Kellogg's Cornflakes and Pepsi models are to be found with three or two rivet bases.

Sub-base. The first production run of the van had 'MB75' on the sub-base. This was soon removed from the mould and examples of the model with this base are now very hard to find. The size of the lettering on English bases also varies. In 1988 the lettering on the sub-base was altered to read 'Matchbox Int'l Ltd' instead of 'Matchbox Toys Ltd'. The word 'Superfast' was also removed.

Window. The colour of the window used in the saloon had been green, but was changed to amber before production of the van began. Two distinct shades of amber are to be found, the window was then changed to clear plastic. Since production moved to Macau the window has only been produced in clear plastic, sometimes these can be found with a very slight amber tint, due to impurities in the plastic.

Liveries. The first issues of the Pepsi model had the words 'Come Alive' on the front doors. These were removed at the request of the Pepsi company who advised Matchbox that this slogan was not in use during 1930s.

The 'Speed Shop' model featured larger wheels on the front and rear. These wheels had been used on other models in the range. Some early issues had chrome lettering on the tyres.

Decoration is often applied to the rear doors as well as the sides. Tampo print is generally used, although labels are often needed for promotional models with intricate designs. During production the shades of tampo printed inks produced can vary between models.

The majority of factory produced promotional models have consisted of only 10,000 models, this being the minimum order the factory will accept.

Listing. This listing does not cover every permutation of all the variations in components. This would involve extensive listings and the individual collector is left to choose to what extent to take his or her collection.

The special livery vans have been offered in many different ways. Often they are easy to obtain and sometimes almost impossible! The various methods are outlined here:

A. Many models have now been used by companies in the U.K. as on-pack offers. With this type of promotion the consumer has to send proofs of purchase from the products and sometimes a small payment. The 'Kellogg's Cornflakes' model was a huge success for both Kellogg's and Matchbox with over 1.9 million vans being produced. The models were offered in France in 1985 and in Denmark in 1987. The models produced for Denmark used the later body casting.

B. The 'Matchbox on the Move in 84' model was given away to customers at the New York Trade Toy Fair in February 1984. 5,000 'Champion' vans were sent from Macau without labels and then labelled by Matchbox Toys U.S.A. Some vans also featured a 'Toy Fair 84' label on the roof.

C. The 'Matchbox U.S.A.' and 'Ben Franklin – Better Quality for Less' models were made at the same time by Matchbox Toys U.S.A. utilising 'Pepsi' models supplied from Macau without tampo print. 2,600 'Matchbox U.S.A.' vans were made for the American collectors' club members. The 'Ben Franklin' is now one of the rarest and most sought after Matchbox Miniatures. 1,000 vans were made and the majority given away at a convention of Ben Franklin store managers. Managers not attending the event were sent models. Very few vans were made available to collectors.

D. Matchbox Toys Australia have issued many models aimed directly at the collectors market. It has been their policy that any models used for on-pack offers are made available to collectors after the offer has finished.

E. There have been a number of vans produced for a particular event or promotional use by a U.K. company. Often a quantity has been set aside for collectors to purchase.

F. The Matchbox International Collectors Club have produced some excellent models for their members. The first was for the 1987 U.K. Convention. 450 models were made in Macau and then labelled by the U.K. Research and Development Department. Each model had five labels and was packed in a special Moko-Lesney style box.

G. Two models have been produced for the W.H. Smith 'On The Road' book club in the U.K. First with a red body then with a yellow body. The models were only available via mail order when consumers joined the book club. These models were packed in white cardboard boxes, with black printing.

H. The 'Silvo Silver Polish' van was produced for Reckitt & Colman Plc to celebrate seventy five years of their polish. The models were given away by salesmen to retailers, to advertise the new style of can used for the polish. The complete range of polishes produced by Reckitt & Colman were mounted in a display pack with the boxed model. After the salesmen's presentation, the van was given to the retailer. Matchbox also issued a number of the vans in the blue window box for collectors.

I. Late in 1987 Matchbox Toys produced 5,000 vans with the livery 'Matchbox This Van Delivers!'. It was packaged in a copy of a large matchbox with an inner tray. The majority of models were then packed with a CY8 Convoy truck and mailed to companies throughout the U.K. to advertise the use of Matchbox toys for promotional use. During 1988 Matchbox in Hong Kong did a similar promotion using the 'This Van Delivers' model. The Hong Kong model was different in two ways: the base was the latest version without Superfast and the tampo print was also

These models have proved popular with collectors, and many have been made for on pack offers and promotional use by companies.

different. The U.K. issue featured their telephone number on the door 01-805-4567, whilst the Hong Kong model did not have any printing on the door.

J. The 'Mervyn Wynn' and 'Manx Cattery' models were produced as a combined order of 5,000 of each. They were made using a batch of models which were to have been used for the first issue of the 'Isle of Man Post Office' model.

The first samples produced of the 'Post Office' model were made using tampo printing on the front doors and labels on the sides of the body. Labels were used by the Macau factory because they felt that tampo printing would not achieve the detailed design, but these labels did not feature the required black and gold border. While the first samples were being checked by the customer in the U.K., the factory went ahead and made the rest of the 10,000 models. These models were not acceptable to the customer and the production run was repeated using tampo print. The factory then put the labelled models into storage.

A further run of the 'Post Office' model was made in 1988 with two modifications to the tampo print. The island on the front doors was in black instead of gold and the rear doors featured a telephone number.

K. The 'Uniroyal Tyre Company' in Canada had 10,000 models produced by Matchbox. Two versions of the van exist. The majority of them had a label applied to the rear doors by Uniroyal. This Code 3 model was used by Uniroyal salesmen. The remaining Code 1 models without the rear labels, were made available to the collectors.

THE SO HIGH RANGE

In 1986 the Superchargers range was launched in the U.S.A., and then in the U.K. during 1987 called Super Trucks. The range consists of models from the miniature range with chrome plated plastic bases and huge wheels and tyres. The Model 'A' Van was introduced into the range in 1987 as number SC3 with the name So High. The model had a yellow body and black base and roof.

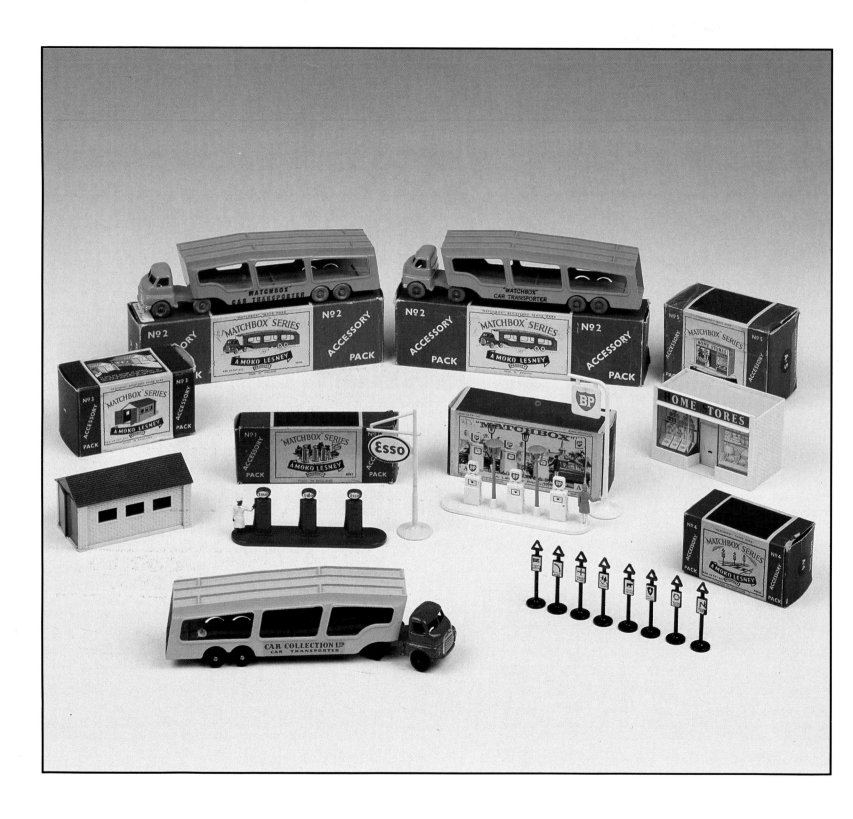

11 The Other Ranges

THE REST OF THE STORY

Early Moko Lesney Accessories - note three versions of the A2.1 Car Transporter.

This section is not intended to be a definitive chapter on all the other ranges not previously mentioned so far. It is, however, designed to enlighten the reader about some of the products that came and went as the company grew. These products and ranges have been mostly forgotten by the vast majority of today's collectors and indeed the research necessary to uncover them has been difficult. Archive material has never been a strong point in the company's history. However, these more obscure ranges are worthy of inclusion as, nostalgia aside, they reveal the development of the company and its expansion into the widening toy market of the 1960s, 1970s and 1980s.

ACCESSORY PACKS

The first accessory to appear in the range arrived in late 1956 and consisted of a set of three 'Esso' Petrol Pumps (A1.1) accompanied by the then familiar sight of an attendant and was completed by a forecourt Esso sign. The set was packaged as the traditional "Matchbox" Series in four different boxes, three describing it as 'A MOKO LESNEY' and the last as 'A LESNEY'. The sides of the carton were blue at either end with 'No. 1 ACCESSORY PACK' on the blue area. The Esso Signs were of the waterslide transfer type and it is very common to find the forecourt sign transfer damaged on later models, as there was a casting fault in the metal behind the transfer. Both the castings for this accessory were supplied

in one box without any internal packaging and so it is common to find them scratched or marked. The colour of the forecourt sign was later changed from cream to white.

The Esso set was replaced in 1963 by an improved version which now featured the logo of British Petroleum (A1.2). This modernised version also featured two overhead lamp fittings and featured an attendant moulded into the casting to the knees with a plastic upper body. The set and sign were packaged in a larger colour illustrated box and were discontinued in 1967.

The third category of the No. 1 Accessory Pack was a Service Ramp made especially to fit in with the large MG1.3 Service Station (this garage is described subsequently). The A1.3 Service Ramp first appeared in 1970 priced at 4s. 6d (22.5p). Lesney felt that as the first two Service Stations had had their own self-contained ramp and the third station could not because of its more simple design, there was a need for a separate ramp. The 1971 catalogue described this accessory as follows: "Run your car onto the ramp, pull the lever and the model is ready to be serviced. Castrol Oil and grease guns on pull-out cables will help you finish the job in record time..." The ramp was always painted in gold and featured red nozzles and pipes and a Castrol label. The ramp then fitted on to the large cardboard base supplied with the Service Station in a space specifically designated for the Lesney Service Ramp.

The next accessory pack undoubtedly became the largest seller. The A2.1 Matchbox Car Transporter was a simple but sturdy articulated vehicle featuring the S Type Bedford cab and was introduced in 1957. The model had no apparent means of entry to either the top or bottom deck. In spite of the large numbers produced, this model contained only two minor casting changes confined to strengthening the inner faces of the transporter. Several variations can be found in connection with the wheels and the trailer advertisement.

Early versions of the model had a large 'MATCHBOX CAR TRANSPORTER' sign stamped in dark blue or black indelible ink. This gave way to a slightly smaller, but shorter in length version of the same sign around the time when the wheels were changed from grenodised metal to grey plastic. By 1960 the stamp technique had been replaced by the use of waterslide transfers which bore the description 'CAR COLLECTION LTD CAR TRANSPORTER' on two lines in either red or orange shades. The grey plastic wheels were soon replaced by black plastic versions but it is possible to find models with grey wheeled cabs and black wheeled trailers, combinations caused in the main by factory errors.

The rarest version is the final run model made in 1962. The model was recoloured to combine a bright

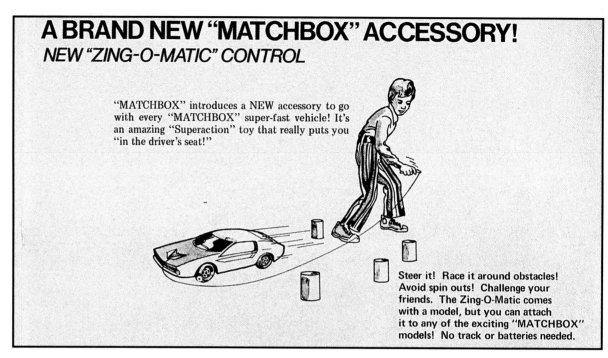

A BRAND NEW "MATCHBOX" ACCESSORY!
NEW "ZING-O-MATIC" CONTROL

"MATCHBOX" introduces a NEW accessory to go with every "MATCHBOX" super-fast vehicle! It's an amazing "Superaction" toy that really puts you "in the driver's seat!"

Steer it! Race it around obstacles! Avoid spin outs! Challenge your friends. The Zing-O-Matic comes with a model, but you can attach it to any of the exciting "MATCHBOX" models! No track or batteries needed.

red cab with a light grey trailer. The model features black plastic wheels and the later transfer. It was packaged in the final colour picture box, whereas earlier versions were packaged in either 'A MOKO LESNEY' or 'A LESNEY' box.

In 1971 the Matchbox 'Auto Sales' (A2.2) was introduced. Made from plastic it encouraged youngsters to enter the world of dealing in cars. The 1971 *Collectors' Catalogue* featured this accessory, "Do you want a new car? Or perhaps arrange a trade-in? Then go along to the 'Matchbox' Auto Sales and find out the value of your present model."

The expansion of the range to include items which would complement vehicles led to the introduction of some buildings. The first of these was an attractive model of a Lock Up Garage (A3.1) introduced in 1958 in the evocative colours of maroon, yellow and green. During its six years of availability this model was subject to a host of small casting changes. One interesting feature of this model was that each one was packed with a metal clip which enabled the enthusiastic owner to

clip several garages together. With a retail price of 2s. 6d (12.5p) prospective mews owners were faced with the unpleasant fact that the cost of each garage was some 60% more than the cost of the car to put in it! The garages came in three different boxes – 'A MOKO LESNEY', 'A LESNEY' and a colour picture box.

In common with Dinky and Triang Spot-On, Lesney were to issue a set of Road Signs (A4-1) in 1960. These consisted of eight contemporary signs and each was marked with the inscription 'Lesney' and 'England' on their bases. The signs were sold in the standard box at a scale of 77:1 and priced at 1s. 6d (7.5p) for the set.

The Zingomatic (Brroomstick) (A3.2) was released as an accessory in 1972. Each orange coloured Zingomatic (a simple plastic handle shaped like a shoe horn) was packaged with a Matchbox car, a piece of elastic and a label that was used to fix the elastic to the bonnet of the car. By pulling the handle the car would set off at a fast speed! The whole package cost 5s. 0d (25 pence) and was only available for one year.

While most cars packed with the Brroomstick were standard items from the normal Superfast Range, the first two cars were painted in special colours:

MB20 Lamborghini Marzal – lemon
MB68 Porsche 910 – white

In 1961 Lesney introduced the Home Stores Accessory (A5.1). This double-fronted shop was fitted with clear plastic windows behind which were paper labels simulating goods on display. Only one major casting change occurred when the location of the Home Stores transfer was altered by the locating ridges being redefined. This last model of the Accessory Series was produced after the take-over of Moko by Lesney, and so the packaging merely reflects the name Lesney. *Railway Modeller* July 1961: "The "Matchbox" Series shop is, however, just right for 00. It retails at 2s. 6d and with modifications . . . several of these could be placed side by side to form the basis of a simple scenic background." Sales of the Home Stores were not as good as Lesney had anticipated. A prototype building with a Cafe decal had been made, but in the light of the Home Stores sales it was never produced.

SERVICE AND FIRE STATIONS

To add further settings and create extra play value Lesney and Matchbox went on to produce over the years a range of Service Stations and a Fire Station. The Matchbox Fire Station (MF.1) was added to the range in 1963. This accessory was described in the 1966 *Collectors' Catalogue* as being 'Made in tough plastic with working double doors, firemen's pole and authentic multi-coloured transfers. Supplied completely assembled in a new full-colour giant 'Matchbox'. The Fire Station was available either as a single item 10s. 6d (52.5p) or as part of the G-10 Gift Set. The station was constructed out of plastic and was released with either a green or red roof, and a grey base which also formed a forecourt. Various labels were applied to add realism to the station. Although an Ambulance Station was developed at the same time in green and white, it was never released and consequently Lesney used up stocks of green roofs by issuing them as part of the Fire Station.

The Matchbox Garage, which was described on its box as a 'Showroom and Service Station for Matchbox toys', was first made in 1957. The design was based on a garage near to one of the Lesney factories. The production was sub-contracted to a plastics firm called Raphael Lipkin Ltd. (L.R.L.) as Lesney at that time did not have the machinery to manufacture it themselves. Early examples of the Matchbox Garage were produced with a red base, yellow building and a clock fascia in red.

The MF 1 Fire Station together with the first version Matchbox Garage- note the LRL trade mark on the box.

The clock recorded the time of twenty two minutes past twelve! The forecourt had a raised area to accommodate the Esso petrol pumps from the No. 1 Accessory Pack. The single-storey building featured clear plastic windows, a sliding door at the front and opening doors at the rear. A bright label was fixed to a plastic panel on top of the building. To boost sales, Lesney then produced the same garage but in the reversed colours of a red building with a yellow base and fascia. By 1960 the garage base was embossed with the words 'MADE IN ENGLAND' because Lesney were now making the garage themselves. Although the LRL trademark was quickly removed from the box, some of the Lesney-made garages were released in those boxes. The tooling for the original garage was returned to Raphael Lipkin Ltd. who re-issued it with plastic petrol pumps glued in position and was sold as the 'Pippin Toy Flyover Service Station'. In 1961 the first garage was removed from the range and replaced by a newly designed garage – the MG1.1.

This second Matchbox Service Station was introduced in 1961. *Railway Modeller* July 1961: "The new "Matchbox" Series garage at 8s. 11d (44.5p)is also 00 scale and represents the fairly elaborate multi-deck showroom/filling station seen in many towns today . . . this again will add to the scene." The station was of a two-storey design; the base and forecourt were red and the building yellow. A yellow plastic ramp clipped onto the rear to add extra play value. There was a red painted diecast metal fascia board and clock on the roof. The remainder of the garage was made in plastic. The base also featured a red servicing and repair ramp and a yellow plastic manhole cover directly in front. As with the first type of garage an area on the forecourt was moulded to take the No. 1 Esso Petrol Pumps. The recorded clock time was five past four. Various labels featuring Esso, the A.A., R.A.C. and Matchbox adorned the service station. All bases were embossed 'MATCHBOX GARAGE MADE IN ENGLAND BY LESNEY'. In 1963 the service station was re-issued as a B.P. garage and was shown for the first time in the 1963 catalogue. The base became green, whilst the building and rear ramp were in white. The repair ramp was also green with a white plastic manhole cover. The fascia board became lemon-yellow. A small modification was made to the area which originally featured the clock changing it to a B.P. sign. All the Esso markings were replaced by a combination of B.P. and Matchbox signs. The area on the forecourt remained constant to hold in position the new A1.2 Accessory Pack B.P. Petrol Pumps. Due to this change of livery there are four different boxes, the first a line drawing

piece Giant and the 124 piece Super Set." In 1974 the Super Station was produced exclusively for the American department store – Sears, Roebuck & Co.

Further service stations/garages followed in 1979 and 1980. The MG-2 (Shell theme) featured two filling pumps, a car wash, lift and service ramp, whereas the MG-3 (Texaco theme) was much larger and came with a realistic cardboard drive-in and car park area. Further realism was added with the inclusion of a hamburger shop next to the garage. The new MG.4 was launched in 1980. Shaped as a 'V' it featured a double storey car park on top of the Parts and Service Department. A multi-storey car park

Below: The MG-1 Service Station beside the later B.P. version from 1968. The cardboard roadway is from the earlier gift set.

Above: An advertisement from the Railway Modeller 1962.

with Esso, the second a colour picture with Esso, the third in colour with B.P. and the fourth once again in colour with B.P. in the background. The B.P. Double Storey Service Station remained in production until 1967.

In 1968 Lesney produced their third Matchbox Garage MG1.2. a single storey garage that still retained its B.P. livery. It was also available as part of the gift set G-1, which included the Service Station and three models. This Gift Set was priced at £1.2s. (£1.10p) The white plastic station featured three removable flags on the roof, a central kiosk on a white base with a large white roof and yellow and white plastic pumps. Labels reflecting B.P. and Matchbox were affixed to various parts. Early stations came with a cardboard forecourt, which in 1970 was enlarged. As described earlier this enlarged version

accommodated the Accessory Pack A1.3 Service Ramp.

In 1971 a new garage accessory was introduced just for the American market. *Matchbox Collectors' Club* 1971: 'Station Maker is the newest entry into the ever expanding line of

accessories designed to make collecting "Matchbox" Models more fun. Each set contains platforms, pillars and ramps that can be easily assembled in hundreds of different ways . . . Station Maker comes in three sizes: the 47 piece Regular, 84

and petrol pumps (Esso) was released as the new MG-6 garage in 1983. This was quickly followed by a new Matchbox Garage, MG-7, which was a compact version of MG-6 but included extras such as the car ramp and car wash.

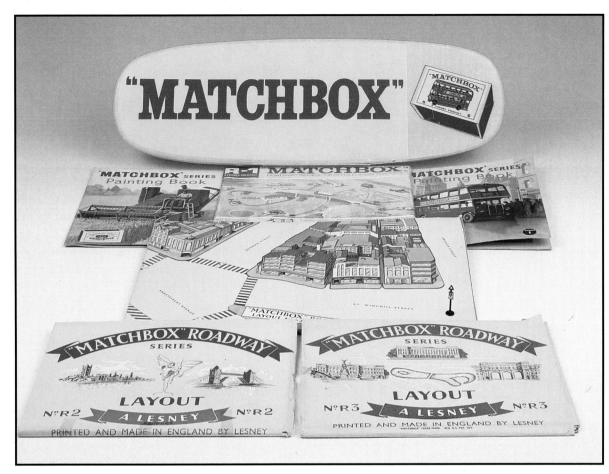

An illuminated shop sign, circa 1966, together with a display of roadways and Lesney painting books from the early 1960s.

The MG-8 Truck Stop Garage was introduced in 1983 to add further scope to the Convoy range. 1986 saw the further addition of the new MG-9 Gear Shift Garage – a battery operated accessory that enabled the user to raise barriers, lift ramps, and open garage doors by moving the simulated driver's gear-stick.

Several other forms of garage have been made by Matchbox Toys such as the Station Maker Series of 1972 and the Play Track Series garages of the 1980s.

ROADWAYS AND MOTORWAYS

Most of the major diecast vehicle manufacturers have at some time turned their attention to the manufacture of model roadways and Lesney were no exception. Model roadways at a first glance appear to be an easy item to produce and a natural extension for the cars that travel on them. In reality they are much more complex, as consideration of items such as curves, bridges, scale and other detailing can be difficult and add to the cost of manufacture and packaging. A roadway is by necessity bulky but yet cannot be expensive to purchase if it is to stand much chance of success.

Lesney entered this market in a modest way with the introduction of a cardboard mat Roadway in 1960. The layout measured 53.5" x 19.75" (1.35 metres x 50.2 cms) and cost a mere 1s. 11d (9.5p) at this time. This roadway was of a most simple design. It was a triangular shape and featured a central connecting road. Within a year Lesney had produced a series of four roadways to replace it. These were entitled R-1 'Main Roadway'; R-2 'The Heart of London'; R-3 'Buckingham Palace' and R-4 'Racing Track'. R-1, R-3 and R-4 featured cardboard cut-out buildings which added a three dimensional effect. In the case of R-2 the third dimension was something of an optical illusion as the buildings were drawn assuming an elevated perspective. The major disadvantage of these road sets was that as they were of folded cardboard it was impossible to lay them out completely flat as the ridge folds were permanent. In 1964 a new R-1 Roadway was introduced featuring amongst other things stand-up cut-outs, along with a new R-4 Grand Prix Race Track. Set R-3 was discontinued in 1965 and R-2 in 1966. These initial sets are extremely hard to find today in complete condition as they were very fragile.

The concept of roadways was relaunched in 1968. The new R-1 Roadway was updated to include a cut-out flyover. R-2 became a construction site. A further construction site layout was also produced in 1969. R-3 became a farmyard. The catalogue illustrations of these sets rather oversold them as they were always depicted with trees, figures and surrounding countryside, all of which was in sharp contrast to the rather meagre pieces of cardboard contained in the package!

In 1967 'Build-a-Road' was introduced into the American market only. Three different sets existed – small, medium and large. Each set comprised interlocking plastic pieces, including straights, curves, junctions and barriers.

1968 heralded a big development in roadway systems when the company launched the 'Matchbox Motorised Motorway' (M-2) priced at £5.2s.6d (£5 12.5p) This was a most ingenious system and undoubtedly first in its field as it did not require any modification to standard Matchbox cars. The system worked by producing a clip-together roadway which contained two slots in its surface. A continuous spring was then laid into each channel and clips were provided which attached to the underside of any standard car and engaged with the spring. The spring was then rotated by an electrically powered motor, causing the vehicle to be pushed forward by the motion of the spring moving in the same manner as an Archimedes screw. The electrical components were bought in from outside suppliers and assembled at the Edmonton factory. The high initial demand for the product soon meant that additional premises adjacent to Edmonton were developed. One immediate advantage of the system was that the second lane could be made to travel in the opposite direction by altering the polarity of the motor drive. The system could be either battery or mains powered via a specially produced transformer. Production began in July 1968 and by November the factory was producing twelve thousand sets a week. *Lister:* "The Motorised Motorway was an excellent product, its only technical failing being the spring and that could have been developed. On a practical level, there were perhaps

too many parts and once these became lost the system was rendered unusable. The Essex Police used to come around and cadge sets for use in traffic demonstrations of road safety at the Essex county show. They would do anything to avoid actually paying for them!" *Lesney News* September 1969: "When I.T.V. and B.B.C.1 challenge the B.B.C.2 dominance on the colour screen in November, Lesney Products will be among the first companies to advertise in this new colour television medium – the commercial will be seen by seven million children and nine million mums and dads several times, and will dramatise the uniqueness of the Motorway. The Motorway was voted the 'Toy of the Year' boys' award in 1968, and

Today - extremely hard to find but in 1968, 12,000 sets a week were made.

a trophy was presented to Mr Smith on the opening day of the International Toy Fair on the 26th January 1969."

The system was added to by the availability of a motorway extension set, and latterly by a comprehensive series of accessories which included driving pins, motor housings, controllers, bridge supports and spare clips. Sales of the Motorised Motorway were high initially and indeed went some way to justify the enormous development costs involved. Several small factors, however, were to undermine the popularity of the concept. The weight of the models was really too much for the spring and as there was nothing to stop an enthusiastic child or adult from loading up all his vehicles onto one spring they were quickly stretched. As soon as the spring stretched the system was ren-

dered useless. Replacement springs were certainly available, but only through selected outlets, unlike the cars which could be purchased almost anywhere by this time. *Ward:* "I remember the regular wheels stayed on the track but the early Superfasts skidded all over the place . . . maybe it was the Super-fasts that killed them." Early tracks had grey roads with green edging, whilst later ones had blue roads and yellow edging. By 1974 the Motorised Motorway was off sale. Examples of the set, though not considered valuable by collectors, are hard to find these days.

Launched in 1969, but using many of the same components as the motorway, was the Matchbox 'Switch A Track'. This development of the motorway featured a roundabout in the middle of a figure eight which could be used to switch models into different lanes. Considered now to be a premature development, sales and the set's reliability could not justify the price of just under £6 in 1970. The set was withdrawn in 1973.

As described elsewhere, the launch of the Superfast range was to have a dramatic effect on the miniatures. The conversion of the range to low-friction wheels led to the development of a gravity powered 'Superfast Track' range of accessories. In its simplest form the range consisted of sections of preformed polythene track which could be affixed to any suitable object by a clamp. The cars could then travel down the slope at great speed. The system was quickly developed from its introduction in 1969 to include many accessories such as 'daredevil leaps, boosters and finishing gates'. These sets were much cheaper than the motorised versions and they sold well. The range was re-developed and re-named to become known as Streak Sets in 1975.

During the mid 1970s intro-

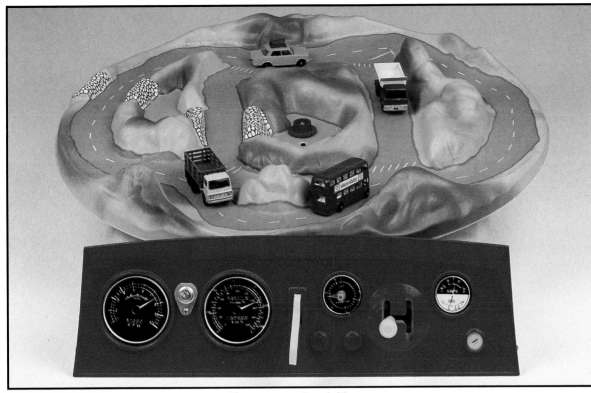

of which were the Y16 Spyker and the Y2 Renault. The game was based on dice and cards. The models of Yesteryear cars (Spyker, Renault or Y15 Rolls Royce) had a hole drilled into the baseplate and were then fitted onto a moving roadway. This game was sold only at Mobil Oil Company petrol stations.

THE GIFTWARE SERIES

There are three main categories of giftware. The first category featured standard first series painted Models of Yesteryear and models from other Matchbox ranges. The second category featured later Models of

duced a new motor racing system – "Power Track" – a system which featured a new range of plastic performance cars. *Tekerian:* "It was another diversified range outside the diecast toy area . . . It was modelled very much on the lines of Scalectrix but it actually incorporated brand new concepts . . . the way in which the track fixed together and instead of using large scale cars we used very much smaller scaled cars and originally a six volt transformer." The track itself was a licensed item but the overall concept of Power Track was developed entirely by Lesney's Research and Development Department. Power Track was made at the Rochford factory. Just before receivership the original six volt transformer was up-graded to twelve volts. Generally, sales of Power track were good with the best figures being achieved in France. With receivership in 1982 Power Track was discontinued. *Tekerian:*

The prototype Steer'n'Go, an ingenious toy which rotated to simulate a moving road layout. Alternative scenes could be purchased. Circa 1970.

"Universal did not buy the system or the stocks. The receivers had the job of selling the whole 'Power Track' and A.M.T. inventory – we then sold them off cheaply."

GAMES

A boardgame called 'Traffic Game' was developed and introduced in 1968. The game was given further play-value with the incorporation of a rotating turntable and a complex traffic signal. Both skill and chance were big features in the game which was suited for either two or four players. Each game came with two "Matchbox" Series models.

In the mid 1960s an English company called Furnel Develop-

ments Ltd. from Hailsham in Sussex, produced a game called 'The London to Brighton Veteran Car Game'. It was packaged in a box similar in size to a Monopoly boardgame, the top of the box showing three vintage cars, two

Yesteryear which were plated either silver or gold. Both categories were fitted to a vast range of non-Lesney produced ornaments. The third category comprised souvenirs and the Heritage Series.

NEW TRAFFIC GAME ANNOUNCED

The latest item of interest to Club members is the new "Traffic Game," developed for use with "MATCHBOX" models. The game has exciting action and motion, as it has a rotating turn-table and a tricky traffic signal. Both choice and chance add to the excitement of the game, which is for two to four players. Two "MATCHBOX" models come with each Game. Suggested retail is $5.00.

Publicity for two Lesney games both incorporating diecast models.

CATEGORY ONE

The idea of incorporating a current model with an ornament was conceived by Richard Kohnstam, who was acting as a distributor for the Wade Pottery Company based in Stoke-on-Trent, Staffordshire. He believed that this would expand the market for Lesney models by selling them in gift and hardware shops whilst earning Moko extra revenue via Wades. Kohnstam organised the supply of Wades merchandise to Lesney. Only four Models of Yesteryear were initially modified to be attachable to the ornaments – the Y2 'B' Type Bus; the Y12 Horse Drawn Bus, the Y13 Santa Fe Locomotive and the Y14 Duke of Connaught. It should be noted that these mounted Yesteryears were not boxed. An MB5b Bus with 'Players Please' advertisement was also issued to employees only in an early promotion with the John Player tobacco company. This bus featured grey plastic wheels and was secured by a single screw to a green earthenware ashtray. The idea of attaching these unplated models to ornaments was then abandoned for several years, the main reason being that because the baseplates were so small, only one securing screw could be fitted, with the result that the model often came away from its base.

CATEGORY TWO

Lesney had successfully completed their electro-plating experiments in the early 1960s with the Y8/2 Sunbeam Motorcycle. Although this particular model was never released as an ornament, Lesney realised that not only was the finish attractive and innovative but also the new larger second series Yesteryears could accept two more stable fixing screws because of the larger baseplates. Plated collars were produced to disguise the locating screws. Later on these collars were to form an integral part of the baseplate. All the electro-plated Yesteryears were originally produced at the factory in Waterden Road, London, E15, directly behind the Eastway factory. However, much of the plating was sub-contracted out to a firm called V.M.C. in Surrey. In 1969 total production moved to the Homerton factory at the end of Lee Conservancy Road. The Giftware Department became part of the commercial diecast business (Lesney Industries Ltd.). *Grundy:* "They were not part of the toy group as such. They borrowed the Yesteryear moulds, put on their own inserts to fix them onto ashtrays." The porous casting was placed in a drum to which a pellet of aluminium was added – an electrical flash caused the aluminium to attach itself to the diecast model component. If the plated model was to be given a silver finish a clear lacquer was added, and if it was to be gold, then an amber lacquer was added. The electro-plated model was then air dried to give an excellent glittering finish. From 1969 Lesney did all their own electro-plating.

Although the Y13-1 Santa Fe and the Y14/2 Duke of Connaught locomotives were used as part of the electro-plating experiments, they were never included in the Giftware range due to their disadvantageously small size. Instead, experiments centred around the newly released Y6/2 1922 Bugatti. A plated version was produced for a short time only without an ornament. In the same year (1962) Lesney printed an attractive brochure devoted entirely to plated Models of Yesteryear. 'A New Range for the Connoisseur – Finely detailed and true-to-scale, these six models from the golden age of motoring are diecast in zinc and finally plated with a long-lasting silver finish. Porcelain trays and boxes will be available featuring these cars.' The brochure announced the arrival of six current models and added some interesting information on the actual vehicles.

Smith: "It really all started after we had gone public. It was important to us, if people came to visit, that we could give them a gift. So we thought, 'well let's take, for example, the old Silver Ghost, plate it and put it on one of Kohnstam's ashtrays . . . there's a gift for you' . . . It was very nice."

By the mid-1960s, Wades could see the potential of the Lesney Giftware. *Smith:* "People then said to us 'I wouldn't mind getting one of these, where can I get them from?'" They began to order finished plated models from Lesney, fitted them to their own ornaments and distributed them via their own network. Collectors to this day can still find an abundance of obsolete stock in shops in and around Stoke.

The plated models, however, were not seriously taken up by diecast collectors. Although Lesney published a catalogue every year, it was only between 1967 and 1971, and finally in 1976, that the catalogue featured

A small selection from the vast range of Lesney Giftware. Note the second Queen's Award to Industry souvenir issued to the Lesney staff, in 1968.

the plated models. They were also harder to find as in most cases they were only on sale in gift shops, and these in the main had been sold via Wades and not Lesney. *Smith:* "It was expensive buying someone else's goods in ... Wades got a cut, Lesney had a cut and so did the wholesaler and retailer . . . expensive."

Please note: For a fuller account of different Models of Yesteryear variations please refer to the Gift Ware series in the No. 2 Supplement to The Collection.

Other models that were plated include: MB17 Londoner Bus (1977) in silver or gold with 'Carnaby Street' or 'Berger Paints' on the hoardings. The K37

Sandcat with an orange base and gold plated body was issued mounted on a sand coloured ashtray. The K50 Street Rod in orange and gold was also issued, attached to a perpetual calendar stand.

CATEGORY THREE

During the 1970s Lesney Products produced a vast range of plated ornaments in addition to their Giftware Series. In 1976 Lesney introduced their Heritage

Series – silver plated miniature pub signs, dogs affectionately named 'Pips', regimental badges, magnetic board games and souvenirs, such as engraved stainless steel boxes. It should be remembered that gold plated models can become silver in appearance after being subjected to sunlight. The underneath of the item will always indicate its original colour.

British Inn Signs

These eighteen paperweights measuring 2.5" (63 mm) high were packaged individually in a see-through box. Generally the signs were finished in chrome with black shading. However, a small quantity were produced in a silver plated finish and some were gold plated such as the Mermaid and George and the Dragon. A final run of the signs were attached to ceramic ashtrays and the finish altered to a bronze colour. A red painted lion sign was used for a time by the Cameron brewery.

The list of signs is shown below:
The Lion
The Pig and Whistle
The Cock
Elephant and Castle
George and Dragon
The Unicorn
The Swan
Sherlock Holmes
Rose and Crown
The Bull
Dick Turpin
The Volunteer
The Mermaid
The Spread Eagle
Britannia
Prince of Wales
The Smugglers
The Dolphin

Originally the signs retailed at 75p. The price was later increased to £1.25.

Miniature Dog Figurines
This range of six dogs is known as the Pips Series. The standard finish was chrome but a small run was also made in silver plating:

Labrador Retriever
French Poodle
Alsatian
Scottie
Rough Collie
Cocker Spaniel

Regimental Badges
This range of two sets of six different badges of famous Regiments and Corps within the British Armed Forces were silver, or gold plated and issued with plastic bases in 1978. Each badge

was packaged in a blister bubble pack:

Set One:
Royal Marines
Coldstream Guards
17th/21st Lancers
Black Watch
Royal Artillery
Argyll and Sutherland
Highlanders

Set Two:
14th/20th Hussars
Royal Engineers
Royal Tank Regiment
Royal Air Force
Parachute Regiment
1st Dragoons

It is known that two more badges were made but it not known of which regiment or corps.

Souvenirs
This was a comprehensive range and included antique-pistols and plated airplanes including a Boeing 747, a Concorde and a Spitfire. These were fitted to ceramic trinkets or bookends. Two interesting souvenirs were made in 1977. Lesney were awarded their fifth Queen's Award to Industry in 1977. The previous years were 1966, 1968, 1969 and 1970. To honour the Queen's Jubilee the Industrial Division at Lesney designed and produced a silver plated memento – a Heraldic Majestic Crest, mounted on a Wade ashtray. This crest was also fitted on a Wade desk-tidy (a dish to hold pens, pencils etc) and as a free-standing paperweight. A label was applied to the base of the crest with the legend '1952 Silver Jubilee 1977'. These crests were mounted onto the porcelain dishes by two screws. To record their own personal achievement the Industrial Division then used this Jubilee memento to commemorate their own award. This particular award was not for general release, unlike the Queen's Jubilee

memento which was sold in retail shops. On the underneath of the Queen's Award for Export Achievement memento was the legend: 'Presented by Lesney Products to mark the occasion of the Queen's Award in Silver Jubilee Year'.

In 1978 a souvenir item (No. 127) of the Heritage Giftware range was introduced. This featured a cutaway diecast bus with a Bisto label, similar in design to the then unreleased Y23 Bus, it was attached to the lid of the wooden trinket box. It was discontinued by early 1980. Other souvenirs included three bronze or aluminium finished paperweights showing different famous London landmarks – Tower Bridge, St Paul's and Big Ben. Further paperweights were also made – a set of five figures finished in a gold colour. These paperweights were first made in 1975. In 1985 Lesney Industries (now no longer part of Lesney or Matchbox) re-issued them.

London Policeman/St Paul's
Beefeater/Tower of London
Horse Guardsman/Buckingham Palace Monument
Scottish Piper/Edinburgh Castle
Guardsman/Unidentified monument

Wooden trinket boxes were also issued in the late 1970s fitted with car badges such as Rolls Royce, Jaguar and Mercedes.

It was worth noting that not all of the giftware range had Lesney on the bases. Lesney also made a golfer figure, a fisherman and a footballer, all in gold and mounted on blue ceramic ashtrays.

Finally, the reader should be aware that there are many examples of Yesteryears in either a painted state or plated finish that have been, for example, embedded in clear acrylic shapes or bottles but these are not Lesney/Matchbox produced

items. From time to time Matchbox may give a licence to another manufacturer such as a soap company to make Matchbox novelty soap bars.

MATCHBOX GIFT SETS 1957–1988

The first thought of grouping individual Matchbox toys together and retailing them as a boxed set came about in early 1957 at which time the "Matchbox" Series had become firmly established in the toy market and Lesney started to examine different ways to market their toys. Gift Sets had long been sold by other diecast model manufacturers with the pre-war Dinky sets being particularly well known. Lesney naturally set about applying an already proved marketing technique to their range of Matchbox toys.

The idea was first implemented in the United States when, in May of 1957, the American importer, Fred Bronner Corporation advertised 'Presentation Sets'. These sets consisted of a large version of the normal 'Matchbox' and during 1957 three different such sets were marketed, and numbered PS.1, PS.2 and PS.3. Each set consisted of eight Matchbox toys all packed in normal boxes and then packed within the large Presentation Box. No attempt was made to sort these models into any kind of thematic collection, rather the sets contained all the current Matchbox models in number sequence, such that PS.1 contained models 1 to 8, PS.2 contained numbers 9 to 16 and PS.3 contained 17 to 24. The retail price of the U.S. Presentation Sets was a fraction more than eight times the normal 49c, at $3.98. These sets were never marketed outside the United

Three of the 1959 "Matchbox" Series Gift Sets.

bearing the name 'A Moko Lesney Product'. On the underside of each set was a listing of the models in the "Matchbox" Standard Series which interestingly included the number 76 Cadillac which was eventually released replacing the Bedford Low Loader model as the No. MB27. There was also a brief listing of Major Series 1 to 6, Accessory Series 1 to 4 and Yesteryear Series 1 to 14. Like the U.S. sets the name 'Presentation Sets' were applied to these sets with a 'PS' number being rubber stamped on the underneath of the box. The models included in these P.S. sets were grouped into themes rather more imaginatively than in the U.S. Sets. Five such sets were advertised in the September 1959 issue of *Games & Toys*. They were declared as '5 Star Winners for the peak selling period!'. Mention was also made that 'for the first time Matchbox are advertising in the big circulation children's magazines. Order your Matchbox presentation sets right away. Now is the time to start your Christmas till bells ringing!'. PS.1 was a Private Owner Set containing three cars and the A.3 Lock-up Garage; PS.2 was a Car Transporter Set with four cars; PS.3 was a Car Transporter Set with six cars; PS.4 a Commercial Vehicle Set and PS.5 an Army Transport Set. The last three of these five sets, whilst rare, do seem to occasionally appear in the collectable toy market, while PS.2 is distinctly rarer and no example of the PS.1 set is currently known to exist in any of the many Matchbox collections throughout the world! It is also worth noting that these Presentation Sets were available in German speaking countries with the boxes printed in the German language.

The first series of Gift Sets proper (as opposed to Presentation Sets) appeared in July and August 1960. These featured a

States. Most youngsters even if they were inclined to keep the individual boxes were not so interested in keeping the outer set box, so most were lost or destroyed and as a result today these sets are the rarest of the Matchbox Gift Sets.

In 1958 three more sets were added to the U.S. Presentation Sets range so that all the current Matchbox toys could be bought in these sets of eight. PS.4 contained models numbered 25 to 32, PS.5 contained models 33 to 40 and PS.6 contained models 41 to 48.

In 1959 further models were added to the "Matchbox" Series and once again these were available in sets of eight. PS.7 contained models numbered 49 to 56 and PS.8 contained models numbered 57 to 64. After this point the Presentation Set series was discontinued so that models numbered 65 onwards were not available in this way. Existing sets were phased out by mid 1960.

The first gift sets to be sold in Europe were advertised shortly before Christmas of 1959 and in keeping with the season the emphasis was on the 'gift' idea with the models nicely displayed in an attractive but rather flimsy box. The models were all inserted into a card inner section with cut-out spaces for the models and with the model name printed below the cut-out. The lid lifted and folded back to complete the display. The boxes were printed in a similar style to the current "Matchbox" Series boxes with blue outer edges, excepting two sides which had the black 'striker' surfaces and with a yellow and red drawing on the lid which showed the models grouped together under the heading "Matchbox" Series. Under the drawing was the usual scroll new, more robust, box with an inner section containing the models and an outer, sliding sleeve which showed an arrangement of individual box illustrations surrounding a larger picture of a prominent model from the set. The underside of the box listed the contents. The colouring of this series of box was prominently yellow and red rather than the blue and yellow of the earlier Presentation Set series. As mentioned above these sets were known for the first time as 'Gift Sets' and the series were given 'G' numbers. Also these sets were available in all countries where Matchbox models were exported. Although they were originally intended to be a limited issue, due to their success they became standard issue and were illustrated as such in the 1961 catalogue. Like the European Presentation Sets, the Gift Sets contained models packed in themes. G.1 was a Commercial

Motors Set; G.2 a Car Transporter Set with six cars; G.3 a Building Constructors Set; G.4 a Farm Set and G.5 an Army Set.

In 1961, although the sets remained basically the same, the artwork was altered slightly. The word 'Moko' having been deleted on boxes for the new Matchbox models of 1961, was also deleted from the small box illustrations on the front face of the gift sets.

The main box display had declared, even in 1960 that the sets were 'By Lesney' so this required no alteration. Other changes to the box design included the addition of the set number on the front face and on the box ends the words 'Gift Set G-' were printed in white on a red panel with the name of the set printed underneath in red where this name had previously been printed to the right of the words 'Set Number G-', all in red print. At the same time the sets were updated to include new Matchbox models,

with the artwork being changed as appropriate. G.4 now included the No. 50 Commer Pickup as an additional model where there had previously been a card filler in a blank space. The box design was accordingly changed to show this model where previously it had illustrated two No. 12 Landrovers (although only one had been in the set).

In addition, for 1961, two new sets were added, G.6 and G.7 both of which contained a selection of Yesteryear models available in gift sets for the first time.

A further series of gift sets also appears to have been available around the 1960/1961 period. Very little is known about these sets apart from a 'Gift Set C' which is known to exist. This set consists of upper and lower parts, the upper lid fitting over the lower part. The box is marked as a 'Matchbox Garage Gift Set' and in similar fashion to the original U.S. presentation sets

individually boxed Matchbox models are contained within. The box lid contains a selection of Matchbox models from this period all drawn in full colour. The notation 'Gift Set C' is included on a slip of paper which is found inside the set and which also notes that the box contains: Sales and Service Station, Roadway R.1, A.1 Esso Pumps, A.2 Car Transporter, M.6 Pickfords Low Loader and eight selective Matchbox Toys.

Continuing with the standard issue gift sets, in 1962 the line-drawing style of boxes were changed to full colour illustrations showing the models contained arranged on a plain yellow background. The change to this style of illustration took place across all the series of the Matchbox range and included the gift sets. The box ends showed a large white 'G' on a blue background and within the 'G' listed the contents of the set. At the same time the interior of the gift set boxes was changed to a

A selection of Models of Yesteryear gift sets from the 1960s, highlighting the development of packaging techniques.

The full colour illustration Gift Sets introduced in 1962.

cardboard 'steps' style in place of the 'pigeon holes'. Formerly all gift sets had only showed the sides of the models when opened as each model was snugly fitted into its own hole which was designed to take the appropriate model. Now for the first time the models could be properly viewed resting on angled steps although a card inner lid was positioned to keep the models in place and had to be removed on opening the box. Some of the 1962 gift sets contained the same themes as the previous sets but some had models changed. G.1 remained a Commercial Vehicle Set but had several models updated, G.2 remained a Car Transporter Set but two of the four cars were replaced by a Crane and a Sports boat; G.5 remained a Military Set with some withdrawn models deleted and replaced by models still currently available; G.6 and G.7 remained as a Yesteryear Set but the selections were divided into cars for G.6 and commercial

vehicles for G.7. Three new sets were introduced: G.8 Civil Engineering Set containing five King Size models; G.9 Major Pack Set containing five Major Pack models and G.10 Garage and Service Station Set containing the MG.1 plastic Service Station in red and yellow with Esso Pumps and three vehicles. Furthermore G.3 and G.4 were still listed in the 1962 catalogue as 'Building Contractors Set' and 'Farm Set' respectively, but these are now known to exist in the 1962 style box.

These two last mentioned sets were, in fact, changed in the 1963 catalogue to G.3 Farm and Agricultural Set and G.4 Grand Prix Race Track Set. However, the two sets are not known in the 1962–1963 style so they were probably not issued until 1964 at which time the packaging of gift sets had changed style again. The only other gift set changes to occur in 1963 were the updating

of G.6 Veteran and Vintage Cars Set to replace the now obsolete Y.10/1 Mercedes with the Y5/2 Bentley and G.10 where the MG.1 Esso Service Station was changed to the new B.P. Station in green and white. Both the G.6 and G.10 box illustrations were changed to show these new models.

1964 saw the illustrations on the outer sleeve covers of all gift sets change again. In keeping with the box illustrations for the Yesteryear, Major Pack and King Size series, a background was added showing the models grouped in an action setting. The large words 'Matchbox Series' emblazoned on the lid was changed simply to 'Matchbox' with the lower edge stating the name of the gift set with the set number to left and right in place of the words 'A Lesney Product'. The inner section of the sets remained as for 1962 and 1963. Apart from the new G.3 and G.4

sets mentioned above other changes were made to the series. G.1 now became a Motorway Set including a card roadway layout and nine vehicles; G.2 remained a Car Transporter Set but included the new Major Pack M.8 in place of the previous Accessory Pack A.2 Car Transporter and the number of accompanying vehicles was reduced to four; G.6 was now the Commercial Truck Set; G.7 was a Veteran & Vintage Set with five Yesteryear car models; G.8 remained a Construction Set but included all new King Size models; G.9 was the Service Station Set with G.10 becoming a Fire Station Set which included the MF.1 Fire Station with two Fire Engines, an Ambulance and a Fire Chief Car.

In 1965 the outer appearance of these sets remained as for 1964, but the inner section were changed to plastic for the first time, being vacuum-formed in yellow with slots for the models.

No new sets were introduced in 1965 although, again, as models that were included in sets became obsolete in the "Matchbox" Series, so they were changed in the gift sets.

In 1966 the outer lids of the Matchbox Gift Sets had a large clear cellophane covering – the first 'window' box gift sets – so that the models could be viewed inside the box. From a marketing viewpoint this had the advantage that the models contained in the set could be seen without opening the box; indeed the sets were shrink wrapped such that they could not be opened without ripping the plastic covering. Another first for 1966 was a gift set which contained Matchbox models painted in different colours specially for the set, this being the G.4 Racetrack Set. This set included six racing car models, No. 19 Lotus in the standard colour of green and a new gift set colour of orange; No. 41 Ford G.T. in the standard white and also in yellow; No. 52 B.R.M. in the standard blue and new colour of red. The latter colours were all special in that these cars were only available in this set. Strangely, the decals remained the same on the special gift set colour as they were on the standard issues, so that both Lotus models showed No. 3, both Ford G.T.s were No. 6 and both B.R.M.s were No. 51. Other new sets for 1966 were as follows: G.1 was a Service Station Set; G.3 was a Vacation Set with leisure associated models such as boats and caravans; G.5 was the Fire Station Set which now included only one instead of two fire engines; G.8 became known as the King Size Set with models no longer necessarily associated with construction work; numbers G.9 and G.10 were no longer used with the gift set series which reduced to eight.

These sets remained unchanged for 1967. Some sets were changed in 1968 although the style remained basically the same. The set numbers were now printed very boldly in white on a blue panel in the top right corner of the set. The new sets were as follows: G.1 Service Station Set now containing the

The attractive box of the G4 Grand Prix Gift Set rather belied its flimsy cardboard contents.

new MG.1 single-storey service station with card layout and No. 56 Fiat 1500 in red, another special gift set coloured model; G.3 Farm Set containing many current farm type models from the "Matchbox" Series; G.4 Race 'n'Rally Set replaced the previous Racetrack Set, the Racing Car Transporter now being deleted in favour of more cars. Two saloon cars were fitted with roof tracks and not being available in the regular series in this way are now quite collectable, these being the No. 25 Ford Cortina and No. 67 the Volkswagen 1600TL with yellow and purple roof-racks respectively; G.5 was now the Famous Cars of Yesteryear Set while G.7 and G.8 were withdrawn, these numbers being unused in 1968.

All gift sets remained the same in 1969 but with the introduction of Superfast models, these were naturally included in the gift set range for 1970. Although the format of these sets remained as before with a number of models contained in a plastic inner section within a flat box and viewed through a clear cellophane covering, new artwork was designed for these Superfast sets in keeping with the 'Fast Wheel' image and, of course, the name Superfast was displayed prominently on the boxes. In fact, the sets now became known as Supersets and the box illustrations showed models in 'Superfast action'. New sets for 1970 mostly reflected the Superfast theme with G.3 being a Racing Specials Superset which contained the first six models available with superfast wheels all in normal colours but with one or two additional labels affixed. Further labels were also included in the set for application by the purchaser, these labels mainly consisting of stripe designs and a guide to assist in application was shown on the box; G.4 became a Truck Superset including eight trucks

which had previously been fitted with regular wheels now in their new Superfast converted form; G.6 was an unallocated number in 1970 so that the gift set range for that year was reduced to five. No changes were made in 1971 to the gift set range while all company resources were ploughed into developing the Superfast range of models.

In 1972 two new sets were added to the series. G.6 was a Drag Race Set with six of the new Superfast models complete with a Thunder Bolt Launcher for play value. G.7 was a Car Ferry Set which included a plastic car ferry which accommodated four Matchbox models which were included in assorted groups, these models being packaged in their individual boxes. The box for G.7 was different in style from other gift sets of the period, in that it was not a window box but a normal card box with opening end flaps. Illustrations on the box showed the Car Ferry in action.

In 1973 existing sets remained unchanged but new sets comprising commercial vehicles reverted back to drawings showing the models in real life settings with the word Superfast not being featured quite so prominently. New sets for 1973 were: G.3, named the Wild Ones and containing five of the new dragster style models; G.4 was the Team Matchbox Superfast Champions Set which was issued at a time when Matchbox ran a team in Formula 2 motor racing and this set included the four current racing cars in the "Matchbox" Series, two each of No. MB24D Team Matchbox and No. MB34D Formula 1, the former being in the standard colour of red with the second model in the special colour of green. The Formula 1 was painted in blue and in orange, both colours special to the gift set. The set was completed with the current Superking K.7 Racing Car Transporter.

Apart from the 1957 Presentation sets, the first sets which were issued specifically for the American market appeared in 1974. These consisted of carry cases, each containing five models grouped together in themes. These sets were known as Carry Case Gift Sets, and three were initially issued, a Rola-matics Case, a Rescue Case and a Cross Country Case. These were joined by a Streakers Case in 1975.

No further changes to the gift set range took place in 1974 and 1975, apart from the deletion of the G.1 Service Station Set. New sets for 1976 started to show the face of a driver, fireman or pilot, associated with the theme of the set as the most prominent drawing on the box. Whilst no changes took place to existing sets in 1976, several new sets were added to the range starting with G.9 (leaving G.1 and G.8 unallocated). G.9 was a Commando Task Force Set making use of the Car Ferry from G.7 as a landing craft and including three of the new Rola-matic military vehicles and a selection of plastic Commando figures

This set was packaged in the same style of box as the G.7 set mentioned above; G.10 was the Thunder Jets Set containing Sky-Buster aircraft models; G.11 was the Strike Force Set with six military models, being the same as those issued in the new military 'Two Packs' of 1976; G.12 was a Rescue Set with six emergency vehicles; G.13 was a Construction Set with five suitable models accompanying a plastic 'Load-a-Vator' which could be used to load the trucks with the plastic coal included in the set; G.14 was a Grand Prix Set with four racing car models and the Superking Racing Car Transporter; G.15 was a Transporter Set with five cars and a Superking Car Transporter. In addition G.100 was issued as the Twin Thunderbolt Launcher Set with

two Superfast models and the Launcher previously issued in the G.6 Drag Race Set of 1972.

The American Carry Case Gift Sets were re-issued in 1976 to contain six models in slightly revised sets and were given GC-numbers. The sets issued were GC.1 Rola-matics Case, GC-2 Rescue Case and GC.3 Keep on Trucking Case.

Many of the new gift sets for 1976 duplicated earlier sets available at that time such that there were now two car transporter sets and two racing car sets in the range. This situation existed with the old and new sets being sold side by side throughout 1976 but by 1977 the older sets were withdrawn leaving the series starting with G.9 and with the G.7 Car Ferry Set being renumbered G.17. Another Sky-Buster set was issued as G.16 Sky Giants.

In America a further Carry Case set was issued in 1977 as GC.4 Military Case. The first special gift set for Japan was issued in 1977 and consisted of four models from the Japanese series and which were re-issues of older models. The set was numbered SP.20 and consisted of a blue card box with central clear window. The models were positioned in a foam plastic inner section.

No changes were made to the gift sets in 1978 and 1979. Although the style of boxes was little changed, more sets started to feature additional items to accompany the models such as farmyard buildings and buildings on fire. Several new sets were issued in 1979 and these were allocated the earlier numbers unused since 1976. G.1 was the Auto Transporter Set which continued like the earlier Car Transporter sets with five cars and a Super King Transporter; G.2 was a Railway Set, the first time such a set had appeared in the range using the new railway models from the "Matchbox" Series. Also included was plastic track, a platform and a level crossing. G.3 was the Racing Car Set virtually the same as the old G.14; G.4 was a Military Assault Set which included six military vehicles along with the plastic landing craft and Commando figures also issued in G.9; G.5 was the same Construction Set as the old G.13, re-numbered; G.6 was a Farm Set including plastic farm buildings; G.7 was an Emergency Set including plastic buildings; G.8 was a renumbered issue of the G.10 Thunder Jets. All other numbers were withdrawn at this time except G.9 Commando Task Force Set, G.17 Car Ferry Set and G.18 Sky Giants.

In 1980 the American Carry Case sets were changed again and reverted back to including only five models and the sets were issued as GC.6 Street Classics, GC.8 Emergency Services, GC.9 Keep on Truckin' and GC.10 Off the Road, these four sets replacing the previous cases GC. to GC.4.

In 1981 the G.4 Military Assault Set and the G.9 Commando Task Force Set were deleted as military models were proving unpopular at this time. No new sets were introduced in either 1980 or 1981 except in the U.S.A.

The American market saw a new series of sets in 1981, these being known as 'Super Sets' and were in a different format to previous sets in that the models were mounted on their wheels on a card base and covered by a large cellophane window. These 1981 sets contained all the new models issued specially for the U.S. market in that year and these models were divided between three such sets: Thunder Road, Sundown Drive and Midnight Boulevard. Each set contained five models.

In 1982 G.3 Racing Car Set, G.8 Thunderjets, G.17 Car Ferry and G.18 Sky Giants were all withdrawn. A new G.4 Convoy Set was issued accompanying the new

'Convoy' series of truck models. The box matched the Convoy series with a silver box with red, white and blue stripes. The set contained three Convoy models, two Matchbox models and a plastic 'Truck Stop'.

In America the Super Sets series was added to in 1982 with Workin Wheels, Off Road Riders, Classy Classics and Pace Setters, all with five Matchbox models each, and Truckin Speed Trap, 18 Wheelers and N.A.S.A. Countdown, these three being Highway Express Sets (Convoy in Europe). These 1982 Super Sets differed from the 1981 sets by including a large header card to illustrate the models.

In 1983 the gift sets series became known as 'Action Packs' and once again featured drawings of vehicles rather more prominently than drivers. This represented the first real change for gift set artwork since 1976. G.1 remained as before the Car Transporter Set and G.7 remained as the Emergency Set; all other gift sets were deleted except the new G.4 Convoy Set issued the previous year.

One further new set was added in 1984, G.8 Turbo Charged Action Pack featuring five Matchbox models along with a plastic launcher.

In 1984 Matchbox issued the Connoisseur's Collection. It featured six obsolete models in new colours:

Y1 1911 Model 'T' Ford
Y3 1910 Benz Limousine
Y4 1909 Opel
Y13 1911 Daimler
Y11 1912 Packard Landaulet
Y14 1911 Maxwell

Each set of six models was packaged in a beautiful hardwood display box There were only 50,000 sets made and so confident were Matchbox about the set, that they offered a buy back guarantee after five years.

Gift Sets resumed in Japan in 1984 with the introduction of the new Japanese issue models in the

1–100 Miniature range. The sets were called 'Collect' and were not numbered, although due to the low rate of inflation in Japan, it was possible to print the price prominently on the box. The smaller sets each contained four models although there were also some larger sets including Convoy models. The boxes were larger versions of the yellow boxes that the Japanese Miniature range was packed in. All the models in these Japanese sets were also standard to the Japanese miniature series with no special colours or markings.

In 1985 two new types of sets were introduced. The first was called 'Team Matchbox' and had TM– numbers. These sets featured the Convoy Kenworth Transporter previously issued as CY.10 with the 'Superboss' Truck. Included in each set were two 1-75 Miniature models, all three were then painted in matching team colours. The packaging was similar to the Convoy series but in a longer, silver window box. Six such sets were issued in 1985 although two of these were only available in the U.S.A.

The second new type of set for 1985 was the 'Convoy Action Pack' which featured CY- numbers with three digits. These sets continued the theme started in 1982 with G.4 having a selection of Convoy and Matchbox models packaged together. Some of these sets contained models painted in special colours but many models were standard issue. The packaging was again similar in colour to the Convoy series, being silver but was in the large gift set type of format. Three Convoy Action Packs were issued in 1985 numbered CY.201 to CY.203.

The Action Packs were joined in 1986 by a rather plainer type of Action Pack. These sets were printed in blue with the current Matchbox logo featuring a red, yellow and white stripe. They had an airline theme and most of the models included were paint-

ed in special colours for the sets with one Sky-Buster aircraft also included. G.10 was a Pan Am Set with G.11 in Lufthansa colours.

Also in 1986 a 7-Up Team joined the Team Matchbox Sets as TM.5 and a new Convoy N.A.S.A. Set was CY.204.

Further Action Packs were issued in 1987 with G.5 Federal Express and G.6 Virgin Airways, although these had new box artwork with rather more attractive designs than the 1986 sets. Also in 1987 appeared Team Matchbox Set TM-6 Duckhams QXR Team and Convoy Sets CY.205 Farm Set and CY.206 Telecom Set.

In the United States 3-pack Gift Sets were issued in 1987 each containing three Miniatures blister-packed on a large backing card and including action cut-outs and buildings. Set 1101 was Metro Police Dept. which included a white and red Plmouth police car not available elsewhere, 1102 was Metro Fire Dept. and 1103 was Sports Racers.

Also in 1987 changes were made to the Japanese gift sets. These were recoloured from yellow to white and included an illustration on the front face. The sets were at the same time given C- numbers. Some new sets were issued but many remained as for 1984 but in the new style box. In the C.6 Emergency Set some Miniature models were included which were not available individually. These included the Snorkel Fire Engine, the Extending Ladder Fire Engine (No. 18 in the U.K.) and the Helicopter all of which had Japanese lettering printed on the models.

A radical change of gift sets occurred with the 1988 range. For the first time since 1960 the G-numbers were no longer used and most new gift sets were issued under the label of 'Motor City Gift Sets'. Motor City was a name introduced in 1986 to cover a series of accessories. Two large

A further selection of Gift Sets featuring the 40th Anniversary Set produced in 1988.

sets were MC.7 Farm Set and MC.8 Construction Set which each contained eight models, one of which was a Convoy and most models were recoloured for these sets. Sets MC.11, MC.12 and MC.13 were much smaller containing one Convoy and two Miniatures in each set, these being a Car Transporter Set, and Aerobatic Team Set and a Police Set respectively.

Another series issued in 1988 was the 'Miniatures Theme Packs' consisting of six different sets each containing three Miniatures, some recoloured. Also for

1988 a series called 'Team Convoy' was introduced, each set consisting of one Convoy model and one or two Miniatures, similar to the previous 'Team Matchbox' series. In fact, the 'Team Matchbox' series was renumbered as Team Convoy at this time and included in the new series.

Finally, for 1988 a unique set was due for Christmas release. Once again numbered G-1 the set contained reproduced castings of five of the first series Matchbox

models in a box styled as for the 1960 series of Gift Sets. The set was called the '40th Anniversary Collection' to commemorate forty years since the start of toy manufacture by Lesney Products & Co. Ltd The castings were virtually exact replicas of the originals although inevitably marked with the country of origin as 'China' rather than 'England'. The boxes were also printed in German and French for export. However the French set was not produced and the German ver-

sion was made in much smaller numbers than the English edition.

Today the early Gift Sets of the 1950s and 1960s are eagerly sought after by collectors. By their very nature they are extremely hard to find as the flimsy boxes are prone to wear and many were discarded by their original owners. A complete early set in perfect condition is generally worth several hundred pounds particularly if it contains models in rare or unique colours. These early Gift Sets are slightly easier to find in America than in the rest of the world.

MATCHBOX DEALER DISPLAYS

One of the more interesting but frequently overlooked areas in the field of Matchbox collecting are the Dealer Displays. Many

The attractive 1963 dealer display stand. The featured MB6 Quarry Truck, had long been out of production by this time.

collectors do not pursue displays as they often occupy too much space in a toy room and at best, are difficult to store properly. Also, most collectors wish to display all variations of a given model together, something that displaying the toys in dealer displays does not permit. For those collectors whose preference lies with a wider variety of series than model

variations, collecting dealer displays can be a very enjoyable part of the Matchbox experience.

Most collectors are undoubtedly familiar with the more recent Superfast display units along with several of the more popular older ones (most notably the white plastic circular units with the red top). The earliest displays were,

however, made of cardboard and given away to dealers free of charge up until 1969 when the last cardboard display was phased out. Many variations of displays exist and while describing each and every one would be beyond the scope of this sub-chapter, the more popular dealer displays will be described for the benefit of the reader.

A later version of the dealer display stand, circa 1968.

CARDBOARD DISPLAYS

In one of the first dealer catalogues (Fred Bronner, 1963), some of the earliest displays can be seen. No-charge dealer displays for the Regular, Accessory/Major Pack, Yesteryear and King Size series were offered and all were flat cardboard which, when assembled provided shelves on to which models were fastened using the supplied small fabric covered wires. All displays were printed in the three basic colours of a Matchbox red, blue

and yellow. The regular wheel display of 1963 pictured the 6b Quarry Truck, a price of 49 cents and listed the proper model at each location on the stand. This last feature was eliminated with the 1964 Regular display due to the increasing discontinuance of models and their subsequent replacement. In 1964 the price was still 49 cents, but the model pictured was the 53b Mercedes. The price changed to 55 cents in 1966 and remained that way until a new display was offered

in 1968. In 1968, the familiar colour scheme was changed to white and yellow, offering a more contemporary look for the series.

The Accessory/Major Pack display in 1963 featured all five accessories and nine Major Pack models. The M-4 Excavator Shovel is pictured and in 1964, the numbering on the display was changed to reflect the only remaining Accessory model (A-1 Petrol Pumps). As it turned out, 1964 would be the last year for

any sort of accessory display and the second to the last year for a Major Pack display, the 1965 version being all blue with the M-9 box displayed prominently on the top header.

Early Yesteryear displays (produced prior to 1963) can be found occasionally, the most common one displaying only fifteen models and picturing the Y13 Locomotive. Other major variations include several free-standing types which support the models on a series of tiered steps. These took more than

MODELS OF YESTERYEAR

HISTORICAL STORY OF MODEL ON BACK OF EACH BOX

MADE IN ENGLAND

MODELS OF YESTERYEAR
Nº15
SERIES
BY LESNEY
Nº15
MADE IN ENGLAND REGD.

DIE-CAST ALL METAL

AUTHENTIC SCALE MODELS

TOY IMPORTS

Y-1 $.75   Y-2 $.75   Y-3 $.75   Y-4 $1.25

Y-5 $1.25   Y-6 $.75   Y-7 $1.25   Y-8 $1.25

Y-9 $1.50   Y-10 $.75   Y-11 $1.00   Y-12 $1.00

Y-13 $1.00   Y-14 $1.00   Y-15 $1.25   Y-16 $1.25

HISTORIC BREATH OF YESTERDAY!

their fair share of counter space and were probably phased out for the standard type which could hang or stand freely. The Models of Yesteryear display of 1963 – 1967 were primarily blue, had space for all sixteen models and depicted the Y15 Rolls Royce. Several variations of this display can be seen if two or more are placed side-by-side. In 1968, the Yesteryear display went from all blue to the more contemporary white and yellow colour scheme.

Another "Matchbox" range which was changing rapidly was the King Size series of models. From 1963 to 1968, the displays totally changed each year! In 1963, the K-6 Earth Scraper was pictured. In 1964, it was the K-10 Excavator. The 1965 display featured a place to insert a K-15 Fire Engine and its box in the top header of the display while in 1966, room for the K-16 Hopper Train was provided. 1967 saw the elimination of the place for the model and the picture as did the 1968 version, which was now white and yellow.

An interesting aside to these displays is a set of three cardboard displays made for the European market. These displays, when assembled, formed step-type counter-top exhibits. The Regular wheel display featured a street scene as did the Yesteryear version. The King Size stand featured the K-16 Twin Tipper. No dates are available on these displays.

In addition to the cardboard displays produced for the Major Pack series from 1963 – 1968, several seldom encountered displays can occasionally be found. These include a 'Military' stand-type display

(1963), shelf-type 'Matchies' display (1965) and various counter-type displays for the direct merchandising of boxed models.

WOODEN DISPLAYS

From 1964 until 1967 when the plastic displays were introduced, dealers could purchase nice wooden displays to hold either the Regular series or the majority of the remaining series'. These wooden stands resemble bleachers at a football stadium, but are totally closed on the front, are painted bright yellow and have a glass cover. A metal or wooden backboard provided ample promotion. Several variations of style, construction and printing, as well as varying uses of wood/metal can be found.

PLASTIC DISPLAYS

The first plastic displays were offered in 1967 and again the dealers had to pay for these units. The first of the familiar round Regular series towers was offered as well as flat stand-type, both promoting the 55 cent price. The Yesteryears could be merchandised in a sixteen model 'picture frame' display as it is often called. A rather attractive gold border surrounded the flat wall mounted display for this series. 1968 offered the dealer two types of flat Regular wheel displays (vertical and horizontal format) as well as the ever popular round unit. Several variations of the round display can be found. The King Size and Yesteryear series could also now be presented to the customer in bright plastic, protected by a clear cover. These displays remained basically unchanged until 1971 when the Superfast era dawned.

A stand to hold the second series of models circa 1967.

THE 'SUPERFAST' ERA

In 1971, a revolving square-sided display was introduced for the Regular series featuring the Superfast logo and related graphics. This display was to be the mainstay of the Superfast line until it was re-designed in 1977. During the Superfast era, the only other plastic displays available included the Yesteryear radiator-style display and a few different styles of vacuum-formed wall displays. The reason for the demise of the diverse dealer displays can be summed up in two words – 'blister pack'. In the 1970s, the trend away from full service hobby and toy shops was in force and the majority of Matchbox models were being merchandised through self-service establishments to keep retail costs down. The blister pack was now the standard package and simple wire racks, some available from Lesney but most supplied by the retailer, were the agent by which the models were displayed.

While most collectors were sorry to see the demise of the models displayed so nicely and sold with their original Matchbox, Lesney had to change with the times. New displays are often encountered even to this day, but few are seen in the average retail environment and are usually only encountered in the more expensive shops. The extreme growth of the company in the 1960s had ended and along with it, the need for displays fitting a type of retailing long forgotten. It was the end of an era when the cardboard displays were traded for the vacuum-formed ones and then again traded for the wire racks. These displays represent a bit of Matchbox history that will probably never again be experienced.

CHARACTER TOYS

Lesney were never to involve themselves in the dynamic field of manufacturing character toys. This was in sharp contrast to Corgi Toys for example, who were particularly adept at producing cars which had attracted the public. James Bond's Aston Martin and Chitty Chitty Bang Bang were two famous successes for the company in the 1960s.

It was not until 1978 that Lesney received permission from Walt Disney Productions to produce an attractive range of Walt Disney characters fitted to Matchbox Miniatures. Originally these models were to be made at the Lesney factories in England, but Lesney almost immediately discovered that the time needed to produce the range of models would be nearly two years and even if they could produce them, Lesney would not show a profit. Lesney contacted Peter Olsen, their Managing Director in Hong Kong, and briefed him to pass the project over to Universal Toys. David Yeh of Universal took the job and the first six models and figures were in the shops by early 1980. The model baseplates credited them to Lesney Products and that they were all made in Hong Kong.

The Lesney Catalogue of 1979 and 1980 heralded the arrival of the new Walt Disney series. "From the Wonderful World of Disney all your favourite characters are faithfully re-produced in this new and exciting range

from 'Matchbox' – Minnie Mouse in her luxury Lincoln, Donald Duck having fun in his Buggy and Mickey Mouse ready to give chase in his Police Jeep ensure a feast of fun and excitement." The first six models WD1 to WD6 were quickly followed by WD7 to WD9 and by late 1980 the series was completed with the arrival of WD10 to WD12. Each model was packaged in the American style blister pack. Although the toys were aimed at 'aged 18 months and over', they quickly became collectable. *Lister:* "The best quality products we have ever produced . . .not one single customer complaint." In 1981 the series was increased to fifteen with the arrival of Popeye, Bluto and Olive Oyl. These characters were not Walt Disney ones; instead they were licensed by the King Features Syndicate Inc. The 1981/82 Catalogue featured the new toys "A new exciting range of diecast products from the POPEYE Series. We have Popeye in his Spinach Wagon, Bluto in true character aboard his Road Roller on the trail of our hero – and the heroine of the story, Olive Oyl in her luxurious Sports Car . . . "

One rare Walt Disney model exists. The Goofy figure in WD3 was initially issued with unattached flapping ears. Quality Control soon discovered that the ears broke during production. The tools were modified so that the ears were fixed permanently in position.

An attractive carton was also produced as a point of sale item in overall yellow and showing a picture of Mickey Mouse and Donald Duck on the lid. Later issues of WD1 to WD12 were released with Macau baseplates.

A further range of Walt Disney figures were developed by the Lesney Products Corporation in New Jersey in the early 1980s. The success of the pre-school Shufflies toys inspired the Research and Development team

CODE	FIGURE	VEHICLE	COLOUR	BASEPLATE DATE
WD1	Mickey Mouse	Fire Engine	Red	1979
WD2	Donald Duck	Beach Buggy	Orange	1979
WD3	Goofy	VW Beetle	Yellow	1979
WD4	Minnie Mouse	Lincoln Convertible	Blue	1979
WD5	Mickey Mouse	Jeep	Blue	1979
WD6	Donald Duck	Police Jeep	White	1979
WD7	Pinocchio	Travelling Theatre	Green/yellow	1979
WD8	Jiminy Cricket	Old Timer Sport	Red/yellow	1979
WD9	Goofy	Sports Car	Blue	1979
WD10	Goofy	Train	Red	1980
WD11	Donald Duck	Ice Cream Van	White	1980
WD12	Mickey Mouse	Corvette	Red	1980
CS13	Popeye	Spinach Wagon	Yellow/red	1980
CS14	Bluto	Road Roller	Blue/yellow	1980
CS15	Olive Oyl	Convertible	White	1980

in the USA to design a new set of Walt Disney characters which were attached to Shufflies baseplates. The characters would then shuffle along being propelled only by gravity. A set of four figures were designed but with the receivership of Lesney in 1982 these prototype figures were discarded and eventually disposed of by the receivers. At the same time, consideration was also given to a range of Roger Hargreaves' 'Mr Men' and 'Little Miss' characters. Early prototypes were made, but this project too was abandoned due to Lesney being placed in receivership.

Neither project has been taken up by Universal Matchbox, although it is believed that the original Walt Disney figures may be re-introduced at a later date.

MATCHBOX SPECIALS

In 1984 Matchbox decided to fill the gap between their Superking and Miniature ranges. Rival diecast companies such as Burago and Solido were seen to be dominating a particular part of the market with their highly

coloured range of 1/43rd competition cars. *Tekerian:* "We wanted to produce a low priced item in terms of selling price." The Matchbox Specials were launched in 1984, early models were made at the Rochford factory but by 1987 they were all made in China. The very high standard of tampo printing ensured that they would be attractive to youngsters. *Tekerian:* "One of the advantages that Matchbox International inherited when Universal International bought out Lesney in 1982 was the development of a tampo printing process of the very highest standard."

The 1984 Catalogue first reported the launch of the new range: 'Matchbox' has added a new meaning to the word specials with the new range of twelve diecast models; special high performance cars; special racing and rally cars; super special colourful decoration specially designed for you. The 1984 catalogue only showed six models. In fact, twelve liveries were released that year, i.e. two liveries per model. Each unique liveried model was catalogued between SP1 and SP12. The price in 1984 was high at £1.79.

By 1988 this price had been reduced to under one pound in order to maintain their sales targets. *Hickmore:* "Originally the models were going to be 1/43rd scale. However, it was found that the cars chosen came out at varying lengths . . .the SP5 and SP6 Lancia was a small car, but the SP3 and SP4 Ferrari S12BB were quite long." Although the scales vary between 1/35 and 1/45 the actual bases are inscribed 1/40! A new range of one-piece racing wheel was specifically designed for the Specials. There were three different sizes and the chrome lettering on the tyre related to the actual diameter of the wheel in inches, i.e. .620, .680 and .750. It is of interest to note that in 1984 the .620 sized wheel was also used on some of the Miniatures.

In 1985, as part of the Matchbox policy to keep the range new and exciting, six of the models were reliveried, i.e. SP1; SP4; SP5; SP8; SP10 and SP11.

In 1986 a new casting was added to the range – the SP13 Porsche 959 ED Racing and SP14 Porsche Turbo 959. *Hickmore:* "The Porsche 959 was designed and developed at the same time as the Matchbox Miniature MB7 Porsche 959 – the same master pattern was made to produce the separate mould tools."

In the same year, to keep the range at twelve liveries, two were withdrawn – the SP6 Lancia Rally and the SP9 Pro-Stocker.

In 1987 further new designs were given to the SP2; SP3; SP7 and SP12. In 1988 the range was renamed as Super GT Sports. Twelve models were shown in the 1988 catalogue – all with new liveries. In the U.S.A. they were issued as 'L.A. Wheels' and distributed through U.A.C. (Universal Associated Companies).

Simultaneously with the development of the Porsche 959, work

NO..	YEAR	MODEL	LOGO	COLOURS	LENGTH
SP1	1984	Grand Prix Porsche CK5	Kremer # 22	Red/white	114 mm
SP1	1985	Grand Prix Porsche CM5	Kremer # 35	Two tone blue/white	114 mm
SP1	1988	Grand Prix Porsche CK5	Kremer # 35	Two tone blue/black	114 mm
SP2	1984	Porsche CK5 Turbo	Dunlop/Shell # 19	White/silver/green	114 mm
SP2	1987	Porsche CK5 Turbo	Shell # 2	White/green/yellow	114 mm
SP2	1988	Porsche CK5 Turbo	Shell # 2	White/red/yellow	114 mm
SP3	1984	Ferrari 512 BB	Pioneer # 71	Blue/white	118 mm
SP3	1987	Ferrari 512 BB	Shell # 147	Yellow/red/green	118 mm
SP3	1988	Ferrari 512 BB	Shell # 147	White/red/green	118 mm
SP4	1984	R J Racing Ferrari 512 BB	European University # 46	Red	118 mm
SP4	1985	R J Racing Ferrari 512 BB	Michelin # 88	Black/yellow/red	118 mm
SP4	1988	R J Racing Ferrari 512 BB	Michelin # 88	Line green/yellow/red	118 mm
SP5	1984	Lancia Rally	Auto Systems # 102	Yellow/red	112 mm
SP5	1985	Lancia Rally	Pirelli # 116	Green/yellow	112 mm
SP5	1988	Lancia Rally	Pirelli # 116	Purple/yellow	112 mm
SP6	1984	Lancia Rally	Martini # 1	White	112 mm
SP7	1984	Zakspeed Mustang	Ford # 16	White/blue	128 mm
SP7	1987	Zakspeed Mustang	Duckhams # 38	Blue/yellow	128 mm
SP8	1984	Zakspeed Mustang Turbo	N/A	White	128 mm
SP8	1985	Zakspeed Mustang Turbo	Avon # 83	Black	128 mm
SP8	1988	Zakspeed Mustang Turbo	Michelin # 20	Yellow/red/blue	128 mm
SP9	1984	Pro-Stocker	NGK # 12	Yellow/blue	120 mm
SP10	1984	Pro-Stocker	Mambo	Metallic blue/yellow	120 mm
SP10	1985	Pro-Stocker	Heuer # 9	Dark green	120 mm
SP10	1988	Pro-Stocker	Heuer # 9	Yellow	120 mm
SP11	1984	Camaro	Goodyear # 18	White/green	117 mm
SP11	1985	Camaro	Total # 7	White/black/red	117 mm
SP11	1988	Camaro	Total # 7	Gold	117 mm
SP12	1984	Camaro Turbo	N/A # 56	Red	117 mm
SP12	1988	Camaro Turbo	Michelin # 3	White/yellow	117 mm
SP13	1986	Porsche 959 ED Racing	Michelin # 44	Red/yellow	110 mm
SP13	1988	Porsche 959 ED Racing	Michelin # 44	Black/yellow	110 mm
SP14	1986	Porsche Turbo 959	Cibie/Bosch # 53	White/blue	110 mm
SP14	1988	Porsche Turbo 959	Cibie/Bosch # 53	Yellow/blue	110 mm

was also done on a Ford RS200. However, this vehicle only made it as far as the drawings and prototype model stage. The RS200 did appear later in the Miniature range as the new MB34 in 1988.

A further sub range was also introduced in 1985 – Turbo Specials. These were based on four of the existing Specials. *Hickmore:* "The Turbo range used the body casting and windows from the Specials, but we had to make new bases and interiors to house the motor."

The Turbo Specials were powered forward by simply pulling the model backwards which activated a motor inside, the car started off slowly but quickly accelerated to a high speed. The models did not need batteries and the motor was a two-speed mechanism. A new wheel was also developed for better grip rubber tyres.

NO.	YEAR	MODEL	LIVERY	COLOURS	LENGTH
TS1	1985	Chevrolet Camaro	Firestone # 4	White/blue	117 mm
TS1	1987	Chevrolet Camaro	Firestone # 4	White/blue	117 mm
TS2	1985	Zakspeed Ford Mustang	Michelin # 20	Yellow/red/blue	128 mm
TS3	1985	Kremer/Porsche	Michelin # 15	Red	114 mm
TS4	1985	Chevrolet Pro-Stocker Turbo	Goodyear # 5	White/black	120 mm
N/A	1986	Lancia Rally	Martini # 1	White	112 mm
N/A	1986	Ferrari 512 BB	Pioneer # 48	White/blue	118 mm
N/A	1986	Porsche 959	Bosch # 27	White	110 mm
N/A	1984	Porsche CK5 Turbo	Shell # 70	Red	114 mm

Above: A complete set of this collectable range. Note the figure of Goofy with the flying ears centre foreground.

SKY-BUSTERS

Sky-Busters came into being as direct competition to the then popular Dinky range of diecast aircraft. The bulk of the sales was to larger chains of stores and in particular the souvenir shops in airport terminals.

The profitability to the manufacturer has, however, been erratic and consequently the range has often been regarded as a poor cousin to the opposition.

This range, comprising both military and civilian aircraft, was launched in 1973. The 1974 Catalogue: "Matchbox' Sky-Busters – 16 fabulous die-cast model

aircraft, complete with striking colours and authentic decals, and each fitted with Superfast wheels for split–second take-offs and landings . . ." In fact the wheels used on the Sky-Busters were never of the Superfast variety – they have always stayed similar to the regular wheels type. Of the first sixteen models, six were civilian, seven were post-war military and three were World War II vintage. All of the original sixteen models were shown in the catalogues, and were issued with single wheels on wire axles. These axles were later changed to double wheel assemblies on longer metal axles. *Hickmore:* "It was found that the wheel could be pulled from the axle exposing a sharp point . . . so we had to develop a new axle housing."

Further new models were issued in 1976 and 1977.

Below: An early press release illustrating four of the first Sky-Busters.

New! SKY-BUSTERS

INTRODUCING NEW DIE-CAST METAL "MATCHBOX" SKY-BUSTERS

"MATCHBOX" takes to the air for 1973 with all die-cast metal aircraft made with the same fantastic detail and quality that made "MATCHBOX" the vanguard in the miniature model field.

Skybusters feature a broad range of aircraft styles from a World War II Prop Corsair to a present day Lear Jet.

★ Fantastic detail with accurate full-color decals and paint jobs, props that spin, wing tanks, and much, much more!

★ Skybusters really move down the runway because they all feature "superfast" wheels.

Not illustrated are four other finely detailed models: Lear Jet, A300B, Mirage F1 and Spitfire.

MIG 21

STARFIGHTER F-104

JUNKERS 87B

CORSAIR A7D

Two models were deleted from the range in 1979 – the SB3 A300 and the SB12 Skyhawk A4F. These were replaced by the new SB3.2 N.A.S.A. Space Shuttle and the SB12.2 Pitts Special respectively. Four new models were issued in 1979.

In 1980 Lesney produced two large Sky-Buster Gift Sets. Each set comprised of four current models:

G-8 'Thunder Jets'
SB24 F16
SB21 Lightning
SB22 Tornado
SB5   Star Fighter

G-18 'Sky Giants'
SB10 Lufthansa
SB13 Swissair
SB23 Air France
SB10 British Airways

These two Gift Sets had been withdrawn by the end of the year. Between 1980 and 1982 the Sky-Buster Range was still shown in the catalogues but, in fact, the production had ceased in order to run down stocks.

Three further models were added in 1981. The Falklands War of 1982 certainly pushed up sales of the military planes within the range and especially the SB27 Harrier Jet, which had been used so successfully by the British Forces. When it was realised that the Harrier had the potential to be a good seller, several small decorative modifications were made to the model including the removal of the American flag on the tail. During the transition between Lesney and Matchbox the range was not shown in the 1983 catalogue.

By 1985 many of the models had been deleted from the range with the result that the Sky-Buster range from 1985 up to 1988 consisted of only sixteen models for the UK market.

With the exception of the SB3, SB13 and SB23 the range was entirely recoloured in 1986. This policy was repeated in 1988 with a further extensive recolouring programme.

Three Sky-Busters were also electro-plated and included as part of the souvenir range of the late 1970s. These were:

SB7   Junkers 87D in gold
SB8   Spitfire in gold
SB10 Boeing 747 in gold/white or silver

It should be noted that a Concorde similar to SB23 was also plated; it was, however, a smaller size and featured no casting marks.

BASIC SKY-BUSTER LISTING

SB NO.	MODEL	COLOUR	LIVERY	PLACE OF MANUFACTURE	REMARKS
SB1	LEAR JET	Yellow/white		England	Introduced 1973 Clear or dark windows. Labels or tampo
SB1	LEAR JET	Lemon/white		Macau	
SB1	LEAR JET	Red	'Datapost'	Macau	
SB1	LEAR JET	Purple/white	'Federal Express'	Macau	
SB1	LEAR JET	White	'US Air Force'	Macau	(USA only)
SB2	CORSAIR A7D	Dark green/white		England	Introduced 1973
SB2	CORSAIR A7D	Dark blue/white		England	
SB2	CORSAIR A7D	Silver blue/white		England	
SB2	CORSAIR A7D	Beige/green/ brown/white	'USAF'	Macau	(USA only)
SB3	A300 AIRBUS	White/silver	'Air France'	England/Macau	Introduced 1973 Labels or tampo
SB3	A300 AIRBUS	White/silver	'Lufthansa'	Macau	Tampo
SB3	SPACE SHUTTLE	White/grey		England	Introduced 1979
SB3	SPACE SHUTTLE	White/silver grey		Macau	
SB4	MIRAGE F1	Red		England	Introduced 1973 Small or large labels
SB4	MIRAGE F1	Red/white	'USAF'	Macau	(USA only – issued as SB8)
SB4	MIRAGE F1	Light orange/brown		Macau	
SB4	MIRAGE F1	Yellow/red/blue		Macau	(USA only – issued as SB3)
SB4	MIRAGE F1	White/blue		Macau	
SB4	MIRAGE F1	Dark orange/brown		Macau	
SB5	STARFIGHTER F104	White/silver grey		England	Introduced 1973
SB5	STARFIGHTER F104	Red/silver grey		England	Deleted 1985
SB6	MIG21	Blue/white		England	Introduced 1973 Star in circle or star without circle – labels
SB6	MIG21	Black/yellow		Macau	(US only – issued as SB4)
SB6	MIG21	Silver blue/white		England	Deleted 1985
SB6	MIG21	Frosted silver		Macau	(US only – issued as SB5)
SB7	JUNKERS	Metallic green		England	Introduced 1973 Small/large Swastika
SB7	JUNKERS	Gold plated		England	Souvenir Range
SB7	JUNKERS	Black/silver grey		England	

SB NO.	MODEL	COLOUR	LIVERY	PLACE OF MANUFACTURE	REMARKS
SB7	JUNKERS	Black/beige/brown		Macau	Re-issue 1987
SB8	SPITFIRE	Dark brown/gold		England	Introduced 1973 Blue or clear canopy
SB8	SPITFIRE	Metallic green/gold		England	
SB8	SPITFIRE	Gold plated		England	Souvenir Range
SB8	SPITFIRE	Tan/khaki tan		Macau	Re-issue 1987
SB9	CESSNA 402	Light green/white		England	Introduced 1973 Clear or blue windows
SB9	CESSNA 402	Dark green/white		England	Labels or tampo
SB9	CESSNA 402	Pea green/white		England	
SB9	CESSNA 402	Metallic dark green/white		Macau	
SB9	CESSNA 402	Brown/beige		Macau	
SB9	CESSNA 402	White/red	'DHL'	Macau	
SB10	BOEING 747	White/dark blue	'BOAC'	England	Introduced 1973 Label
SB10	BOEING 747	White/dark blue	'British Airways'	England	Label or tampo
SB10	BOEING 747	White/dark blue	'Qantas'	England	Tampo
SB10	BOEING 747	White/silver grey	'United States'	England	Tampo
SB10	BOEING 747	White/silver grey	'MEA'	England	Tampo
SB10	BOEING 747	White/silver plated	'BOAC'	England	Souvenir Range
SB10	BOEING 747	White/gold	'British Airways'	England	Souvenir Range
SB10	BOEING 747	White/dark blue	'British'	Macau	Tampo
SB10	BOEING 747	White/silver	'Cathay Pacific'	Macau	Tampo
SB10	BOEING 747	White/silver	'British Caledonia'	Macau	Tampo
SB10	BOEING 747	White/silver	'Lufthansa'	Macau	Tampo
SB10	BOEING 747	White/silver	'Pan-Am'	Macau	Tampo
SB10	BOEING 747	White	'Virgin'	Macau	Tampo
SB10	BOEING 747	White	'Nippon'	Macau	Tampo (only in 1988 Japanese Airport Set)
SB10	BOEING 747	Silver/blue	'KLM'	Macau	
SB11	ALPHA JET	Metallic red/white		England	Introduced 1973
SB11	ALPHA JET	Blue/red		England or Macau	
SB11	ALPHA JET	White/red		Macau	
SB12	SKYHAWK A-4F	Dark blue/white	'Navy'	England	Introduced 1973
SB12	SKYHAWK A-4F	Dark blue/white	'Marines'	England	Deleted 1979
SB12	PITTS SPECIAL	Metallic red/white		England	Introduced 1979 Red Chequers on wing
SB12	PITTS SPECIAL	Metallic red/white		England	Red Flares on wing
SB12	PITTS SPECIAL	Blue/white	'Matchbox'	Macau	
SB12	PITTS SPECIAL	Red	'Virgin'		
SB12	MISSION HELICOPTER	Olive/tan		Macau	(MB57 issued as a Skybuster, USA only)
SB13	DC-10	White/red	'Swissair'	England	Introduced 1973
SB13	DC-10	White/silver grey	'Swissair'	England/Macau	
SB13	DC-10	White/silver grey	'United'	England	
SB13	DC-10	White/silver	'Lufthansa'	Macau	
SB13	DC-10	White/silver	'Alitalia'	Macau	
SB13	DC-10	White	'Thai'	Macau	
SB13	DC-10	Silver/red	'Aero Mexico'	Macau	
SB14	CESSNA 210	Orange/white		England	Introduced 1973 Deleted 1985 labels or tampo
SB15	PHANTOM F4E	Metallic red/white Red/blue or red/white/blue		England	Introduced 1973
SB15	PHANTOM F4E	Bright red/white		England	Labels
SB15	PHANTOM F4E	Metallic red		Macau	Re-issued 1987
SB15	PHANTOM F4E	Grey/orange		Macau	(US only – issued as SB6)
SB16	CORSAIR F4U	Metallic blue		England	Introduced 1973

SB NO.	MODEL	COLOUR	LIVERY	PLACE OF MANUFACTURE	REMARKS
SB16	CORSAIR F4U	Orange		England	
SB16	CORSAIR F4U	Light orange		Macau	Re–issue 1987
SB17	RAMROD	Red/white		England	Introduced 1976/77
SB18	WILDWIND	Lime green/white		England	Introduced 1976/77 7 or Star label
SB18	WILDWIND	Lime green/white		Macau	Re–issue 1987

Reaching for the sky in 1973.

SB NO.	MODEL	COLOUR	LIVERY	PLACE OF MANUFACTURE	REMARKS
SB19	PIPER COMMANCHE	Red/yellow	'N246'	England	Introduced 1976/77
SB19	PIPER COMMANCHE	White	'XP'	Macau	
SB19	PIPER COMMANCHE	Tan/dark blue		Macau	
SB20	HELICOPTER	Olive green	'Army'	England	Introduced 1976/77
SB20	HELICOPTER	White/blue	'Coast Guard'	England	
SB20	HELICOPTER	White/red	'Police'	England	
SB20	HELICOPTER	Dark blue/white	'Air–Aid'	Macau	
SB20	HELICOPTER	Blue	'RAF Rescue'	Macau	
SB21	LIGHTNING	Olive/grey		England	Introduced 1976/77
SB21	LIGHTNING	Silver/grey		England	
SB21	LIGHTNING	Silver		England	
SB21	LIGHTNING	Bright silver/grey		Macau	Re–issue 1987
SB22	TORNADO camouflage	Light grey/white	Pale grey	England	Introduced 1979 Label or tail-stripe or '01'
SB22	TORNADO camouflage	Dark grey/white	Light grey	England	
SB22	TORNADO	Dark grey/white	Cream camouflage	England	
SB22	TORNADO	Mid grey/white	F132	Macau	(US only – issued as SB7)
SB22	TORNADO	Light grey/white		Macau	
SB22	TORNADO	White/red		Macau	
SB23	SUPERSONIC JET	White	'Air France'	England or Macau	
SB23	SUPERSONIC JET	White	'Singapore'	Macau	
SB24	F16 FIGHTER	White/red	'US Air Force' (side decal)	England	Introduced 1979 Star or USAF decal on wings
SB24	F16 FIGHTER	White/red (no side decal)	'US Air Force'	England	
SB24	F16 FIGHTER	White/red	'US Air Force'	Macau	
SB24	F16 FIGHTER	Grey/blue/grey/white	'US Air Force'	Macau	(US only–issued as SB9)
SB24	F16 FIGHTER	Red/white	'US Airforce'	Macau	Tampo
SB24	F16 FIGHTER	White/black	'USAF'	Macau	
SB25	HELICOPTER	Yellow	'Rescue'		Introduced 1979 Black or chrome exhausts
SB25	HELICOPTER	White/red/white	'Los Angeles Fire Dept'		Code Red Model
SB25	HELICOPTER	White/blue			Deleted 1985
SB26	CESSNA FLOAT WING	Red/white	N264H	England or Macau	Introduced 1981
SB26	CESSNA FLOAT WING	Black/white	C210F	Macau	
SB26	CESSNA FLOAT WING	Red	'Fire'	Macau	
SB27	HARRIER JET	White/red	'Marines'	England or Macau	Introduced 1981
SB27	HARRIER JET	Light grey/white		Macau	Camouflage (Issued as SB10-USA)
SB27	HARRIER JET	Metallic blue/white	'Royal Navy'	Macau	
SB27	HARRIER JET	Green/grey/white	'US Marines'	Macau	(US only – issued as SB11)
SB28	A300 AIRBUS	White/silver	'Lufthansa'		Introduced 1981
SB28	A300 AIRBUS	White	'Alitalia'	Macau	
SB28	A300 AIRBUS	White	'Air France'	Macau	
SB28	A300 AIRBUS	Blue/silver	'Korean Air'	Macau	

THE DINKY COLLECTION

Matchbox Toys announced to the toy world in April 1987 at the opening of the Matchbox Room at the Chester Toy Museum the successful acquisition of the Dinky trademark. Shortly afterwards six models from the Miniature range, MB7 VW Golf, MB9 Fiat Abarth, MB44 Citroen 150V, MB51 Pontiac Firebird, MB60 Toyota Supra and the MB69 Corvette, were packaged in a Dinky bubble pack and sold through retail outlets. This was not an attempt to pass off these Miniatures as Dinky but more a means of protecting the Dinky trademark.

Resin models of the first three proposed all new Matchbox Dinkys were made by a model maker in Southend and were shown to the trade for the first time at the Harrogate Toy Fair in 1988, the DY1 'E' Type Jaguar, the DY2 Chevrolet Bel Air 1957 and the DY3 M.G.B. G.T. A press release issued in January 1988 announced: "A major re-launch of one of the biggest names in diecast history will be taking place in 1988. Matchbox Toys will be restoring DINKY to its original glory. Matchbox purchased the rights to the famous brand name last year reinforcing the company's leadership and total commitment to the diecast market. Research has shown that Dinky still has one of the highest consumer recall of any toy brand in the U.K. and Matchbox will be using its acquisition to extend the company's market share in the diecast market. Gerry Tekerian the Marketing Manager for Matchbox Toys said: 'Dinky had been static for eight years and there were no original moulds in existence. Matchbox had to start completely from scratch. The company has invested in an extensive research and development programme, talking to the trade and the consumer on an international basis to find out exactly what the users really want from Dinky.' The initial aim is to introduce a range of models for an era for which the Dinky name has the greatest meaning. Not only will the avid collectors be purchasers of this exclusive range, but also it will appeal to those people who grew up in the 1950s and 1960s who appreciate the nostalgic value of these models."

Matchbox Toys had considered launching a new mini Yesteryear series before the Dinky brand name was acquired. They had investigated ways in which to incorporate into the Models of Yesteryear series subjects such as the Volkswagen Beetle, Morris 1000 and 'E' Type Jaguar; but the management were reticent about extending the Yesteryear date up to the 1950s and 1960s. Of course, there had been exceptions such as the four classic racing cars, but these were regarded as one-offs. The Research and Development team even made a plastic model of an 'E' Type Jaguar for this considered mini-range. Tools were also made of a 1955 B.M.W., which was eventually placed in the Yesteryear range even though it was regarded by some as being too contemporary, but as its scale was not 1/43rd it could not be included in the Dinky Collection.

The return of Dinky, early prototypes, 1988.

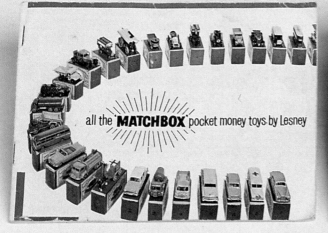

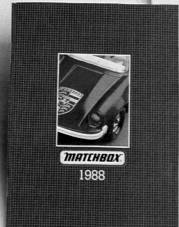

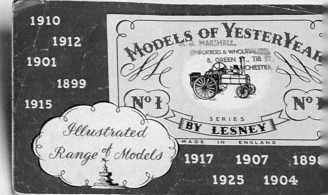

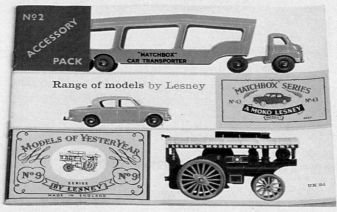

Publications
12 and Clubs

FURTHER READING

The first Lesney catalogues were larger than those of the 1960s which were produced in a smaller, standard size.

This final chapter offers the reader advice on where to turn to next for further information.

There are several good publications already available, some of which offer the collector easy-to-follow tables and listings. There are also two international collectors' clubs, which provide further reading material for their members. For collectors in the U.K., your local retailer should also be able to give you an abundance of up-to-date information. Matchbox Toys Ltd (U.K.) have established a network of over seven hundred Appointed Stockists, who endeavour to keep in stock an excellent range of Matchbox products. To obtain a listing of these retailers the reader is advised to write to: Consumer Services, Matchbox Toys Ltd, Swaines Industrial Estate, Ashingdon Road, Rochford, Essex, SS4 1RH, enclosing a Stamped Addressed Envelope for a speedy reply. Collectors in Australia and New Zealand should be aware that Matchbox Toys (Australia) has established a similar system and are encouraged to write to: The Product Manager, Matchbox Toys Ltd, 5 Leeds Street, Rhodes, Sydney, NSW 2138, Australia, for further information.

Lastly there are the Matchbox Catalogues produced by the company annually for over 30 years and these are reviewed in some detail below.

MATCHBOX CATALOGUES

Up until 1957 Lesney had not published any catalogues or brochures for the toy trade, although some of the toy factors and importers had produced simple trade sheets. J. Kohnstam & Co. Ltd, in 1957 produced a trade sheet in colour, and from then on Lesney and Matchbox have continued to publish a catalogue every year. It has proved to be a successful way in which to demonstrate their many ranges to the buying public. The huge growth in collecting has had the effect of making these trade sheets, brochures and catalogues collectable in their own right, but it should not be assumed that this is because they form an accurate pictorial history of the company. For many years models have appeared in the catalogues which were not destined for the public in their illustrated form, and equally for many years the enthusiastic collector has been haranguing bemused shopkeepers to order models in certain colours that do not exist!

The reason for the confusion is simple; it takes months of preparation, photography and artwork to produce a catalogue and during this time the models are still in their infancy and simply not ready for photography. A catalogue cannot be sent to the printers until it is absolutely complete, so for the sake of expediency a mock-up or drawing is substituted for the real thing. It can take quite some months to print and distribute a catalogue, so by the time the collector receives it, some of the illustrated models are bound to differ from the production versions.

Catalogues were a useful means of opening up new foreign markets to Lesney in their early years, and it is common to discover them with the word 'catalogue' in the language of the country where the catalogue was to be distributed.

Old catalogues today offer the reader a charming trip back in time. Not only do the catalogues reflect a change in design and graphic style but they chart the move from a purely descriptive document to a 'hard sell'.

Between 1957 and 1959 Lesney used both fold-out sheets and booklet catalogues. In 1957 J. Kohnstam & Co. Ltd. published a fold-out sheet, which when opened up measured 12.25" x 12.5" (31.1 cms x 31.8 cms). On one side of the sheet, "Matchbox" Series models No. 1 through to No. 24 were illustrated, and on the other side the cover picture of the No. 1 Road Roller was shown along with No. 25 through to No. 42. This fold-out sheet did not feature any Models of Yesteryear. All of the catalogues from this date until 1971 employed the technique of photographing each model in black and white then hand-colouring and separating it from its background and highlighting and retouching it. This gave the reader the impression of a drawing rather than a photograph and was a means of highlighting the detailing of the miniature. Photography has come a long way since

those early days and this process is now largely obsolete.

In 1958 a Models of Yesteryear fold-out sheet and a separate catalogue were published. The former measured 5" x 8" (12.7 cms x 20.3 cms) when folded, and it featured the first nine Yesteryears. The catalogue also measured 5" x 8" (12.7 cms x 20.3 cms). The front cover was yellow and pictured the No. 44 Rolls Royce and its carton. The contents included "Matchbox" Series numbers 1 to 60, Accessory Packs numbers 1 to 3 and Major Packs numbers 1 and 2.

In 1959 another fold-out sheet featuring the first fourteen Yesteryears was published. As with the 1958 sheet, the length of the models was shown in inches and millimetres as well as the scale of the models. The 1959 sheet was the same size as its predecessor. There were two different catalogues published as well in 1959. The first catalogue (the Kohnstam edition) had the same front cover as the 1958 catalogue except that the words '1959 EDITION' were printed on the upper right corner. It measured 8" x 5" (20.3 cms x 12.7 cms). The second 1959 catalogue measured 7.25" x 5.25" (18.4 cms x 13.3 cms) and had a new front cover showing the A2 Car Transporter, the No. 43 Hillman Minx and the Y9 Showman's Engine. This second 1959 catalogue was produced by Lesney Products after the take-over of J. Kohnstam & Co. Ltd and illustrated the Yesteryear range, a sure reflection of the growing popularity of these models.

The 1960 catalogue measured 7" x 5" (17.8 cms x 12.7 cms). It was good value for money as it cost only 3d (1.5p) and covered all the available ranges. *Ward:* "It is understood that these catalogues were free to retailers and were intended to be given free to customers. The price tag was to discourage children and collectors taking handfuls." Although the catalogue cost money in the U.K. it

cost nothing in the U.S.A. Catalogues were free in the U.S.A. except for one or two years in the late 1970s. This edition was very typical of its time using the then current craze for plain uneven lettering on the cover and arrowed signposts to direct the eye to its contents. This edition was also the first to notify the buyer of new models soon to be released by means of single colour line drawings. One, in fact, erroneously described the Y4 Shand Mason Fire Engine as a 'Merryweather'!

This catalogue also listed the scale of every model. This is interesting as previous catalogues seldom mentioned scales because at that time a high import duty was applicable to models (as opposed to toys) brought into the U.S.A. Lesney Products were well aware, however, that many of their products, the Y1 Allchin being a particular example, were being bought by model railroad and railway enthusiasts. The absolute accuracy of these printed scales is very much open to question. *Odell:* "We used to call them any scale that would suit railway modellers."

The 1961 and 1962 catalogues were of much smaller dimensions, 5" x 4" (12.7 cms x 10.2 cms), and retailed at 2d (1p). They were now entitled 'International Pocket Catalogue' and included complex price tables in their back pages (as did the 1960 edition). The growing internationalism of the company was reflected by price lists which included Kenya, Malta, Malaya and Hong Kong on the reverse of the 1961 catalogue. The 1961 catalogue illustrated the "Matchbox" Series No. 5 Routemaster bus on the cover, while the 1962 catalogue showed the new 65b Jaguar 3.4 litre. From 1962 onwards the year was always quoted on the catalogues.

The 1963 catalogue was of a similar style to the previous year's editions and used many of the pictures from those editions.

1964 saw the introduction of a full colour illustration of a real car on the cover. The phrase 'pocket money toys by Lesney' was abandoned and for the first time the word 'Collector' was introduced. The 1964 version also featured spaces for the collector to tick off his or her purchases, although the catalogue was still only relying on brief descriptions to sell its products. The first truly international catalogue was published in 1964; prices for the models in seventeen countries were shown on the rear cover of the International Edition.

The 1965 issue featured a motor racing scene. These front covers were beautifully drawn though highly inaccurate. The 1965 edition illustrated a Ferrari (No. 73) in turquoise while a year later an American Fire Chief's Car could be seen cruising around Parliament Square in London. The U.S.A. market released the international catalogue with a pasted in price sheet reflecting dollar currency, as stocks of the 1965 U.S.A. catalogue had been exhausted.

The 1966 edition expanded on the collecting aspect of Matchbox toys and the catalogue was in some ways a public relations document with features on the company's history, how the toys were made and even a Matchbox quiz with marks out of nine. Significantly 1966 was to be the first year that Lesney won the Queen's Award for Industry.

The brochure impudently informed contestants that, if they scored less than four out of nine 'there is only one answer to the problem – buy more Matchbox models and next time you will know all the answers!' Some might consider that a bit much from a company that pictured a fire fighting illustration involving an L.C.C. Ambulance and an A.E.C. Fire Engine alongside a Denver Fire Pump and the American Fire Chief's Car. The 1966 version had grown in size to become the standard size, and this size remained until the 1980s. 1966 was also the first time that a catalogue was published in the Japanese language.

The 1967 version reflected flags of the countries which were Lesney's main markets. The first two pages highlighted the news that Ford's new Mustang had sold over one million cars in two years, but that Lesney had sold the same quantity of their miniature version in just a few weeks. This catalogue featured a charming period shot of a little boy playing with a huge selection of products, entitled 'Now the fun begins'. Ironically, the fun was soon to begin for Lesney with the arrival of Hot Wheels from Mattel. Lesney produced eight million catalogues in that year. The 1968 catalogue revealed two new regular wheel models, the Foden Concrete Truck and the D.A.F. Tipper Container Truck.

In 1969 two catalogues were published and both illustrated that year's major innovation 'Matchbox Motorways' with three full pages of illustrations and text. It is unlikely that the company would be allowed to advertise the product in this way today because the illustrations show a wealth of trees and other details that were not included with the actual product. The second edition for 1969 included a reference to the Superfast range, but all of the models could plainly be seen with the then current regular wheels. Lesney printed a total of twelve million catalogues, of which six million were the American edition. *Lesney News* 1969: "The catalogues are far more comprehensive than any other of previous years and feature all accessories available for 1969. An added feature is a detailed write-up accompanying a full colour sketch of each of the Veteran and Vintage models. P.S. We need a proof reader for the Japanese 1969

catalogue. This is the first time ever that the Japanese catalogue has been printed in England– usually it is completely handled in Japan."

The 1970 catalogue is most interesting in that it illustrated the entire Miniature range as drawings and not photographs. This was because of the need to show graphically the model in motion and to disguise the fact that the full Superfast range was not ready to photograph. The catalogue was an amazing mish-mash of illustrations from cover to cover with few exceptions; the only items that were photographed were the Superfast track and sets. Close inspection of some of the models used in these photographs reveal them to be regular wheel models.

The 1970s catalogues were to reflect the growth of Lesney as a toy company and their divergence from being just model car manufacturers. The company was about to break into the lucrative pre-school market and early 1970s catalogues revealed an emphasis on the play value of Matchbox produced accessories. The 1970 catalogue had its first fifteen pages devoted to products such as Scorpions and Superfast Race-tracks. The emphasis was centred upon what the models could do rather than a model for model's sake. The exception was Models of Yesteryear which were retained unscathed and presented in their traditional form. The 1971 Catalogue highlighted the book –'Mike and the Model Makers'– and offered to the collector the book at only 25 pence.

1972 featured the introduction of the Big MX series, a range of semi-mechanised toys and clearly a further effort by Lesney to increase play value. It is noticeable that none of the models of this series were photographed; they were all artist's impressions. Further product introductions that year included 'Screamin' Demons', 'Plug Props' and 'Plug Buggies'. The emergence of customised

vehicles in the Superfast range bears witness to the tremendous battle for sales between Matchbox and Mattel in the U.S.A. at this time.

The 1973 catalogue was enlarged to accommodate two new ranges into the series. Two pages were devoted to the Sky-Busters series announced as being available in the spring of 1973. The second range was that of 1/72nd scale Aircraft Kits to be available from April 1973. Models of Yesteryear finally expanded to seventeen models in the series. A Hispano Suiza was photographed but in un-issued colours and the Y11 Lagonda was claimed to be new, although it had, in fact, been launched in 1972.

The next year's edition (1974) gave prominence to plastic kits which by then included military vehicles. The Superfast range was marketed almost as accessories to the Superfast track. Battlekings and the expanded Superkings range made up the bulk of the catalogue, with Models of Yesteryear being relegated to only four pages.

By 1975 the catalogue was giving the clear impression that it was not attaching undue importance to diecast collectors as it was packed with ranges of dolls and additional ranges of plastic kits. The miniature range was retitled as 'Matchbox 75' an indication of concern over the possible loss of identity. A sub-series within the range was titled Rola-matics and these were models with parts that moved as they were pushed along. The Models of Yesteryear pages illustrated a Y2 Vauxhall with bright red seats; this variation did exist but most of the small production run was exported and this model today commands extremely high prices.

Since 1972 Lesney had been producing different versions of the catalogue tailor-made for their various markets. Not every

country would be able to sell all of the ranges, and so the catalogues were altered accordingly. This had the unfortunate effect of diminishing the usefulness of the catalogue to the collector as it no longer reflected all that the company produced. It did, however, have the effect of promoting international collecting and enthusiasts around the world began communicating, mainly through the clubs, some of which had been formed during the mid-1960s.

The catalogues of 1977 and 1978 are only noteworthy in so far as they were all photographed to a high standard and the use of illustrations once so prominent was no longer apparent. The 1979 catalogue must have been the largest ever in terms of content with many products such as the 900 series, Matchbox Motorways, Powertrack, Playmats, Playtrack and Skateboarders. From the catalogue collector's point of view, it is the Models of Yesteryear range which is the most interesting. For the first time two liveries on the same model (the Y12 Model 'T' Ford Colman's Mustard and Coca-Cola) were shown with a note saying 'Available in selected markets only' against the Coca-Cola version. This would undoubtedly prove to be a spur to international collecting.

The catalogues produced up to and including the year of receivership (1982) continued to show the many ranges of toys being marketed by Lesney. Certainly the general public, on glancing through the catalogues, would have been surprised to learn of the financial difficulties of Lesney. 1982 also marked the last year of a U.S.A. catalogue. It is now generally agreed that it was somewhat of a miracle for the newly created Matchbox Toys Ltd. to publish a 1983 catalogue. It usually takes up to six months to have the catalogue ready and that includes planning, photography, artwork, printing and delivery.

The marketing team at Matchbox had to have the trade brochure ready for the Harrogate Toy Fair in early January 1983, only three months after the new company had been formed. The pocket catalogue had virtually the same content and artwork as the trade brochure, but obviously in a much smaller size. *Tekerian:* "It was the sheer timing of the situation with Universal buying Matchbox so late in the year . . . " The 1983 catalogue concentrated solely on the diecast ranges – omitting all the ancillary ranges from previous issues.

Since 1983 the contents of the catalogues have increased to include all of the major ranges such as Miniatures, Superkings, Lasers, Convoy, Motorcity and Models of Yesteryear.

Both the 1987 and 1988 catalogues gave notice of the newly-formed Junior Matchbox Club for youngsters. The 1988 catalogue also publicised details of how to join the Matchbox International Collectors' Association.

PAINTING BOOKS

A set of new A4 sized painting books was first produced in 1961 by Lesney Products. These retailed at 6d (2.5). There were four different books, each with its own theme. They were described in the 1961 catalogue as follows:

P-1 'Popular Lesney 'Matchbox' models shown in action, and in wonderful true colours. Includes a selection of Models of Yesteryear.'

P-2 "Matchbox" Series vehicles are shown in this book in a variety of situations, including some Military and Motor racing scenes.'

P-3 'The farm scene is set with 'Matchbox' agricultural and farming models shown in correct surroundings, and in full colour.'

P-4 'Many of the Commercial vehicles in the 'Matchbox' ranges are featured, and exciting 'action' scenes are illustrated.'

To complement the painting books Lesney also had made a Paint and Crayon Set - No. PC-1, which contained six water paints, a painting brush and six colouring crayons. The painting books and painting set are now extremely difficult to find, especially unused.

MATCHBOX CALENDARS

Matchbox Toys Ltd commissioned their first calendar in July 1983. The black-covered 1984 Calendar was published in late 1983. This Calendar featured twelve attractive photographs of what were then regarded as the twelve rarest Models of Yesteryear. The style of photography and the composition of each picture was highly unusual and acclaimed by both the toy trade and collectors alike. The 1984 Calendar was sold in the United Kingdom through retail outlets and direct from Matchbox Toys. It is of interest to note that the 1984 Calendar was used as a set prop in one of the 'Minder' television programmes.

Further calendars showing Models of Yesteryear were commissioned in 1985, 1986, 1987 and 1988. The 1989 Calendar, however, deviated from showing Models of Yesteryear alone. Instead, it was sold as 'The 1989 Matchbox Calendar' and showed models from many of the Matchbox ranges including an early Lesney toy, Convoys, Miniatures and Models of Yesteryear.

All these Calendars are not only regarded as being excellent references but have also become highly collectable. The older ones now command prices of around £15 to £20 and may be found in mint condition at some of the larger toy fairs or in the better obsolete toy and model shops.

ASPECTS OF COLLECTING

To some extent one can term any Matchbox diecast model as rare if it can no longer be found in a toy shop. Rarity is a question of degree and it can be argued that no obsolete or discontinued model is rare because if a collector is prepared to pay enough he will be able to locate and purchase it. This simple circumstance has developed because of the huge growth in the hobby of collecting diecast model vehicles. Concurrent with this growth has been the emergence of swapmeets, specialist dealers and vintage toy shops and toy museums. The media has also played its part with features on toy fairs, columns in newspapers seeking out alternative investments and even television programmes such as B.B.C. T.V.'s 'The Antiques Roadshow', which often devotes some of its airtime to old toys.

Within the diecast toy collecting hobby in general, collecting Models of Yesteryear is undoubtedly the largest sector and much of this popularity is thought to be because the range is still made today. This allows many enthusiasts to buy the models as they appear without having to search out the older issues at high prices. It is fair to say that there are very few bargains to be had today as all the attendant publicity has ensured that the non-collecting public are

convinced that even badly battered old toy cars are worth a lot of money.

The first aspect of collecting concerns the packaging of the models. Yesteryear models, for example have always been boxed, and today many collectors will not, unless absolutely necessary, purchase a Yesteryear without its box. This trend has grown to the point where a mint and boxed first series model commands a price of roughly three times that of an identical but unboxed example. Many collectors feel that this is a ridiculous situation and it affords them the opportunity to collect mint unboxed models at a fraction of the price of a boxed collection. Supply and demand is, of course, the reason for this trend as the flimsy boxes were nearly always discarded at the time of purchase, hence their rarity. At the time of writing a box for a first series model is worth as much as, if not more, than the unboxed model.

The term 'mint' needs some amplification. In its simplest sense it means perfect condition with no evidence of marking or scratches or indeed any evidence of handling or fading. In reality this is an uncommon condition for what are after all cheap mass-produced toys, many of which are now over thirty years old. It is even doubtful if all of the models left the factory in mint condition and models that were subject to extended travelling may bear evidence of scuffing even if they have never been out of their boxes. The term 'mint' may mean different things to different people. For instance, many otherwise unmarked models may have had their original transfers inaccurately applied. To the purist the model is not mint even though it has never been touched by someone outside the factory.

Fortunately, Matchbox models need very little care or maintenance, but the following suggestions have been included to help the reader maintain his models in the best possible condition:

Storage. Models must be stored in dry, ventilated conditions. Damp will quickly rust plated and bare metal parts, particularly axles. It will also attack the absorbent card of all the early type boxes as it has the effect of delaminating the card material. In extreme cases it can cause the cardboard to attach itself to the model. Most attics

model usually appears silver on top but violet underneath. Red paint will turn pink and light green will become pale blue if exposed for long periods, as revealed in the accompanying photograph.

Dust & Grime. Many early Matchbox models which were bought as ornaments spent their life on top of cupboards or curtain pelmets and may well have become very dirty, possibly

ed using any proprietary brand of metal polish, but excessive cleaning and polishing can result in wearing away the thin coating.

Rust. Can be removed from axles and steering wheels by gently rubbing the blade of a very thin sharp knife across the axle, rotating the axle slowly.

Metal Fatigue. Some early Lesney toys suffer from metal

started, collecting many of the ranges of Matchbox Toys may appear quite daunting because of their price, availability or even their quantity. It is very true to say that some ground-work will pay dividends in the future.

The most immediate decision to be taken is that of which type to collect. These notes have been written to provide an outline of the main characteristics of some of the ranges.

Early Lesney Toys. As there are

These two Y3-2 Benz Limousines were originally in identical colours. The model on the right was exposed to sunlight. The results are clear.

and cellars contain sufficient changes of climate to affect models adversely. Cartons which have been exposed to damp become brittle when dried. If the reader does not want to display his cartons, they should be flat packed and stored away in a dry area of the house.

Sunlight. Even through glass direct sunlight can seriously fade models in a short time. The most famous example in the Yesteryear range is the Y7-2 Mercer in violet. This colour contained a violet pigment which can fade even if not exposed to direct sunlight. A faded

because of tobacco smoke or other atmospheric conditions. With a little care these can be restored by various methods. The most favoured is actually to immerse the models in warm water to which a few drops of liquid dishwashing detergent have been added. Whilst immersed the model can be scrubbed using a soft bristled toothbrush, taking care not to damage the underlying paint or transfers. The model should then be quickly dried using a soft absorbent cloth. The drying must be thorough and reasonably quick.

Metal Plated Parts. Can be clean-

fatigue, caused by impurities such as lead in the zinc alloy. This can result in lifting paint and crazing or crumbling of the metal, sometimes only affecting some of the components. Fatiguing parts will be very brittle, but if handled with care, the condition does not usually get any worse. Fatiguing models should be kept at room temperature and away from currents of hot air (e.g. they should not be kept above a radiator). A very early example of the "Matchbox" Series No. 1 has also been found with metal fatigue.

To the person who is about to start, or perhaps has only just

only fifteen models identified, this may seem to be the most attractive range to collect, but these are without doubt the hardest to find and mint examples are extremely expensive. The Rag and Bone Cart, for example, in mint and boxed condition usually sells at a price in excess of £2,000.00. At the other end of the scale the early Cement Mixer in mint condition is usually less than £100.00. Note also that many of these toys were not boxed and did not have a maker's name prominently cast on their undersides. There is always the chance that they will turn up unidentified at jumble or car boot sales at a fraction of their normal value.

Early Lesney toys are avidly collected and it is estimated that there are well over one thousand active collectors. Patience is probably the key to collecting this series, and it may well pay to buy duplicates of models and then barter with swaps to build the collection. This series is probably the only one where condition is not paramount to possession of a model, as rarity is the over-riding factor.

1-75 Regular Wheels. This series has become very popular with collectors in recent years. Very few children in the U.K. did not possess some of these toys in the 1950s and they undoubtedly possess a strong nostalgic value. The range is, of course, very large and this has led many to specialise in various ways. Some collectors only collect first edition models in first edition colours in mint and boxed condition. Others obtain the whole series, but not always in boxes or even in perfect condition. Still more collect the models according to specific box types, for example only those models bearing the Moko trade-mark or only models featuring a line drawing box.

Prices for this series are currently increasing very quickly and as usual these increases are directed at mint and boxed examples. The collector who chooses to ignore boxed models in favour of unboxed examples will save up to 60% of the total cost of collecting. It has to be noted that this type of collection will be more difficult to sell, but if that is not a prominent consideration, then it is a very good way to begin.

Prices for mint and boxed first series miniatures usually begin in the U.K. at ten pounds currently, with the vast majority available at under twenty pounds. Very rare

models can fetch prices well over one hundred pounds.

Superfast Series. This market is unusual in that there are only a few hundred collectors in the U.K. but several thousand in the U.S.A. The market is also characterised by much lower prices than regular wheels models in both countries, generally around five pounds for a relatively rare model. This is purely a reflection of the forces of supply and demand.

It is worth noting, however, that the first models in this range are now twenty years old and are thus becoming an attractive proposition to many would-be collectors.

Many collectors were originally deterred from collecting as this range originally became very toy-like in appearance as the emphasis was on play and novelty value, as opposed to the nostalgic realism so evident in the regular wheels range.

This realism has returned in the recent years, however, and there are certainly many collectors of the models which are available in shops at current retail values. This is an important factor for the future.

Models of Yesteryear. This group is by far the most collected of all the Matchbox ranges and it is estimated that there may be at least 100,000 collectors in the world today. These numbers far exceed any other collectors of toys of other makes, and part of this appeal is that the range is still being produced. If a range of obsolete models is collected, then inevitably there are only a limited number to obtain and none of them can be readily bought from normal retail shops; hence the collector is restricted to models at elevated prices.

Models of Yesteryear have been available since 1956 and so they offer the collectors scope to specialise. The main categories to which some collectors confine themselves include (1) Com-

mercial vans (2) First Series models (3) All models up to the Woodgrain Series (4) All models after 1973 and up to 1985 (5) Saloon cars (6) Macau-made models. This flexibility enables collectors to specialise in certain variations such as casting changes or wheel colour changes. Listed below are some general guidelines to each range:

(1) Commercial Vans. This category provides much scope for the specialist; for instance there are five variations listed in 'The Collection' on the Y5-4 Talbot 'Lipton's Tea with Royal Crest' and a further five with the 'City Road' version. It is not vital to collect every version and many are content to have just one example of each livery.

The Y12-3 Model T Ford also has many variations, many of which can be obtained for very little money. Inevitably, there are a few which have become very expensive. The most famous is the 'Arnott's Biscuits' livery, which now commands a price in excess of £145.00, this price being purely a reflection of its rarity. In 1982, its year of introduction, these were sold in the U.K. for four pounds.

(2) First Series Yesteryears. This category, produced between 1956 and 1963, has proved to be the most sought after. They certainly have retained the most nostalgic value with their simple execution and now very dated packaging style. It is seldom that any of the first fourteen can be obtained in the U.K. for less than sixty pounds in mint and boxed condition; yet examples of mint but unboxed models seldom fetch half that price. They are generally thought to be a safe investment and their price rises steadily with the passing years. These models seldom attract the attention of the forgers, especially in boxed condition. Many of these models

were prone to breakage, but the replacement parts which are available are cast in white metal which is easily recognisable because it is heavier and softer than the original zinc alloy.

(3) Pre Woodgrain Series. Some enthusiasts do not collect beyond this point (1974/1975) mainly because the packaging and the models underwent noticeable changes. Metallic paint, standardised wheels and tyres and the commonality of the plastic parts tended to rob the models of some of their charm. Although the first series are expensive, the huge growth of Lesney in the 1960s means that there are far more models available and so the second series are more affordable and plentiful. There are, however, some examples which are rare, such as the metallic green Y5-2 Bentley and the Y11-2 Lagonda in purple. There are certainly sufficient variations to satisfy the most avid collector.

(4) Woodgrain Series To Date. Newer collectors are quite happy to pursue this range, one of the main reasons being that many of the models were released with multi-coloured components providing great scope for the variation hunter. Woodgrain models are also relatively in-expensive and this enables the collector to amass a good quantity of perfect models very quickly.

(5) Saloon Cars. This range attracts the collector whose hobby may be centred on the actual vehicles and who finds that Yesteryears form a coherent way to have a vintage transport display. Generally the commercial trucks and lorries have proved to be better sellers than the saloons; yet the current management of Matchbox is still committed to maintaining a balance of vehicles.

Major Packs, Accessories and Buildings. This range is almost totally overlooked by the majority of collectors, possibly because it is too small in scope and does not possess the strong identity of the other series. The range does, however, have the advantage of offering excellent value for money combined with an unusual choice of subjects. At this time the collector should certainly choose mint and boxed subjects and these normally can be obtained in the U.K. for less than twenty five pounds. This situation is bound to change and their rarity is already becoming evident.

King Size and Superkings. This comprehensive range of vehicles has never really attracted a strong following although the reasons for this are hard to explain. Quite possibly the various other ranges have simply been too desirable and have left these in their shadow. Superkings are also rather too close in appearance to many models from the Dinky Range and may suffer as a result. The range also went through a period in the 1970s when the emphasis was placed too much on play value and in doing so lost their identity as models of vehicles which could be seen on the road.

CLUBS

The UK Matchbox Club. This efficiently run club was founded in 1977 by Mr Ray Bush, a long standing authority on Matchbox products.

For their annual subscription members received magazines, originally every month and later every two months which were most informative and of a high standard. With the demise of Lesney Products, Mr Bush decided to close down the club in 1985. Back issues of Mr Bush's magazine are well worth reading, but are increasingly hard to find.

The Matchbox International Collectors' Association (M.I.C.A.). With the demise of the U.K. Matchbox Club, a new Association was formed in January 1985. M.I.C.A. members, for their annual subscription receive six magazines each year at regular two month intervals. These are of an excellent standard, in full colour and frequently cover the following subjects: Models of Yesteryear – past, present and future, an in-depth feature on an obsolete Model of Yesteryear, news of new Miniatures with regular articles on obsolete 1-75s and Superfast models, Catalogues; early Lesney toys; readers news and views, Collectors Fairs, overseas news from Australia and the U.S.A and a classified advertisements section, which enables M.I.C.A. members to buy, sell or exchange models or to obtain back issues of the magazine. These advertisements are free of charge to members and receive worldwide distribution.

To further the social aspects of Matchbox collecting, M.I.C.A. holds annual conventions which in the past have attracted members from all over the world. The management of Matchbox Toys also attend the conventions and regularly show the new releases for the following year, as well as answering members' questions on matters related to collecting Matchbox, which adds to an already lively and enjoyable evening.

You are encouraged to join M.I.C.A. Please send an S.A.E or two I.R.C.'s to your own regional representative:

U.K. or Europe. The Membership Secretary, MICA, 42 Bridge Street Row, Chester CH1 1NN, England.

U.S.A or Canada. The Membership Secretary, M.I.C.A. N.A., 585 Highpoint Avenue, Waterloo, Ontario, Canada, N2L 4Z3.

Australia or New Zealand. M.I.C.A. Co-Ordinator, Matchbox Toys Pty Ltd, 5 Leeds Street, Rhodes, Sydney, N.S.W. 2138, Australia.

When you join, you will receive the back issues of the magazine relating to the Club year of joining.

Matchbox U.S.A. This well-run club produces twelve monthly magazines each year for its members with black and white photographs. The emphasis is on Matchbox Miniatures and Models of Yesteryear, but there is also coverage of Matchbox diecast and non-diecast toys, past, present and future. Once a year Mr Charles Mack runs a Club convention in the U.S.A. For further information please write to: Matchbox U.S.A., Rural Route 3, Box 216, Saw Mill Road, Durham, Connecticut 06422, U.S.A. For $1 or 2 I.R.C.'s Mr Mack will send a sample issue of the magazine. Mr Mack has also produced several booklets covering Superfast, Convoy, Sky-busters and Catalogues.

THE MATCHBOX ROOM

The Toy Museum in Chester, England, was opened on the 4 May 1983 by Her Grace the Duchess of Westminster. As a privately-owned museum it attracts thousands of members of the public each year.

The first five rooms are devoted to a comprehensive display of antique dolls, tinplate and clockwork vehicles, novelty tinplate toys from the early 1900s up to the early 1950s, pedal cars, trains, lead figures and games. The museum is, however, now most famous for its enormous collection of Matchbox toys, thought to be the largest collection of its type on public

display in the world. The collection is an amalgamation of several hitherto privately-owned collections and necessitated the construction of a special room to display them all adequately. The room was named The Matchbox Room and was opened to the public on 10 April 1986 by Mr Michael Hind, the then Managing Director of Matchbox Toys Ltd. The walls of the room have been filled with display cases featuring the early Lesney toys, Models of Yesteryear, Miniatures, Major Packs, King Size, Plated Models, Gift Sets and Display Stands. On average some five models are added to the display each week. An audio-tape adds extra interest to the display and collectors and the public alike can spend several hours in the room checking and verifying models and/or shades of colour or variations which have been announced in many of the well-read collectors' journals.

The Museum and the Matchbox Room have been visited by many well-known and respected collectors throughout the world, including Mr Jack Odell O.B.E. The Museum is open seven days a week, each day of the year, with the exception of Christmas Day and Boxing Day.

Further information can be obtained by writing direct to The Curator, The Chester Toy Museum, 42 Bridge Street Row, Chester CH1 1NN, England, enclosing a Stamped Addressed Envelope or two International Reply Coupons, telephone 0244 46297.

THE MATCHBOX CAR MUSEUM

This exhibition is located at the Children's Palace of China Welfare Institute, 64 Yan An Road West, Shanghai, China. The display has over one thousand Matchbox models and will be increased each year. The exhibition is run by Universal International and was established to illustrate the history of car manufacturing and to enhance the cultural history of China.

The China Welfare Institution is a charitable organisation and was founded by Madame Sun Yi-Xian in the 1930s. She established the Children's Palace in 1953 and by locating the Matchbox Car Museum in the palace it is envisaged that the name Matchbox will become a household name with an excellent reputation all over China.

THE POWERHOUSE MUSEUM

In 1984 Matchbox Toys (Australia) bought a 2,500 Matchbox collection from an ex-Lesney manager, Mr David Leeman, a picture of whom appears in the Australian issue of the 1984 pocket catalogue. Matchbox Toys (Australia) have since added to this collection and finally put it on permanent public display in 1987 at the Power House Museum in Sydney, Australia. It is well worth a visit and is up-dated regularly by Matchbox Toys. In 1988 a special MB38 van was issued by Matchbox Toys (Australia) to commemorate the Matchbox display. The Power House Museum is open every day of the year between 10 a.m. and 5 p.m., except Christmas and New Year. It is located on the corner of Harris and MacArthur Street, Ultimo, Tel (02) 2170111.

RECOMMENDED FURTHER READING

'MATCHBOX' 1 - 75 SERIES.

1953 - 1969 Collectors' Catalogue
by MICHAEL J STANNARD
ISBN: 0-951036-70-X

The definitive book on this particular range of Matchbox die-casts was written in 1985. Highly recommended, and avaiable from: Mr Graham Ward, Promod Ltd., Vivian Road, Fenton, Stoke-on-Trent ST4 3JG, England.

'MATCHBOX' MODELS OF YESTERYEAR – THE COLLECTION

by KEVIN McGIMPSEY
and Stewart Orr
ISBN: 0-951088-50-5

This looseleaf book is annually up-dated in the form of supplements. All of the known and recognised variations, colour changes and new models have been recorded. Excellent colour photographs have been used to assist Yesteryear collectors to catalogue their own collection. The book is available from all good toy and model shops. If you have difficulty obtaining a copy please send an S.A.E./2 IRC's to the publishers Major Productions Ltd, 42 Bridge Street Row, Chester CH1 1NN.

This book has also been published in German and copies may be obtained direct from: Matchbox Toys GmbH, Siemenstrasse 23, 8759 Hosbach, West Germany.

Matchbox Miniatures 1 to 75 1953-1958

Early Lesney Toys 1948 – 1957

Matchbox Major and

Accessories Packs 1957 – 1973

Matchbox Gift Sets 1957 – 1988

These, the first four in a series of yellow-backed pamphlets, are highly recommended listings for the enthusiast. Much information in the form of tables and notes has been incorporated by the author, Mr Philip Bowdidge.

Available direct from Mr Bowdidge at: 8 Melrose Court, Ashley, New Milton, Hants BH25 5BY, England.

MIKE AND THE MODELMAKERS

by: M LASEK
First Edition:1970

In this book the author captured in colour the vast range of 'Matchbox' through the eyes of a young boy. It related in a very simple but charming way how 'Matchbox' models are made. Although now out of print, this book can often be seen for sale in second-hand book shops. *Lesney News* February 1970: "The new 'Matchbox' book was shown for the first time at Harrogate and has had a good reception, with copies going to Italy and other export markets where they are going to be used in schools to teach English. There is also the interesting story of the Iron Curtain countries buying the book."

'MATCHBOX TOYS'

by NANCY SCHIFFER
ISBN: 0-916838-74-9

A complete book filled with photographs and listings of many of the collectable Matchbox ranges up to 1982. The book was published in 1982 and is still available from the publishers Schiffer Publishing Limited, Box E, Exton, Penn. 19341, U.S.A.